MikroTik

MTCNA

Ehab Abo Elazm

ISBN: 978-1-7397931-2-8

Publisher: CAN for Learning and Development Ltd

Registered office address: 27 Old Gloucester, London, WC1N 3AX, United Kingdom

Tel: +44 (0)204 577 22 82 +44 (0)744 144 71 75

Email: info@canukltd.uk URL: https://www.canukltd.uk

Warning and Disclaimer

This book is designed to provide information about the MikroTik MTCNA exam using the latest versions available at the time of publishing this book, v7.18 & v6.49. Every effort has been made to make this book as complete and as accurate as possible, but no warranty or fitness is implied. The information is provided on an as is basis. The authors, and CAN for Learning and Development Ltd. shall have neither liability nor responsibility to any person or entity with respect to any loss or damage arising from the information contained in this book.

Trademark Acknowledgments

All trademarks mentioned in this book are the property of their respective owners.

All terms mentioned in this book that are known to be trademarks or service marks have been appropriately capitalized. CAN for Learning and Development Ltd. cannot attest to the accuracy of this information. Use of a term in this book should not be regarded as affecting the validity of any trademark or service mark.

بسم الله الرحمن الرحيم

Introduction

Praise be to Allah, the Lord of the worlds, and peace and blessings be upon Prophet Mohammed, his family, and companions.

The MTCNA (MikroTik Certified Network Associate) is the first step in the MikroTik certification path. It is a foundational certification required before studying any other MikroTik certifications.

This book is designed to help you understand the official MTCNA certification syllabus, covering the fundamentals of MikroTik technologies in a simple and clear way. It includes step-by-step explanations, diagrams, and practical examples and labs in both GUI and CLI, using the latest version of RouterOS.

Whether you are new to MikroTik technology and want to learn it or are aiming to get certified, this guide is the right start. It will help you understand the course content and pass the exam with confidence.

I wish you all the best in your learning journey and success in your certification.

Ehab Abo Elazm

Istanbul, 2025

MIKROTIK | MTCNA

1

Module

INTRODUCTION

MTCNA

Module 1

This module provides an introduction to MikroTik technology, introducing its products, exploring RouterBOARD and RouterOS, how to access the device, make simple configurations, manage the device, update it, and save a backup.

This module covers the following course content topics:

- About MikroTik
  - What is RouterOS
  - What is RouterBoard
- First time accessing the router
  - WinBox and MAC-WinBox
  - WebFig and Quick Set
  - Default configuration
- RouterOS command line interface (CLI)
  - Null Modem cable
  - SSH and Telnet
  - New terminal in WinBox/WebFig
- RouterOS CLI principles
  - <tab>, double <tab>, "?", navigation
  - Command history and its benefits
- Upgrading RouterOS
  - Package types
  - Ways of upgrading
  - RouterBOOT firmware upgrade

- Router identity
- Manage RouterOS logins
- Manage RouterOS services
- Managing configuration backups
  - Saving and restoring the backup
  - Difference between a backup and an export (.rsc) file
  - Editing an export file
- Resetting a RouterOS device
- Reinstalling a RouterOS device (Netinstall)
- RouterOS license levels
- Sources of additional information
  - wiki.mikrotik.com
  - forum.mikrotik.com
  - mum.mikrotik.com
  - Distributor and consultant support
  - support@mikrotik.com

Introduction

1.1 About MikroTik

MikroTik is a networking company established in Riga, Latvia, in 1996. It provides a wide variety of networking products.

These products and equipment are used by ISPs, companies, and individuals.

MikroTik mission is to make Internet technologies faster, more powerful, and more affordable for a wider range of users. (Source: MikroTik official website)

1.2 Historical Background

- In 1996, MikroTik was established.
- In 1997, MikroTik launched an operating system called RouterOS.
- In 2002, MikroTik introduced a hardware product called RouterBOARD.
- In 2006, MikroTik started organizing a meeting for its users called the MikroTik User Meeting (MUM).

1.3 MikroTik Products

MikroTik develops and produces both hardware and software for networking devices.

1.4 Hardware Products

In general, the main hardware devices or hardware solutions that MikroTik produces are called RouterBOARD.

These devices range from small SOHO (Small Office/Home Office) solutions designed for home users to carrier-class, heavy-duty devices designed for companies and ISPs.

MikroTik products are categorized into several groups:

- Ethernet routers.
- Switches.
- Wireless systems.
- Wireless for home and office.
- RouterBOARDs.

Plus, additional categories like:

- Interfaces.
- Accessories.
- Antennas.

For detailed and up-to-date information about MikroTik products and categories, visit the MikroTik website.

https://www.mikrotik.com

1.5 Product Naming

MikroTik products follow specific naming rules, making it easier to understand the product specifications by simply reading the product code name. Currently, at the time of publishing this book, these codes are divided into three categories:

- Naming codes for RouterBOARD products.
- Naming codes for CloudCoreRouter products.
- Naming codes for CloudRouterSwitch and CloudSmartSwitch products.

1.5.1 RouterBOARD Products

For RouterBOARD (RB) products the following coding structure is used:

<board name> <board features>-<built-in wireless> <wireless card features>-<connector type>-<enclosure type>

<band><power_per_chain><protocol><number_of_chains>

- Board Name

  There are three types of board names, so far,:

  - 3-symbol Name
    - The first symbol represents the series. It can be a number or a letter.
    - The second digit represents the number of wired interfaces (Ethernet, SFP, SFP+).
    - The third digit represents the number of wireless interfaces.

      For example: **RB951**Ui-2HnD
      - RB: RouterBOARD.
      - 9: 9th series board.
      - 4: 4 wired (ethernet) interfaces.
      - 1: wireless interface.
  - Word

    The name of the Board can be a word. , like cAP (ceiling Access Point) , or hAP (home Access Point).

      For example: **hAP**
      - hAP: Home Access Point

- Exceptional Naming

  The name of the Board can be a number represents a product series, like 600, 800, 1000, 1100, 1200, 2011, 3011, 4011.

  For example:**RB1100**AHx4

  - RB: RouterBOARD
  - 1100: 1100 series.

- Board Features

  The board features are letters represent specific features, for example U means the device has USB port, H means the device has more powerful CPU, A means the device has more memory and ,or, higher license level, i means single port power injector.

  For example: RB951**Ui**-2HnD

  - U: USB port
  - i: single port power injector.

  RB1100**AHx4**

  - A more memory or higher license level.
  - H more powerful CPU.
  - x4: 4 CPU cores.

- Built-in Wireless

  If the device has built-in wireless, the wireless feature codes will be in the following structure:

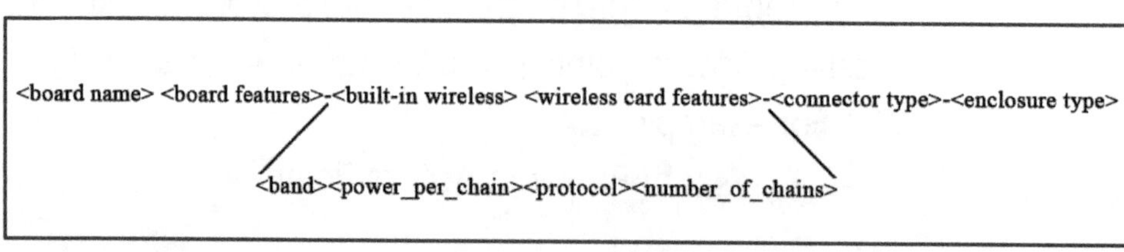

- Band

  Band represents the supported frequency band, like 5 for 5Ghz, 2 for 2.4Ghz , 52 for dual band 5Ghz and 2.4Ghz

  For example: RB951Ui-**2**HnD

    - 2 means 2.4Ghz.

  RB952Ui-**5**ac**2**nD

    - 2 means 2.4Ghz.
    - 5 means 5Ghz.

- Power per chain

  Power per chain is a symbol represents the supported chain power, for example H means High power.

  For example: RB951Ui-2**H**nD

    - H: High power.

- Protocol

  Protocol represents the supported wireless protocol, like n, ac, ax.

  For example: RB951Ui-2H**n**D

    - n: means 802.11n support.

- Number of Chains

  This symbol represents the number of chains in the device, like D which means dual chain, T which means triple chain.

  For example: RB951Ui-2Hn**D**

    - D means dual chain.

- Connector Type

  The connector type on the wireless interface. If there is no symbol that means only one connector option on the model. The MMCX means the device uses MMCX connector type. u.FL means the device uses u.FL connector type

- Enclosure Type

  A symbol represents the enclosure type, like RM means rack-mount enclosure, TC means tower case.

  For example: RBD52G-5HacD2HnD-**TC**

  - TC means tower case.

Example

RB941-2nD

- RB
  - RB (RouterBOARD)
- 941
  - 9th series board
  - 4 wired (ethernet) interfaces
  - 1 wireless interface.
- 2nD
  - 2 means 2.4GHz band.
  - n means 802.11n support
  - D means dual chain.

1.5.2 CloudCoreRouter Products

To name CloudCoreRouter (CCR) products the following coding structure is used:

<4 digit number>-<list of ports>-<enclosure type>

- 4-digit number
  - The first digit represents the series.
  - The second digit is reserved.

- The third and fourth digits represent the number of CPU cores.

  For example: **CCR2004**-16G-2S+PC

  - CCR: Cloud Core Router
  - 2: Series 2
  - 0: reserved
  - 04: 4 CPU course.

- List of Ports

  The second part of the name represents the number of ports and its type.

  For example: CCR2004-**16G-2S+**PC

  - 16G: 16 one-gigabit ethernet interfaces.
  - 2S+: 2 ten-gigabit ethernet interfaces.

- Enclosure Type

  The third part of the name represents the enclosure type, like RM means rack-mount enclosure, TC means tower case, PC means passive colling enclosure.

  For example:CCR2004-16G-2S+**PC**

  - PC: Passive Cooling enclosure

Example

CCR2004-16G-2S+PC

- CCR2004
  - CCR: Cloud Core Router.
  - 2: Series 2.
  - 0: reserved.
  - 04: 4 CPU course.
- 16G-2S+
  - 16G: 16 one-gigabit ethernet interfaces.
  - 2S+: 2 ten-gigabit ethernet interfaces.

- PC
  - PC: Passive Cooling enclosure.

1.5.3 CloudRouterSwitch & CloudSmartSwitch Products

To name a CloudRouterSwitch (CRS) and CloudSmartSwitch (CSS) products the following coding structure is used:

<3 digit number>-<list of ports>-<built-in wireless card>-<enclosure type>

- 3-digit Number
  - The first digit represents the series.
  - The second and third digits represent the number of wired interfaces.

    For example: **CRS326**-4C+20G+2Q+RM
    - CRS: Cloud Router Switch
    - 3: Series 3
    - 26: 26 wired interfaces (Ethernet+Fiber)
- List of Ports

  The second part of the name represents the number of ports and its type.

  For example: CRS326-**4C+20G+2Q+**RM
  - 4C: 4 combo 10G Ethernet/SFP ports
  - 20G+ : 20 of 2.5G Ethernet ports
  - 2Q+ : 2 40G QSFP+ ports
- Built-in Wireless Card

  If the device has built-in wireless, the third part of the name represents built-in wireless interface card details.

- Enclosure type

  The fourth part of the name represents the enclosure type, like RM means rack-mount enclosure, TC means tower case, PC means passive colling enclosure.

  For example: CRS326-4C+20G+2Q+**RM**

  - RM: rack-mount enclosure.

Example

CRS326-4C+20G+2Q+RM

- CRS326
  - CRS: Cloud Router Switch
  - 3: Series 3
  - 26: 26 wired interfaces (Ethernet+Fiber)
- 4C+20G+2Q+
  - 4C: 4 combo 10G Ethernet/SFP ports
  - 20G+ : 20 of 2.5G Ethernet ports
  - 2Q+ : 2 40G QSFP+ ports
- RM
  - RM: rack-mount enclosure.

For detailed and up-to-date information about product naming, visit the MikroTik website.

1.6 Software Products

At the beginning, MikroTik introduced an operating system called RouterOS.

Later, MikroTik developed another operating system called SwitchOS.

1.7 RouterOS

RouterOS is an operating system based on the Linux kernel. This operating system enables the device to function as a router with multiple features, such as:

- Full support for 802.11 a/b/g/n/ac standards, LTE, and 60GHz wireless technologies.
- Flow control, firewall filtering, and bandwidth shaping.
- Creating VPNs or tunnels using various protocols (PPPoE, SSTP, PPTP, OpenVPN, L2TP+IPsec).
- Running services like DHCP, Hotspot, and User Manager (RADIUS).
- And many more.

There are three version types of this operating system that can be installed on:

- MikroTik hardware devices (RouterBOARD) — RouterOS version.
- PCs — x86 version.
- Virtual Machines (VMs) — CHR version.

1.8 SwitchOS

MikroTik developed the SwitchOS operating system for specific products to provide enhanced switching and Layer 2 capabilities.

You will learn more about this operating system in the MTCSWE course.

1.9 Accessing RouterOS

To configure RouterOS to perform the required operations in the network, you can use either the Command Line Interface (CLI) or the Graphical User Interface (GUI) and execute the appropriate commands.

To access the CLI or GUI, you need two things:

- Media.
- Software.

1.10 Media

You can access the RouterOS by using:

- Ethernet cable, connecting it to the Ethernet interface.
- Null modem cable, connecting it to the serial interface.
- WiFi, if the device has a wireless interface.

1.11 Software.

After choosing the connection media, you can use one of the following software to access RouterOS:

- WinBox.
- WebFig.
- Telnet and SSH.
- Terminal emulator.

1.11.1 WinBox

WinBox is a software developed by MikroTik to access the RouterOS GUI. It is a free software and can be downloaded from the official MikroTik website:

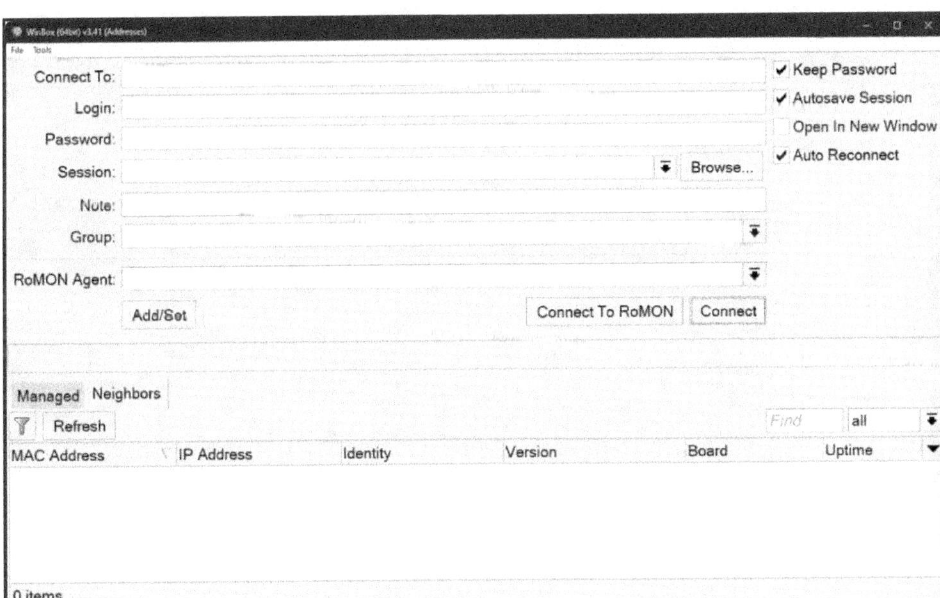

To access RouterOS, enter the device address in the **Connect To** field, the username in the **Login** field, and the password in the **Password** field. Then, click the **Connect** button.

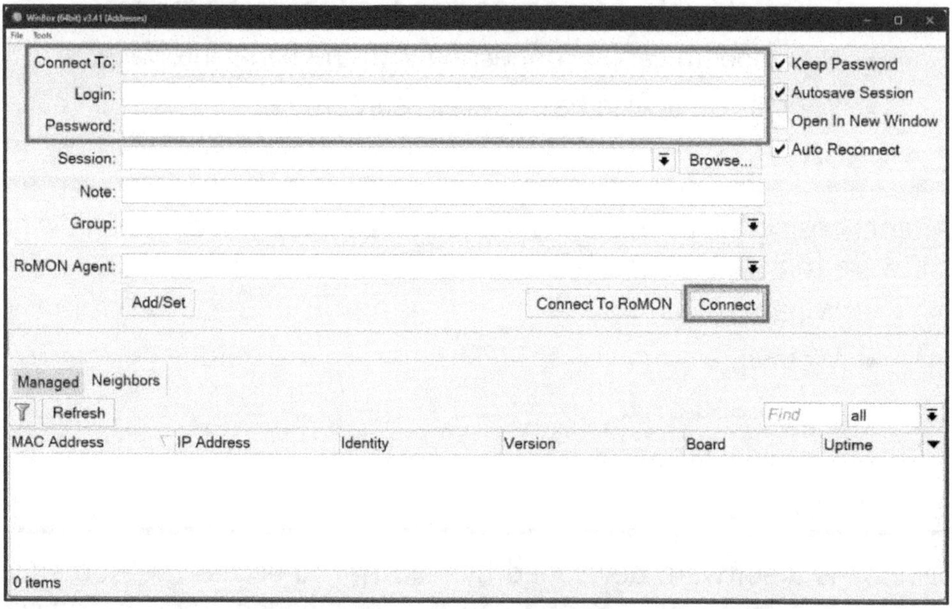

After connecting to the device, the RouterOS GUI will appear.

WinBox Supports both IP address and MAC address, that means you can enter the device IP address in the **Connect To** field, or its MAC address.

If you want to use the IP address to connect to the device, the IP address should be reachable from your PC. Or you can use the MAC address if the device is in the same broadcast domain and does not have an IP address, or if the IP address is not in the same subnet.

It is recommended to use an IP address whenever possible. A MAC session uses network broadcasts and is not fully reliable.

In the default configuration:

- IP address (LAN side): 192.168.88.1
- User: admin
- Password: (printed on the back of the device).

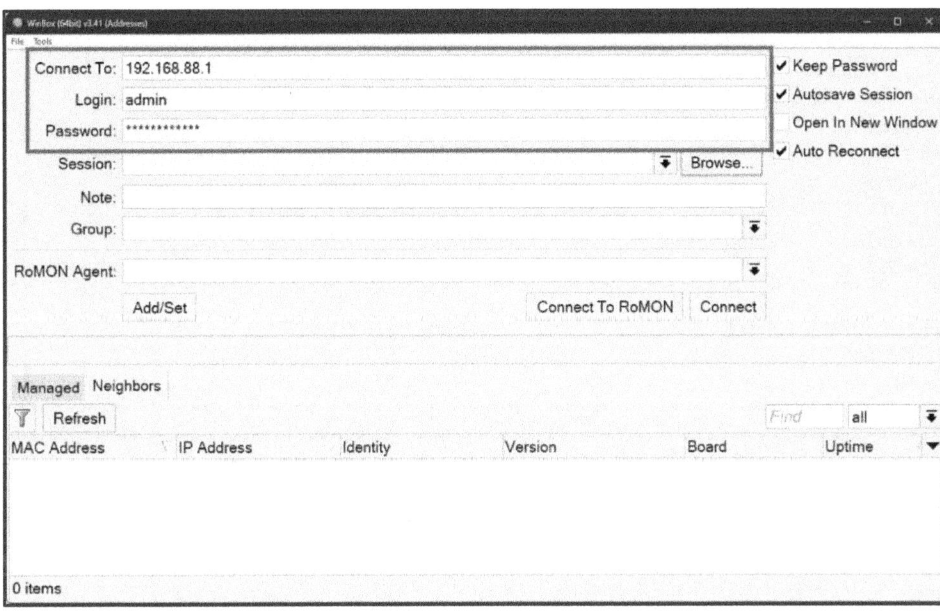

MikroTik devices used to be shipped with a default configuration that did not have a password. Nowadays, all new devices are shipped with a password that is printed on the back of the device.

Instead of entering the address manually in the **Connect To** field, you can use the **Neighbors** tab for an easier way to access devices that are in the same broadcast domain.

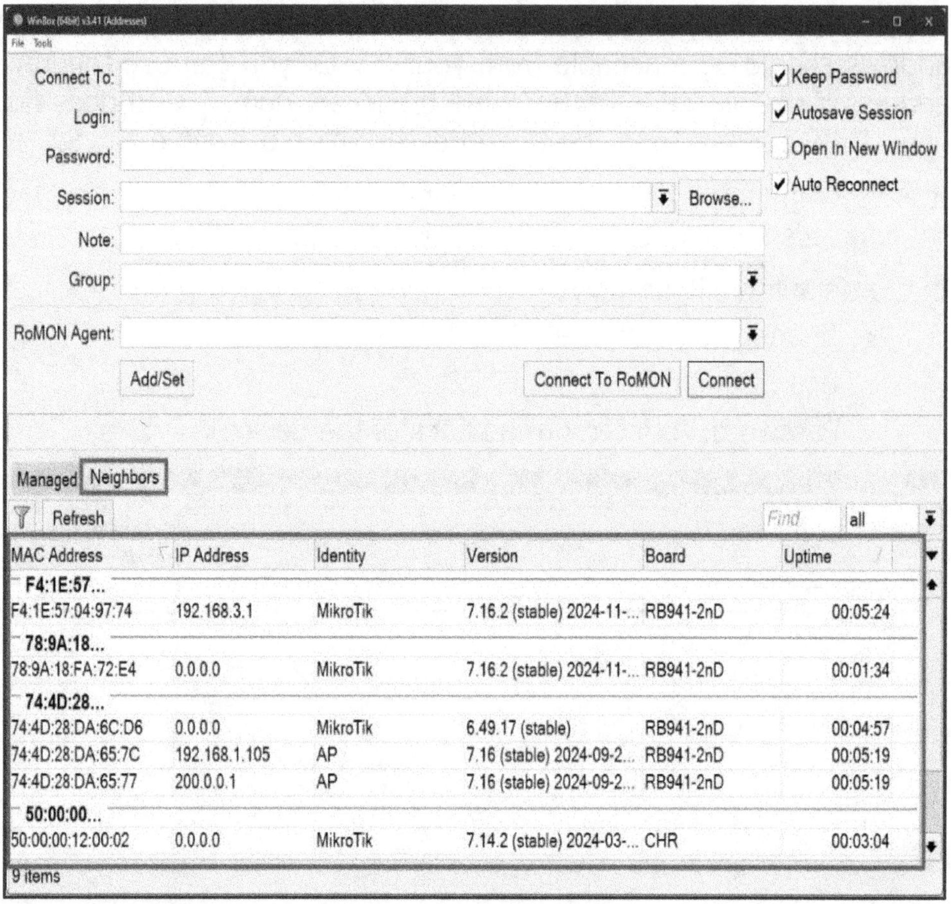

In the **Neighbors** tab, WinBox displays a list of MikroTik devices that can be connected to, along with some information about each device, such as the IP address, MAC address, etc.

To connect to any of these devices, click the IP address or MAC address of the desired device from the list. The address will automatically appear in the **Connect To** field.

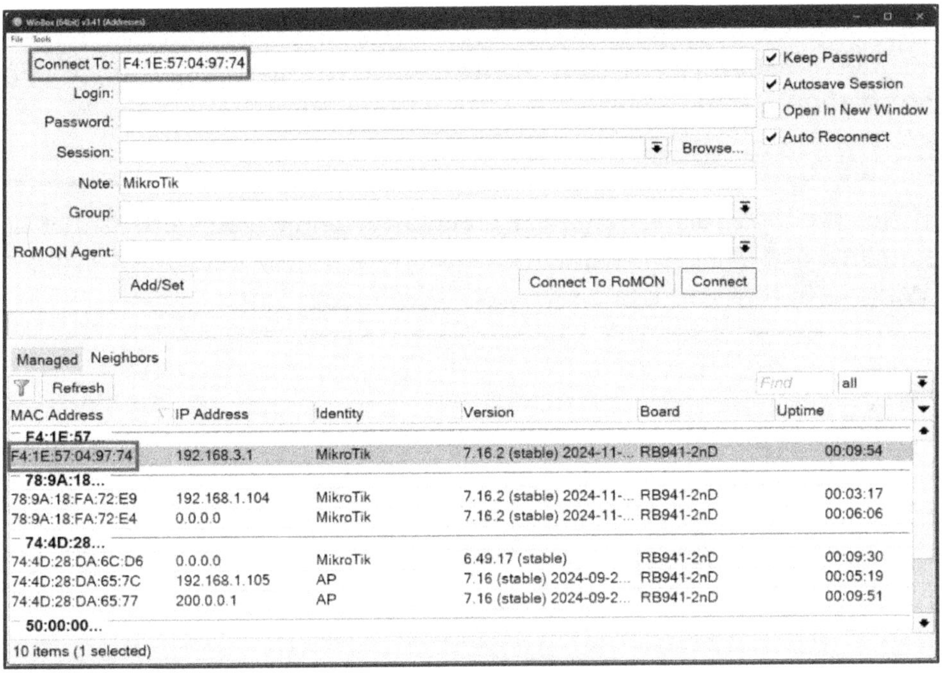

Then, enter the username in the **Login** field, the password in the **Password** field and click the **Connect** button.

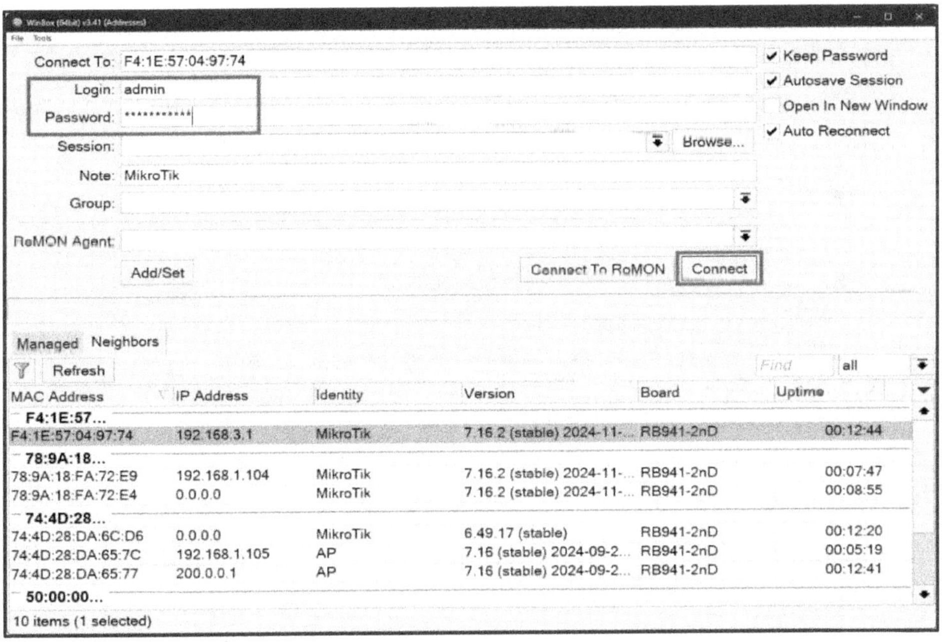

WinBox uses TCP port 8291 to operate, and it uses the MikroTik Neighbor Discovery Protocol (MNDP) over UDP port 5678 to display information about devices.

1.11.2 MAC-WinBox

In the past, to run WinBox on macOS or Linux, you had to use an emulator like Wine software. Now. there is a new version of WinBox (WinBox 4) that can run directly on macOS and Linux.

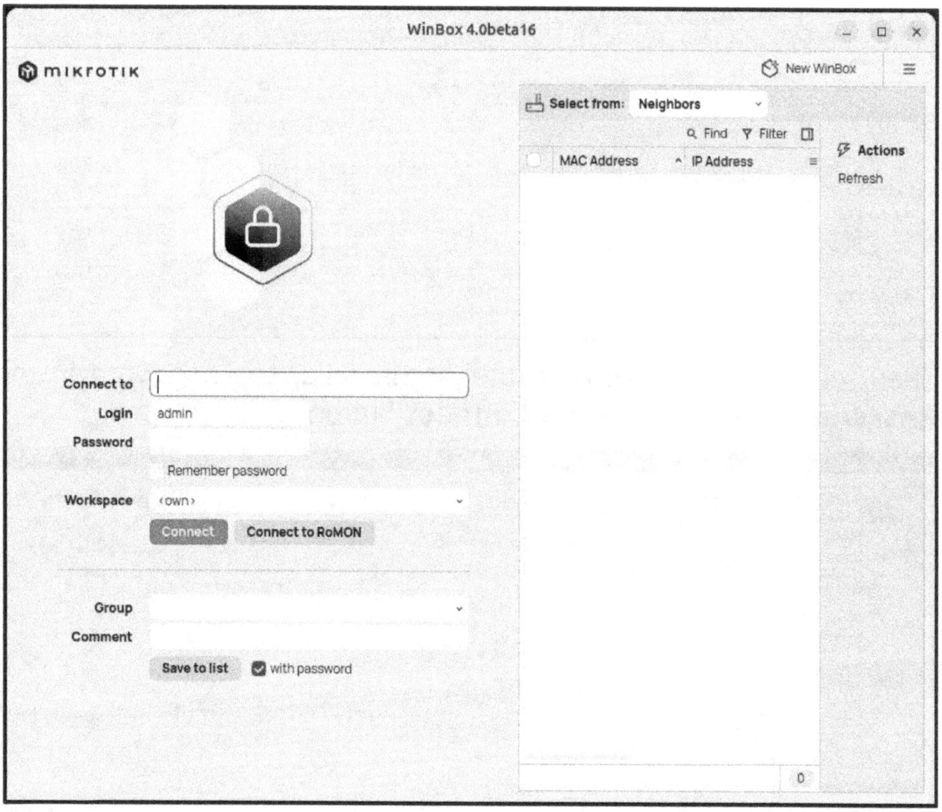

1.11.3 WebFig

WebFig is an application installed in RouterOS that allows access to the RouterOS GUI through any web browser.

To access RouterOS, simply enter the device IP address in the browser.

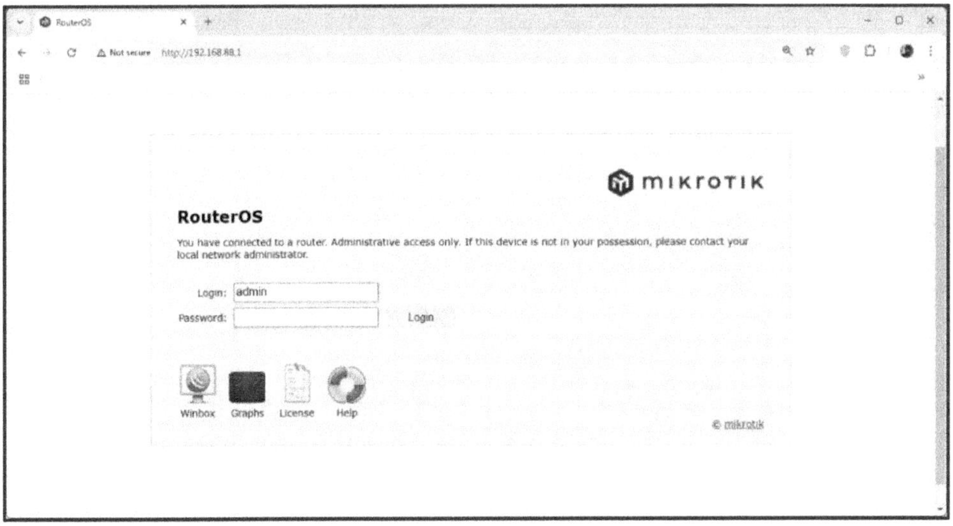

Then, enter the username in the **Login** field, the password in the **Password** field and click **Login** to access the WebFig GUI.

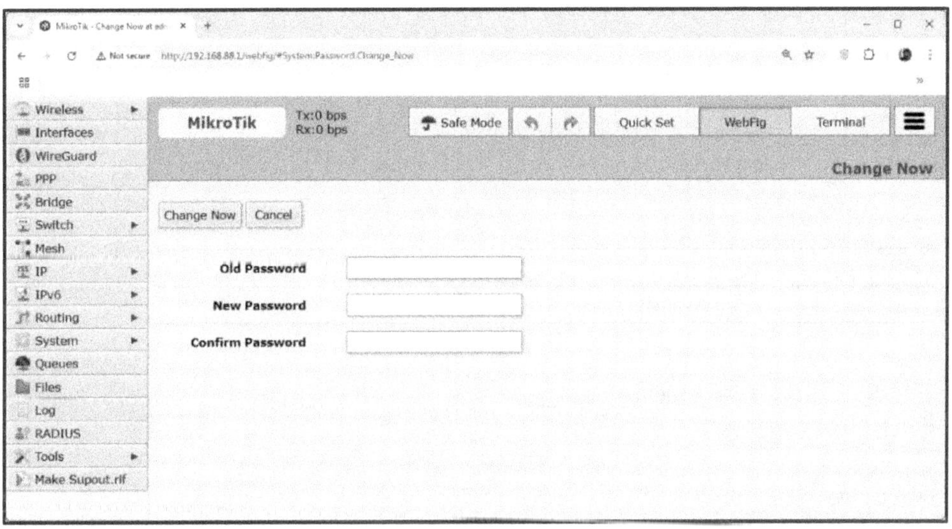

If the device does not have an IP address, you should use WinBox to access the device by MAC address.

1.12 RouterOS GUI

After using WinBox or WebFig to access RouterOS, the main window of the RouterOS GUI will appear.

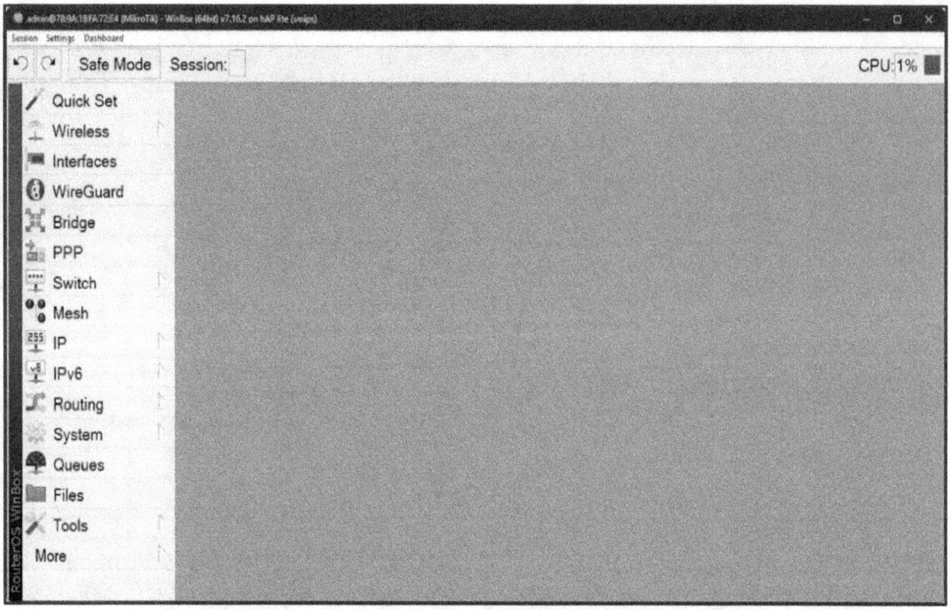

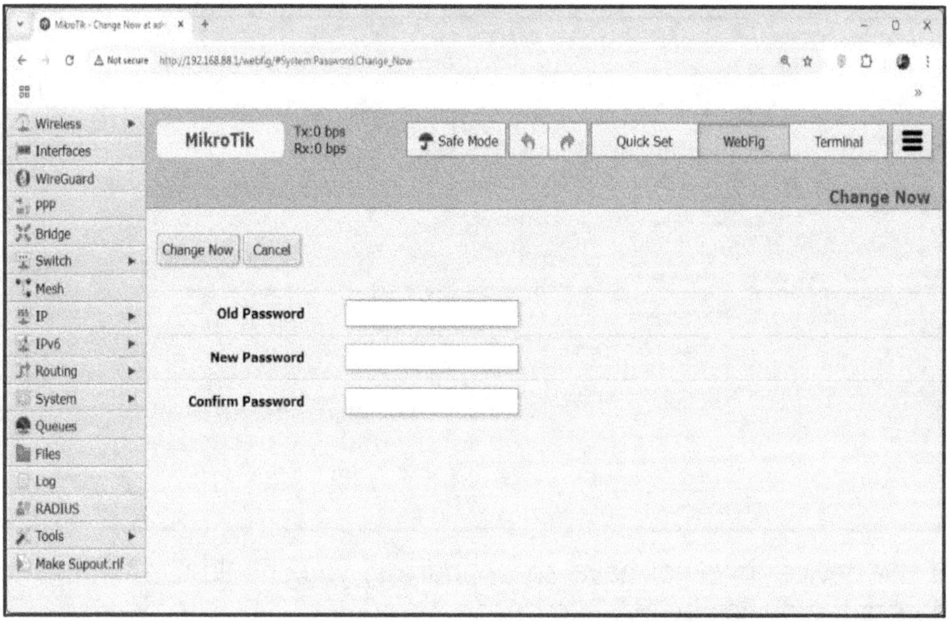

On the left-hand side of the RouterOS GUI, you will find a set of menus containing commands and other submenus.

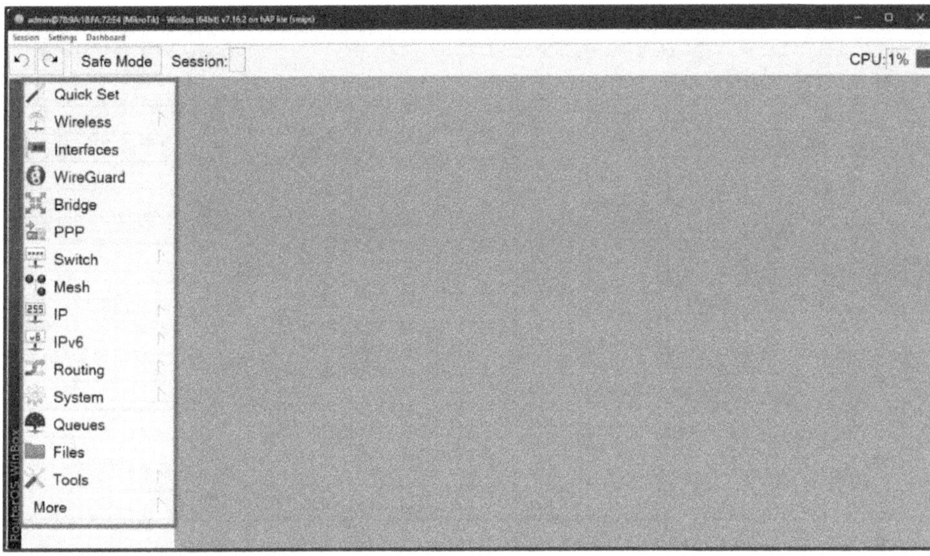

You can configure the device by clicking the menus, buttons, checkboxes, and other elements that appear in the GUI.

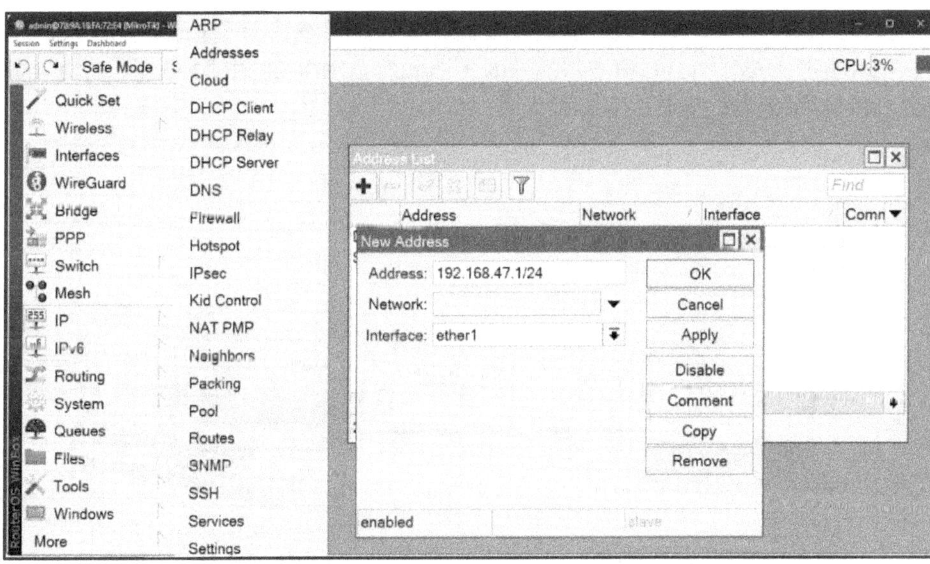

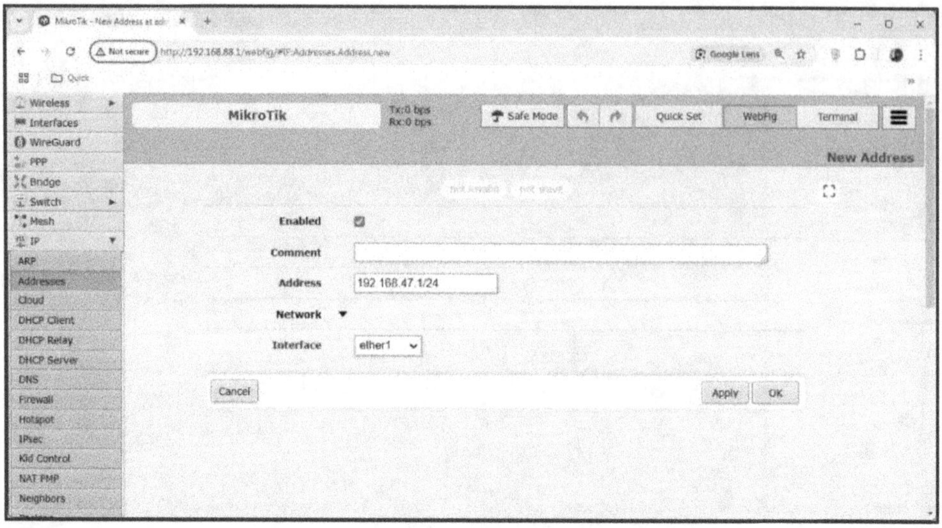

Let's study the following simple lab to learn how to configure a MikroTik RouterOS using GUI.

LAB

In this lab, you have a MikroTik device connected to a PC via the ethernet interface ether1.

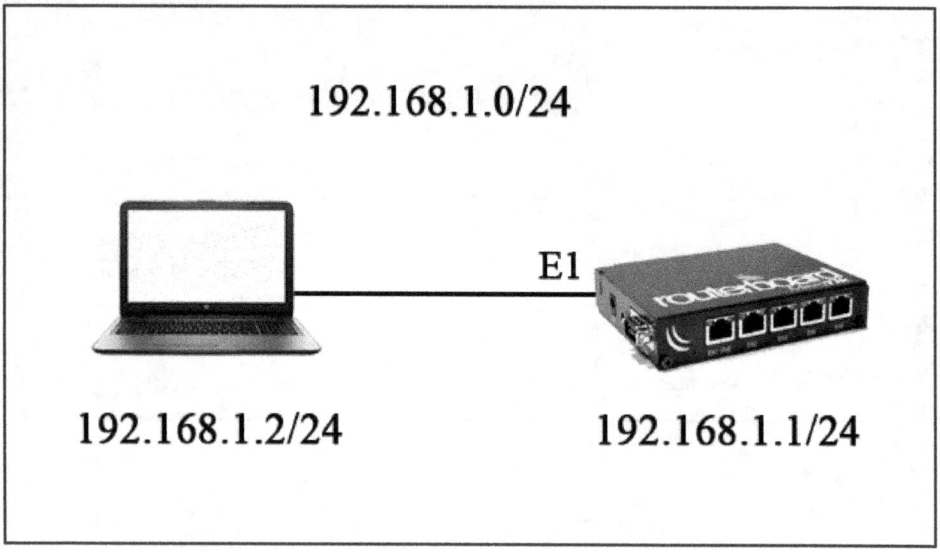

You want to assign the IP address 192.168.1.1/24 to the interface ether1 of the MikroTik device, and the IP address 192.168.1.2/24 to the PC. Then, you will check the connectivity between the two devices using the ping command.

In this lab, you will use the GUI to configure the MikroTik device and assign an IP address to its interface. The device has no configuration and has the default username (admin) without a password.

To access the MikroTik GUI:

- First: download WinBox from the MikroTik website and connect your PC to the MikroTik device using the interface ether1.
- Then: run WinBox and wait until the MikroTik device appears in the **Neighbors** tab of the WinBox window. Click the MAC address of this device in the **Neighbors** tab and make sure it appears in the **Connect To** field. Enter the username admin in **Login** field, leave the **Password** field empty, and click the **Connect** button.

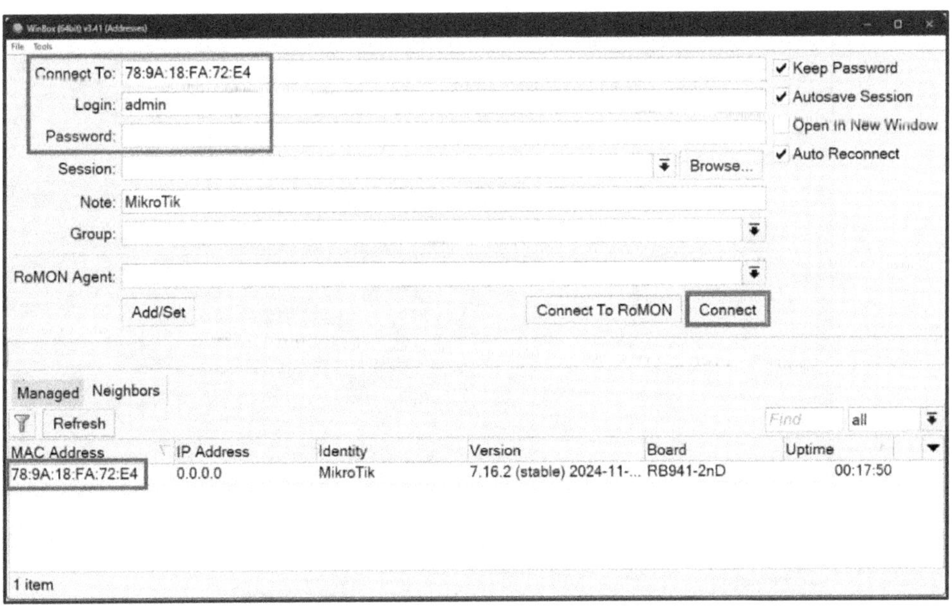

To assign an IP address to a MikroTik device interface using the GUI, you will use the **Address List** window.

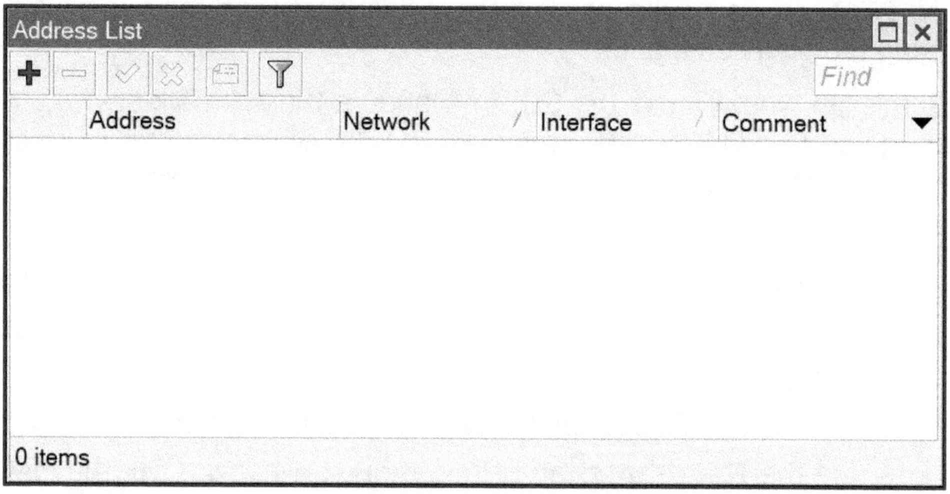

To open the **Address List** window:

- Click the **IP** menu to open it.
- From the **IP** menu, click **Addresses** to open the **Address List** window.

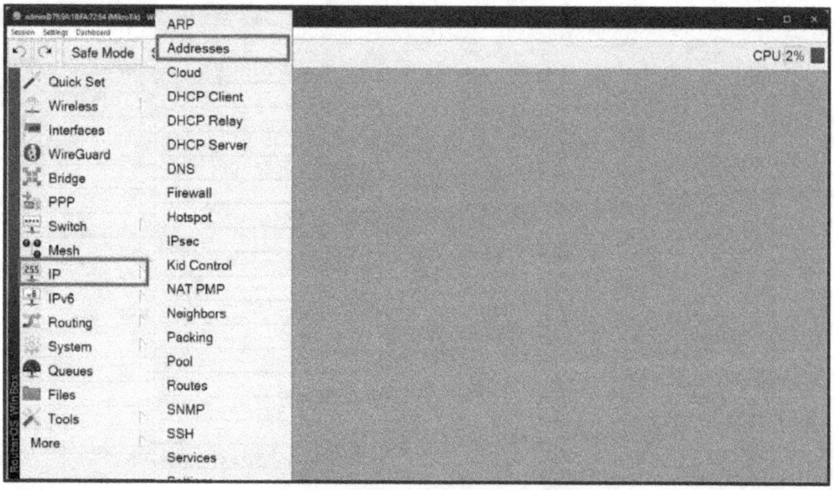

You can use the **Address List** window to assign IP addresses to the MikroTik device interfaces.

- From the **Address List** window, click the **Add** button to open the **New Address** dialog box.

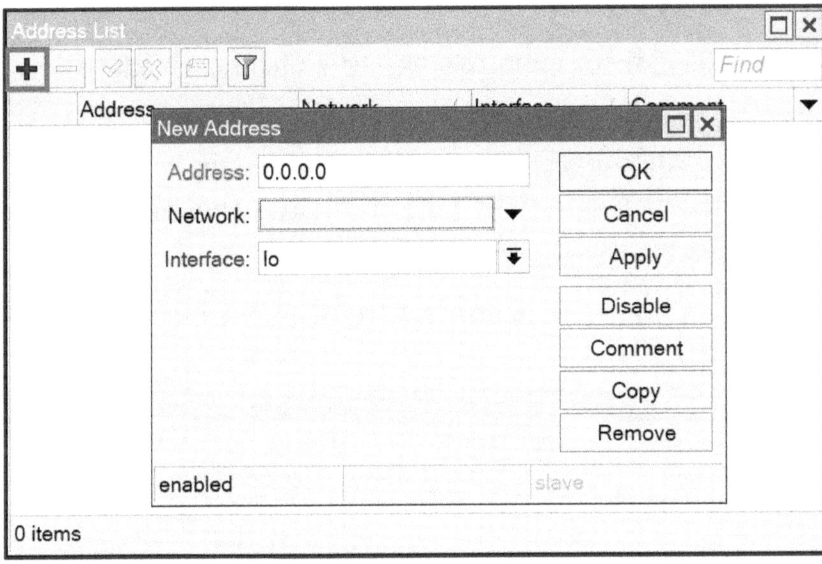

- In the **New Address** dialog box, enter the IP address along with the subnet mask 192.168.1.1/24 in the **Address** field, and select ether1 from the **Interface** field.

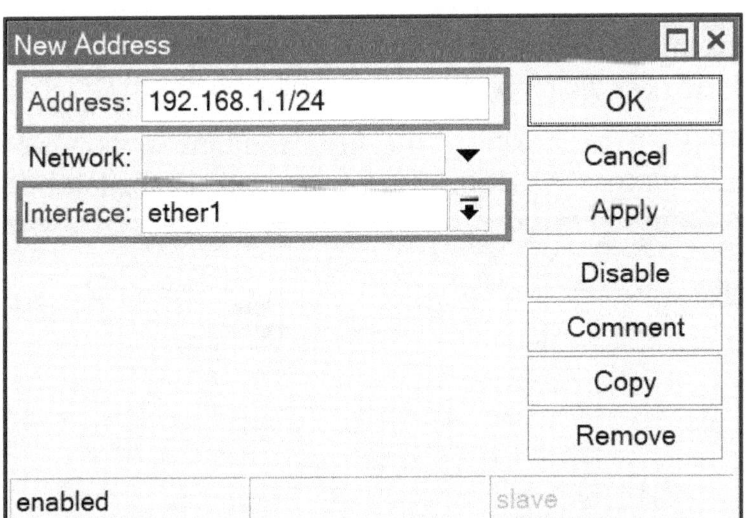

Note that you should enter the IP address along with the subnet mask as follows:

192.168.1.1/24

It is a common mistake to write the IP address without the subnet mask, like this:

192.168.1.1

- Then click the **OK** button to close the dialog box and assign the IP address to the interface.

Now, when you look at the **Address List** window, you will see the new IP address.

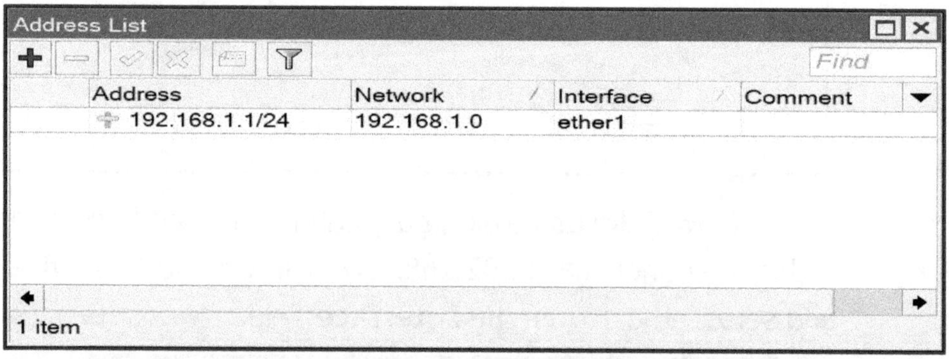

It is very important to learn how to read the information from this window to know which IP address is assigned to which interface.

Here in this lab, by looking at the **Address List** window, you can see that the IP address 192.168.1.1/24 is assigned to the interface ether1.

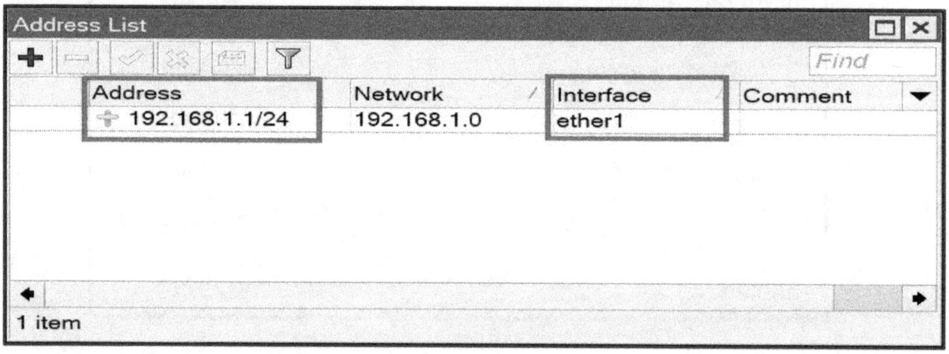

If you want to edit or change this address, (in case you entered the wrong number or forgot to enter the subnet mask for example), double-click it to open the **Address** settings dialog box and make the required changes.

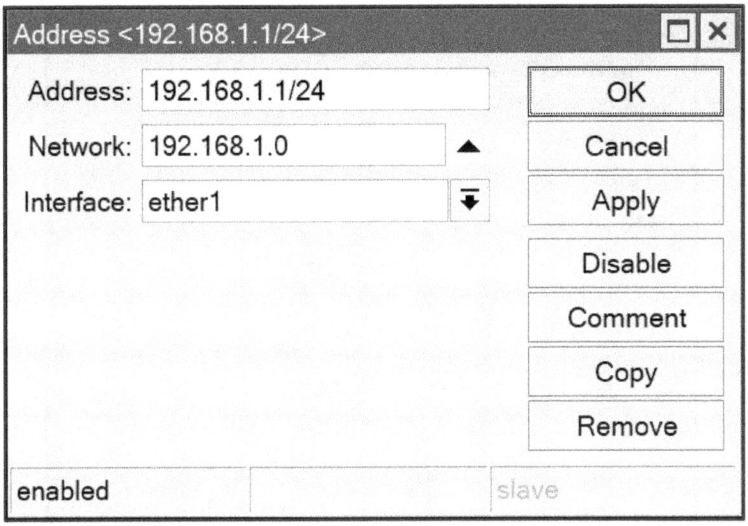

If you want to delete or remove this address, select it by single-click, and click the **Remove** button from the **Address List** window.

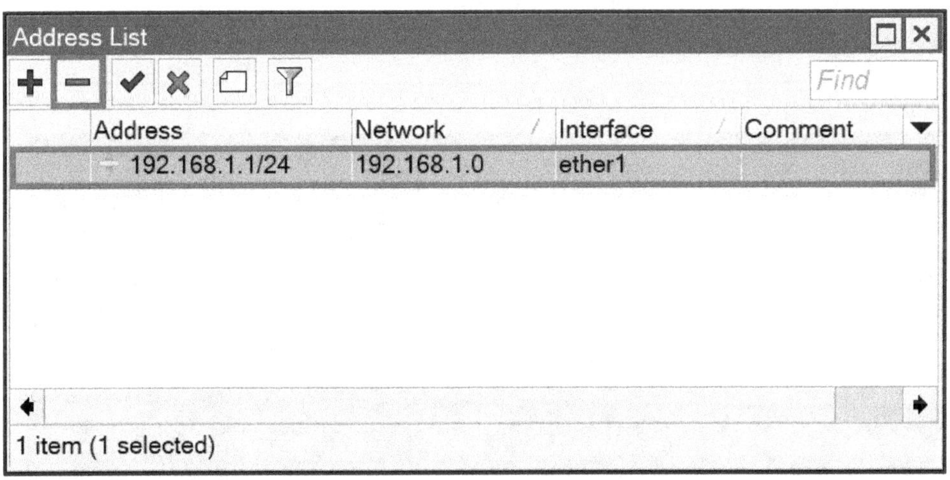

After finishing the configuration on the MikroTik device, assign the IP address 192.168.1.2/24 to your PC.

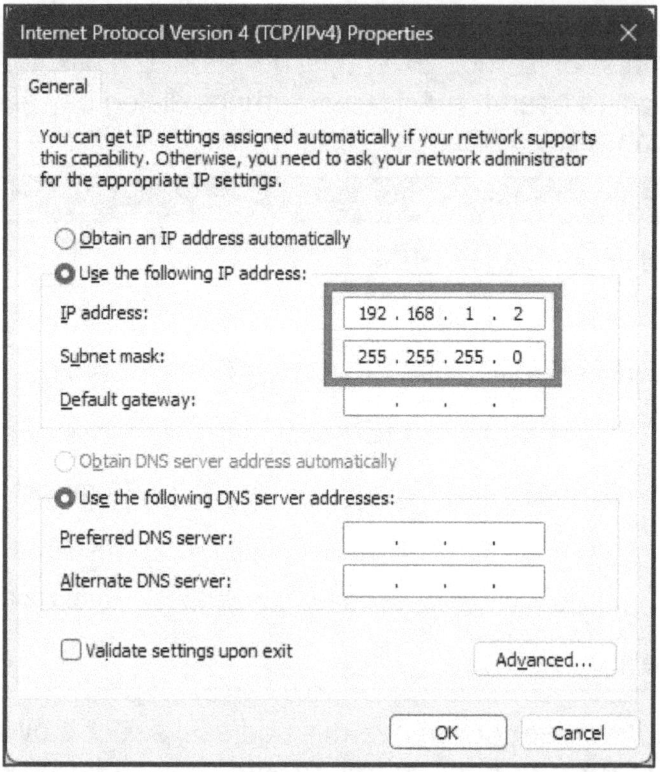

Now, check the connectivity by pinging the IP address 192.168.1.1 from your PC CLI.

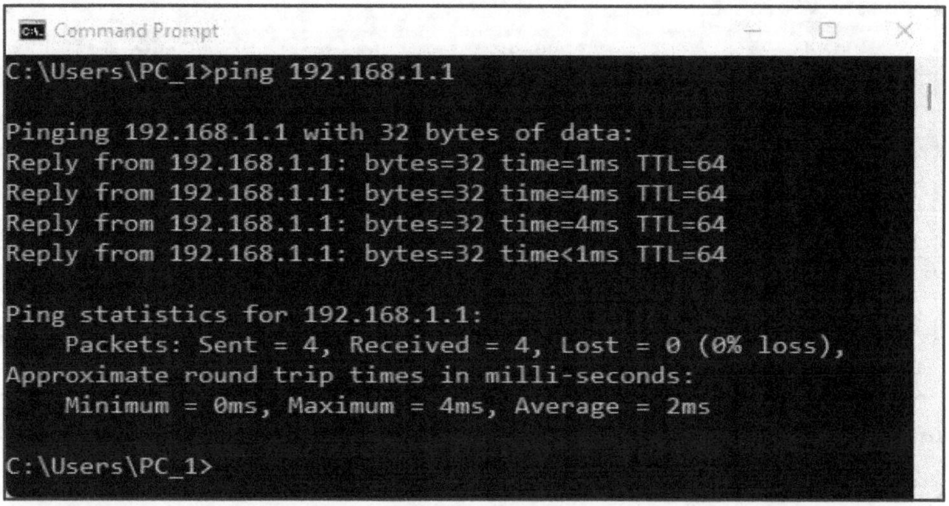

1.13 RouterOS GUI Principles

As mentioned, you can configure the device using the RouterOS GUI by clicking menus, buttons, checkboxes, etc. There are some common buttons you will see in most windows and dialog boxes.

1.14 Common Buttons

1.14.1 Add Button

This button is used to add a new item or configuration, (like adding a new IP address to the Address List window, as you did in the previous lab).

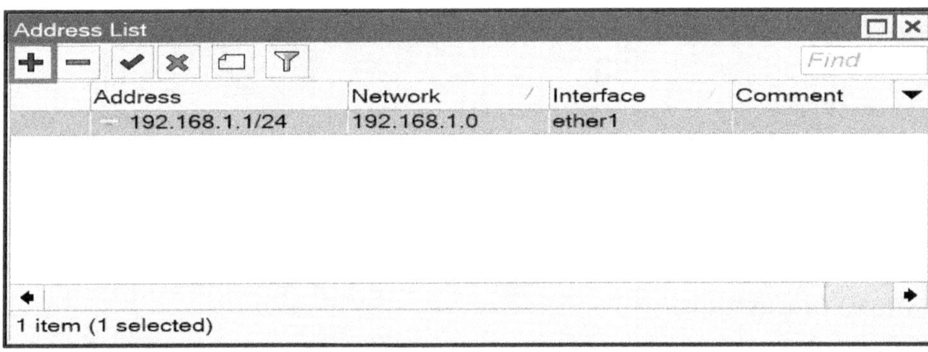

1.14.2 Remove Button

This button will remove the item or the configuration. For example, if you want to delete or remove the IP address assigned to an interface, select this IP address by single-click in the **Address List** window, then click the **Remove** button.

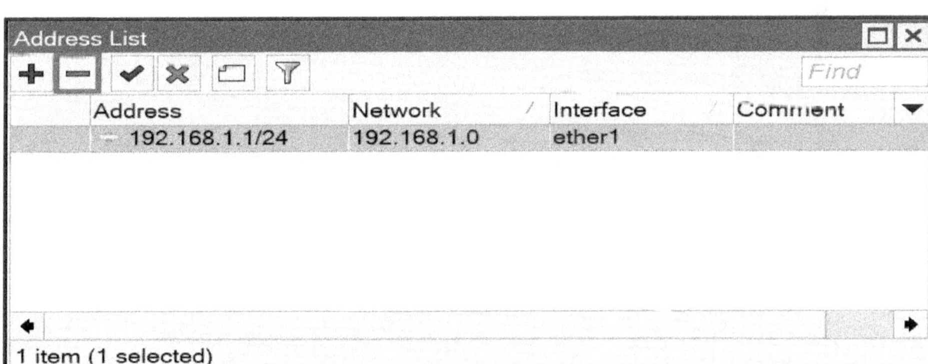

Or you can use the **Remove** button from the **Address** settings dialog box.

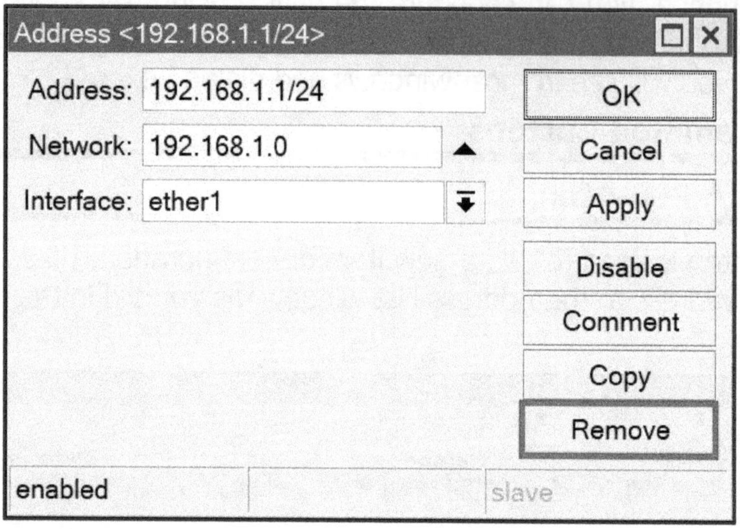

1.14.3 Disable Button

This button disables the item or the configuration, but does not remove or delete it.

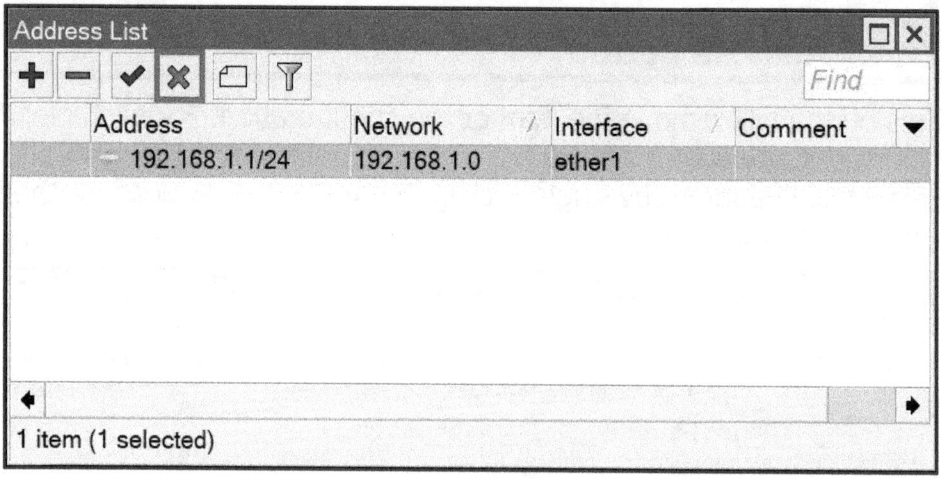

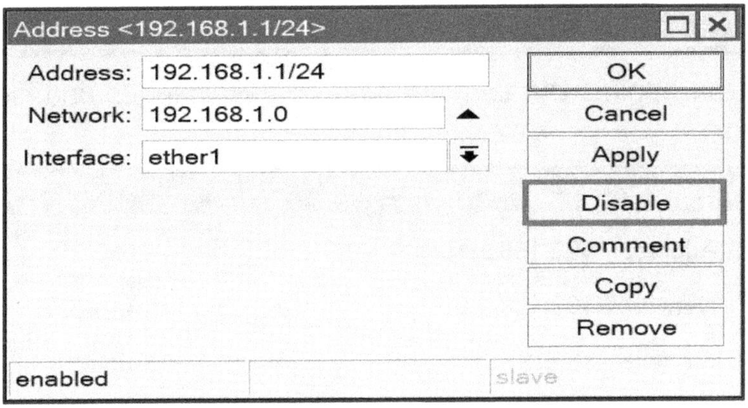

1.14.4 Enable Button

This button will re-enable the item which was disabled using the **Disable** button.

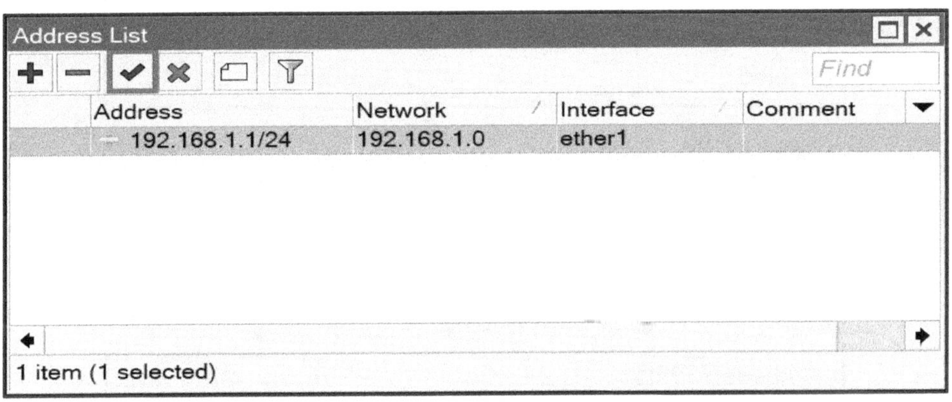

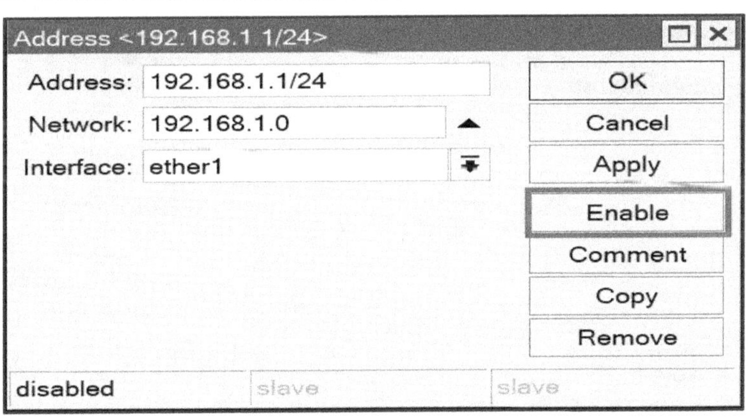

1.14.5 OK Button

This button applies the configuration or the changes and closes the dialog box.

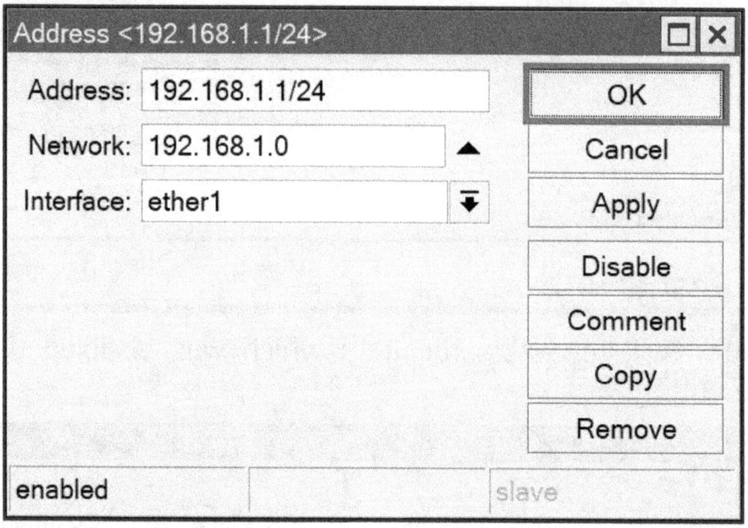

1.14.6 Cancel Button

This button will close the dialog box without applying any configuration or changes.

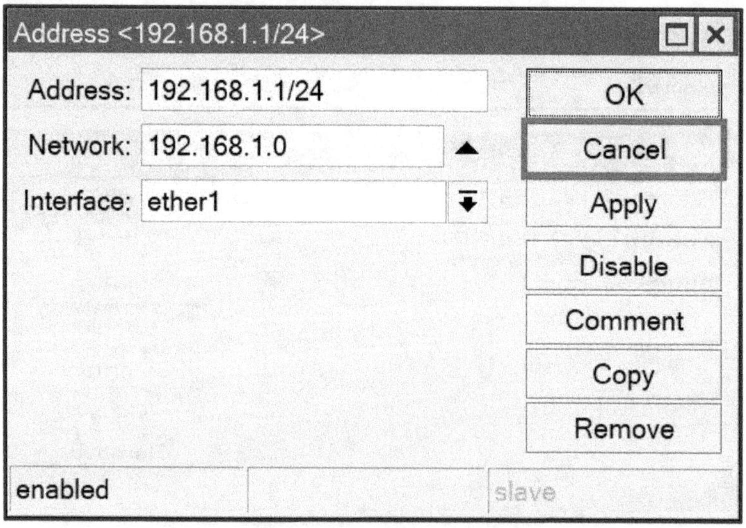

1.14.7 Apply Button

This button will apply the configuration and does not close the dialog box.

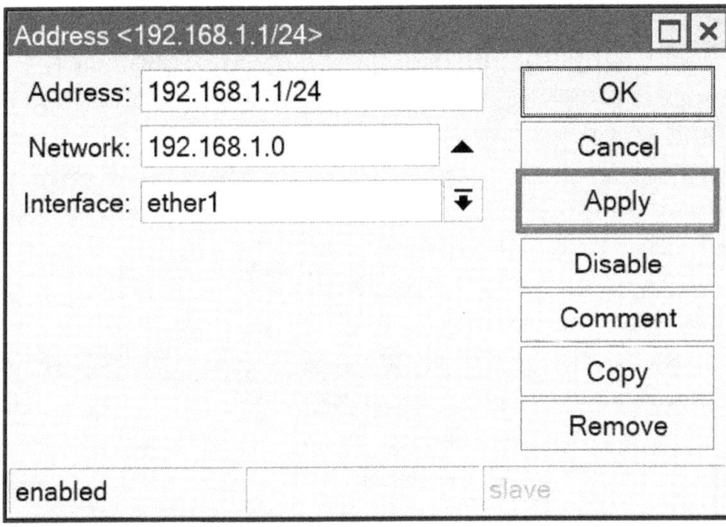

1.14.8 Copy Button

This button makes a copy of the current dialog box.

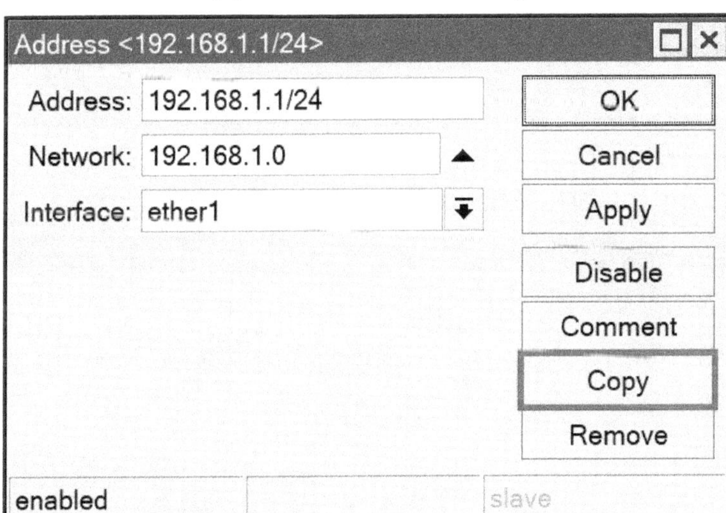

You can use this button when you need to configure multiple settings or add several items. For example, instead of repeating clicking the **Add** button to open the **New Address** dialog box, entering the IP address, clicking **OK** to close it, and then clicking **Add** again for the next IP address, you can click the **Apply** button to add the first IP address while keeping the dialog box open. Then, click the **Copy** button to open a new dialog box where you can enter the second IP address, and so on.

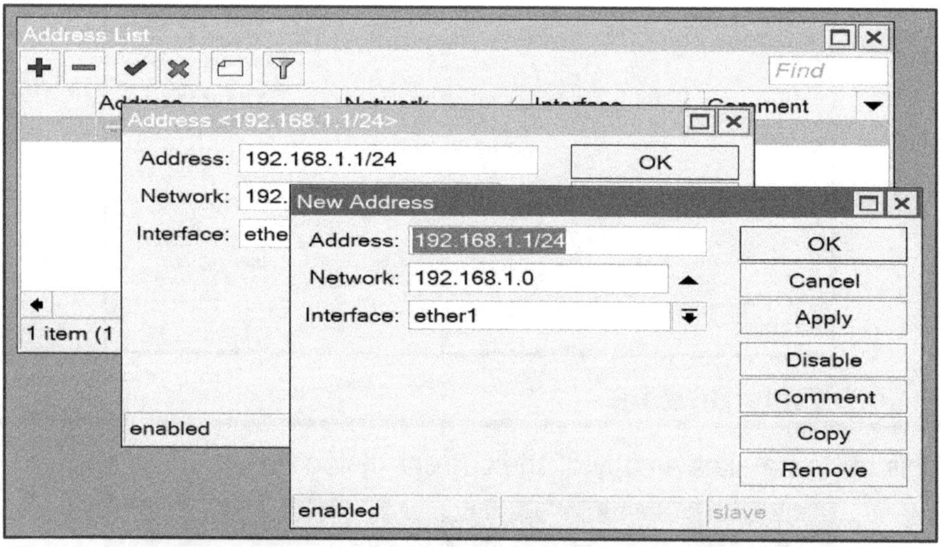

1.14.9 Comment Button

This button allows you to add helpful comments to remind you of the configuration you are making.

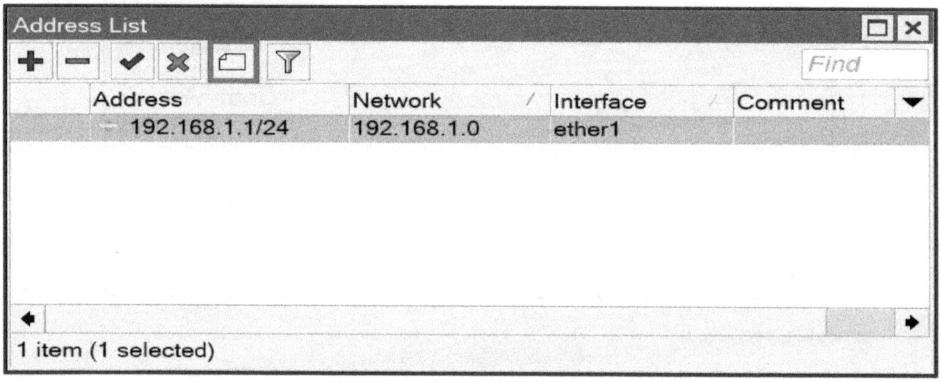

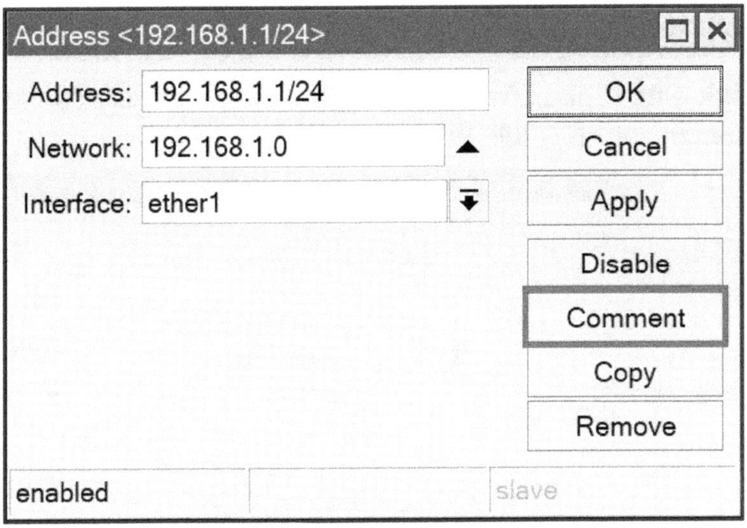

For example, when assigning an IP address to the interface ether1, you can add a comment like (This interface is connected to my PC), and ether2 is connected to a server or printers, and so on.

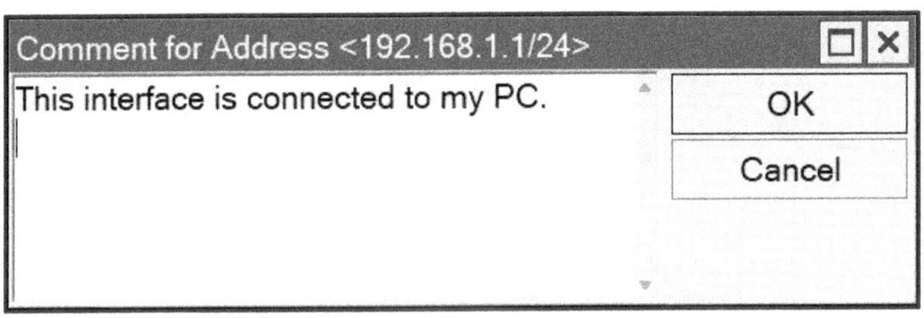

This comment will appear in the **Address List** window, making it easier for you to identify which interface is connected to which device.

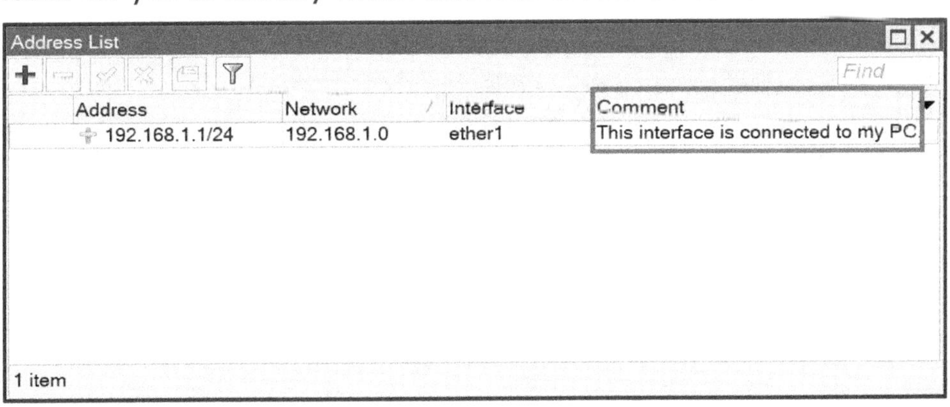

1.15 Quick Set

The **Quick Set** tool allows you to apply simple, basic configurations to the device from a single window.

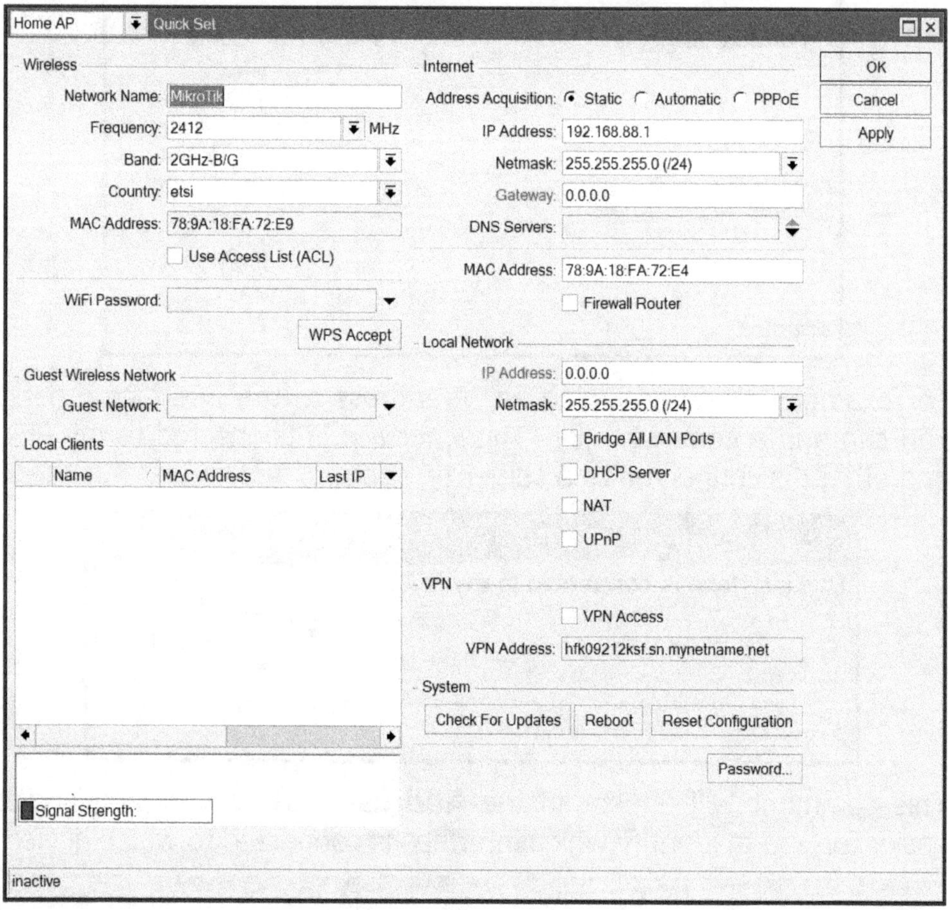

You can select a pre-set collection of configurations from the **Quickset** dropdown menu, based on the device model and its desired role in the network.

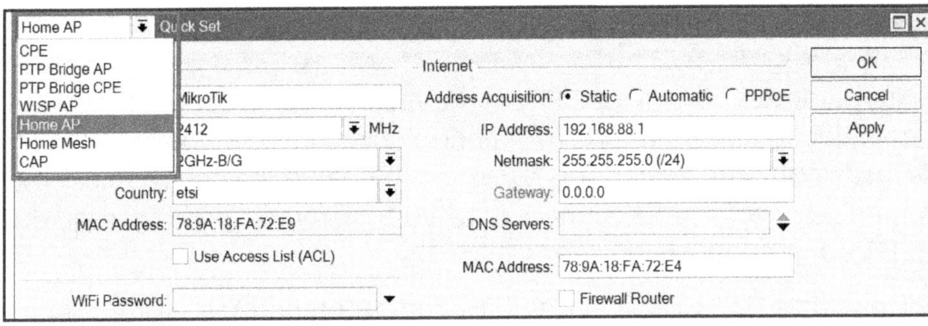

You can access this tool from WinBox and WebFig.

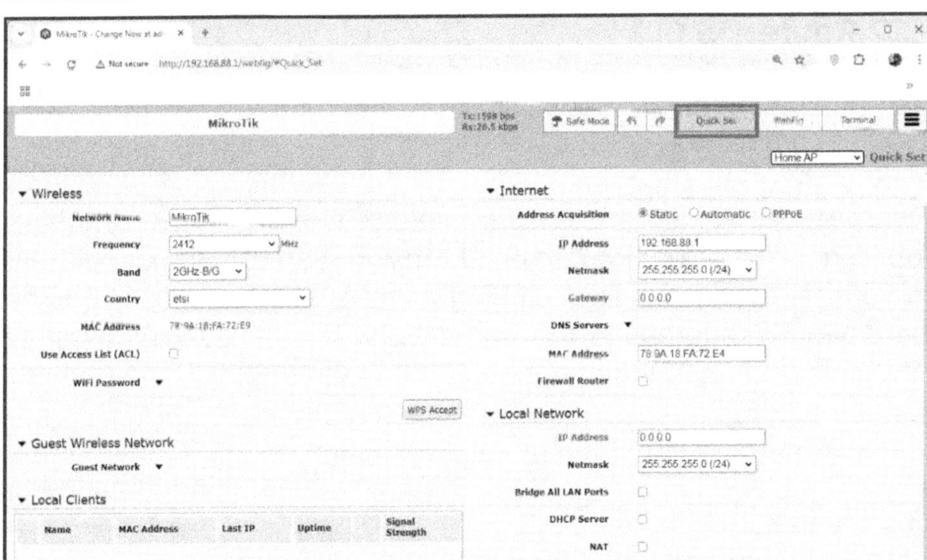

1.16 Default Configuration

MikroTik devices are shipped from the factory with a configuration that varies depending on the device model. This configuration is called the **default configuration**. It is designed to enable the device to operate immediately after you connect it to your network, without requiring additional setup.

For example, in SOHO devices (like the hAP model), a DHCP client is preconfigured on ether1, while a DHCP server is configured on the remaining interfaces and WiFi, using the subnet 192.168.88.0/24.

This means that when you connect the internet source to ether1, the device will obtain an IP address from the ISP and share the internet connection through the other interfaces.

In most cases, you may need to add additional configurations or remove the default configuration to configure the device according to your network specific requirements.

Note: In the default configuration, you cannot use interface ether1 to connect to the device using WinBox. You can use any other interface instead.

1.17 RouterOS CLI

You can configure MikroTik RouterOS using the CLI by executing the relevant commands.

1.17.1 SSH and Telnet

You can access the RouterOS CLI using SSH or Telnet with an appropriate application like PuTTY. To access the RouterOS CLI, enter the device IP address in the application. This IP address must be reachable from your PC.

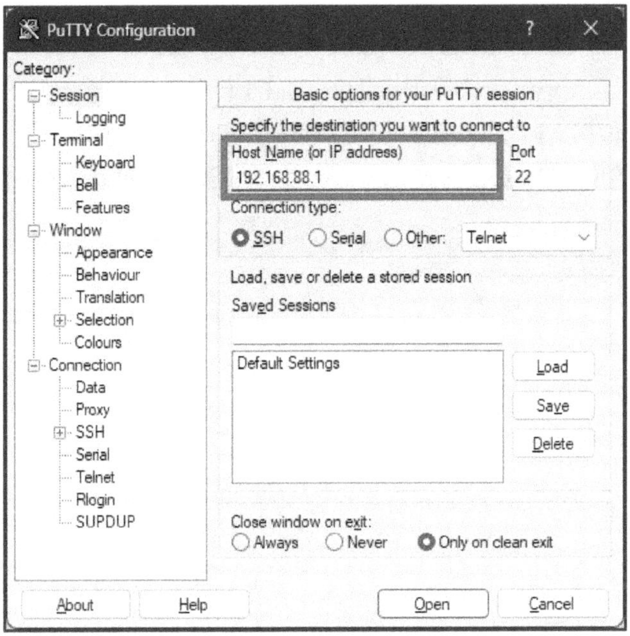

If the device does not have an IP address, you should first use WinBox to access the device by its MAC address. Then, assign an IP address to one of the device interfaces to enable access to the CLI using SSH or Telnet.

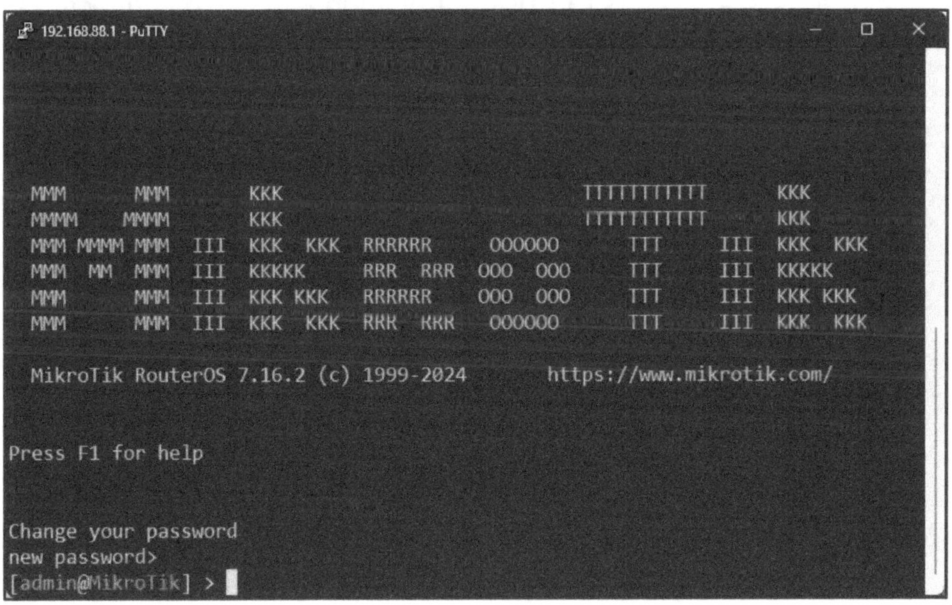

1.17.2 New Terminal in WinBox and WebFig

You can also access the RouterOS CLI from the GUI when using WinBox or WebFig by using the **New Terminal** tool.

1.17.3 Null Modem Cable

You can access RouterOS CLI using a null modem cable connected to the device serial port, along with a terminal emulation program like HyperTerminal on Windows.

This method is primarily used for initial setup or recovery configuration.

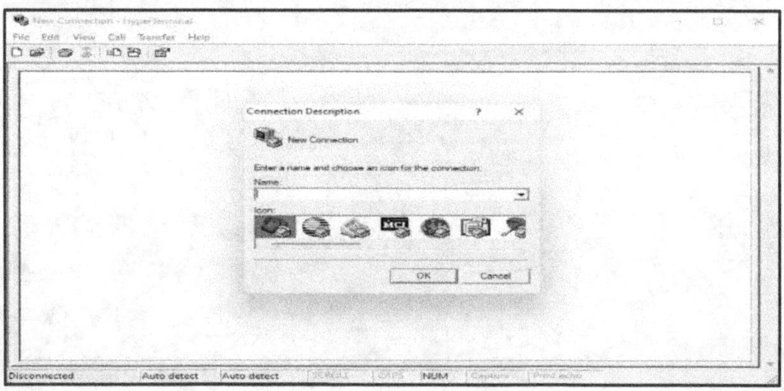

The default settings of MikroTik RouterBOARD serial port:

- 115200 bits/s (for x86 default is 9600 bits/s).
- 8 data bits.
- 1 stop bit.
- No parity.
- Hardware (RTS/CTS) flow control.

1.18 RouterOS CLI Principles

To execute commands in the RouterOS CLI, enter the commands in the correct order with the required parameters.

Let's study the following lab to learn how to configure a MikroTik device using the CLI.

LAB

In this lab, you have a MikroTik device connected to a PC via the interface ether1.

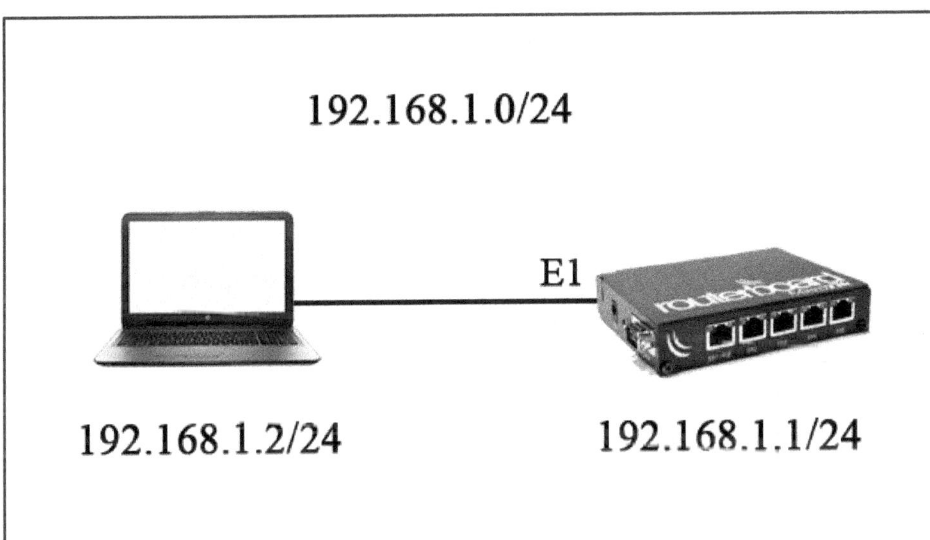

You want to assign the IP address 192.168.1.1/24 to the interface ether1 of the MikroTik device, and the IP address 192.168.1.2/24 to the PC. Then, you will check the connectivity between the two devices using the ping command.

In this lab, you will use the CLI to configure the MikroTik device and assign an IP address to its interface. The device has no configuration and has the default username (admin) without a password. So you have to use WinBox and access GUI first, and click the **New Terminal** Menu to open the **New Terminal** window to access the CLI.

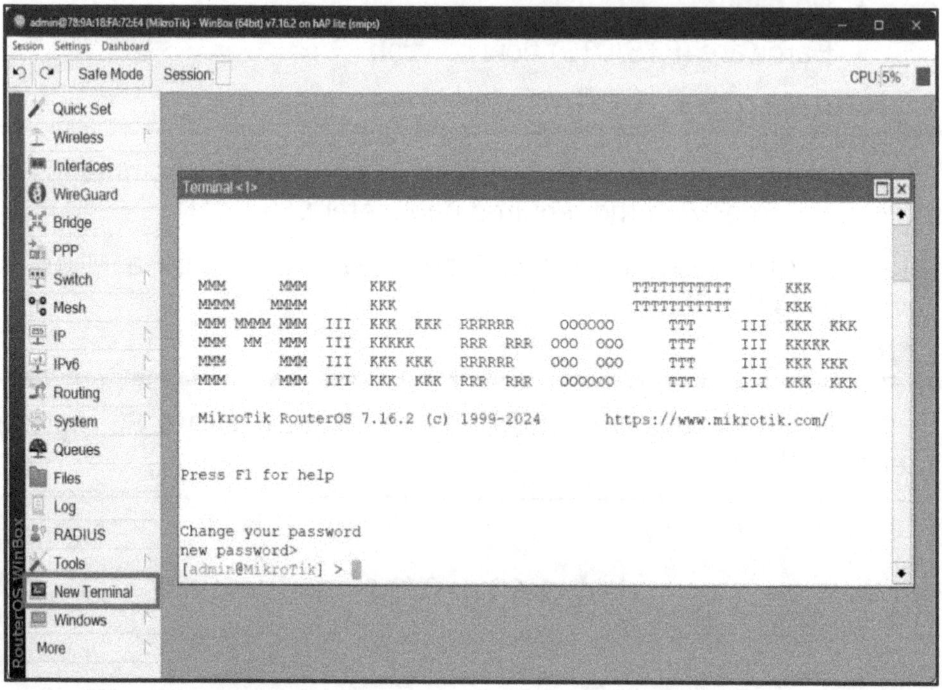

To assign an IP address to a MikroTik device interface using the CLI, you will follow steps similar to those used with the GUI. When assigning an IP address to an interface using the GUI, you followed these steps:

- Clicked on the **IP** menu.
- Clicked on **Addresses**.
- Clicked on the **Add** button from the **Address List** window.
- Entered the IP address in the **Address** field and selected ether1 in the **Interface** field in the **New Address** dialog box.

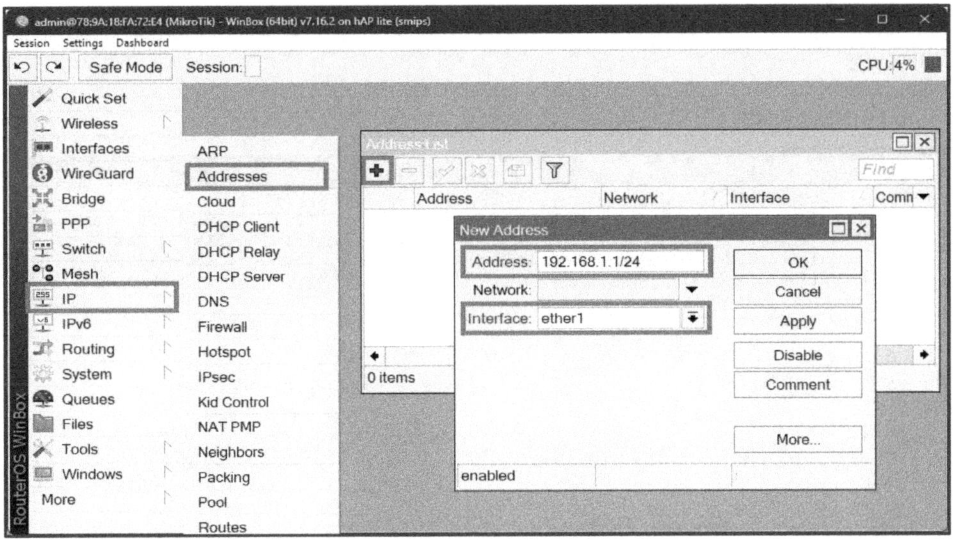

So, when assigning an IP address using the CLI, you will enter the command in a similar order:

- Type **ip**.
- Then type **addresses**.
- Then type **add**.
- After that, write the IP address using the **address=** command and specify the interface using **interface=** command.

The full command will be as follows:

```
ip address add address=192.168.1.1/24 interface=ether1
```

Then press Enter to execute the command.

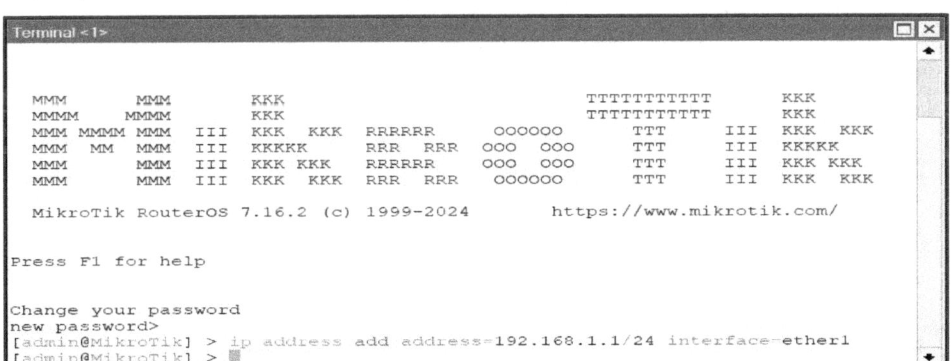

To display the address list from the CLI, use **Print** command as follows:

```
ip address print
```

```
  MMMM    MMMM       KKK                          TTTTTTTTTTT      KKK
  MMM MMMM MMM  III  KKK  KKK  RRRRRR     OOOOOO      TTT     III  KKK  KKK
  MMM  MM  MMM  III  KKKKK     RRR  RRR  OOO  OOO     TTT     III  KKKKK
  MMM      MMM  III  KKK KKK   RRRRRR    OOO  OOO     TTT     III  KKK KKK
  MMM      MMM  III  KKK  KKK  RRR  RRR   OOOOOO      TTT     III  KKK  KKK

  MikroTik RouterOS 7.16.2 (c) 1999-2024       https://www.mikrotik.com/


Press F1 for help


Change your password
new password>
[admin@MikroTik] > ip address add address=192.168.1.1/24 interface=ether1
[admin@MikroTik] > ip address print
Columns: ADDRESS, NETWORK, INTERFACE
# ADDRESS         NETWORK      INTERFACE
0 192.168.1.1/24  192.168.1.0  ether1
[admin@MikroTik] >
```

From the output of this command, you can see that the IP address 192.168.1.1/24 is assigned to the interface ether1.

```
new password>
[admin@MikroTik] > ip address add address=192.168.1.1/24 interface=ether1
[admin@MikroTik] > ip address print
Columns: ADDRESS, NETWORK, INTERFACE
# ADDRESS         NETWORK      INTERFACE
0 192.168.1.1/24  192.168.1.0  ether1
[admin@MikroTik] >
```

1.19 Hierarchical Structure

The commands in RouterOS CLI are organized in hierarchical groups, like menu levels. For example, to display the IP address list, you can write the command in one line as follows:

```
ip address print
```

```
[admin@MikroTik] >
[admin@MikroTik] >
[admin@MikroTik] >
[admin@MikroTik] >
[admin@MikroTik] > ip address print
```

Or you can break it down step by step:

- First: move to the IP level by typing the **ip** command and pressing Enter.

```
Terminal <1>
[admin@MikroTik] >
[admin@MikroTik] >
[admin@MikroTik] >
[admin@MikroTik] > ip
[admin@MikroTik] /ip>
```

- Then: in the IP level prompt, move to the Address submenu by typing **address** and pressing Enter.

```
Terminal <1>
[admin@MikroTik] >
[admin@MikroTik] >
[admin@MikroTik] > ip
[admin@MikroTik] /ip> address
[admin@MikroTik] /ip/address>
```

- Finally: in the Address level prompt, execute the **print** command to display the address list.

```
Terminal <1>
[admin@MikroTik] >
[admin@MikroTik] >
[admin@MikroTik] > ip
[admin@MikroTik] /ip> address
[admin@MikroTik] /ip/address> print
```

```
Terminal <1>
[admin@MikroTik] >
[admin@MikroTik] > ip
[admin@MikroTik] /ip> address
[admin@MikroTik] /ip/address> print
Columns: ADDRESS, NETWORK, INTERFACE
# ADDRESS          NETWORK       INTERFACE
0 192.168.1.1/24   192.168.1.0   ether1
[admin@MikroTik] /ip/address>
```

To move up to the main level, you can use the forward slash **/** symbol.

```
Terminal <1>
[admin@MikroTik] /ip/address>
[admin@MikroTik] /ip/address>
[admin@MikroTik] /ip/address>
[admin@MikroTik] /ip/address> /
[admin@MikroTik] >
```

To move up one level, you can use the two dots **..**.

```
Terminal <1>
[admin@MikroTik] /ip/address>
[admin@MikroTik] /ip/address>
[admin@MikroTik] /ip/address>
[admin@MikroTik] /ip/address> ..
[admin@MikroTik] /ip>
```

You can also use the forward slash / symbol to execute commands from other levels without having to move to that level.

For example, if you are at the system level and want to display the IP address list, you would normally need to move to the IP address level first and then use the **print** command.

```
Terminal <1>
[admin@MikroTik] /system>
[admin@MikroTik] /system> /
[admin@MikroTik] > ip
[admin@MikroTik] /ip> address
[admin@MikroTik] /ip/address> print
```

If you want to avoid moving to the IP address level, you can simply use the forward slash **/** to execute the command directly in system level

```
Terminal <1>
[admin@MikroTik] /system>
[admin@MikroTik] /system>
[admin@MikroTik] /system>
[admin@MikroTik] /system>
[admin@MikroTik] /system> /ip address print
```

1.20 Tips for Using CLI

You can use some techniques to help you write commands more easily in the RouterOS CLI.

When you write a command, you can use the **Tab** key on the keyboard to autocomplete the command.

For example, if you are at the IP address level and want to execute the print command, you can type the first letter of the command, **p** :

```
Terminal <1>
[admin@MikroTik] /ip/address>
[admin@MikroTik] /ip/address>
[admin@MikroTik] /ip/address>
[admin@MikroTik] /ip/address>
[admin@MikroTik] /ip/address> p
```

Then press the **Tab** key to autocomplete the command.

```
Terminal <1>
[admin@MikroTik] /ip/address>
[admin@MikroTik] /ip/address>
[admin@MikroTik] /ip/address>
[admin@MikroTik] /ip/address>
[admin@MikroTik] /ip/address> print
```

You can use the double tab to display the available commands, arguments, or parameters.

```
Terminal <1>
[admin@MikroTik] /ip/address>
add          edit          find          reset
comment      enable        print         set
disable      export        remove
[admin@MikroTik] /ip/address>
```

For example, if you are at the IP address level and want to know which commands can be executed at this level, you can press the **Tab** key twice to see those commands.

You can use the **F1** key on the keyboard in RouterOS v7, or the **F1** key and the question mark **?** in RouterOS v6, to display quick help about commands.

```
Terminal <1>
[admin@MikroTik] /ip/address>
[admin@MikroTik] /ip/address>

.. -- go up to ip
add -- Create a new item
comment -- Set comment for items
disable -- Disable items
edit --
enable -- Enable items
export -- Print or save an export script that can be used to restore configuration
find -- Find items by value
get -- Gets value of item's property
print -- Print values of item properties
remove -- Remove item
reset --
set -- Change item properties

Press F1 for general console usage help
[admin@MikroTik] /ip/address>
```

You can also navigate through previous commands using the **Up** ↑ and **Down** ↓ arrow keys.

1.21 Common Commands

1.21.1 Add Command

This command is used to add a new item or configuration, (like adding a new IP address as you did in the previous lab).

To use this command, first move to the CLI menu level where you want to add the new item or configuration, then type the command and follow it with the other parameters you want to add, depending on the item or configuration.

For example, to add or assign the IP address 192.168.1.1/24 to interface ether1, write the command as follows:

```
ip address add address=192.168.1.1/24 interface=ether1
```

```
Terminal <1>
[admin@MikroTik] >
[admin@MikroTik] >
[admin@MikroTik] > ip address add address=192.168.1.1/24 interface=ether1
```

1.21.2 Sequence Number.

When adding a new item or configuration, it will be listed with a sequence number starting from 0. To edit this item from the CLI, its sequence number will be used to select it.

For example, when you add or assign an IP address to an interface, this IP address will be listed in the address menu with sequence number 0.

```
Terminal <1>
[admin@MikroTik] >
[admin@MikroTik] >
[admin@MikroTik] > ip address print
Columns: ADDRESS, NETWORK, INTERFACE
# ADDRESS          NETWORK       INTERFACE
0 192.168.1.1/24   192.168.1.0   ether1
[admin@MikroTik] >
```

If you add or assign another IP address to another interface, this IP address will be listed with sequence number 1, and so on.

```
Terminal <1>
[admin@MikroTik] >
[admin@MikroTik] > ip address print
Columns: ADDRESS, NETWORK, INTERFACE
# ADDRESS          NETWORK       INTERFACE
0 192.168.1.1/24   192.168.1.0   ether1
1 192.168.2.1/24   192.168.2.0   ether2
[admin@MikroTik] >
```

To edit an IP address, you will use its sequence number to select it.

1.21.3 Print Command

This command displays information about items or configurations in RouterOS.

To use this command, first move to the CLI menu level where you want to display its configuration, then type the command.

For example, if you want to display the current IP address configured on the device, write the command as follows:

```
ip address print
```

```
Terminal <1>
[admin@MikroTik] >
[admin@MikroTik] > ip address print
Columns: ADDRESS, NETWORK, INTERFACE
# ADDRESS          NETWORK       INTERFACE
0 192.168.1.1/24   192.168.1.0   ether1
1 192.168.2.1/24   192.168.2.0   ether2
[admin@MikroTik] >
```

1.21.4 Remove Command

This command is used to remove the item or the configuration.

To use this command, first move to the CLI menu level where the item or configuration exists, then type the command and follow it with the sequence number of the item.

For example, if you want to delete or remove the IP address assigned to interface ether1, write the command as follows:

```
ip address remove numbers=0
```

```
Terminal <1>
[admin@MikroTik] >
[admin@MikroTik] >
[admin@MikroTik] > ip address remove numbers=0
```

You can find the sequence number of the item by using the Print command.

```
ip address print
```

```
Terminal <1>
[admin@MikroTik] >
[admin@MikroTik] > ip address print
Columns: ADDRESS, NETWORK, INTERFACE
# ADDRESS          NETWORK       INTERFACE
0 192.168.1.1/24   192.168.1.0   ether1
1 192.168.2.1/24   192.168.2.0   ether2
[admin@MikroTik] >
```

1.21.5 Disable Command

This command disables the item or the configuration, but does not remove or delete it.

To use this command, first move to the CLI menu level where the item or configuration exists, then type the command and follow it with the sequence number of the item.

For example, if you want to disable the IP address assigned to interface ether1, write the command as follows:

```
ip address disable numbers=0
```

```
Terminal <1>
[admin@MikroTik] >
[admin@MikroTik] >
[admin@MikroTik] > ip address disable numbers=0
```

1.21.6 Enable Command

This command will re-enable the item which was disabled using the **Disable** command.

To use this command, first move to the CLI menu level where the item or configuration exists, then type the command and follow it with the sequence number of the item.

For example, if you want to enable the IP address which you disabled before, write the command as follows:

```
ip address enable numbers=0
```

```
Terminal <1>
[admin@MikroTik] >
[admin@MikroTik] >
[admin@MikroTik] > ip address enable numbers=0
```

1.21.7 Comment Command

This command allows you to add helpful comments to remind you of the configuration you are making.

To use this command, first move to the CLI menu level where the item or configuration exists, then type the command and follow it with the sequence number of the item and the parameter command=, followed by the comment you want to add.

For example, if you want to add a comment to the IP address assigned to interface ether1, write the command as follows:

```
ip address comment numbers=0 comment="This interface is connected to
my PC"
```

```
Terminal <1>
[admin@MikroTik] >
[admin@MikroTik] >
[admin@MikroTik] > ip address comment numbers=0 comment="This interface is connected to my PC"
```

This comment will also appear when using print command.

```
Terminal <1>
[admin@MikroTik] > ip address print
Columns: ADDRESS, NETWORK, INTERFACE
# ADDRESS           NETWORK      INTERFACE
;;; This interface is connected to my PC
0 192.168.1.1/24  192.168.1.0  ether1
1 192.168.2.1/24  192.168.2.0  ether2
[admin@MikroTik] >
```

1.21.8 Set Command

This command allows you to edit or change the item or the configuration settings.

To use this command, first move to the CLI menu level where the item or configuration exists, then type the command and follow it with the sequence number of the item and the parameter of the property or setting you want to change, followed by the new value for that setting.

For example, if you want to change the IP address assigned to interface ether1, write the command as follows:

```
ip address set numbers=0 address=192.168.10.1/24
```

```
Terminal <1>
[admin@MikroTik] >
[admin@MikroTik] >
[admin@MikroTik] > ip address set numbers=0 address=192.168.10.1/24
```

If you want to change the interface to ether3, write the command as follows:

```
ip address set numbers=0 interface=ether3
```

```
Terminal <1>
[admin@MikroTik] >
[admin@MikroTik] >
[admin@MikroTik] > ip address set numbers=0 interface=ether3
```

1.22 Router Identity

The Identity property is used to give RouterOS a name to identify it in the network.

You can change RouterOS Identity by using the **Identity** dialog box.

To open the **Identity** dialog box, click the **System** menu, then select **Identity**.

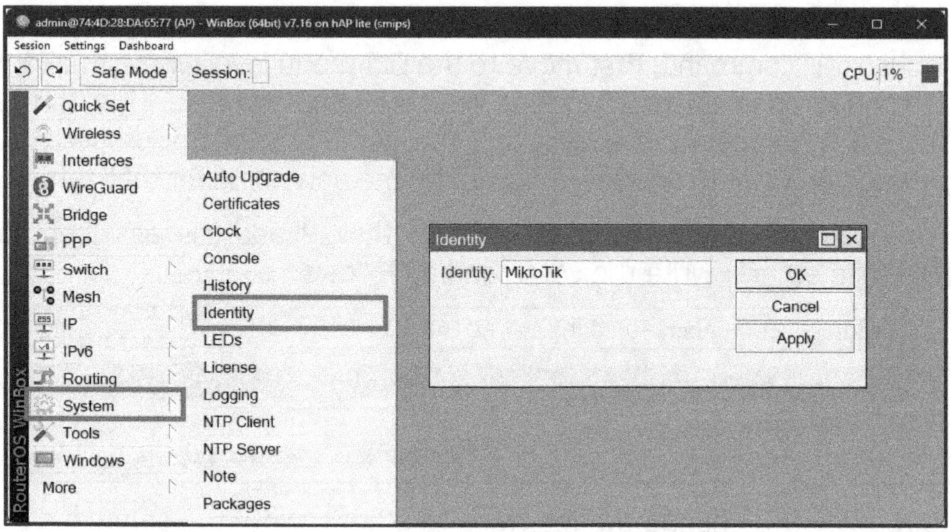

To change the name or the identity of RouterOS, enter the desired name in the **Identity** field in this dialog box and click the **OK** button.

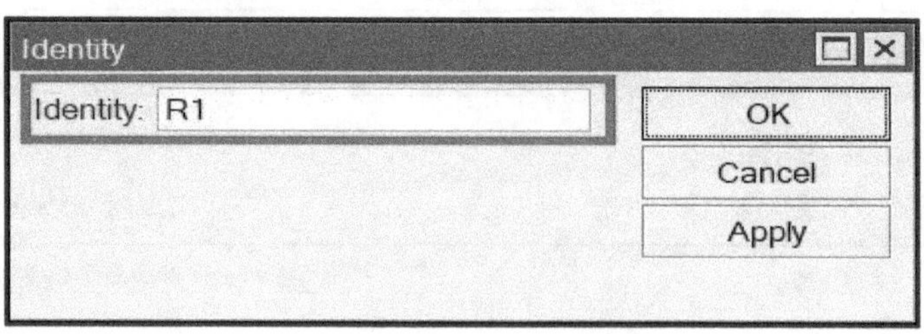

After changing the identity, the new identity will appear in the WinBox window, title bar, and in the CLI prompt as well.

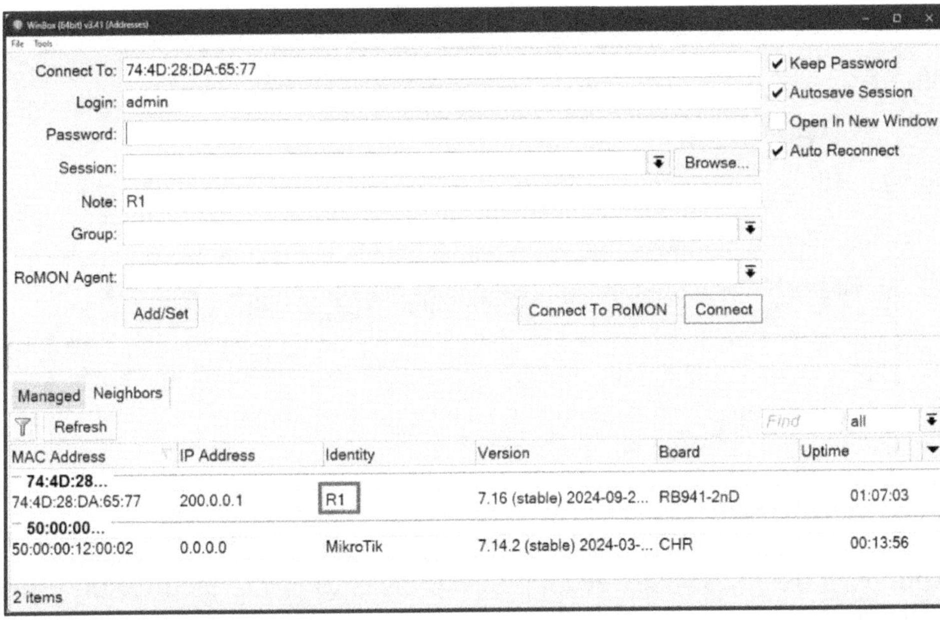

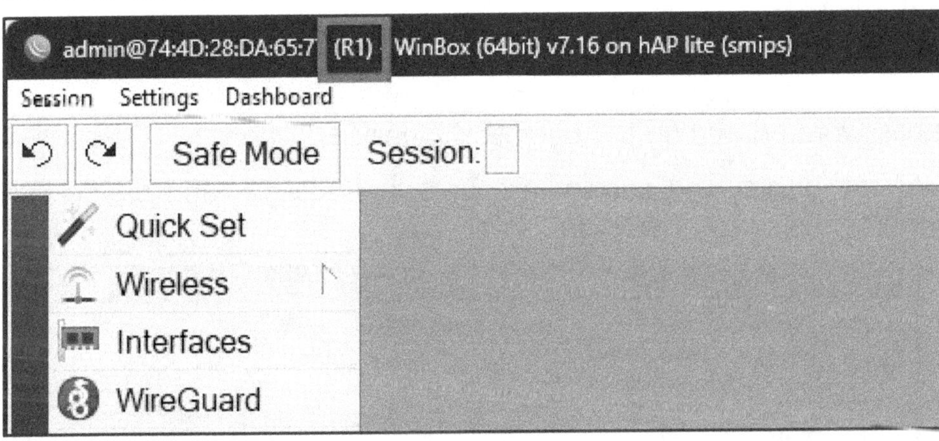

You can also change RouterOS identity from the CLI using the following command:

```
system identity set name=[name]
```

Where:

- [name] is the desired name.

For example:

```
system identity set name=R1
```

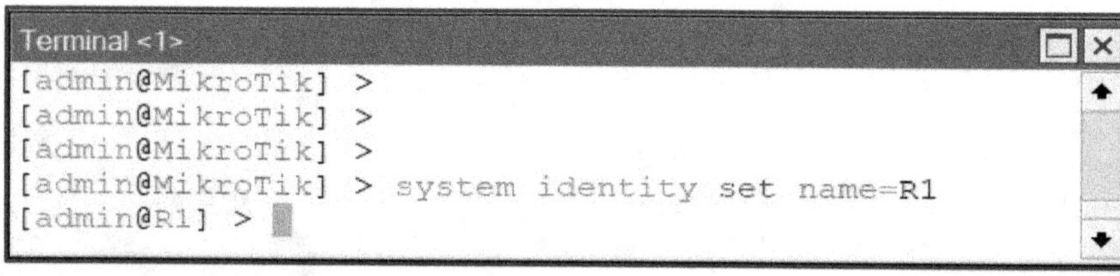

1.23 RouterOS User Accounts

RouterOS users, or user accounts, are used to log in to the RouterOS GUI and CLI.

The default account uses the username admin. In the past, this account had no password. but recently, new devices are shipped with a password printed on the back of the device.

You can display the current accounts in RouterOS and create new accounts using the **User List** window.

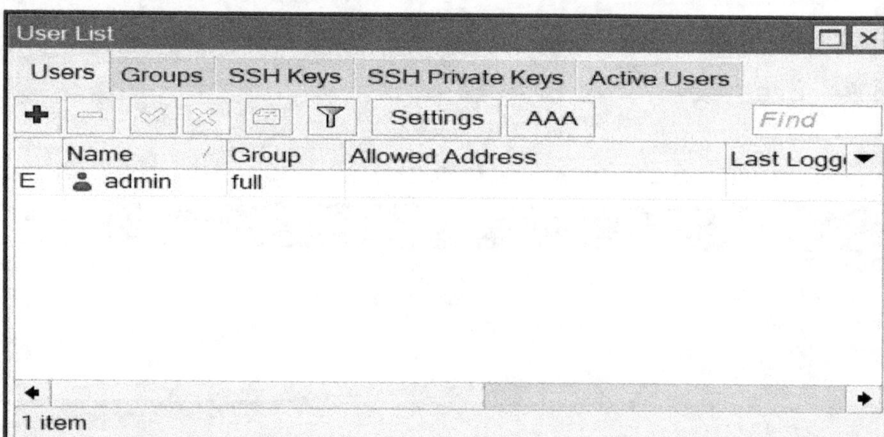

To open the **User List** window, click the **System** menu then select **Users**.

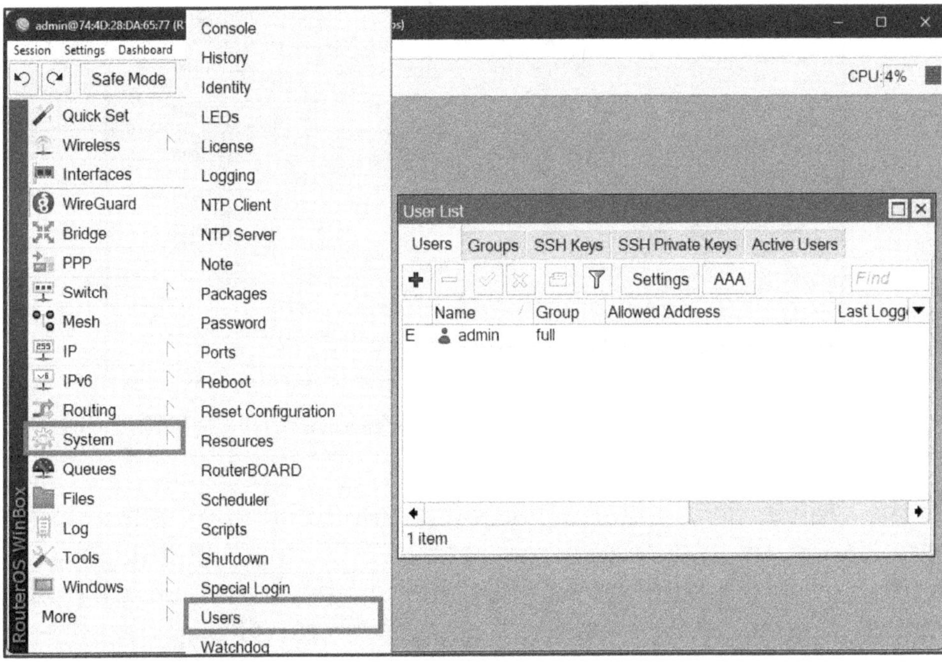

You can also display the current accounts in RouterOS from the CLI using the following command:

```
user print
```

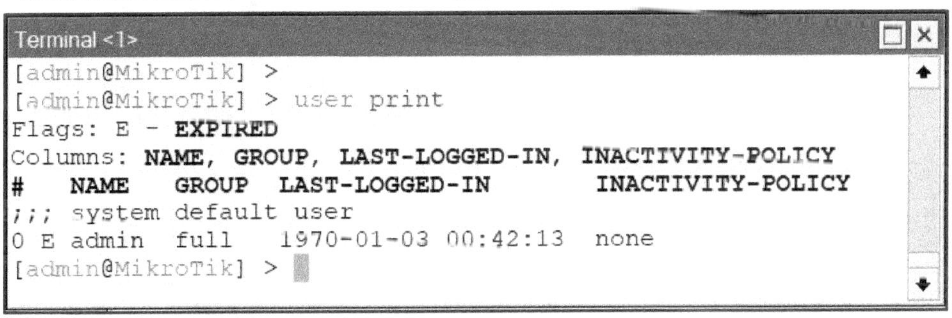

To create a new user account, click the **Add** button in the **Users** tab of the **User List** window to open the **New User** dialog box.

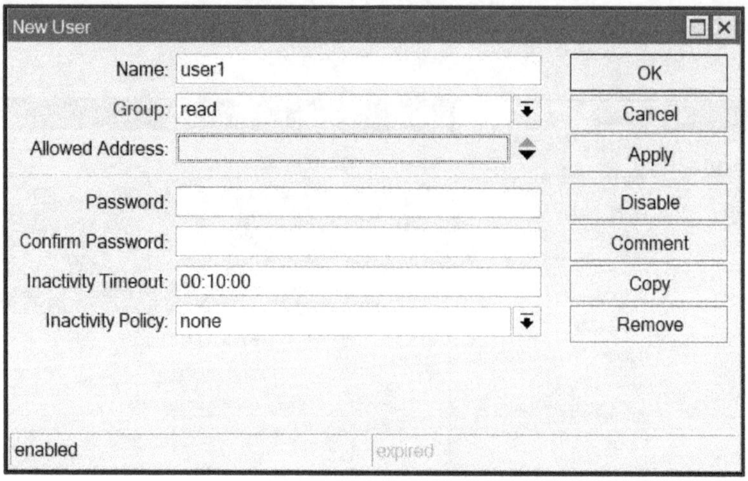

You can use this dialog box to add a new account and configure its different properties.

In the **Name** field, enter a name for the account. You can assign permissions to this account to **read**, (or display information), or **write**, (or modify settings but not manage other users), or **full** (to full control the device) by choosing a group from the **Group** field. In the **Password** and **Confirm Password** fields, enter the password for the account.

Note: both the **Name** and the **Password** are case-sensitive.

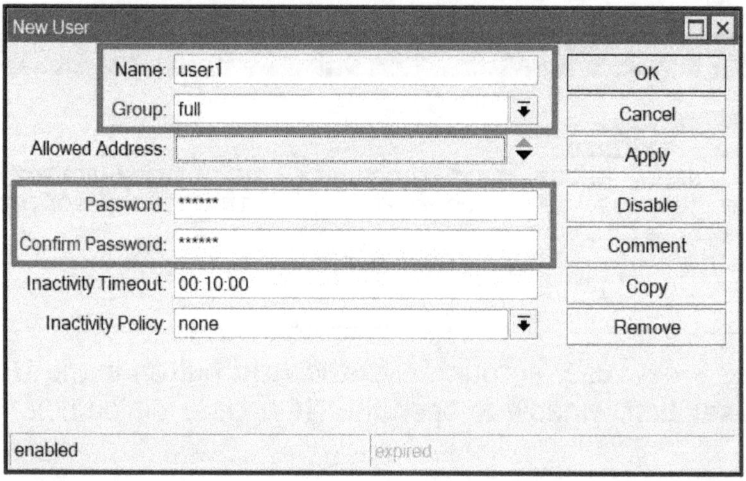

You can also create a new set of permissions by creating a new group and choosing the desired permissions.

To create a new group, click the **Add** button in the **Groups** tab of the **User List** window to open the **New Group** dialog box. Then, choose the desired settings for the group.

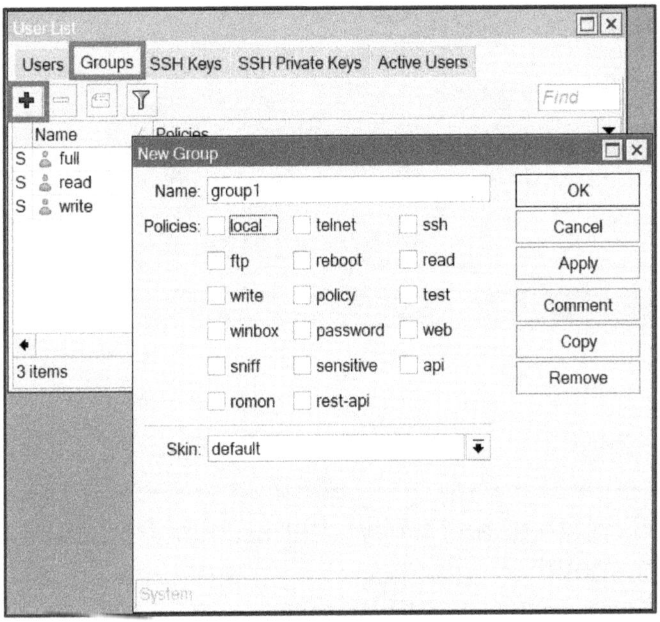

After creating the account, it will appear in the **User List** window.

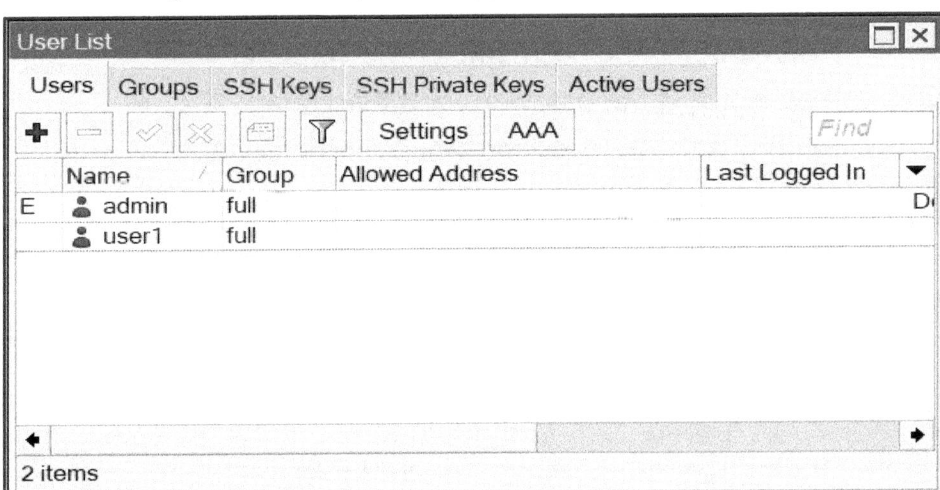

When using this account to log in to RouterOS, the username will appear in the title bar of the WinBox window and in the CLI prompt as well.

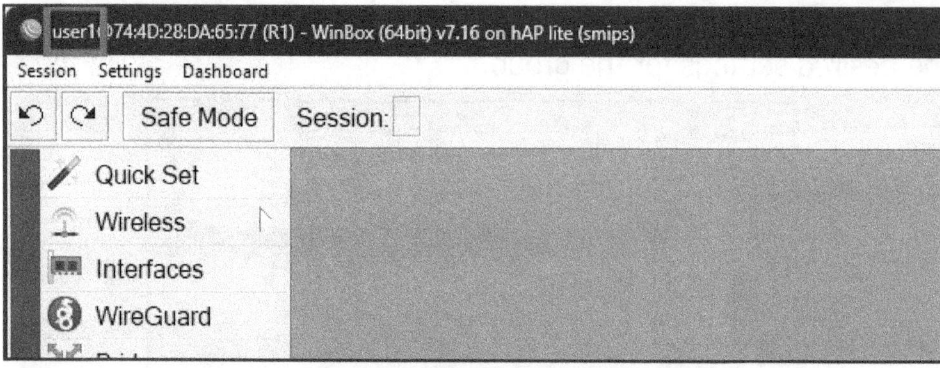

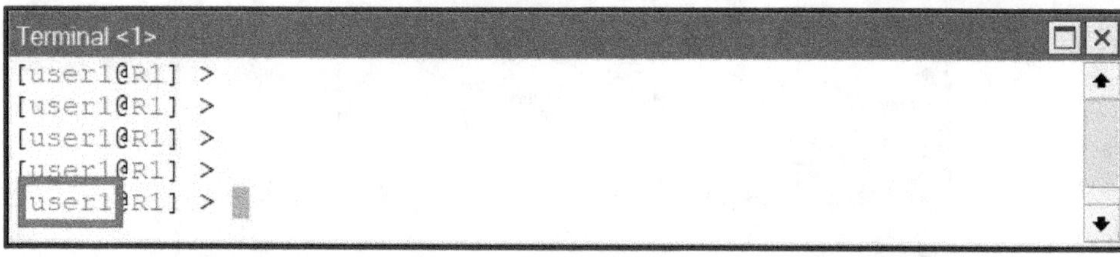

You can also create or add a new user account from the CLI using the following command:

```
user add name=[username] password=[password] group=[group]
```

Where:

- [username] is the username of the account.
- [password] is the password of the account..
- [group] is the permissions group for the account.

For example:

```
user add name=user1 password=1234 group=read
```

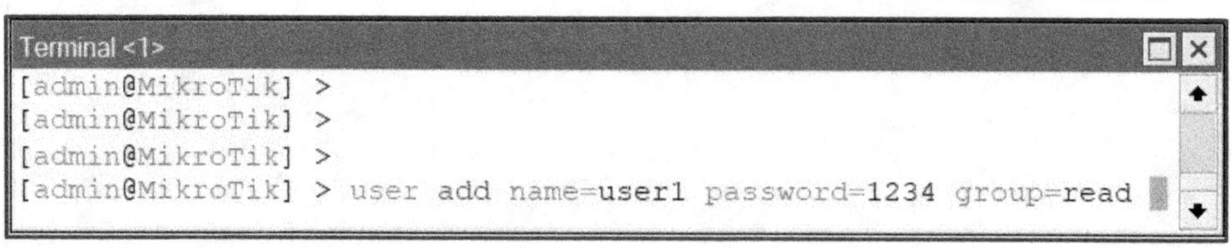

1.24 RouterOS Services

The **IP Services list** window displays the services that RouterOS is using, along with the corresponding protocols and ports, such as FTP or Telnet services.

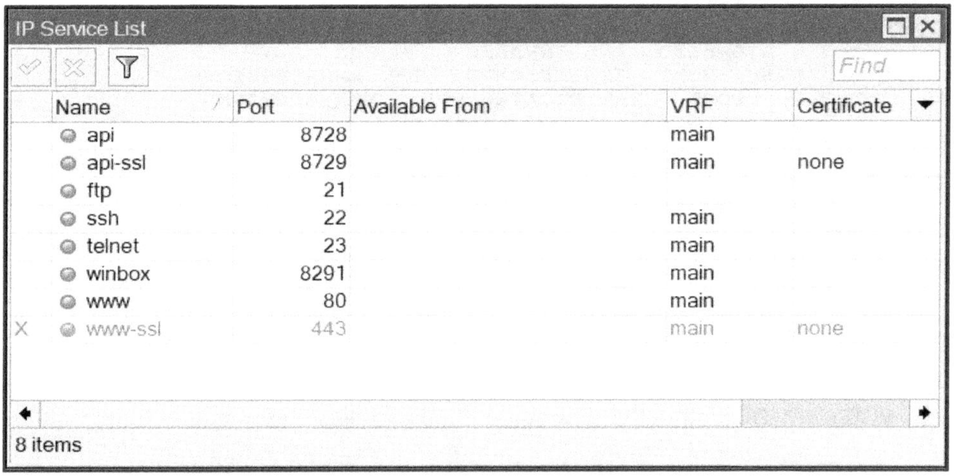

To open **IP Service List** window, click the **IP** menu, then select **Services**

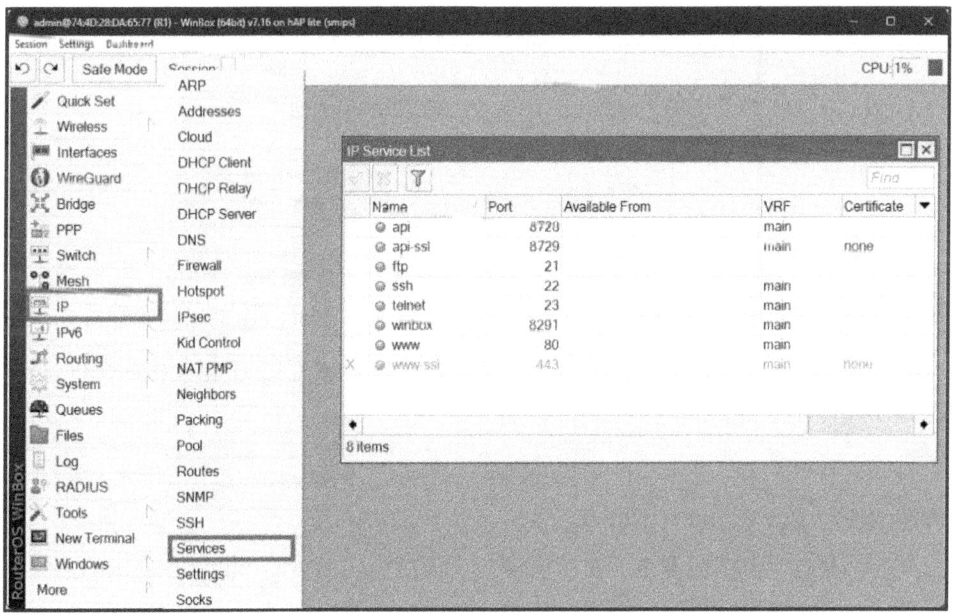

You can also display the IP services in RouterOS from the CLI using the following command:

```
ip service print
```

```
Terminal <1>
[admin@MikroTik] >
[admin@MikroTik] > ip service print
Flags: X - DISABLED, I - INVALID
Columns: NAME, PORT, CERTIFICATE, VRF, MAX-SESSIONS
#   NAME      PORT  CERTIFICATE   VRF   MAX-SESSIONS
0   telnet      23                main            20
1   ftp         21                                20
2   www         80                main            20
3   ssh         22                main            20
5   api       8728                main            20
6   winbox    8291                main            20
7   api-ssl   8729  none          main            20

[admin@MikroTik] >
```

You can disable or enable any of these services or change their ports, but you cannot add a new service to this list.

For example, if you want to change the port number of the www service, double-click the service in **IP Service List** window to open the service dialog box.

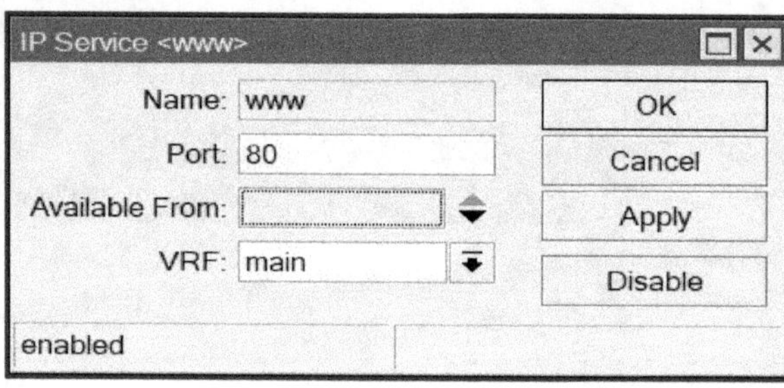

In the **Port** field, enter the desired port number, then click **OK**.

You can also change the port number from the CLI using the following command:

```
ip service set [service] port=[number]
```

Where:

- [service] is the service you want to change its port number.
- [number] is the desired number.

For example:

```
ip service set www port=8080
```

1.25 Configuration Backups

When configuring RouterOS and applying different settings and commands, you do not need to do any additional steps to save these settings; the configuration is automatically saved.

After configuring RouterOS, you can create a backup of these configurations to use it whenever needed. For example, you can take these configurations and apply them to another device or re-apply them to the same device if something happens or if you change the configuration and want to restore the old configuration back.

There are three methods to create a backup of the settings:

- Create a backup file.
- Create a script.
- Store the backup online.

1.25.1 Create a Backup File

To create a backup file, use the **File List** window.

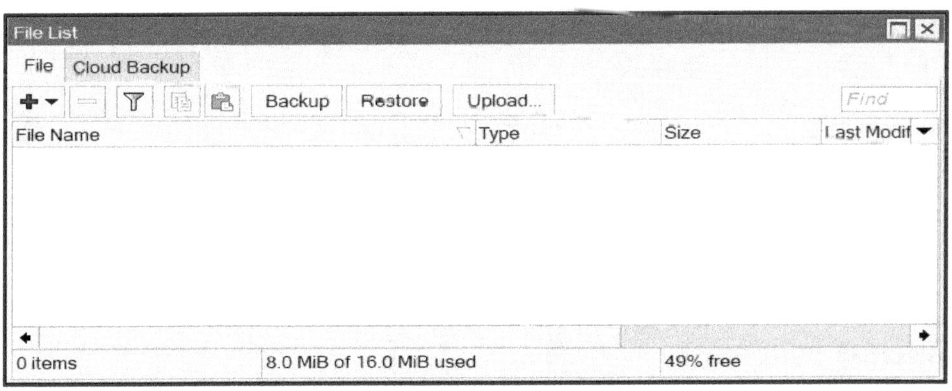

To open the **File List** window, click the **Files** menu.

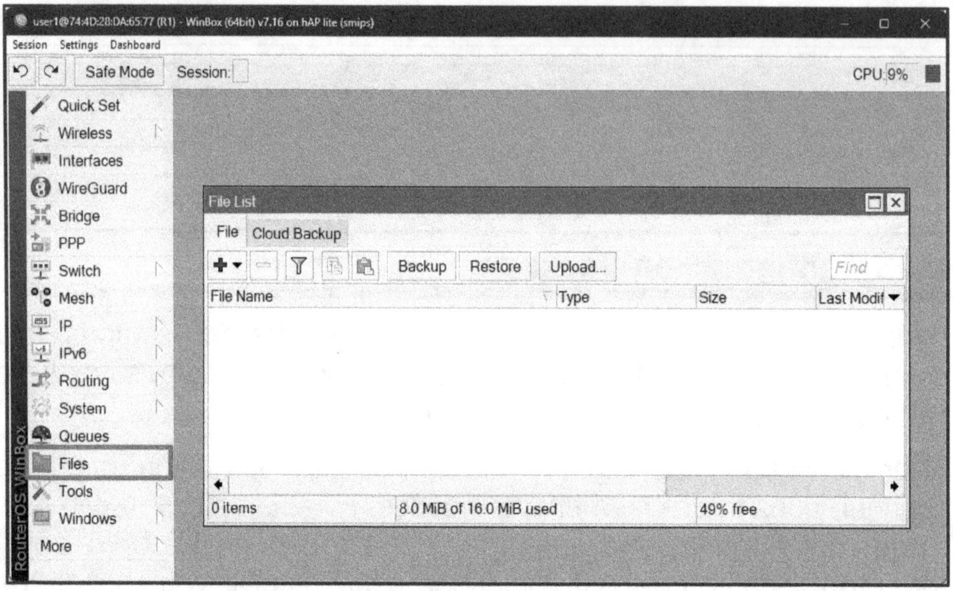

To create a backup file, click the **Backup** button in the **File** tab of the **File List** window to open the **Backup** dialog box.

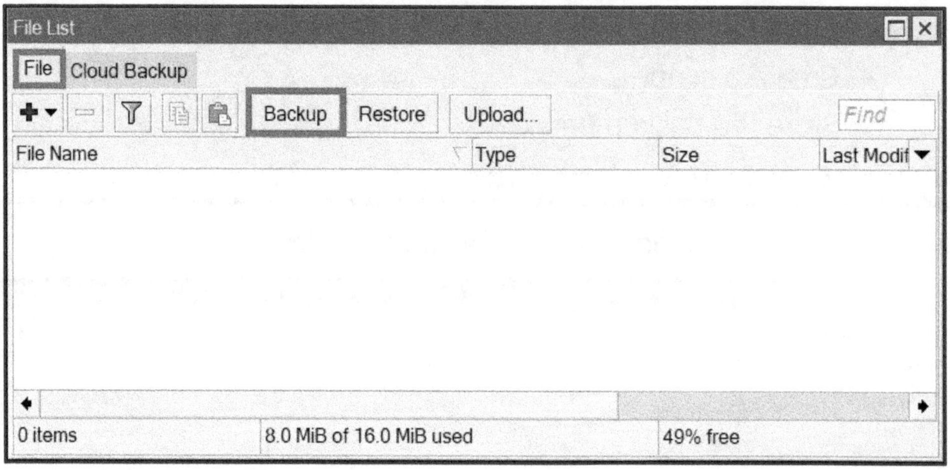

In the **Name** field, enter a name for the backup file. In the **Password** field, enter a password to protect the file, so that only authorized people who know the password can restore it later. Then, click the **Backup** button.

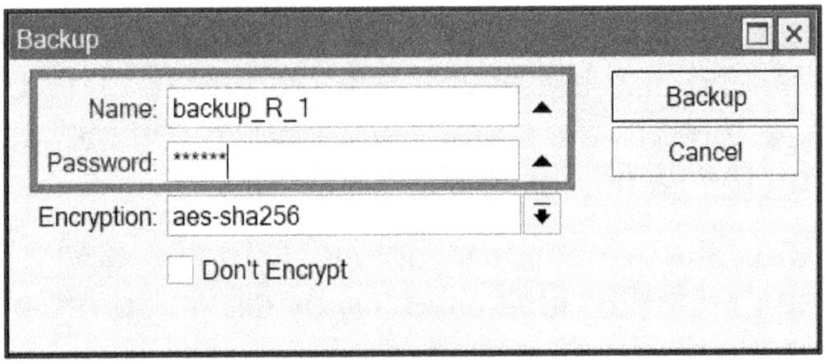

After creating the backup file, it will appear in the **File** tab of the **File List** window with the extension .backup.

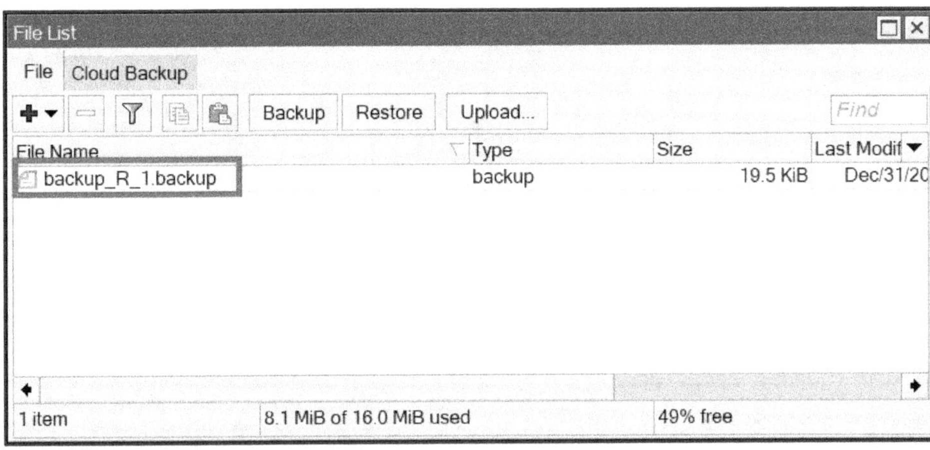

You can save this file on your computer by dragging and dropping it or by right-clicking the file and selecting **Download**.

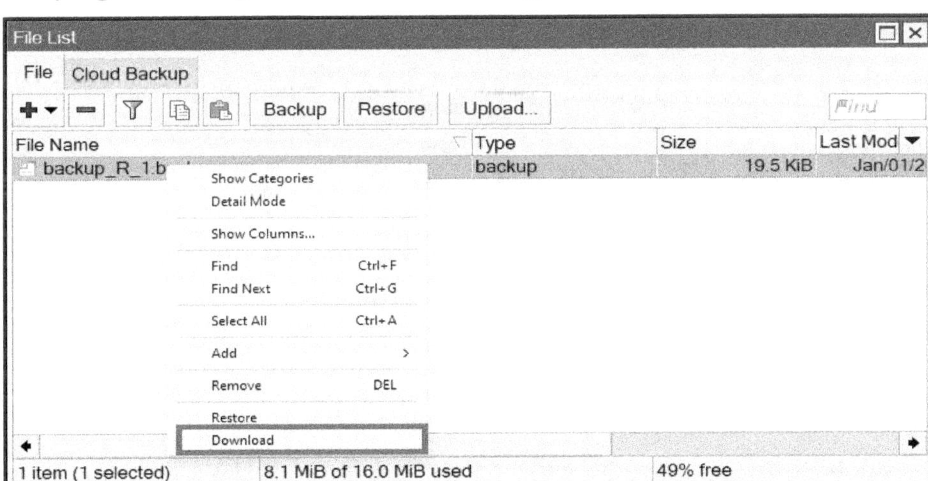

This file contains the device configuration in binary format, including user accounts, and also the device MAC addresses. This backup file is meant to be restored to the same device. It is recommended to restore the backup on the same version of RouterOS.

To restore the backup file, first upload it to the device (if it is not already saved in the **File List** window) by clicking the **Upload** button and selecting the file from your computer.

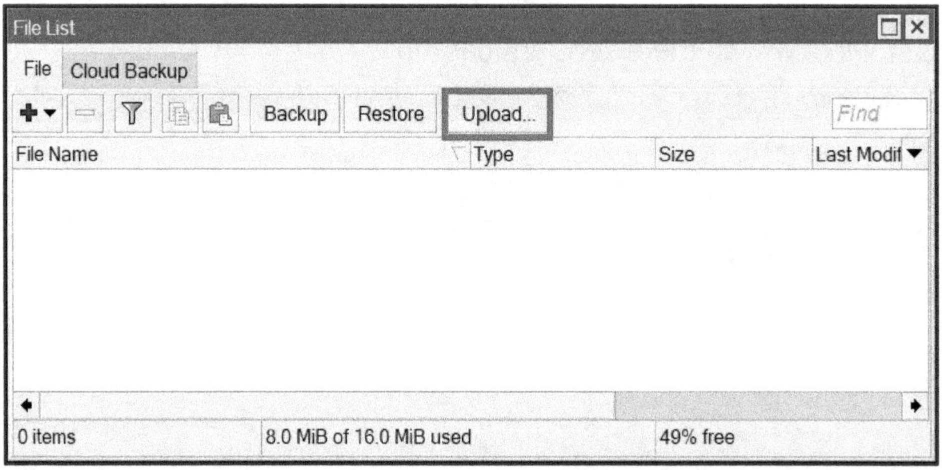

Then, click the **Restore** button to open the **Restore** dialog box. Enter the password for the file in the **Password** field in this dialog box and click the **Restore** button.

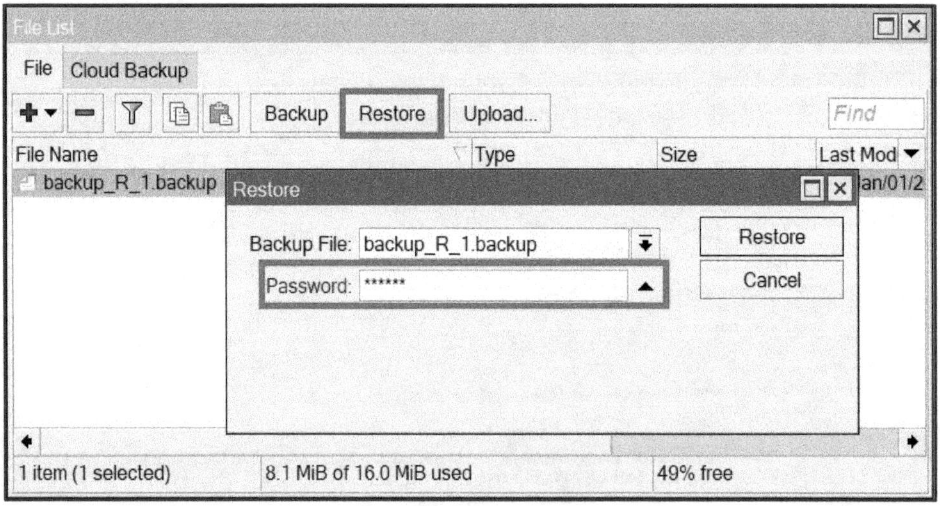

Then, accept the next message to restore the configuration and reboot RouterOS.

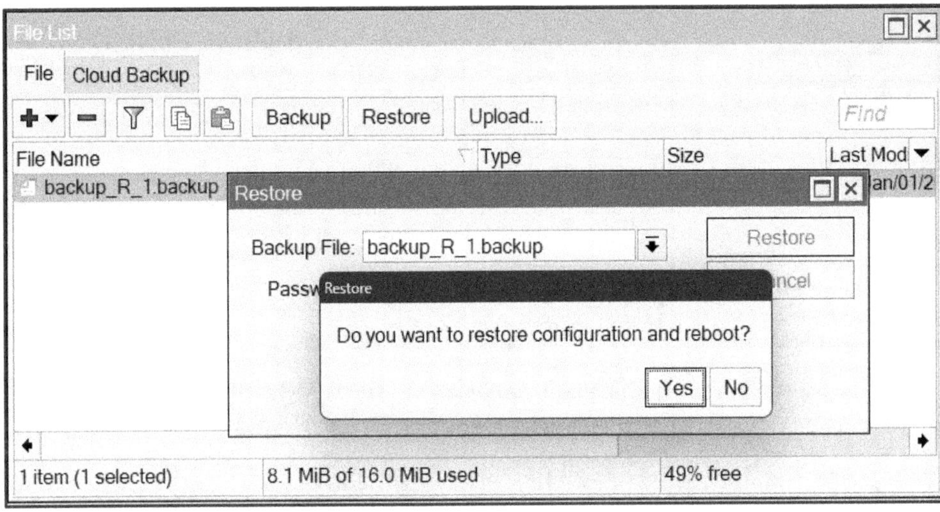

1.25.2 Create a Script.

To create a script containing the device configuration, you can use the **export** command as follows:

```
export file=[name]
```

Where:

- [name] is the name for the script file.

For example:

```
export file=script_R_1
```

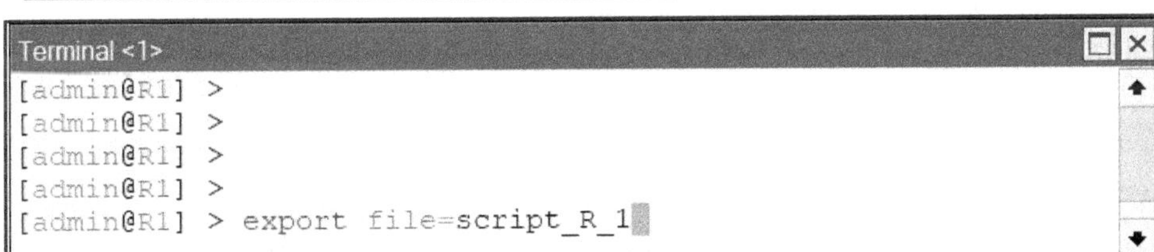

After creating the script file, it will appear in the **File** tab of the **File List** window with the extension .rsc.

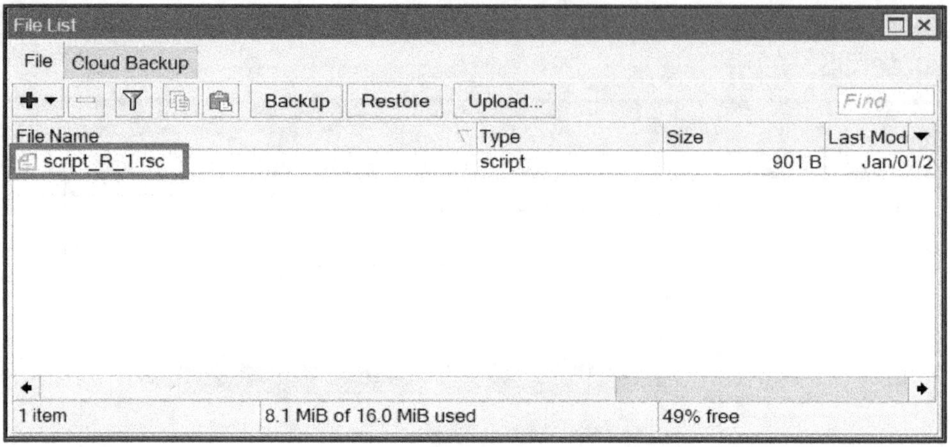

You can save this file on your computer by dragging and dropping it or by right-clicking the file and selecting **Download**.

This script file is a plain text file and is editable. You can open it with any text editor application and modify its content.

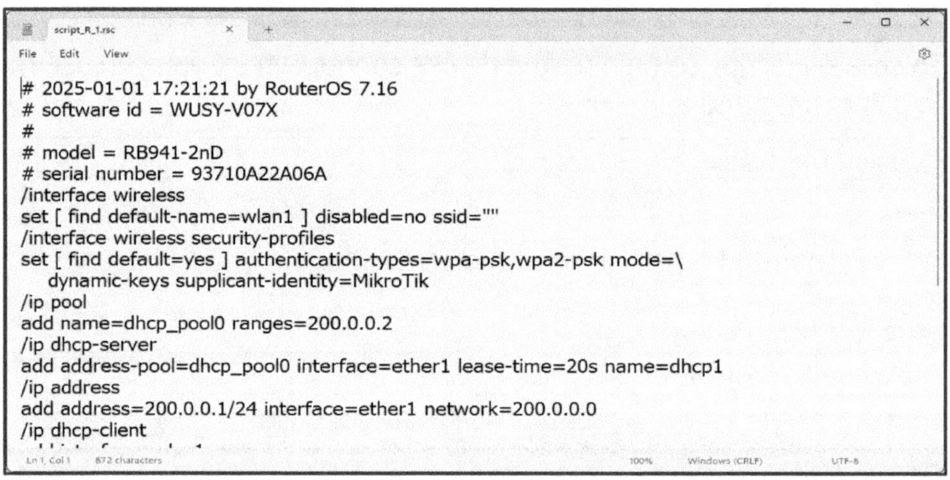

This file does not contain the user accounts, passwords or the MAC addresses, unlike the backup file.

You can also save a partial configuration by executing the **export** command in the menu level you want to save. For example, if you want to save the IP addresses configuration only, you can first move to the IP addresses menu level in the CLI, then execute the **export** command.

```
Terminal <1>
[admin@R1] >
[admin@R1] >
[admin@R1] >
[admin@R1] >
[admin@R1] > ip address export file=script_addresses_R_1
```

On the other hand, if the **export** command is executed without the **file=** parameter, it will display the configuration in the CLI and will not save it to a file.

```
Terminal <1>
[admin@R1] >
[admin@R1] > export
# 2025-01-01 17:37:15 by RouterOS 7.16
# software id = WUSY-V07X
#
# model = RB941-2nD
# serial number = 93710A22A06A
/interface wireless
set [ find default-name=wlan1 ] disabled=no ssid=""
/interface wireless security-profiles
set [ find default=yes ] authentication-types=\
    wpa-psk,wpa2-psk mode=dynamic-keys supplicant-identity=\
    MikroTik
/ip pool
add name=dhcp_pool0 ranges=200.0.0.2
```

To restore or re-apply the script file, first upload it to the device (if it is not already saved in the **File List** window) by clicking the **Upload** button and selecting the file from your computer. Then use the **import** command followed by the name of the script file as follows:

```
import [name]
```

Where:

- [name] is the name for the script file.

For example:

```
import script_R_1.rsc
```

```
Terminal <1>
[admin@R1] >
[admin@R1] >
[admin@R1] >
[admin@R1] >
[admin@R1] > import script_R_1.rsc
```

1.25.3 Store the Backup Online.

To create a backup file and store it online, use the **Cloud Backup** tab of the **File List** window. This feature was added to RouterOS starting from version 6.44.

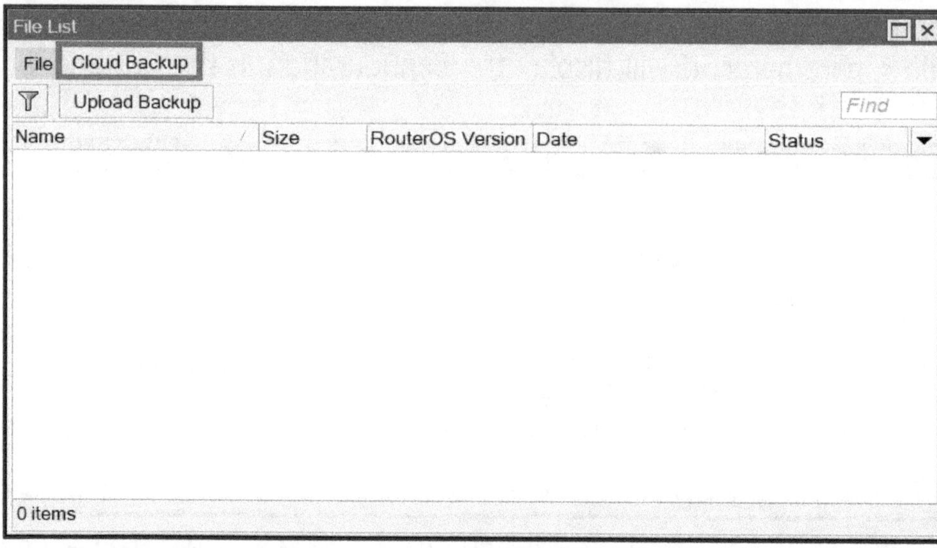

To create a backup file, click the **Upload Backup** button in the **Cloud Backup** tab of the **File List** window to open the **Upload Backup** dialog box.

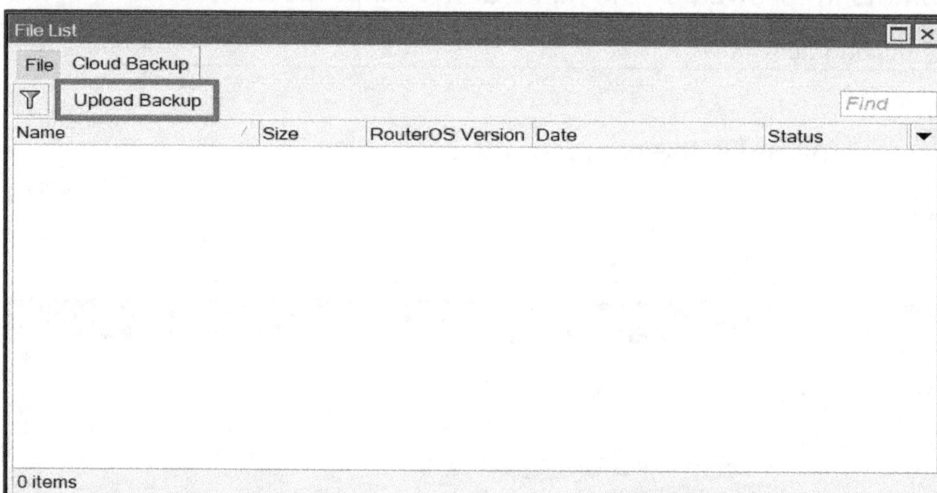

In the **Action** field, make sure the **Create and Upload** action is selected. In the **Name** field, enter a name for the backup file. In the **Password** field, enter a password to protect the file, so that only authorized people who know the password can restore it later. Then, click the **Start** button.

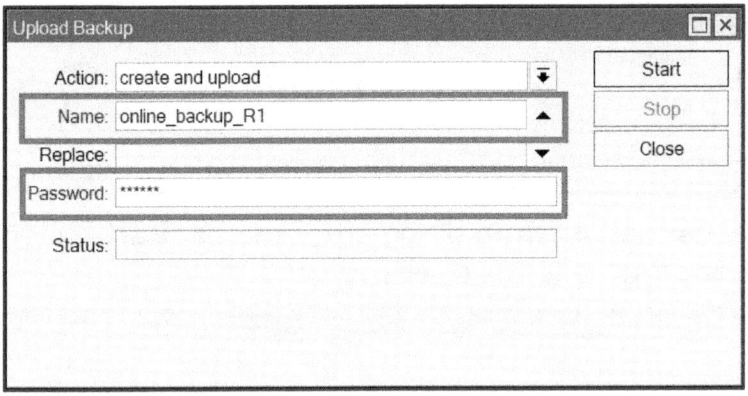

After creating the backup file, it will be saved online and it will appear in the **Cloud Backup** tab of the **File List** window.

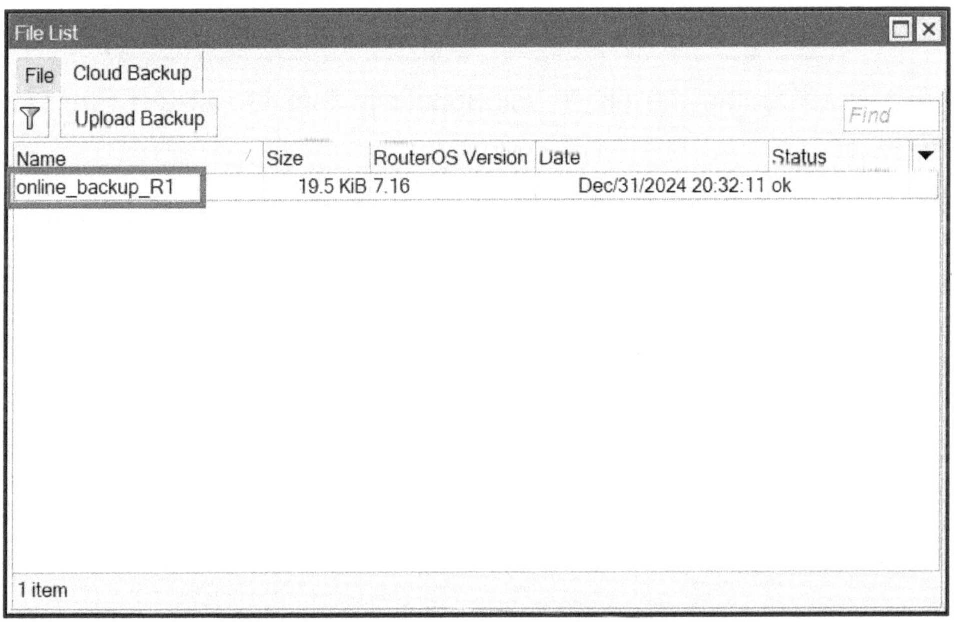

To restore the backup file, first download the file to the device by double-clicking it in the **Cloud Backup** tab to open the **Cloud**

Backup dialog box, which displays information about the file. Then, click the **Download** button in this dialog box to open the **Download Backup** dialog box.

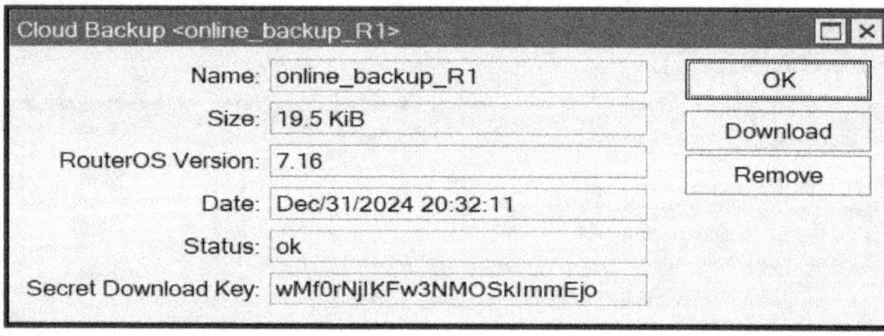

In the **Download Backup** dialog box, click the **Start** button to start downloading the file to the device.

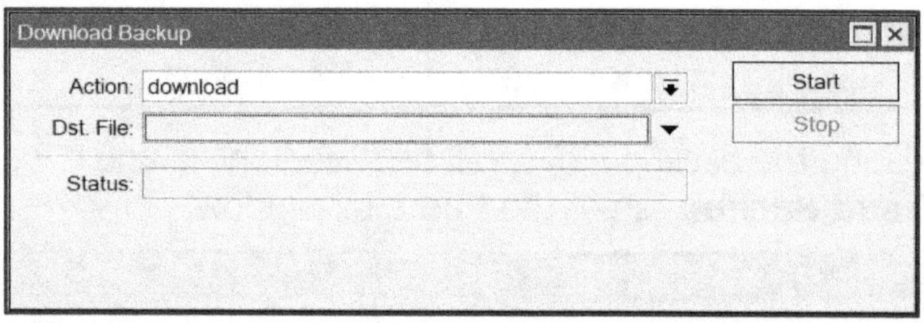

After downloading the file, it will appear in **File** tab of the **File List** window.

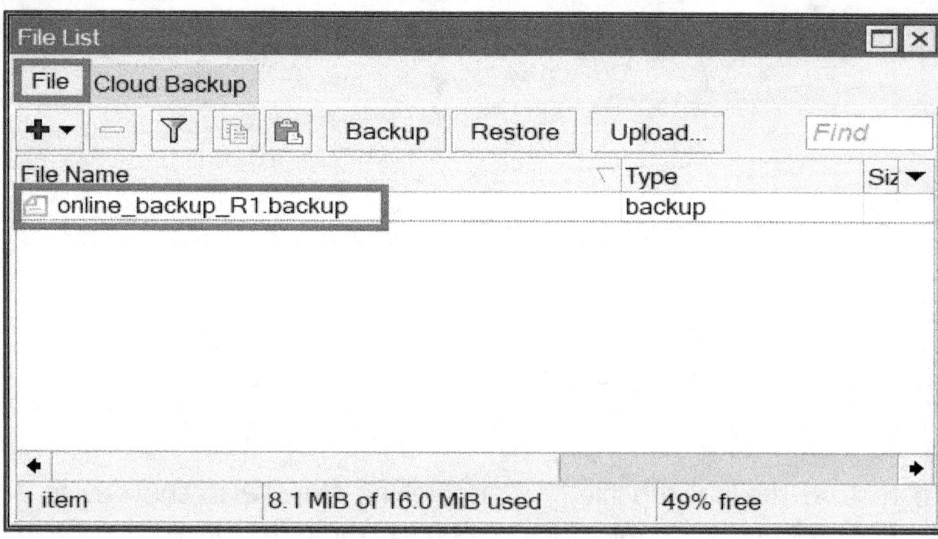

Now, you can click the **Restore** button to open the **Restore** dialog box and enter the password for the file in the **Password** field and click **Restore** button.

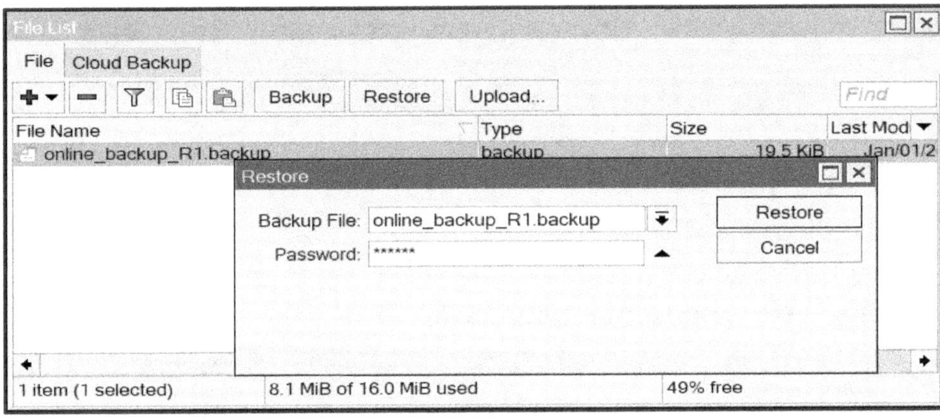

1.26 RouterOS Packages

RouterOS comes with multiple tools, capabilities, and features, which are provided in form of packages.

Each package adds specific functionality to RouterOS. For example, the DHCP package enables the RouterOS to function as a DHCP server or a DHCP client. So, to configure the RouterOS as a DHCP server, you need to install the DHCP package and then use the appropriate commands provided by the package. And to configure the device to function as an access point (AP), you need to install the Wireless package.

There is a main package (RouterOS package or system package) that contains the standard features of RouterOS, combining sub packages such as DHCP, hotspot, wireless, PPP, security, MPLS, advanced-tools, ipv6, routing packages.

And there are Extra Packages that provide additional optional features can be installed as needed.

In RouterOS v7, the main features are combined in one package (routeros package).

You can display the currently installed packages in RouterOS from the **Package List** window.

Package List window in RouterOS v7

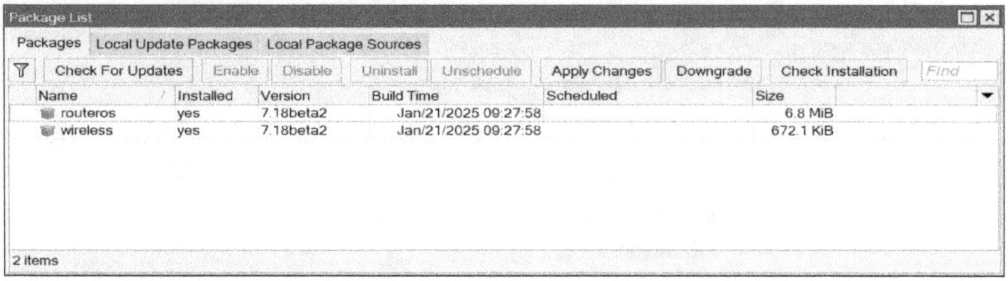

Package List window in RouterOS v6

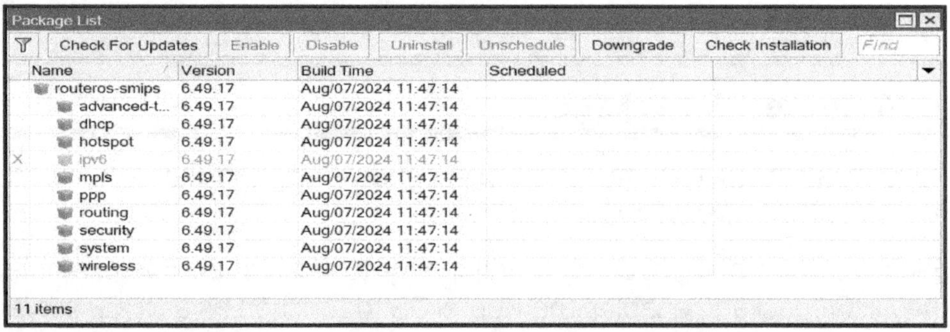

To open the **Package List** window, click the **System** menu, then select **Packages**

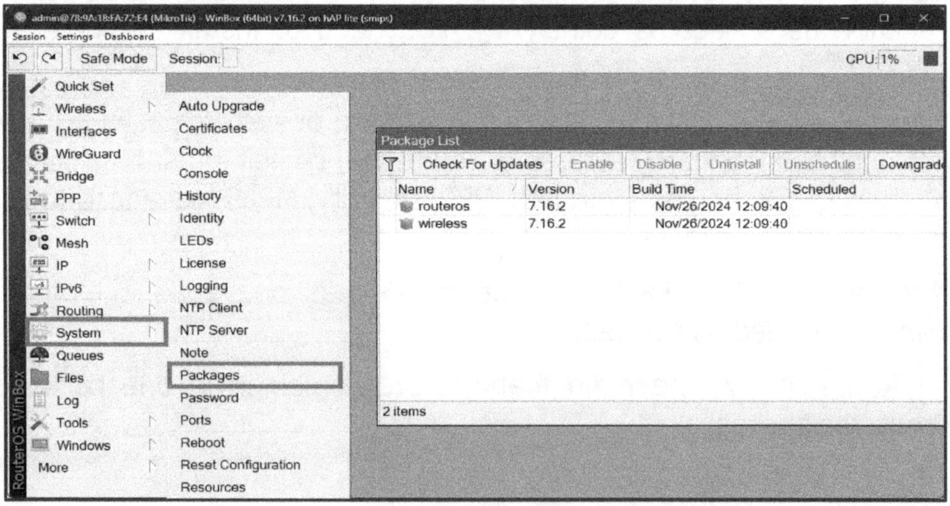

You can enable or disable specific RouterOS functions by enabling or disabling the corresponding packages using the **Enable** or **Disable** buttons from **Package List** window.

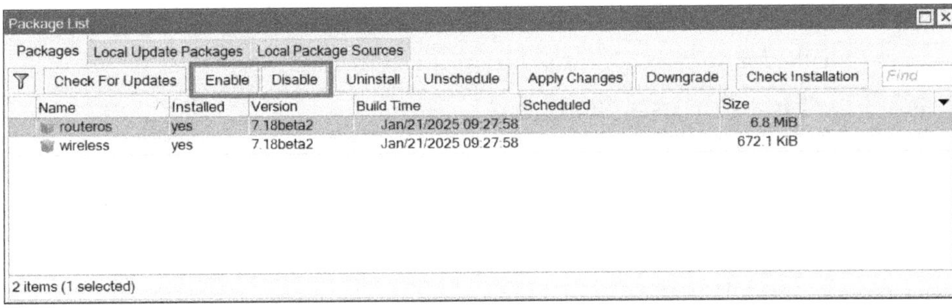

You can also display the currently installed packages in RouterOS from the CLI using the following command:

```
system package print
```

RouterOS v7

```
Terminal <1>
[admin@MikroTik] >
[admin@MikroTik] > system package print
Columns: NAME, VERSION, BUILD-TIME, SIZE
# NAME        VERSION     BUILD-TIME           SIZE
0 routeros    7.18beta2   2025-01-21 09:27:58  6.8MiB
1 wireless    7.18beta2   2025-01-21 09:27:58  672.1KiB
[admin@MikroTik] >
```

in RouterOS v6

```
Terminal <1>
[admin@MikroTik] >
[admin@MikroTik] > system package print
Flags: X - disabled
 #    NAME                  VERSION                SCHEDULED
 0    routeros-smips        6.49.17
 1    system                6.49.17
 2 X  ipv6                  6.49.17
 3    wireless              6.49.17
 4    hotspot               6.49.17
 5    mpls                  6.49.17
 6    routing               6.49.17
 7    ppp                   6.49.17
 8    dhcp                  6.49.17
 9    security              6.49.17
10    advanced-tools        6.49.17
[admin@MikroTik] >
```

1.26.1 Package Update

There are two methods to update RouterOS packages:

- Online method.
- Offline method.

1.26.1.1 The Online Method.

This is the easiest method to update the current packages. First, you need to connect the device to the internet, then click the **Check for Updates** button in the **Package List** window to open **Check For Updates** dialog box.

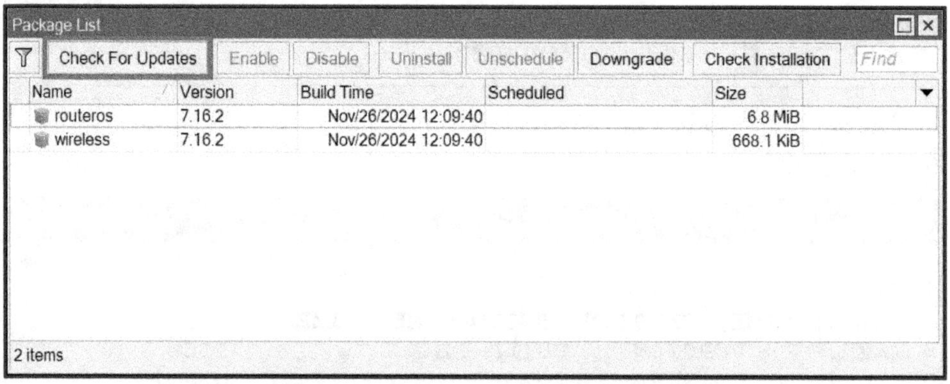

Then click the **Check for Update** button in this dialog box.

RouterOS will check for the latest versions to update the current packages (the main package and any extra installed packages). Select the desired version, then click the **Download & Install** button. No additional packages will be installed.

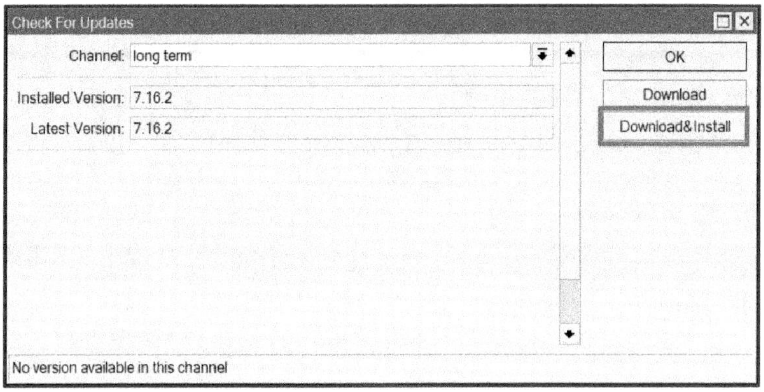

By using this method, you can:

- Update the currently installed packages (the main package and any extra packages).

1.26.1.2 The Offline Method

You can download the package file from MikroTik website and upload it to the device manually.

By using this method, you can:

- Update the currently installed packages (the main package and any extra packages).
- Add new extra packages.

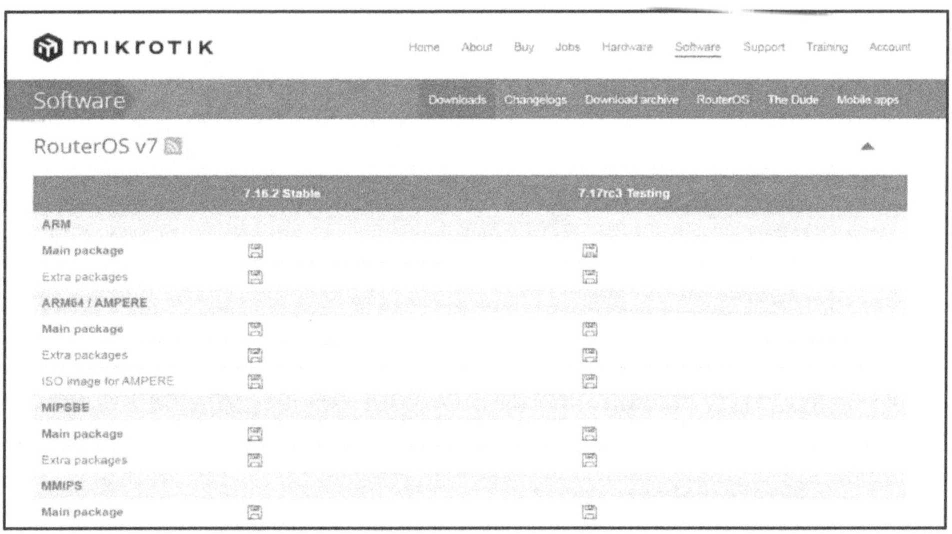

1.26.1.2.1 Update the Main Package

To update the main package:

- First: download the main package file from MikroTik website.

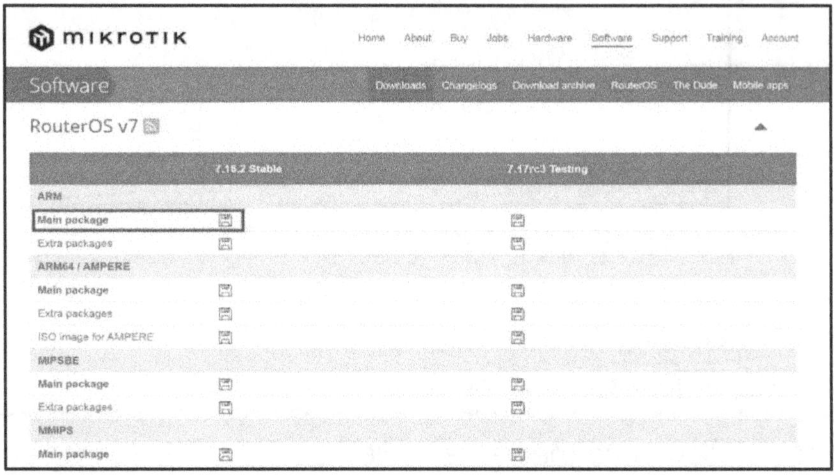

This package should match the architecture of the device (ARM, ARM64 / AMPERE, MIPSBE, SMIPS, etc.)

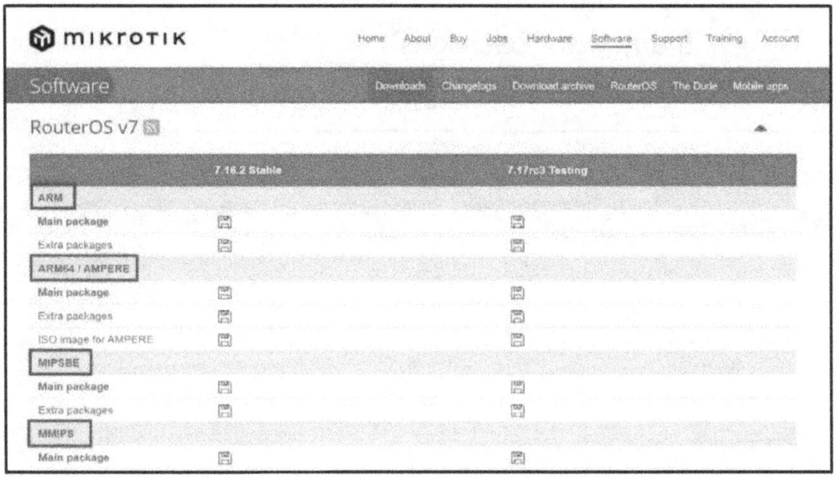

To know the architecture of your device, you can open the **Resources** dialog box by clicking the **System** menu and selecting **Resources**.

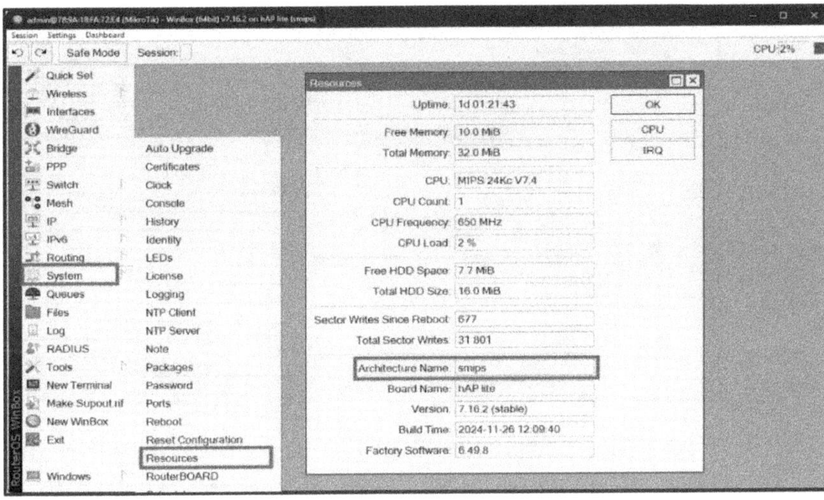

Or, you can check the architecture by simply looking at the title bar in the WinBox window.

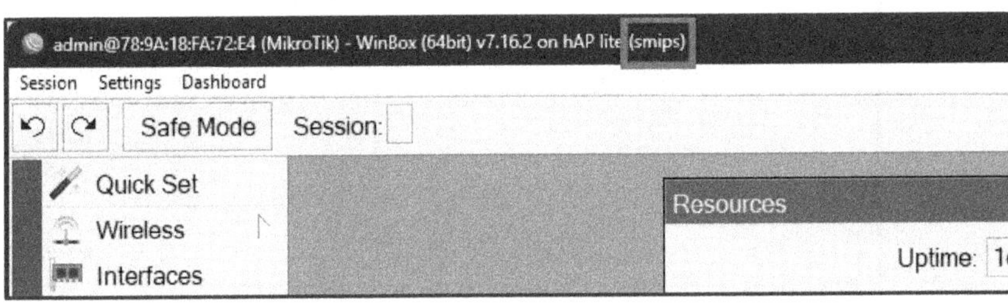

- Second: after downloading the package, upload it to RouterOS by using the **File List** window.

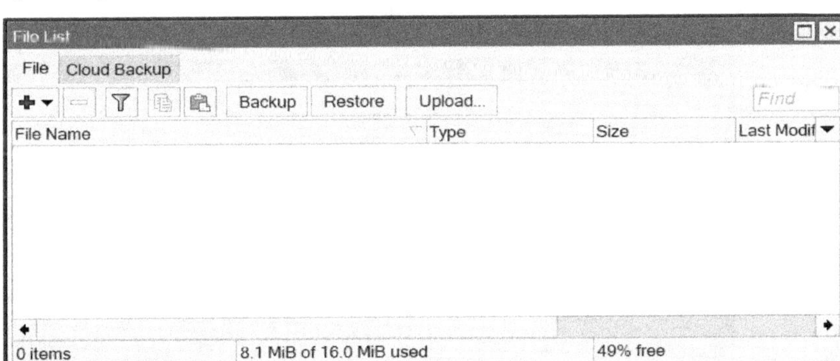

To open **File List** window, click the **Files** menu.

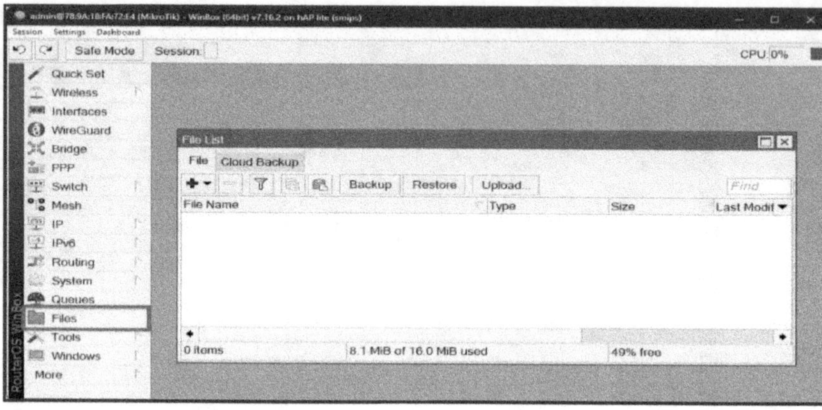

To upload the package file to RouterOS, click the **Upload** button in this window and choose the file.

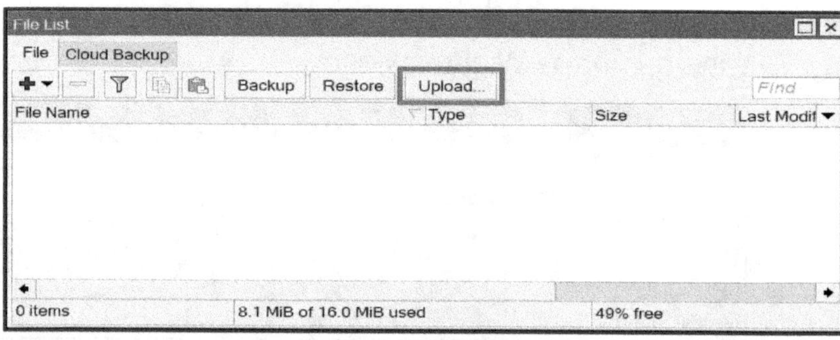

- Third: after uploading the package file to the **File List** window, reboot RouterOS to install the package by clicking the **System** menu and selecting **Reboot**.

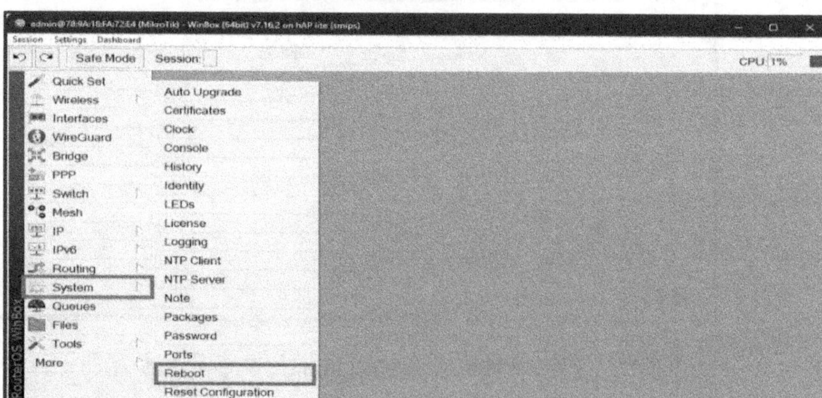

After the RouterOS rebooted, the new package will be installed.

1.26.1.2.2 Add a New Package

To add a new package:

- First: download the extra packages file from MikroTik website.

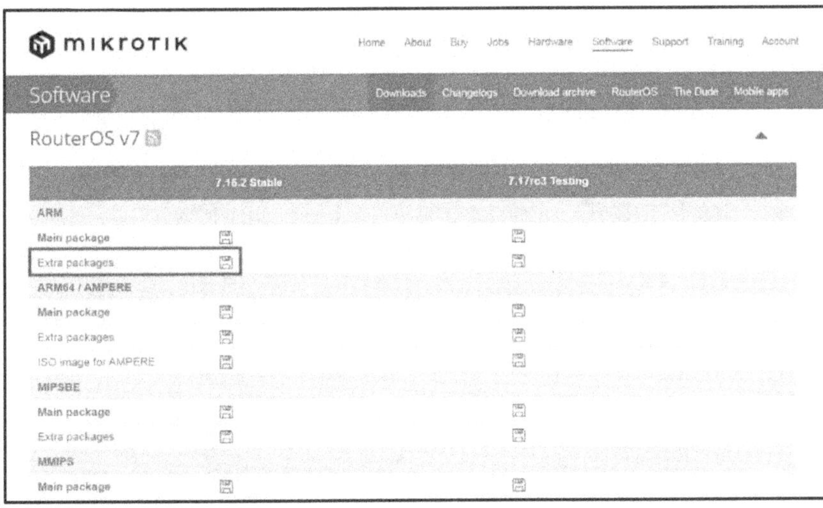

This package should match both of the architecture of the device (ARM, ARM64 / AMPERE, MIPSBE, SMIPS, etc.) and the version of the main package installed on this device.

To check the current version of RouterOS installed on your device, you can open the **Package List** window.

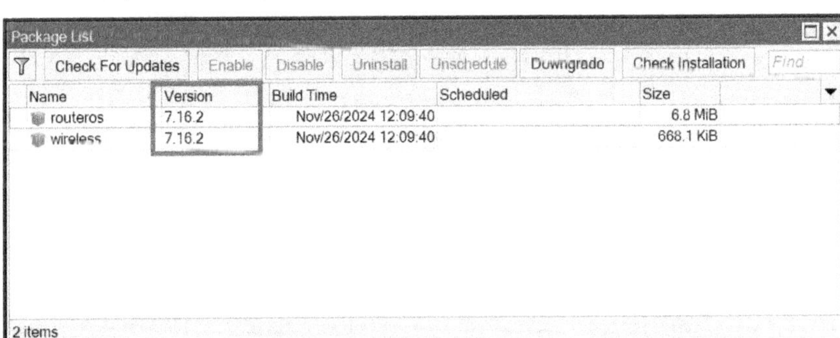

Or, you can check the RouterOS version by simply looking at the title bar in the WinBox window.

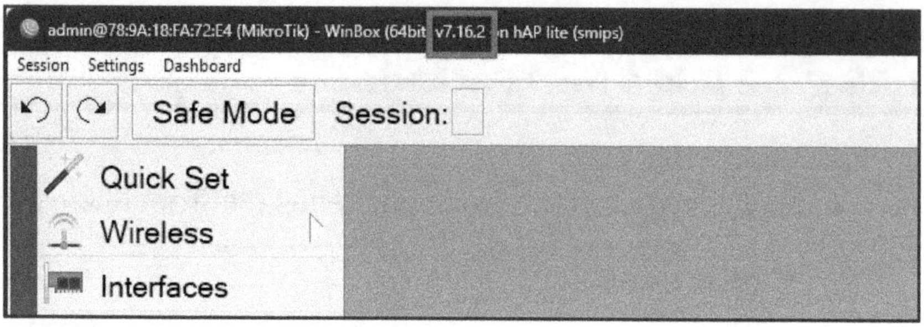

- Second: after downloading the extra packages file, unzip the file, choose the package file you want to install and upload it to RouterOS using the **File List** window.
- Third: after uploading the package file to the **File List** window, reboot RouterOS to install the package by clicking the **System** menu and selecting **Reboot**.

1.26.1.2.3 Update the Main and the Extra Packages

You can also use this method to update the main package and the currently installed extra packages, as well as install new packages in one step, by downloading the main and extra packages files, which should be the same version and match the architecture of the device (ARM, ARM64/AMPERE, MIPSBE, SMIPS, etc.). Then upload the main package file to the device along with the desired extra packages (whether they are currently installed or new packages).

Note: if you have extra packages currently installed and you upload only the main package file, the old extra packages will be removed.

1.26.2 RouterOS Release Chains

When updating RouterOS, you can choose a release chain:

- Long-term : this release contains fixes, without new features
- Stable: this release contains fixes and new features
- Testing: this release is considered as a beta version
- Development: this release contains raw changes and new features.

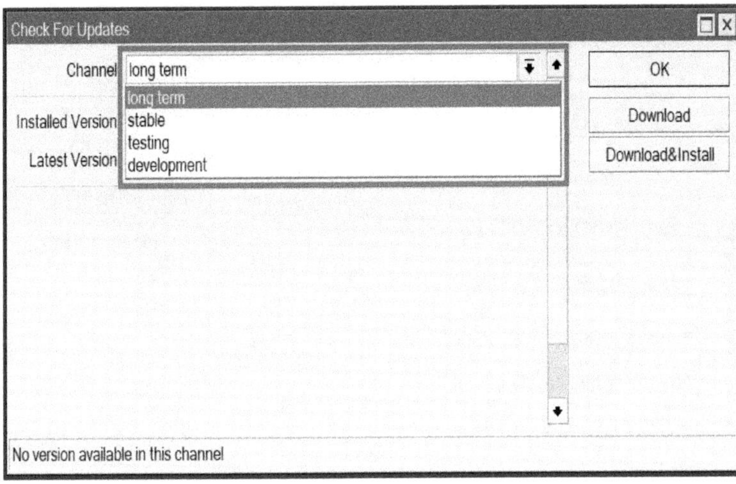

1.26.3 New Names

In RouverOSv6, Since v6.43/v6.44, the old release names have been changed as follows:

- Bugfix to Long-term
- Current to Stable
- Release candidate to Testing

1.27 RouterBOOT Firmware

The firmware of MikroTik RouterBOARD devices which is responsible for starting the device is called boot loader, or loader or RouterBOOT.

There are two boot loaders:

- Main boot loader
- Backup boot loader

The Main boot loader or the main firmware can be updated, while the Backup loader can be used if needed.

When updating the package, the updated version of the firmware will be downloaded as well, but it will not be installed automatically. To install this update, use the **RouterBOARD** dialog box.

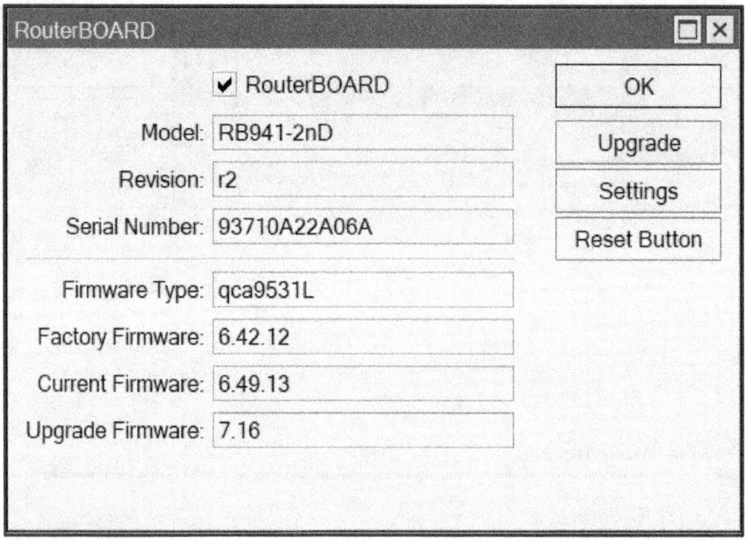

To open the **RouterBOARD** dialog box click the **System** menu, then select **RouterBOARD**

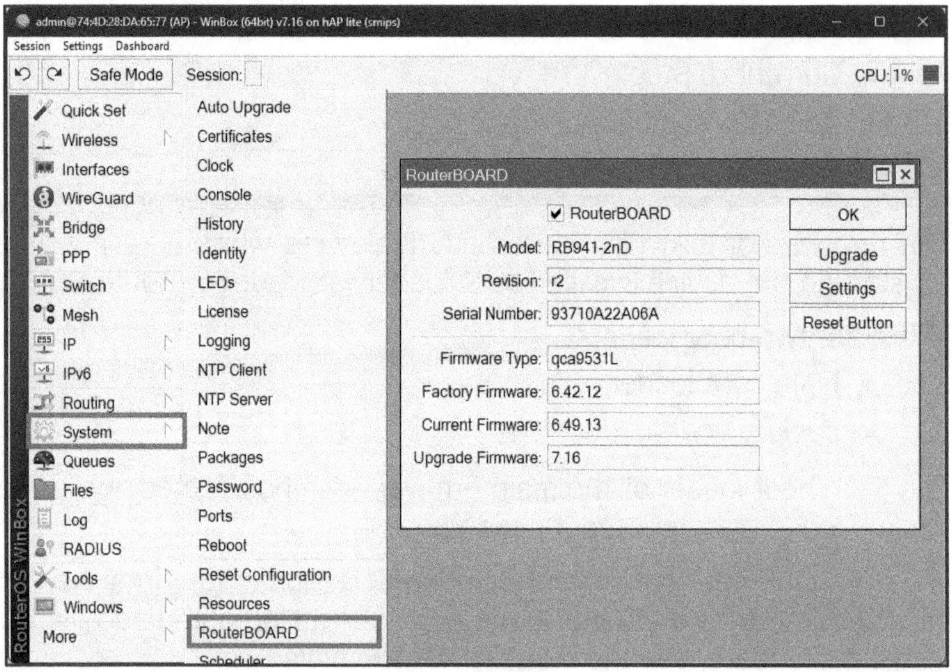

To update the firmware, click the **Upgrade** button from this dialog box.

1.28 Reset Configuration

If you want to remove all the configurations from RouterOS, in other words, if you want to reset the configuration, you can use the **Reset Configuration** dialog box.

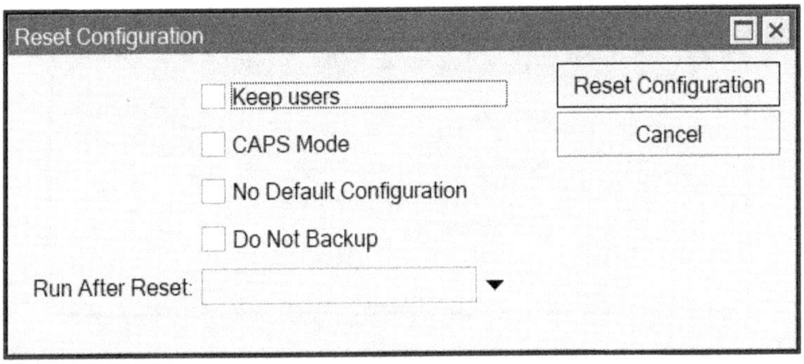

To open the **Reset Configuration** dialog box, click the **System** menu, then select **Reset Configuration**.

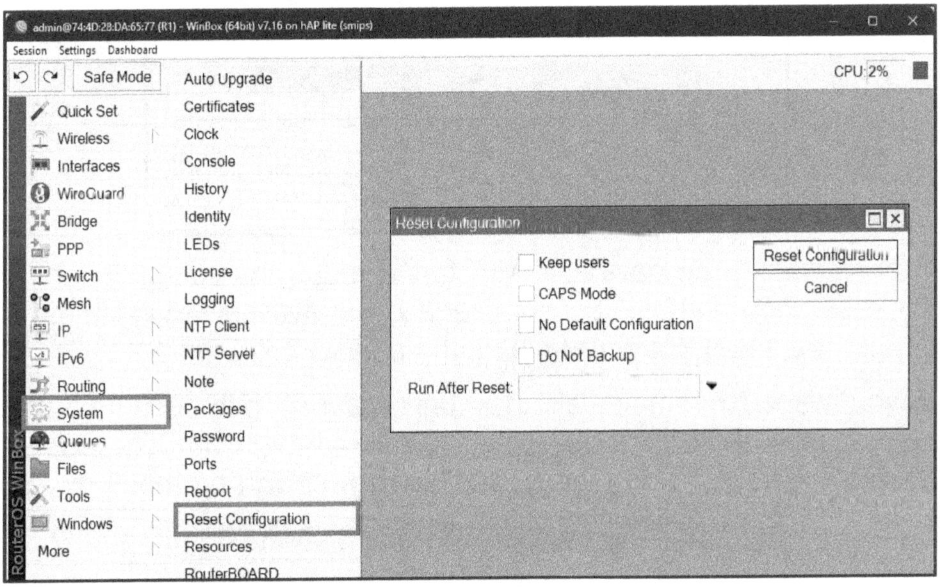

You can use the **Reset Configuration** dialog box to:

- Reset the RouterOS configuration.
- Restore the default configuration.
- Put the device in CAPs Mode.

1.28.1 Reset the RouterOS Configuration

To reset the configuration and remove all the settings from the device, open the **Reset Configuration** dialog box, make sure to check the **No Default Configuration** checkbox, and click the **Reset Configuration** button.

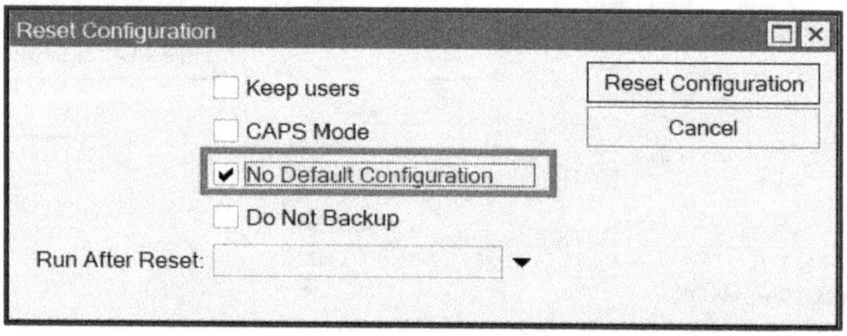

Accept the next message to reset the configuration and reboot RouterOS.

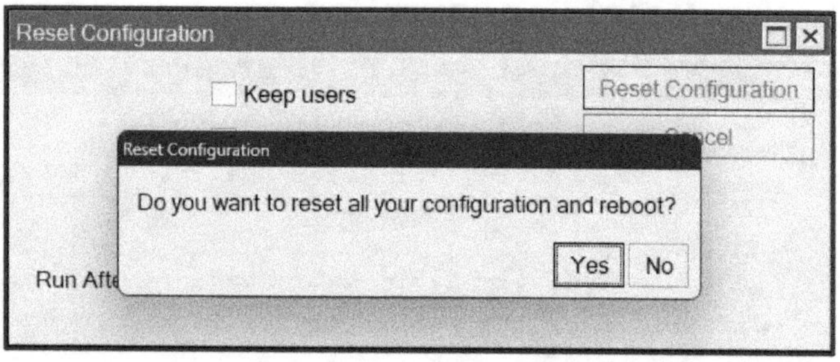

After rebooting the device, it will start without any configuration. In this case, there will be a default user account available to log in to the device: the username is (admin) with no password.

If you want to remove all the configurations but keep the user accounts created on the device, make sure to check the **Keep Users** checkbox before clicking the **Reset Configuration** button.

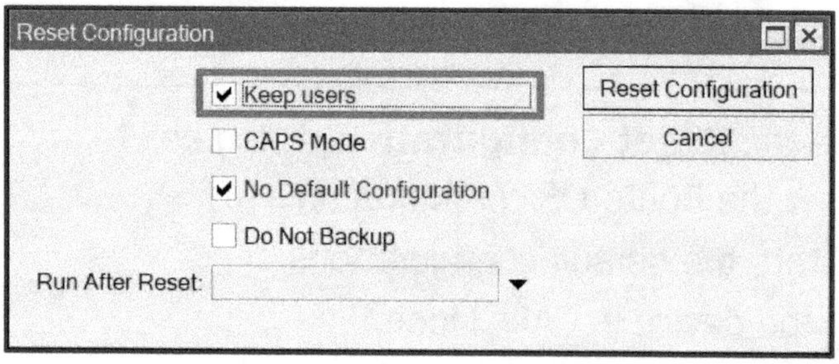

When resetting the configuration, the device will automatically create a backup file of the current configuration in case you want to restore it. This file will be saved on the device and will appear in the **File List** window with the name **auto-before-reset**.

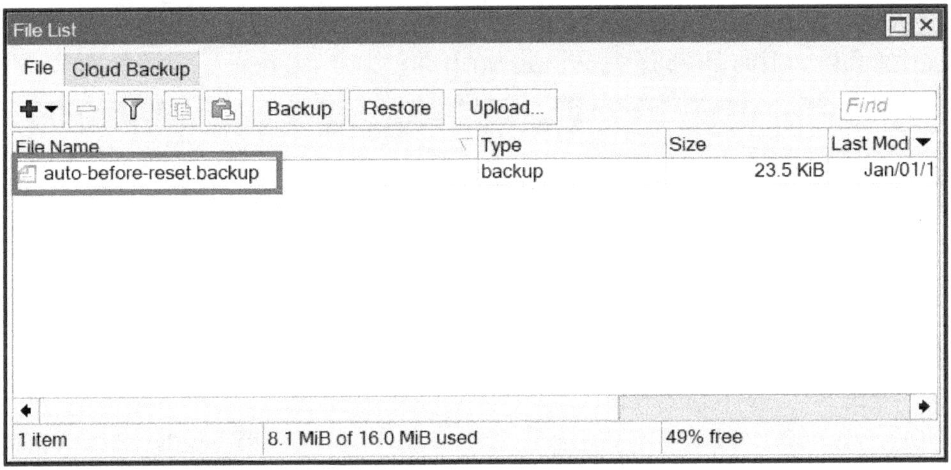

If you do not want the auto backup, make sure to check the **Do Not Backup** checkbox before clicking the **Reset Configuration** button.

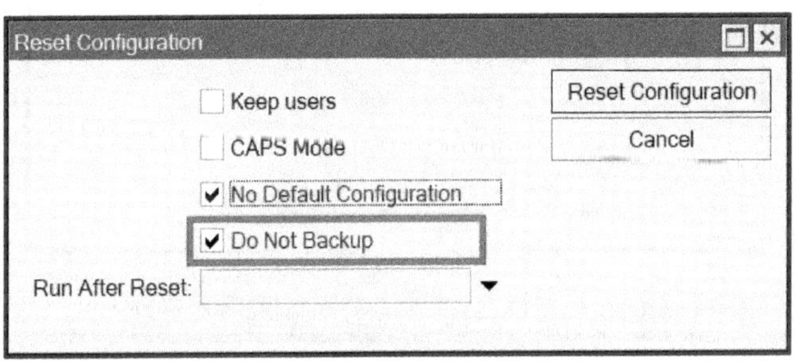

You can also run a script after resetting the device by choosing the script from the **Run After Reset** field.

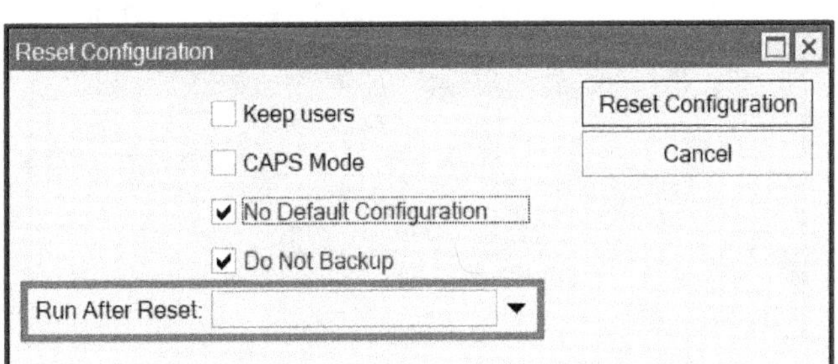

You can use this option to reset the configuration and remove all the current settings of the device, then apply a script containing other configurations that you have taken from another device.

For example, if you create a script containing the configuration of a device using the **export** command as learned earlier, and upload this script file to the **File List** window on another device.

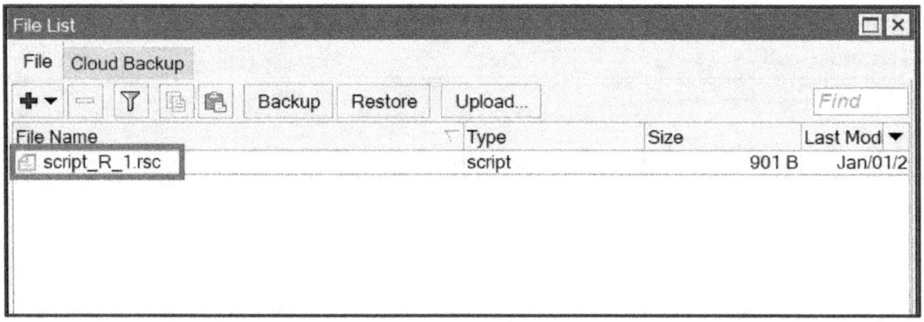

Now, you can reset the current configuration on this device and apply this script by selecting it from the **Run After Reset** field.

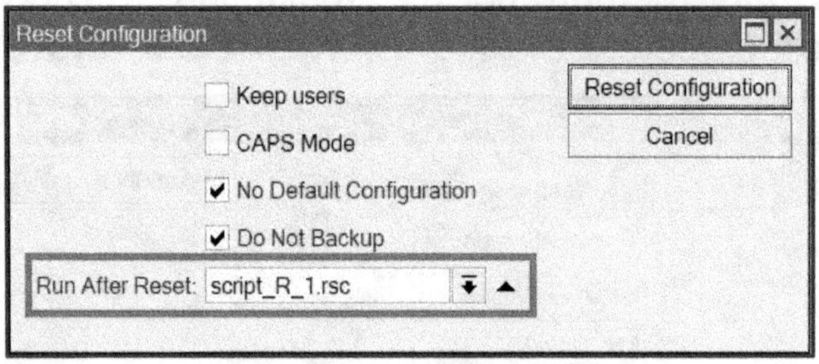

1.28.2 Restore the Default Configuration

To restore the default configuration, open the **Reset Configuration** dialog box, make sure to uncheck the **No Default Configuration** checkbox, and click the **Reset Configuration** button.

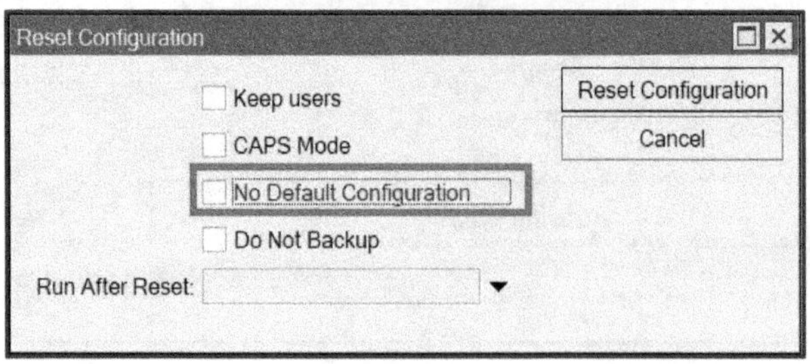

Accept the next message to reset the configuration and reboot RouterOS.

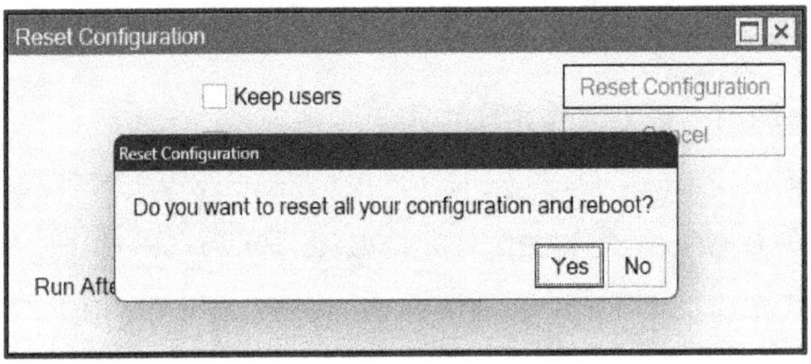

After rebooting the device, it will start with the default configuration.

1.28.3 Put the Device in CAPS Mode

You can configure the device to function as an access point (AP), and you can control this access point (AP) using a central device for easier network management.

In this case, the access point (AP) device is called a Controlled Access Point (CAP) (or, as other vendors call it, a lightweight access point). The device that controls this access point (AP) is called the Access Point Controller or Access Point System Manager (CAPsMAN), (or as other vendors refer to it, the wireless controller).

To put the device in CAPs Mode to be controlled by an Access Point Controller, open the **Reset Configuration** dialog box, check the **CAPs Mode** checkbox, and click the **Reset Configuration** button.

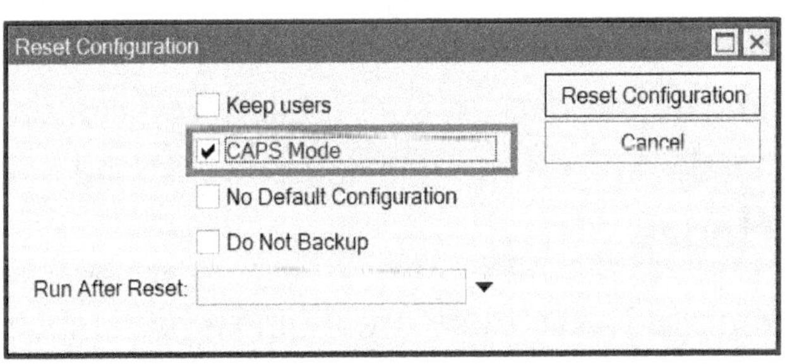

You will learn more about CAPs and CAPsMAN in the MTCEWE course.

1.29 The Reset Button

The reset button is a Multi-function button that can be used to perform three actions:

- Resetting the configuration

  If you press the button immediately after switching the device on and keep holding it for 5 seconds until the LED light starts flashing, that will reset the configuration.
- CAPs mode

  If you press the button immediately after switching the device on and keep holding it for 10 seconds until the LED light turns solid, that will put the device in CAPs mode.
- Etherboot mode

  If you press the button immediately after switching the device on and keep holding it for 15 seconds until the LED light turns off, that will put the device in Etherboot mode, also called Netinstall mode.

On the other hand, as mentioned before, there are two boot loaders: the main boot loader and the backup boot loader.

- If you press the reset button immediately after switching the device on (within 3 seconds) it will use the main boot loader.
- If you press the reset button before switching the device on, it will recall the backup boot loader. You can use the backup boot loader in case there is an issue with the main loader.

1.30 Boot Modes

In MikroTik RouterBOARD, there are multiple boot modes, each used for a specific purpose.

- NAND Mode

  This is the normal boot mode to load RouterOS from the internal memory.

- Ethernet Mode

  This mode is used to boot from the ethernet. It is also called Etherboot Mode or Netinstall Mode.
- Flash Boot Mode

  This mode is used with the FlashFig app, (which is a special application that allows you to quickly apply configurations to the device). It is also called FlashFig Mode.
- CAPs Mode

  This mode is used to connect the device to Wireless Controller CAPsMAN.

To choose the boot mode, use the **RouterBOARD Settings** dialog box.

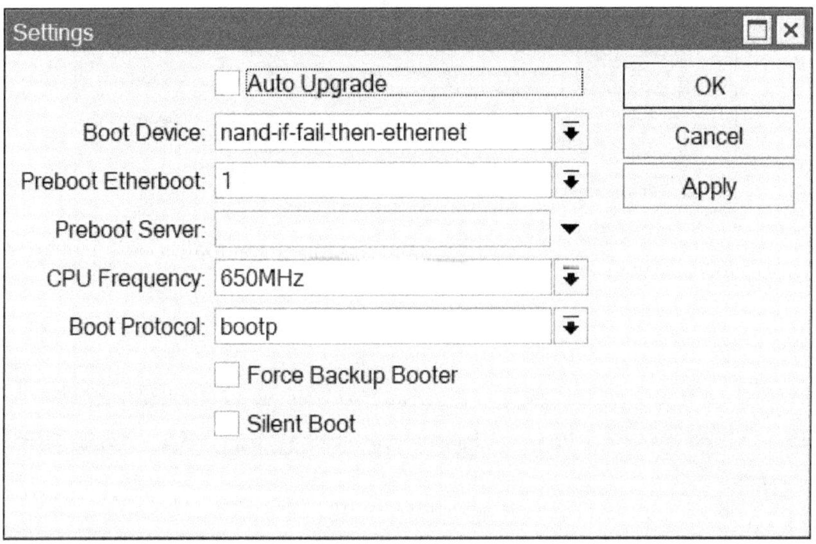

To open the **RouterBOARD Settings** dialog box, first open **RouterBOARD** dialog box by clicking the **System** menu, selecting **RouterBOARD**, then clicking the **Settings** button.

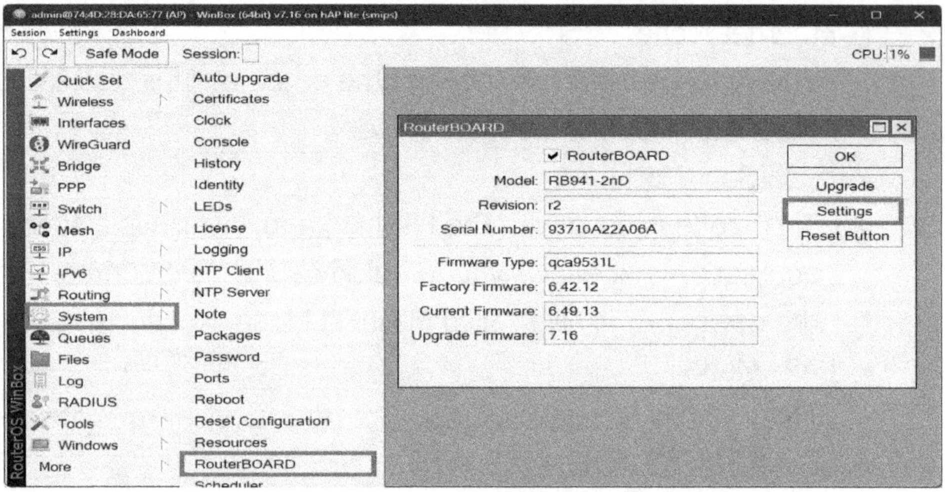

Then select the boot mode you want from the **Boot Device** field.

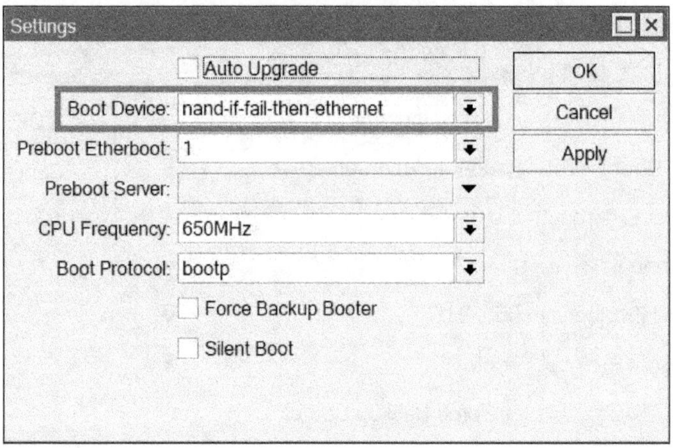

You can also choose some boot modes using the reset button as mentioned.

1.31 Netinstall

In some cases, you may need to reinstall RouterOS on a MikroTik RouterBOARD device if it does not work properly. To do this, you can use a specific application called Netinstall.

Netinstall is software developed by MikroTik that allows you to install RouterOS on the device. It is available in two versions: a GUI (Graphical user interface) version for Windows and a CLI (Command

Line Interface) version for Linux. It is free software and can be downloaded from the official MikroTik website:

To reinstall RouterOS using Netinstall, perform five steps:

- Step One: Download the required files.
    - Netinstall Application

      Download Netinstall from MikroTik website.

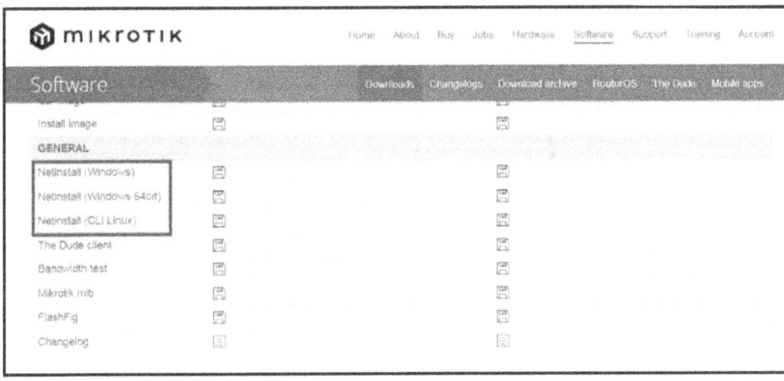

    - RouterOS Operating System File

      This is the main package file. It must match the device architecture type, or you can download a special version of this package called the RouterOS Universal Package, which is compatible with all architectures.

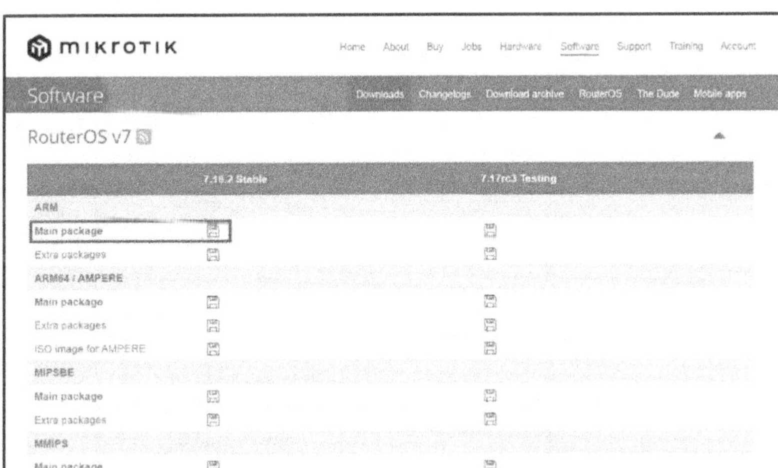

- Step Two: Prepare Your PC
    - Use One Ethernet Adapter

      Netinstall will only work with one active network interface with the highest priority. so, it is recommended to disable all other network adapters to ensure that the Ethernet interface is the only active one.

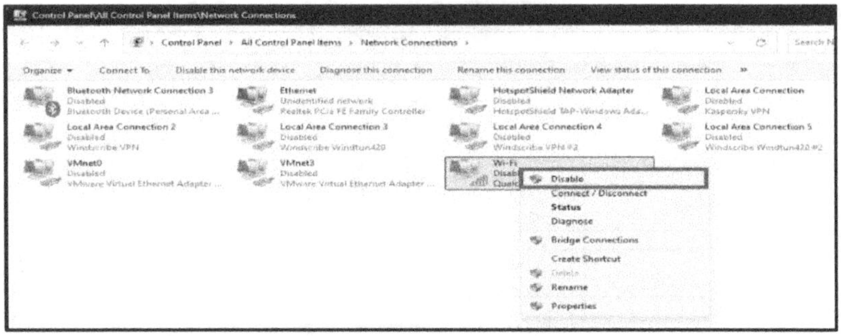

You can also configure the Ethernet adapter to have the highest priority by opening the **Internet Protocol Version 4 (TCP/IPv4) Properties** dialog box and clicking the **Advanced** button.

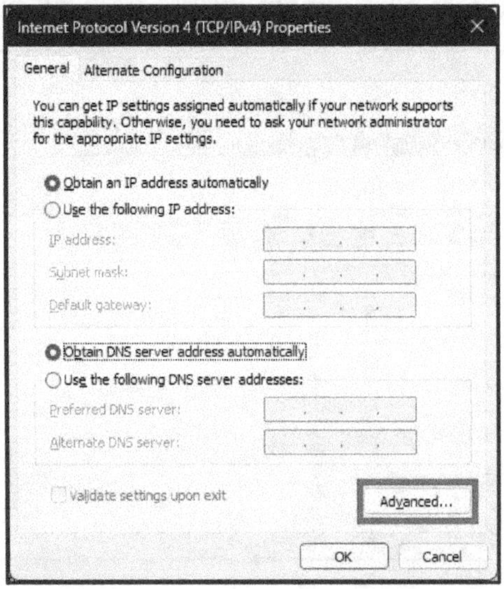

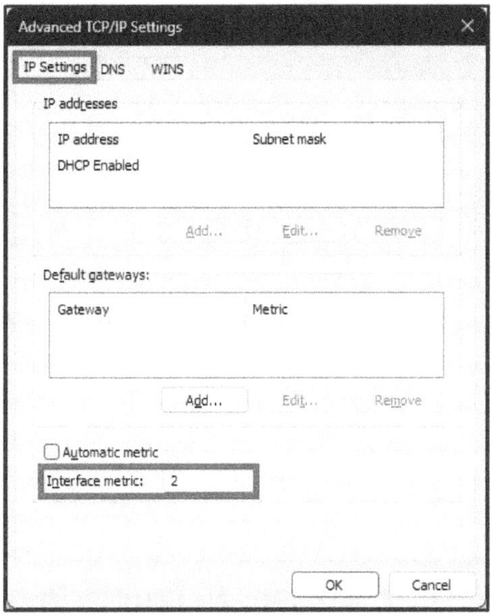

In the **Interface Metric** field in the **IP Settings** tab, increase the value of the metric.

In most cases, it will work; however, it is recommended to disable all other adapters.

- Assign an IP Address

  Assign the following IP address, default gateway, and DNS to the Ethernet adapter:

  - IP Address: 192.168.88.2/24
  - Default Gateway: 192.168.88.1
  - DNS: 192.168.88.1

- Open Netinstall Application

  Open the Netinstall application with administrator rights by right-clicking on the application and selecting **Run as Administrator.**

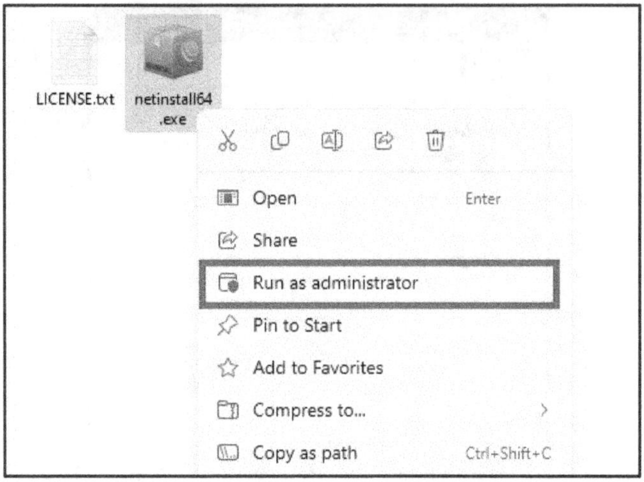

Then click the **Net Boot** button in the application window to open the **Network Booting Settings** dialog box. Check the **Boot Server Enabled** check box in this dialog box, and in **Client IP address** enter the IP address 192.168.88.3 and click the **OK** button to close this dialog box.

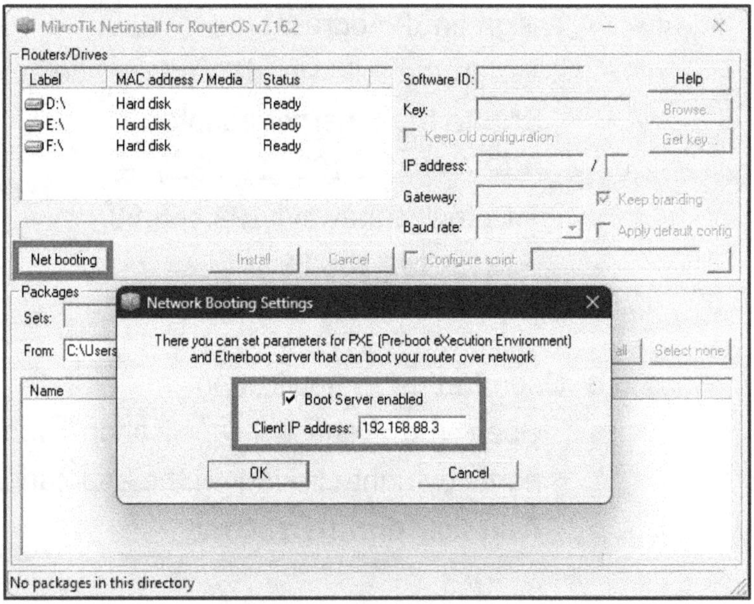

- Step Three: Connect the PC to MikroTik RouterBOARD
  Connect your PC to the MikroTik RouterBOARD using the **Boot** interface, which is the Ether1 interface on most devices. Or you can check the interface marked with **BOOT**. If you are unsure which interface is the boot interface, check the device manual.
- Step Four: Prepare MikroTik RouterBOARD
  Prepare the MikroTik RouterBOARD by putting it into Etherboot mode.
  First, switch the device off. Then, switch it on and immediately press the reset button, holding it for 15 seconds until the LED turns off.
- Step Five: Use the Netinstall Application to Install RouterOS
  Wait until the device appears in the Netinstall window, then click the **Browse** button and select the folder where you downloaded the RouterOS file.

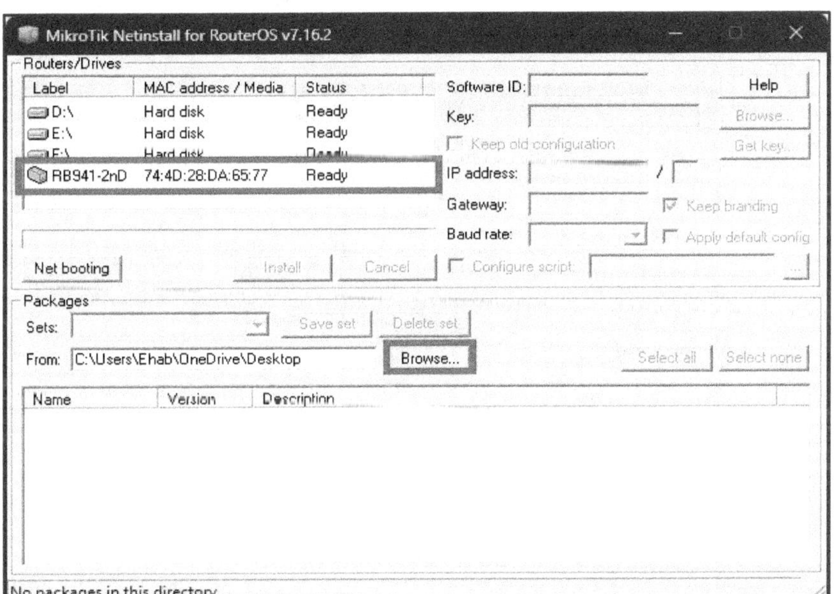

After selecting the folder, the RouterOS file will appear in the Netinstall window.

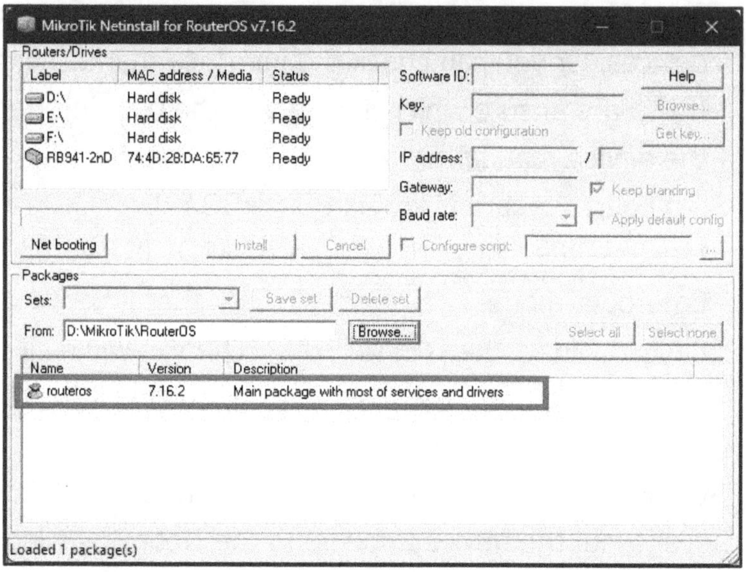

Click the MikroTik device in the Netinstall window to select it, select the RouterOS file you want to install, and click the **Install** button to begin installing RouterOS on the device.

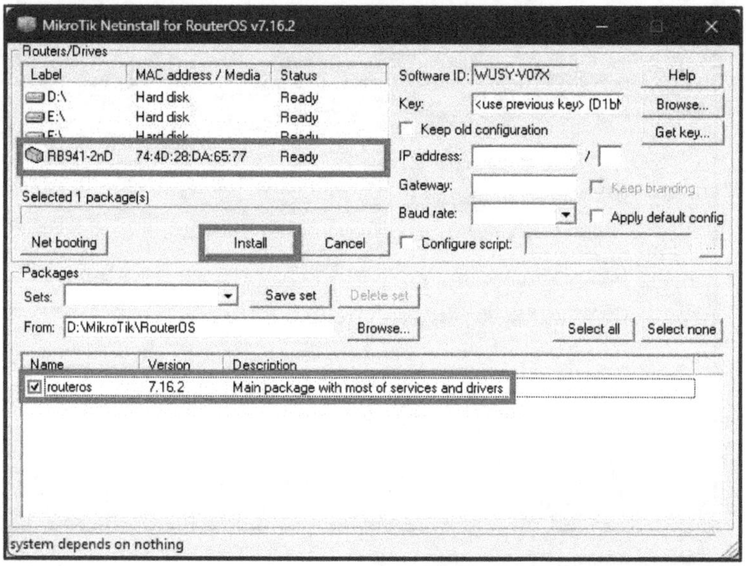

After completing the installation successfully, you can reboot your MikroTik device in normal mode.

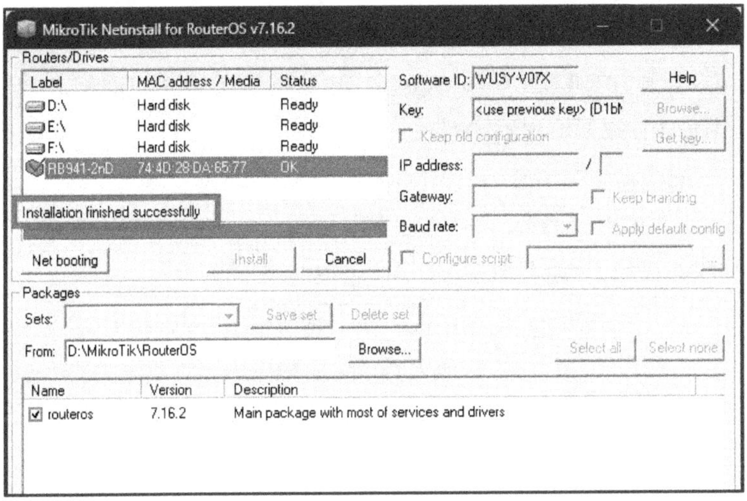

1.32 FlashFig

FlashFig is a special application developed by MikroTik that allows you to quickly apply configurations to a device. This configuration will become the device default configuration. It is free software and can be downloaded from the official MikroTik website.

To apply a configuration to a device using FlashFig, perform six steps:

- Step One: Download FlashFig Application.

  Download FlashFig from MikroTik website.

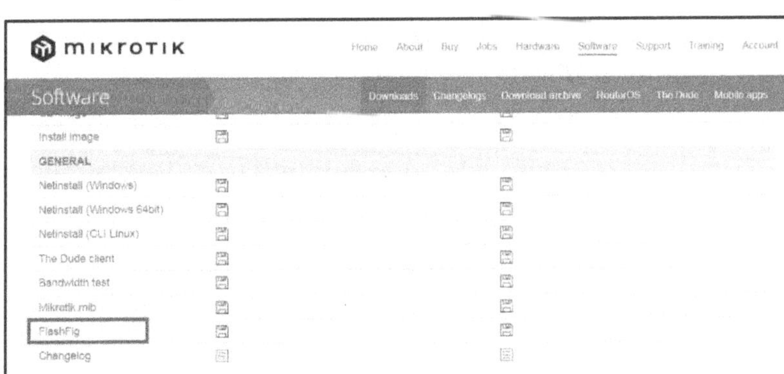

- Step Two: Create the Configuration File

  Create the configuration file you want to apply to the device in .rsc format. You can prepare the file manually by writing the desired code or script, or you can configure a device and then use the **export** command to export its configuration to a script .rsc file. Then download this file to your PC.

- Step three: Prepare Your PC
  - Use One Ethernet Adapter

    FlashFig is similar to Netinstall, it will only work with one active network interface with the highest priority. so, it is recommended to disable all other network adapters to ensure that the Ethernet interface is the only active one.

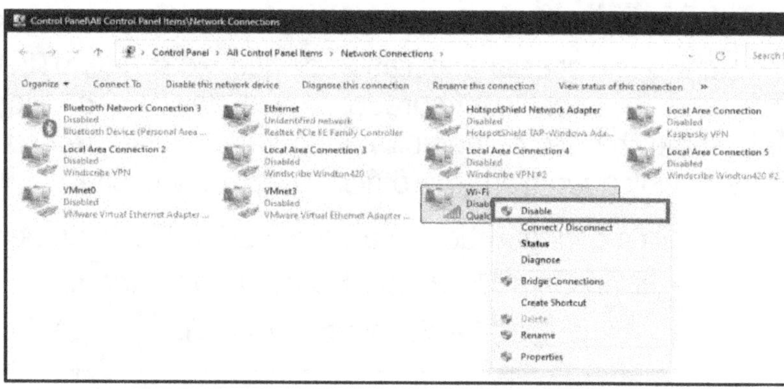

  - Assign an IP Address

    Assign an IP address to your ethernet interface. You can use your own network IP address range or use the following IP address, which is the default subnet for MikroTik devices:

    - IP Address: 192.168.88.2/24
    - Default Gateway: 192.168.88.1
    - DNS: 192.168.88.1

- Step Four: Open FlashFig Application

  Open the **FlashFig** application. In **Boot Client Address** field enter an IP address from the same subnet of your PC, which in this case is 192.168.88.1, then click the **Browse** button to select the configuration file you want to apply.

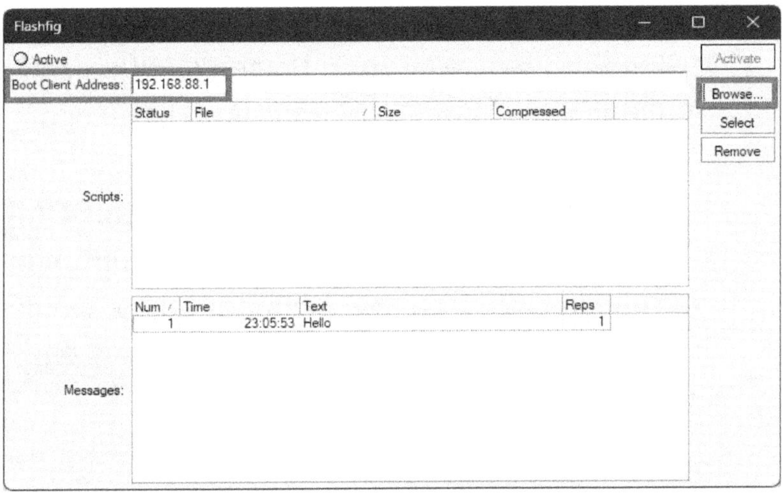

After the file appears in the application window, select it by single click, and click the **Select** button, then click the **Activate** button.

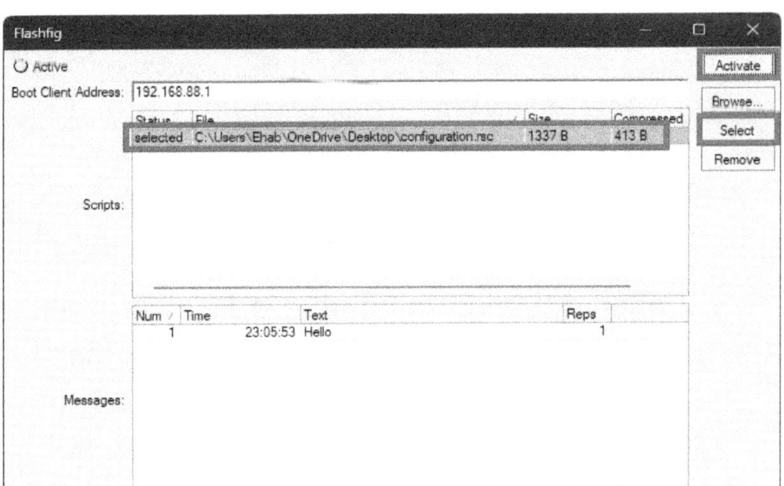

- Step Five: Connect the PC to MikroTik RouterBOARD

  Connect your PC to the MikroTik RouterBOARD using the **Boot** interface, which is the Ether1 interface on most devices. Or you can check the interface marked with **BOOT**. If you are unsure which interface is the boot interface, check the device manual.
- Step Six: Prepare MikroTik RouterBOARD

  Prepare the MikroTik RouterBOARD by putting it into FlashFig mode.

  Click the **System** menu, select **RouterBOARD**, click the **Settings** button, then choose **flash-boot** mode from **Boot Device** field. After that restart or reboot the device.

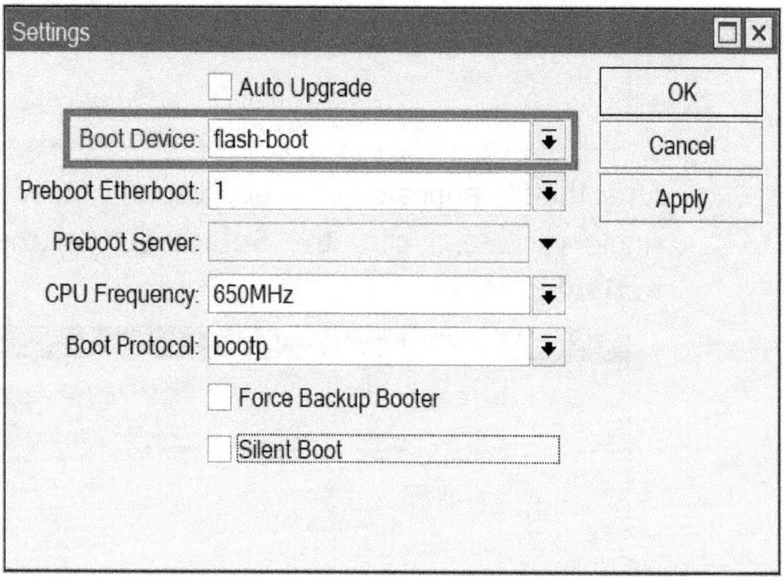

After restarting the device in FlashFig mode, the FlashFig application will apply the configuration, then it will display a message saying the device is FlashFigged successfully.

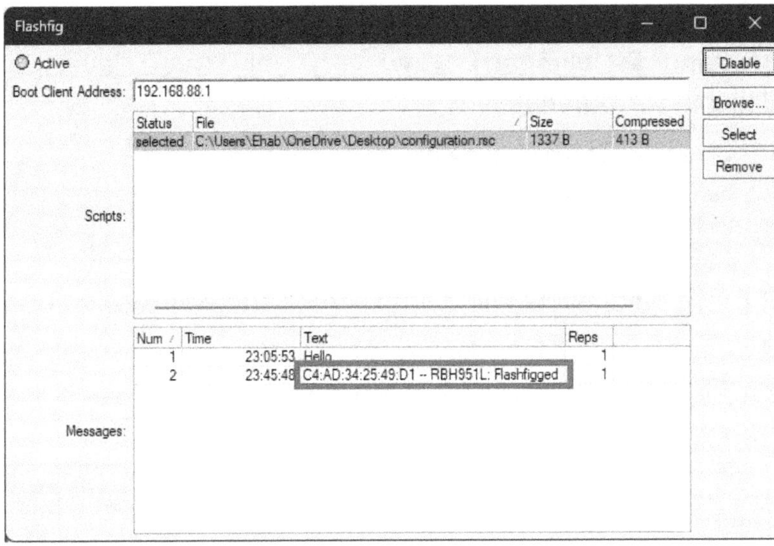

After completing the FlashFig process, you can reboot your MikroTik device in normal mode. This configuration will now become the default configuration on the device. Whenever you use the **Reset Default Configuration** option, this configuration will be restored.

1.33 RouterOS License

To use RouterOS, you need to have a valid license. As mentioned beforc, there are three types of RouterOS, depending on the platform it is installed on:

- RouterOS version for MikroTik hardware devices (RouterBOARD devices)
- x86 version for PCs
- CHR version for Virtual Machines

All MikroTik devices that run RouterOS version are shipped with a license. For x86 and CHR versions, you need to purchase a license to use them.

There are multiple levels of licenses, each level provides specific capabilities.

For RouterOS and the x86 versions, there are 7 license levels (level 0 to level 6), while for the CHR version, there are 4 levels, plus a trial version for 60 days that provides access to the paid levels (Free, P1, P10, and P-Unlimited). However, only three levels are currently available for purchase:

- Level 4/P1 45 USD
- Level 5/P10 95 USD
- Level 6/P-Unlimited 250 USD

All these paid levels will work forever and will receive updates forever too.

The following tables provide a quick overview of each license level.

RouterOS and x86 License Levels

Level	Type	Price
0	Trial Mode, runs for 24 hours only	Trial
1	Free demo after registering the trial license	Free
2	It was a transitional license, no longer available	-
3	Wireless Station, CPE	-
4	AP (Access Point), WISP, Home, Office	45 US$
5	ISP, have more capabilities than Layer 4	95 US$
6	Controller, Unlimited RouterOS Features	Price

CHR License Levels

Level	Speed limit	Price
Free	1Mbit	Free
P1	1Gbit	45 US$
P10	10Gbit	95 US$
P-Unlimited	Unlimited	250 US$

To check the license level on RouterOS and access license settings, use the **License** dialog box.

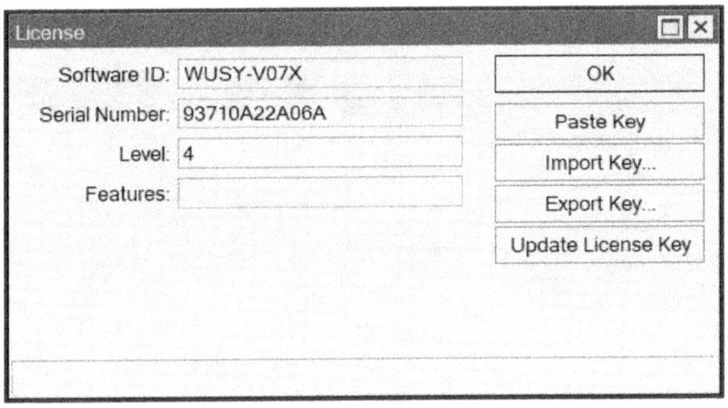

To open the **License** dialog box, click the **System** menu and then select **License**.

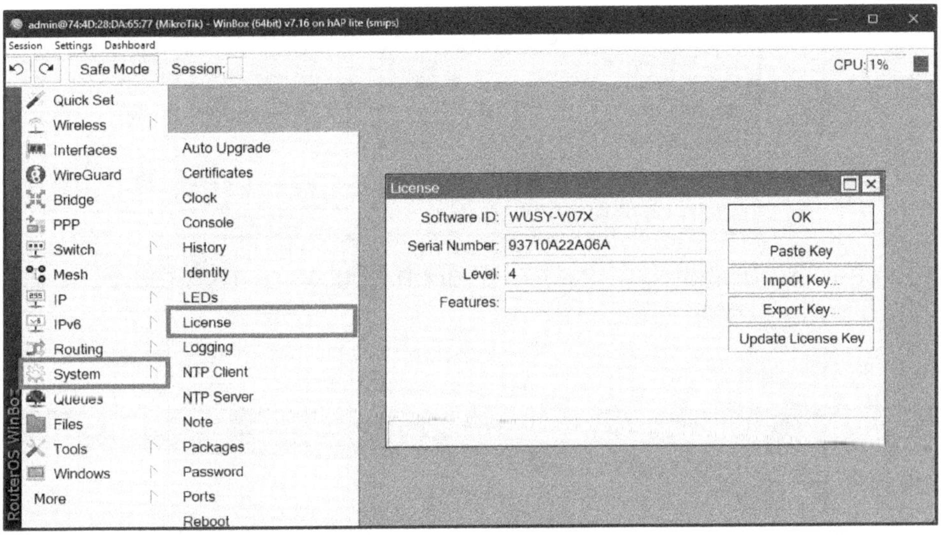

Here you can see the license level is Level 4, which is the default level in most SOHO models of MikroTik RouterBOARD devices.

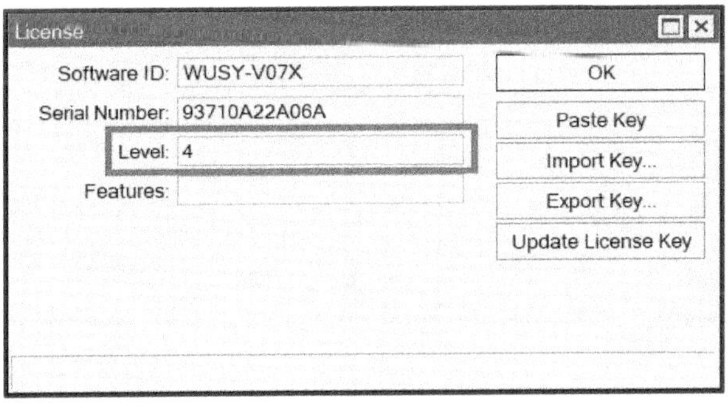

In the x86 version, the default level is Level 0.

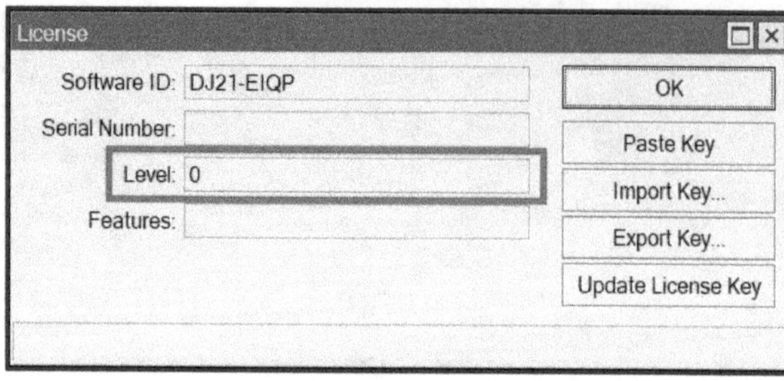

In the CHR version, the default level is Level Free.

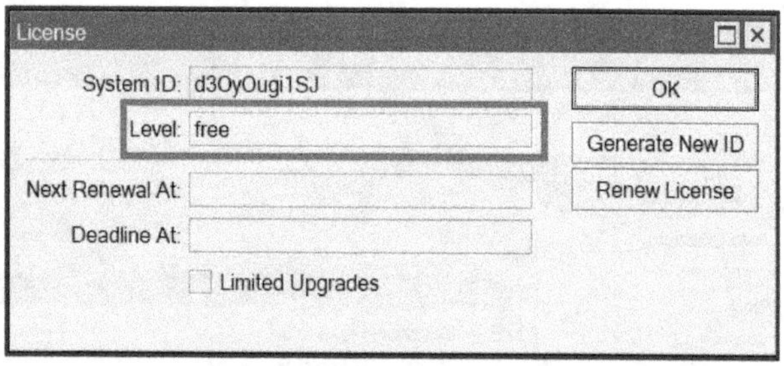

You can also display the license level on RouterOS from the CLI using the following command:

```
System license print
```

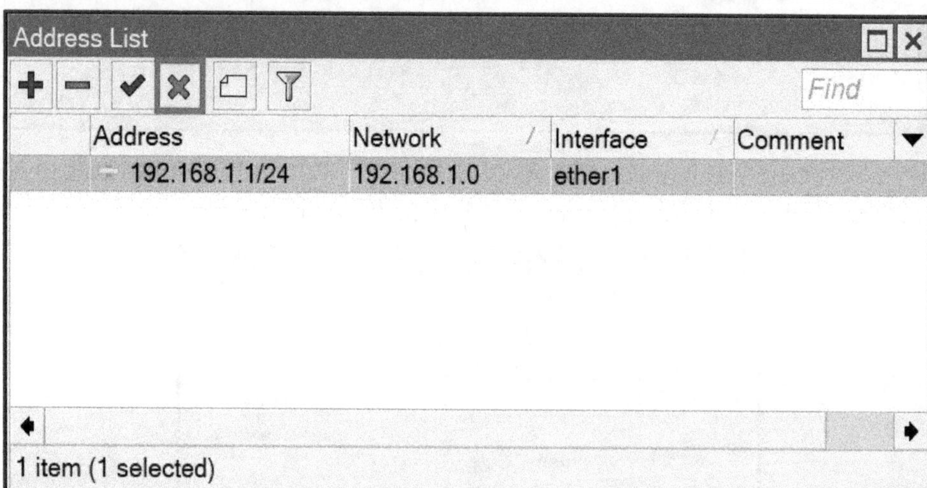

1.33.1 x86 Version

When installing the RouterOS x86 version, it will run in trial mode at level 0, which means it will work only for 24 hours. You can register the version to use the free demo level 1, or purchase levels 4, 5, or 6. Level 2 was a transitional license, and level 3 is not available for purchase.

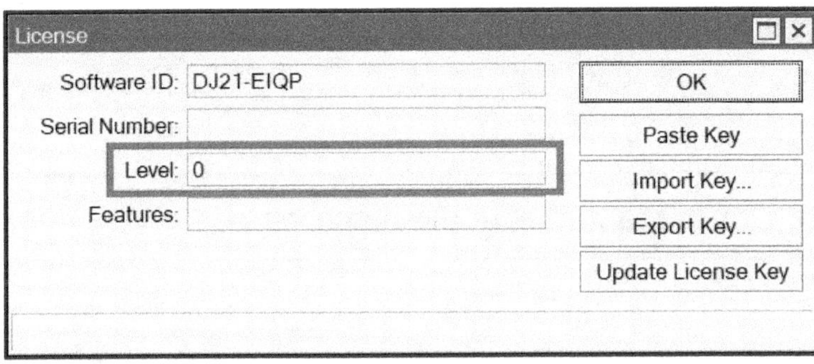

1.33.1.1 Free Demo Level 1

To use the free demo level 1 license of RouterOS x86 version, first log in to your MikroTik account and click **Make a Demo Key**.

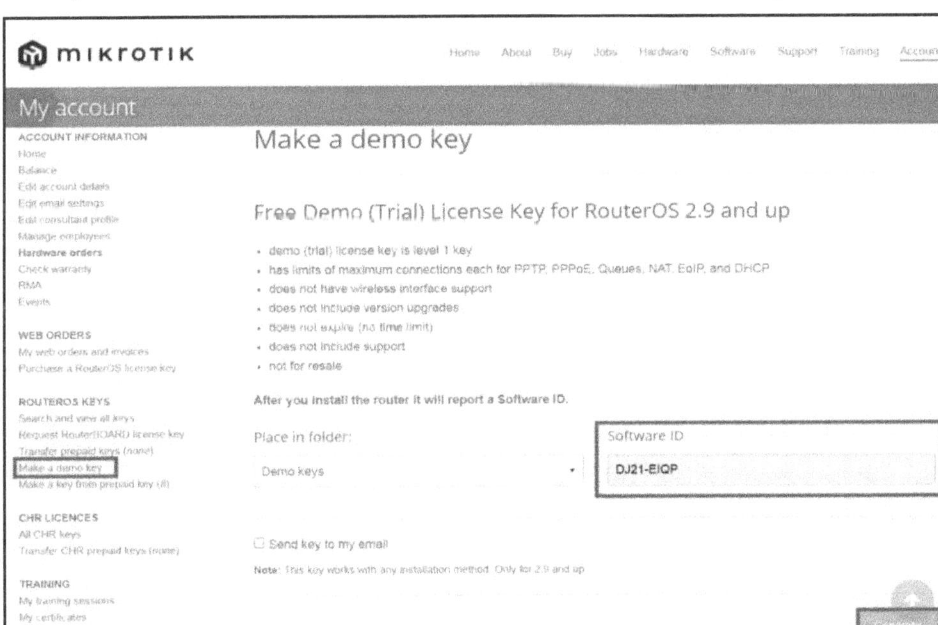

Then, in the **Software ID** field, enter the Software ID of your RouterOS x86 version, which appears in the **License** dialog box.

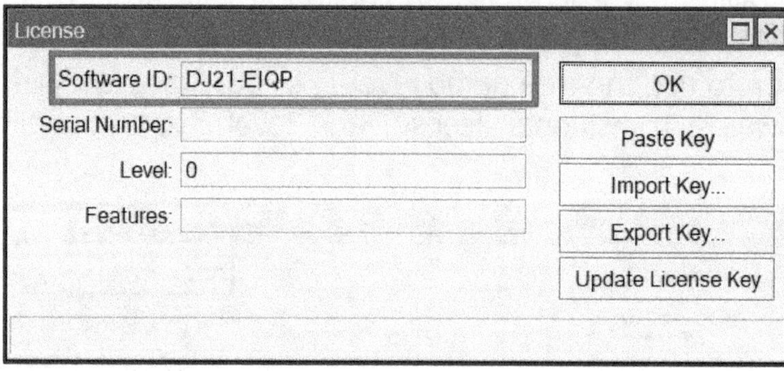

Then click **Generate** to create the demo key.

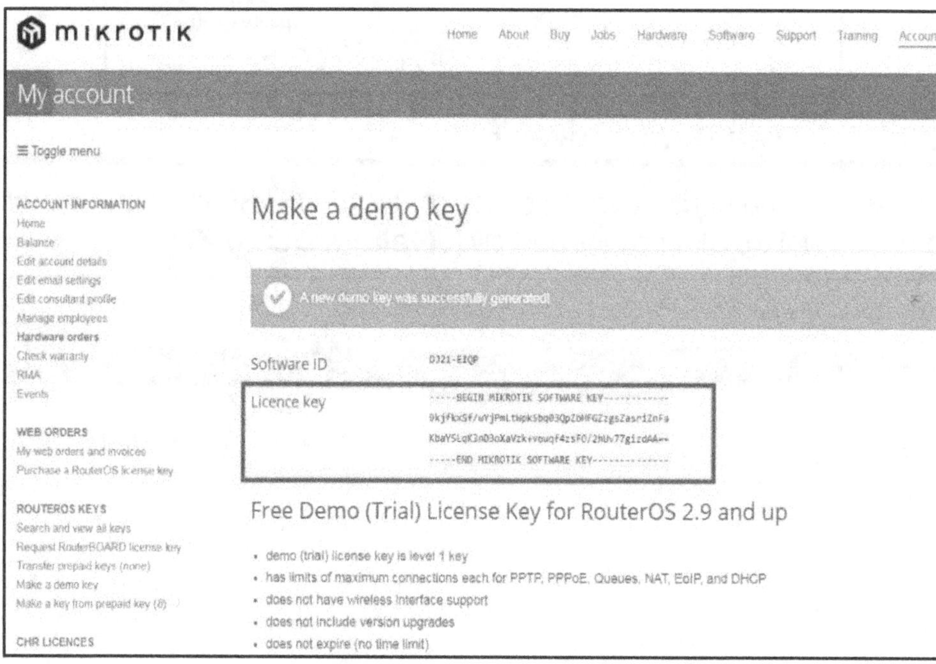

Now, copy this license key and paste it in the **License** dialog box on the device by clicking the **Paste Key** button.

Or you can choose to receive the key by email, download the key file, and import it by clicking the **Import Key** button.

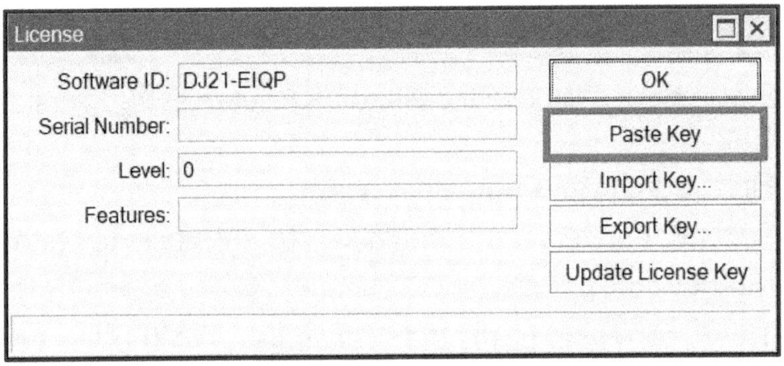

Accept the following message to reboot the RouterOS and use the license.

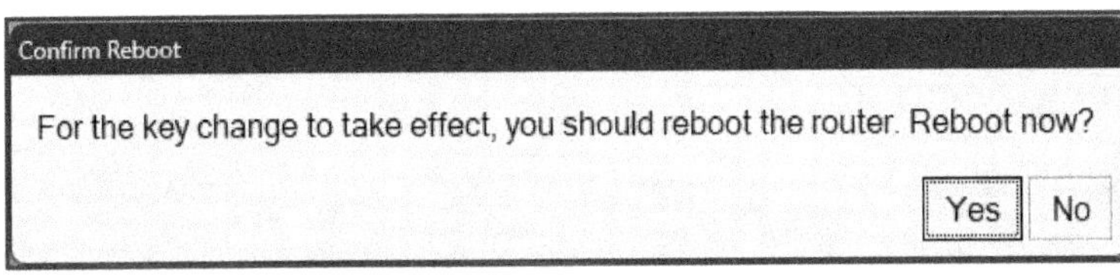

After rebooting the device, the free demo level 1 will appear in the **License** dialog box.

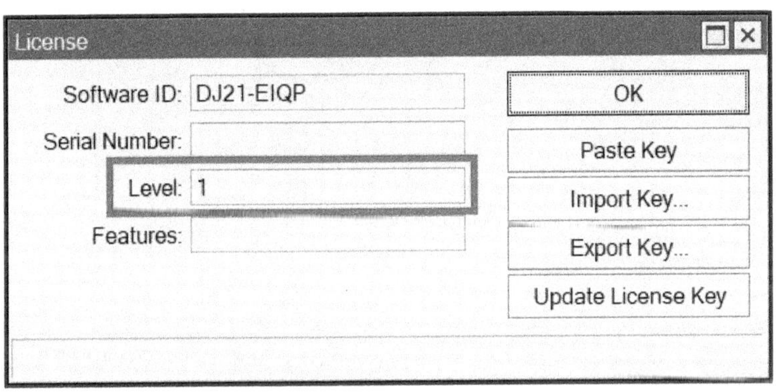

The demo level 1 will not expire, but it is meant to be just for demo to try the operating system. It has a limit of only one connection for PPTP, PPPoE, Queues, NAT, EoIP, and DHCP. It also does not support wireless interfaces and does not allow downloading the updates. Therefore, it can be used for basic testing or training but not in a production network.

1.33.1.2 Purchase a License for x86

To buy or purchase a license for MikroTik RouterOS x86 version, follow these steps:

- First: purchase a prepaid key.
- Second: convert the prepaid key to a license key and link it to the device.
- Third: copy and paste the license key into the device.

To purchase a prepaid key, log in to your MikroTik account and click **Purchase a RouterOS License Key**.

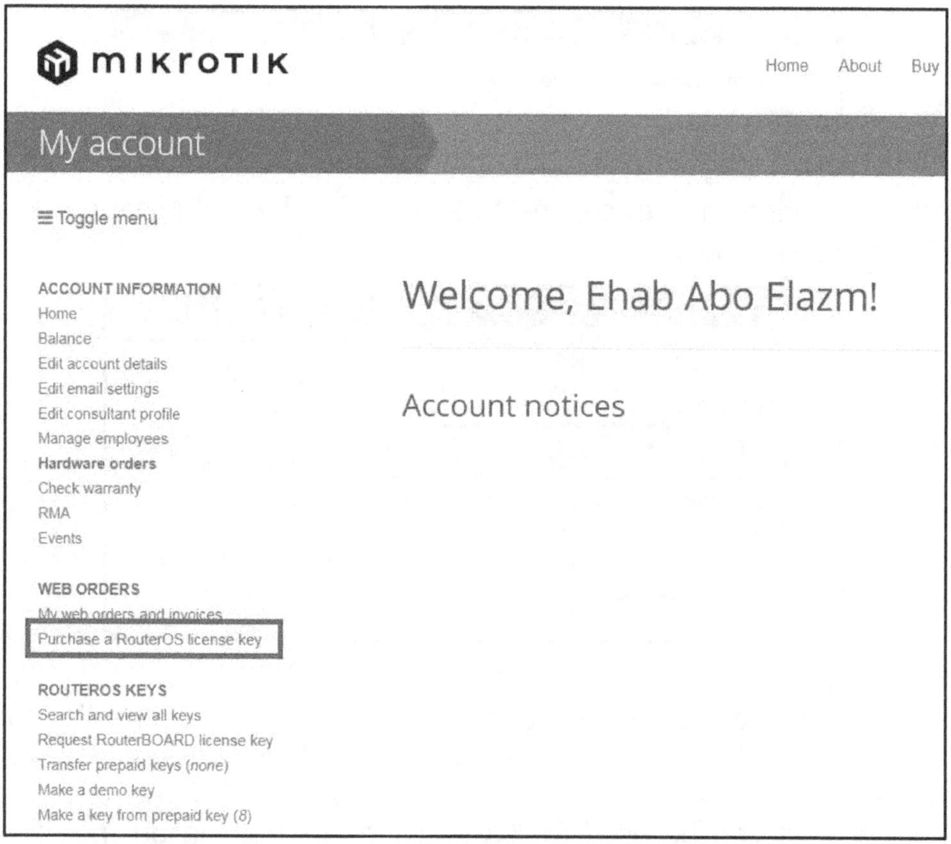

From the **Select Key Level** section, choose the license level you want to buy: L4/P1, L5/P10, or L6/Pu.

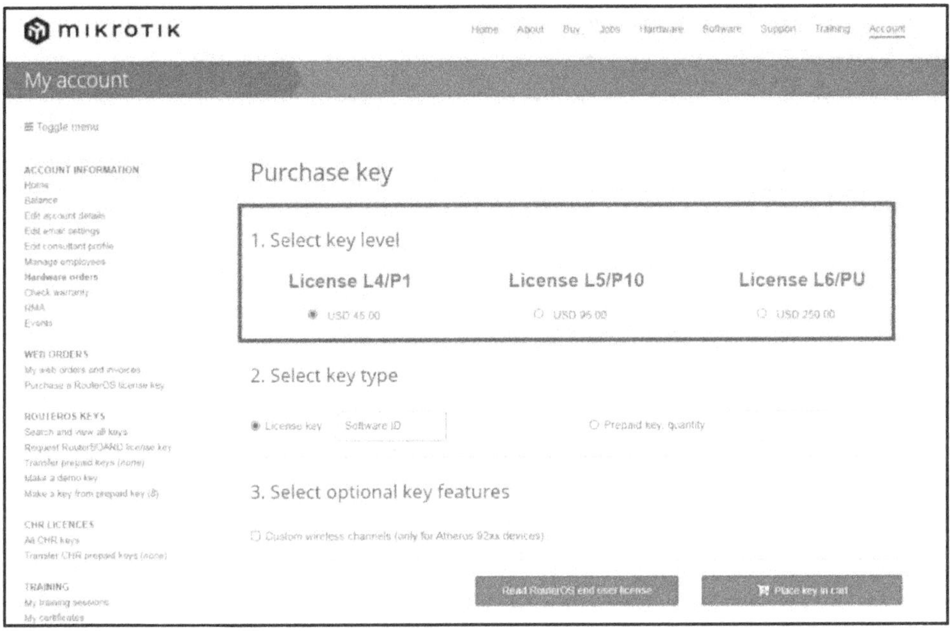

From the **Select Key Type** section, choose to buy a license key using the device software ID or a prepaid key that can be applied to any device.

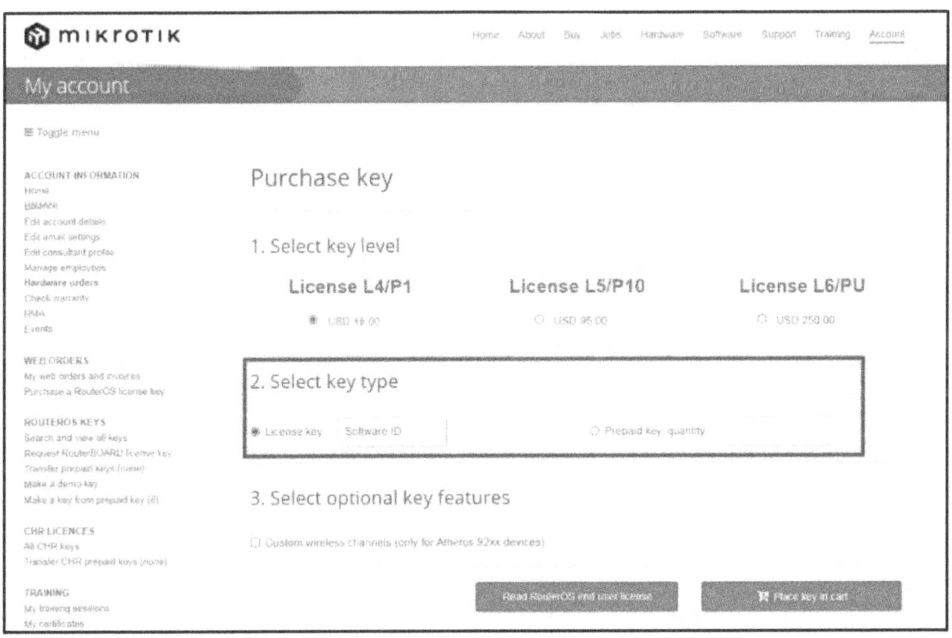

Here, you will buy one level 4 prepaid key by entering the quantity in the **Prepaid Key Quantity** field and clicking **Place Key in Cart.**

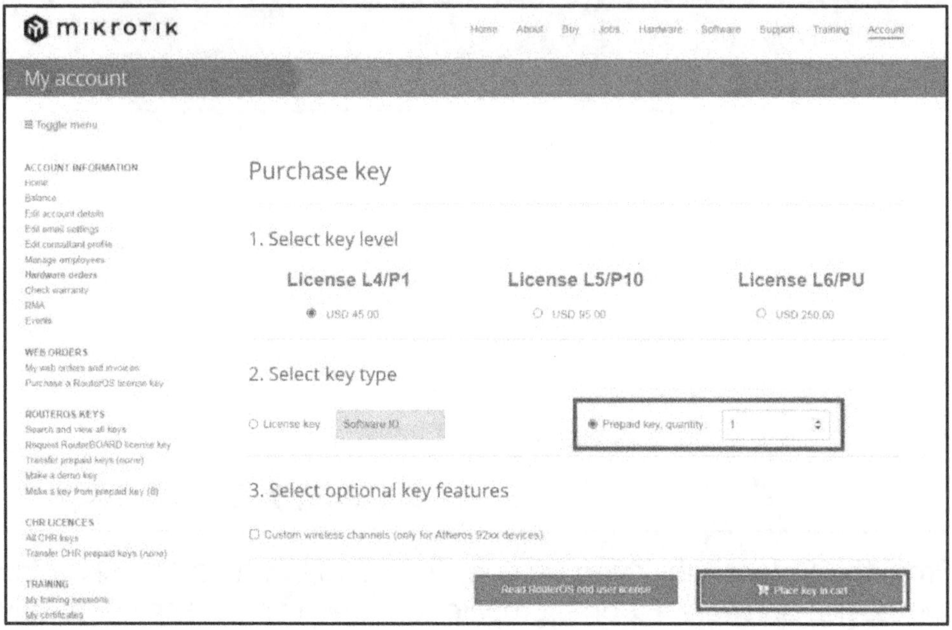

Then, click **Proceed to Checkout**.

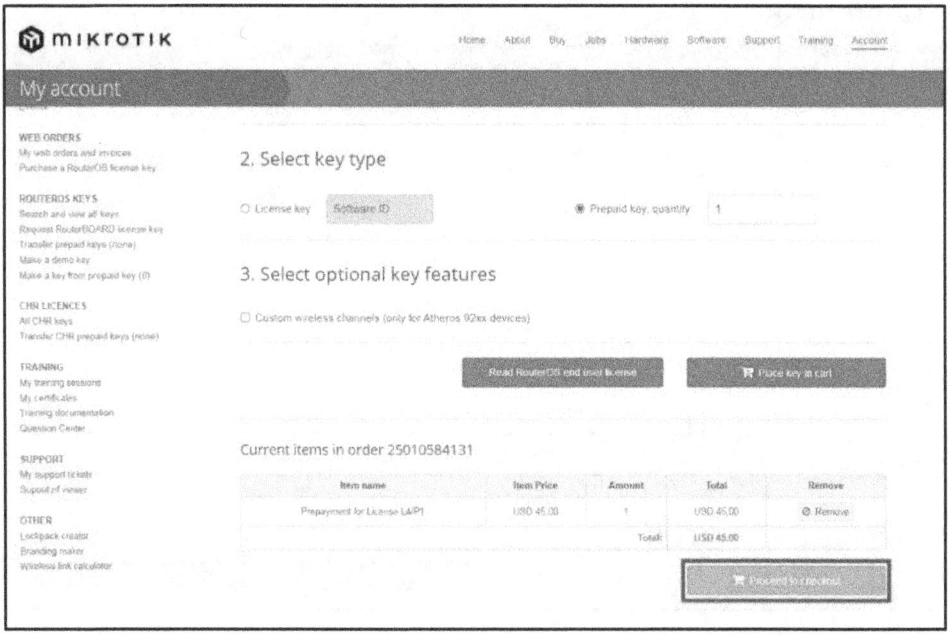

Review your order and complete the payment.

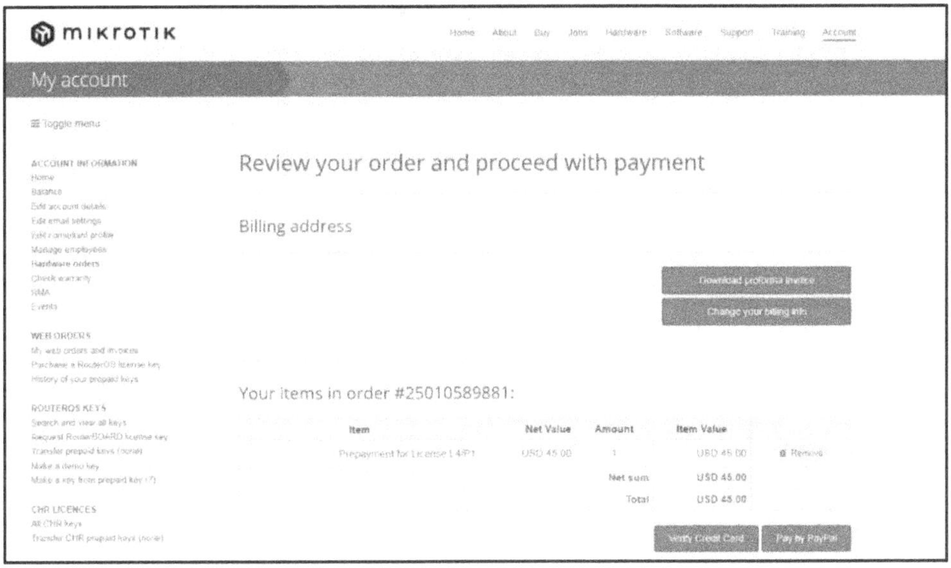

Now, after purchasing the prepaid key, convert it to a license key and link it to the device by clicking **Make a Key from Prepaid Key**. In the **Prepaid Keys** field, select the prepaid key you've just purchased.

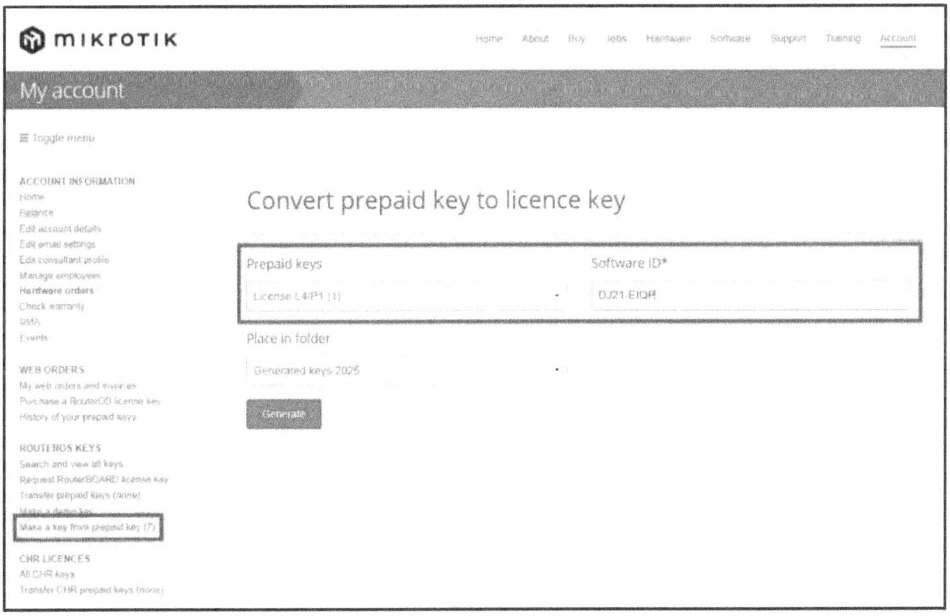

In the **Software ID** field, enter the Software ID of your RouterOS or x86 version, which appears in the **License** dialog box.

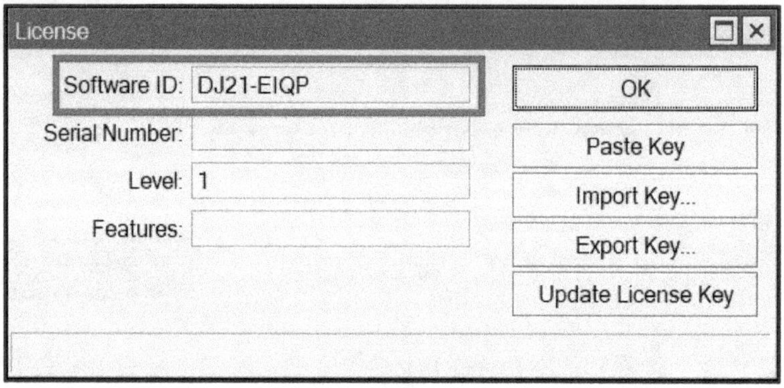

Then click **Generate** to create the license key.

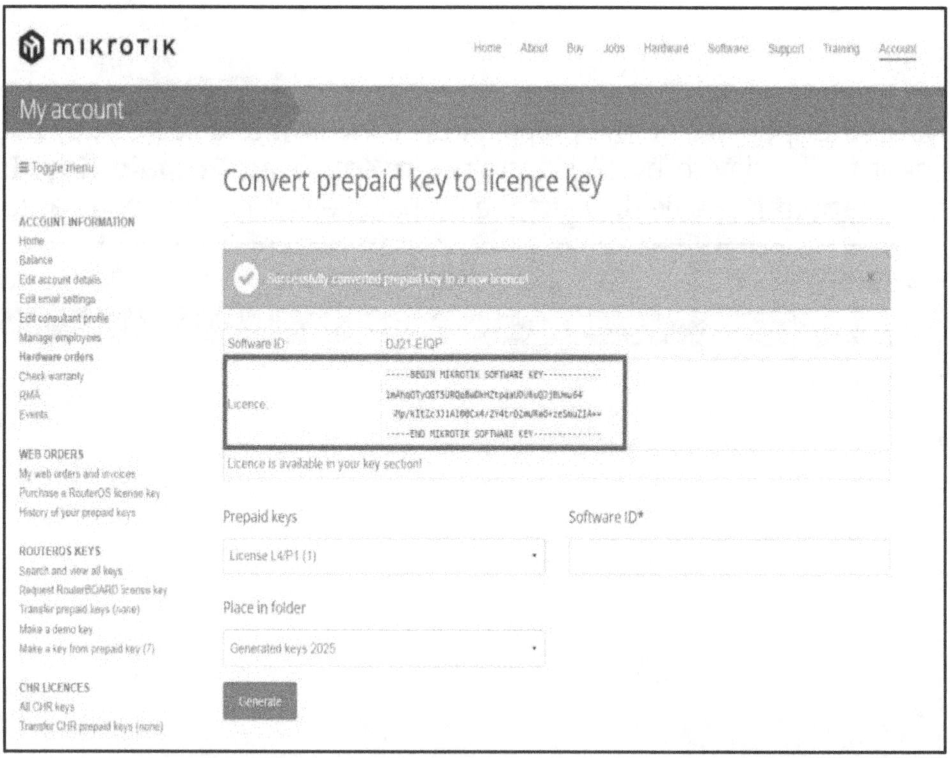

Now, copy the license key and paste it into the **License** dialog box by clicking the **Paste Key** button.

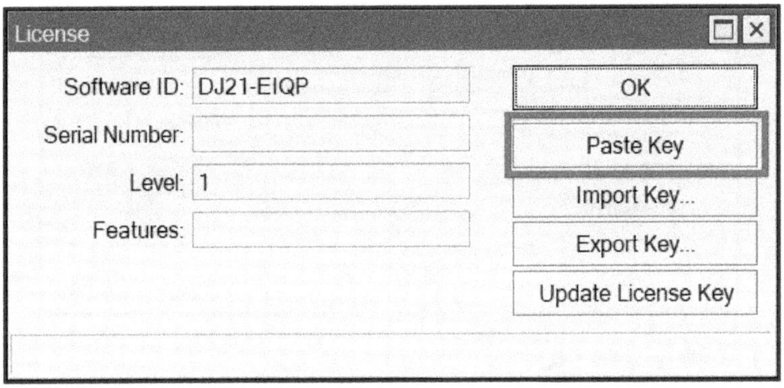

Accept the following message to reboot the RouterOS and use the license.

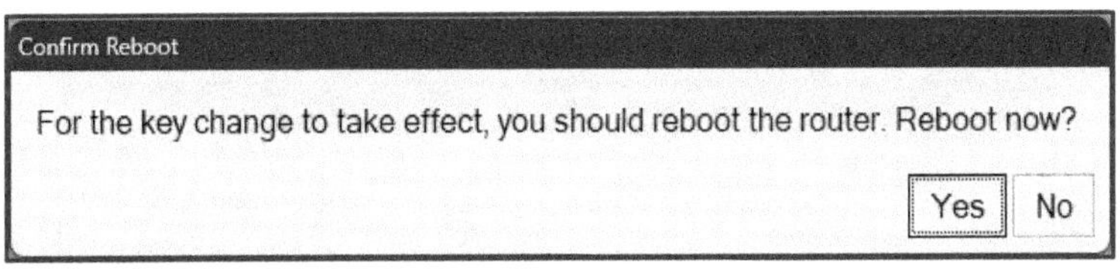

After rebooting the device, license level 4 will appear in the **License** dialog box.

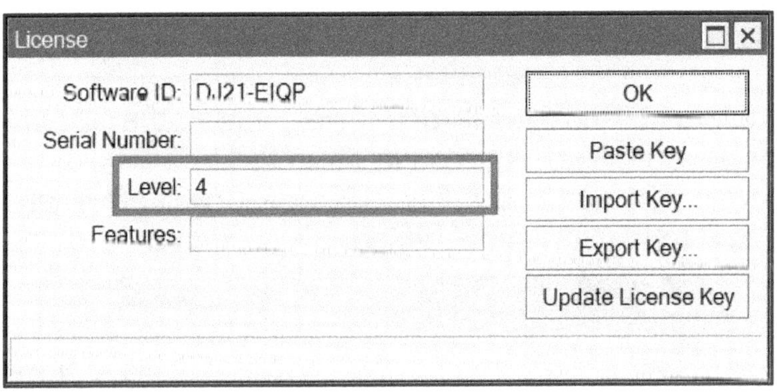

1.33.2 CHR Version

When using the CHR version, it will run in free mode level, which means it will not expire, but the bandwidth is limited to 1 Mbps. You can try a free trial version, or purchase P1, P10, or P-Unlimited level. The CHR license can be transferred from one CHR to another.

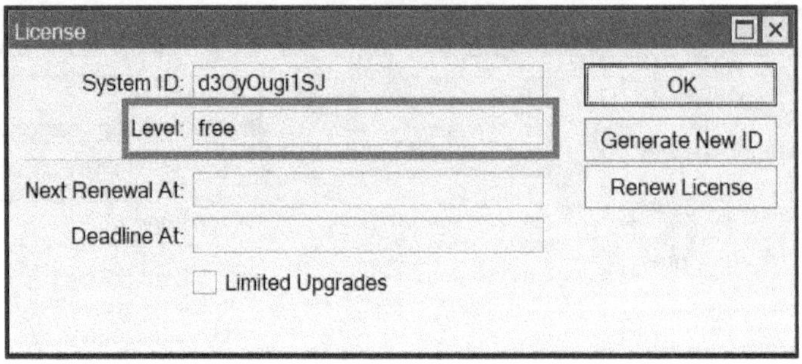

1.33.2.1 Trail Version

To use the trial version of the paid CHR license levels, click the **Renew License** button in **License** dialog box to open the **Renew License** dialog box.

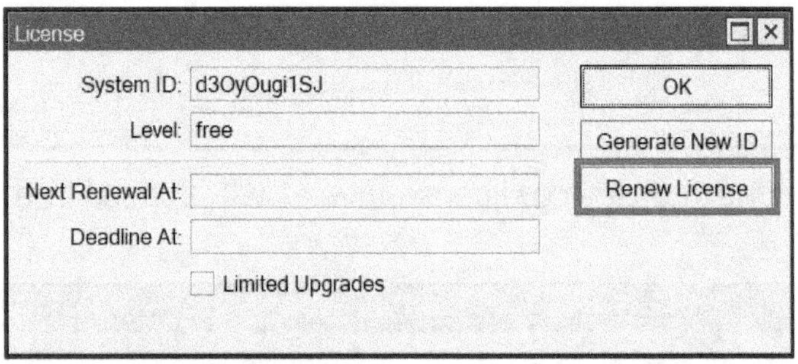

In the **account** and **password** fields, enter the username and password of your MikroTik account. From the **Level** field, choose the license level you want to try: P1, P10, or P-Unlimited. Then click the **Start** button to begin the trial period.

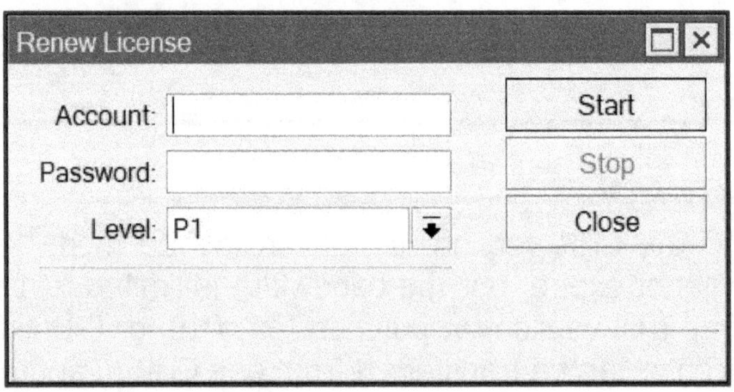

When starting the trial period, the chosen level will appear in the **License** dialog box.

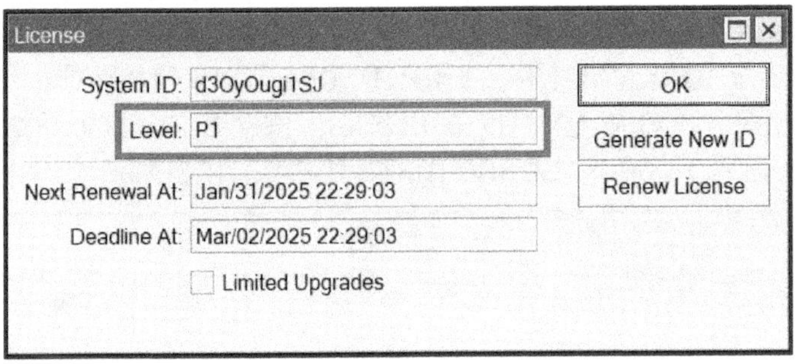

The CHR will be linked to your MikroTik account and will appear on the **All CHR Keys** page by its System ID, allowing you to manage it later.

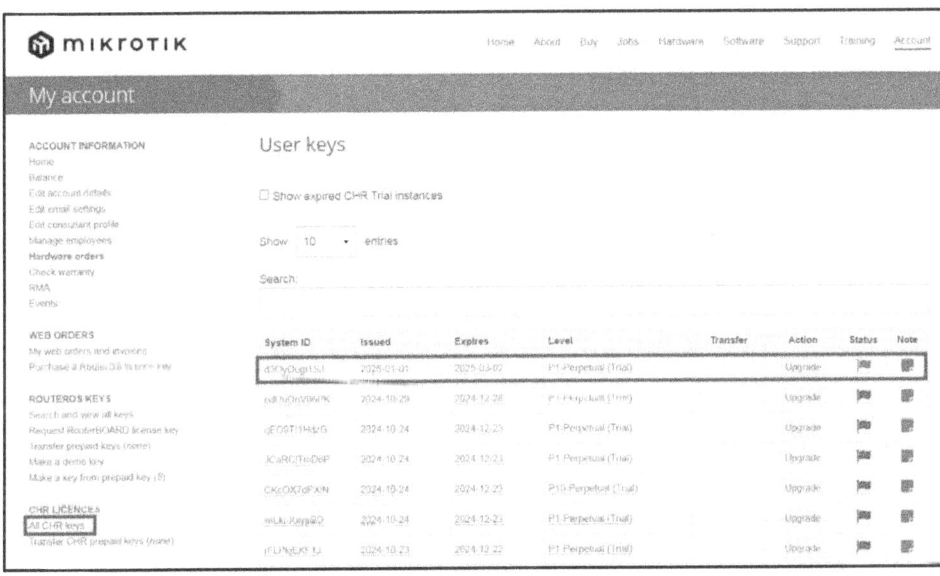

1.33.2.2 Purchase a License for CHR

To buy or purchase a license for MikroTik RouterOS CHR version, follow these steps:

- First: purchase a prepaid key.
- Second: link the device to your account.
- Third: upgrade the device to use the prepaid key.

To purchase a prepaid key, follow the same steps explained earlier.

(Log in to your MikroTik account and click **Purchase a RouterOS License Key**. From the **Select Key Level** section, choose the license level you want to buy: L4/P1, L5/P10, or L6/Pu. From the **Select Key Type** section, choose to buy a prepaid key and click **Place Key in Cart**. Proceed to checkout and make the payment).

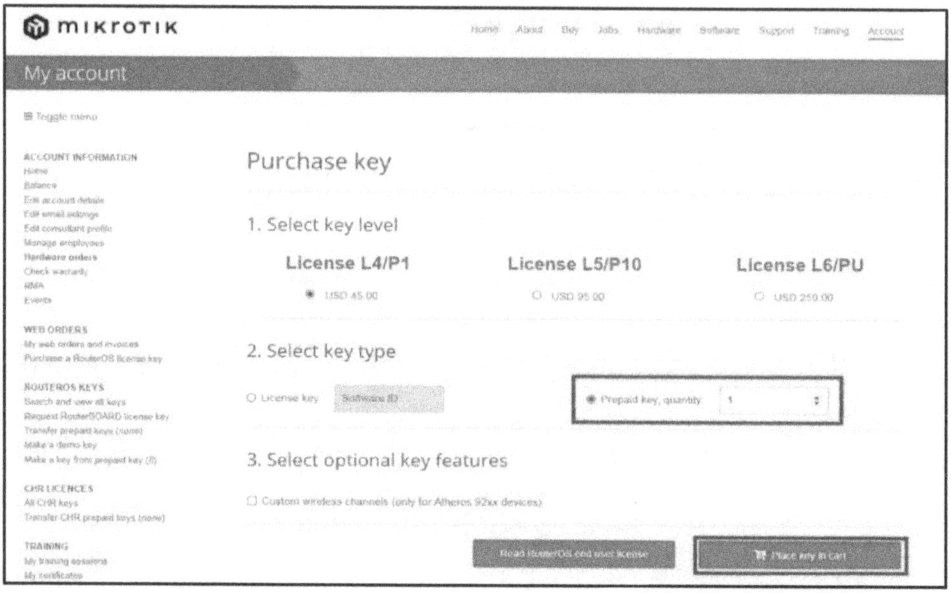

Now, after purchasing the prepaid key, link the device to your account by activating a trial version, following the same steps explained earlier.

(Click the **Renew License** button in **License** dialog box, enter the username and password of your MikroTik account, choose any license level and click the **Start** button to start the trial period).

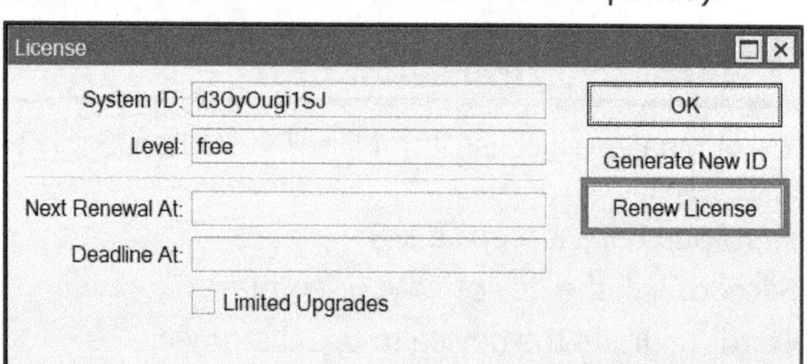

In your MikroTik account, click **All CHR Keys** and make sure that the device is linked to your account by checking its system ID.

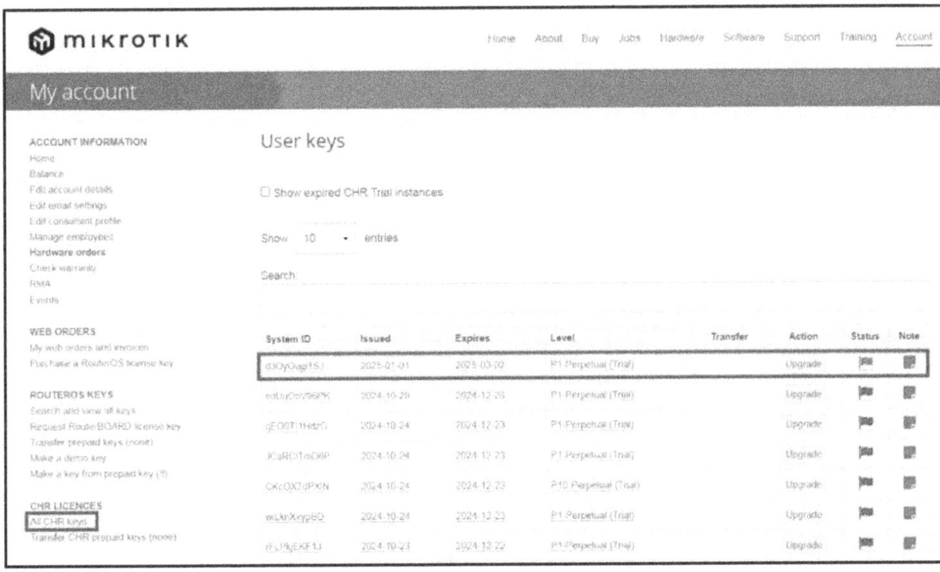

To upgrade the device and use the prepaid key, select the device and click **Upgrade** on the **All CHR Keys** page in your MikroTik account.

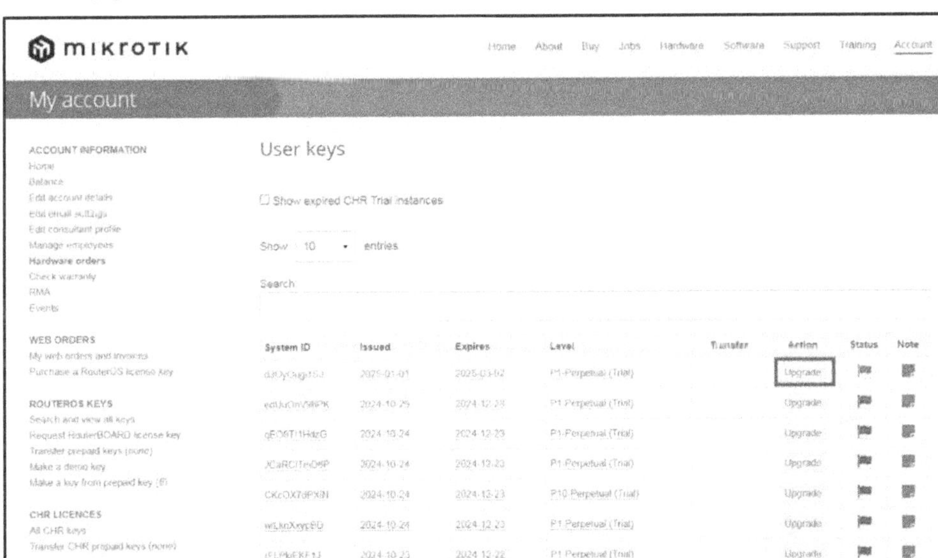

In the **Level** field on the **Upgrade License** page, choose the license level you've just purchased and click **Upgrade**.

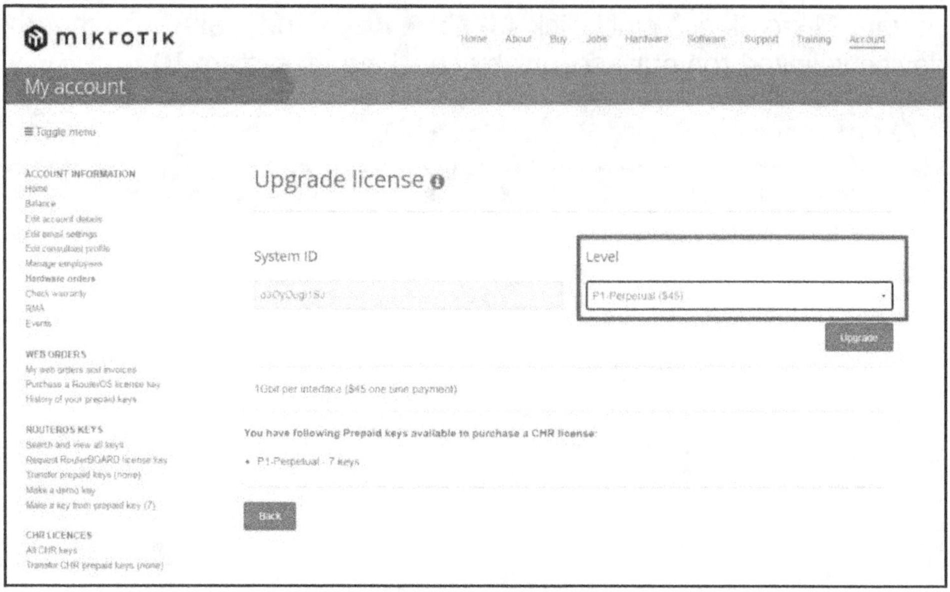

On the **Payment** page, click **Pay Using Prepaid Key**. Or you can click **Proceed to Checkout** if you haven't completed the first step to purchase the prepaid key.

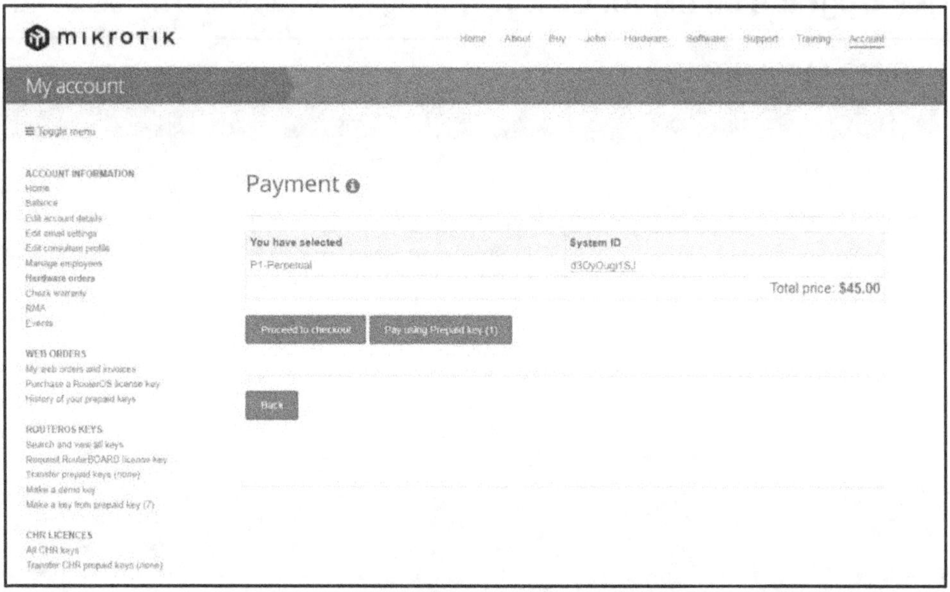

After upgrading the license, the device will now appear with an unexpired license.

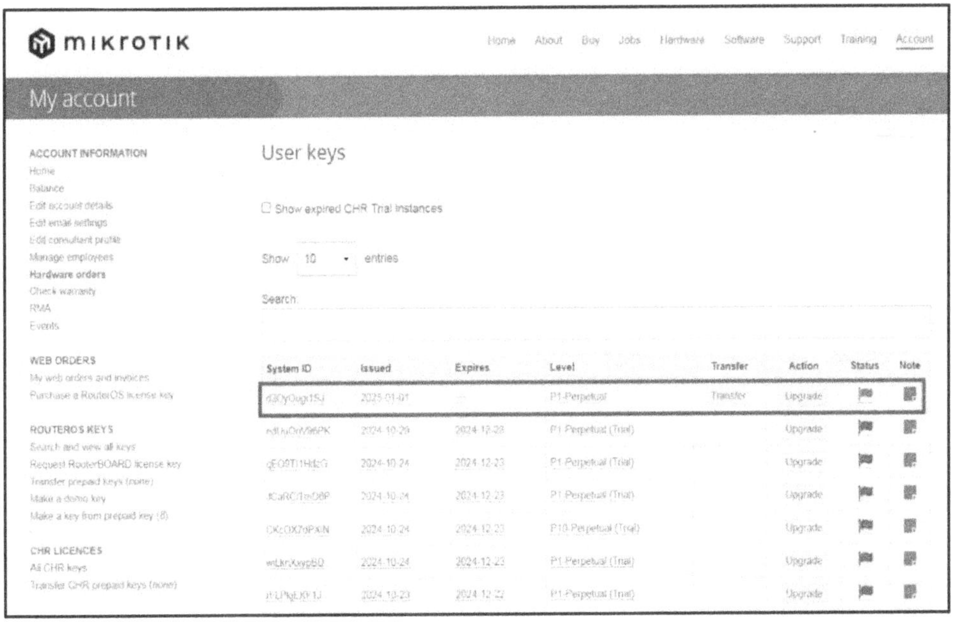

Now, to activate the license on the device, click the **Renew License** button in the **License** dialog box, enter the username and password of your MikroTik account, select the license level you've just purchased, and click the **Start** button to activate the paid license.

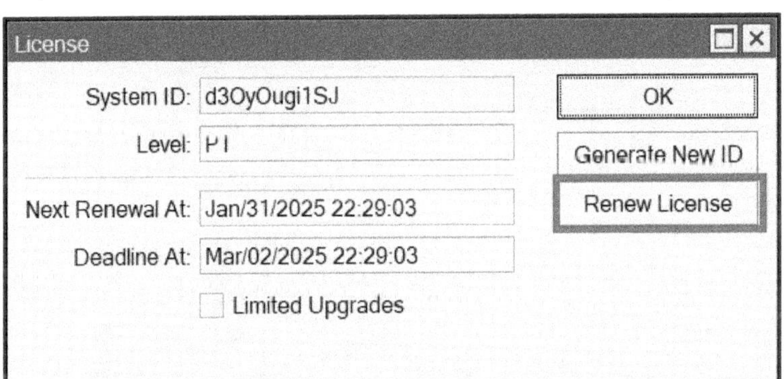

Note: this CHR license can be transferred to any other CHR device linked to your account by clicking **Transfer** on the **All CHR Keys** page in your account and selecting the device you want.

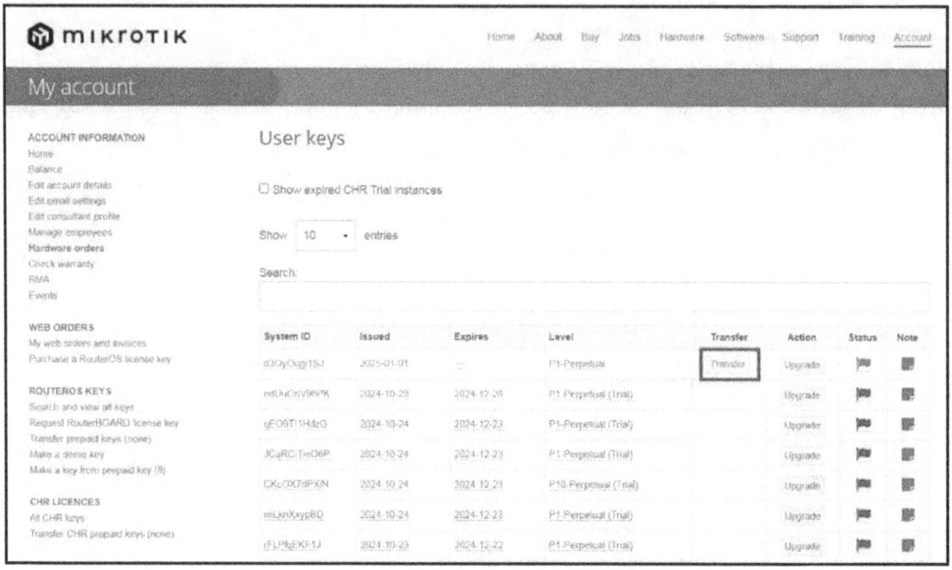

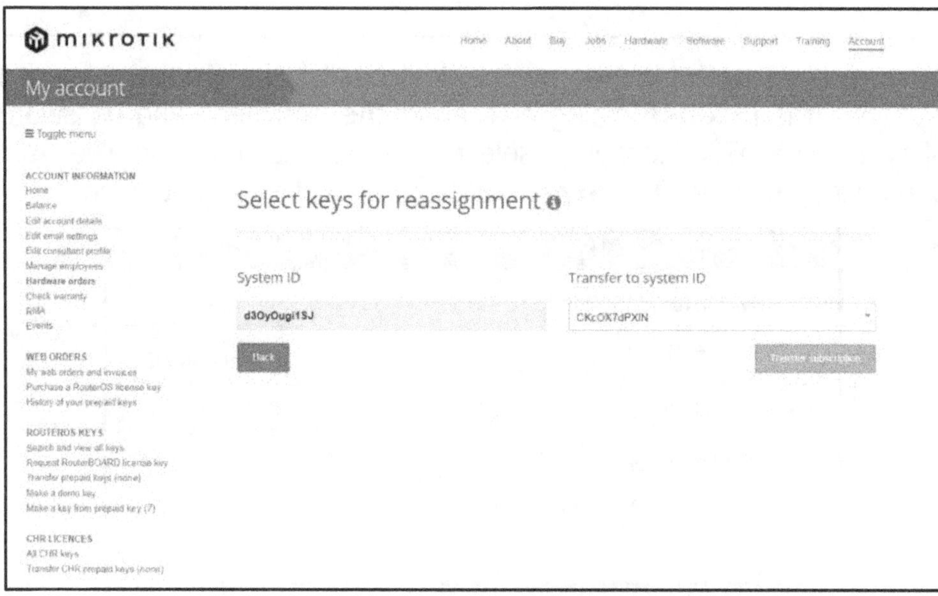

It is very important to understand that since the CHR license can be transferred to another device, the device will continue contacting the MikroTik license server when it reaches the date indicated in the **Next Renewal At** field in the license dialog box to keep the license active.

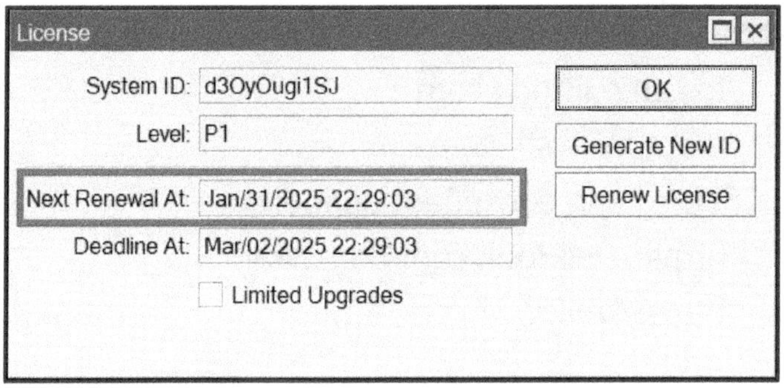

If the **Deadline At** date is reached without successfully contacting the server, the device will consider the license expired. It will continue working normally but will not receive updates. The **Limited Upgrades** checkbox will be checked to indicate that the license has expired.

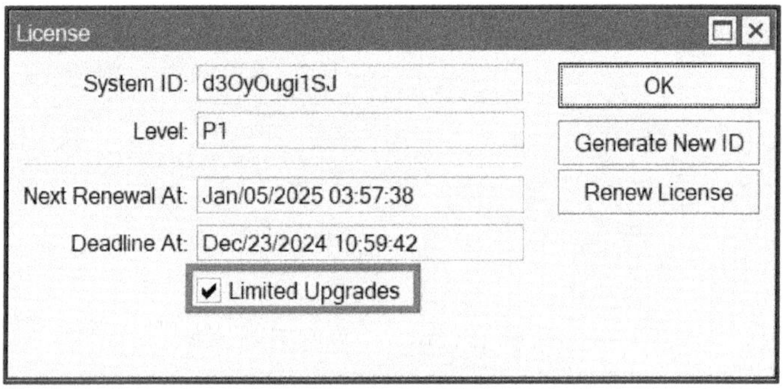

1.34 Sources of Additional Information

MikroTik provides several channels to obtain information about its products and their usage:

- MikroTik official website:
  - www.mikrotik.com
- MikroTik official documentation and information center:
  - wiki.mikrotik.com
  - help.mikrotik.com
- MikroTik official support
  - •support@mikrotik.com

- User and trainer forums:
    - forum.mikrotik.com
    - mum.mikrotik.com
- Distributor and consultant support
    - https://mikrotik.com/consultants
    - https://mikrotik.com/buy

Module 2

DHCP

Module 2

This module provides simple information about the DHCP protocol and how to configure it in MikroTik RouterOS quickly and easily using the setup wizard. It explains the IP pools tool and its use in MikroTik and also provides a brief overview of the ARP protocol.

More advanced information about the DHCP protocol is available in the MTCTCE course, and more advanced information about the ARP protocol is available in the MTCSWE course.

This module covers the following course content topics:

- DHCP Server and Client
    - DHCP Client
    - DHCP Server Setup
    - Leases Management
    - DHCP Server Network Configuration
- Address Resolution Protocol (ARP)
    - ARP Modes
    - RouterOS ARP table
- IP pool
    - Creating Pool
    - Managing Ranges
    - Assigning to a Service

DHCP

2.1 DHCP Overview and Key Concepts

To connect a computer, or a host, to a computer network, the host must have an IP address.

you can assign an IP address to a host in two ways:

- Statically: By manually assigning the IP address to the host
- Dynamically: By using a protocol called DHCP (Dynamic Host Configuration Protocol).

2.2 DHCP Protocol

The Dynamic Host Configuration Protocol (DHCP) is a protocol used to automatically distribute IP addresses to hosts, instead of manually assigning static IP addresses to them.

2.3 How DHCP Protocol Works

The concept of using DHCP is as follows: Configuring a device on the network to be responsible for providing IP addresses to other devices that need one. This device is called a DHCP Server, and the devices that request IP addresses are called DHCP Clients. The process of distributing IP addresses is known as IP address leasing.

The IP address leasing process happens in four steps:

- The client sends a message called DHCP Discover.
- The server replies with a message called DHCP Offer.
- The client sends a message called DHCP Request.

- The server replies with a message called DHCP Acknowledgement.

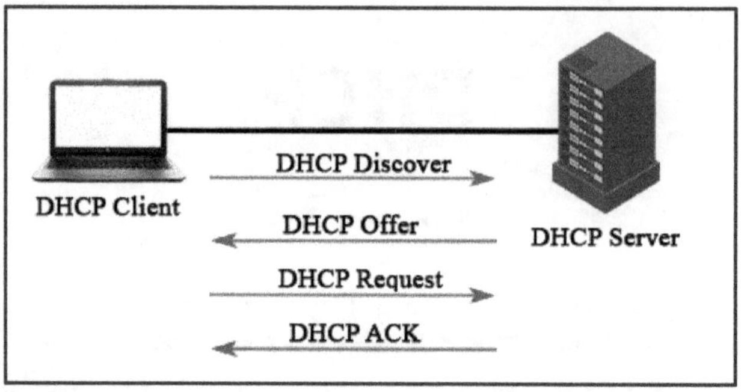

The DHCP server can provide the DHCP client with the following:

- IP address
- Subnet mask
- Default gateway
- DNS server address
- Additionally, it can provide other configuration options.

You can configure RouterOS to function as either a DHCP Server or a DHCP Client.

2.4 DHCP Server Configuration

To configure a DHCP Server on RouterOS to function as a DHCP server and distribute IP addresses to DHCP clients, you must first assign an IP address to the interface where the DHCP Server will be installed. Then, use the **DHCP Server** window to configure the server.

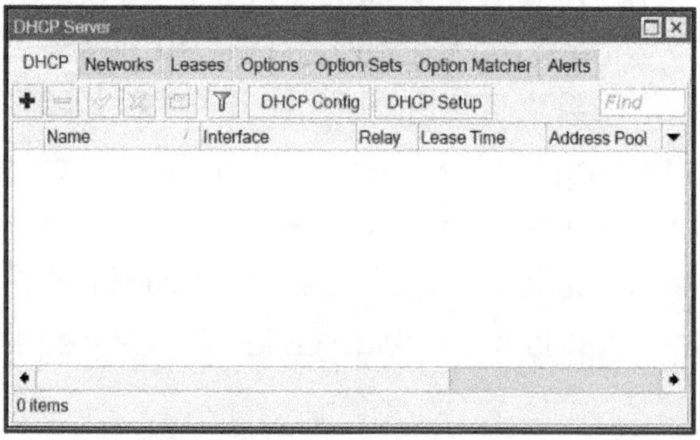

To open the **DHCP Server** window, click the **IP** menu, then **select DHCP Server**.

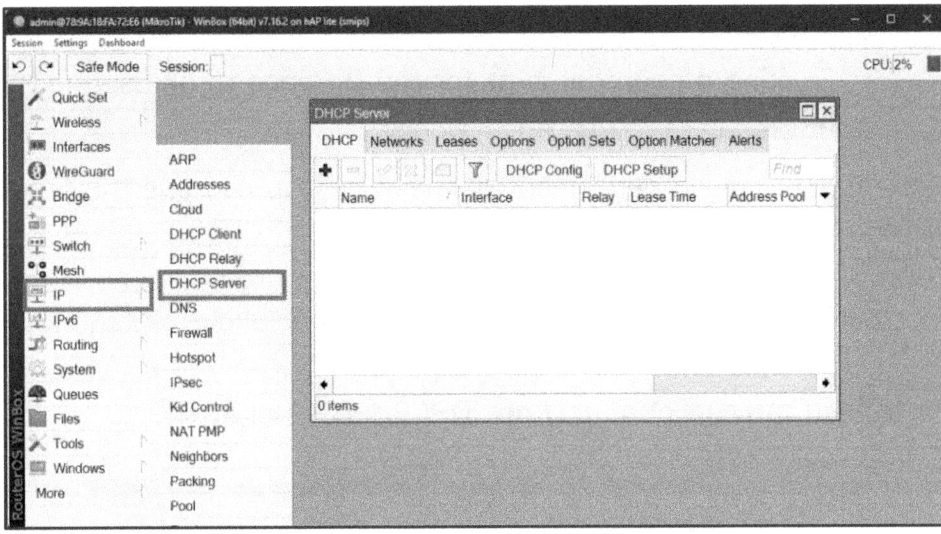

Note: In RouterOS v6, before configuring DHCP, make sure that the DHCP package is installed. In RouterOS v7, this package is already included in the main package.

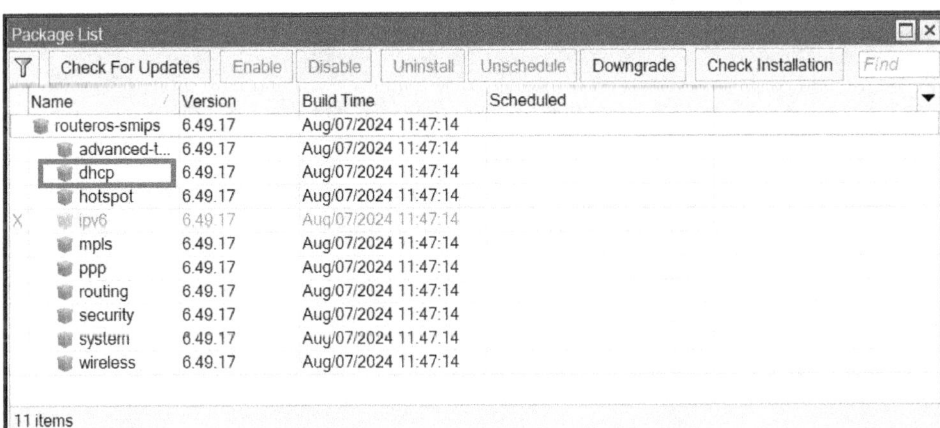

To configure a DHCP server, perform three steps:

- Creating a server on an interface in the **DHCP** tab of the **DHCP Server** window.

- Creating a network that contains the information to be distributed to clients in the **Network** tab of the **DHCP Server** window
- Creating a pool that contains the IP range to be used in the **Pools** tab of the **IP Pool** window

These steps can be performed manually, or you can use the Setup Wizard to configure them automatically.

For the objectives of the MTCNA course, you will use the Setup Wizard to create a DHCP Server. You will learn more about DHCP in the MTCTCE course.

Note: you can configure only one DHCP server per interface.

2.5 DHCP Setup

you can use the **DHCP Setup** to automatically create a DHCP server on an interface in RouterOS.

To start the setup, click the **DHCP Setup** button in the **DHCP** tab of the **DHCP Server** window.

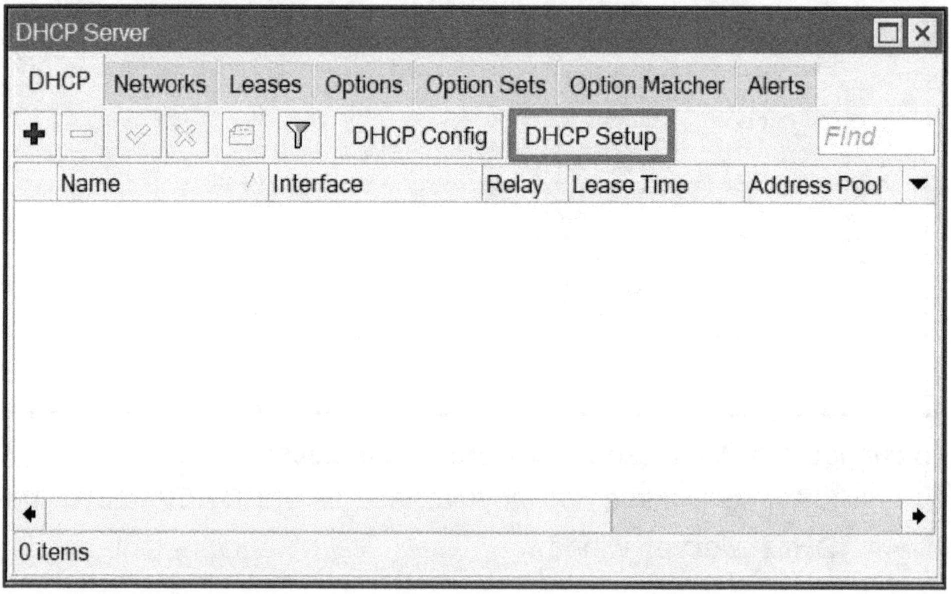

In the first message, select the interface on which you want to configure the DHCP server, then click the **Next** button.

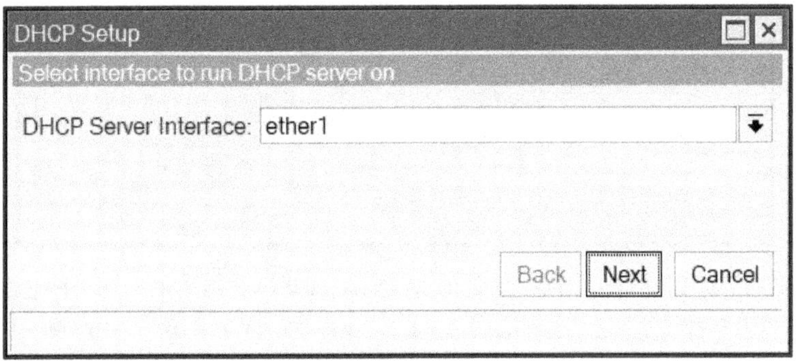

The setup wizard will check the IP address of the selected interface to automatically gather information for the DHCP server, such as the network address, gateway, and the range of IP addresses to distribute to clients. It will then display this information in the following messages, allowing you to modify any of them if needed.

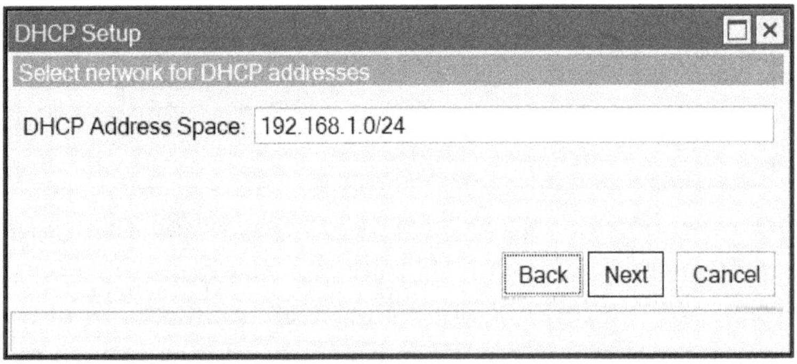

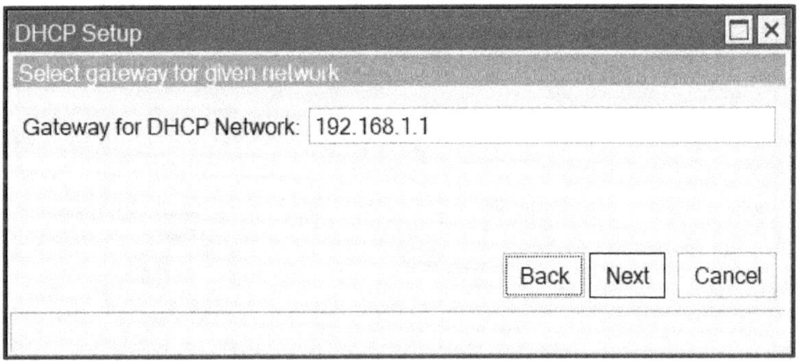

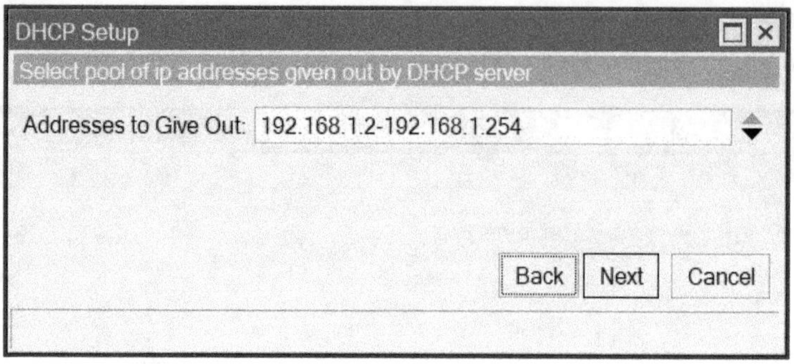

In the next message, the setup wizard will ask for the IP address of the DNS server to be distributed to clients. If a DNS server is already configured on RouterOS, it will appear here, or you can enter the IP address of the DNS server you want to use.

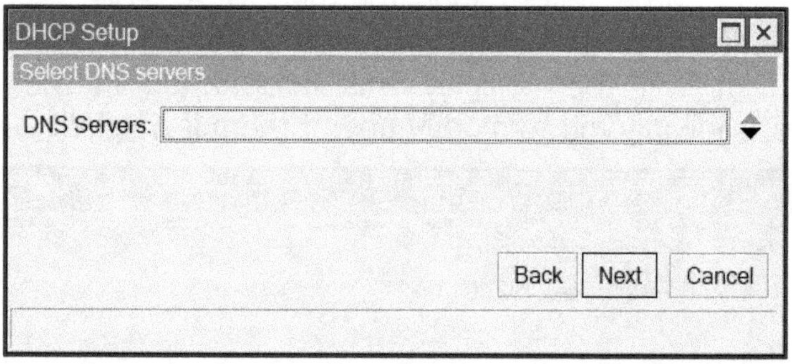

In the last message, it will ask for the lease time. The default is 30 minutes in RouterOS v7, and 10 minutes in RouterOS v6 (as of the latest versions at the time of publishing this book: v6.49 and v7.18). .

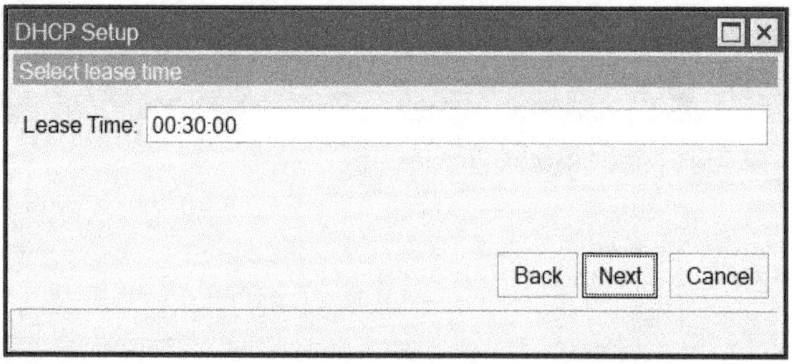

After clicking next, if everything is ok, the setup wizard will tell you that Setup has completed successfully.

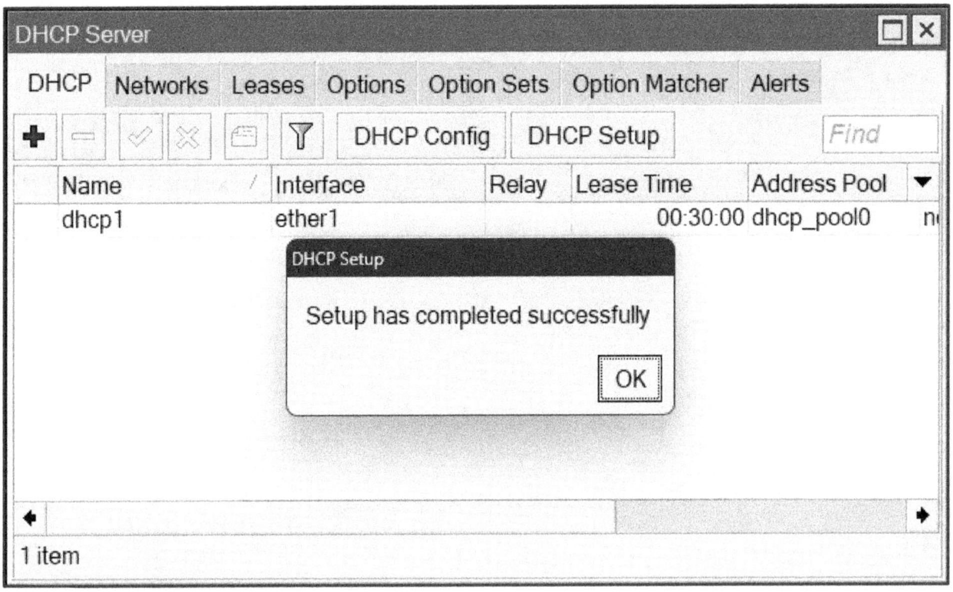

The setup wizard will add:

- The server in the **DHCP** tab.
- A network in the **Network** tab of the **DHCP Server** window.
- A pool in the **IP Pool** window.

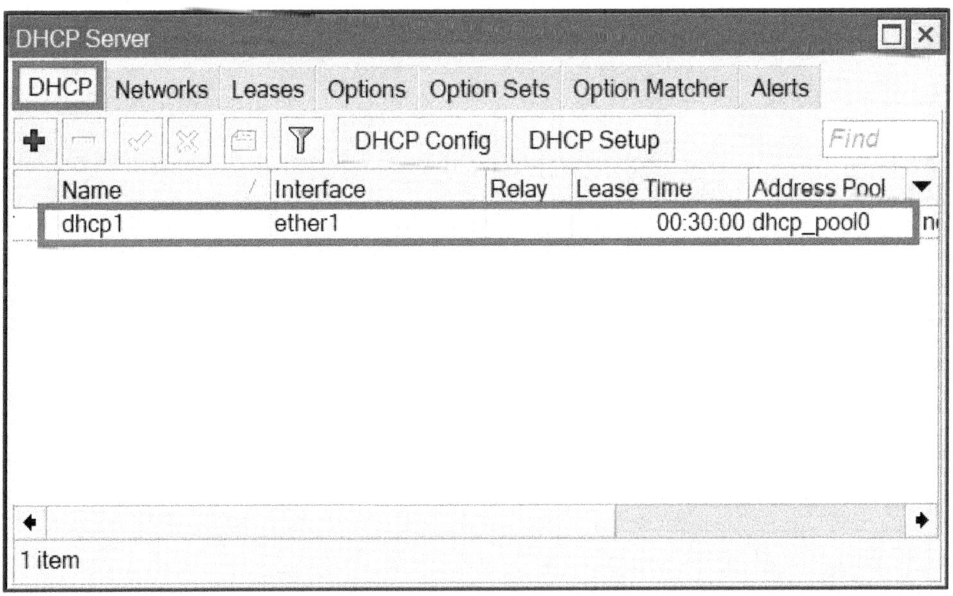

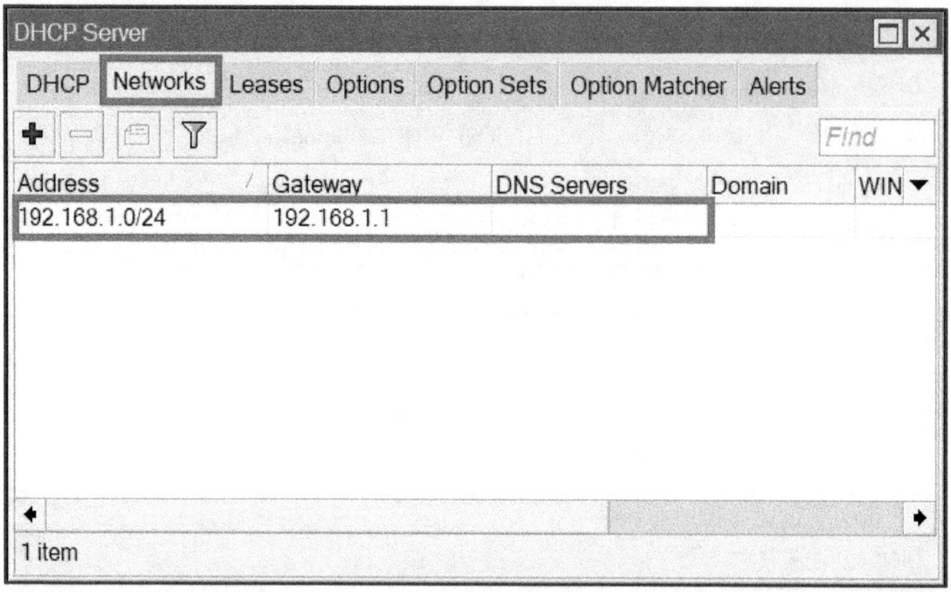

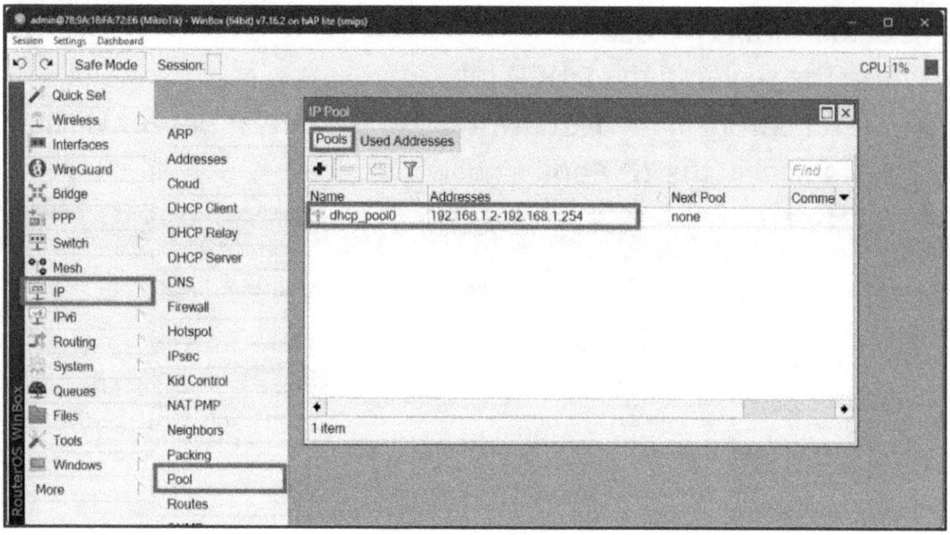

Now, any device connects to this interface will receive an IP address from the server.

You can also configure the DHCP server from the CLI using the following command:

```
ip dhcp-server setup
```

Then enter the information or accept the displayed settings by pressing Enter each time the setup wizard asks for input

```
Terminal <1>
[admin@MikroTik] >
[admin@MikroTik] > ip dhcp-server setup
Select interface to run DHCP server on

dhcp server interface: ether1
Select network for DHCP addresses

dhcp address space: 192.168.1.0/24
Select gateway for given network

gateway for dhcp network: 192.168.1.1
Select pool of ip addresses given out by DHCP server

addresses to give out: 192.168.1.2-192.168.1.254
Select DNS servers

dns servers:
Select lease time

lease time: 1800
[admin@MikroTik] >
```

To display information about DHCP servers, use the following command:

```
ip dhcp-server print
```

```
Terminal <1>
[admin@MikroTik] >
[admin@MikroTik] >
[admin@MikroTik] > ip dhcp-server print
Columns: NAME, INTERFACE, ADDRESS-POOL, LEASE-TIME
# NAME   INTERFACE  ADDRESS-POOL  LEASE-TIME
0 dhcp1  ether1     dhcp_pool2    30m
[admin@MikroTik] >
```

To display information about DHCP networks, use the following command:

```
ip dhcp-server network print
```

```
Terminal <1>
[admin@MikroTik] >
[admin@MikroTik] >
[admin@MikroTik] > ip dhcp-server network print
Columns: ADDRESS, GATEWAY
# ADDRESS         GATEWAY
0 192.168.1.0/24  192.168.1.1
[admin@MikroTik] >
```

To display information about IP pools, use the following command:

```
ip pool print
```

```
Terminal <1>
[admin@MikroTik] >
[admin@MikroTik] >
[admin@MikroTik] > ip  pool print
Columns: NAME, RANGES
#  NAME        RANGES
0  dhcp_pool2  192.168.1.2-192.168.1.254
[admin@MikroTik] >
```

LAB

In this lab, MikroTik device R1 is connected to PC1 via the interface ether1. You want to configure a DHCP server on this interface to assign an IP address to PC1.

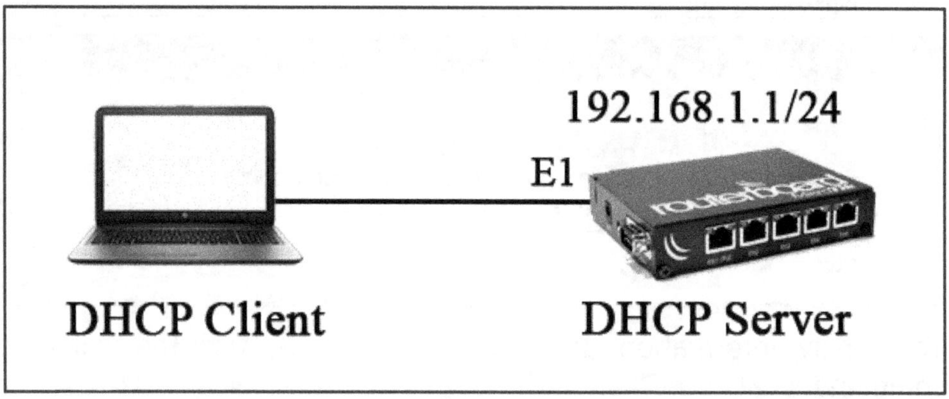

To start the configuration:

- First: start by assigning an IP address to the ether1 interface.

- Second: configure the DHCP server on this interface.

To assign an IP address to the ether1 interface click the **IP** menu, then select **Addresses** to open the **Address List** window.

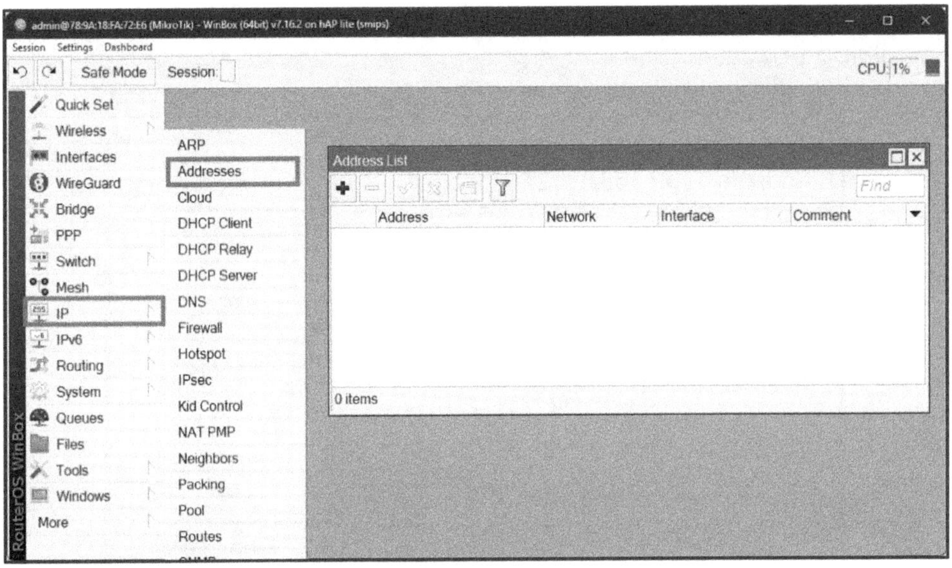

Then click the **Add** button in **Address List** window to open the **New Address** dialog box.

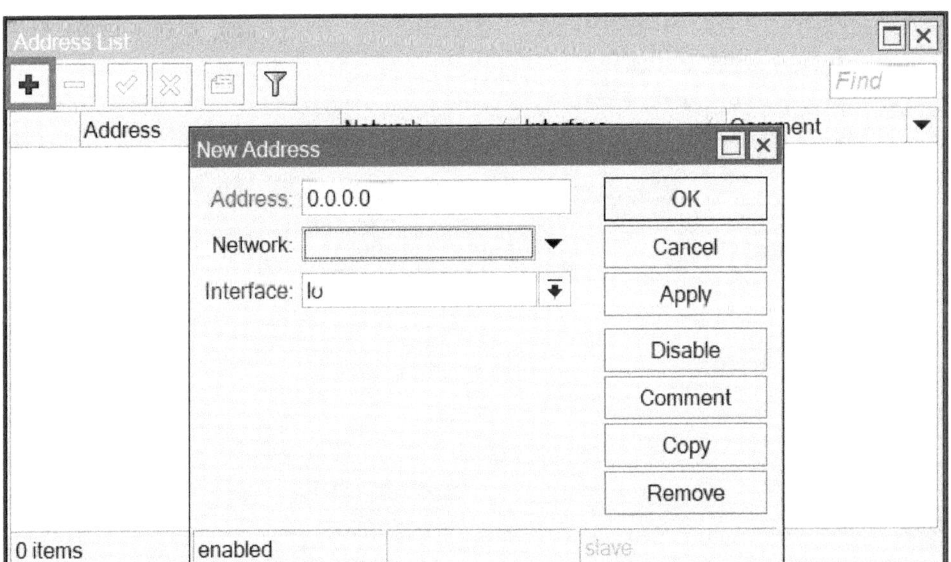

In **Address** field in this dialog box, enter the following IP address and subnet mask:

192.168.1.1/24

In the **Interface** field, select ether1, then click the **OK** button to close the dialog box.

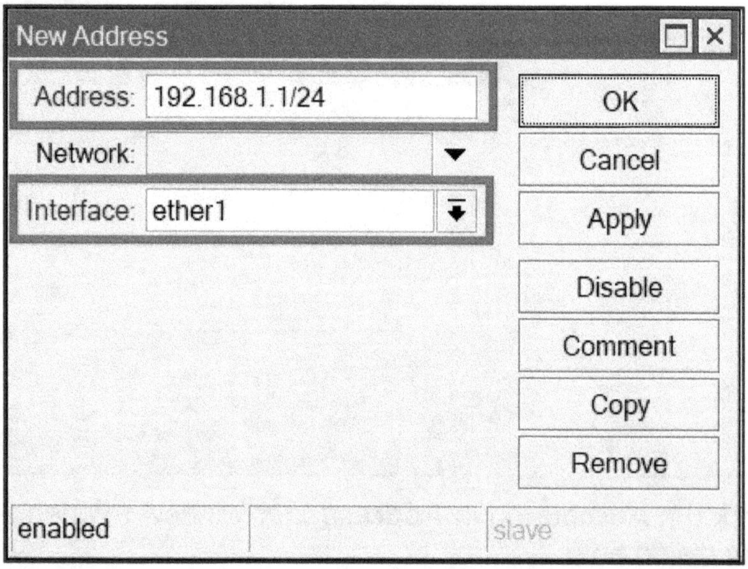

After assigning the IP address to the ether1 interface, it will appear in the **Address List** window.

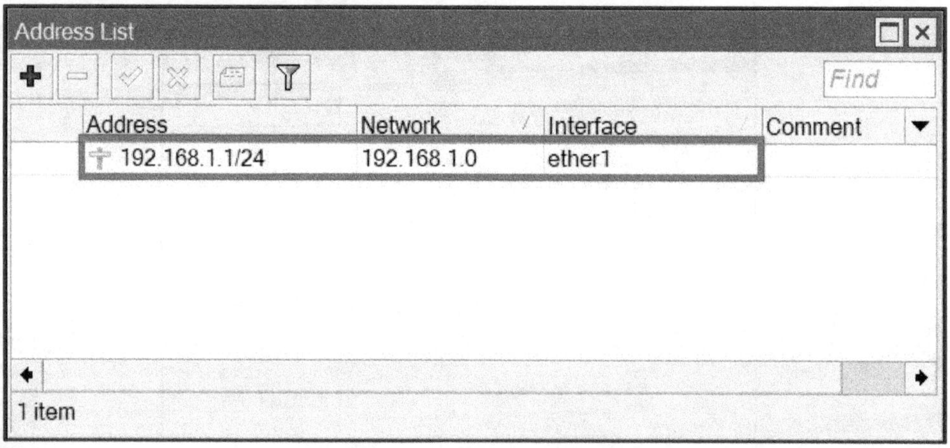

To configure the DHCP server, click the **IP** menu, then select **DHCP Server** to open the **DHCP Server** window.

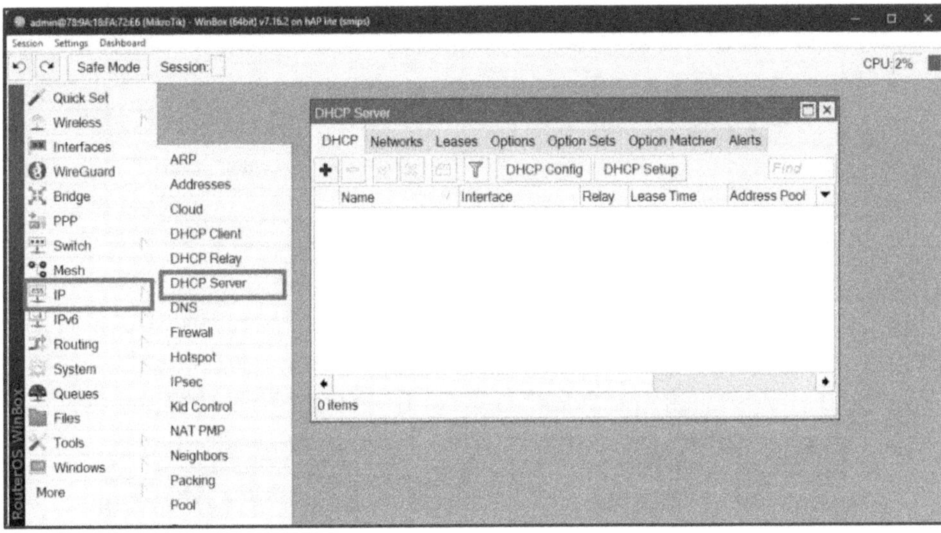

Then, click the **DHCP Setup** button in the **DHCP** tab to open **DHCP Setup** dialog box.

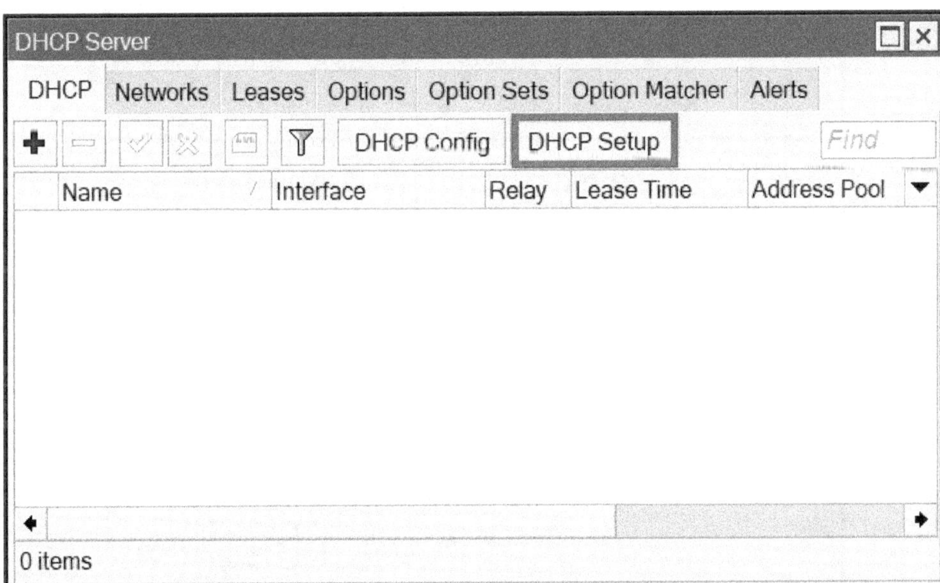

Select the ether1 interface from the **DHCP Server Interface** field, and click the **Next** button.

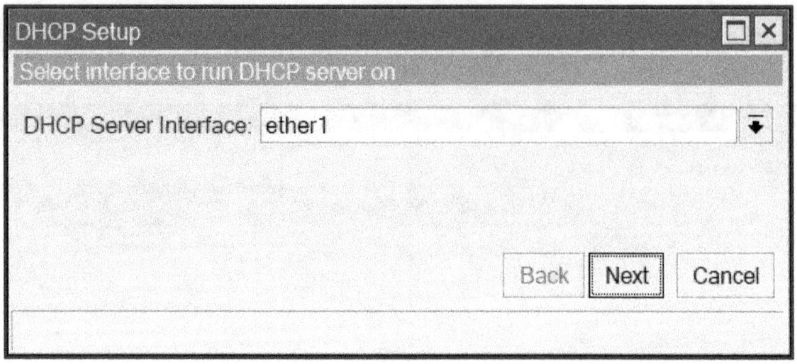

In the next message, the setup wizard will check the IP address of the ether1 interface and automatically display the network ID and the subnet mask in the **DHCP Address Space** field, which in this case is 192.168.1.0/24. Click the **Next** button to accept this setting.

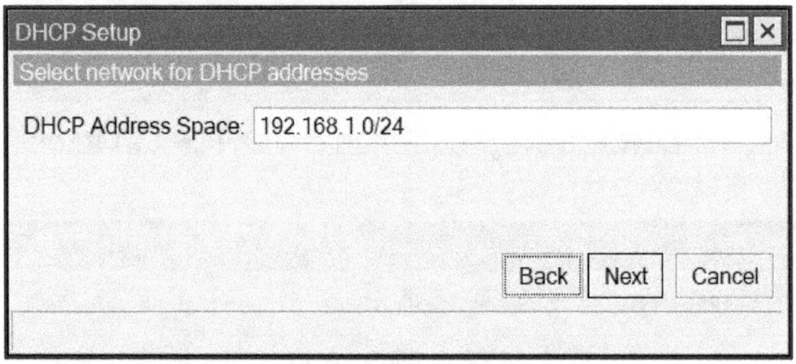

In the next message, the setup wizard will display the gateway, which is the IP address of the interface itself (in this case, 192.168.1.1). Click the **Next** button to accept this gateway.

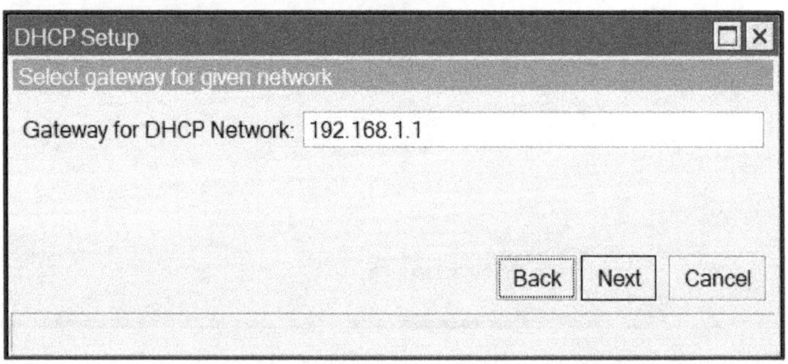

In the next message, the setup wizard will display the range of IP addresses to be used in the **Addresses to Give Out** field, which in this case is 192.168.1.2-192.168.1.254. Click the **Next** button to accept this range.

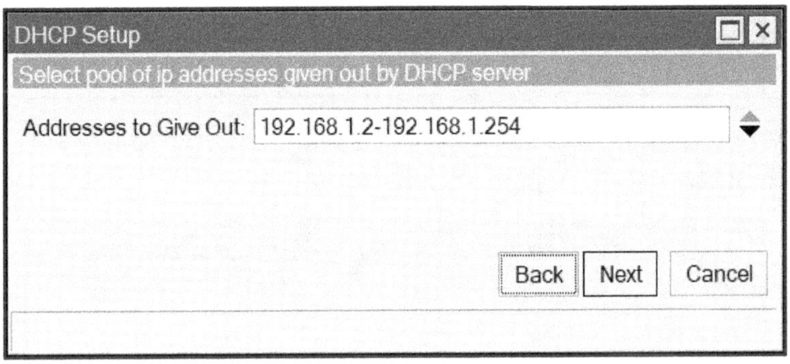

In the next message, the setup wizard will display the DNS server IP address. Since you do not have a DNS server configured on the device now, this field will be empty.

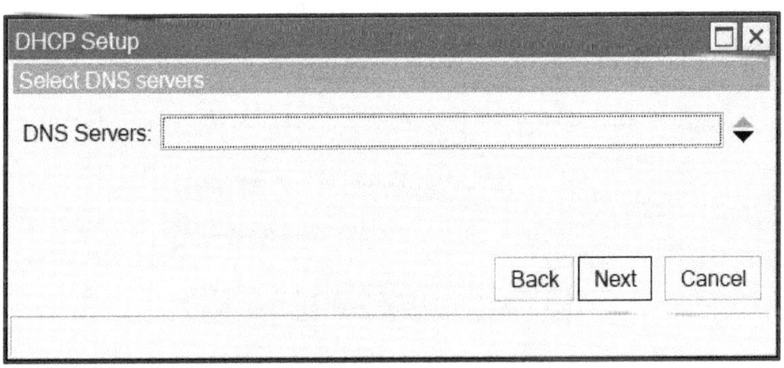

You can enter the address of the DNS server you want to use, for example google DNS server IP address 8.8.8.8, or you can leave this field empty and click the **Next** button.

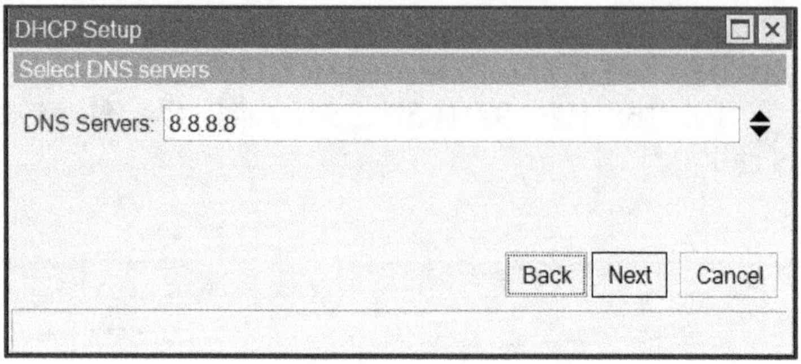

In the last message, the setup wizard will display the lease time. Click the **Next** button to accept the default value.

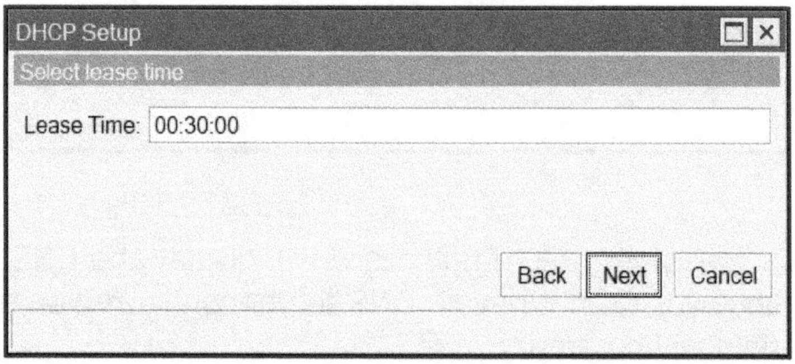

After clicking **Next**, if everything is correct, the wizard will display a message saying that the setup has completed successfully.

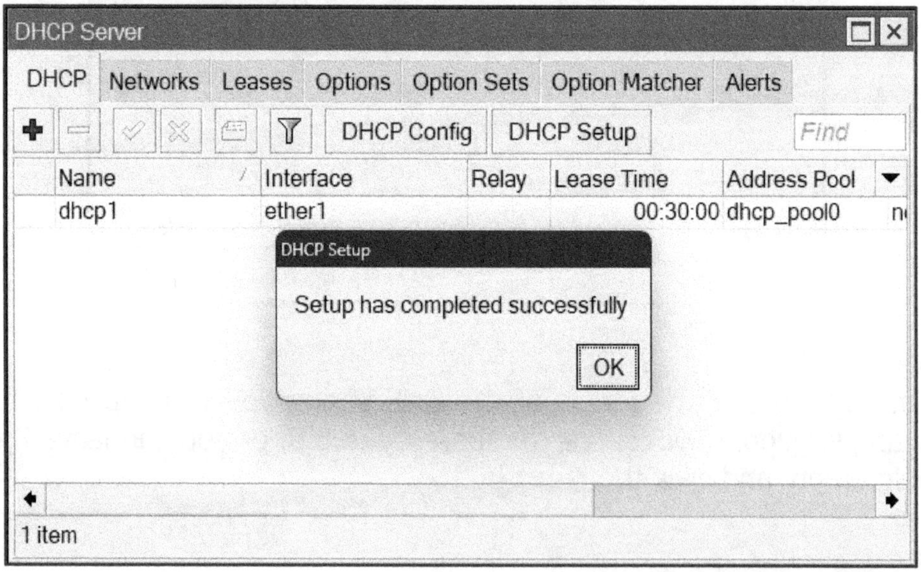

Finally, you will see the DHCP server listed in the **DHCP** tab.

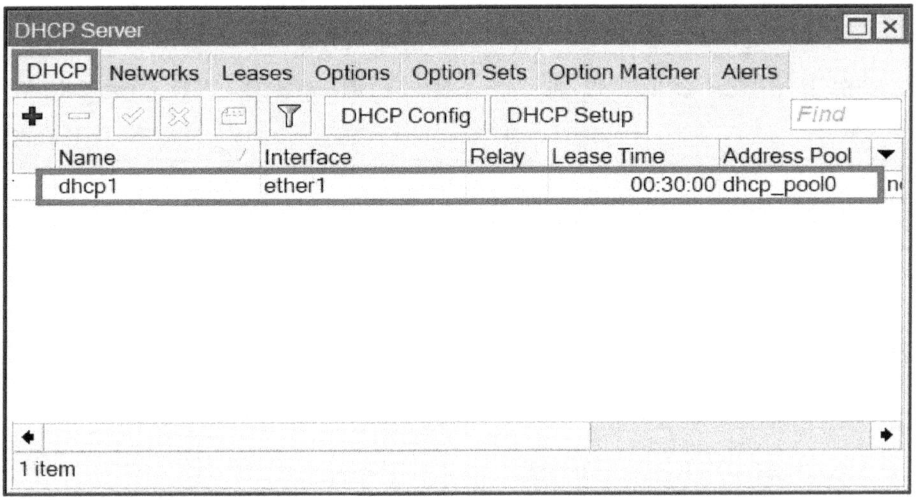

Now, when you connect PC1 to the ether1 interface, it will automatically receive an IP address from the DHCP server.

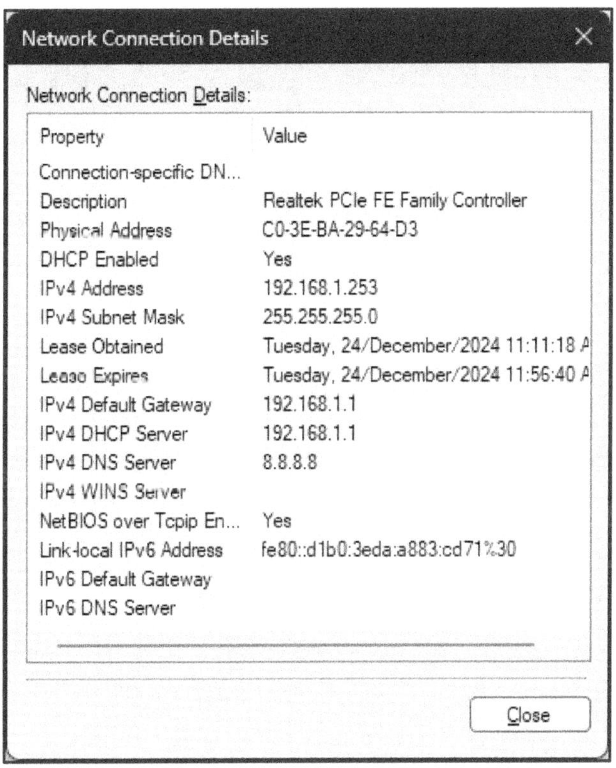

CLI

You can also make the configuration from the CLI.

To assign an IP address to the ether1 interface, use the following command:

```
ip address add address=192.168.1.1/24 interface=ether1
```

To configure a DHCP server on the ether1 interface using the DHCP setup wizard, use the following command, choose ether1 interface and accept the default settings by pressing Enter each time the setup wizard asks for input:

```
ip dhcp-server setup
```

2.6 Leases Management.

When the DHCP server assigns an IP address to a device, this IP will appear in the **Leases** tab of the **DHCP Server** window, along with other information about the device, such as its MAC address.

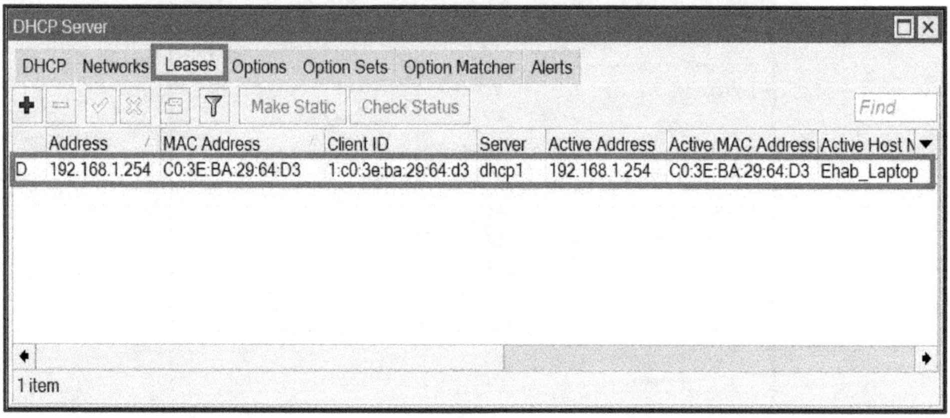

You can also display the leased IP addresses from the CLI using the following command:

```
ip dhcp-server lease print
```

This operation happens automatically. Whenever a device requests an IP address, the DHCP server will assign the next available IP address from the pool. If the device is disconnected and later reconnected to the network again, it will be assigned an IP address, which could be a different one. In some cases, you may want a device to always have the same IP address and prevent any other devices from receiving this IP address. This can be done by statically assigning the IP address through static leases.

2.7 DHCP Static Lease

To create a static lease for a device to always receive the same IP address when it connects to the network, use the **Leases** tab of the **DHCP Server** window.

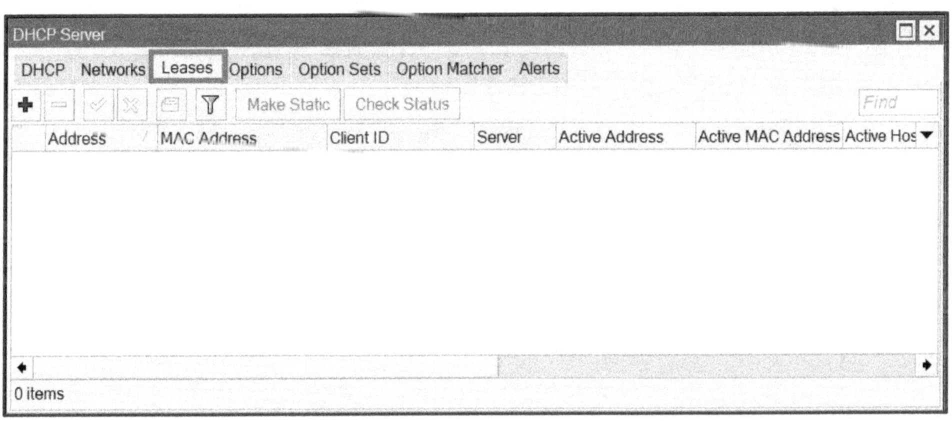

To add a new static lease, click the **Add** button in the **Leases** tab of the **DHCP Server** window to open the **New DHCP Lease** dialog box.

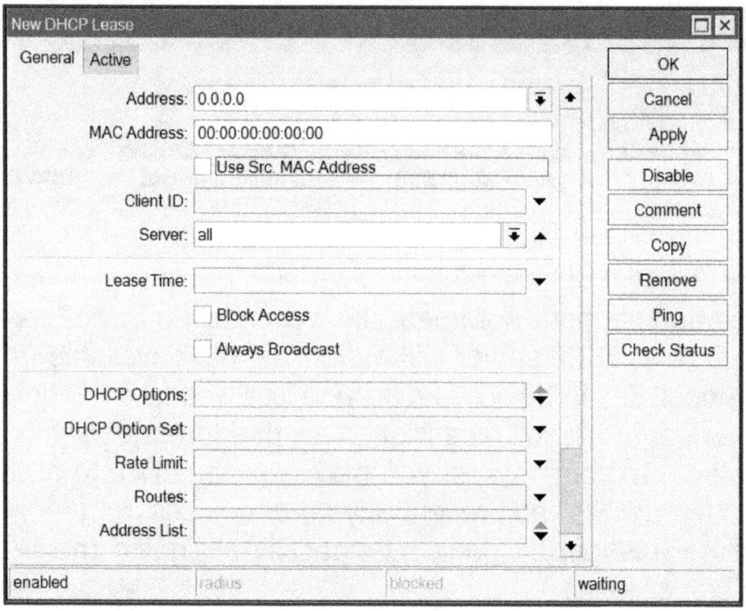

In **MAC Address** field, enter the device MAC address. In **Address** field, enter the IP address you want to assign to this device.

Instead of manually entering the MAC address, you can also connect the device to the network and wait until it dynamically gets an IP address and appears in the **Leases** table. Then, double-click it to open **DHCP Lease** dialog box, and click the **Make Static** button and click the **OK** button to close this dialog box.

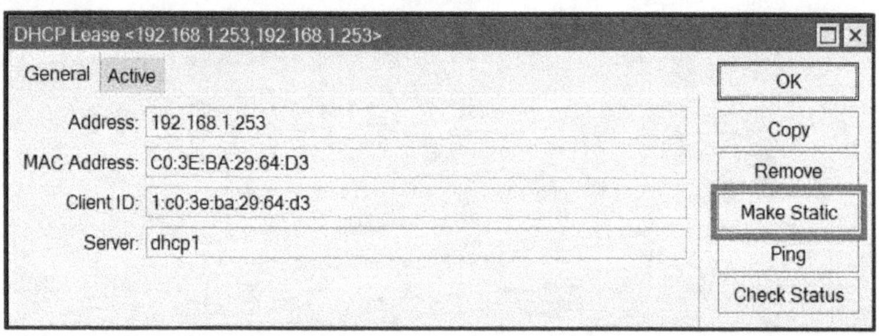

If you want to edit the IP address or any other information, double-click the IP address again to open the **DHCP Lease** dialog box and edit the information you want.

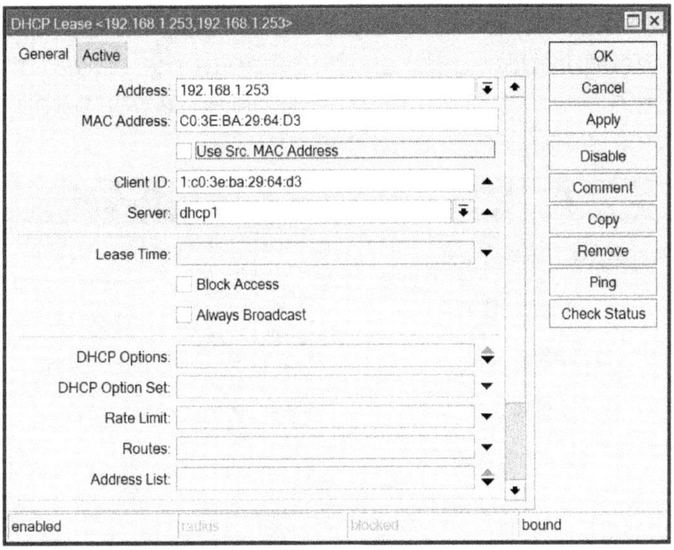

On the other hand, for security reasons, you can use the DHCP server to assign statically configured IP addresses without using a pool. This ensures that only known devices, which you have already added by their MAC address, can connect to the network and obtain an IP address.

2.8 DHCP Server Settings

As mentioned, when configuring the DHCP server, it will appear in the **DHCP** tab of the **DHCP Server** window.

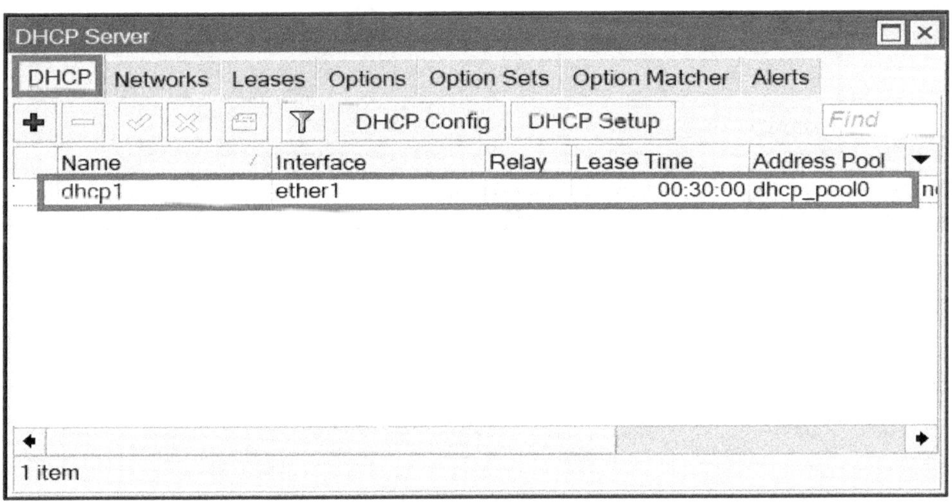

When double-clicking the server, a dialog box will appear displaying the server configuration, such as the name of the server, the interface it is configured on, the lease time, and other server settings. You can change any of these settings if needed.

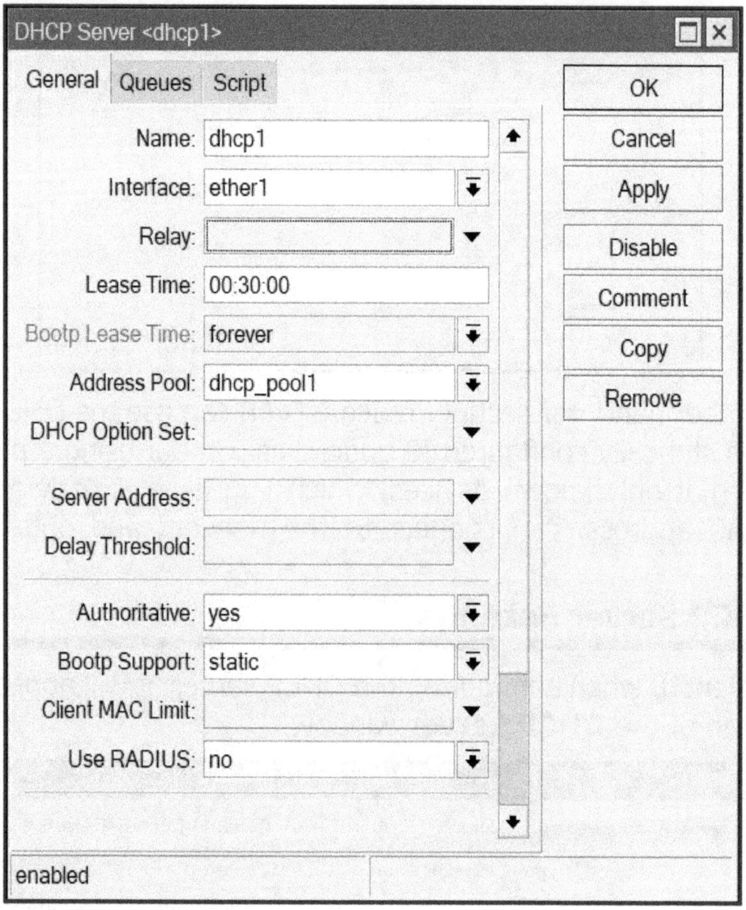

2.9 DHCP Network Settings

The DHCP server provides DHCP clients with an IP address and other information such as the subnet mask, default gateway, DNS server IP.. etc. These details are stored in the **Network** table in the **DHCP Server** window.

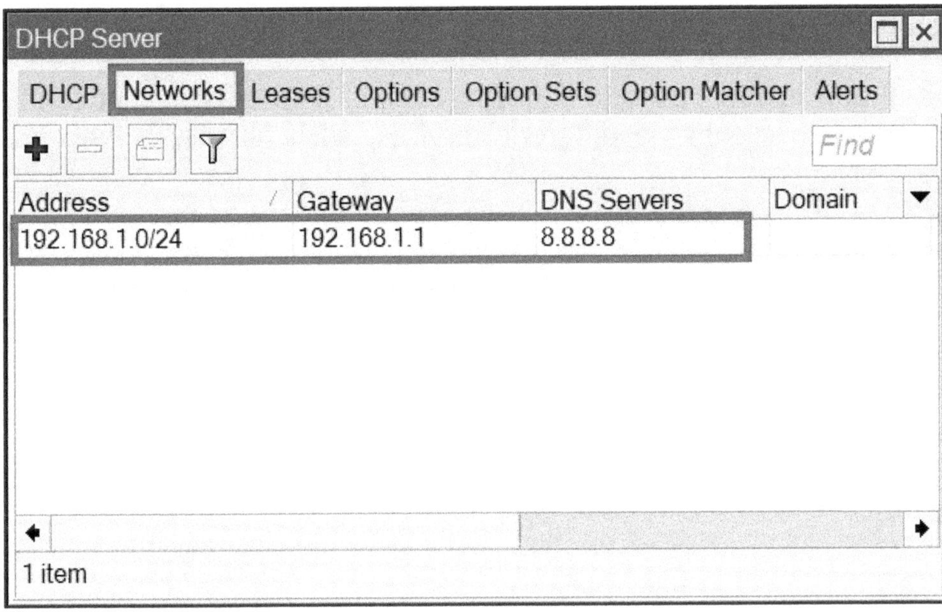

When double-clicking the network, a dialog box will appear displaying the network configuration. You can change any of these settings if needed.

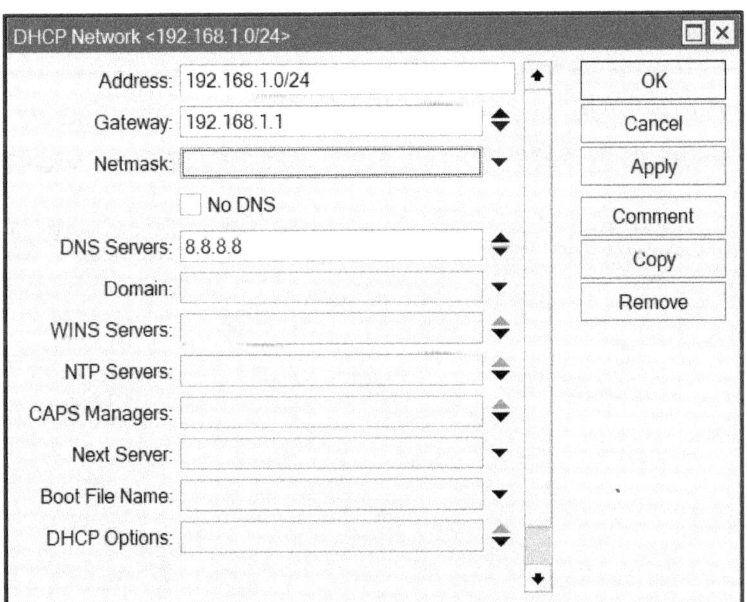

2.10 IP Pool

An IP pool is a tool used to define a range of IP addresses that can be assigned to clients via different services, such as DHCP, PPP, and hotspot.

2.10.1 Create IP Pool

To create an IP pool, use the **IP Pool** window.

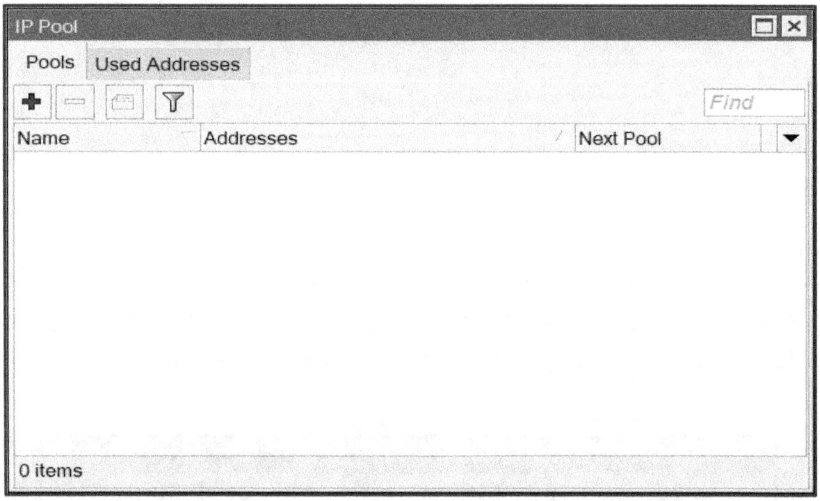

To open the **IP Pool** window, click the **IP** menu, then select **Pool**.

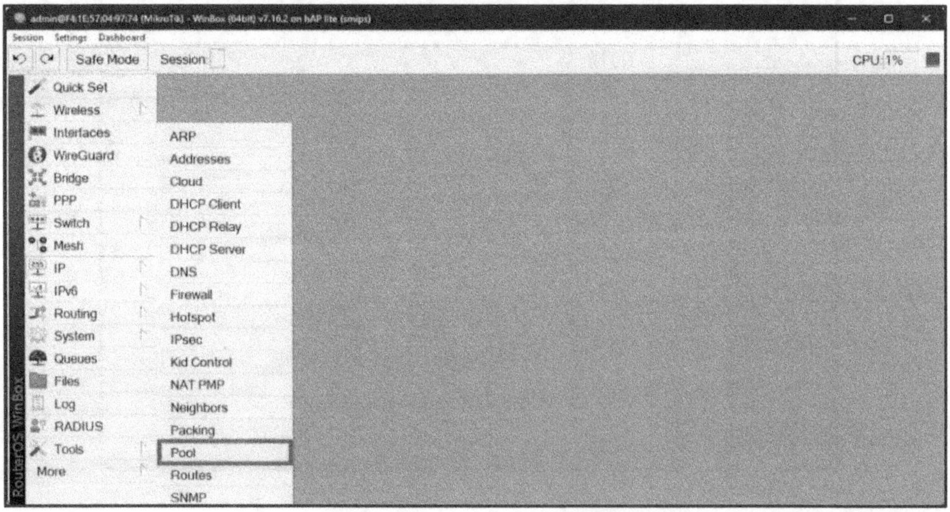

To add a new pool, click the **Add** button in the **Pools** tab of the **IP Pool** window to open the **New IP Pool** dialog box.

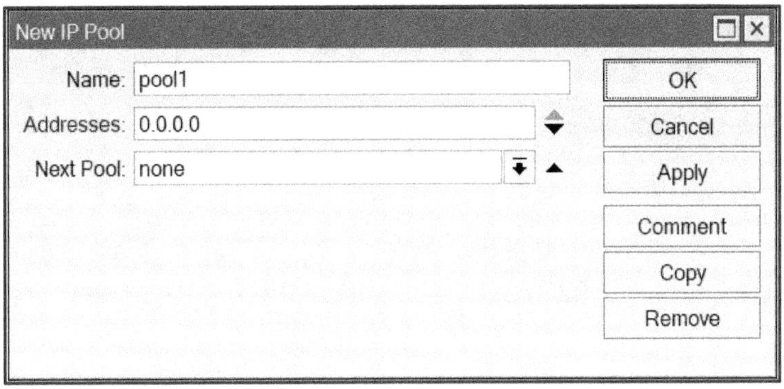

You can use this dialog box to create a new IP pool and configure its settings.

In the **Name** field, enter a name for the pool, or leave the default name.

In the **Addresses** field, enter the range of IP addresses for the pool.

You can write a subnet ID as follows:

192.168.1.0/24

Or you can write the first IP address, then a dash (–), followed by the last IP address

For example, to specify the range of IP addresses from 192.168.1.10 to 192.168.1.19, write the range like this:

192.168.1.10 – 192.168.1.19

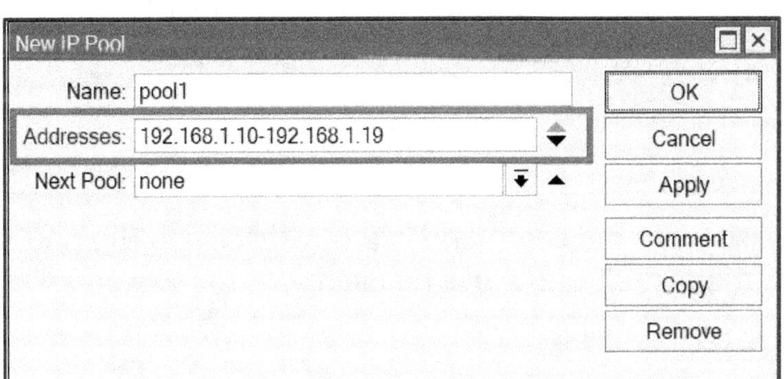

Click the **OK** button to close this dialog box and create the pool.

The new pool will now appear in the **IP Pool** window.

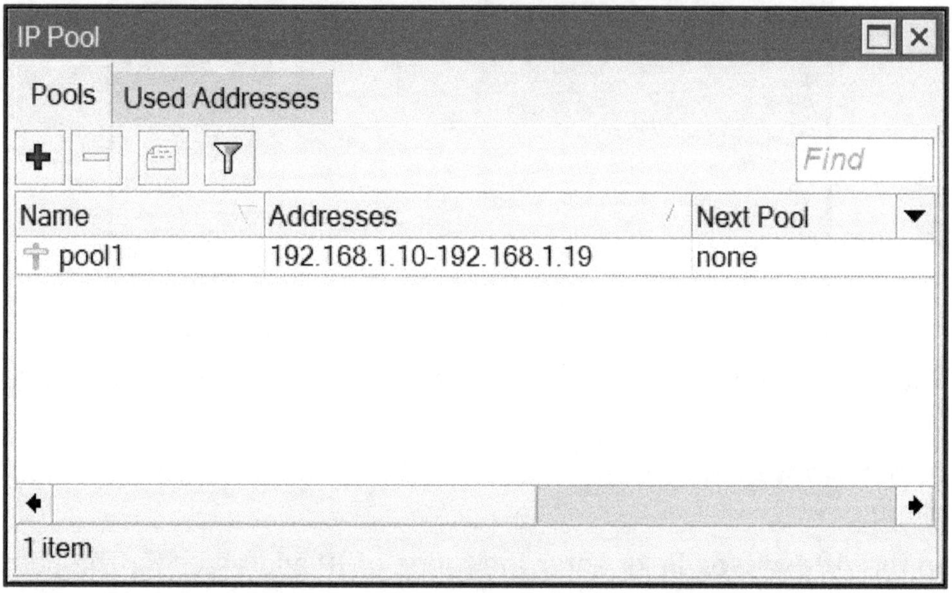

You can also create a pool from the CLI using the following command:

```
ip pool add name=[name] ranges= [range]
```

where:

- [name] is the name of the pool.
- [range] the range of IP addresses

For example:

```
ip pool add name=pool1 ranges=192.168.1.10-192.168.1.19
```

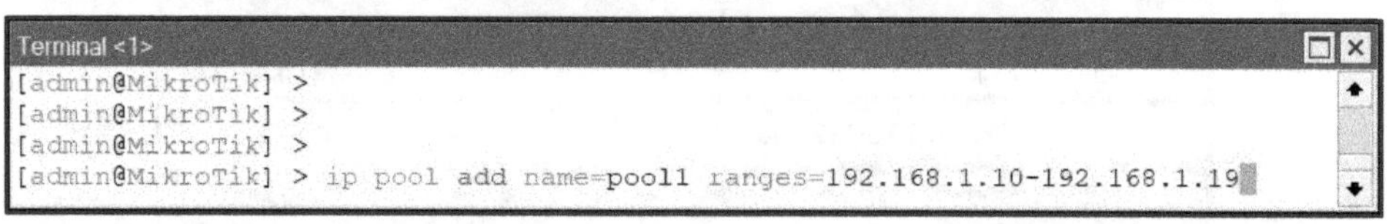

You can also write the command without specifying the pool name. In this case, the default name will be used.

```
ip pool add ranges= [range]
```

To display the current IP pools in RouterOS from the CLI use the following command:

```
ip pool print
```

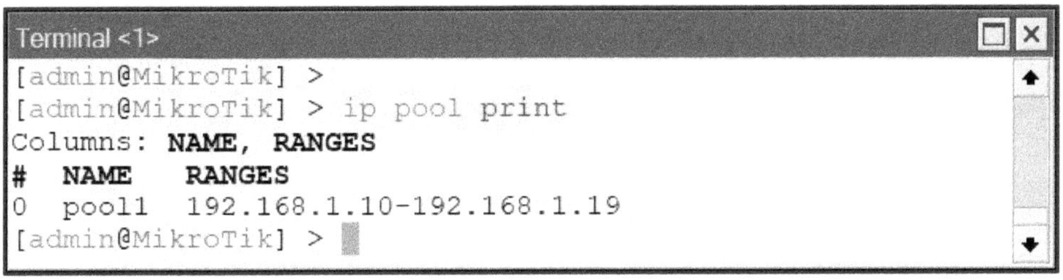

2.10.2 Managing IP Ranges

You can add a new range of IP addresses to the same pool by clicking on the small arrow next to the **Addresses** field to add a new field, then, enter the range in this new field.

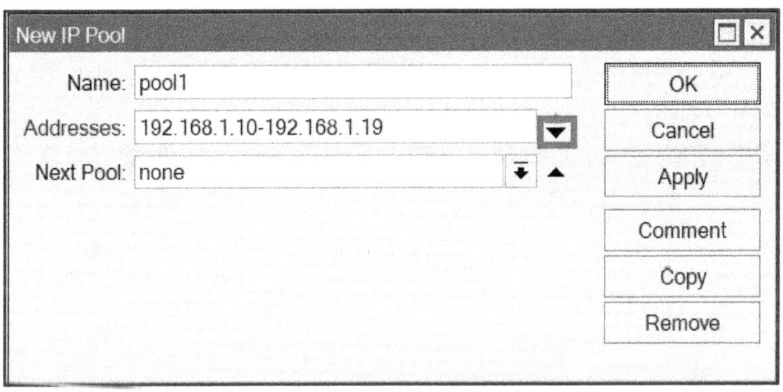

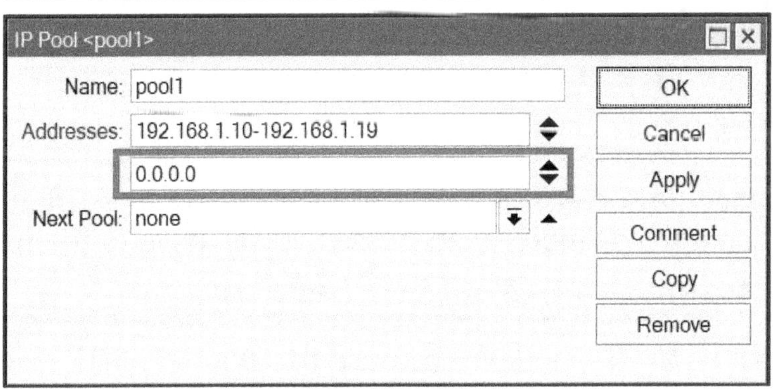

For example, if you created a range of IP addresses from 192.168.1.10 to 192.168.1.19, but later you want more IP addresses, you can add another range, (such as 192.168.1.50 to 192.168.1.59), by entering the range in the new **Addresses** field like this:

192.168.1.50-192.168.1.59

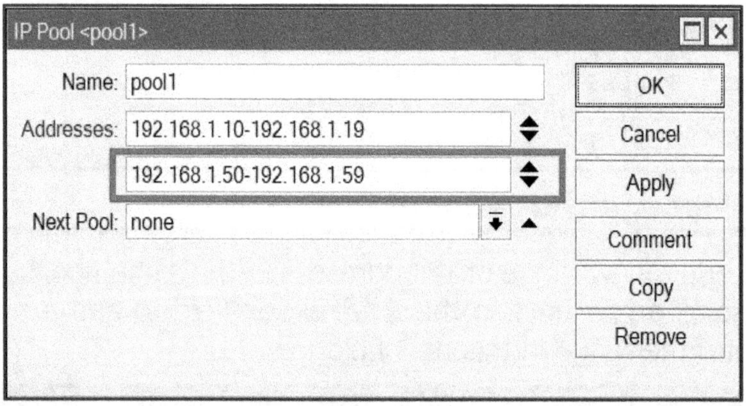

You can also create a new IP pool and link it to this pool by using the **Next Pool** field.

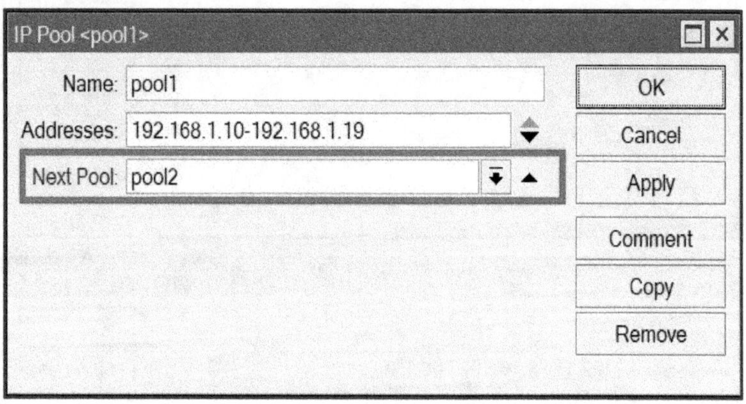

In this case, the server will start assigning IP addresses from the first pool. When it needs more IP addresses, it will move to the next pool.

2.10.3 Assign the IP Pool to a Service

After creating an IP pool, you can use this pool in multiple RouterOS services, such as DHCP, PPP, and hotspot.

2.11 DHCP Client Configuration

To configure a DHCP client on a RouterOS interface to get an IP address from a DHCP server, use the **DHCP Client** window.

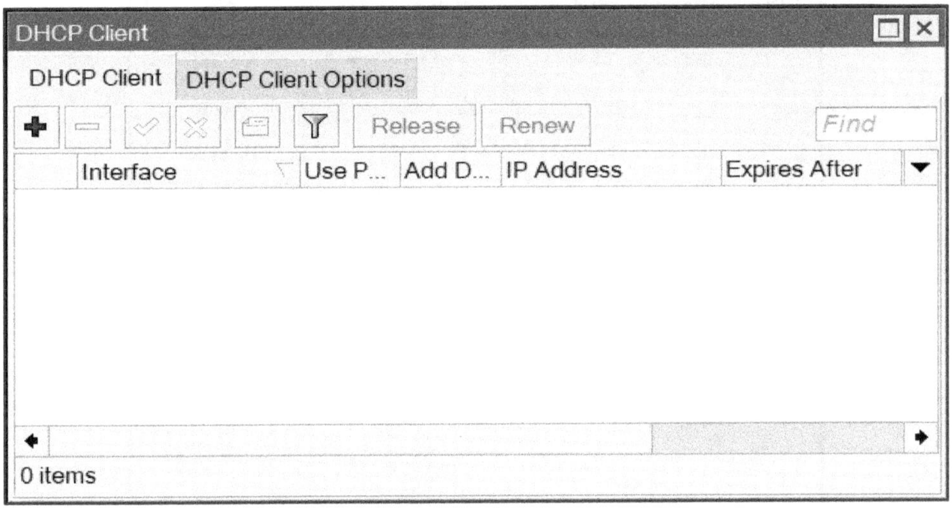

To open the **DHCP Client** window, click the **IP** menu and then select **DHCP Client**.

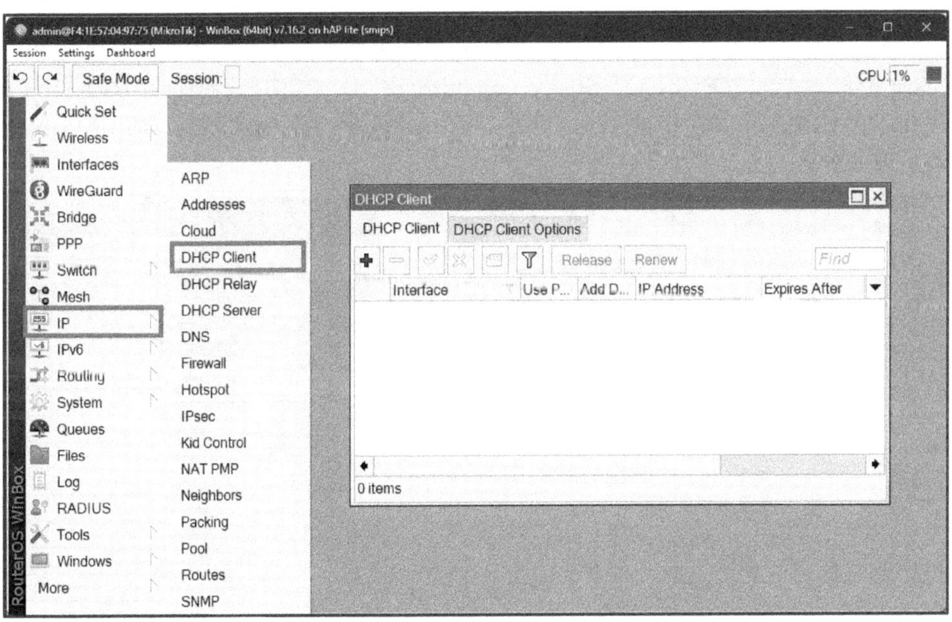

To configure a DHCP client on an interface, click the **Add** button in the **DHCP Client** window to open the **New DHCP Client** dialog box.

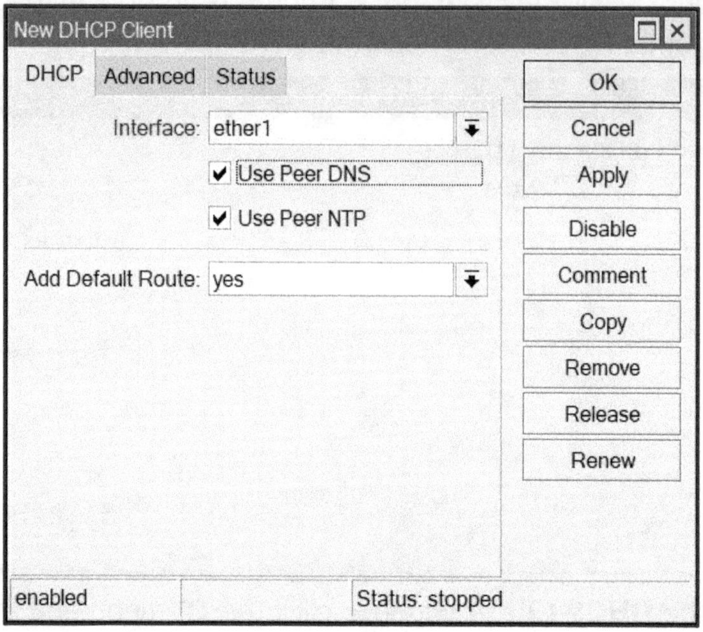

In **interface** field, select the interface on which you want to configure the DHCP client. Then, click the **OK** button to close this dialog box.

After the interface successfully obtains an IP address from the DHCP server, this IP will appear in the **DHCP Client** tab with other information.

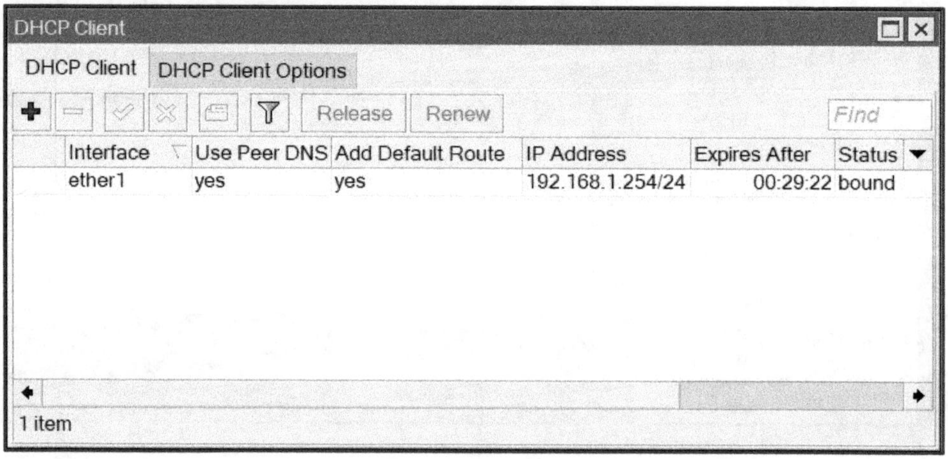

A DHCP client receives four main pieces of information from the server:

- The IP address
- The subnet mask
- The default gateway
- The DNS

You can see the IP address and subnet mask in the **Address List** window.

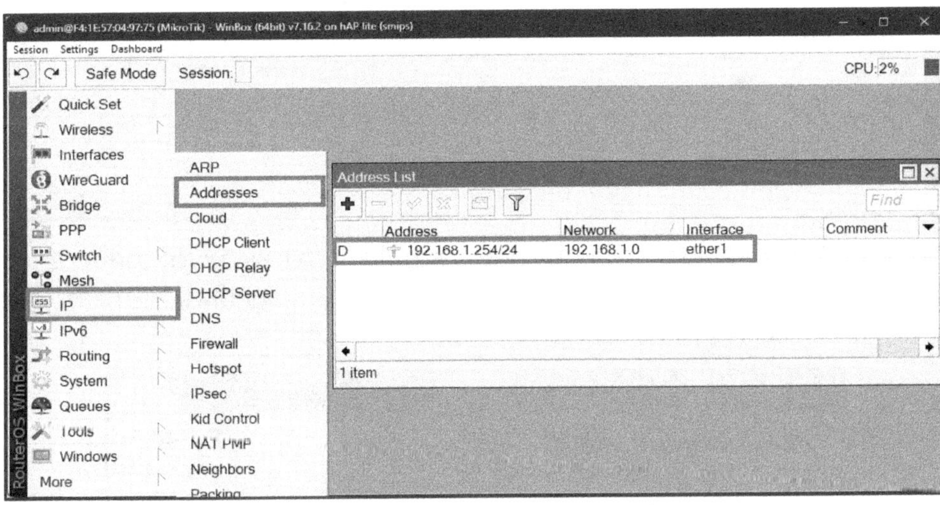

The default gateway is listed in the **Routing Table**.

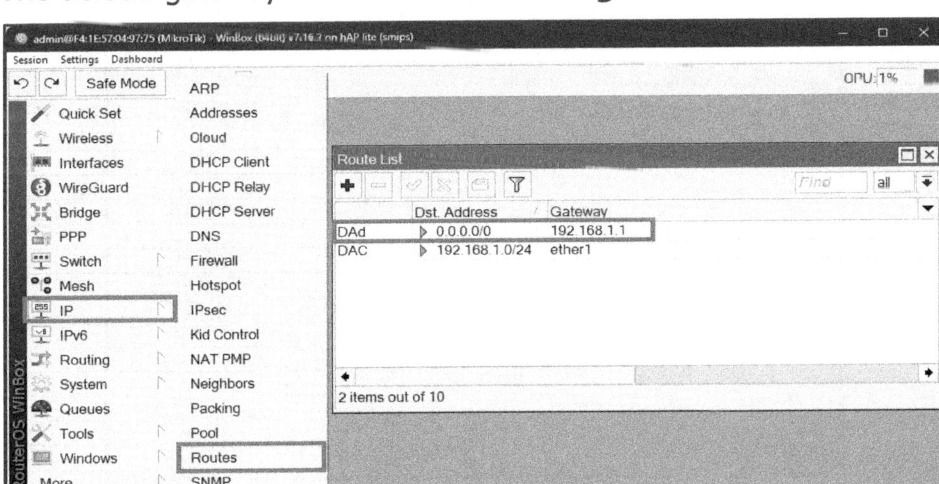

The DNS can be seen in the **DNS** window.

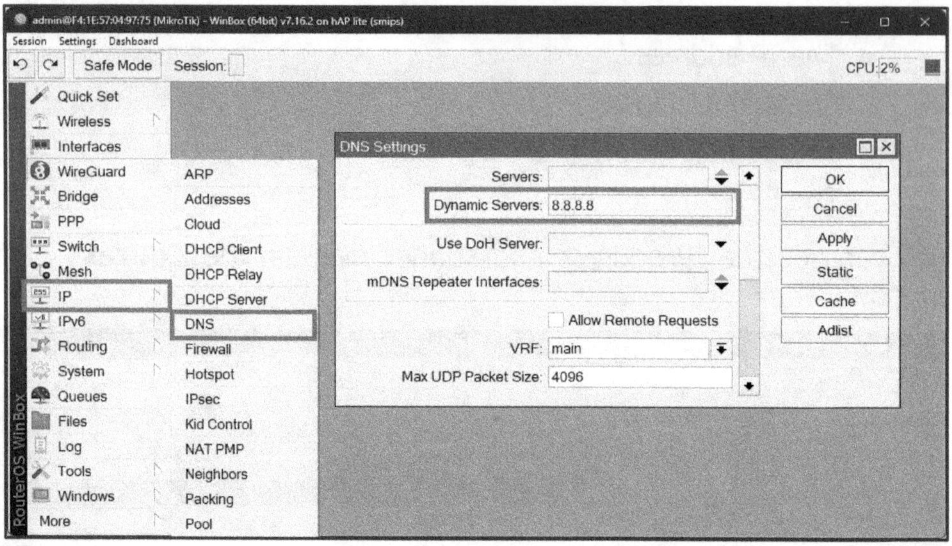

You can choose whether or not you want to receive the default gateway and DNS from the DHCP server by selecting the required settings in the **New DHCP Client** dialog box.

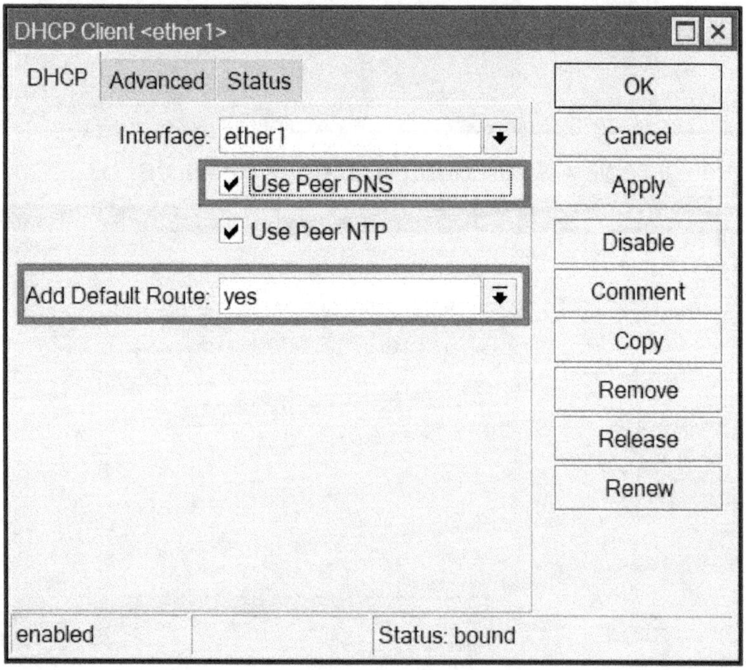

You can also configure a DHCP client on an interface from the CLI using the following command:

```
ip dhcp-client add interface=[interface]
```

Where:

- [interface] is the desired interface.

For example:

```
ip dhcp-client add interface=ether1
```

```
Terminal <1>
[admin@MikroTik] >
[admin@MikroTik] >
[admin@MikroTik] > ip dhcp-client add interface=ether1
[admin@MikroTik] >
```

To display the information about DHCP client use the following command:

```
ip dhcp-client print
```

```
Terminal <1>
[admin@MikroTik] >
[admin@MikroTik] >
[admin@MikroTik] > ip dhcp-client print
Columns: INTERFACE, USE-PEER-DNS, ADD-DEFAULT-ROUTE, STATUS, ADDRESS
# INTERFACE  USE-PEER-DNS  ADD  STATUS  ADDRESS
0 ether1     yes           yes  bound   192.168.1.254/24
[admin@MikroTik] >
```

LAB

In this lab, MikroTik device R1 is configured as DHCP Server and connected to MikroTik device R2 via the interface ether1. You want to configure R2 as DHCP Client to get an IP address from the server.

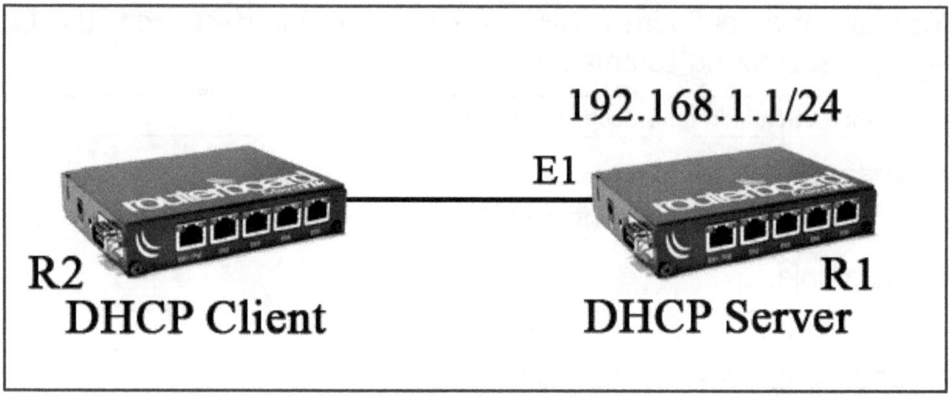

To configure the DHCP Client on interface ether1 in R2, click the **IP** menu, then select **DHCP Client** to open the **DHCP Client** window.

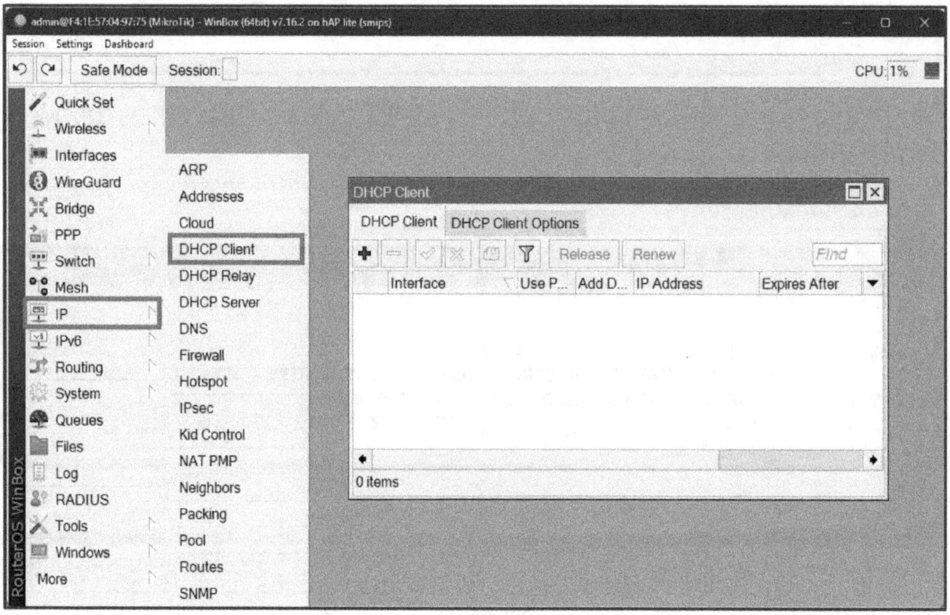

Then, click the **Add** button in the **DHCP Client** window to open the **New DHCP Client** dialog box.

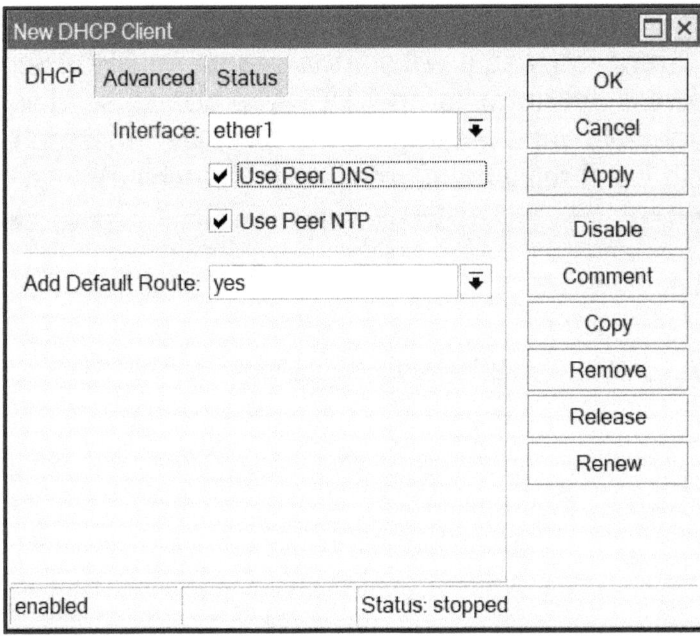

In the **interface** field, select the ether1 and click the **OK** button to close this dialog box.

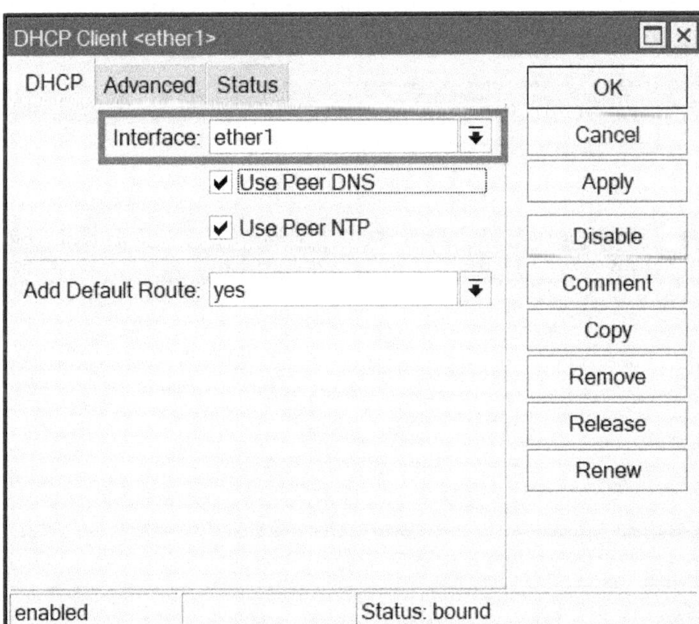

After configuring the DHCP Client on the interface ether1, it will appear in **DHCP Client** tab, and it will start to search for DHCP Server to get an IP address, performing the DORA process, sending a DHCP Discover message and waiting for DHCP Offer message. And the **Status** field will display the current state (searching).

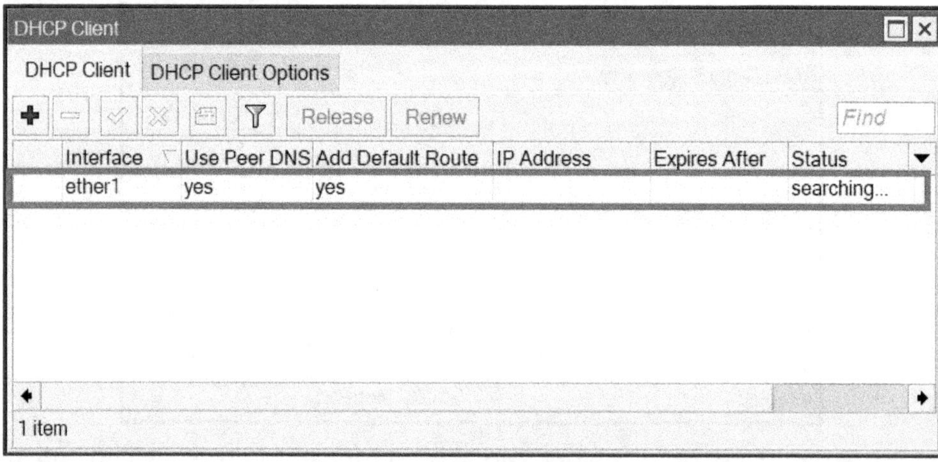

After the interface successfully obtains an IP address from the DHCP server, this IP will appear in the **DHCP Client** tab with other information. The **Status** field will change to (Bound).

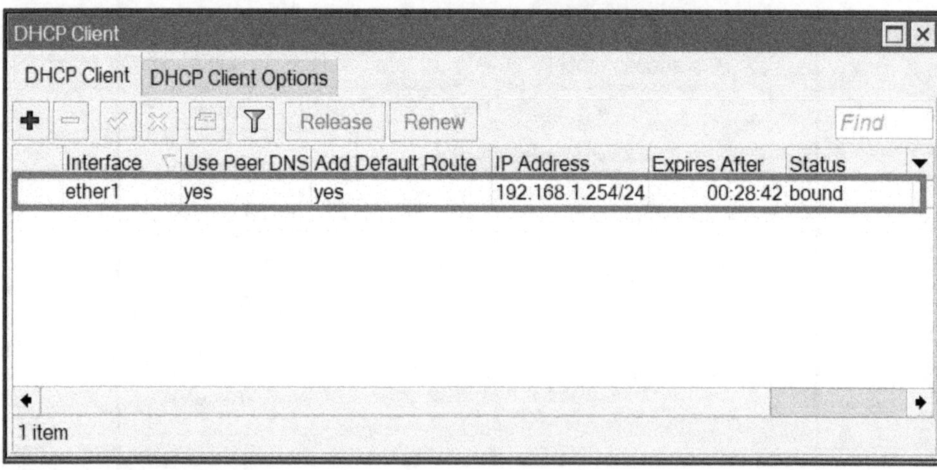

CLI

You can also make the configuration from the CLI.

To configure a DHCP client on the ether1 interface, use the following command:

```
ip dhcp-client add interface=ether1
```

ARP

2.12 ARP Overview and Key Concepts

If a computer, or a host, wants to send data to another computer, it must know the MAC address of the other computer. This can be achieved using a protocol called ARP (Address Resolution Protocol).

2.13 ARP Protocol

The Address Resolution Protocol (ARP) is a protocol used to get the destination MAC address.

2.14 How ARP Protocol Works

The concept of using ARP is as follows: when a device wants to know the MAC address of another device, it sends a message called an ARP request, asking the device with a specific IP address to reply and send its MAC address. When the device with this IP address receives the message, it will reply by sending an ARP reply containing its MAC address.

So, the process happens in two steps:

- The source device sends an **ARP request** message.
- The destination device replies with an **ARP reply** message.

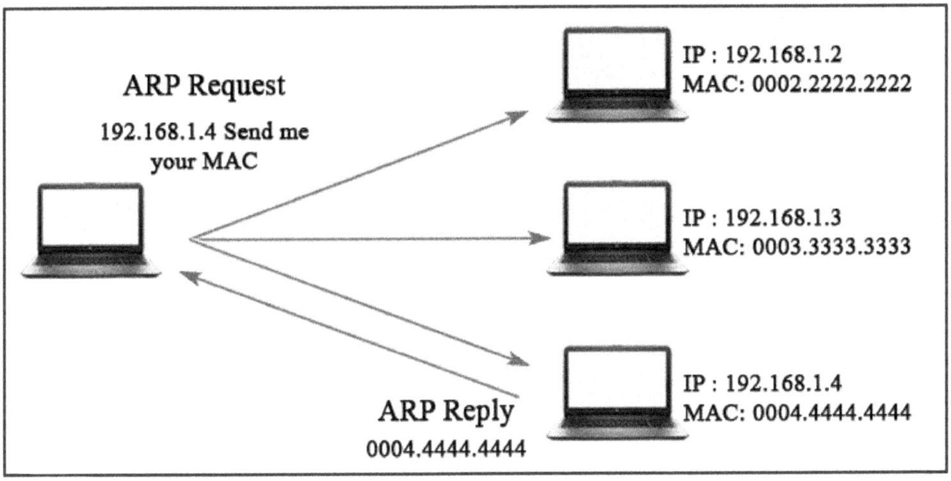

This process happens automatically, and the device will store the received MAC address in a table called the **ARP cache** or **ARP table**.

2.15 RouterOS ARP Table

To display the ARP table, click the **IP** menu and then select **ARP**.

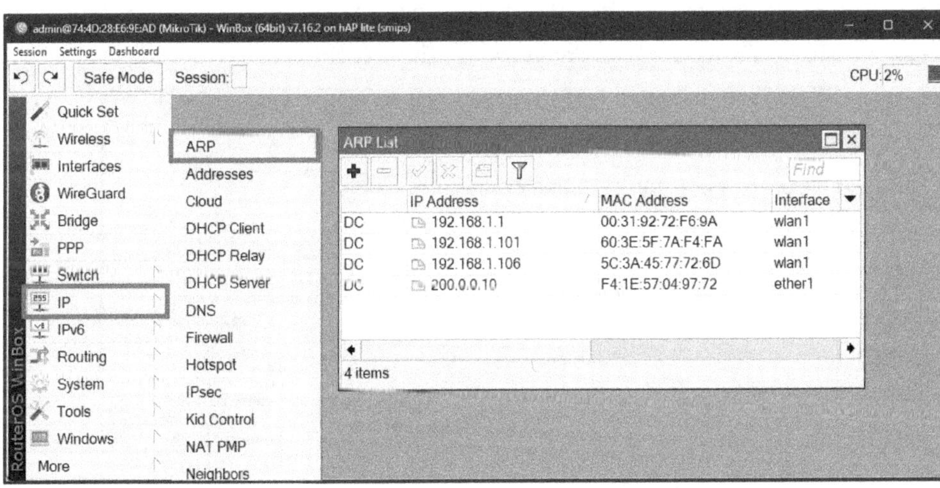

The **ARP List** window displays the MAC address, the corresponding IP address, and the interface that received this MAC address.

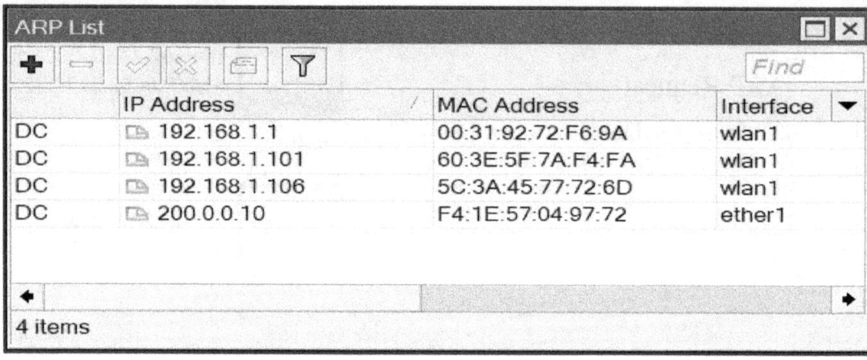

You can also display the ARP table in RouterOS from the CLI using the following command:

```
ip arp print
```

2.16 ARP Static Entry

Instead of sending an ARP request and waiting for the reply to get the MAC address of a device, you can add a static entry to the ARP table.

To add a static entry to the ARP table, click the **Add** button in the **ARP List** window, to open the **New ARP** dialog box.

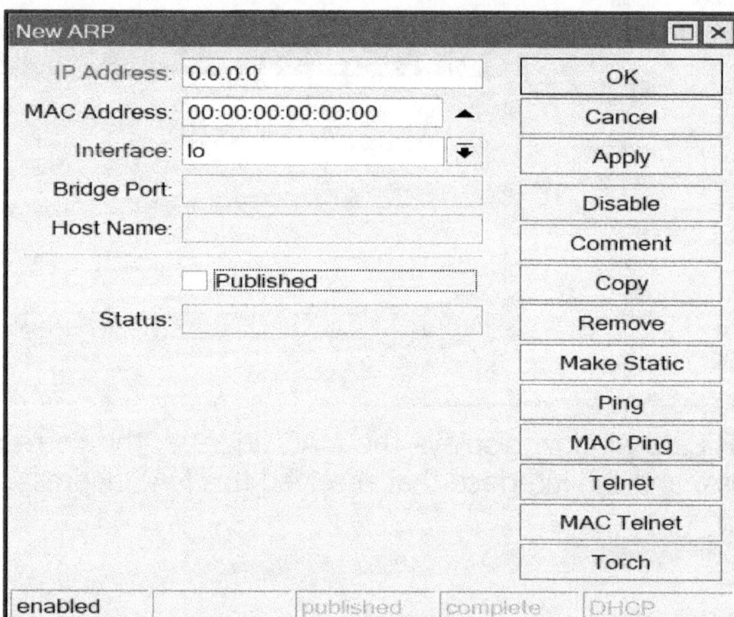

Enter the **IP address**, the **MAC Address**, and the **Interface** to which this device is connected, then click **OK** button.

Instead of manually entering the MAC address, you can wait until the device dynamically appears in the ARP table, (or ping its IP address to accelerate the process), then double-click the address in the **ARP List** window, and click the **Make Static** button.

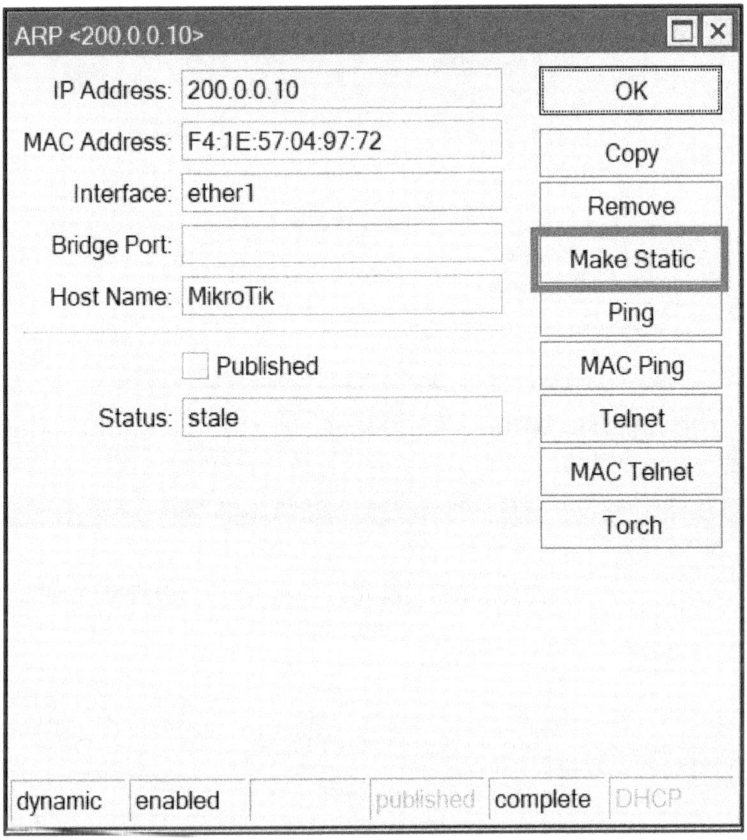

2.17 ARP Timeout

In the default settings, the dynamic entries in the ARP table will stay in the ARP table for 30 seconds, after that they will be deleted. These entries will also be deleted when the device is rebooted. Static entries will not be deleted.

You can change the default ARP timeout using the **IP Settings** dialog box.

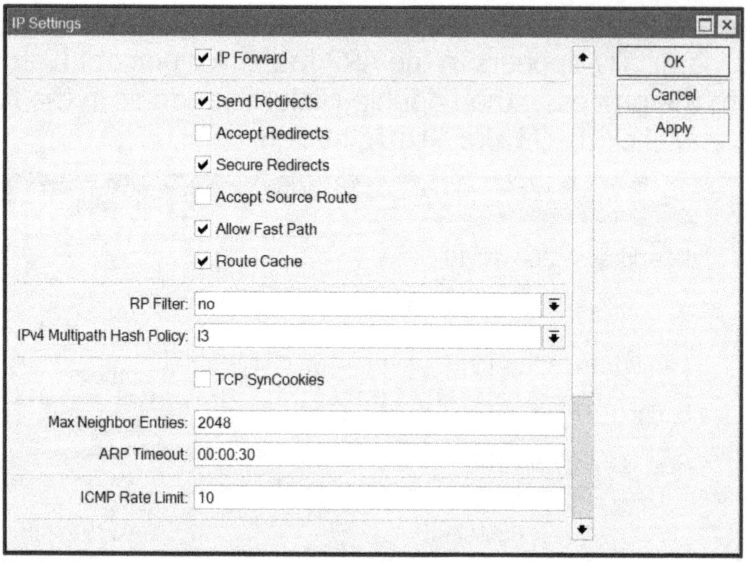

To open the **IP Settings** window, click the **IP** menu, then select **Settings**.

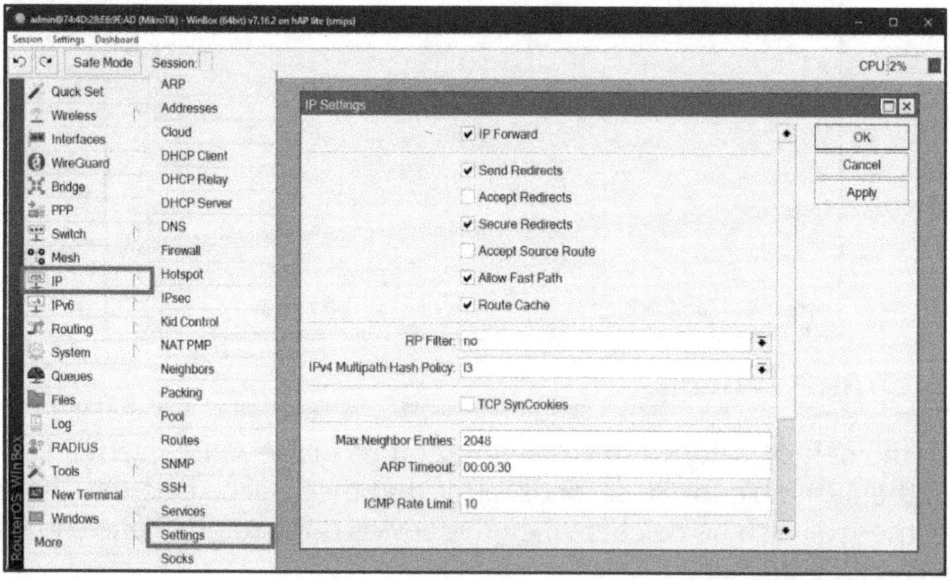

To change the ARP timeout, enter the required period in the **ARP Timeout** field.

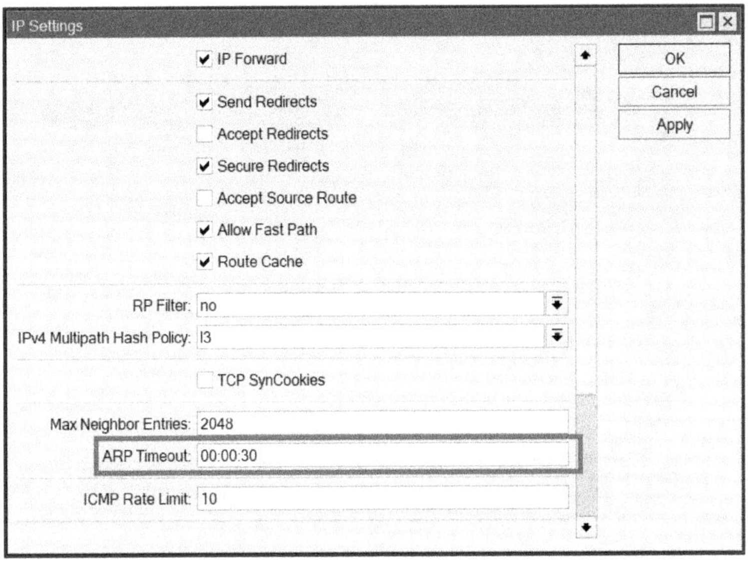

You can also modify the ARP Timeout for each interface separately, by using the **Interface** settings dialog box.

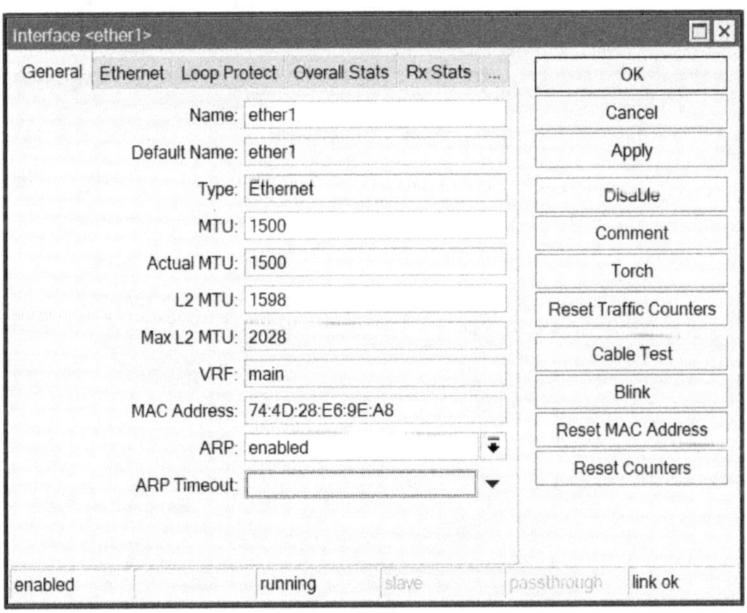

To open the **Interface** settings dialog box, first open the **Interface List** window by clicking the **Interfaces** menu.

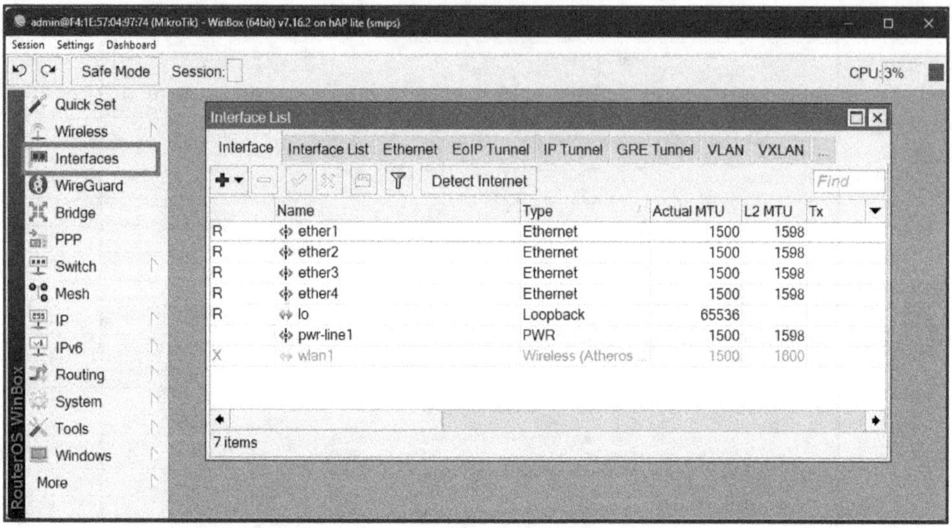

Then, in the **Interface** tab, double-click the required interface to open its settings dialog box.

To change the ARP timeout, enter the required period in the **ARP Timeout** field.

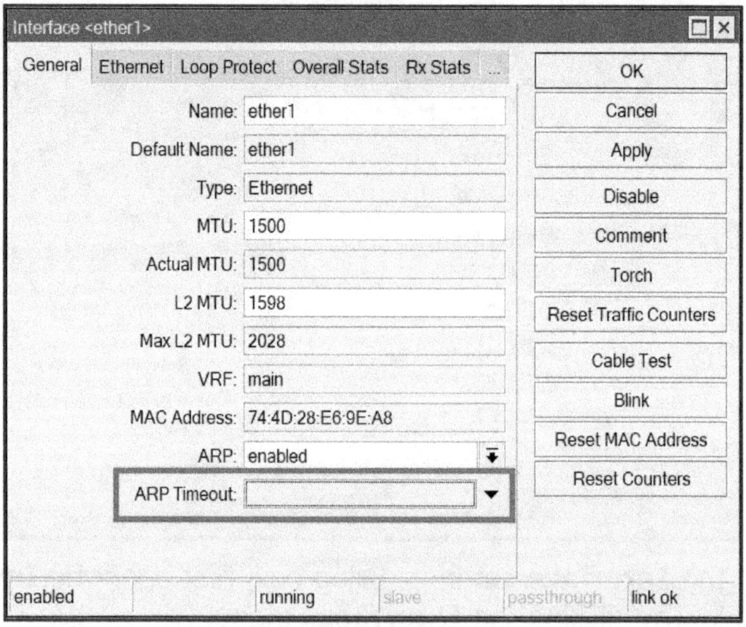

2.18 ARP Modes

As mentioned, there are two types of ARP messages:

- ARP Request
- ARP Reply

The default behavior of an interface is to send an ARP request when the device needs to know the MAC address of another device.

And when the interface receives an ARP request from another device asking for its MAC address, it will respond by sending an ARP reply.

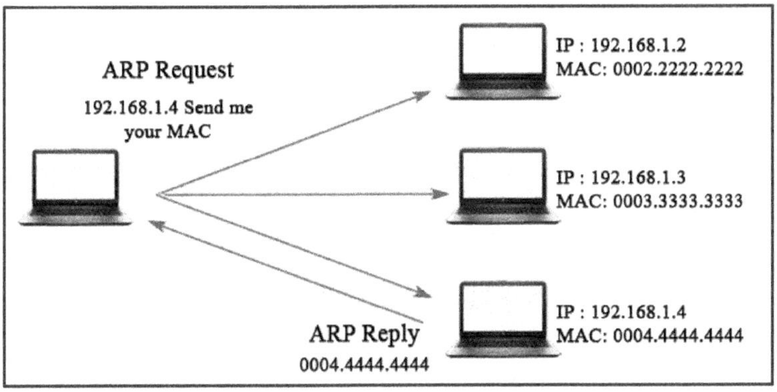

You can control this behavior by changing the ARP modes of the interface using **interface** settings dialog box.

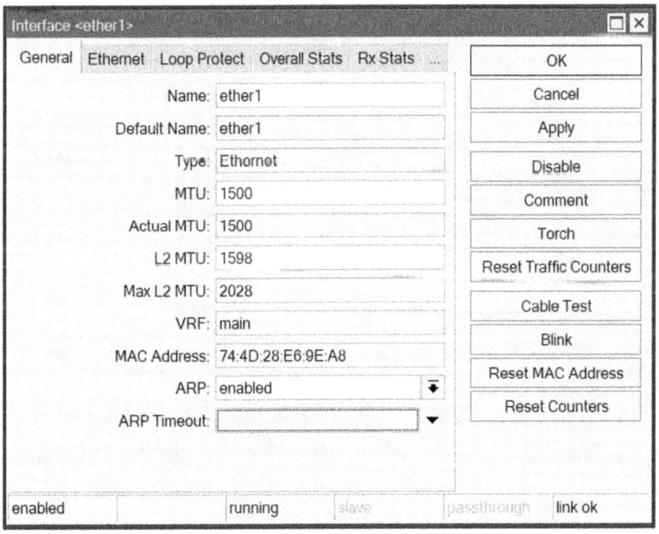

To open the **Interface Settings** dialog box, double-click the desired interface in **Interface** tab of the **Interface List** window.

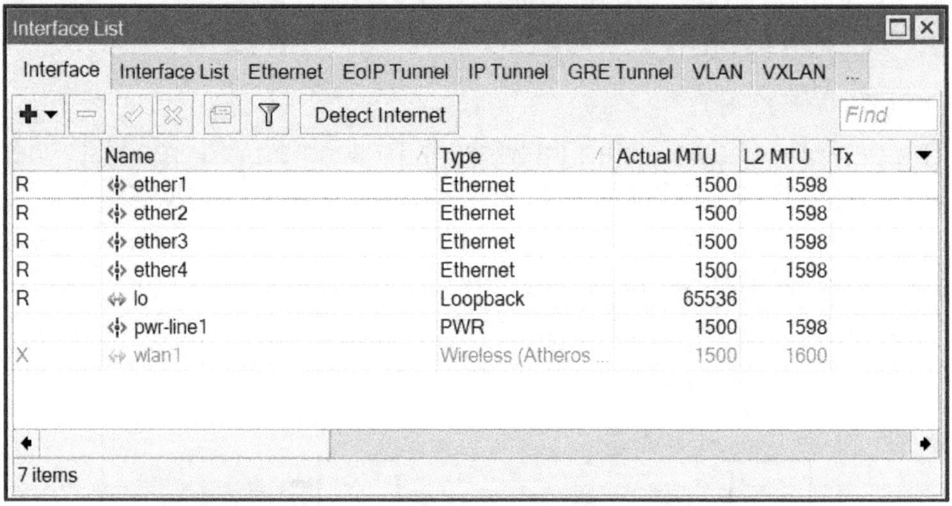

Then, in the **ARP** field, select the desired mode.

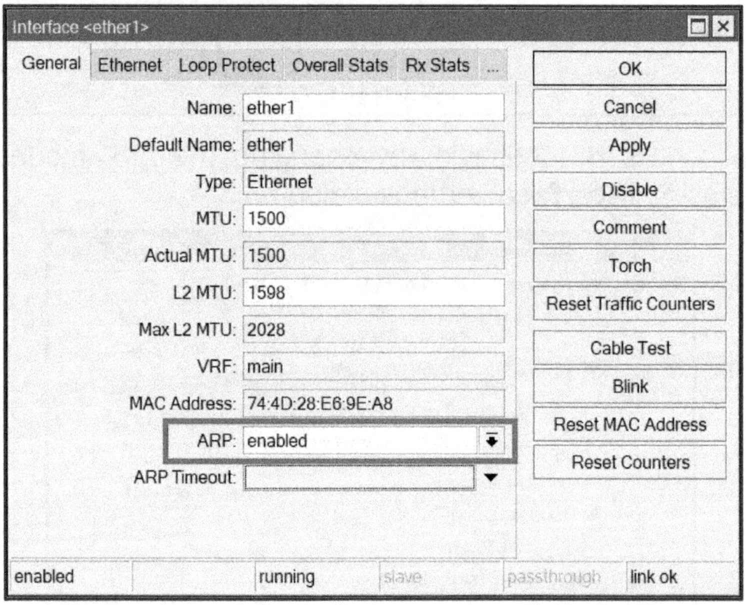

For example, you can allow the interface to send both ARP request and ARP reply messages by selecting the Enabled mode.

To prevent the interface from sending ARP requests or ARP replies, select the Disabled mode. In this case, you should rely on static entries in both devices to communicate.

To allow the interface to send ARP replies but prevent it from sending ARP requests, select the Reply Only mode.

In this case, you should rely on static entries in this device, while the other device will dynamically get the MAC address.

In some cases, you may want the interface to respond to ARP requests for IP addresses other than its IP address. In this case, you can use **Proxy ARP**. You will learn more about ARP in the MTCSWE course.

3

Module

BRIDGING

Module 3

This module provides an introduction to Layer 2 technology in MikroTik devices, introducing the concept of using the Bridge tool to configure the device as a switch.

More advanced information about Layer 2 technologies, such as VLANs, wireless bridging, and Layer 2 VPNs, is available in the MTCSWE, MTCRE, MTCUME, and MTCWE courses.

This module covers the following course content topics:

- Bridging overview
    - Bridge concepts and settings
    - Creating bridges
    - Adding ports to bridges
- Bridge wireless networks
    - Station bridge

Bridging

3.1 Bridging Overview and Key Concepts

To connect computers, or hosts, together within the same subnet, a device called a switch is used.

3.2 Switch

The switch is a device that connects hosts in the same subnet and forwards the data between them.

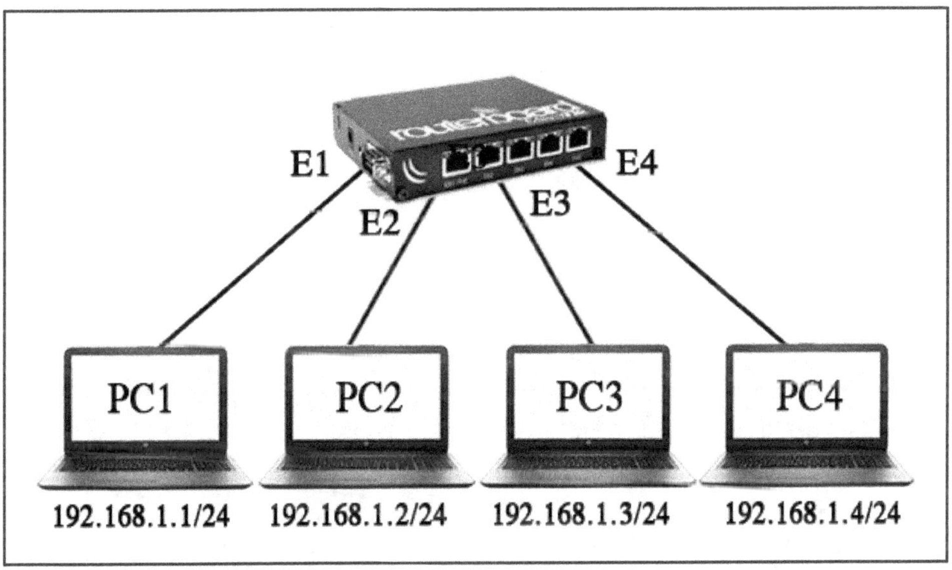

3.3 How Switch Works

When a device wants to send data to another device in the same subnet, it creates a frame and writes its own MAC address as the source MAC address in this frame and the MAC address of the other device as the destination MAC address. It then sends the frame to the switch.

When the switch receives the frame, it will:

- First: check the source MAC address of the frame and save this address in a table along with the interface it came from.
- Second: check the destination MAC address of the frame and look up this address in the table to determine which interface it should forward the data through.

This table is called the MAC address table

MAC Address	Interface
00:11:11:11:11:11	E1
00:22:22:22:22:22	E2
00:33:33:33:33:33	E3
00:44:44:44:44:44	E4

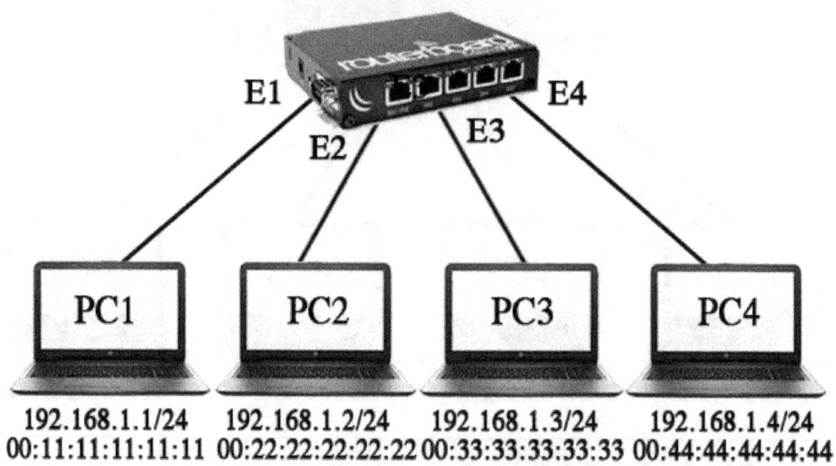

You can configure RouterOS to function as a switch to connect hosts in the same subnet by using a tool called Bridge

3.4 MAC Address Table

The MAC address table is a table that contains the MAC addresses of hosts in the subnet and the interfaces connected to those hosts.

The switch can add the MAC addresses of hosts to the MAC address table, (or build the MAC address table), by checking the source MAC address of incoming frames it receives whenever a host sends data.

3.5 MikroTik Bridge

MikroTik Bridge is a software tool that connects interfaces together to function as a switch and forward data based on Layer 2. This software bridge consumes CPU resources.

You can bridge different types of interfaces, (or add different types of interfaces to a bridge), such as ethernet, wireless, SFP, and tunnel interfaces.

3.6 Bridge Configuration

To configure RouterOS to function as a switch, use the **Bridge** window.

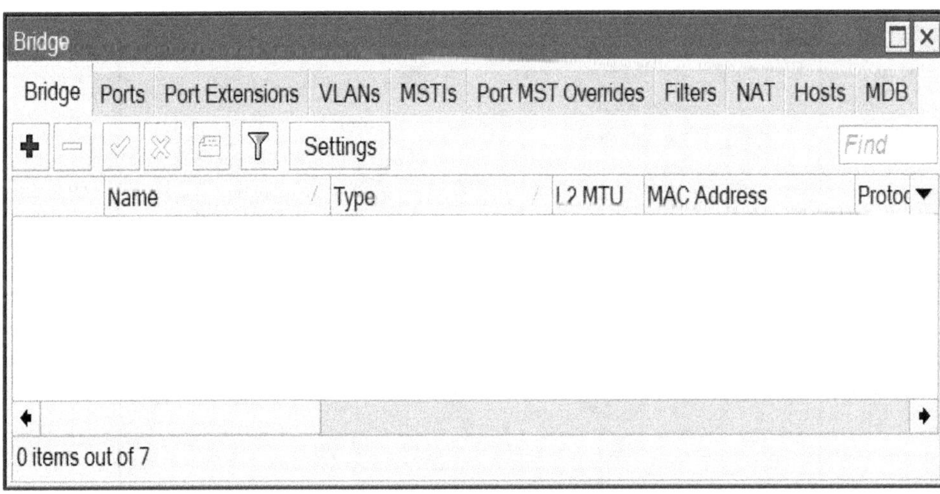

To open the **Bridge** window, click the **Bridge** menu.

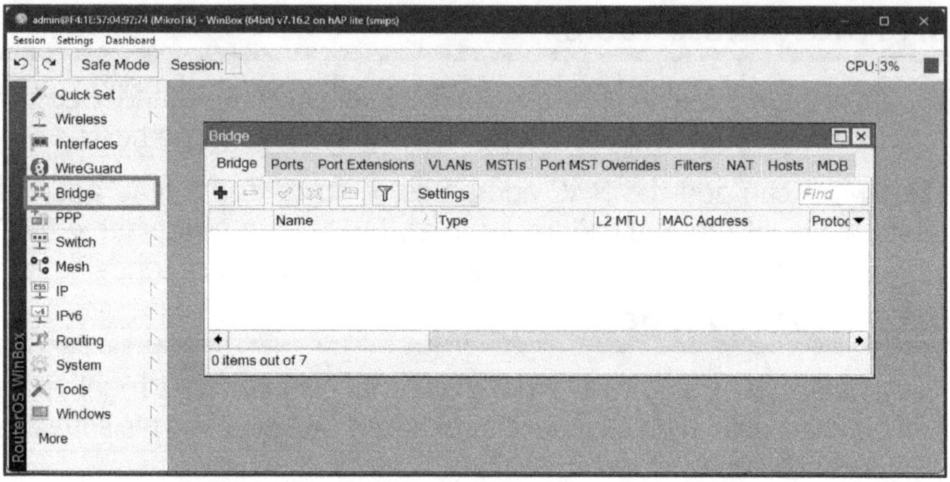

To configure the Bridge, follow two steps:

- Create a bridge.
- Add ports to the bridge.

3.6.1 Creating a Bridge

To create a bridge, click the **Add** button in the **Bridge** tab of the **Bridge** window to open the **New Interface** dialog box.

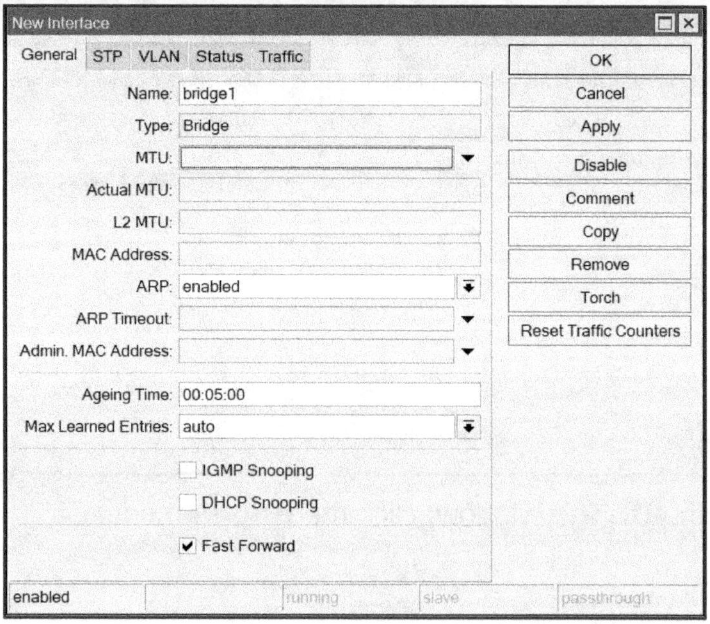

You can use this dialog box to create a bridge and configure its different properties.

In the **Name** field, you can enter a name for this bridge, or you can leave the default name.

Click the **OK** button to close this dialog box and create the bridge.

The new bridge will now appear in the **Bridge** tab.

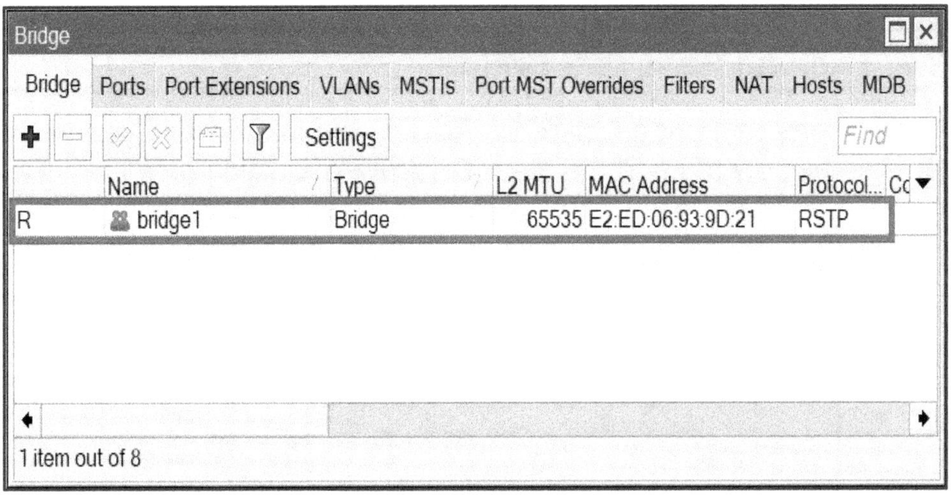

You can also create a bridge from the CLI using the following command:

```
interface bridge add
```

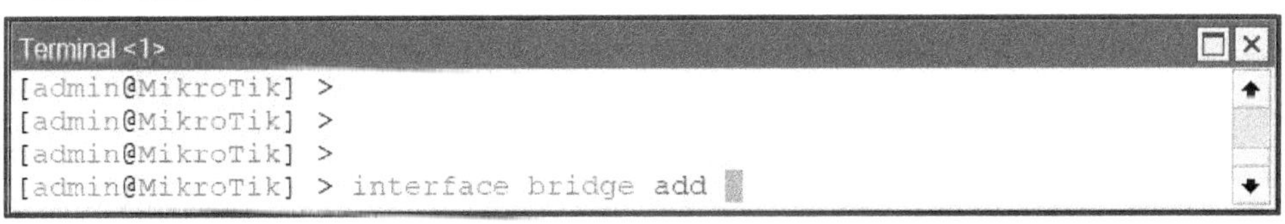

That will create a bridge by the default name.

To display the current bridges in RouterOS from the CLI use the following command:

```
interface bridge print
```

```
Terminal <1>
[admin@MikroTik] >
[admin@MikroTik] > interface bridge print
Flags: X - disabled, R - running
 0 R name="bridge1" mtu=auto actual-mtu=1500 l2mtu=65535 arp=enabled
     arp-timeout=auto mac-address=C6:21:9D:00:C9:62
     protocol-mode=rstp fast-forward=yes igmp-snooping=no
     auto-mac=yes ageing-time=5m priority=0x8000 max-message-age=20s
     forward-delay=15s transmit-hold-count=6 vlan-filtering=no
     dhcp-snooping=no port-cost-mode=long mvrp=no
     max-learned-entries=auto
[admin@MikroTik] >
```

3.6.2 Adding Ports to a Bridge

To add ports to a bridge, click the **Add** button in the **Ports** tab of the **Bridge** window to open the **New Bridge Port** dialog box.

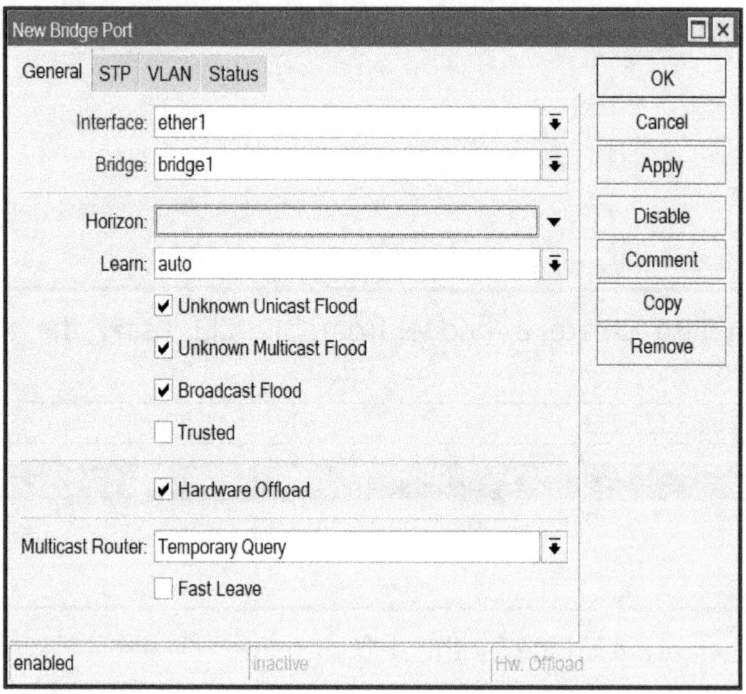

You can use this dialog box to add ports to a bridge and configure different properties of these ports.

In the **Interface** field, select the interface or the port you want to add, and in the **Bridge** field, select the bridge to which you want to add this interface.

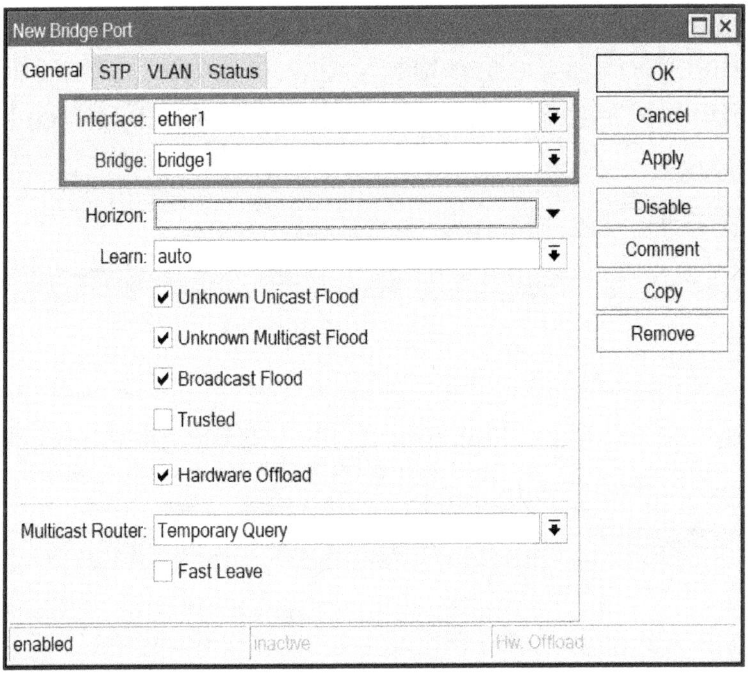

Then click the **OK** button to close this dialog box and add the interface to the bridge.

The new interface will now appear in the **Ports** tab.

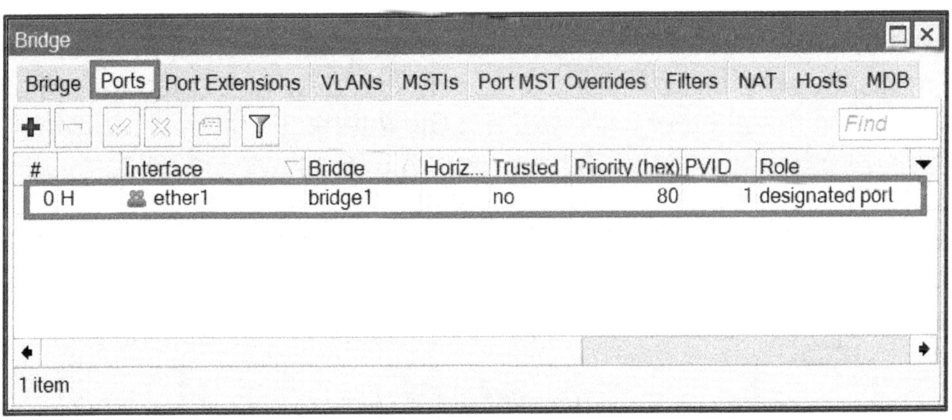

You can also add ports to a bridge from the CLI using the following command:

```
interface bridge port add interface=[interface] bridge=[bridge]
```

Where:

- [interface] is the interface you want to add to the bridge.
- [bridge] is the bridge you want to add this interface to.

For example:

```
interface bridge port add interface=ether1 bridge=bridge1
```

```
Terminal <1>
[admin@MikroTik] >
[admin@MikroTik] >
[admin@MikroTik] >
[admin@MikroTik] > interface bridge port add interface=ether1 bridge=bridge1
```

To display the current bridge interfaces, use the following command:

```
interface bridge port print
```

```
Terminal <1>
[admin@MikroTik] >
[admin@MikroTik] >
[admin@MikroTik] > interface bridge port print
Flags: H - HW-OFFLOAD
Columns: INTERFACE, BRIDGE, HW, PVID, PRIORITY, HORIZON
#   INTERFACE  BRIDGE   HW    PVID  PRIORITY  HORIZON
0 H ether1     bridge1  yes      1  0x80      none
[admin@MikroTik] >
```

LAB

In this lab, the MikroTik device is connected to two computers: PC1 via the interface ether1 and PC2 via the interface ether2. You want to configure the device to function as a switch, allowing both computers to communicate within the same subnet.

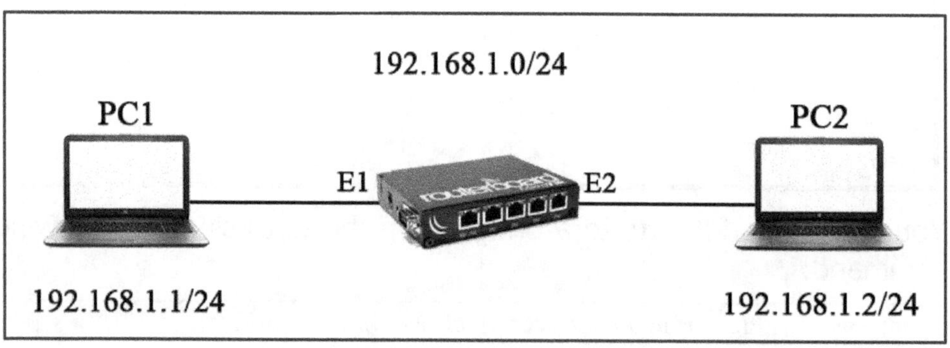

To configure the device to act as a switch, follow two steps as mentioned:

- Create a bridge in this device.
- Add both interfaces, or ports, ether1 and ether2 to the bridge.

To create a bridge, click the **Add** button in the **Bridge** tab of the **Bridge** window to open the **New Interface** dialog box.

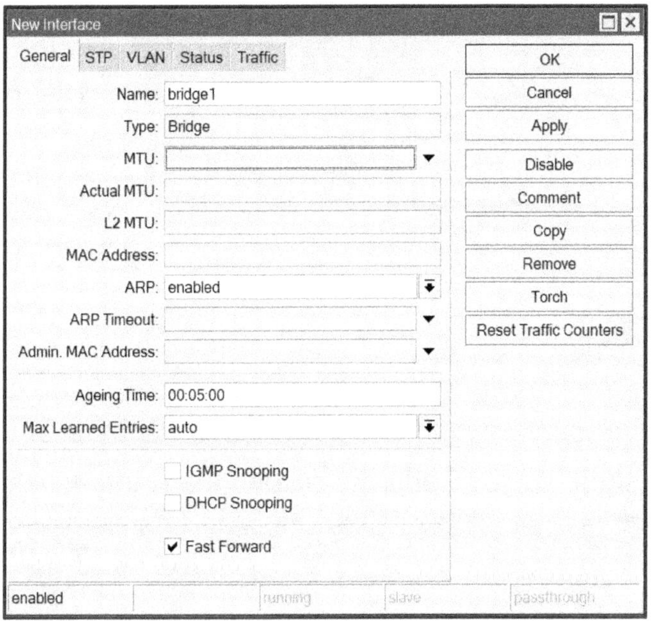

Accept all default settings and just click the **OK** button to close this dialog box. You will see the new bridge in **Bridge** tab.

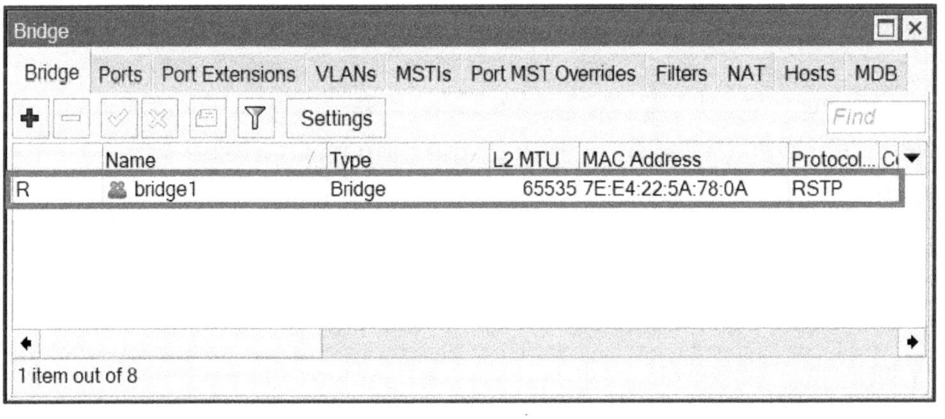

To add the first port or the first interface to the bridge, click the **Add** button in the **Ports** tab to open the **New Bridge Port** dialog box. In the **Interface** field, select ether1, and in the **Bridge** field, select bridge1. Then click the **OK** button.

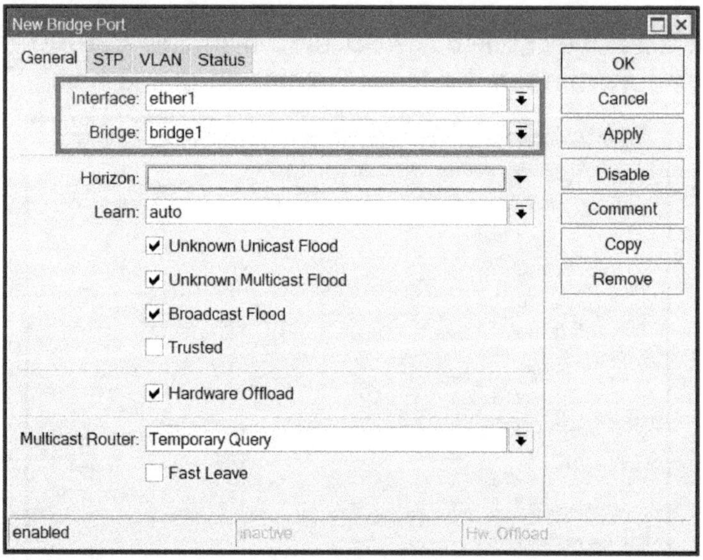

Repeat the same steps to add the second interface, ether2

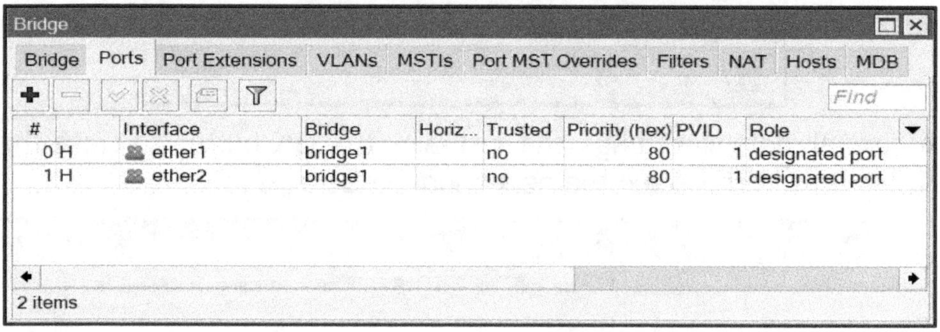

Now, when PC1 tries to ping PC2, the ping will succeed.

CLI

You can also make the configuration from the CLI .

To create a bridge, use the following command:

```
interface bridge add
```

To add ports to the bridge, use the following commands:

```
interface bridge port add interface=ether1 bridge=bridge1
interface bridge port add interface=ether2 bridge=bridge1
```

3.7 Bridging Wireless Networks

As mentioned, you can add wireless interfaces to a bridge, to bridge wireless networks. In this case, you must configure the wireless interface using one of the following modes:

- Station Bridge: This mode is used to connect RouterOS to RouterOS.
- Station Pseudo-Bridge: This mode is used to connect RouterOS to other devices.
- Station WDS: This mode is used to connect RouterOS to RouterOS.

You will learn more about this topic in the MTCWE course.

3.8 Bridge as a Loopback

You can also use the bridge as a loopback interface by creating a bridge and assigning an IP address to this bridge, like any other interface.

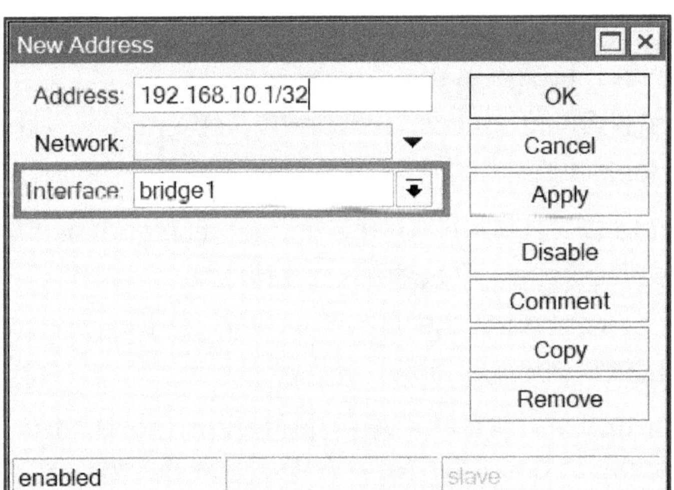

3.9 DHCP on Bridge Interface

You can create a bridge, add interfaces to it, assign an IP address to the bridge, and then configure a DHCP server on this bridge. In this case, the DHCP server will distribute IP addresses to devices connected to any of those interfaces.

LAB

In this lab, the MikroTik device is connected to two computers: PC1 via the interface ether1 and PC2 via the interface ether2. you want to configure the device to function as a switch, allowing both computers to communicate within the same subnet, also to distribute IP addresses to those computers.

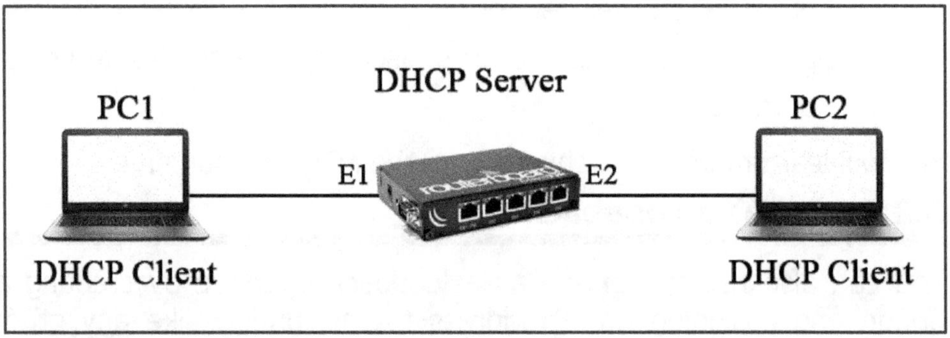

To configure the device to act as a switch, follow two steps as mentioned:

- Create a bridge in this device.
- Add both interfaces, (or ports), ether1 and ether2 to the bridge.

To configure a DHCP server on the bridge, as mentioned also:

- First: assign an IP address to bridge1.
- Then: configure the DHCP server on this bridge using the **DHCP Server** window.

To create a bridge, click the **Add** button in the **Bridge** tab of the **Bridge** window to open the **New Interface** dialog box.

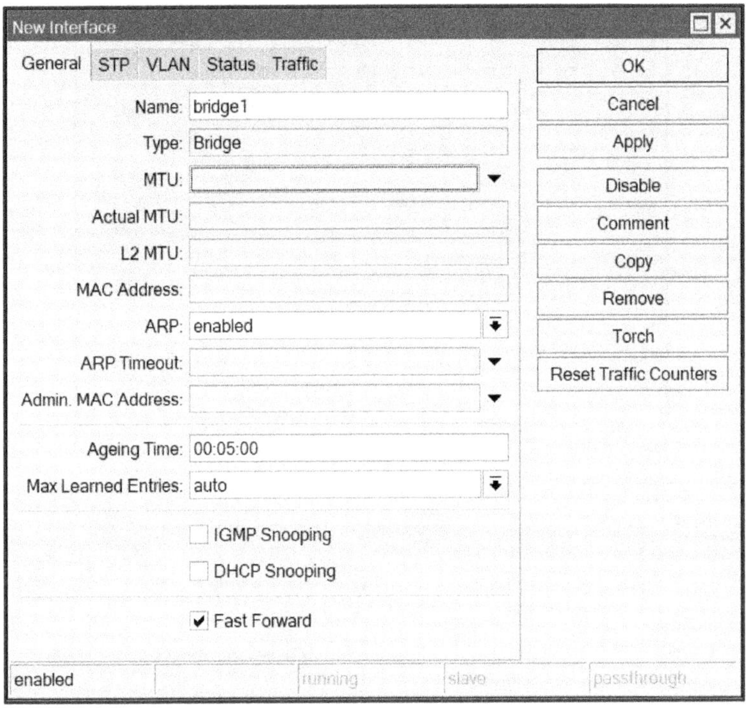

Accept all default settings and just click the **OK** button to close this dialog box. You will see the new bridge in **Bridge** tab.

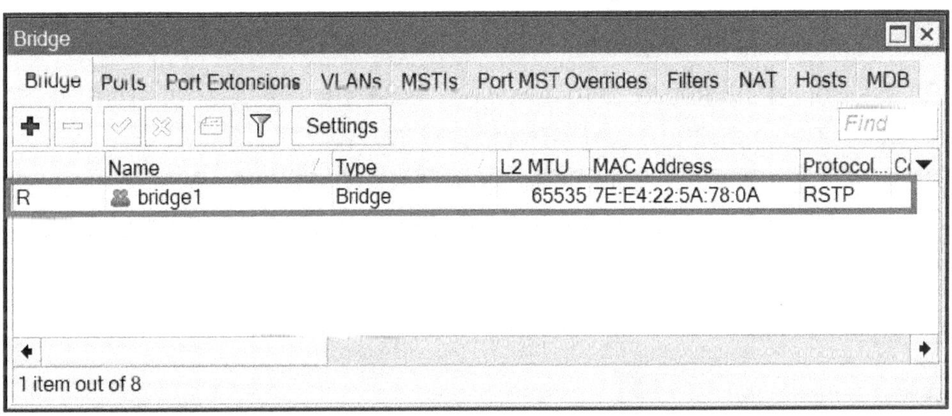

To add the first port or the first interface to the bridge, click the **Add** button in the **Ports** tab to open the **New Bridge Port** dialog box. In the **Interface** field, select ether1, and in the **Bridge** field, select bridge1. Then click the **OK** button.

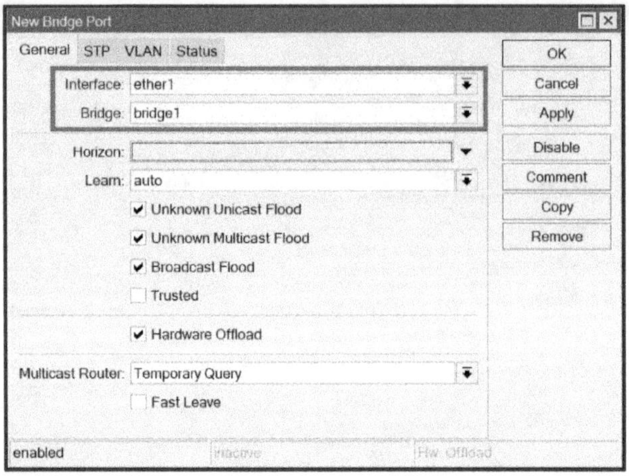

Repeat the same steps to add the second interface, ether2

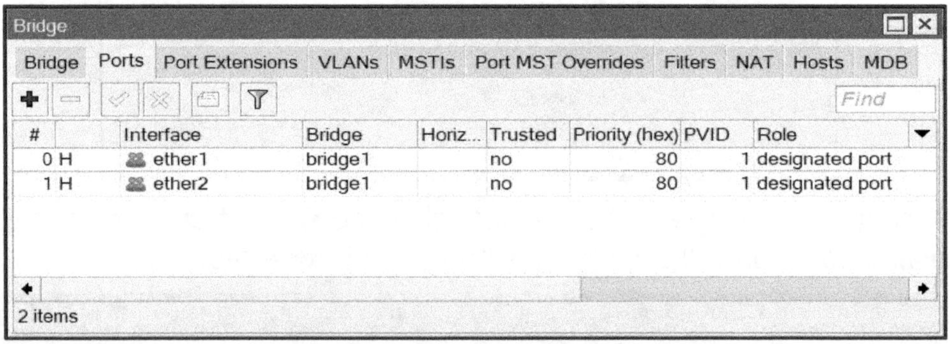

To assign an IP address to bridge1, click the **IP** menu, then select **Addresses** to open the **Address List** window.

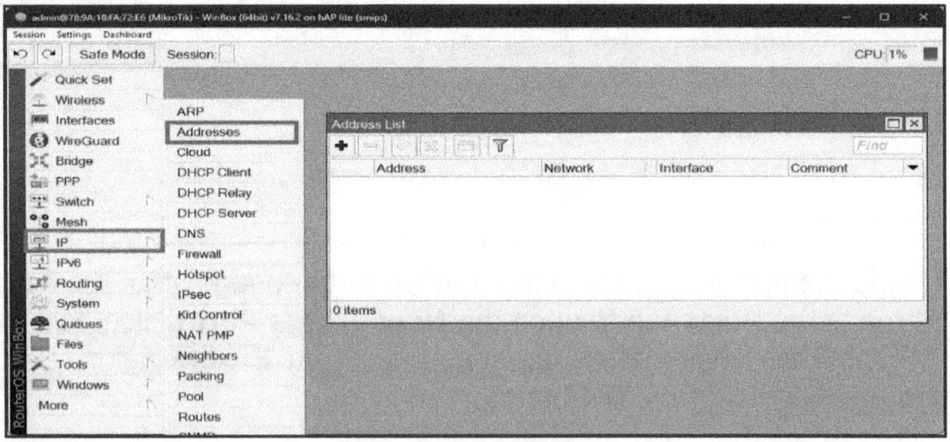

Then click the **Add** button in **Address List** window to open the **New Address** dialog box.

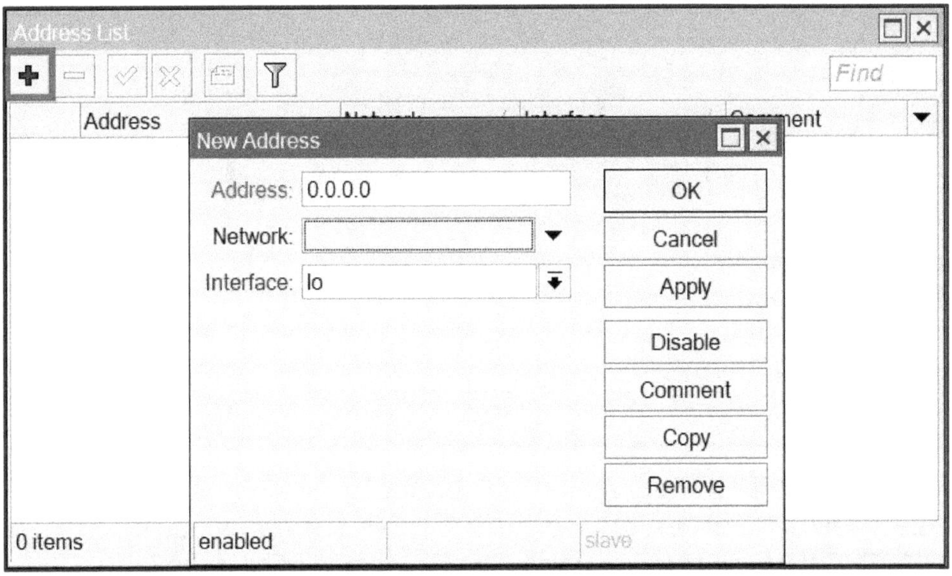

In the **Address** field in this dialog box, enter the IP address and subnet mask 192.168.1.1/24. In the **Interface** field, select bridge1, then click the **OK** button to close the dialog box.

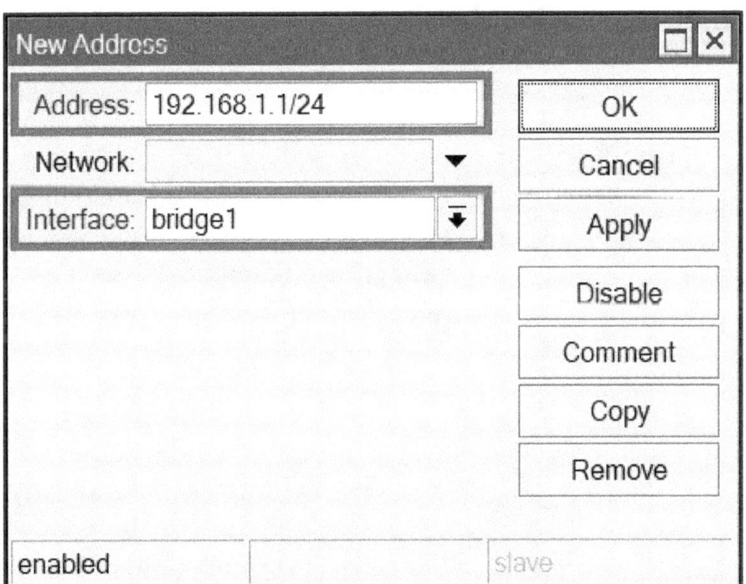

After assigning the IP address to bridge1, it will appear in the **Address List** window.

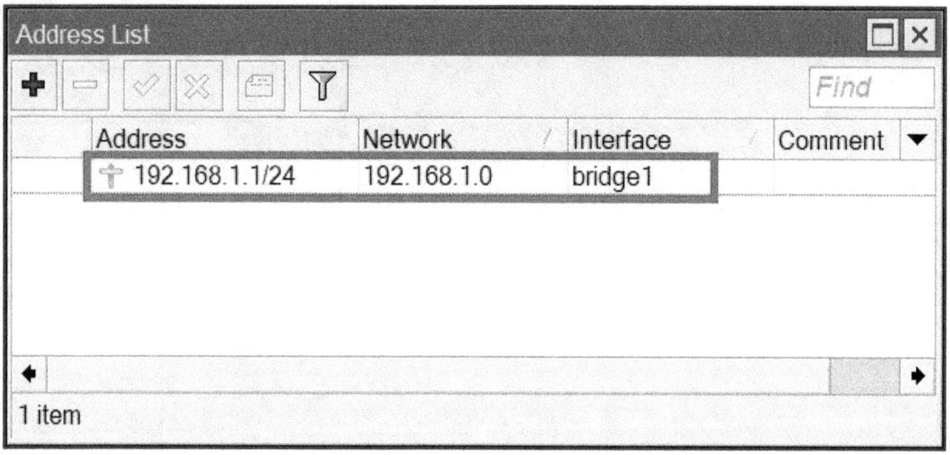

To configure DHCP server on the bridge1, click the **IP** menu, then select **DHCP Server** to open the **DHCP Server** window. click the **DHCP Setup** button to open **DHCP Setup** dialog box. In **DHCP Server Interface** field select the interface bridge1, and click the **Next** button in all other messages to accept the default settings and configure the DHCP Server.

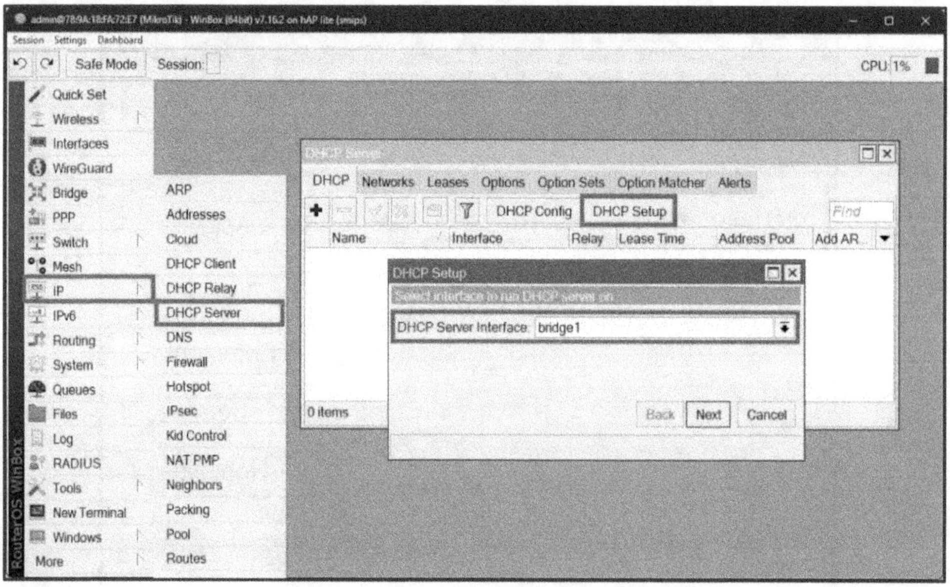

Now, when you connect PC1 and PC2 to the ether1 and ether2 interfaces, they will automatically receive an IP address from the DHCP server.

CLI

You can also make the configuration from the CLI .

To create a bridge, use the following command:

```
interface bridge add
```

To add ports to the bridge, use the following commands:

```
interface bridge port add interface=ether1 bridge=bridge1
interface bridge port add interface=ether2 bridge=bridge1
```

To assign an IP address to the bridge1, use the following command:

```
ip address add address=192.168.1.1/24 interface=bridge1
```

To configure a DHCP server on the bridge1 using the DHCP setup wizard, use the following command, choose bridge1 interface and accept the default settings by pressing Enter each time the setup wizard asks for input:

```
ip dhcp-server setup
```

mikrotik | MTCNA

④

Module

ROUTING

MTCNA

Module 4

This module provides an introduction to Layer 3 technology in MikroTik devices and explains how to configure the device as a router.

More advanced information about Layer 3 technologies, such as static routes and dynamic routing protocols, is available in the MTCRE and MTCINE courses.

This module covers the following course content topics:

- Routing overview
  - Routing concepts
  - Route flags
- Static routing
  - Creating routes
  - Setting default route
  - Managing dynamic routes
  - Implementing static routing in a simple network

Routing

4.1 Routing Overview and Key Concepts

To connect different subnets together, a device called a router is used.

4.2 Router

The router is a device that connects different subnets together and forwards the data between them.

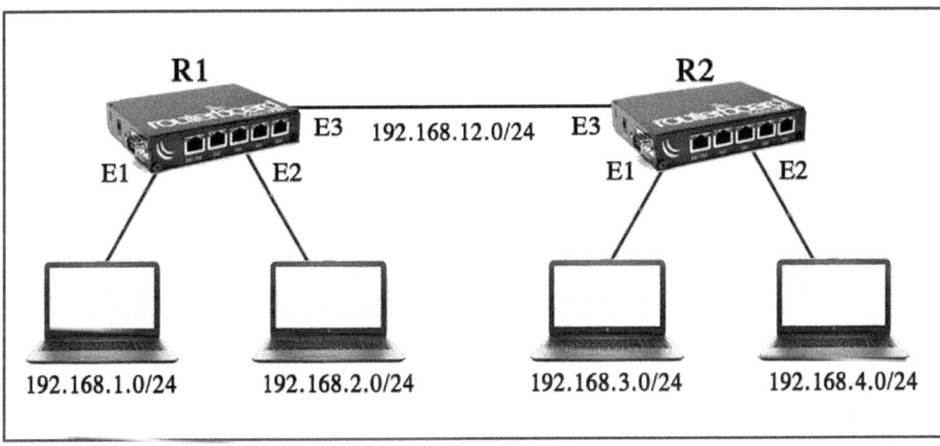

4.3 How Router Works

When a device wants to send data to another device in a different subnet, it creates a packet and writes its own IP address as the source IP address in this packet, and the IP address of the other device as the destination IP address. It then sends the packet to the router.

When the router receives the packet, it will check the destination IP address of the packet and look up this address in a table that contains the IP addresses of the subnets connected to the router, along with the interfaces it is connected to, to determine which interface it should forward the data through

This tale is called routing table.

Network	Port
192.168.1.0/24	E1
192.168.2.0/24	E2
192.168.12.0/24	E3
192.168.3.0/24	E3
192.168.4.0/24	E3

Network	Port
192.168.3.0/24	E1
192.168.4.0/24	E2
192.168.12.0/24	E3
192.168.1.0/24	E3
192.168.2.0/24	E3

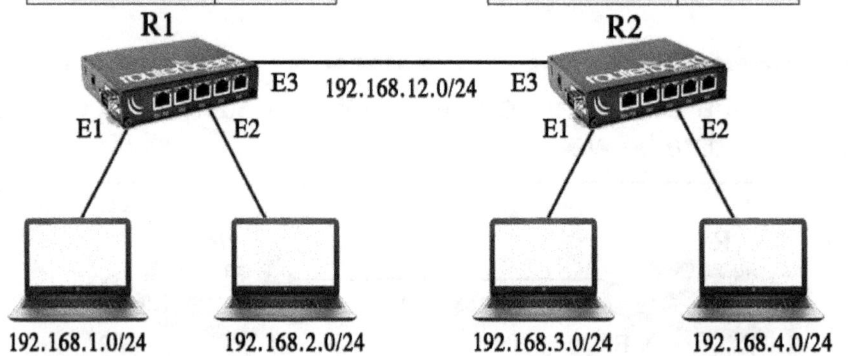

You can configure RouterOS to function as a router to connect different subnets together by assigning an IP address to each interface.

4.4 Routing Table

The routing table is a table that contains the Network ID of subnets in the network, (or the internetwork) and the interfaces connected to those subnets.

Each entry or record in this table is called a route.

The router can add subnets to the routing table depending on the subnet location. From the perspective of the router, these subnets are divided into two categories:

- Directly Connected Subnets:

  Directly connected subnets, (or connected subnets), are subnets directly connected to the router. The router will automatically, or dynamically, recognize these subnets and add them to the routing table without any external help.

- Remote Subnets:

  Remote subnets are subnets connected to another routers. The router cannot recognize these subnets on its own, it needs help to learn about them and add them to the routing table.

You can help the router learn about remote subnets in two ways:

- Statically: By manually adding the remote subnet to the routing table.
- Dynamically: By using protocols called dynamic routing protocols.

4.5 Router Configuration

To configure RouterOS to function as a router, assign an IP address to each interface. By doing this, RouterOS will work as a router without any additional configuration.

To assign an IP address to an interface, use the **Address List** window.

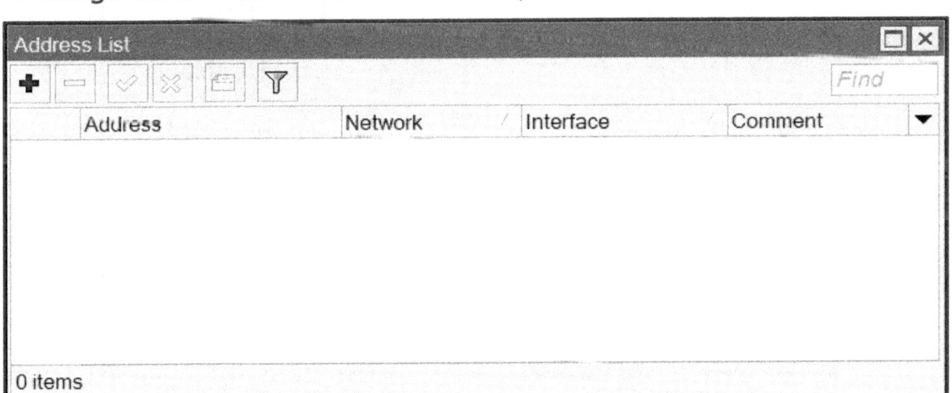

To open the **Address List** window, click the **IP** menu, then select **Addresses**.

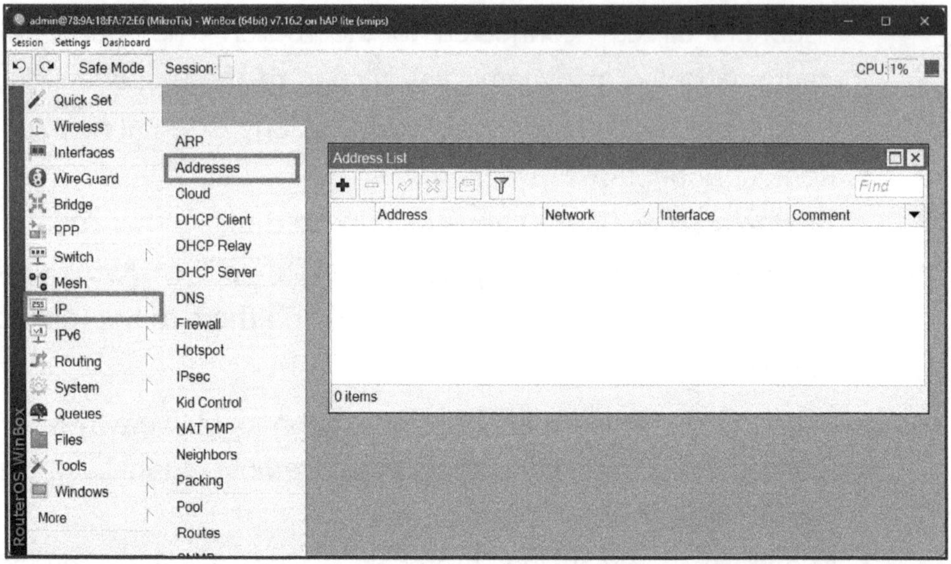

To assign an IP address to an interface, click the **Add** button in the **Address List** window to open the N**ew Address** dialog box.

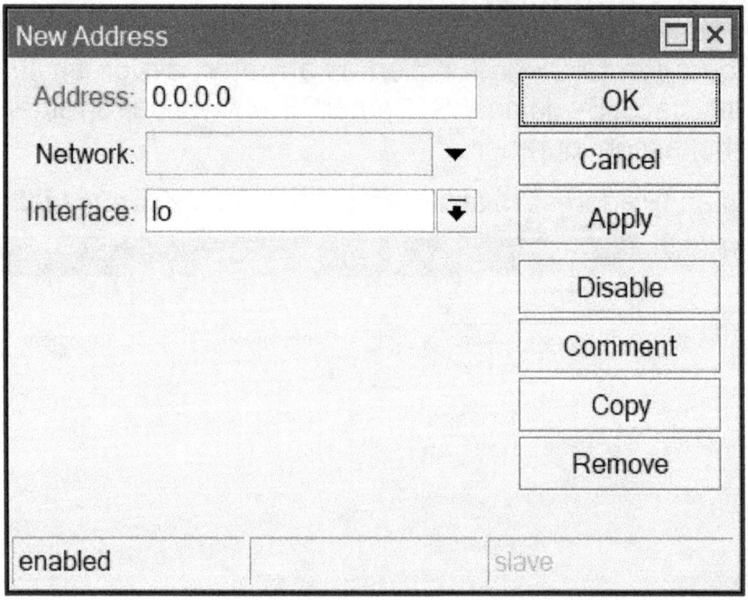

In the **Address** field, enter the IP address along with the subnet mask. In the **Interface** field, select the interface to which you want to assign the IP address.

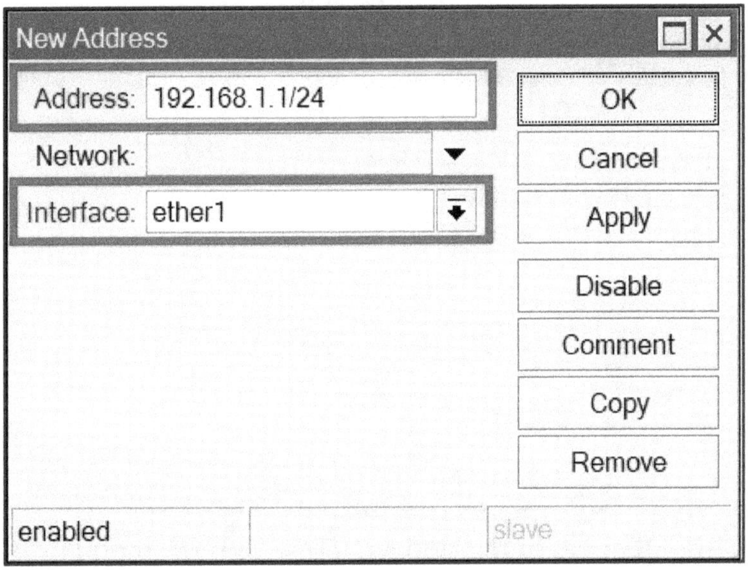

Then click the **OK** button to close this dialog box and assign the IP to the interface.

The new IP will now appear in the **Address List** window.

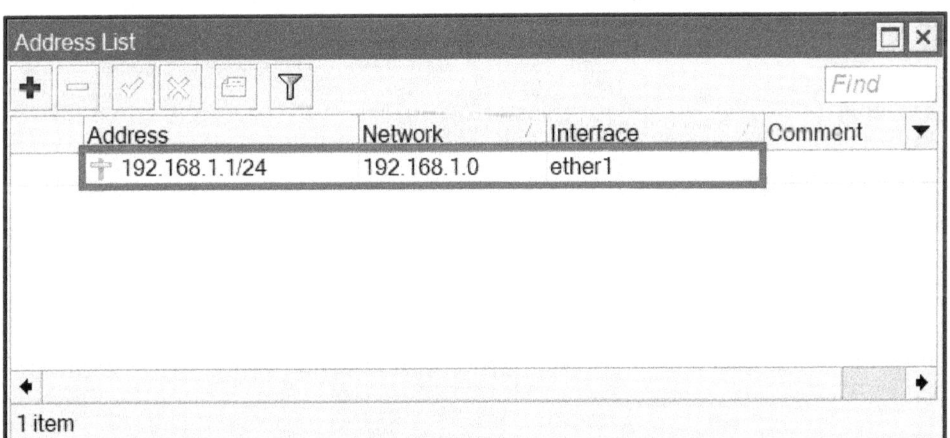

After adding the IP address, the device will recognize this new directly connected subnet and automatically, or dynamically, add it to the routing table, along with the interface it is connected to. A new route will appear in the **Route List** window, which displays the routing table. The device will save the subnet in the **Dst. Address** field, and the interface it is connected to in the **Gateway** field.

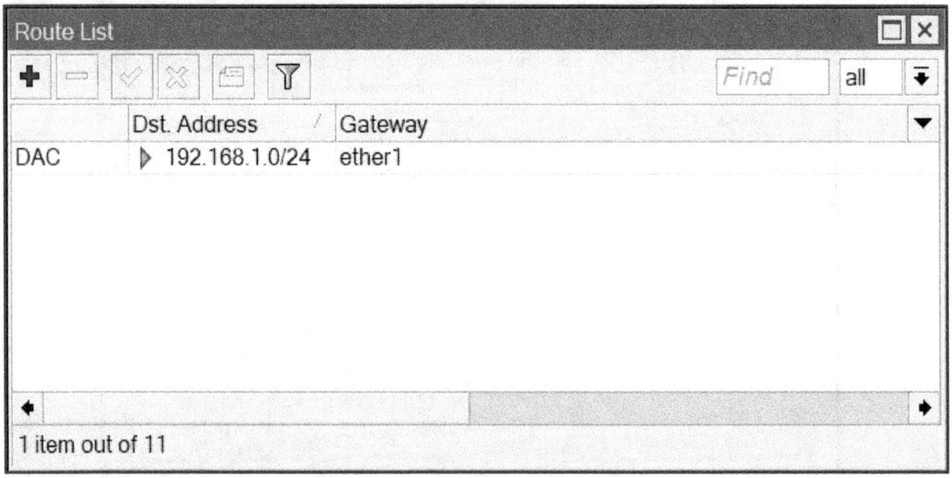

To open the **Route List** window, click the **IP** menu, then select **Routes**.

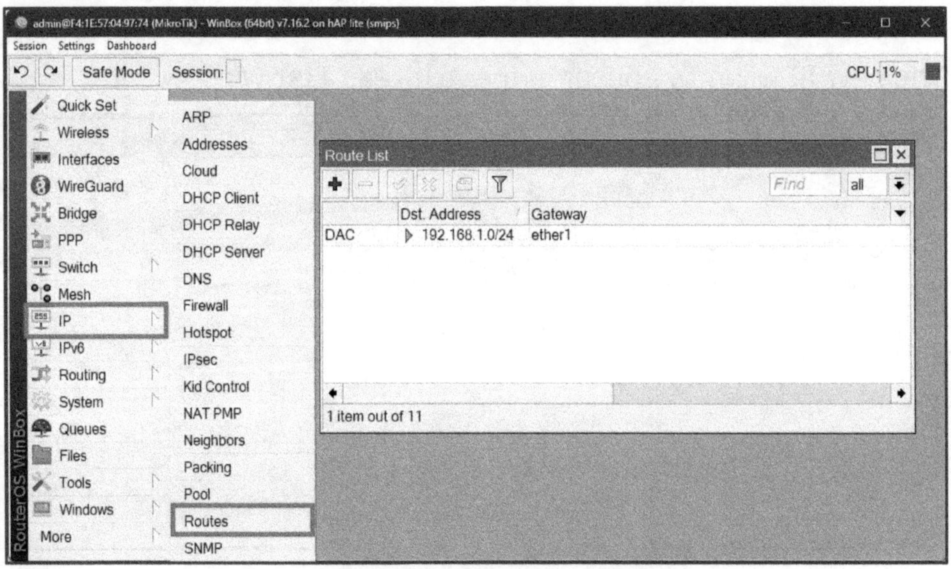

Note: the device will calculate the network ID of the subnet from the IP address and its subnet mask assigned to the interface and save this network ID in the Routing table, in the **Route List** window.

The routing table (or the **Route List** window) contains the network IDs of the subnets, while the **Address List** window contains the IP addresses assigned to each interface on the router.

In this example, the IP address is 192.168.1.1/24. The router will calculate the network ID for this IP address and add it to the routing table as 192.168.1.0/24.

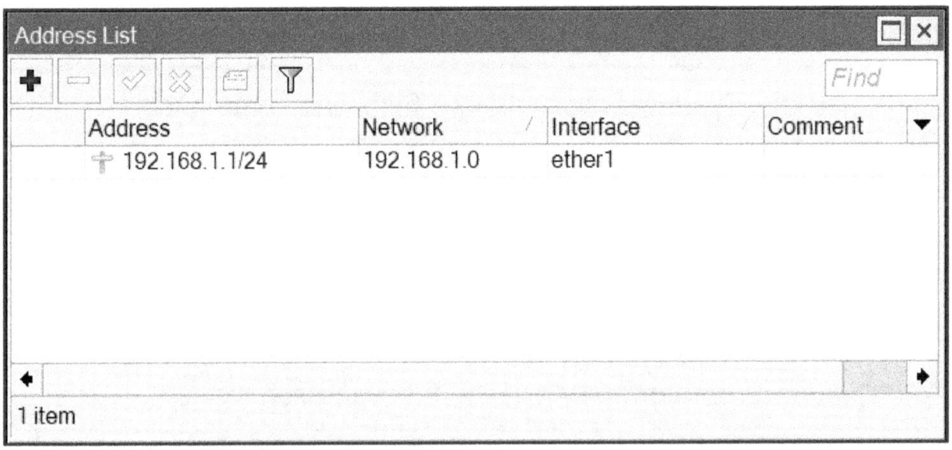

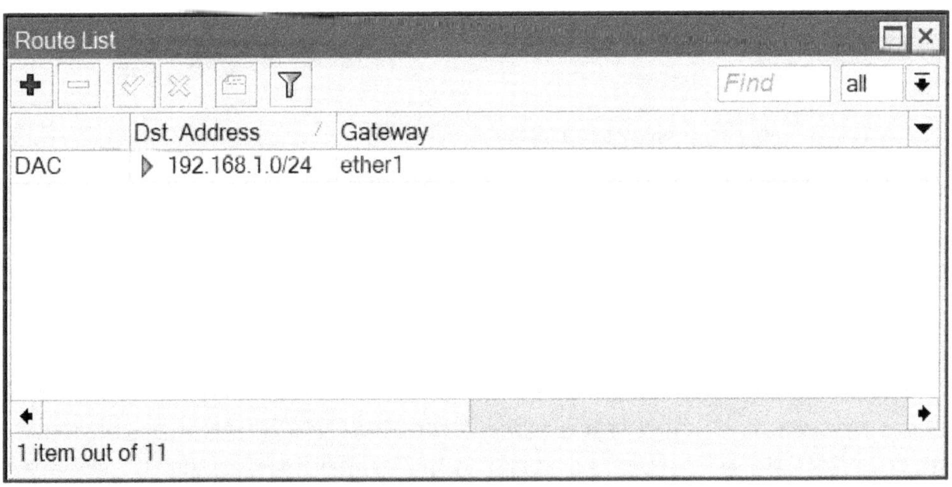

You can also assign an IP address to an interface in RouterOS from the CLI using the following command:

```
ip address add address=[IP/mask] interface=[interface]
```

Where:

- [IP/mask] is the IP address and the subnet mask.
- [interface] is the interface to which you want to assign this IP.

For example:

```
ip address add address=192.168.1.1/24 interface=ether1
```

```
Terminal <1>
[admin@MikroTik] >
[admin@MikroTik] >
[admin@MikroTik] >
[admin@MikroTik] > ip address add address=192.168.1.1/24 interface=ether1
[admin@MikroTik] >
```

To display the IP address list, use the following command:

```
ip address print
```

```
Terminal <1>
[admin@MikroTik] >
[admin@MikroTik] > ip address print
Columns: ADDRESS, NETWORK, INTERFACE
# ADDRESS         NETWORK       INTERFACE
0 192.168.1.1/24  192.168.1.0   ether1
[admin@MikroTik] >
```

To display the routing table, use the following command:

```
ip route print
```

```
Terminal <1>
[admin@MikroTik] >
[admin@MikroTik] > ip route print
Flags: D - DYNAMIC; A - ACTIVE; c - CONNECT
Columns: DST-ADDRESS, GATEWAY, DISTANCE
    DST-ADDRESS      GATEWAY  DISTANCE
DAc 192.168.1.0/24   ether1          0
[admin@MikroTik] >
```

LAB

In this lab, the MikroTik device R1 is connected to two computers, each in a different subnet. PC1, in the subnet 192.168.1.0/24, is connected to the interface ether1, PC2, in the subnet 192.168.2.0/24, is connected to the interface ether2. You want to configure the device to function as a router, allowing both computers in those different subnets to communicate. You will do this by assigning the first IP address of each subnet to the corresponding interface.

- The IP address 192.168.1.1/24 will be assigned to the interface ether1.
- The IP address 192.168.2.1/24 will be assigned to the interface ether2.

And assign the second IP address of each subnet to the corresponding PC:

- The IP address 192.168.1.2/24 will be assigned to PC1.
- The IP address 192.168.2.2/24 will be assigned to PC2

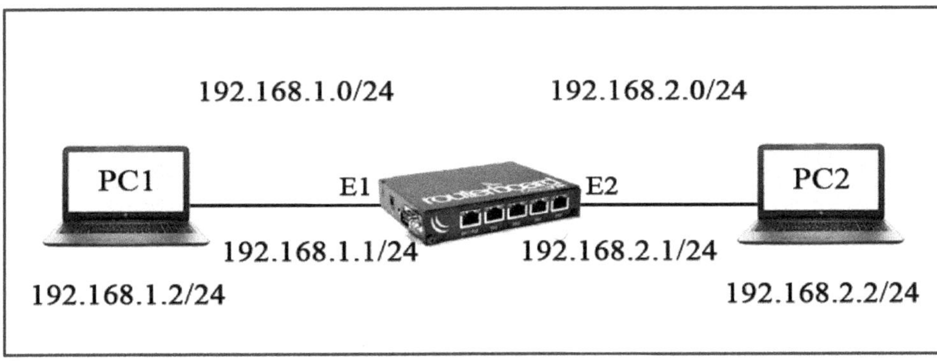

To assign an IP address to an interface, click the **IP** menu, then select **Addresses** to open the **Address List** window.

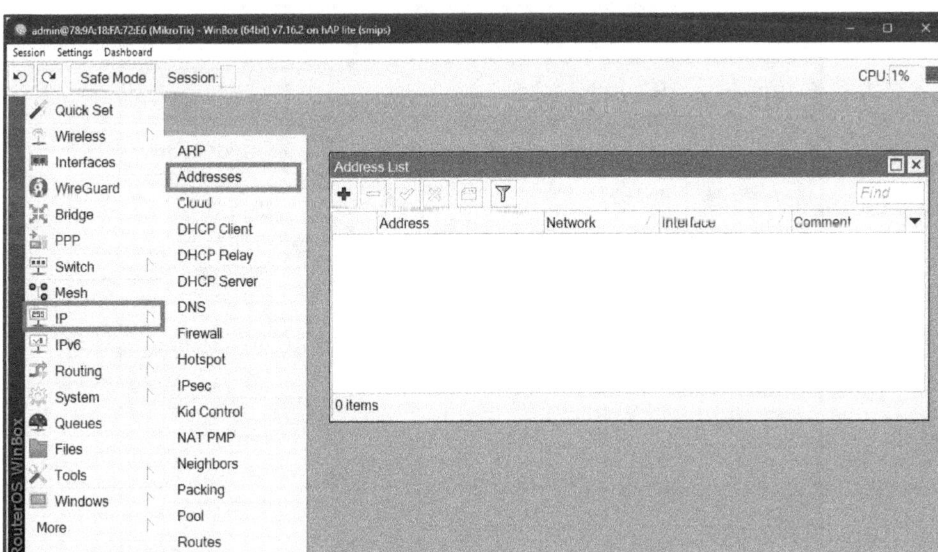

Click the **Add** button in the **Address List** window to open the **New Address** dialog box. In the **Address** field, enter the IP address along with the subnet mask. 192.168.1.1/24 . In the **Interface** field, select the interface ether1. Then click the **OK** button to close this dialog box and assign the IP to the interface.

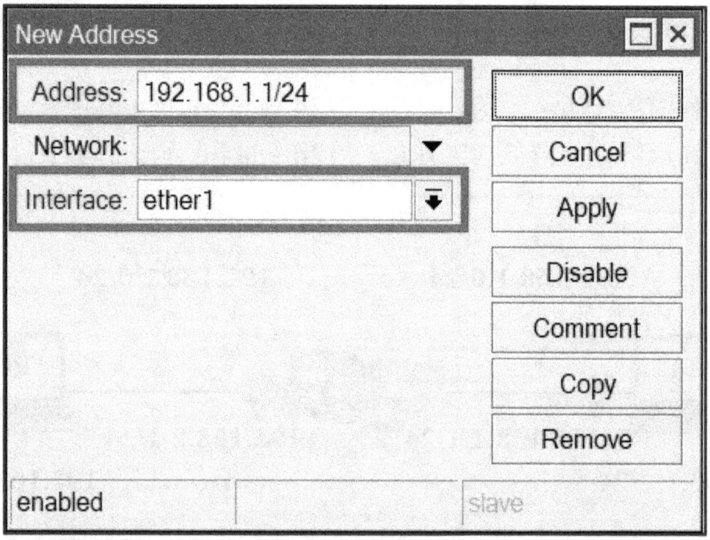

Repeat the same steps to assign the IP address 192.168.2.1/24 to the interface ether2**.**

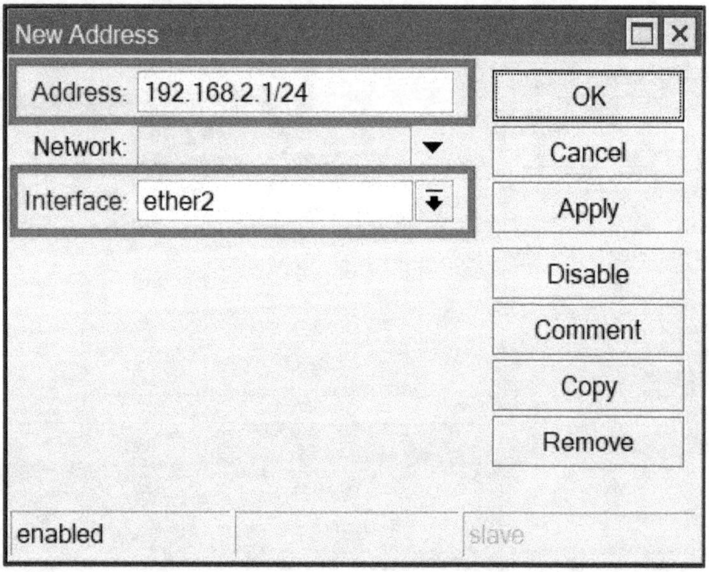

After assigning both IP addresses to each interface, they will appear in the **Address List** window.

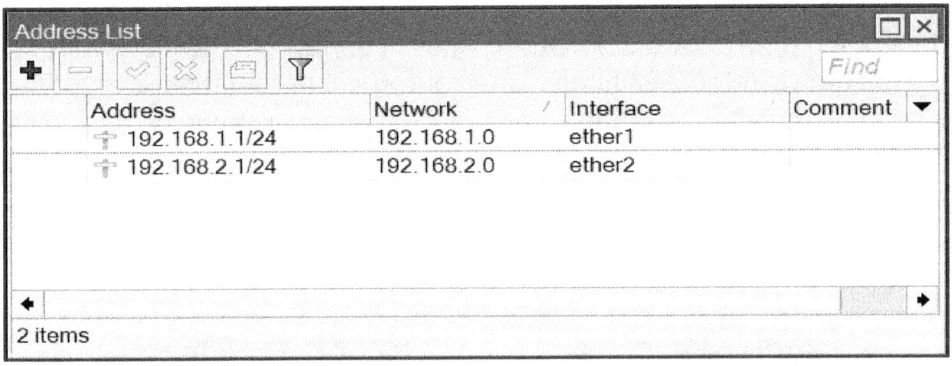

The router will recognize those directly connected subnets and automatically, or dynamically, add them to the routing table, they will appear in **Route List** window.

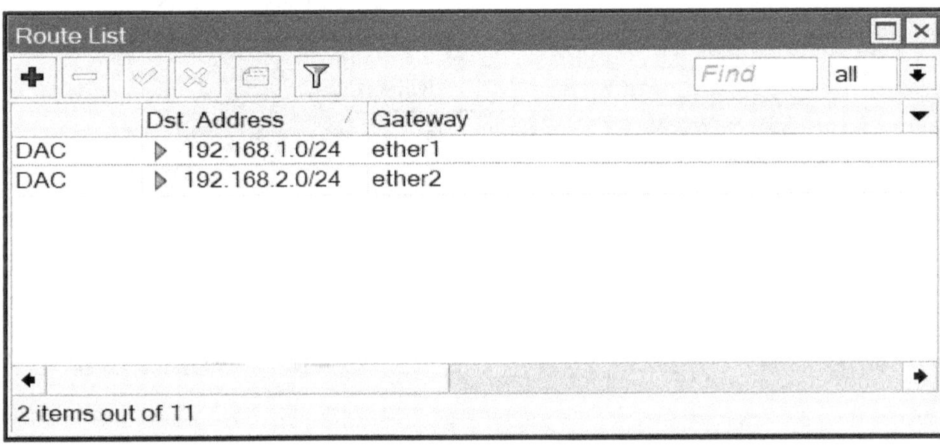

Now, when PC1 tries to ping PC2, the ping will succeed.

CLI

You can also make the configuration from the CLI.

To assign IP addresses to the interfaces ether1 and ether2, use the following commands:

```
ip address add address=192.168.1.1/24 interface=ether1

ip address add address=192.168.2.1/24 interface=ether2
```

4.6 Static Routes

As mentioned before, routers can add subnets to the routing table depending on the subnet location. These subnets can be either directly connected or remote subnets. The router will automatically recognize directly connected subnets without any external help or any extra configuration. However, to learn about remote subnets, the router needs help, or needs extra configuration. This can be done either by manually, (or statically), adding the subnets to the routing table or by using dynamic routing protocols

Dst. Address	Gateway
192.168.1.0/24	E1
192.168.2.0/24	E2
192.168.12.0/24	E3
192.168.3.0/24	192.168.12.2
192.168.4.0/24	192.168.12.2

Dst. Address	Gateway
192.168.3.0/24	E1
192.168.4.0/24	E2
192.168.12.0/24	E3
192.168.1.0/24	192.168.12.1
192.168.2.0/24	192.168.12.1

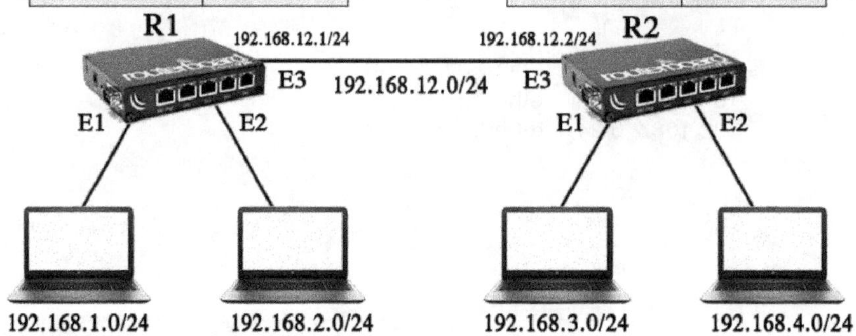

When you add a static route to the routing table to tell the router about a remote subnet, you provide the router with two important pieces of information:

- The network ID of the remote subnet.
- The path, or the gateway, to reach this subnet.

In this case, this route is called a static route.

In general, this path, or gateway, can be the interface connected to the subnet, or the next hop IP address, which is the IP of the other router.

In MikroTik RouterOS, when you add a static route use the next hop IP address as the gateway.

4.7 Create Static Route

To create or add a static route, use the **Route List** window.

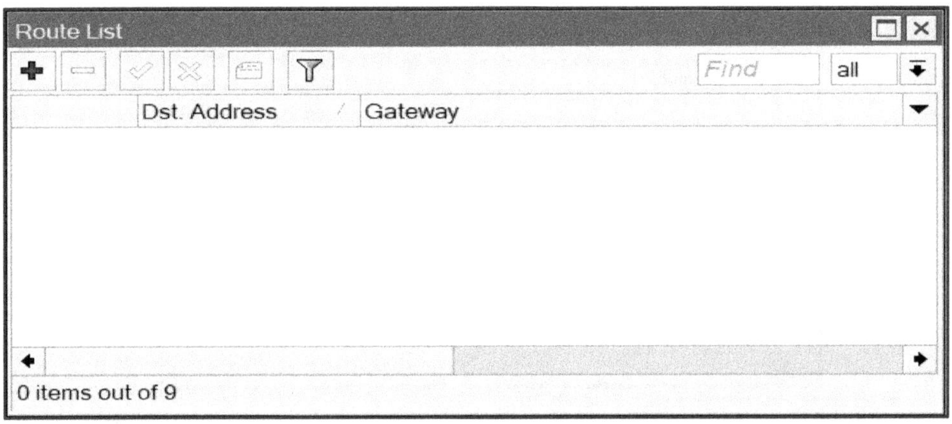

To open the **Route List** window, click the **IP** menu, then select **Routes**.

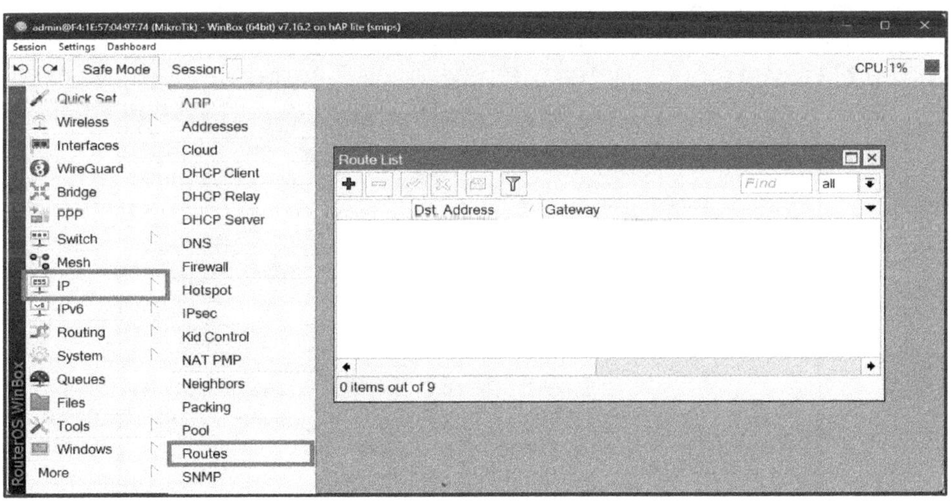

To add a static route, click the **Add** button in the **Route List** window to open the **New Route** dialog box.

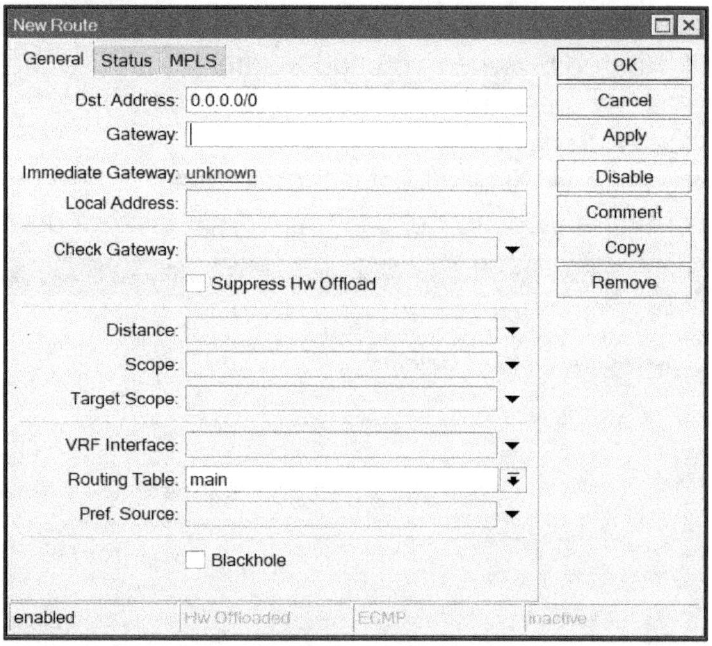

You can use this dialog box to configure different properties of the static route.

In the **Dst Address** field, (or Destination Address) , in the **General** tab, enter the remote subnet network ID along with the subnet mask. In the **Gateway** field, enter the next hop IP address.

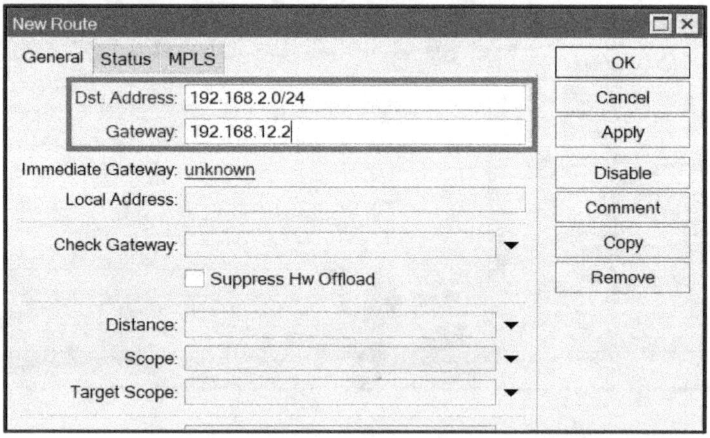

Then click the **OK** button to close the dialog box and create the static route. The new static route will now appear in the **Route List** window.

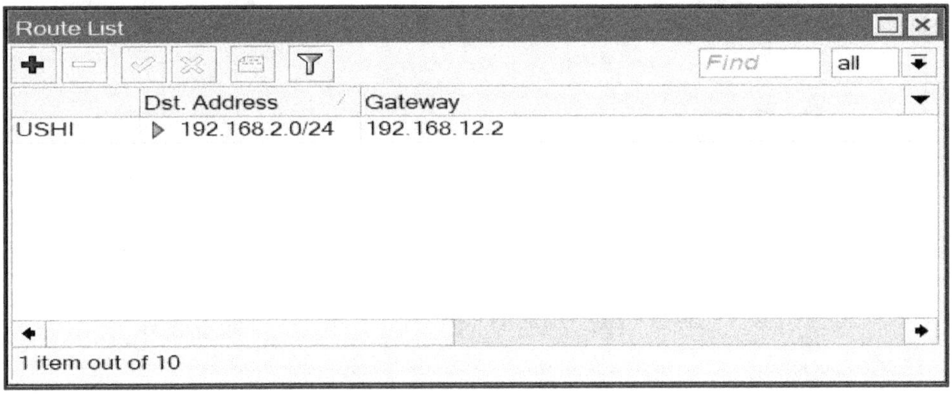

You can also create or add a static route to the routing table in RouterOS from the CLI using the following command:

```
ip route add dst-address=[network ID/mask] gateway=[next hop IP]
```

Where:

- [network ID/mask] is the remote network ID and the subnet mask.
- [next hop IP] is the IP address of the next hop.

For example:

```
ip route add dst-address=192.168.2.0/24 gateway=192.168.12.2
```

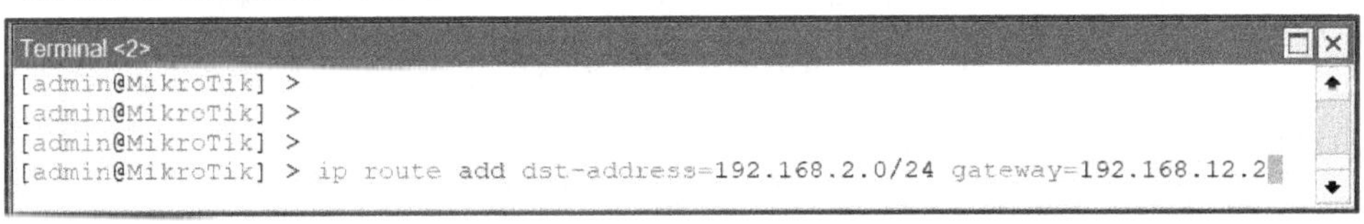

LAB

In this lab, you have two MikroTik devices. R1 is connected to two subnets: subnet 192.168.1.0/24 via ether1, and subnet 192.168.12.0/24 via ether2. Router 2 is connected to two subnets as well: subnet 192.168.2.0/24 via ether1, and subnet 192.168.12.0/24 via ether2. You want to configure these devices to function as routers, allowing computers in these different subnets to communicate.

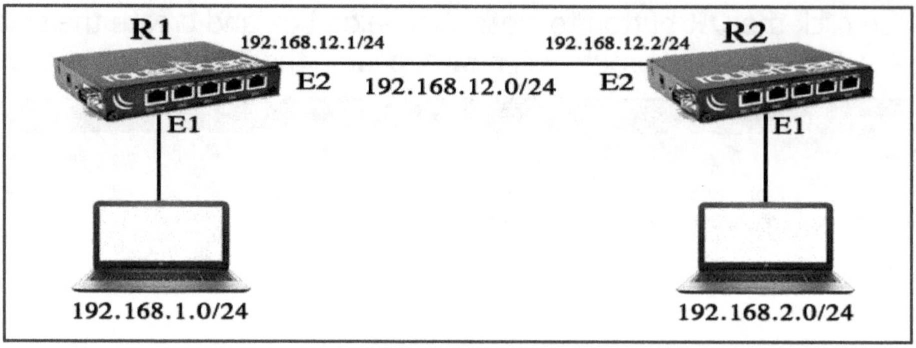

To ensure full connectivity in this lab, every router should have a route, in the routing table, for every subnet in this network, (or this internetwork).

To approach this lab:

- First: start by counting how many subnets exist in the internetwork.
- Then: determine how many subnets are directly connected to each router to identify the remote subnets from the perspective of each router.
- After identifying those remote subnets, they should be added manually (or statically) to each router.
- When the configuration is complete, ensure that each router has a route for every subnet by counting the number of routes in the routing table of each device.

In this lab, there are three subnets:

- 192.168.1.0/24
- 192.168.2.0/24
- 192.168.12.0/24

Router R1 is directly connected to two subnets:

- 192.168.1.0/24 via Ether1
- 192.168.12.0/24 via Ether2

From the perspective of R1, there is one remote subnet:

- 192.168.2.0/24.

So, you will add this subnet statically to R1.

Router R2 is directly connected to two subnets:

- 192.168.2.0/24 via Ether1
- 192.168.12.0/24 via Ether2

From the perspective of R2, there is one remote subnet:

- 192.168.1.0/24.

So, you will add this subnet statically to R2.

To start the configuration:

- First: assign the IP addresses to each interface,
- Second: create the static routes

Assigning the IP addresses:

R1

In Router R1:

- Assign the IP address 192.168.1.1/24 to the ether1.
- Assign the IP address 192.168.12.1/24 to the ether2.

To assign an IP address to an interface, click the **IP** menu, then select **Addresses** to open the **Address List** window.

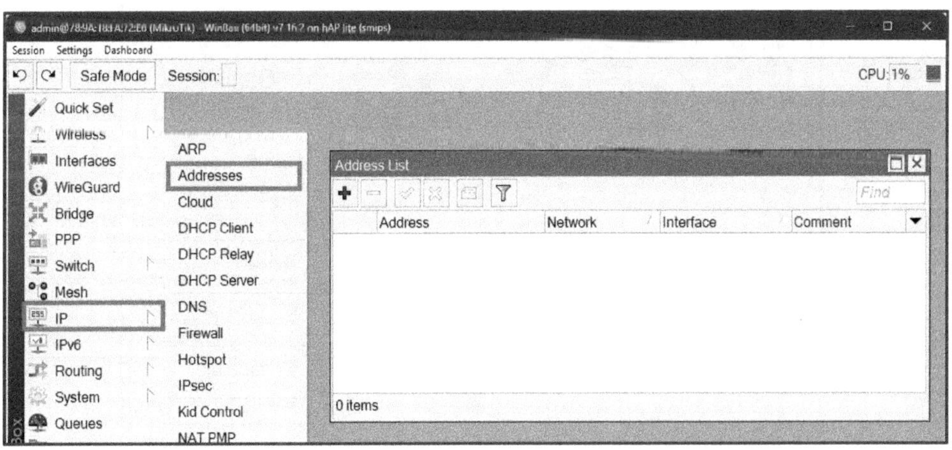

Click the **Add** button in the **Address List** window to open the **New Address** dialog box. In the **Address** field, enter the IP address along with the subnet mask. 192.168.1.1/24 . In the **Interface** field, select the interface ether1. Then click the **OK** button to close this dialog box and assign the IP to the interface.

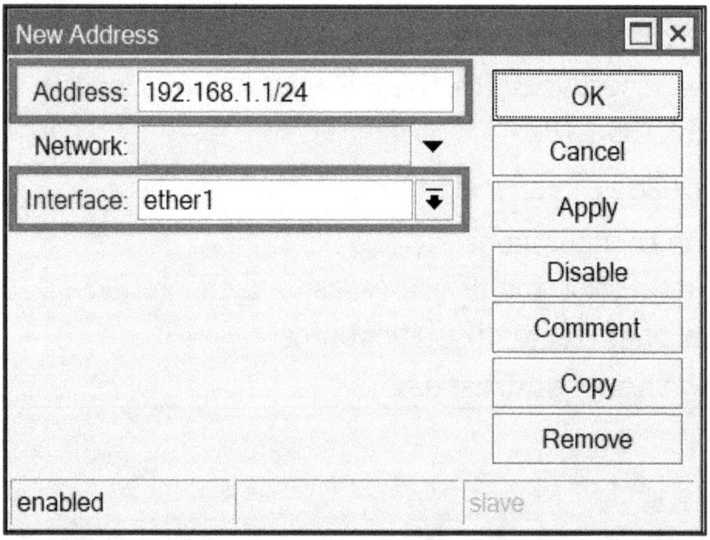

Repeat the same steps to assign the IP address 192.168.12.1/24 to the interface ether2.

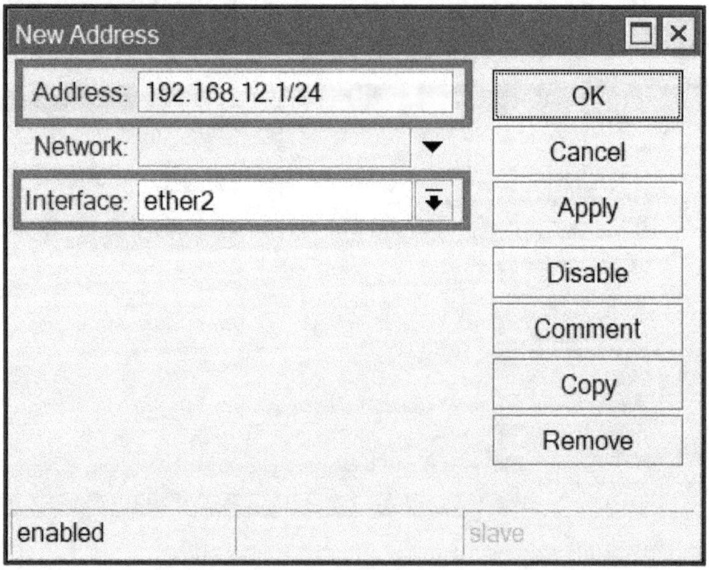

After assigning both IP addresses to each interface, they will appear in the **Address List** window.

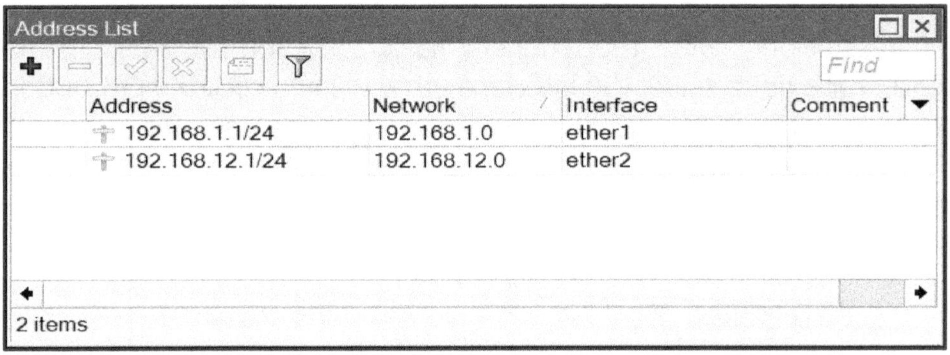

Now, if you open the routing table, you will see routes for those two subnets, because, as mentioned, the router will recognize the directly connected subnets and add them automatically (or dynamically) to the routing table without any external help, or additional configuration.

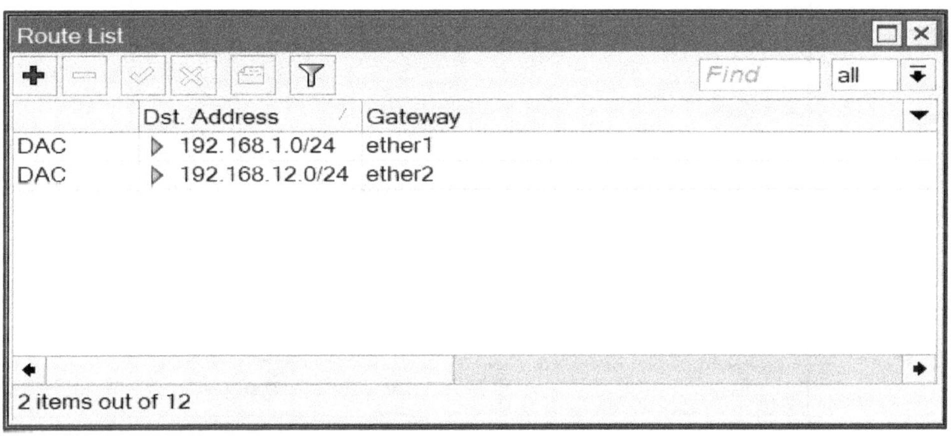

But you will not see any routes for the remote subnet 192.168.2.0/24, because, as mentioned, the router cannot know about the remote subnets by itself alone; it needs help.

R2

In Router R2:

- Assign the IP address 192.168.2.1/24 to the ether1.
- Assign the IP address 192.168.12.2/24 to the ether2.

Click the **IP** menu, then select **Addresses** to open the **Address List** window. Click the **Add** button in the **Address List** window to open the **New Address** dialog box. In the **Address** field, enter the IP address along with the subnet mask. 192.168.2.1/24 . In the **Interface** field, select the interface ether1. Then click the **OK** button.

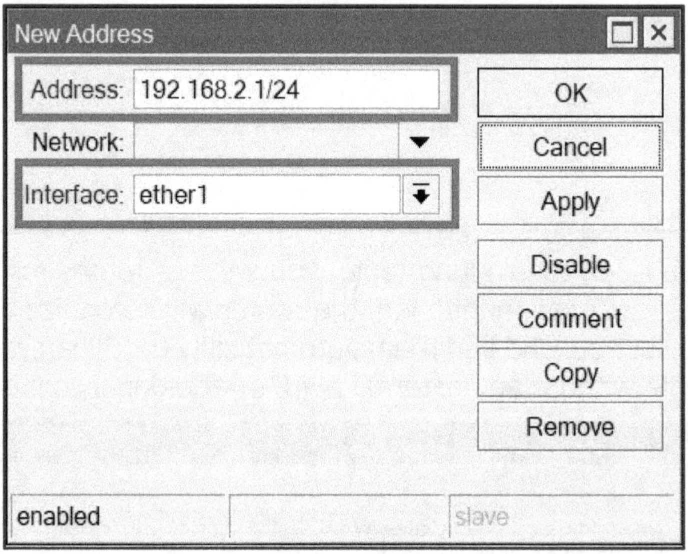

Repeat the same steps to assign the IP address 192.168.12.2/24 to the interface ether2**.**

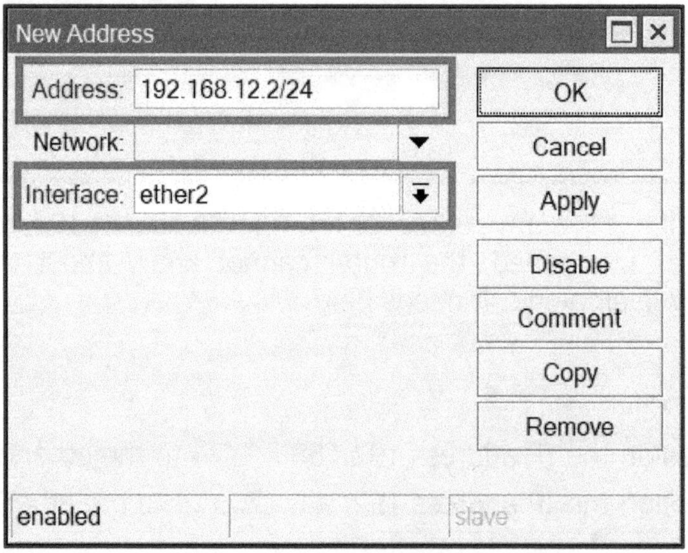

After assigning both IP addresses to each interface, they will appear in the **Address List** window.

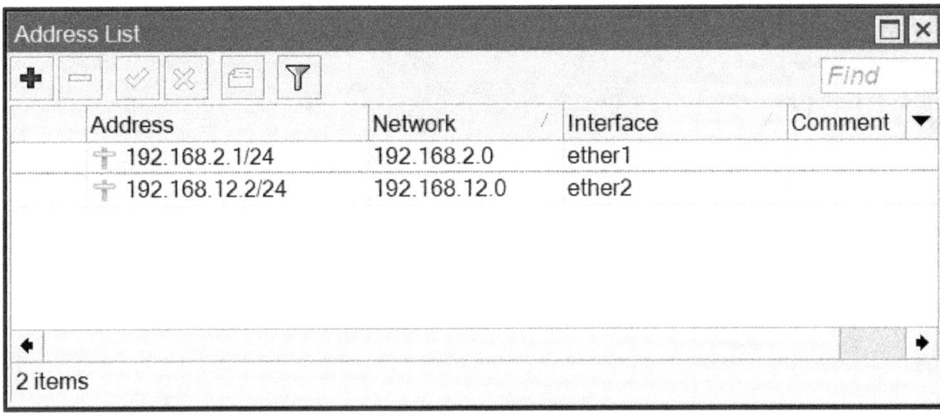

And the router will recognize those directly connected subnets and add them automatically (or dynamically) to the routing table.

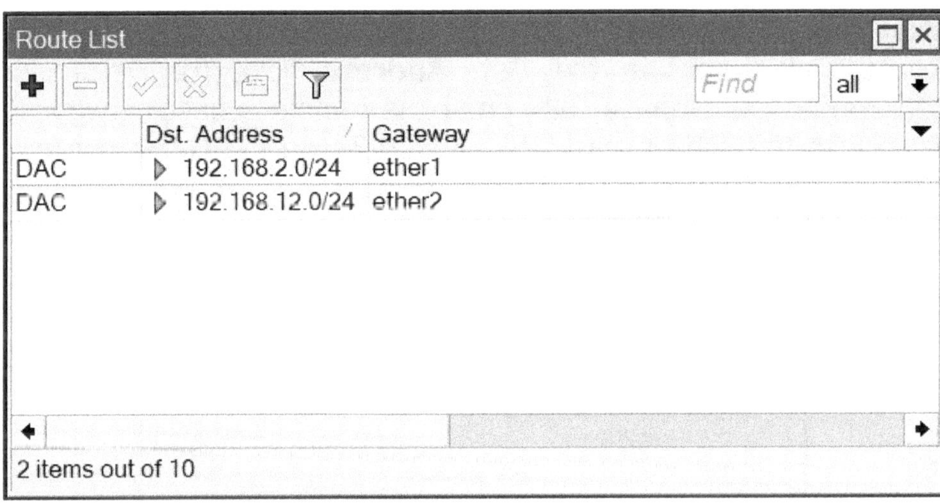

Creating the Static Routes

R1

In Router R1:

- Create a static route for the subnet 192.168.2.0/24 using the next-hop IP address 192.168.12.2, which is the IP address of R2.

To create a static route, click the **IP** menu, then select **Routes** to open **Route List** window.

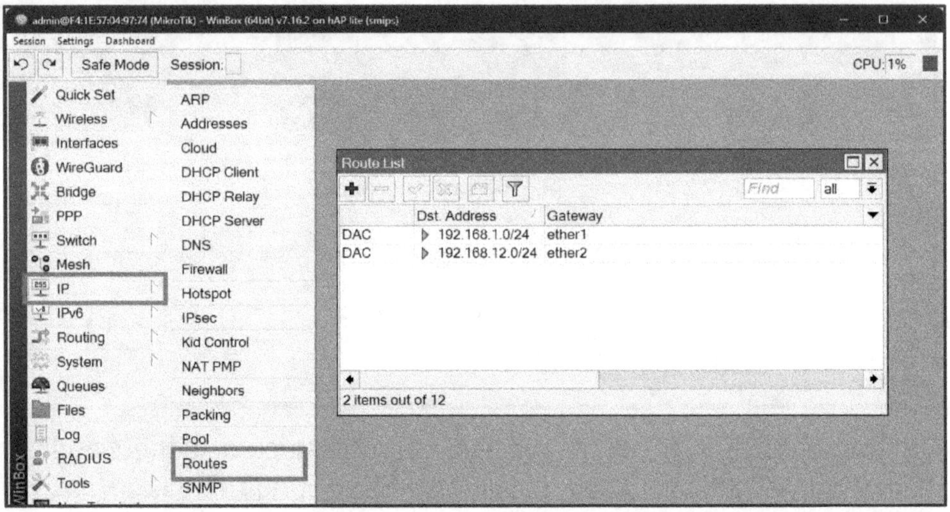

Click the **Add** button in the **Route List** window to open the **New Route** dialog box. In the **Dst. Address** field, (or Destination Address), in the **General** tab, enter the remote subnet network ID along with the subnet mask 192.168.2.0/24. In the **Gateway** field, enter the next hop-IP 192.168.12.2. Then click the **OK** button to close this dialog box and create the static route.

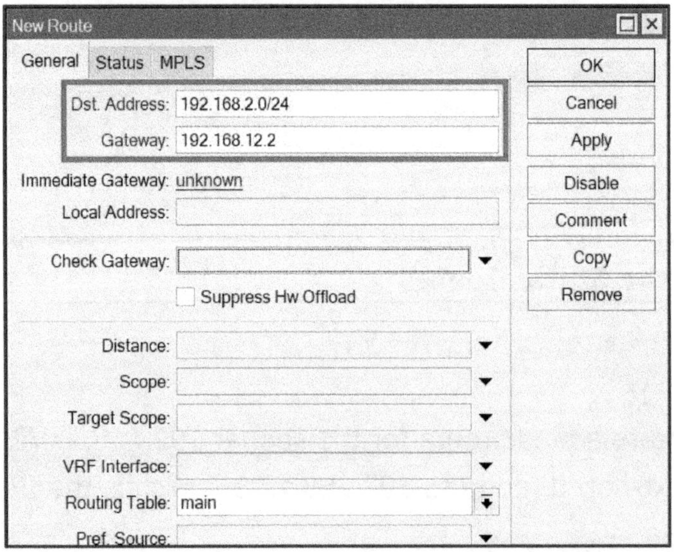

After creating the static route, it will appear in the **Route List** window.

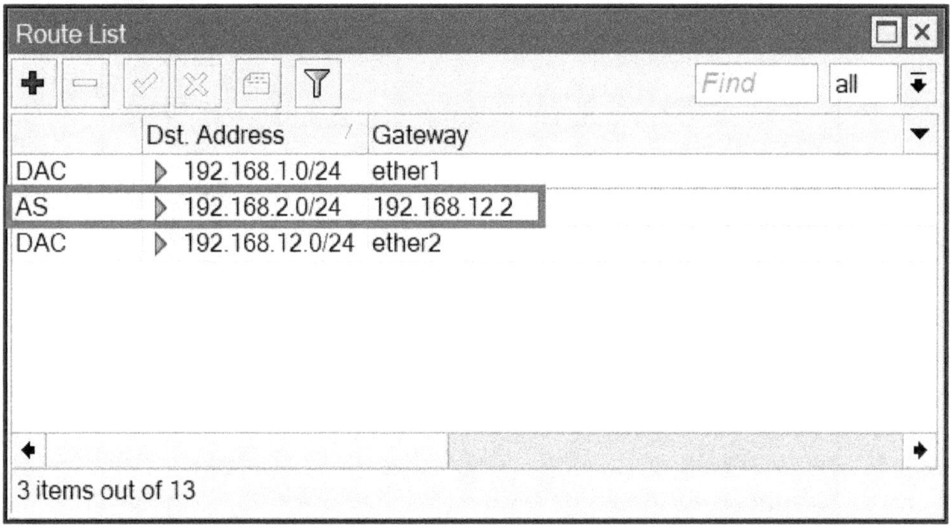

Now, by looking at the routing table (**Route List** window) in R1, you will see three routes for the three subnets you have in this lab. That means R1 now knows about all the subnets that exist in the internetwork.

R2

In Router R2:

- Create a static route for the subnet 192.168.1.0/24 using the next-hop IP address 192.168.12.1, which is the IP address of R1.

To create a static route, click the **IP** menu, then select **Routes** to open **Route List** window. Click the **Add** button in the **Route List** window to open the **New Route** dialog box. In the **Dst Address** field, (or Destination Address), in the **General** tab, enter the remote subnet network ID along with the subnet mask 192.168.1.0/24. In the **Gateway** field, enter the next hop-IP 192.168.12.1. Then click the OK button to close this dialog box and create the static route.

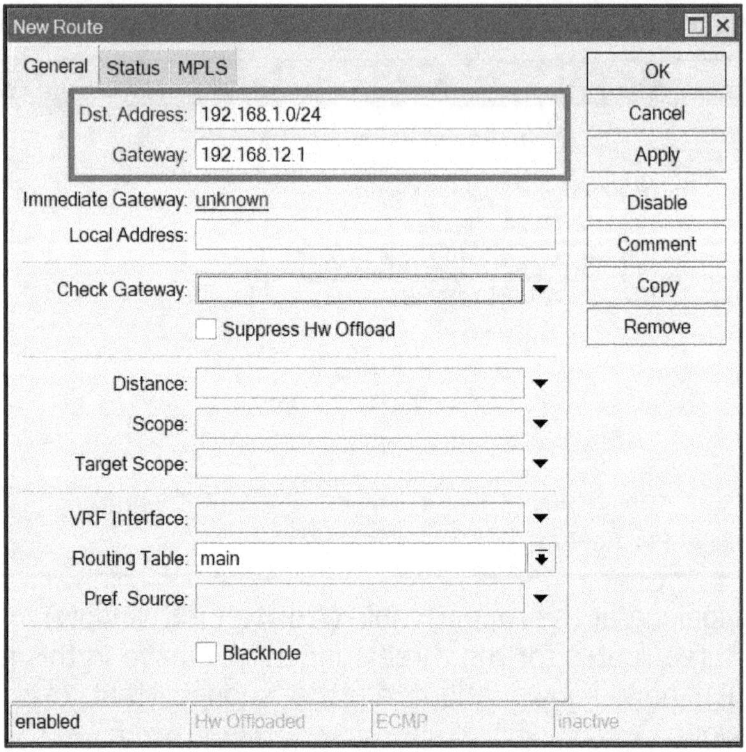

After creatin the static route, it will appear in the **Route List** window.

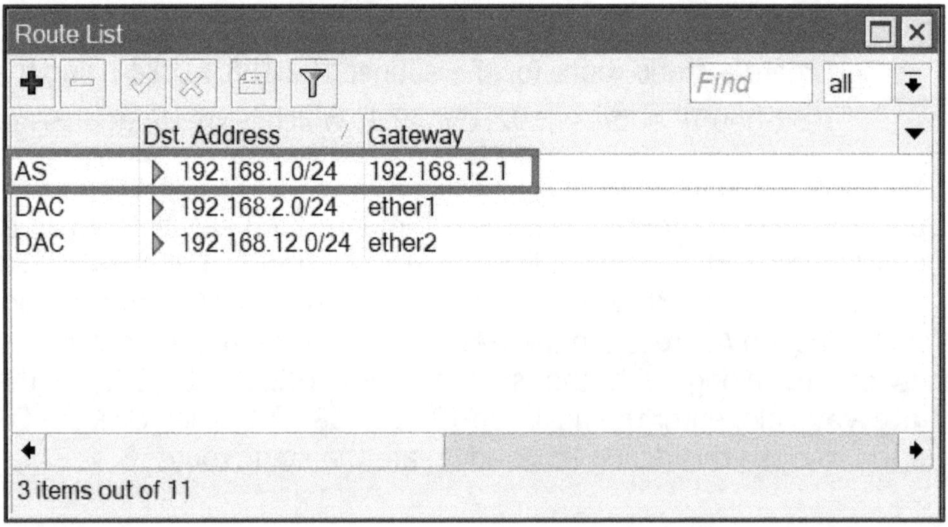

Now, by looking at the routing table (**Route List** window) in R2, you will see three routes for the three subnets you have in this lab. That means both R1 and R2 now know about all the subnets that exist in the internetwork, and you have full connectivity.

Now, when PC1 tries to ping PC2, the ping will succeed.

CLI

You can also make the configuration from the CLI.

To assign IP addresses to the interfaces, use the following commands:

R1

```
ip address add address=192.168.1.1/24 interface=ether1
ip address add address=192.168.12.1/24 interface=ether2
```

R2

```
ip address add address=192.168.2.1/24 interface=ether1
ip address add address=192.168.12.2/24 interface=ether2
```

To create static routes, use the following commands:

R1

```
ip route add dst-address=192.168.2.0/24 gateway=192.168.12.2
```

R2

```
ip route add dst-address=192.168.1.0/24 gateway=192.168.12.1
```

4.8 Default Route

As mentioned before, to achieve full connectivity in the internetwork, all routers should know about all subnets exist in the internetwork and have a route for each in the routing table.

Sometimes, it is hard, or even impossible, to add all subnets to the routing table, for example, when you connect to the internet, because the internet contains many subnets. In this case, you can use a special type of route representing all those subnets. This route is called the default route.

To configure a default route, you simply enter 0.0.0.0/0 in the **Dst. Address** field (or Destination Address) when adding a static route.

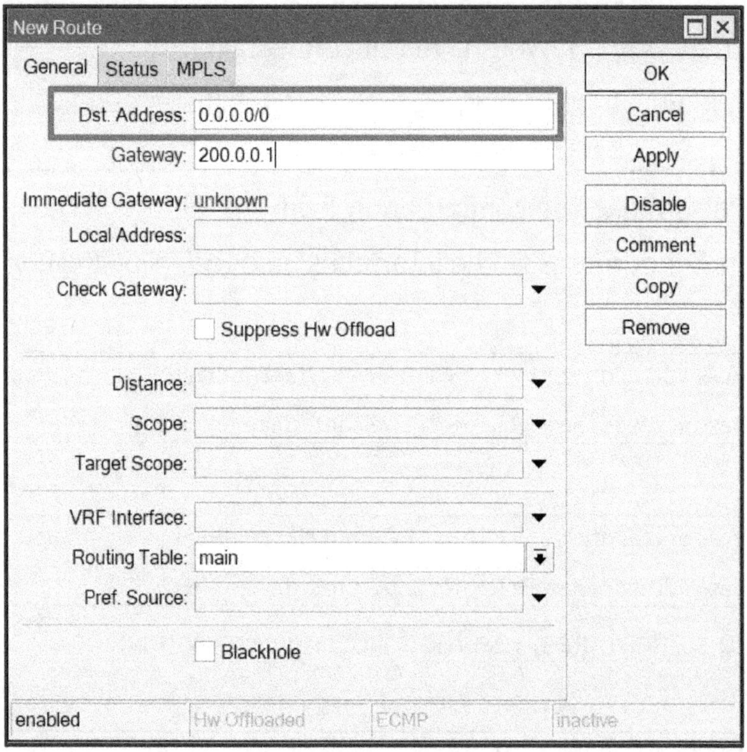

You can also create or add a static default route to the routing table in RouterOS from the CLI using the following command:

```
ip route add dst-address=0.0.0.0/0 gateway=[next hop IP]
```

Where:

[next hop IP] is the IP address of the next hop.

For example:

```
ip route add dst-address=0.0.0.0/0 gateway=200.0.0.1
```

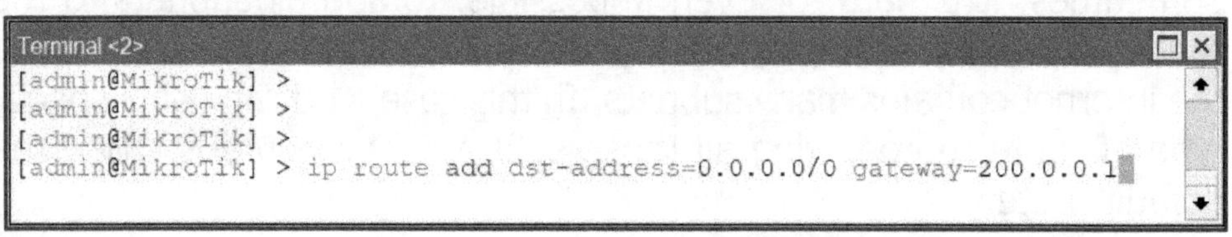

Or you can write the command without specifying the destination address as follows:

```
ip route add gateway=[next hop IP]
```

Where:

- [next hop IP] is the IP address of the next hop.

For example:

```
ip route add gateway=200.0.0.1
```

```
Terminal <2>
[admin@MikroTik] >
[admin@MikroTik] >
[admin@MikroTik] >
[admin@MikroTik] > ip route add gateway=200.0.0.1
```

LAB

In this lab, R1 is connected to two subnets, subnet 192.168.1.0/24 via ether1, and subnet 200.0.0.0/24 via ether2 which is connected to the internet.

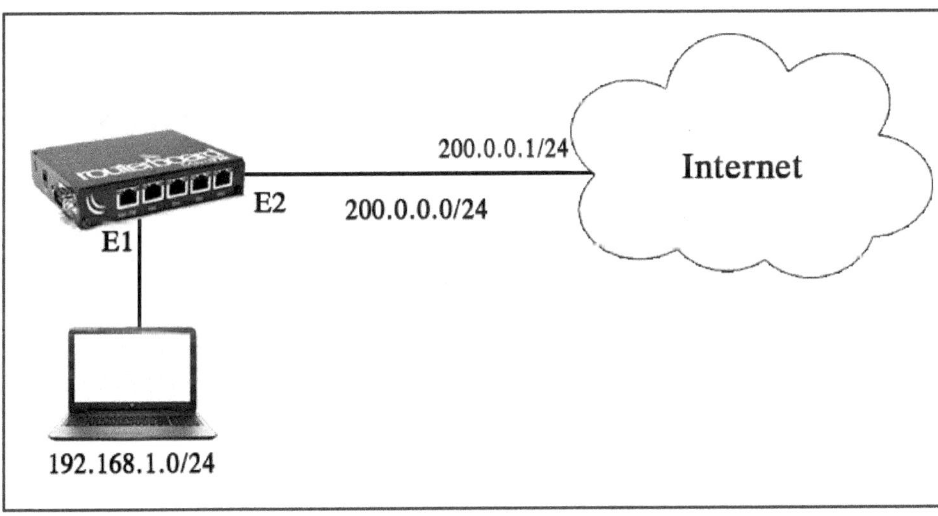

As mentioned, to ensure full connectivity in this lab, R1 should have a route for every subnet in this internetwork.

You will start by counting how many subnets are in this internetwork.

Then check how many directly connected subnets to the router and how many remote subnets that you should add statically

In this lab you have two subnets directly connected to the R1

- 192.168.1.0/24
- 200.0.0.0/24

Also, you have the internet. Because there are many subnets on the internet, you cannot add all of them to the routing table. In this case, you will add only one static default route to the routing table.

To start the configuration:

- First: assign the IP addresses to each interface.
- Second: create the static default route.

Assigning the IP addresses:

In Router R1:

- Assign the IP address 192.168.1.1/24 to the ether1.
- Assign the IP address 200.0.0.2/24 to the ether2.

To assign an IP address to an interface, click the **IP** menu, then select **Addresses** to open the **Address List** window.

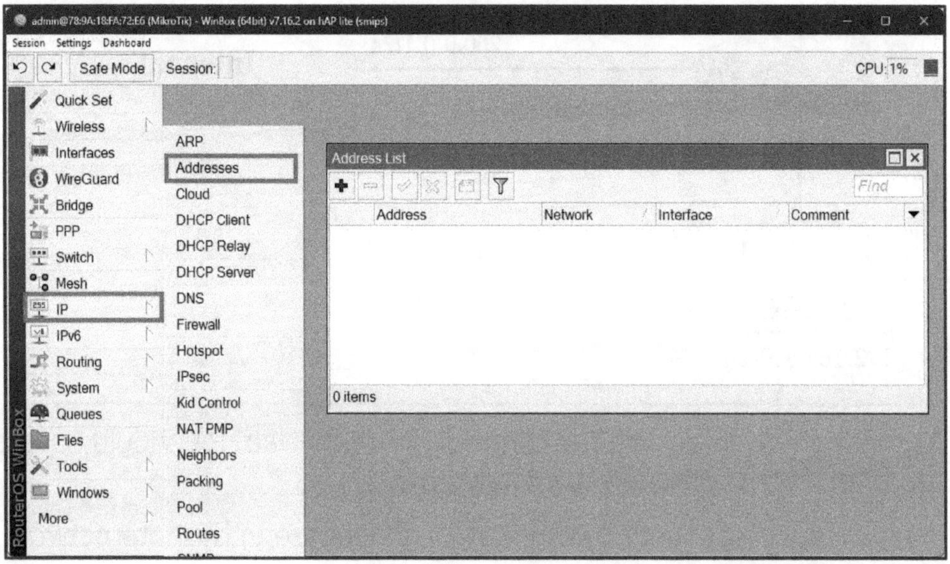

Click the **Add** button in the **Address List** window to open the **New Address** dialog box. In the **Address** field, enter the IP address along with the subnet mask. 192.168.1.1/24 . In the **Interface** field, select the interface ether1. Then click the **OK** button to close this dialog box and assign the IP to the interface.

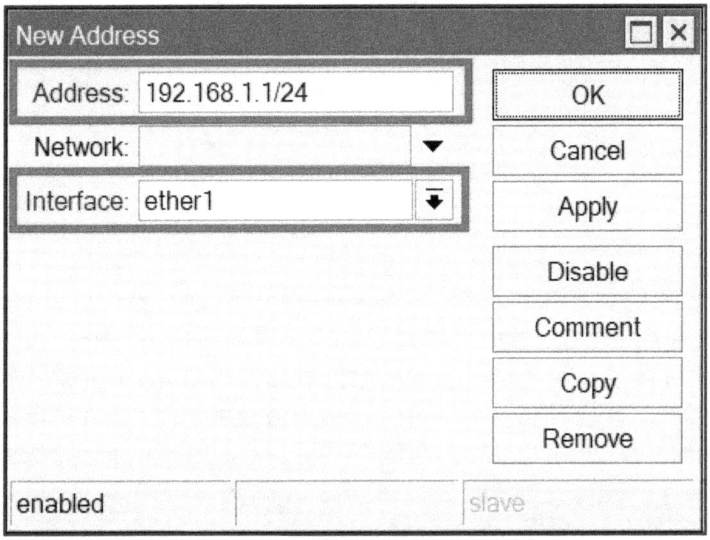

Repeat the same steps to assign the IP address 200.0.0.2/24 to the interface ether2**.**

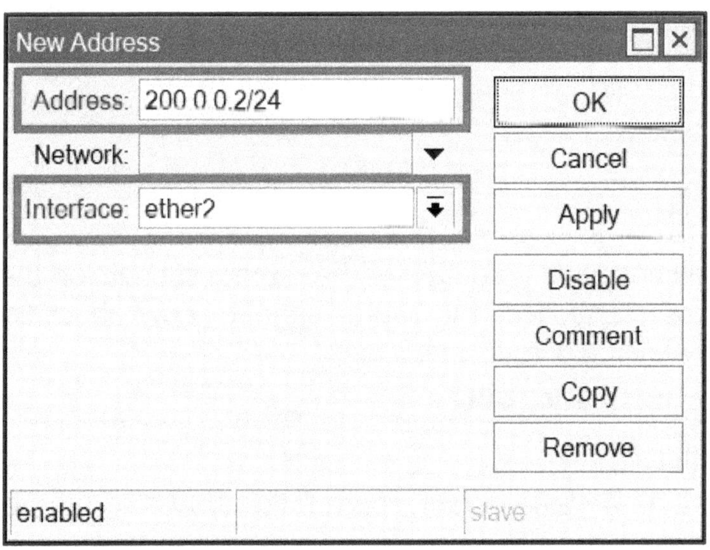

After assigning both IP addresses to each interface, they will appear in the **Address List** window.

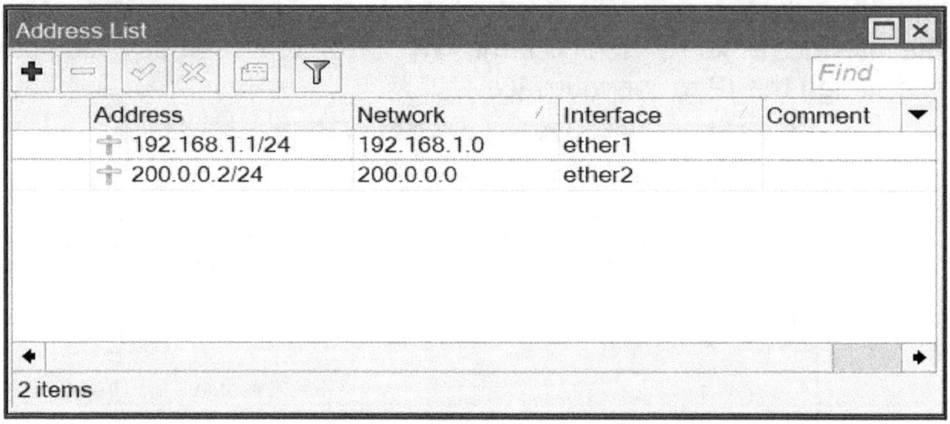

Now, if you open the routing table, you will see routes for those two subnets, because, as mentioned, the router will recognize the directly connected subnets and add them automatically (or dynamically) to the routing table without any external help, or additional configuration.

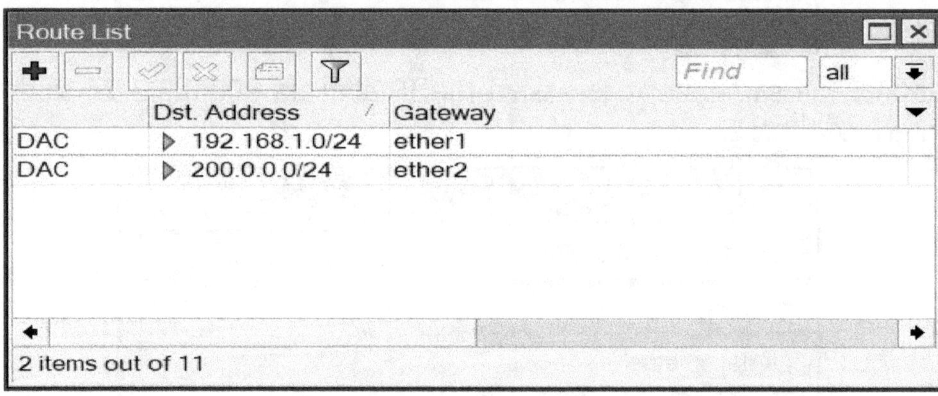

But you will not see any routes for the remote subnets on the internet, because, as mentioned, the router cannot know about the remote subnets by itself alone; it needs help.

Creating the Static routes

In Router R1:

- Create a static default route 0.0.0.0/0 using the next-hop IP address 200.0.0.1, which is the IP address of ISP router.

To create a static default route, click the **IP** menu, then select **Routes** to open **Route List** window.

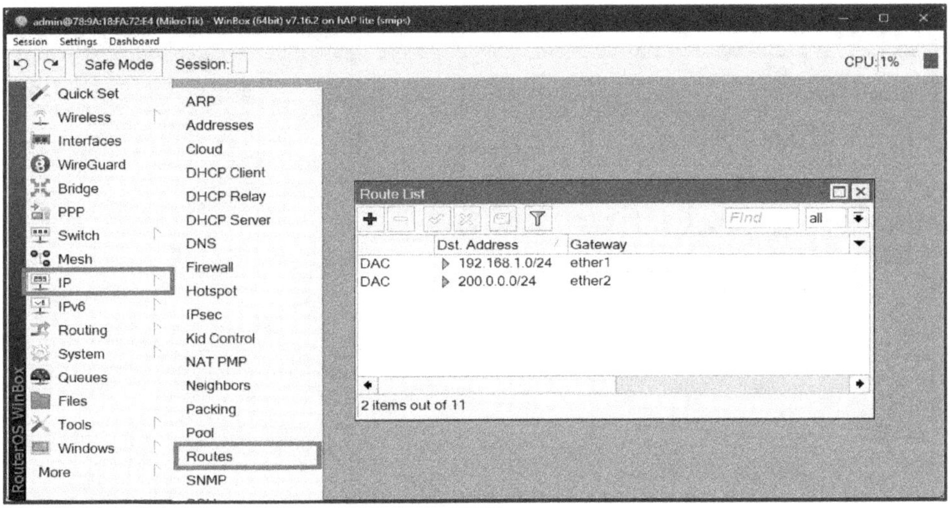

Click the **Add** button in the **Route List** window to open the **New Route** dialog box. In the **Dst. Address** field, (or Destination Address), in the **General** tab, enter 0.0.0.0/0. In the **Gateway** field, enter the next hop-IP 200.0.0.1. Then click the **OK** button to close this dialog box and create the default static route.

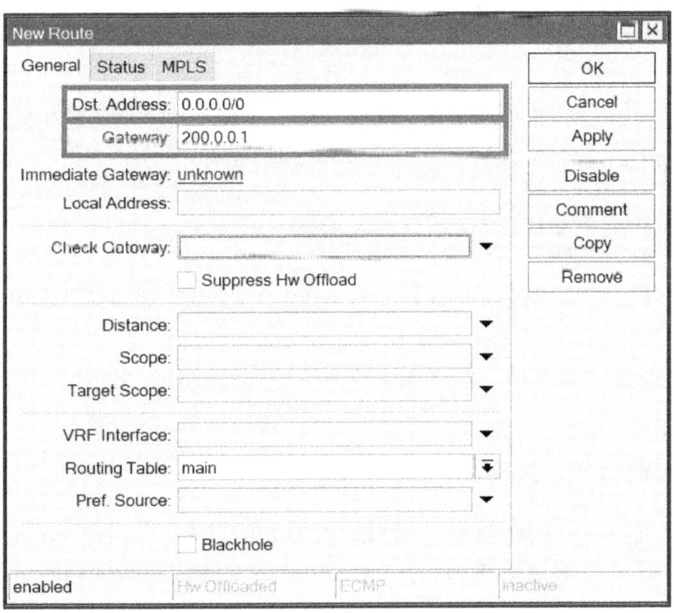

After creating the static default route, it will appear in the **Route List** window.

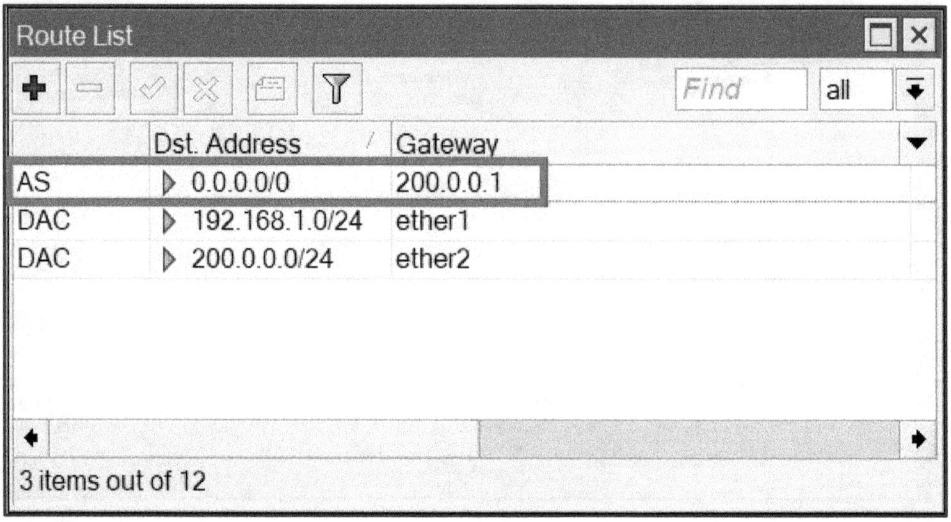

CLI

You can also make the configuration from the CLI.

To assign IP addresses to the interfaces, use the following commands:

```
ip address add address=192.168.1.1/24 interface=ether1
ip address add address=200.0.0.2/24 interface=ether2
```

To create static default route, use the following command:

```
ip route add dst-address=0.0.0.0/0 gateway=200.0.0.1
```

4.9 Dynamic Routing Protocols

As mentioned, you can help the router to learn about remote subnets by:

- Adding those subnets to the routing table manually, or statically.
- Using dynamic routing protocols.

Dynamic routing protocols will inform the router about remote subnets, and if there are multiple paths to those remote subnets, the dynamic routing protocols will choose the best path. If any changes occur in the network, such as adding or removing a subnet, or breaking a path or link, the dynamic routing protocols will automatically update the router about these changes.

There are multiple dynamic routing protocols, which are divided into two main categories:

- Protocols that work within an Autonomous System network

  Such as RIP, OSPF, ISIS, and Cisco proprietary protocol EIGRP.

  These protocols are called Interior Gateway Protocols (IGPs).
- Protocols that work between different Autonomous System networks

  Such as the BGP protocol.

  These protocols are called Exterior Gateway Protocols (EGPs).

You will learn more about dynamic routing protocols in the MTCRE and MTCINE courses.

4.10 Route Flags

When RouterOS adds a route to the routing table, it will also include some additional information about the route and how it learned about it using route flags.

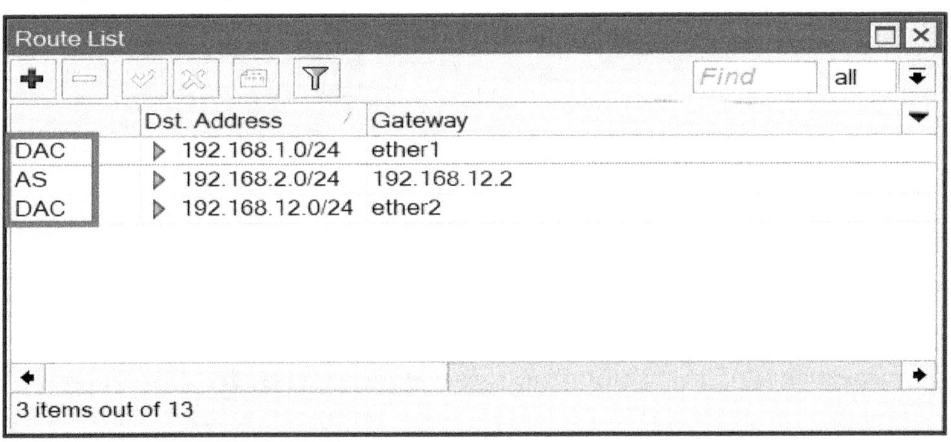

- If the router learns about this subnet automatically, or dynamically, it will add the flag D, which stands for dynamic.
- If you add the route to the routing table manually or statically, it will add the flag S, which stands for static.
- If the subnet is directly connected to the router, it will add the flag C, which stands for connected.
- If this route is the active route to this subnet, the router will add the flag A, which stands for Active.
- If the router learns about this subnet via a dynamic routing protocol, it will add the flag representing this protocol: O for OSPF, R for RIP, B for BGP.

There are some other flags, and there are also some differences in flags between RouterOS v6 and RouterOSv7.

Example

If you have a route that has DAC flags:

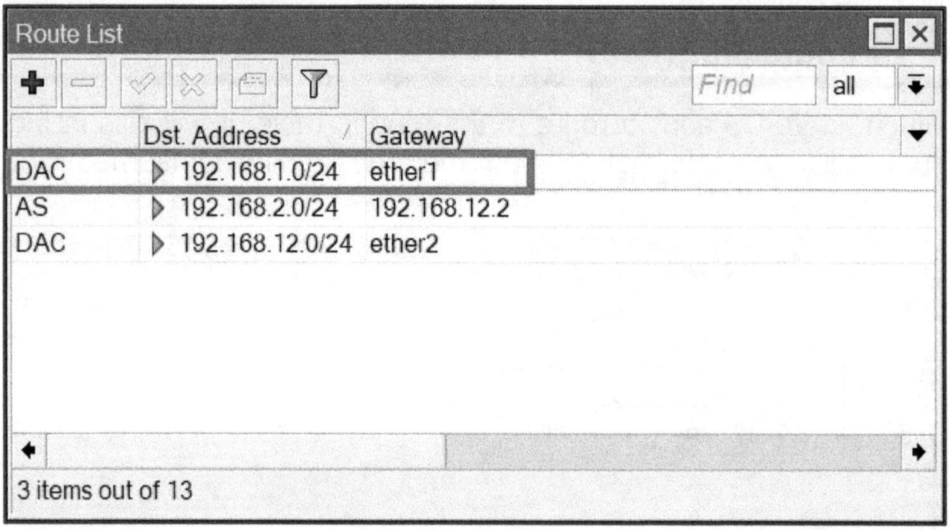

That means the router knows about this route automatically or dynamically (D), this subnet is directly connected to the router (C), and this is the active route (A) that the router will use to send data to this subnet.

Example

If you have a route that has AS flags:

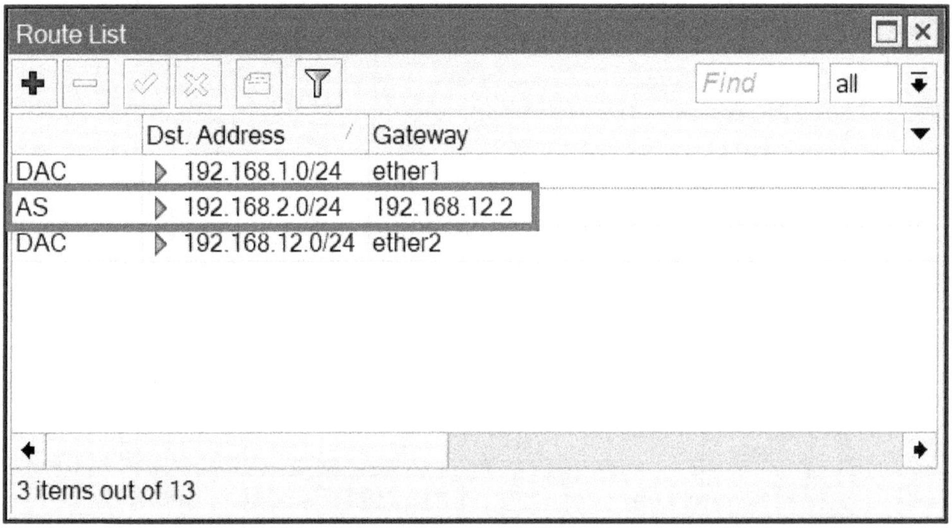

That means the router knows about this route statically, you have added it manually. (S), and this is the active route (A) that the router will use to send data to this subnet.

4.11 Administrative Distance

If a router learns about the same subnet by different methods, it will assign a value to each method, and then it will choose the best route based on this value.

This value is called the administrative distance AD.

For example, if the router learns about a route to a subnet using the OSPF protocol and learns about another route to the same subnet using the RIP protocol, it will use the administrative distance value to choose which route will be the active route to use when sending data to this subnet.

The lowest administrative distance AD value is the most reliable.

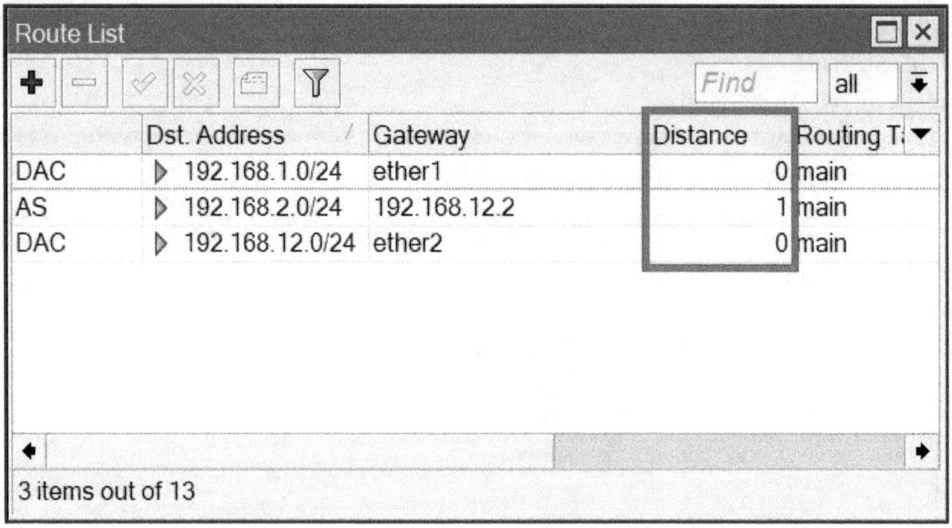

The following table displays the different methods and their corresponding administrative distance (AD) values.

Route Type	Administrative Distance
Direct Connected	0
Static Route	1
BGP (External)	20
OSPF	110
IS-IS	115
RIP	120
BGP (Internal)	200

5

Module

WIRELESS

Module 5

This module provides an introduction to wireless technology in MikroTik devices and explains how to configure the device as an access point (AP) and wireless station, using some security and protection options.

More advanced information about wireless technologies is available in the MTCWE, MTCEWE and MTCUME courses.

This module covers the following course content topics:

- 802.11a/b/g/n/ac Concepts
  - Frequencies (bands, channels) data-rates / chains (tx power,
  - rx sensitivity, country regulations)
- Setup a simple wireless link
  - Access Point configuration
  - Station configuration
- Wireless Security and Encryption
  - Access List
  - Connect List
  - Default Authenticate
  - Default Forward
  - WPA-PSK, WPA2-PSK
  - WPS accept, WPS client
- Monitoring Tools
  - Snooper

- Registration table

Wireless

5.1 Wireless Overview and Key Concepts

To connect computers, or hosts, to a computer network wirelessly, a device called Access Point (AP) is used. In this case, those hosts are called Wireless Stations or Wireless Clients.

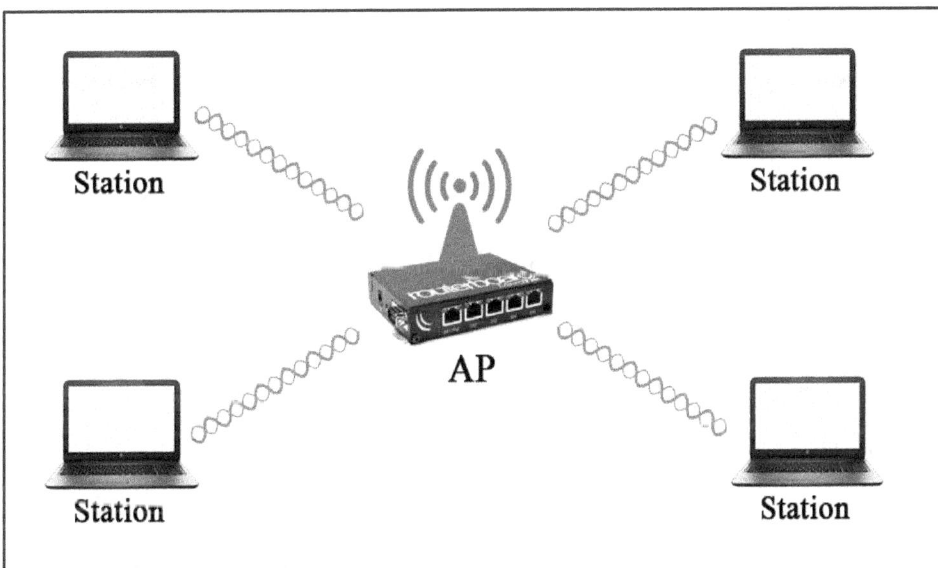

5.2 Access Point (AP)

The Access Point (AP) is a device that connects wireless stations to a computer network.

You can configure RouterOS to function as an Access point (AP) to connect Wireless Stations to the network, also to function as a Wireless Station to connect to Access Point (AP).

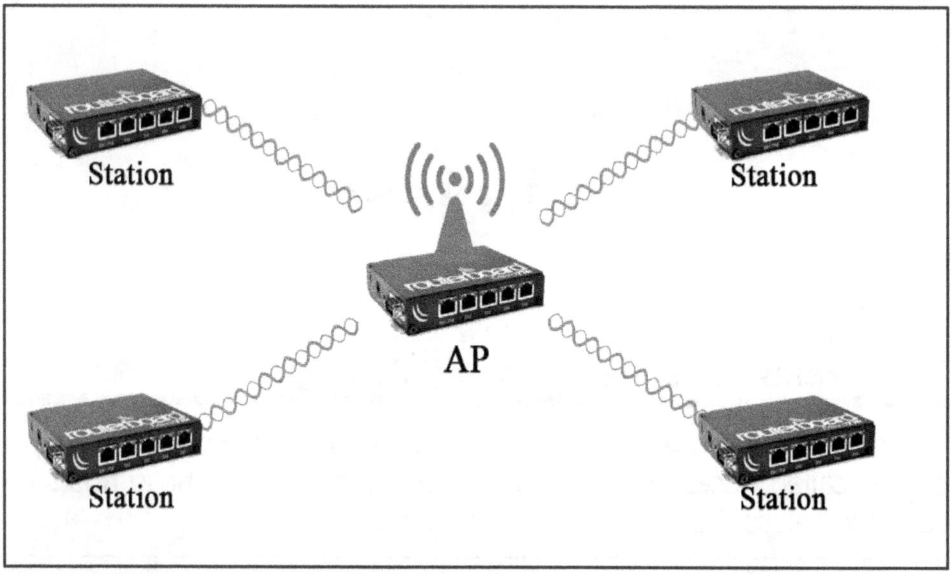

5.3 How Wireless Network Works

Radio frequency is used to connect devices in a computer network wirelessly. Specific ranges of frequencies are used to do this. Each range is called a band, and each band consists of channels.

Currently, MikroTik devices support three bands:

- 2.4 GHz.
- 5 GHz.
- 60 GHz.

The method of sending data using radio frequency is called Wireless Protocol. In computer networks, a protocol called 802.11 is used.

5.4 802.11 Protocol

The 802.11 protocol is used to connect wireless devices in the computer network. There are multiple versions of this protocol. These versions are called revisions, amendments, or standards.

The following table displays some information about different versions of 802.11 and their theoretical speed or data rate.

Standard	Band	Data Rate
802.11 (1997)	2.4GHz	2 Mbps
802.11a	5GHz	54 Mbps
802.11b	2.4GHz	11 Mbps
802.11g	2.4GHz	54 Mbps
802.11n	2.4Ghz & 5GHz	600 Mbps
802.11ac (Wi-Fi 5)	5GHz	6.93 Gbps
802.11ax (Wi-Fi 6)	2.4Ghz & 5GHz	9.60 Gbps
802.11ad	60GHz	6.75 Gbps
802.11ay	60GHz	42 Gbps

5.5 2.4GHz Band

This band is divided into 14 channels. Most countries use 13 channels, the USA uses 11 channels, and Japan uses 14 channels.

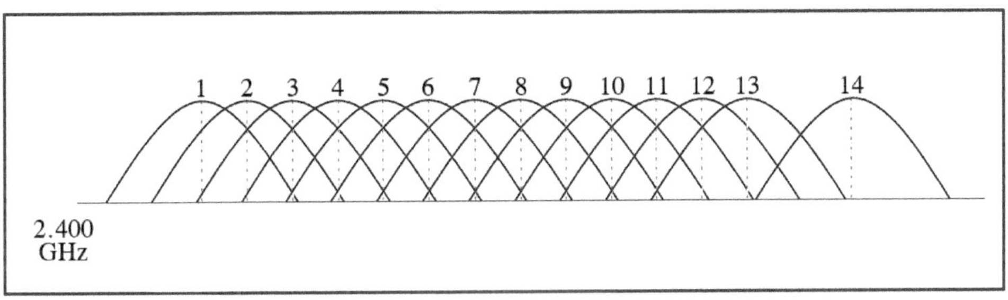

The width of each channel can be 20 MHz, 22 MHz, or 40 MHz, and other width values can also be used.

When using a 20 MHz width, you will have 3 non-overlapping channels: Channel 1, Channel 6, and Channel 11.

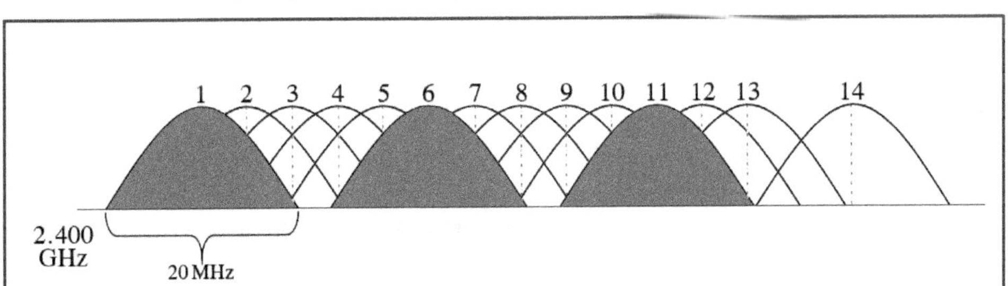

If you use 40 MHz width, you will have only two non-overlapping channels: Channels 3 and 11.

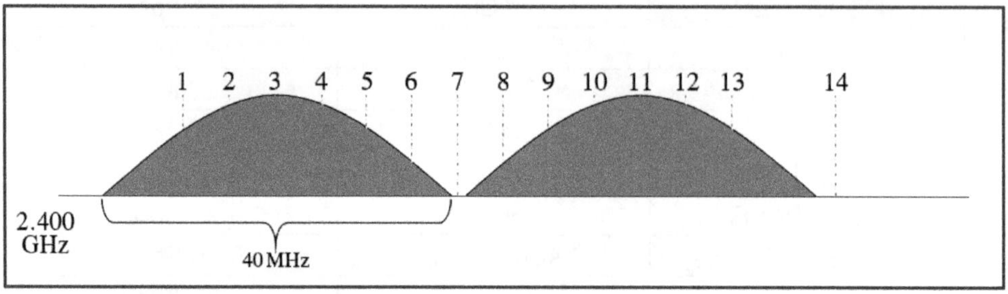

The 2.4 GHz band provides the longest range (or coverage) but offers the slowest speeds compared to the 5 GHz and 60 GHz bands.

5.6 5GHz Band

This band is divided into 24 or more channels, depending on the protocol version, country, and its regulations.

The width of each channel can be 20 MHz, 40 MHz, 80 MHz, or 160 MHz.

These channels do not overlap.

The 5 GHz band provides a shorter range but offers faster speeds compared to the 2.4 GHz band.

5.7 60GHz Band

This band is divided into 4 or 6 channels, depending on the protocol version, country, and its regulations.

The width of each channel is 2160 MHz or 8640 MHz.

These channels do not overlap.

The 60 GHz band provides the shortest range but the fastest speeds compared to the 2.4 GHz and 5 GHz bands.

5.8 Access Point Configuration

To configure a MikroTik RouterBOARD to function as an access point (AP), use the **Wireless Tables** window.

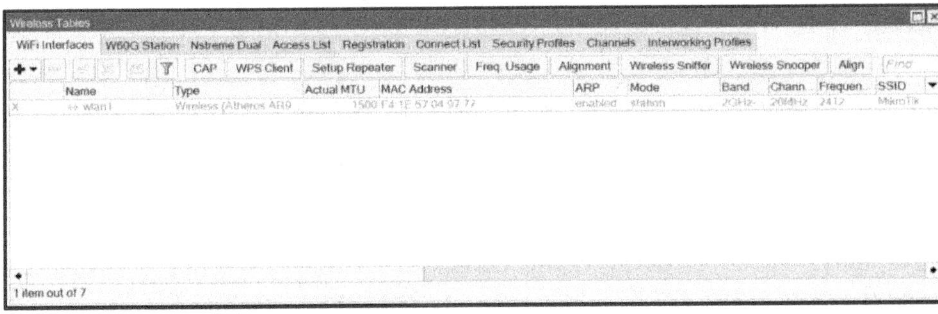

To open the **Wireless Tables** window, click the **Wireless** menu, then select **wireless**.

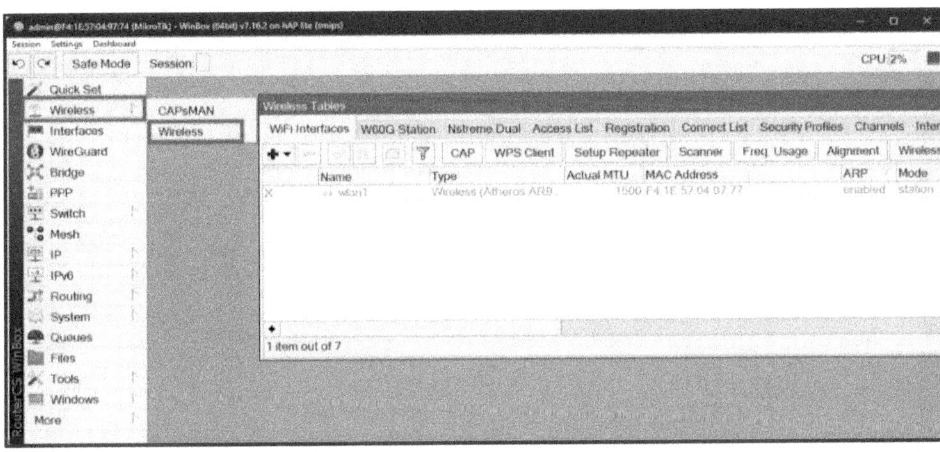

In RouterOS v6, to open the **Wireless Tables** window click **Wireless** menu.

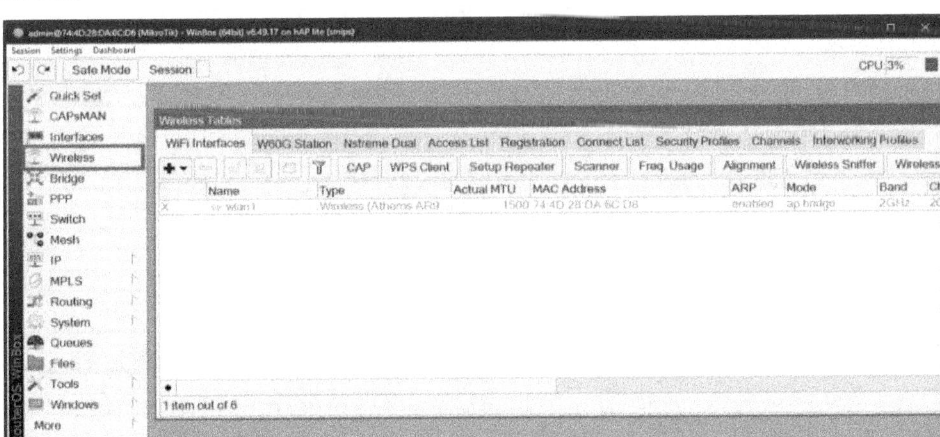

Note: Before configuring the wireless settings on a MikroTik device, make sure you have:

- Physical wireless interface in the device.
- The required wireless package installed.
- The appropriate license level.

To display the interfaces in the device, (including wireless, wired and virtual interfaces too), click the **Interfaces** menu to open the **Interface List** window. This window will display all interfaces in the device.

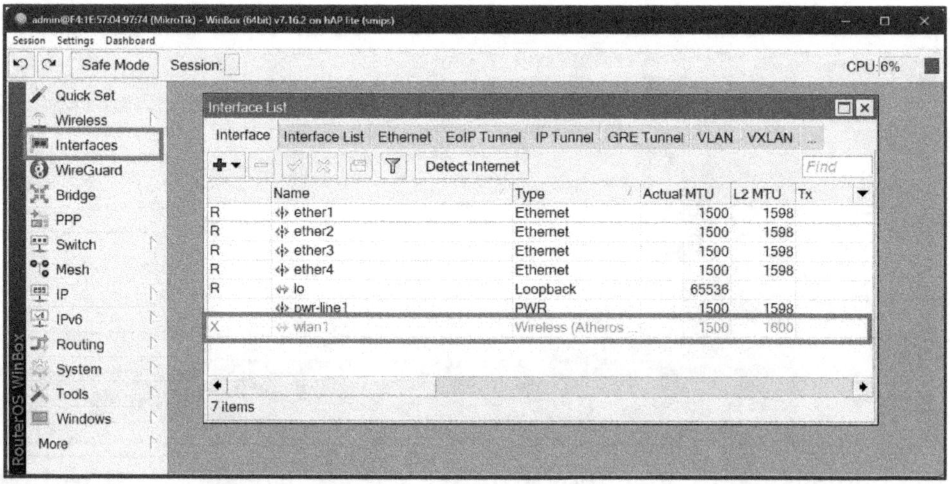

Or, you can click the **Wireless** menu, then select **Wireless** to open the **Wireless Tables** window, which displays only the wireless interfaces.

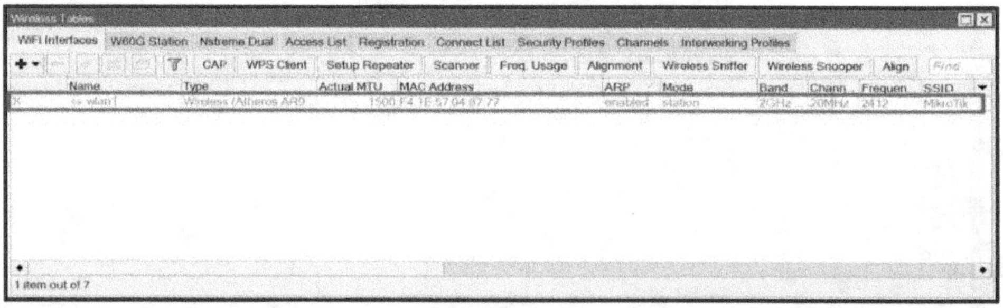

Some devices have one wireless interface, some have two, and others may not have any.

To check if you have the required wireless package, click the **System** menu, then select **Packages** to open the **Package List** window, which displays all the packages installed in RouterOS.

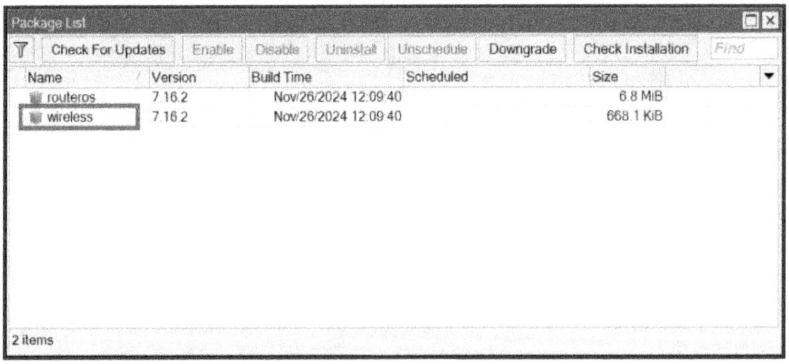

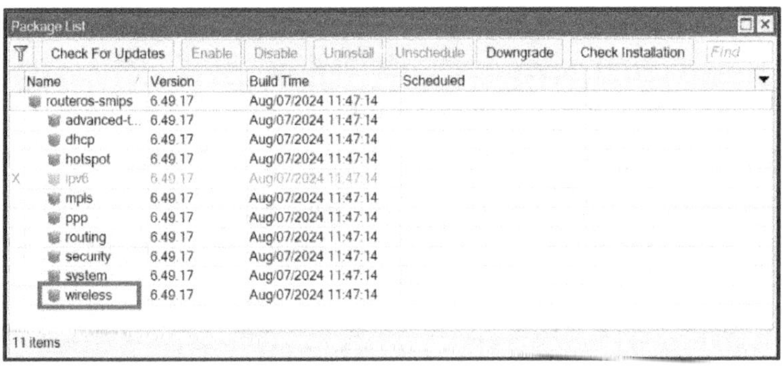

Note: you may need to install different wireless packages depending on the wireless interface installed in your device (wireless, wifiwave2, wifi-qcom, wifi-qcom-ac). Before RouterOS v7.13, the wireless package was included in the main package or system package (routeros package). For 802.11ax support, you needed to use the wifiwave2 package

Since v7.13 (up to the latest version available at the time of publishing this book, v7.18), you need to use the wireless package to configure the wireless settings. For 802.11ax support, you need to use the wifi-qcom package.

To check the license level, click the **System** menu, then select **License** to open the **License** window, which displays the licenses installed in RouterOS.

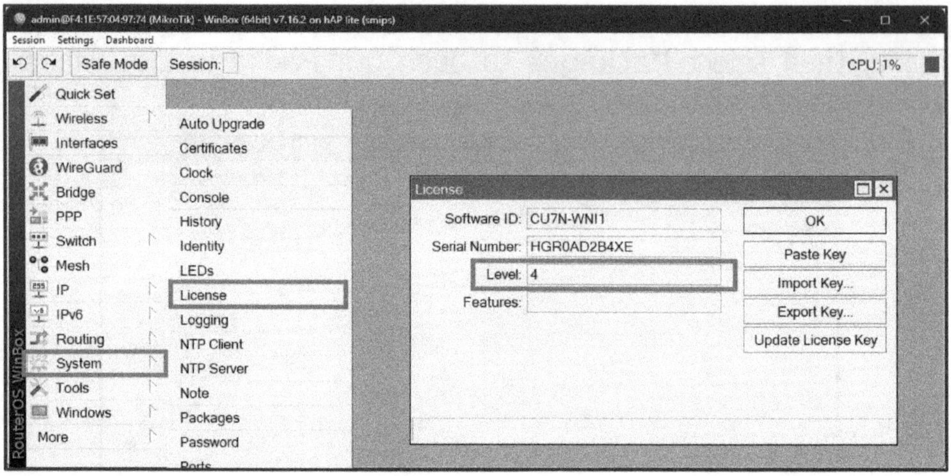

Remember that when using Level 3, you can configure the device as wireless station, and when using Level 4 or higher, you can configure the device as an access point (AP) too.

To configure a MikroTik device to function as an access point (AP), double-click the wireless interface you want to configure in the **Wireless Tables** window to open the wireless **Interface** settings dialog box.

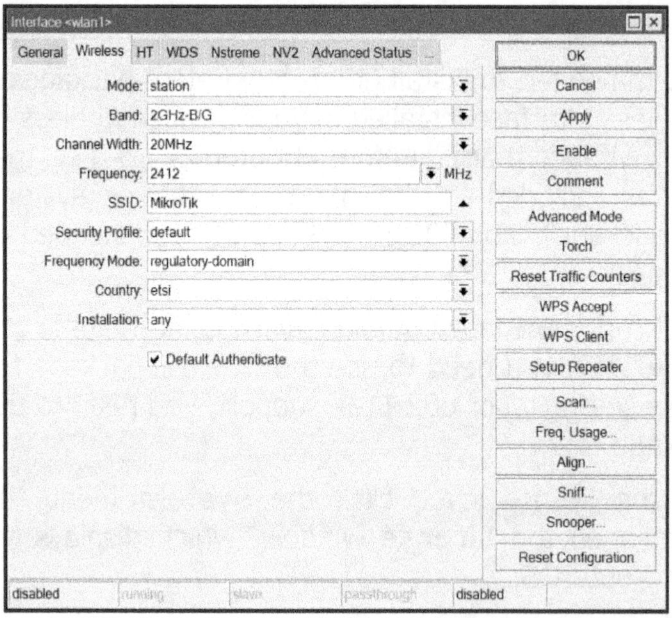

You can use this dialog box to configure different properties of the wireless interface.

From the **Mode** field in the **Wireless** tab, select ap bridge mode.

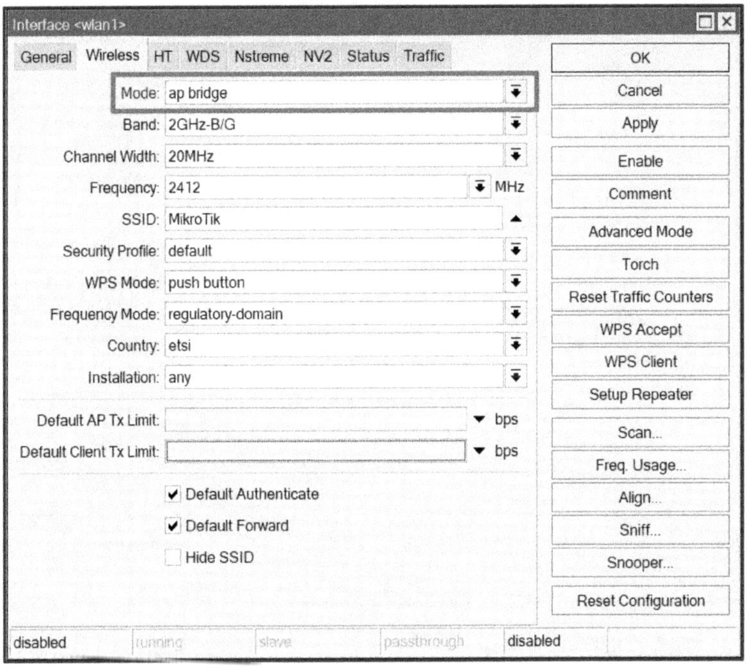

Then click the **OK** button to accept all other default settings, and close the dialog box.

By default, all wireless interfaces are disabled. To enable the wireless interface, select it and click the **Enable** button in the **Wireless Tables** window.

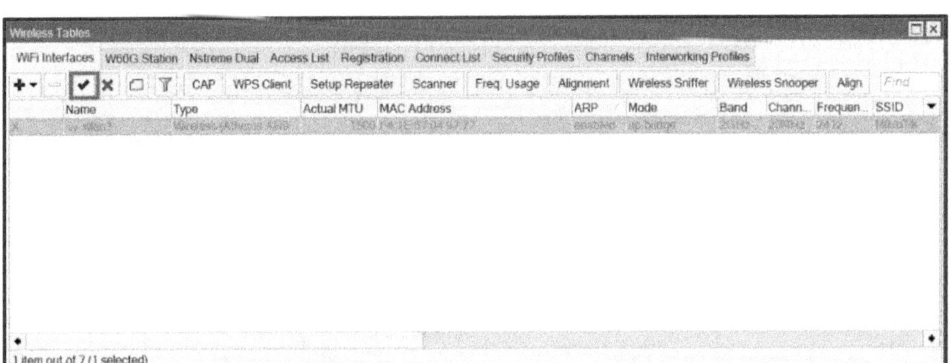

You can also enable the interface by clicking the **Enable** button from the wireless **Interface** settings dialog box before closing it.

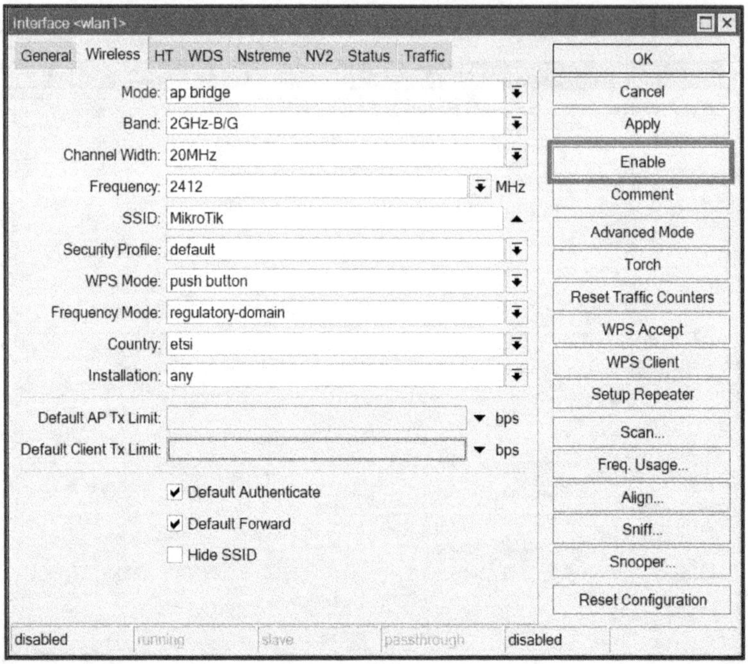

This is the minimum configuration required to set up a MikroTik device to function as an access point (AP) with the default configuration, just set the mode to ap bridge.

You can also configure the MikroTik device to function as an access point (AP) from the CLI using the following command:

```
interface wireless set [interface name] mode=ap-bridge
```

Where:

- [interface name] is the name of the wireless interface.

For example:

```
interface wireless set wlan1 mode=ap-bridge
```

To enable the wireless interface, use the following command:

```
interface wireless enable [interface name]
```

Where:

- [interface name] is the name of the wireless interface.

For example:

```
interface wireless enable wlan1
```

In most cases, the access point (AP) will distribute IP addresses to the wireless stations when they connect to it. To do that, you need to configure a DHCP server on the wireless interface of the access point (AP).

As you have learned before, to configure a DHCP server on an interface:

- First: assign an IP address to the interface.
- Then: configure the DHCP server on this interface using the **DHCP Server** window.

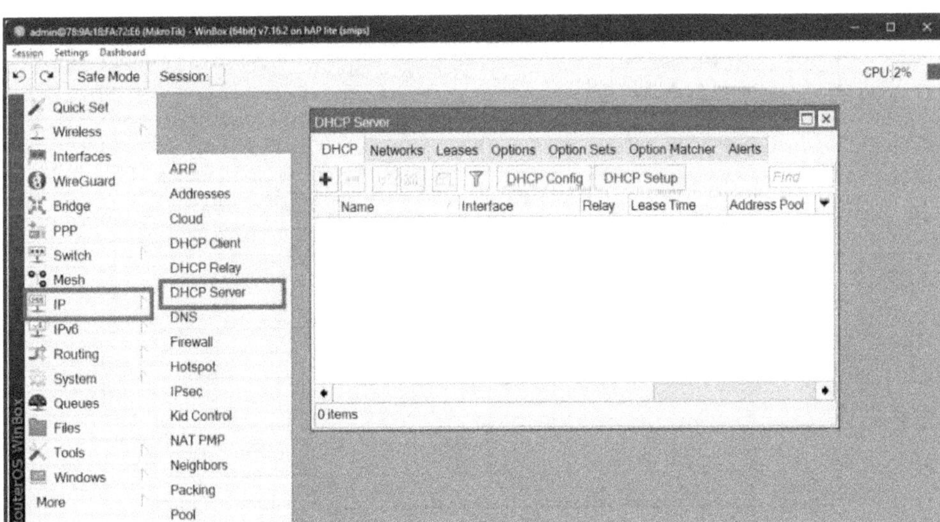

5.9 Station Configuration

To configure a MikroTik device to function as a wireless station, double-click the wireless interface you want to configure in the **Wireless Tables** window to open the wireless **Interface** settings dialog box. From the **Mode** field in the **Wireless** tab, select station mode.

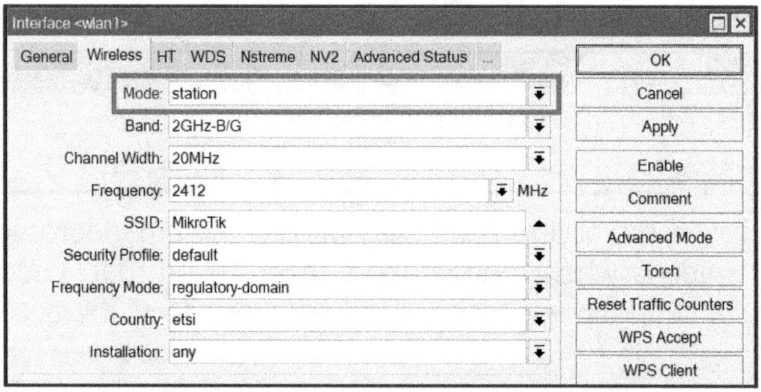

Then click the **Scan** button to open the **Scanner** dialog box.

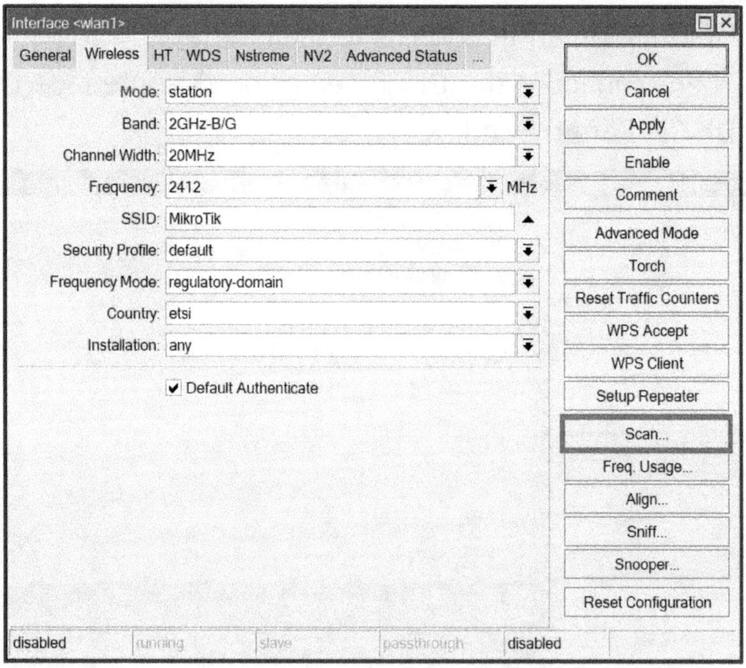

You can use the **Scanner** dialog box to search for the access point (AP) you want to connect to.

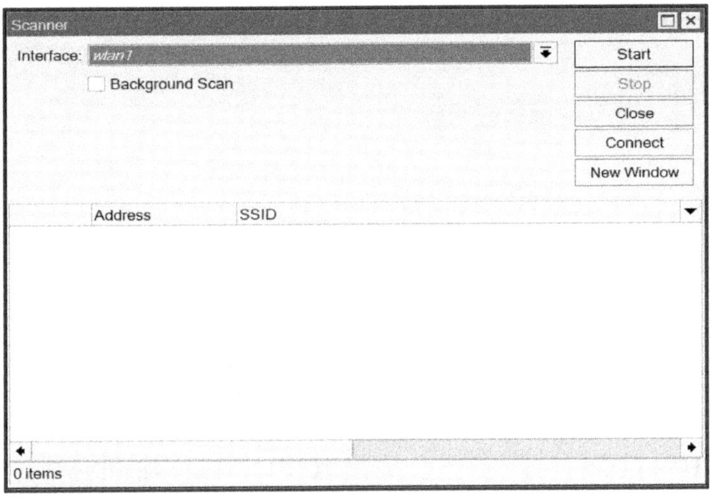

From the **Interface** field, select the wireless interface you are using (in case multiple interfaces are installed on the device). Then, click the **Start** button to begin scanning and searching for available access points (AP).

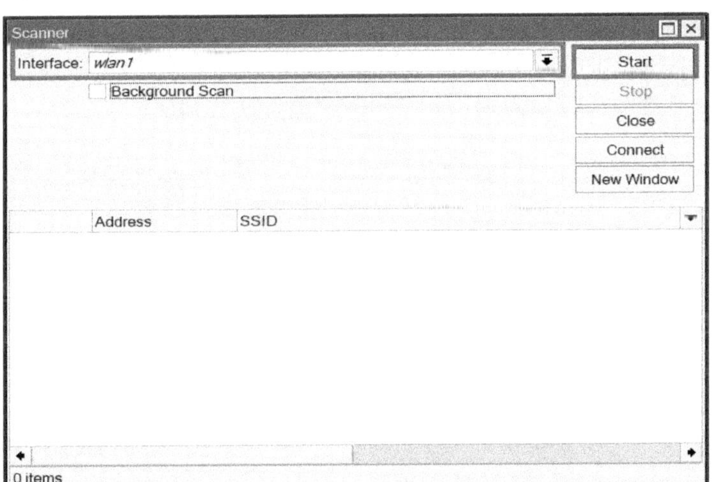

The device will search for all access points (AP) in the area and list them in this dialog box. Select the access point (AP) you want to connect to and click the **Connect** button to connect to it.

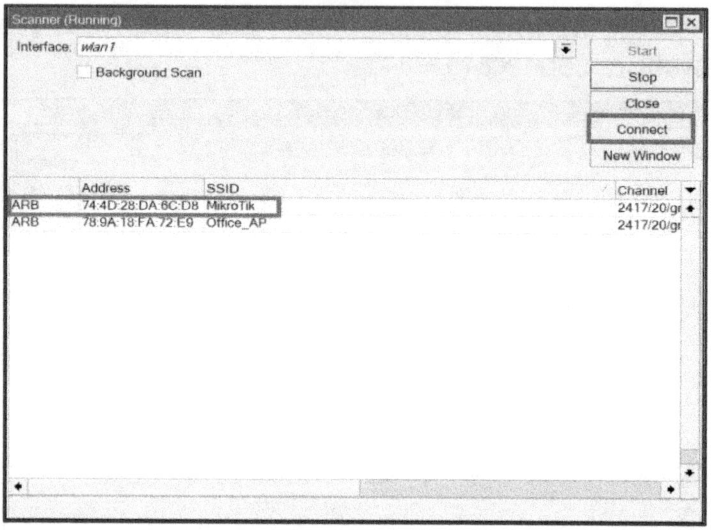

Note: in this case you do not want to manually enable the interface, it will be enabled automatically.

This is the easiest way to configure the device to function as a wireless station and connect it to specific access point (AP): set the mode to station, click the **Scan** button, and select the desired access point (AP).

You can also configure the MikroTik device to function as wireless station from the CLI using the following command:

```
interface wireless set [interface name] mode=station
```

Where:

- [interface name] is the name of the wireless interface.

For example:

```
interface wireless set wlan1 mode=station
```

To scan and search for all access points (AP) in the area use the following command:

```
interface wireless scan [interface name]
```

Where:

- [interface name] is the name of the wireless interface.

For example:

```
interface wireless scan wlan1
```

```
Terminal <1>
[admin@MikroTik] > interface wireless scan wlan1
Flags: A - ACTIVE; P - PRIVACY; R - ROUTEROS-NETWORK; B - BRI>
Columns: ADDRESS, SSID
     ADDRESS            SSID
A RB 74:4D:28:DA:6C:D8  MM3
AP   50:E0:39:B7:50:70  erdem
AP   E8:6E:44:12:0F:00  VODAFONE_4959
AP   48:22:54:83:E2:EC  Telekom_TPE2E6_2.4GHz
AP   4A:22:54:D3:E2:EC
AP   B8:D5:26:C2:AC:85  KAPLAN

[admin@MikroTik] >
```

Later, you will learn how to connect to one of those access points (AP) using some of its properties that have not been explained yet.

In most cases, you want the wireless station device to obtain an IP address automatically or dynamically from the access point (AP). So you need to configure DHCP client on the wireless interface of the wireless station.

To configure DHCP client on an interface, as you have learned before, use the **DHCP Client** window.

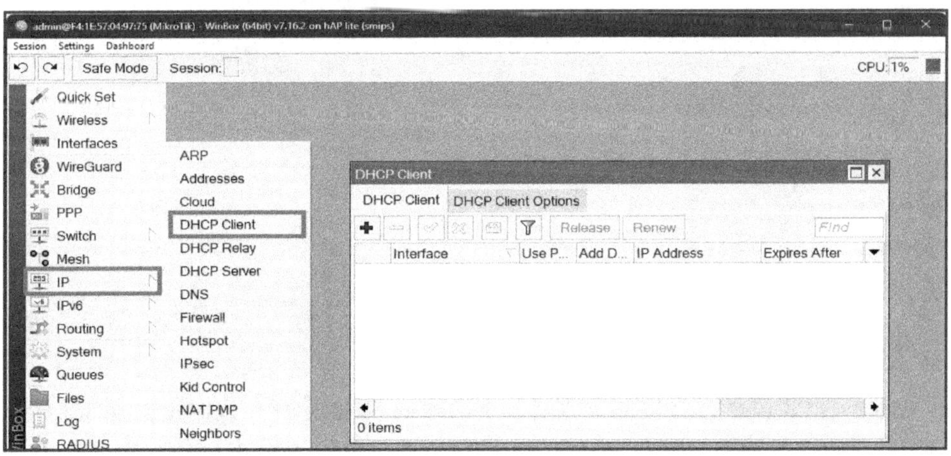

LAB

In this lab, you have two MikroTik devices. you want to configure one device to function as an access point (AP), and the other device to function as a wireless station.

In the access point (AP) device:

- Configure the wireless interface by setting the mode to ap bridge.
- Assign the IP address 192.168.1.1/24 to the wireless interface.
- Configure a DHCP server on the wireless interface.

In the wireless station device:

- Configure the wireless interface by setting the mode to station.
- Configure a DHCP client on the wireless interface.

Access Point (AP):

To configure the first device to function as an access point (AP), click the **Wireless** menu, then select **Wireless** to open **Wireless Tables** window.

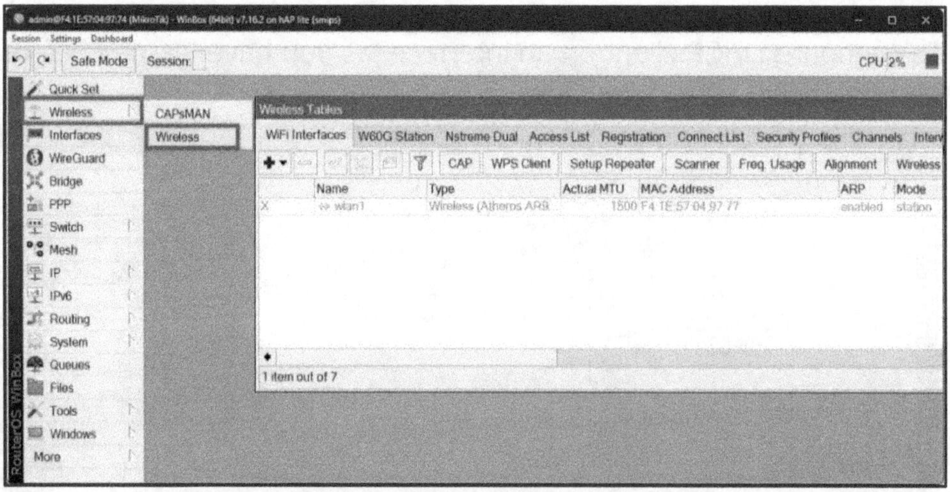

Double-click the wireless interface in the **Wireless Tables** window to open the wireless **Interface** settings dialog box. In the **Mode** field select ap bridge mode. Then click the **OK** button, to close this dialog box.

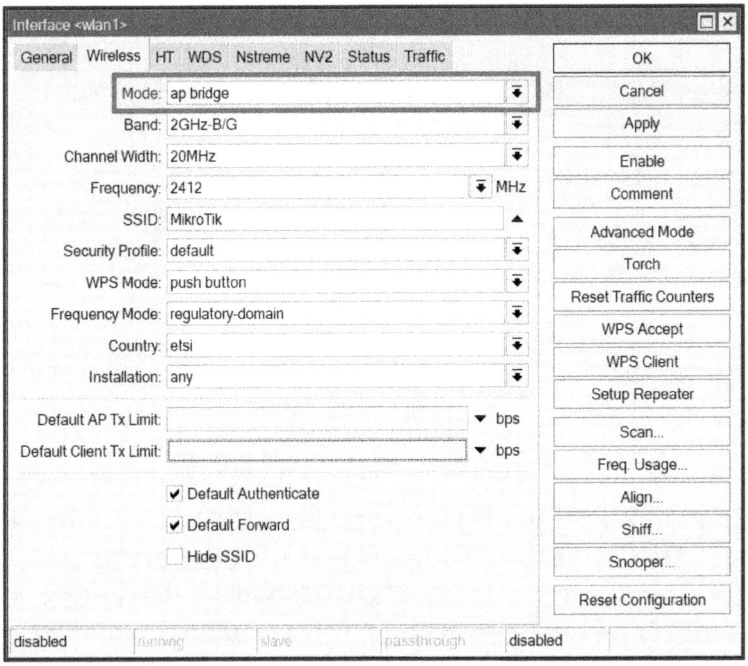

Click the **Enable** button in the **Wireless Tables** window to enable the wireless interface.

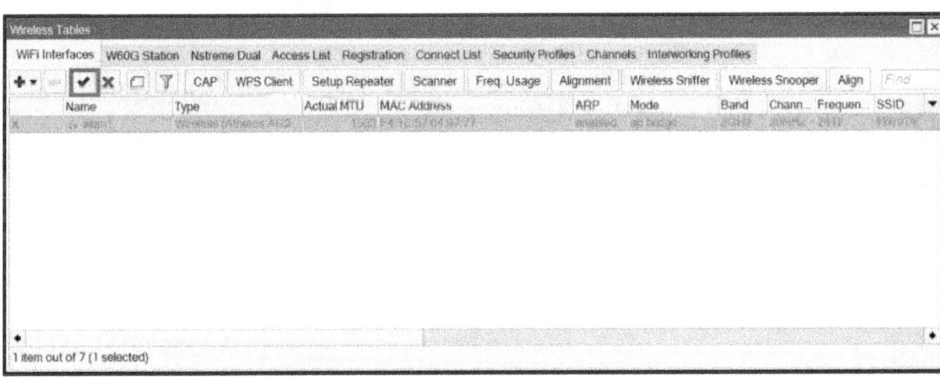

To assign an IP address to the wireless interface, click the **IP** menu, then select **Addresses** to open the **Address List** window. Click the **Add** button to open the **New Address** dialog box. In the **Address** field, enter the IP address along with the subnet mask. 192.168.1.1/24

. In the **Interface** field, select the interface wlan1. Then click the **OK** button to close this dialog box and assign the IP to the interface.

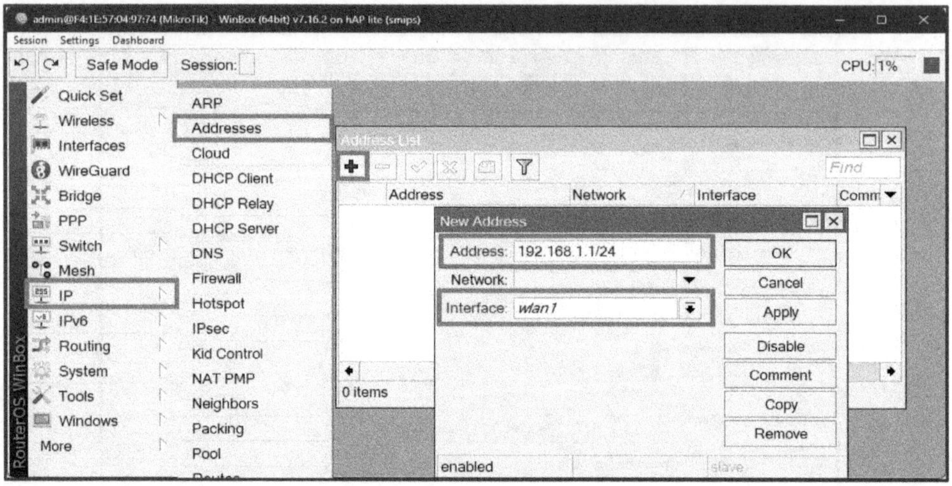

To configure DHCP server on the wireless interface, click the **IP** menu, then select **DHCP Server** to open the **DHCP Server** window. click the **DHCP Setup** button to open **DHCP Setup** dialog box. In **DHCP Server Interface** field Select the interface wlan1, and click the **Next** button in all other messages to accept the default settings and configure the DHCP Server.

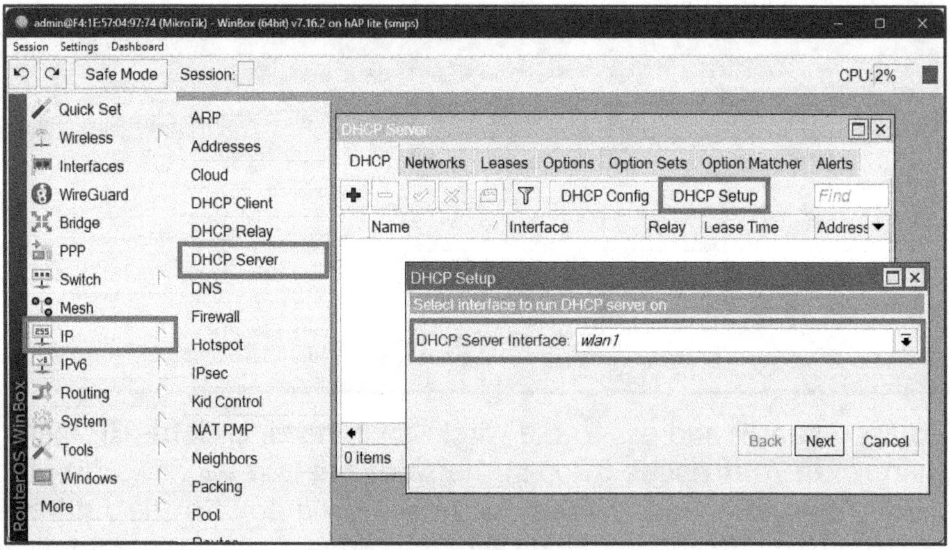

Wireless Station:

To configure the second device to function as a wireless station, click the **Wireless** menu, then select **Wireless** to open **Wireless Tables** window.

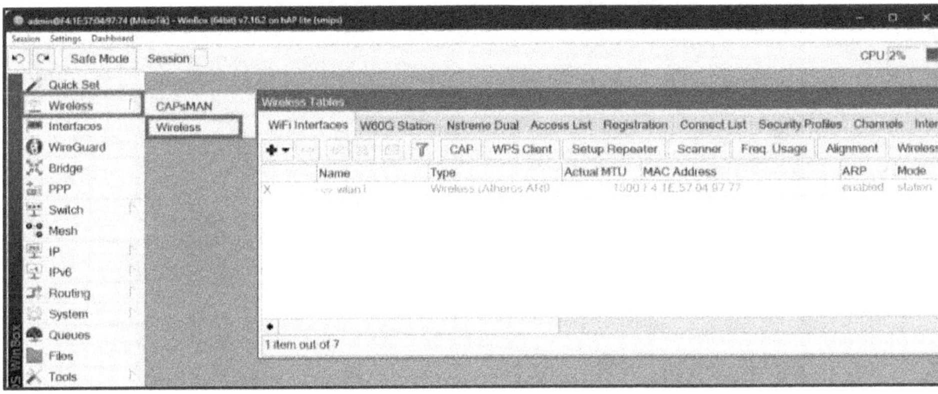

Double-click the wireless interface in the **Wireless Tables** window to open the wireless **Interface** settings dialog box. In the **Mode** field, select station mode. Then, click the **Scan** button to open the **Scanner** dialog box.

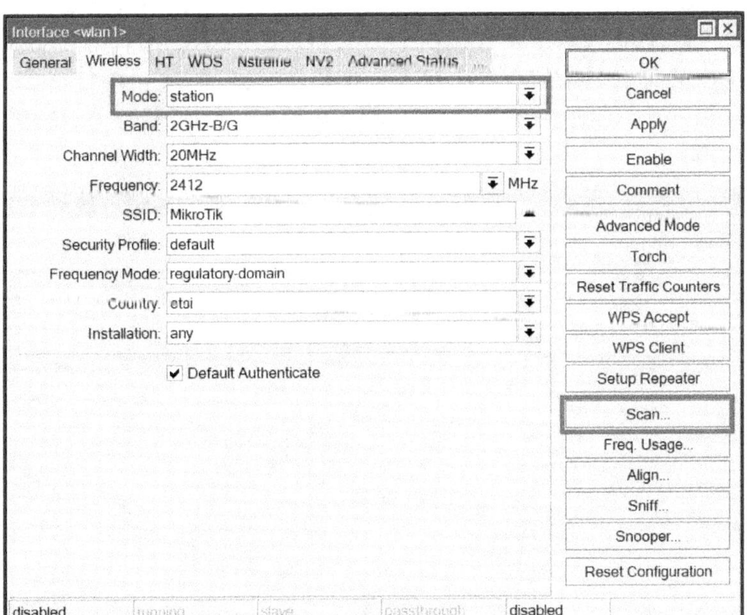

From the **Interface** field, select the wireless interface wlan1 and click the **Start** button to begin scanning and searching for available access points (AP). Then, select the access point (AP) (MikroTik) and click the **Connect** button to connect to this access point (AP).

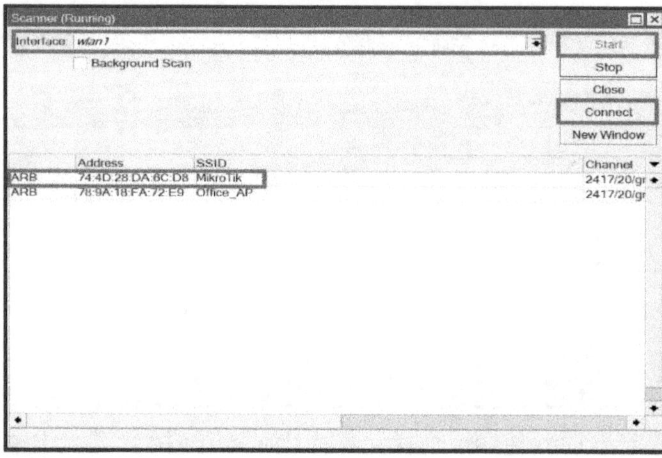

Then click the **OK** button to close the wireless **Interface** settings dialog box.

To configure DHCP client on the wireless interface, click the **IP** menu, then select **DHCP Client** to open the **DHCP Client** window. Click the **Add** to open the **New DHCP Client** dialog box. In the **Interface** field, select the interface wlan1. Then, click the **OK** button to close this dialog box.

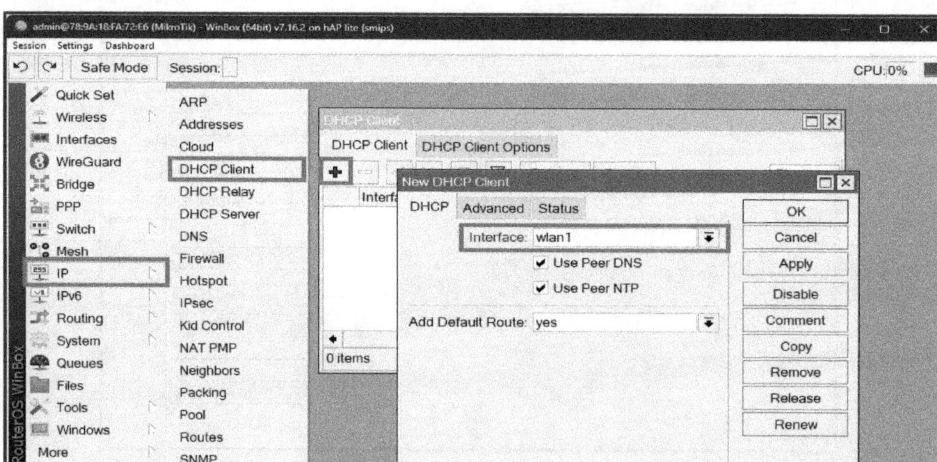

After completing the configuration, the wireless station will connect to the access point (AP), and will get an IP address. This IP address will appear in the **Address List** window.

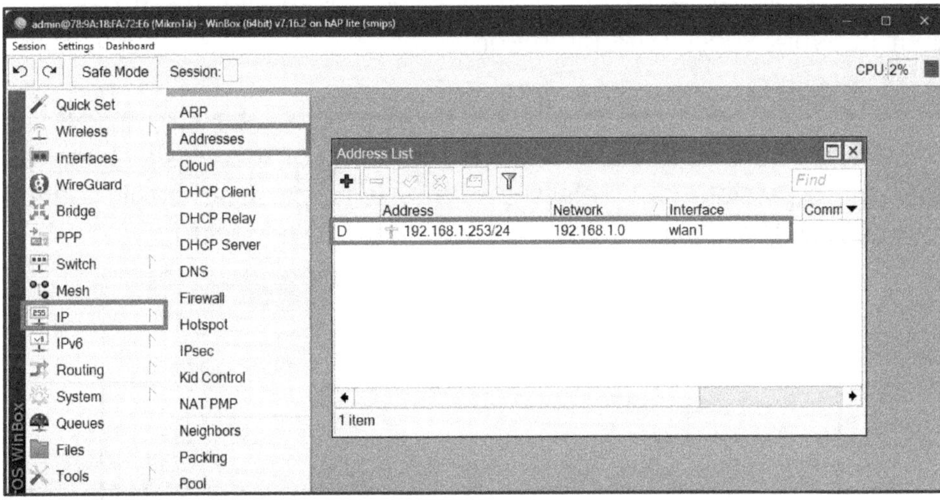

5.10 Registration Tab

The **Registration** table in the **Wireless Tables** window lists the connected devices and displays information about each one. This applies to both access point (AP) devices and station devices.

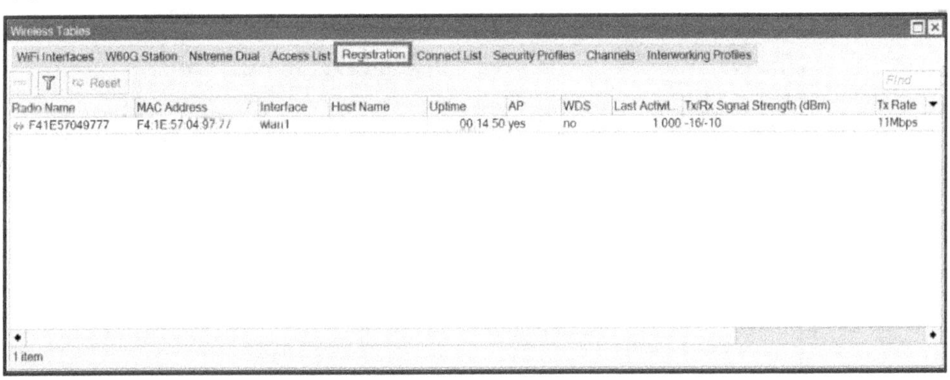

On the access point (AP) device, it will display information about the connected wireless stations.

On the wireless station device, it will display information about the access point (AP) it is connected to.

5.11 Other Configurations.

When you configure the device to function as an access point (AP), you can either accept the default settings or modify them based on your network specific requirements.

5.11.1 SSID

The **SSID** (Service Set Identifier) is the name of the wireless network that will be visible to wireless stations. It helps users easily identify and choose the access point (AP) they want to connect to.

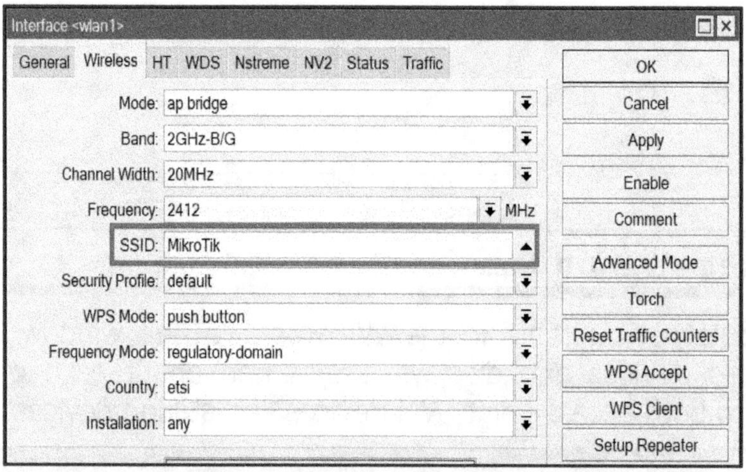

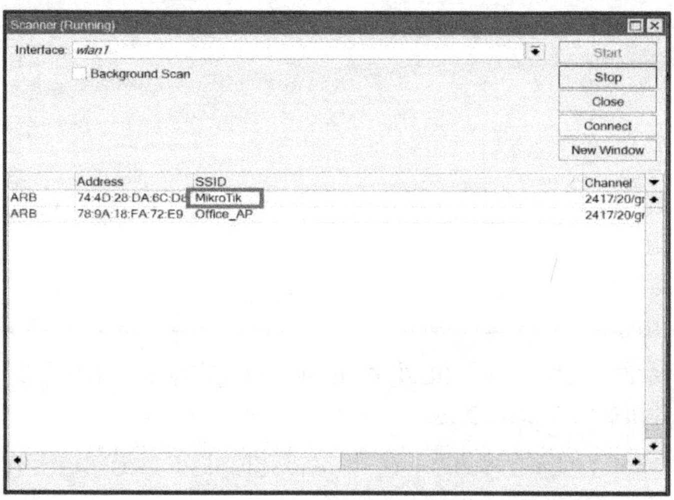

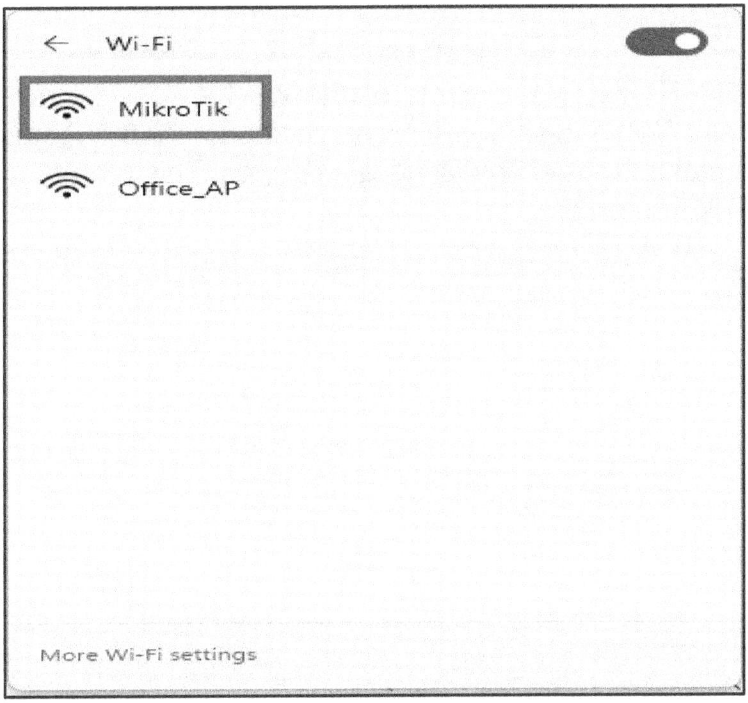

You can enter the desired name in the **SSID** field in the **Wireless** tab of the wireless **Interface** settings dialog box.

You can also set the SSID name from the CLI using the following command:

```
interface wireless set [interface name] ssid=[name]
```

Where:

- [interface name] is the name of the wireless interface.
- [name] is the desired name for SSID.

For example:

```
interface wireless set wlan1 ssid=Office_AP
```

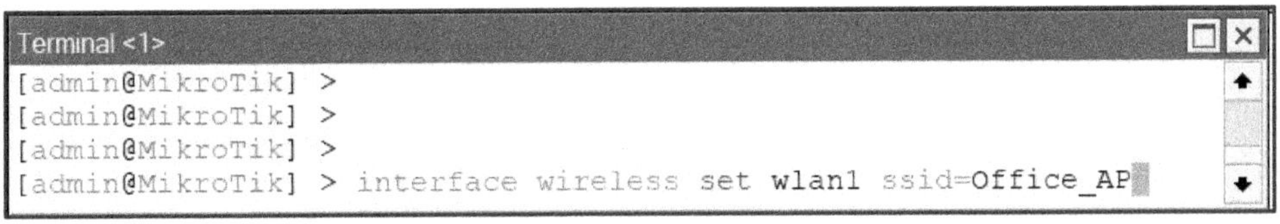

5.11.2 Radio Name

The **Radio Name** is the name of the wireless device for both the access point (AP) and station. This name appears in the **Registration** table, to make it easier to distinguish devices. This feature is specific to MikroTik RouterOS.

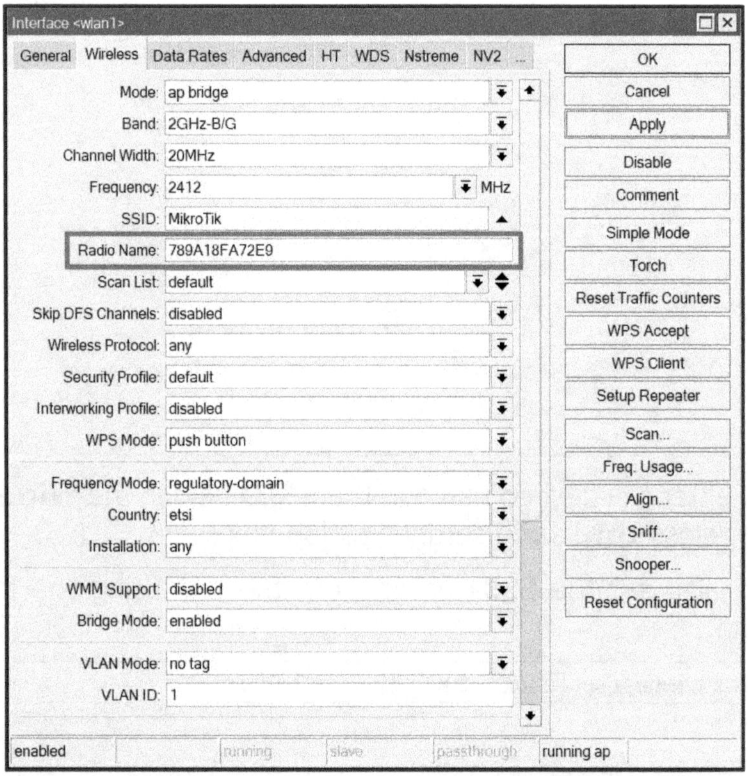

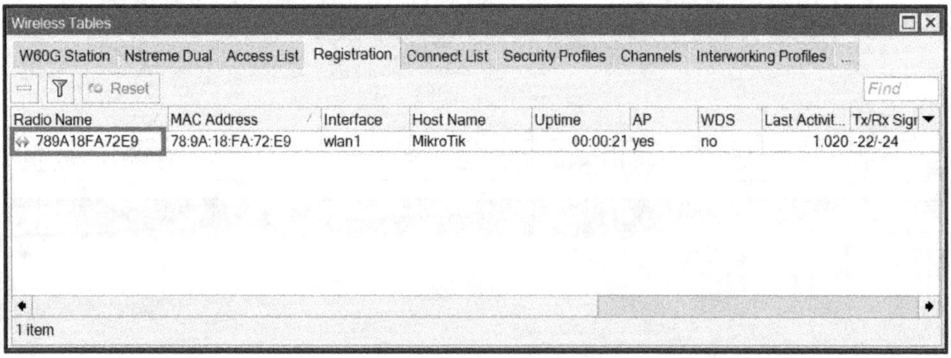

If the **Radio Name** field does not appear in the **Wireless** tab, click the **Advanced** button to display the advanced options, which include the **Radio Name**.

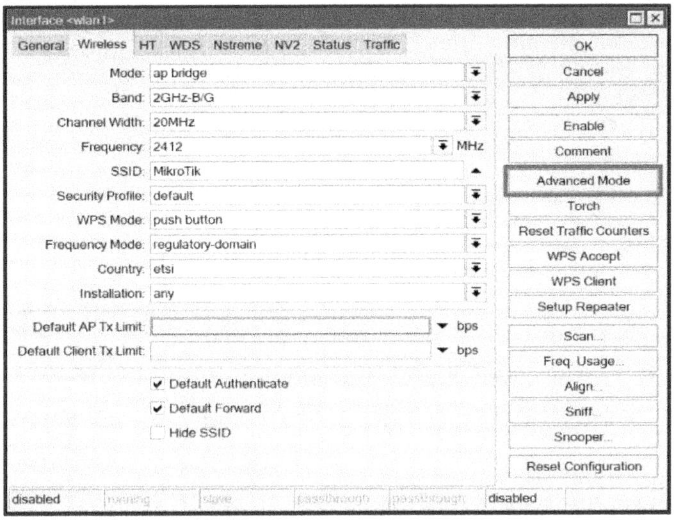

In the default settings, this name is the MAC address of the wireless interface. You can change the radio name to a more understandable one depending on your needs.

For example, if you change the radio name in the Access point (AP) device to (MikroTik_AP).

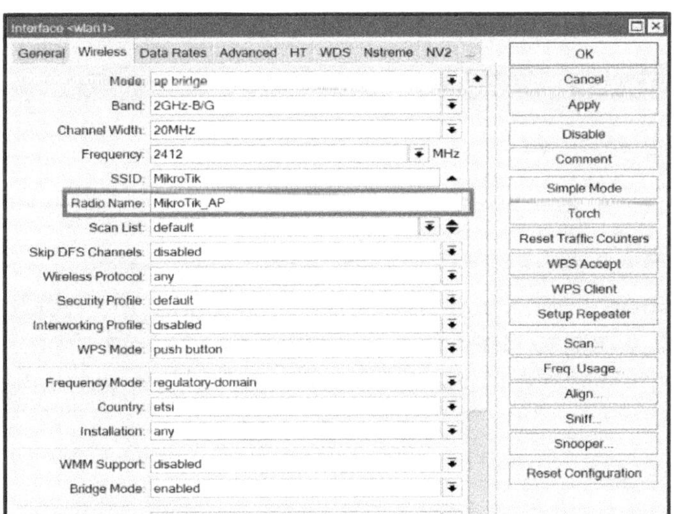

It will appear in the **Registration** tab of the **Wireless Tables** window in the wireless station device.

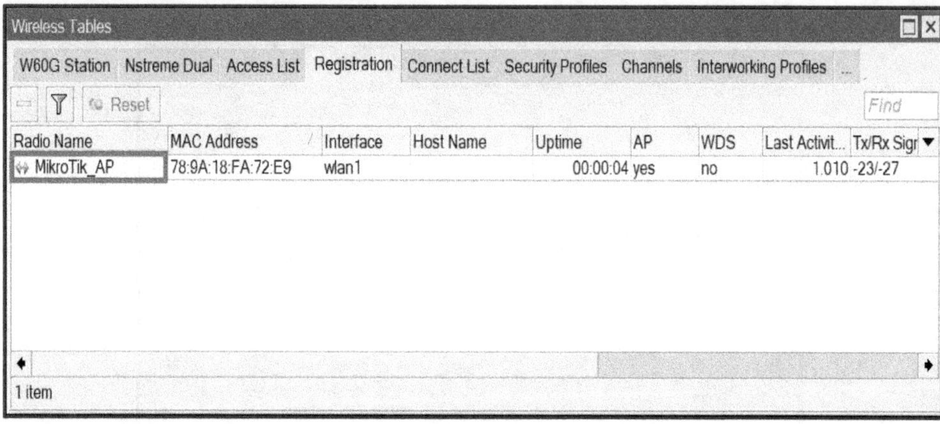

You can also set the radio name from the CLI using the following command:

```
interface wireless set [interface name] radio-name=[name]
```

Where:

- [interface name] is the name of the wireless interface.
- [name] is the desired name for radio name.

For example:

```
interface wireless set wlan1 radio-name=MikroTik_AP
```

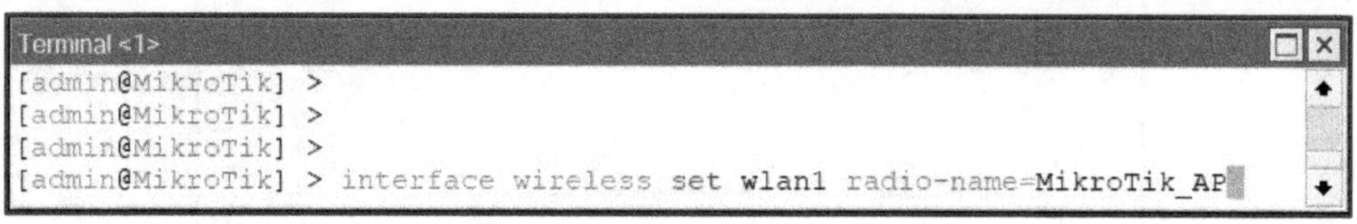

5.11.3 Band

From the **Band** field, you can select which band and wireless protocol version you want to use. The available bands and protocol versions depend on the device model and the installed wireless interface.

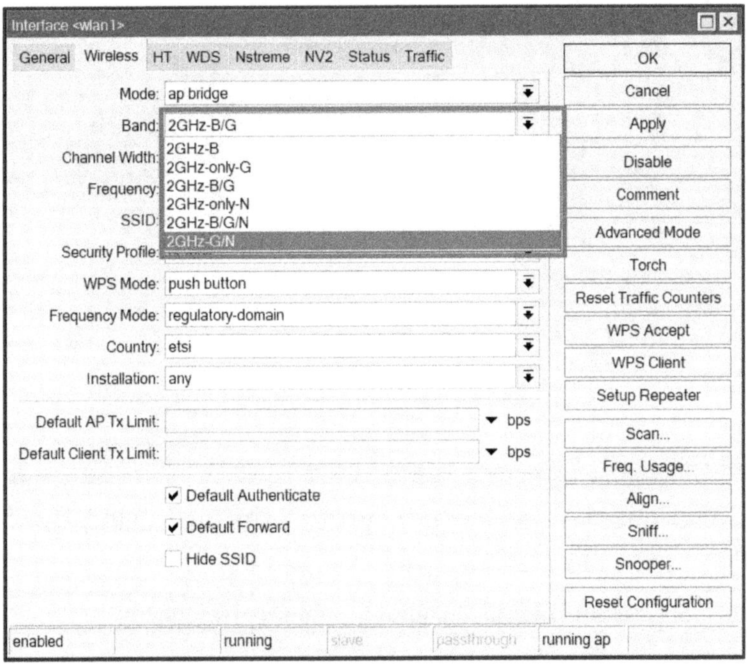

You can also select the band from the CLI using the following command:

```
interface wireless set [interface name] band=[band]
```

Where:

- [interface name] is the name of the wireless interface.
- [band] is the desired band

For example:

```
interface wireless set wlan1 band=2ghz-b/g/n
```

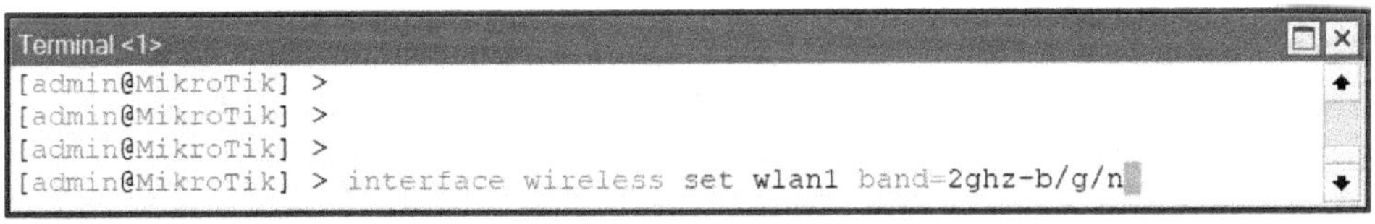

5.11.4 Frequency

From the **Frequency** field, you can choose which frequency (or channel) you want to use.

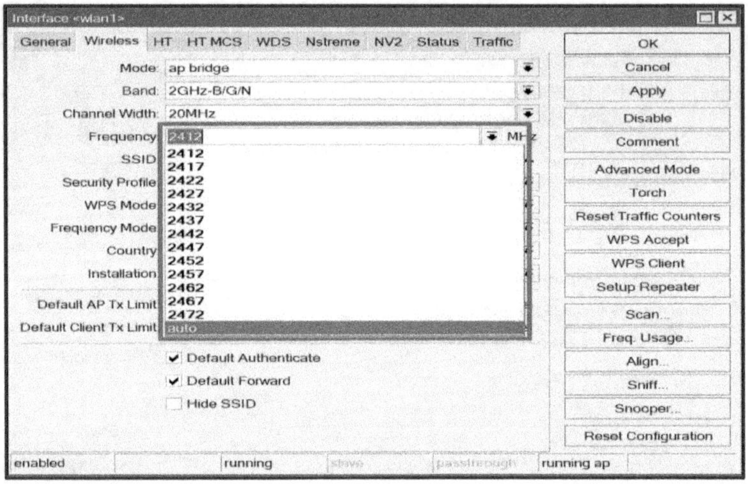

You can also choose the frequency from the CLI using the following command:

```
interface wireless set [interface name] frequency=[frequency]
```

Where:

- [interface name] is the name of the wireless interface.
- [frequency] is the desired frequency

For example:

```
interface wireless set wlan1 frequency=2437
```

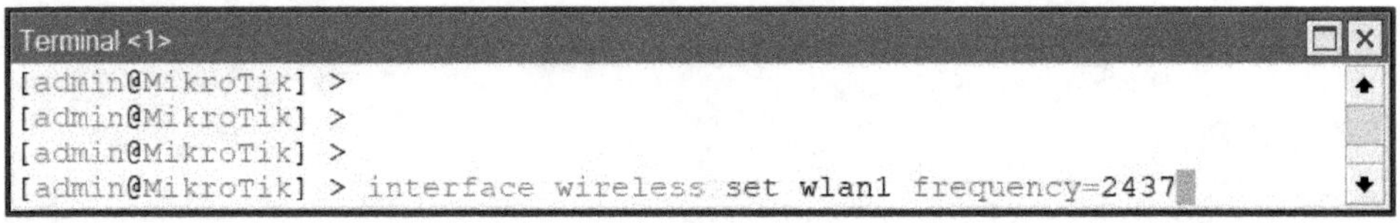

5.11.5 TX Power

The TX Power (Transmission Power) is the strength of the signal transmitted by the wireless interface.

It is measured in dBm (decibel milliwatts)

Higher TX Power generally results in better signal range and penetration, but it can also lead to interference and noise if set too high.

You can change the TX Power mode and values from the **TX Power** tab.

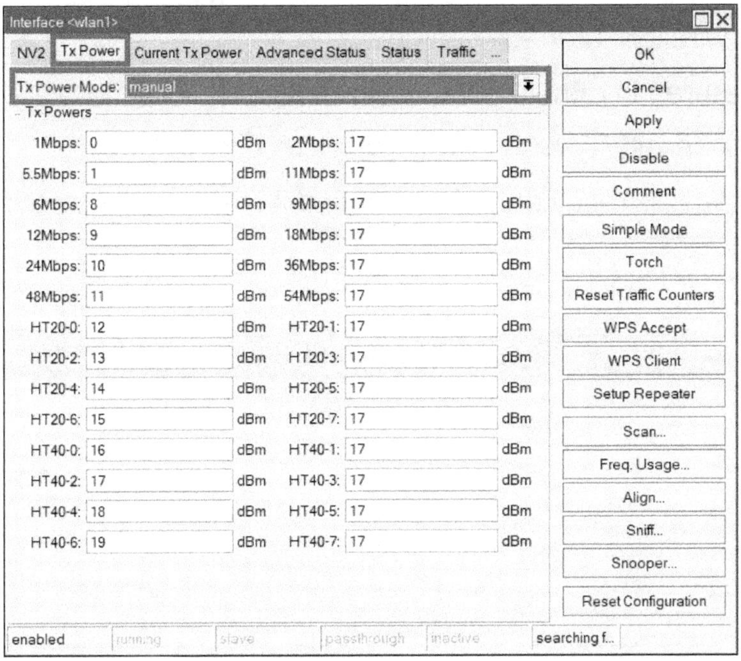

You can also change the TX power from the CLI using the following command:

```
interface wireless set [interface name] tx-power-mode=[mode] tx-
power=[power value]
```

Where:

- [interface name] is the name of the wireless interface.
- [mode] is the desired tx power mode
- [power value] is the desired tx power value

For example:

```
interface wireless set wlan1 tx-power-mode=all-rates-fixed tx-power=8
```

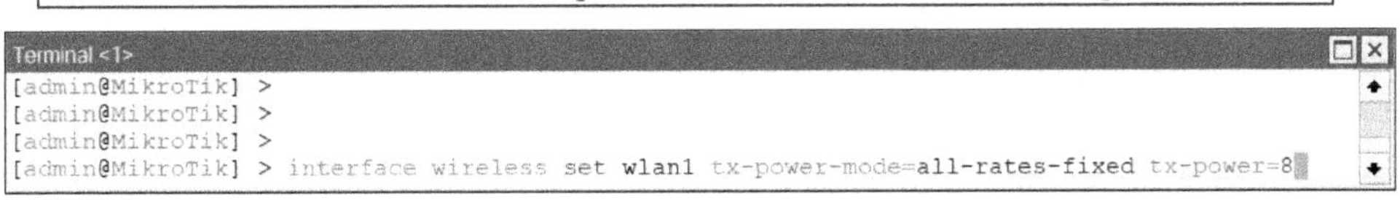

5.11.6 Rx Sensitivity

The RX Sensitivity (Receive Sensitivity) is the minimum signal strength that the wireless interface can detect.

It is measured in dBm (decibel milliwatts)

Lower RX sensitivity results in signal detection.

This property is ready only, you can find it in the device specifications.

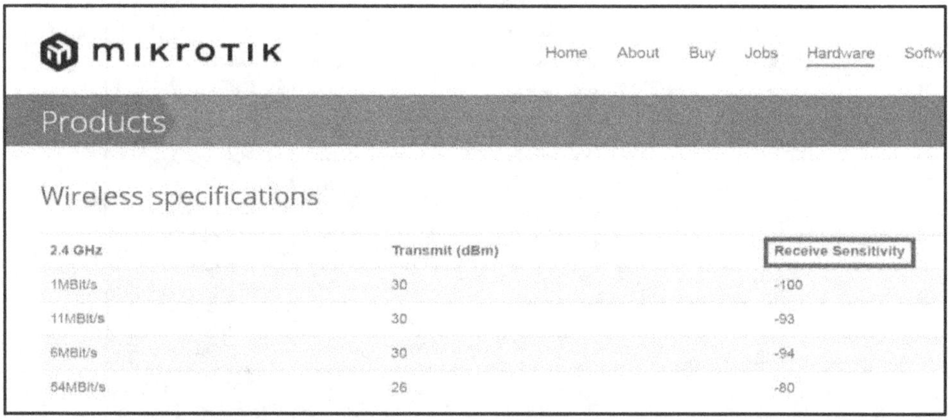

5.11.7 Country

From the **Country** field, you can select the country to follow its regulations regarding frequencies and TX power. When selecting a country from this field, the **Frequency** field will display only the allowed frequencies for that country.

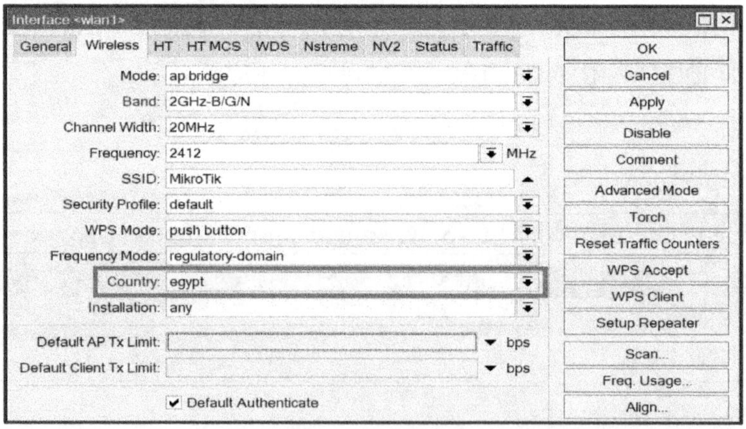

You can also select the country from the CLI using the following command:

```
interface wireless set [interface name] country=[country]
```

Where:

- [interface name] is the name of the wireless interface.
- [country] is the desired country

For example:

```
interface wireless set wlan1 country=egypt
```

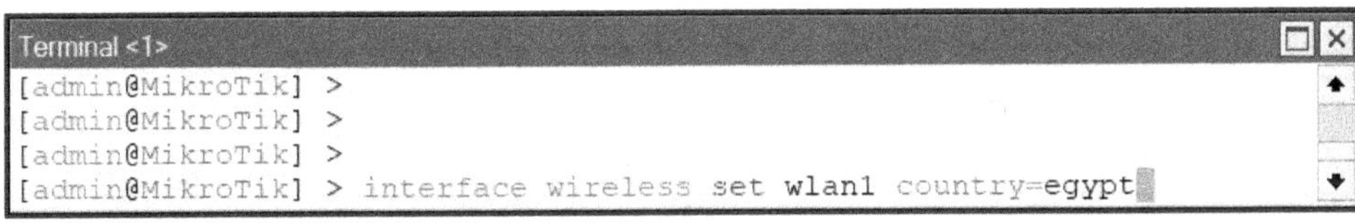

5.11.8 Frequency Mode

From the **Frequency Mode** field, you can select **Regulatory Domain** to follow the country regulations for frequencies and TX power, as specified in the **Country** field.

Or you can choose **Manual TX Power** to manually adjust the TX power, or you can select **SuperChannel** to allow using any frequency and TX power values that the device supports.

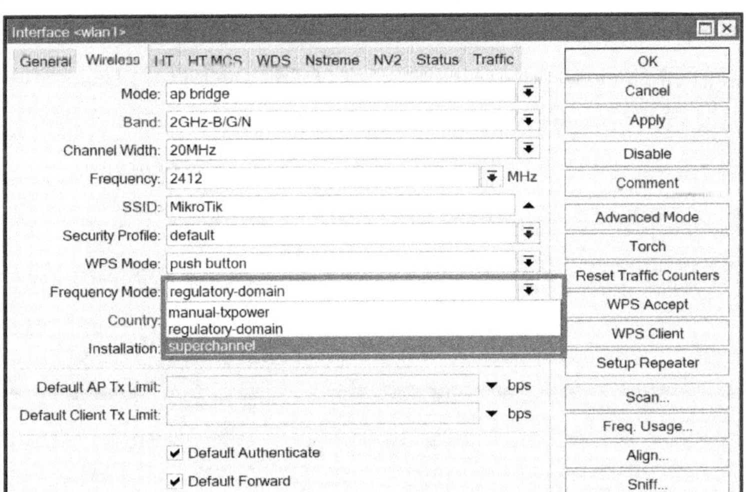

You can also select the frequency mode from the CLI using the following command:

```
interface wireless set [interface name] frequency-mode=[mode]
```

Where:

- [interface name] is the name of the wireless interface.
- [mode] is the desired frequency mode.

For example:

```
interface wireless set wlan1 frequency-mode=superchannel
```

```
Terminal <1>
[admin@MikroTik] >
[admin@MikroTik] >
[admin@MikroTik] >
[admin@MikroTik] > interface wireless set wlan1 frequency-mode=superchannel
```

5.11.9 DFS

The DFS (Dynamic Frequency Selection) feature allows devices using the 5 GHz band to detect radar systems and automatically switch to a different frequency. It works as follows:

- The access point (AP) scans for radar signals on a channel before transmitting.
- If radar signals are detected, the access point (AP) avoids that channel and selects another one dynamically.
- If no radar is detected, the access point (AP) uses the channel but continues to monitor for radar activity.
- If radar is later detected, the access point (AP) stops using the channel and switches to a different one.

To enable this feature, you can use the **Radar Detect** option from this field.

LAB

In this lab, you have two MikroTik devices. you want to configure one device to function as an access point (AP), and the other device to function as a wireless station.

In the access point (AP) device:

- Configure the wireless interface as follows:
    - Set the mode to ap bridge
    - Set the SSID to Office_AP
    - Select 2GHz-only-G band
    - Use the frequency 2437
- Assign the IP address 192.168.1.1/24 to the wireless interface.
- Configure a DHCP server on the wireless interface.

In the wireless station device:

- Configure the wireless interface as follows:
    - Set the mode to station.
- Configure a DHCP client on the wireless interface.

Access point (AP):

To configure the first device to function as an access point (AP), click the **Wireless** menu, then select **Wireless** to open **Wireless Tables** window.

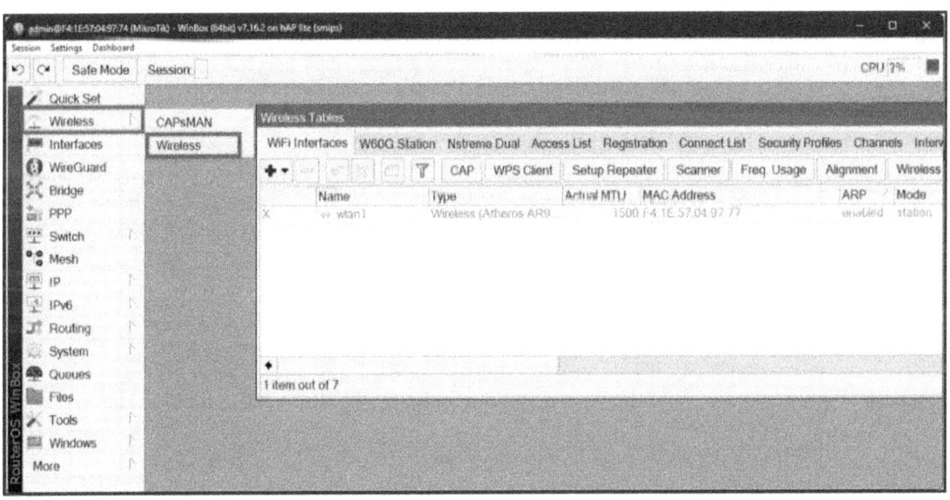

Double-click the wireless interface in the **Wireless Tables** window to open the wireless **Interface** settings dialog box. In the **Mode** field select ap bridge mode. In the **SSID** field enter Office_AP. From the **Band** field select 2GHz-only-G. From the **Frequency** select 2437.

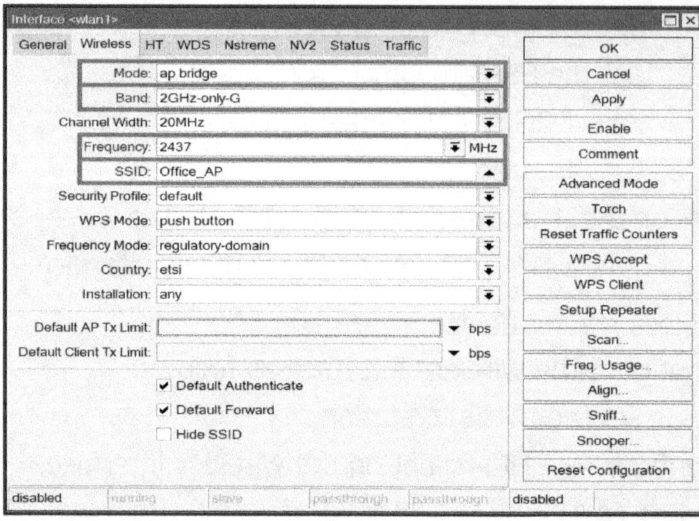

Instead of clicking the **OK** button to close this dialog box and then clicking the **Enable** button in the **Wireless Tables** window to enable the wireless interface. You can directly click the **Enable** button from the **Interface** dialog box, then accept the message to commit or apply the configuration before enabling the interface.

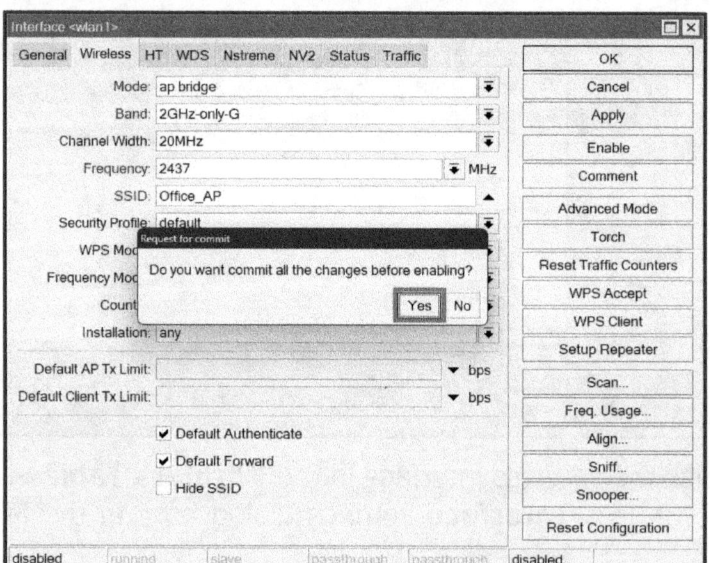

Or you can also click the **Apply** button, before clicking the **Enable** button from the **Interface** dialog box. Then click the **OK** button to close this dialog box

To assign an IP address to the wireless interface, click the **IP** menu, then select **Addresses** to open the **Address List** window. Click the **Add** button to open the **New Address** dialog box. In the **Address** field, enter the IP address along with the subnet mask. 192.168.1.1/24 . In the **Interface** field, select the interface wlan1. Then click the **OK** button to close this dialog box and assign the IP to the interface.

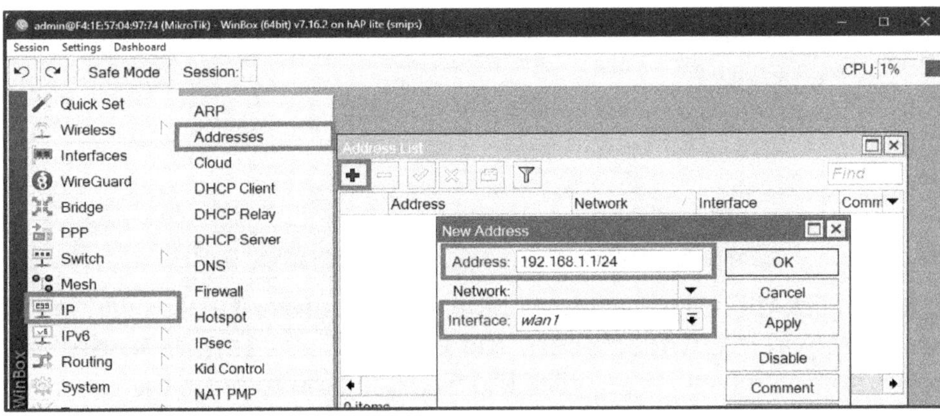

To configure DHCP server on the wireless interface, click the **IP** menu, then select **DHCP Server** to open the **DHCP Server** window. click the **DHCP Setup** button to open **DHCP Setup** dialog box. In **DHCP Server Interface** field Select the interface wlan1, and click the **Next** button in all other messages to accept the default settings and configure the DHCP Server.

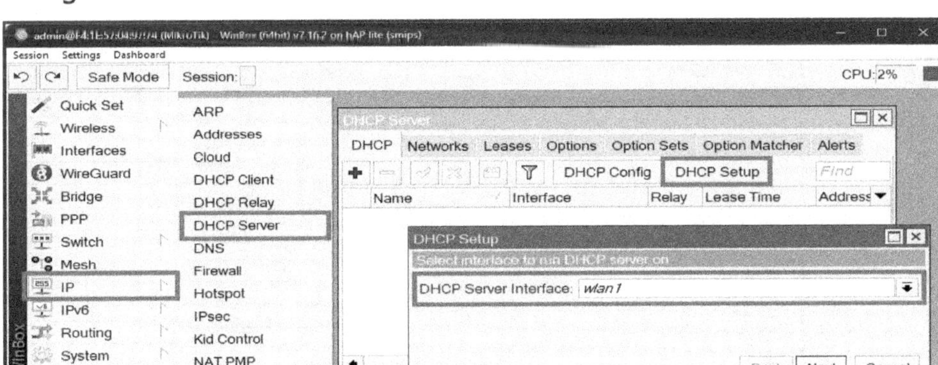

Wireless Station:

To configure the second device to function as a wireless station, click the **Wireless** menu, then select **Wireless** to open **Wireless Tables** window.

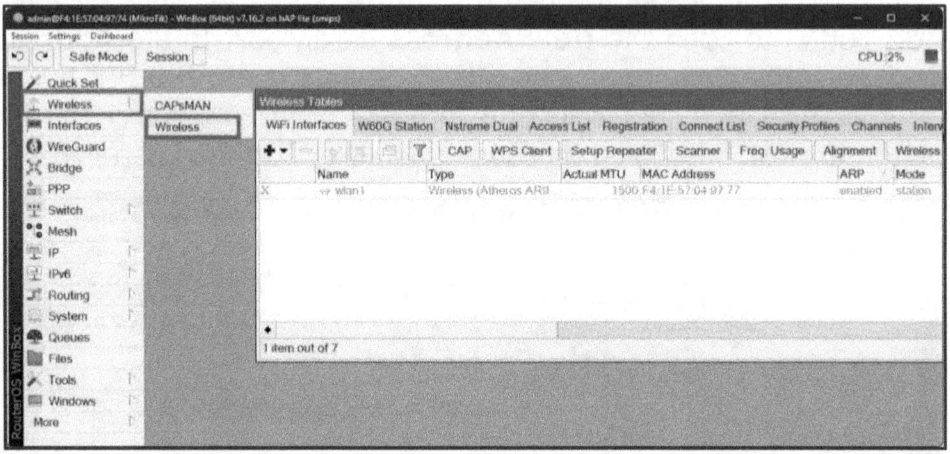

Double-click the wireless interface in the **Wireless Tables** window to open the wireless **Interface** settings dialog box. In the **Mode** field, select station mode. Then, click the **Scan** button to open the **Scanner** dialog box.

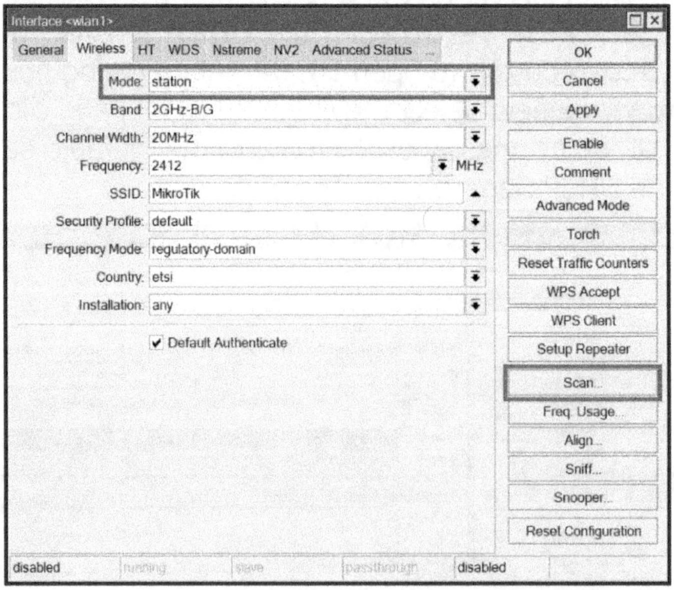

From the **Interface** field, select the wireless interface wlan1 and click the **Start** button to begin scanning and searching for available access points (AP). Then, select the access point (AP) (Office_AP) and click the **Connect** button to connect to this access point (AP).

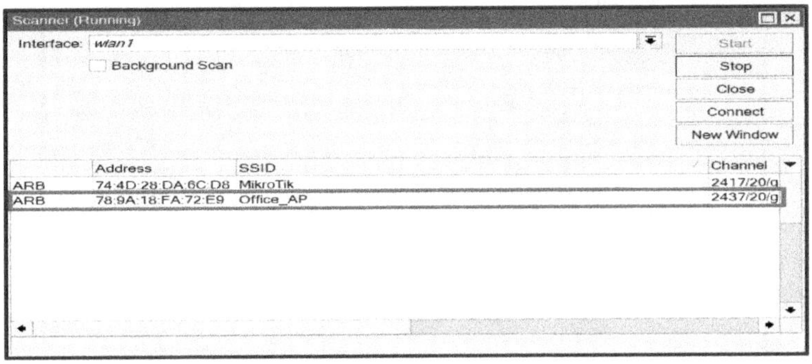

Note: in this case when using the **Scan** button to search for the access point (AP) and connect to it, you do not need to set the SSID or the frequency in the wireless station device, it will get these settings from the access point (AP) after it connects to it.

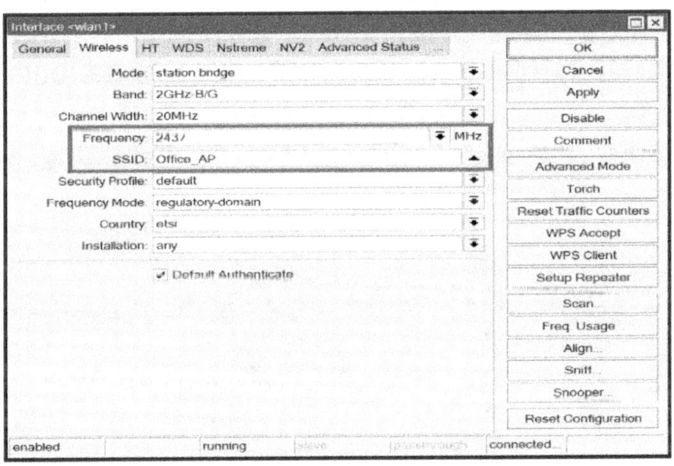

Instead of using the **Scan** button, you can configure the wireless station by setting the **Mode** field to station, the **SSID** field to Office_AP, the **Band** field to 2GHz-only-G, and the **Frequency** field to 2437. Then enable the interface. The wireless station will connect to this access point (AP) automatically.

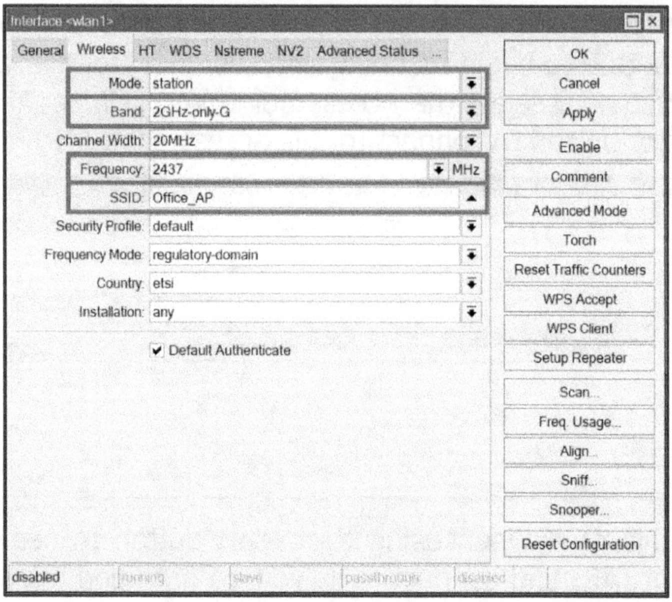

To configure DHCP client on the wireless interface, click the **IP** menu, then select **DHCP Client** to open the **DHCP Client** window. Click the **Add** to open the **New DHCP Client** dialog box. In the **Interface** field, select the interface wlan1. Then, click the **OK** button to close this dialog box.

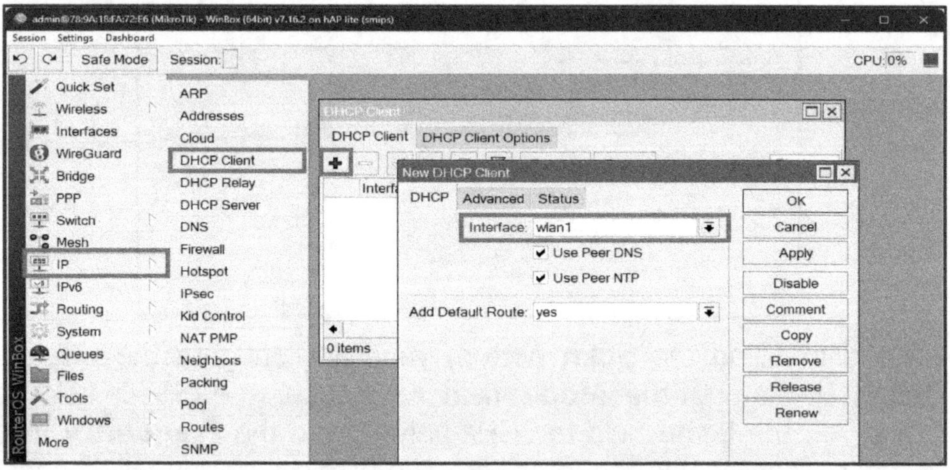

After completing the configuration, the wireless station will connect to the access point (AP), and will get an IP address. This IP address will appear in the **Address List** window.

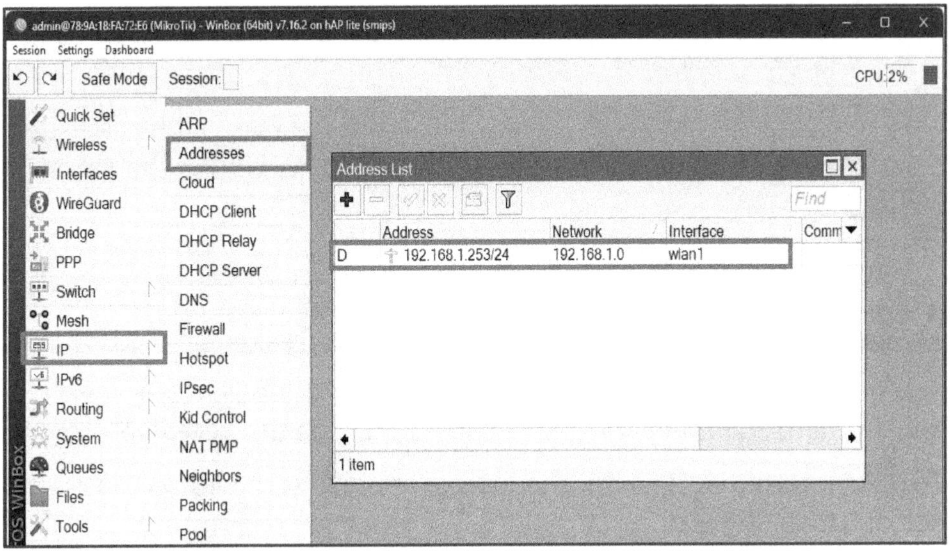

CLI

You can also make the configuration from the CLI .

Access point (AP):

To configure the wireless interface, use the following commands

```
interface wireless set wlan1 mode=ap-bridge ssid=Office_AP band=2ghz-onlyg frequency=2437

interface wireless enable wlan1
```

To assign an IP address to the wireless interface, use the following command

```
ip address add address=192.168.1.1/24 interface=wlan1
```

To configure DHCP server on the wireless interface using the DHCP setup wizard, use the following command, choose wireless interface and accept the default settings by pressing Enter each time the setup wizard asks for input

```
ip dhcp-server setup
```

Wireless Station:

To configure the wireless interface, use the following commands

```
interface wireless set wlan1 mode=station ssid=Office_AP band=2ghz-onlyg frequency=2437

interface wireless enable wlan1
```

To configure DHCP client on the wireless interface, use the following command

```
ip dhcp-client add interface=wlan1
```

5.12 Wireless Security

You can protect the wireless network by using a password or key, so only authorized wireless stations can connect to the access point (AP).

To protect the access to the access point (AP) with a password, perform two steps:

- First: create a password using a security profile.
- Second: select this profile to be used.

To create a password or key, use the **Security Profiles** tab of the **Wireless Tables** window to create a Security Profile and store the password in it.

By default, there is a predefined security profile, you can use it, or create a new profile.

To create a new profile, click the **Add** button in the **Security Profiles** tab to open **New Security** profile dialog box.

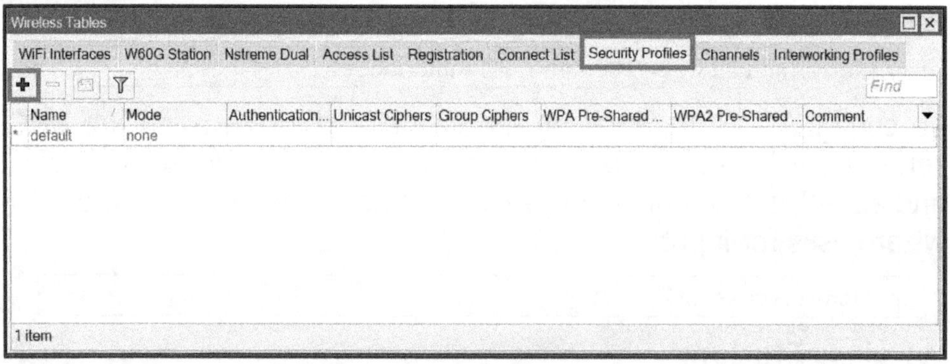

You can use the **Security Profile** dialog box to add a new profile and configure different properties and options for wireless security.

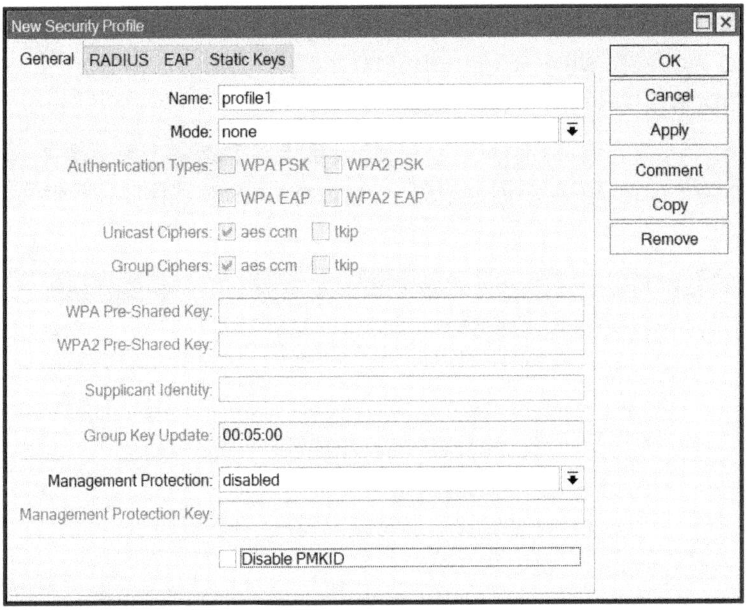

In the **Name** field, enter a name for this profile, or you can leave the default name. From the **Mode** field, choose Dynamic Key.

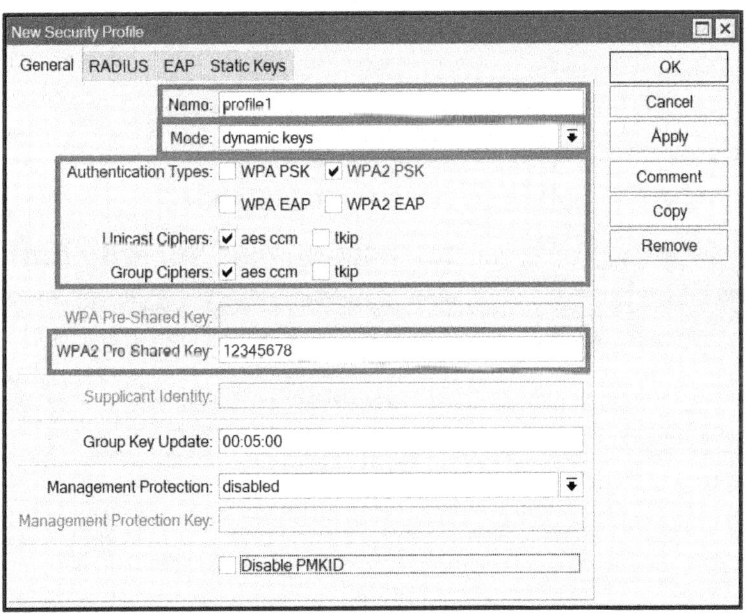

Next, choose the **Authentication Type**, select **WPA PSK** (Wi-Fi Protected Access with a Pre-shared Key), either version 1 or 2, and the encryption method **AES-CCM** or **TKIP**.

Enter the password or the key in the **WPA Pre-Shared Key** field. If you choose both WPA and WPA2, you can set a different password for each version.

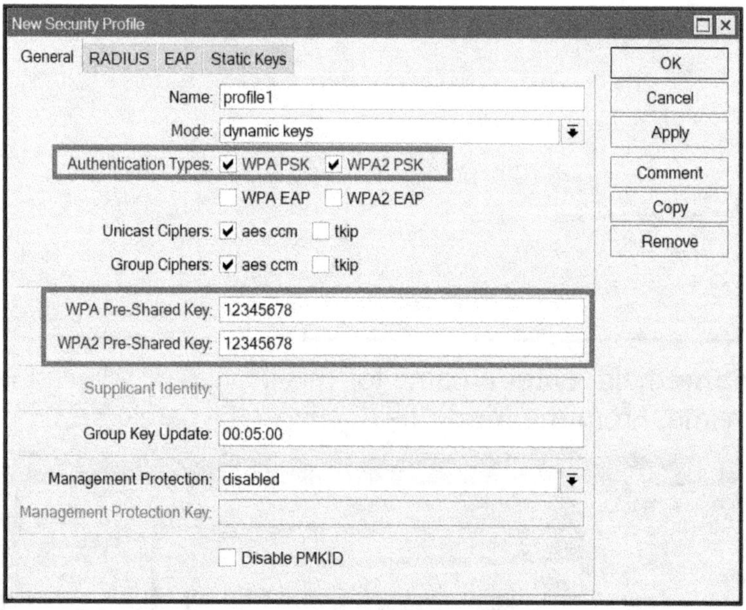

Then click the **OK** button to close the dialog box.

The new security profile will now appear in the **Security Profiles** tab.

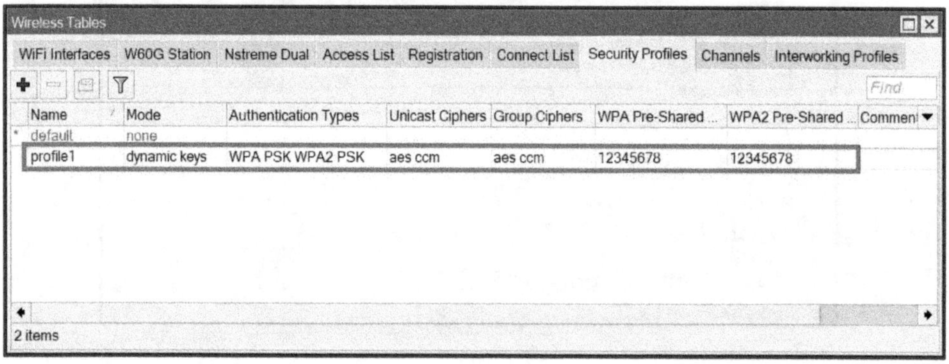

Now, to use this profile on the access point (AP), select the profile from the **Security Profile** field in the **Wireless** tab of the wireless **Interface** settings dialog box.

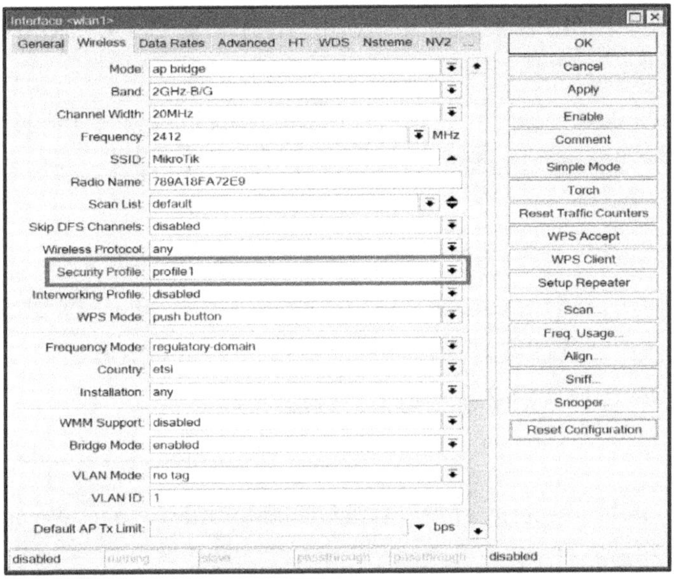

For the station device, do exactly the same: create a security profile, select the same authentication protocols and encryption methods, and enter the same password or key. Then, from the **Wireless Profile** field, select this security profile.

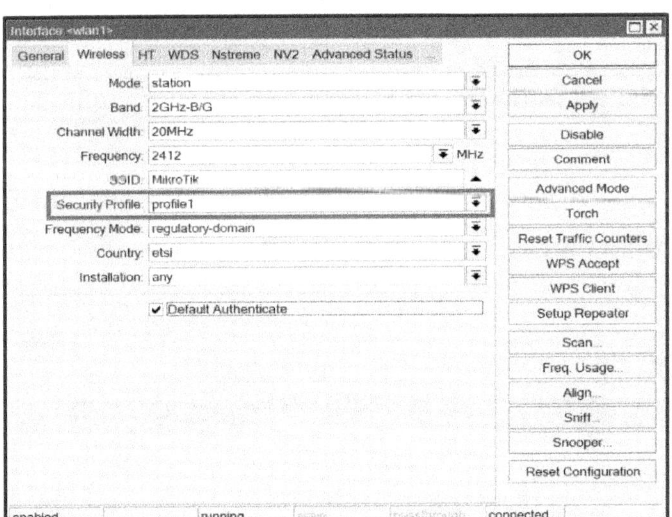

Note: if the **Security Profile** field does not appear in the **Wireless** tab, click the **Advanced** button to display the advanced options, which include the **Security Profile** field.

You can also create a security profile from the CLI using the following command:

```
interface wireless security-profiles add name=[name] mode=[node]
authentication-types=[type] wpa2-pre-shared-key=[key]
```

Where:

- [name] is the name for the security profile.
- [mode] is the encryption mode for the security profile.
- [type] is the authentication type of this profile,
- [key] is the key or the password.

For example:

```
interface wireless security-profiles add name=profile1 mode=dynamic-
keys authentication-types=wpa2-psk wpa2-pre-shared-key=12345678
```

To configure the wireless interface to use this profile, use the following command:

```
interface wireless set [interface name] security-profile=[profile name]
```

Where:

- [interface name] is the name of the wireless interface.
- [profile name] is the name of the profile.

For example:

```
interface wireless set wlan1 security-profile=profile1
```

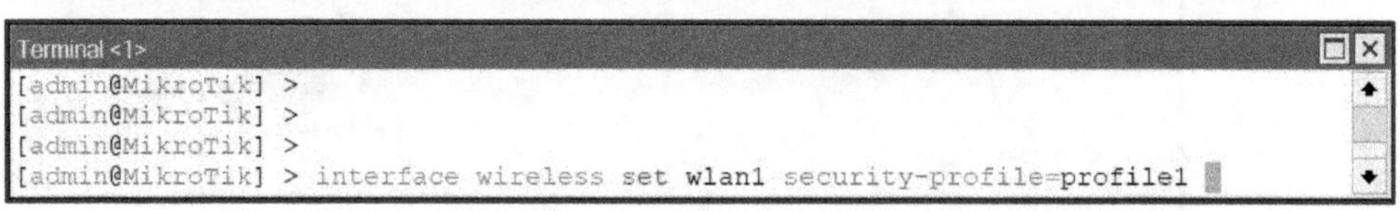

LAB

In this lab, you have two MikroTik devices. You want to configure one device to function as an access point (AP), and the other device to function as a wireless station. You also want to protect the access to the access point (AP) with a password.

To start the configuration:

In the access point (AP) device:

- Create a security profile with an authentication type WPA2 PSK and a key 12345678.
- Configure the wireless interface as follows:
    - Set the mode to ap bridge.
    - Set the SSID to Office_AP.
    - Select the security profile you've created.
- Assign the IP address 192.168.1.1/24 to the wireless interface.
- Configure a DHCP server on the wireless interface.

In the wireless station device:

- Create a security profile with an authentication type WPA2 PSK and a key 12345678.
- Configure the wireless interface as follows:
    - Set the mode to station.
    - Select the security profile you've created.
- Configure a DHCP client on the wireless interface.

Access Point (AP):

To configure the first device to function as an access point (AP), click the **Wireless** menu, then select **Wireless** to open **Wireless Tables** window.

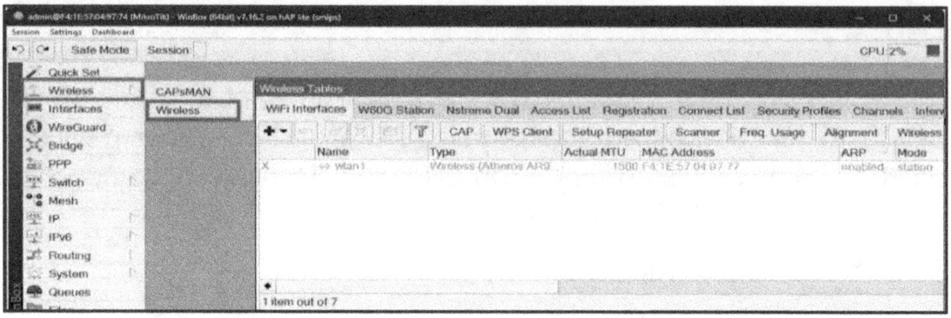

To create a security profile, click the **Add** button in the **Security Profiles** tab of the **Wireless Tables** window to open **New Security** profile dialog box.

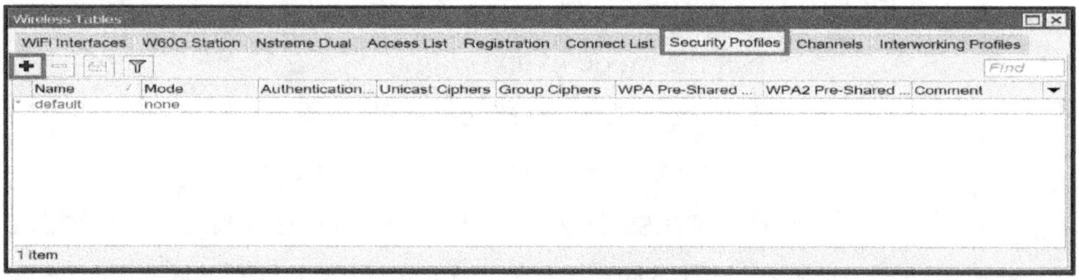

Leave the default name in the **Name** field. From the **Mode** field, choose Dynamic Key. From the **Authentication Type** section select **WPA2 PSK** and enter the password 12345678 in the **WPA Pre-Shared Key** field. Then click the **OK** button to close this dialog box.

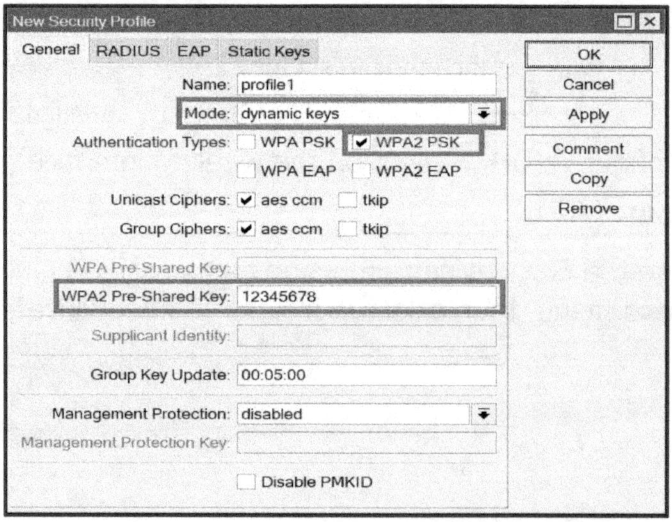

The new security profile will now appear in the **Security Profiles** tab.

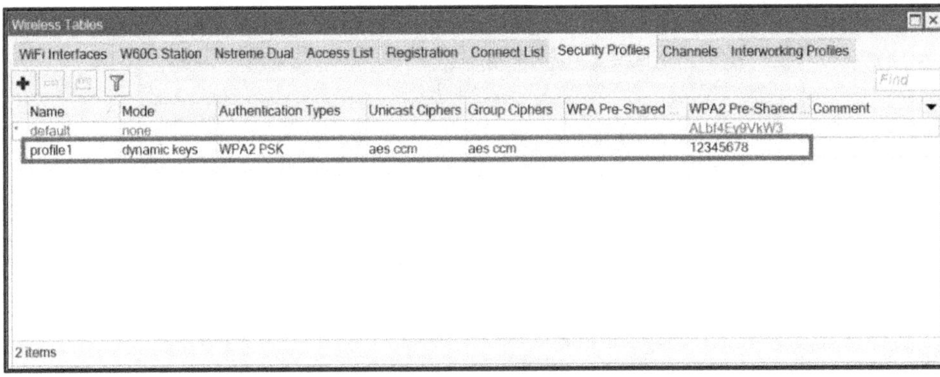

To configure the wireless interface, double-click the interface in the **Wi-Fi Interfaces** tab of the **Wireless Tables** window to open the wireless **Interface** settings dialog box. In the **Mode** field select ap bridge mode. In the **SSID** field enter Office_AP. From the **Security Profile** select Profile1.

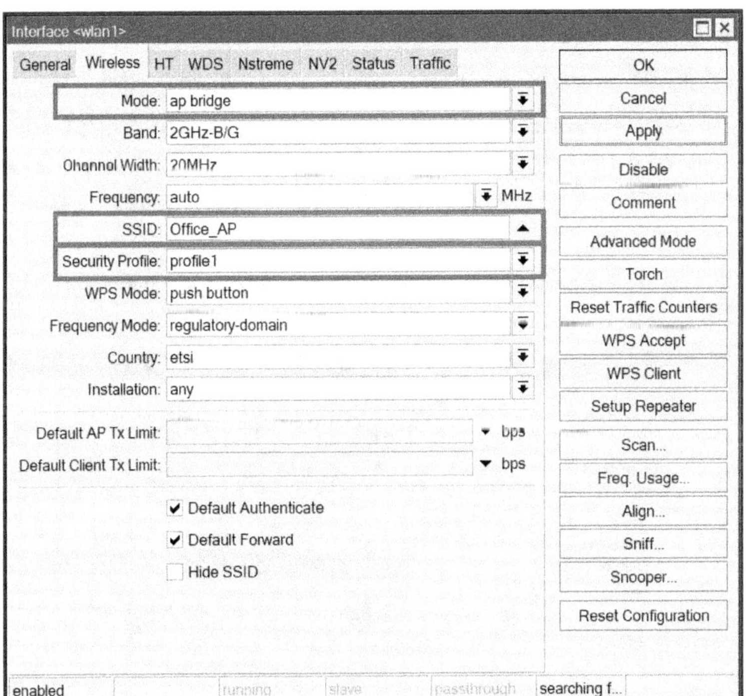

Click the **Enable** button and accept the message to commit or apply the configuration before enabling the interface.

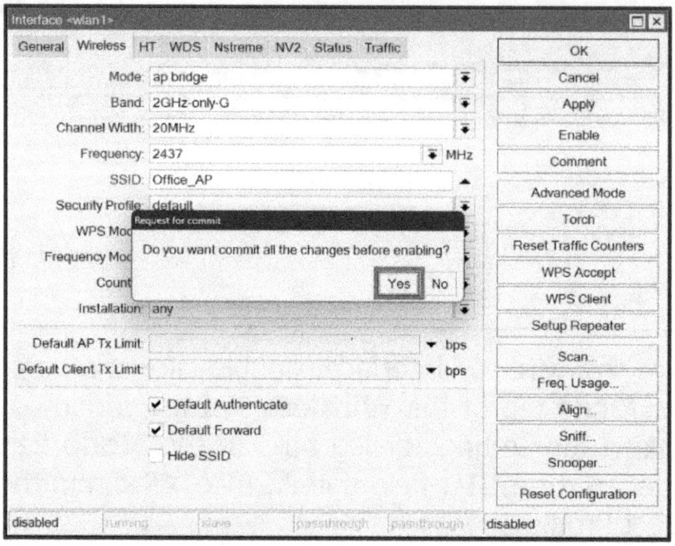

Then click the **OK** button to close this dialog box

To assign an IP address to the wireless interface, click the **IP** menu, then select **Addresses** to open the **Address List** window. Click the **Add** button to open the **New Address** dialog box. In the **Address** field, enter the IP address along with the subnet mask. 192.168.1.1/24. In the **Interface** field, select the interface wlan1. Then click the **OK** button to close this dialog box and assign the IP to the interface.

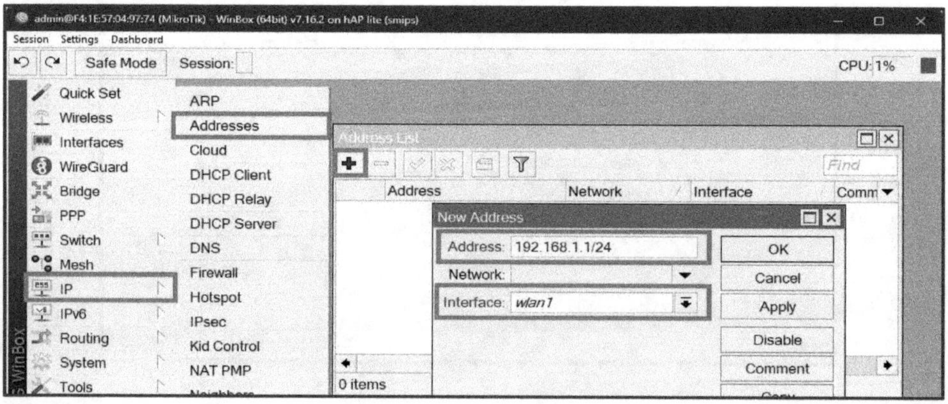

To configure DHCP server on the wireless interface, click the **IP** menu, then select **DHCP Server** to open the **DHCP Server** window. click the **DHCP Setup** button to open **DHCP Setup** dialog box. In **DHCP Server Interface** field Select the interface wlan1, and click the **Next** button in all other messages to accept the default settings and configure the DHCP Server.

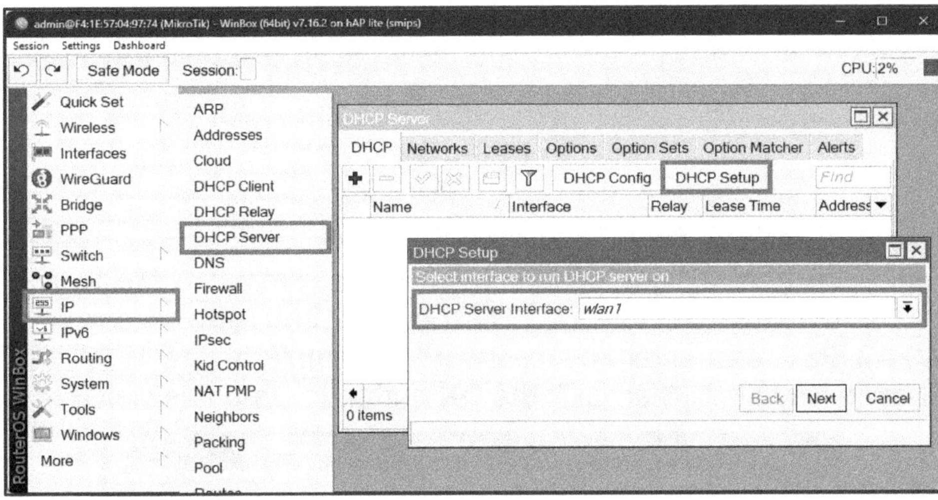

Wireless Station:

To configure the second device to function as a wireless station, click the **Wireless** menu, then select **Wireless** to open **Wireless Tables** window.

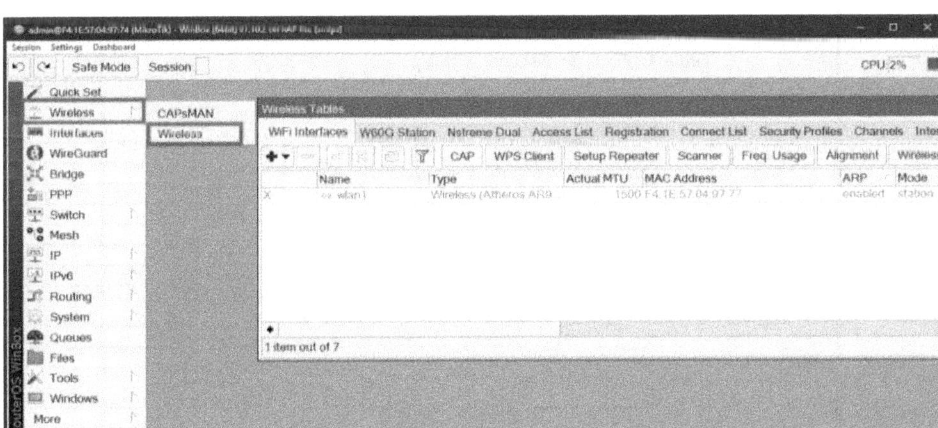

To create a security profile, click the **Add** button in the **Security Profiles** tab of the **Wireless Tables** window to open **New Security** profile dialog box.

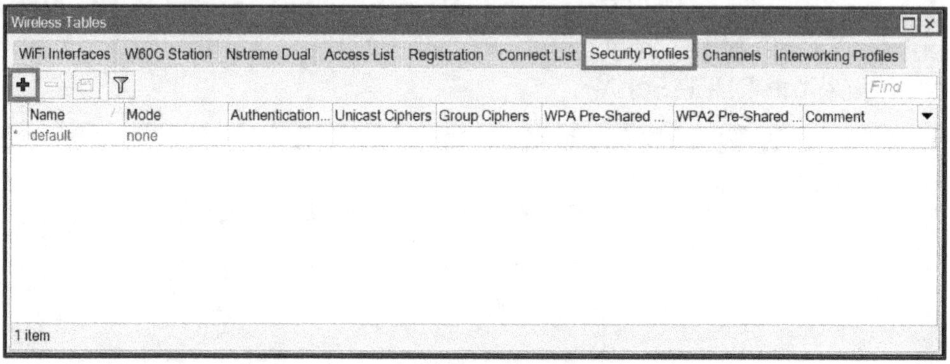

Leave the default name in the **Name** field. From the **Mode** field, choose Dynamic Key. From the **Authentication Type** section select **WPA2 PSK** and enter the password 12345678 in the **WPA Pre-Shared Key** field. Then click the **OK** button to close this dialog box.

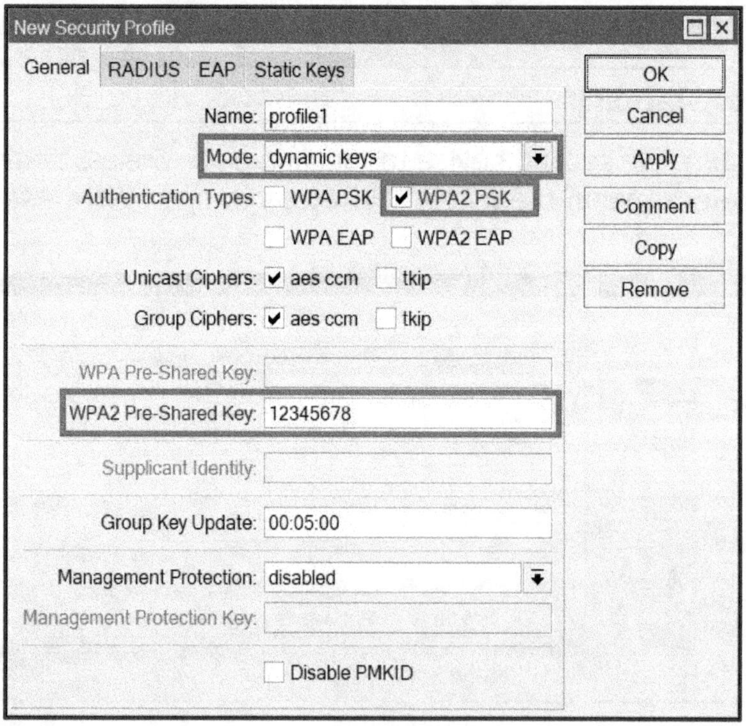

The new security profile will now appear in the **Security Profiles** tab.

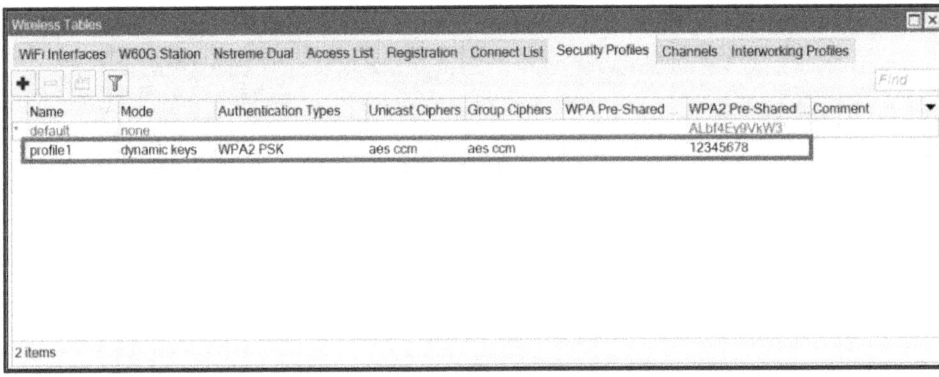

To configure the wireless interface, double-click the interface in the **Wi-Fi Interfaces** tab of the **Wireless Tables** window to open the wireless **Interface** settings dialog box. In the **Mode** field, select station mode. From the **Security Profile** select Profile1. Then, click the **Scan** button to open the **Scanner** dialog box.

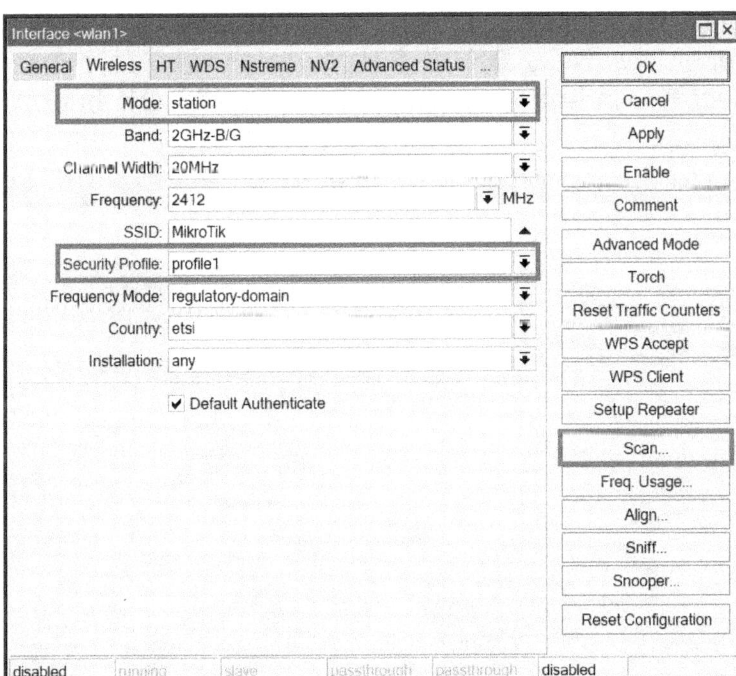

From the **Interface** field, select the wireless interface wlan1 and click the **Start** button to begin scanning and searching for available access points (AP). Then, select the access point (AP) **Office_AP** and click the **Connect** button to connect to this access point (AP).

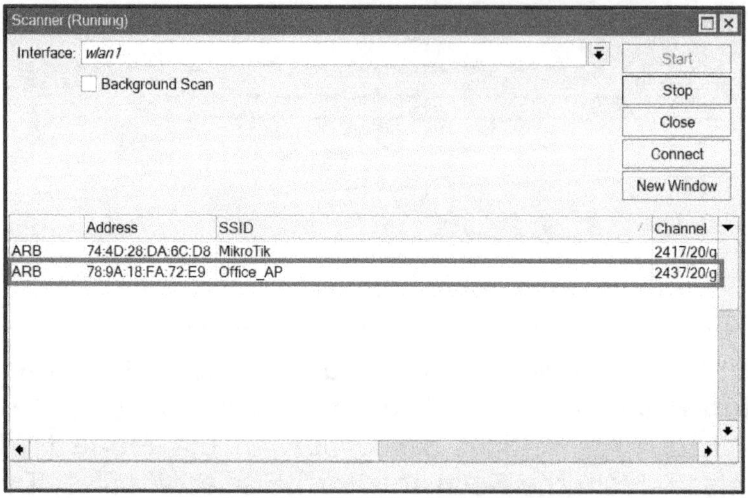

To configure DHCP client on the wireless interface, click the **IP** menu, then select **DHCP Client** to open the **DHCP Client** window. Click the **Add** to open the **New DHCP Client** dialog box. In the **Interface** field, select the interface wlan1. Then, click the **OK** button to close this dialog box.

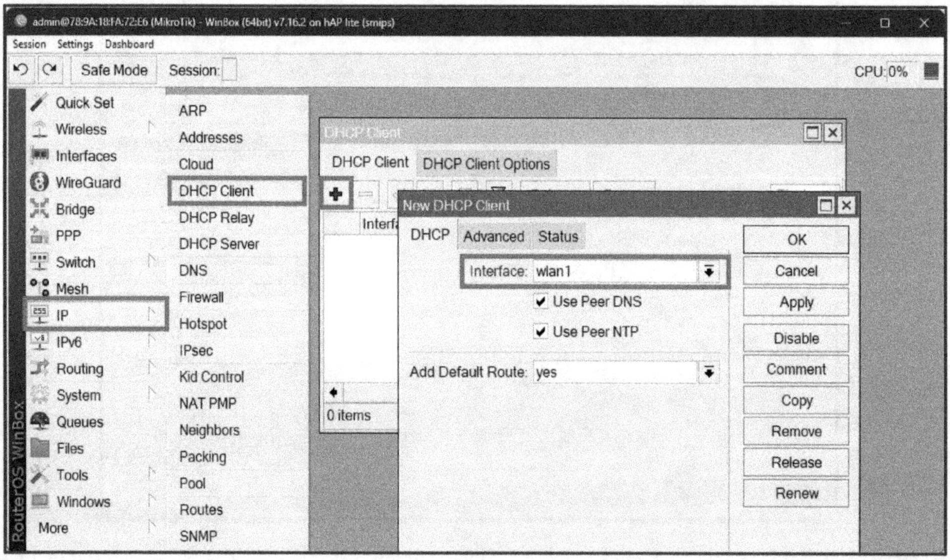

After completing the configuration, the wireless station will connect to the access point (AP) using the password you provide.

CLI

You can also make the configuration from the CLI .

Access Point (AP):

To create a security profile, use the following command:

```
interface wireless security-profiles add name=profile1 mode=dynamic-keys authentication-types=wpa2-psk wpa2-pre-shared-key=12345678
```

To configure the wireless interface, use the following commands

```
interface wireless set wlan1 mode=ap-bridge ssid=Office_AP security-profile=profile1

interface wireless enable wlan1
```

To assign an IP address to the wireless interface, use the following command

```
ip address add address=192.168.1.1/24 interface=wlan1
```

To configure DHCP server on the wireless interface using the DHCP setup wizard, use the following command, choose wireless interface and accept the default settings by pressing Enter each time the setup wizard asks for input

```
ip dhcp-server setup
```

Wireless Station:

To create a security profile, use the following command:

```
interface wireless security-profiles add name=profile1 mode=dynamic-keys authentication-types=wpa2-psk wpa2-pre-shared-key=12345678
```

To configure the wireless interface, use the following commands

```
interface wireless set wlan1 mode=station ssid=Office_AP security-profile=profile1

interface wireless enable wlan1
```

To configure DHCP client on the wireless interface, use the following command

```
ip dhcp-client add interface=wlan1
```

5.13 Access List

The Access List is a tool used by the access point (AP) to control which wireless station is allowed or denied access to the access point (AP).

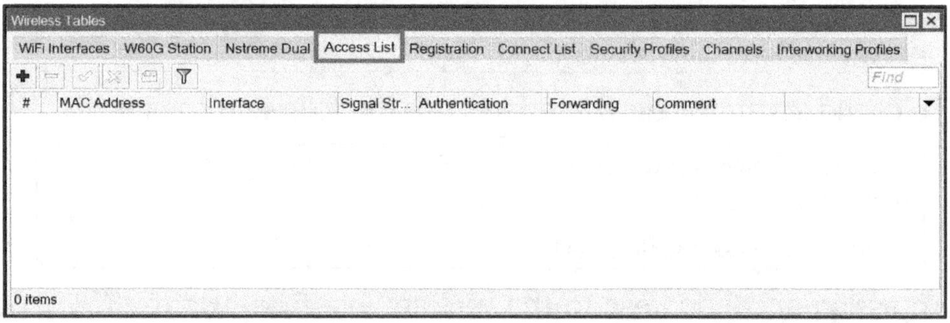

To add a wireless station to the access list, Click the **Add** button in the **Access List** tab of the **Wireless Tables** window to open the **New AP Access** rule dialog box.

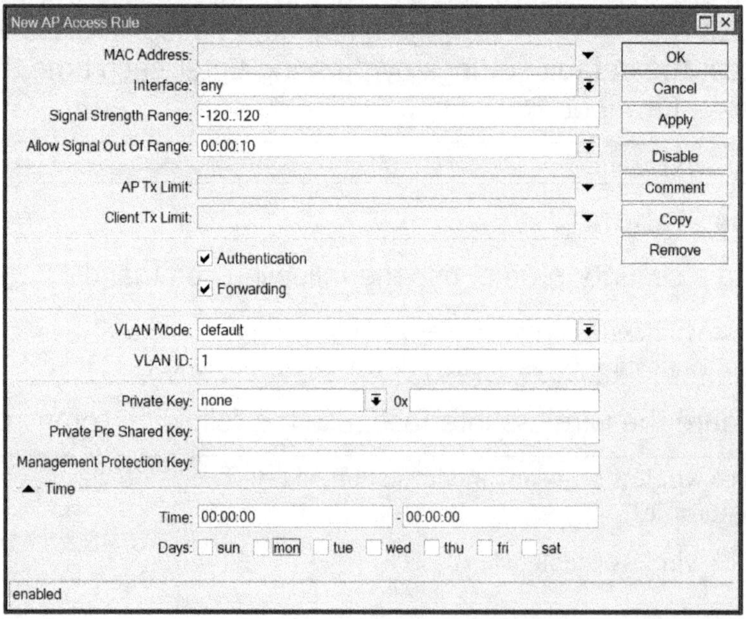

You can use this dialog box to create rules that control the access to the access point (AP), add devices to the list to either allow or deny them, and configure different access options.

To allow a wireless station to connect to the access point (AP), add the wireless station to the access list using its MAC Address, and check the **Authentication** check box, which permits access.

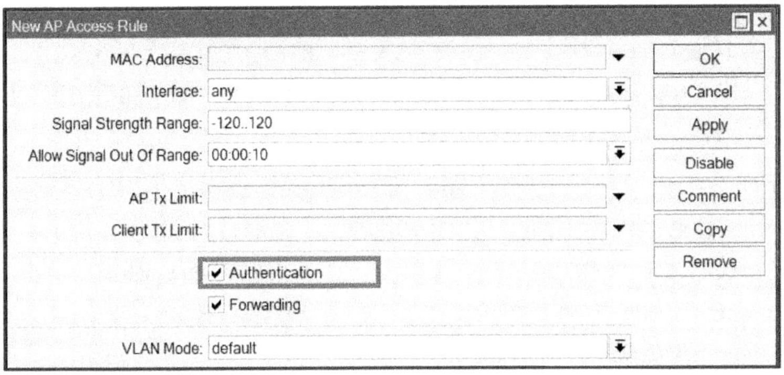

To deny a wireless station, add it to the list and uncheck the **Authentication** check box.

You can also use additional options, like allowing access during specific periods of the day or days of the week, or allowing the access based on the signal strength.

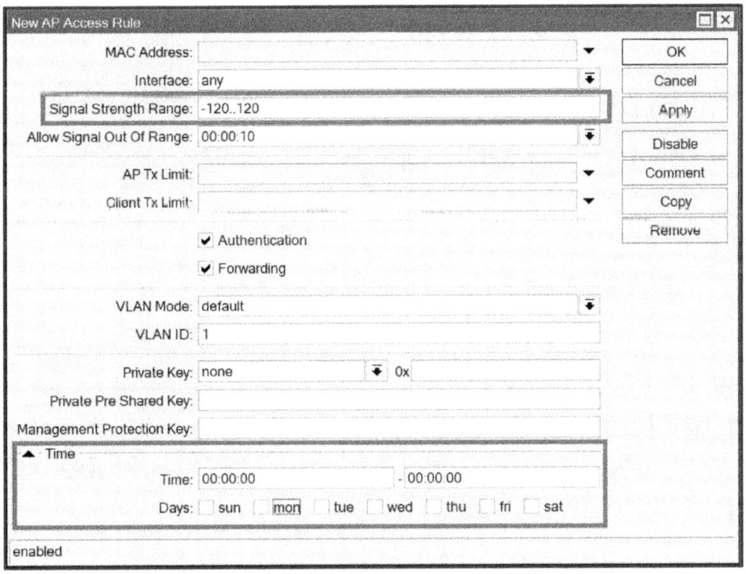

Rules in the Access List are processed in sequential order. This means that RouterOS will start by checking the first rule:

- If the connection matches the rule, the action (allow or deny) will be applied.
- If it does not match, RouterOS will move to the next rule, continuing until it reaches the end of the list.

Therefore, the order of the rules is very important. For example, if the first rule denies the connection and the second rule allows it, the connection will be denied because the first rule will be applied.

When adding an AP access rule, in default settings, this rule will be applied to the matching connections coming from any wireless interface. You can choose to apply the rule to a specific interface by selecting the desired interface from the **Interface** field (if the device has multiple wireless interfaces).

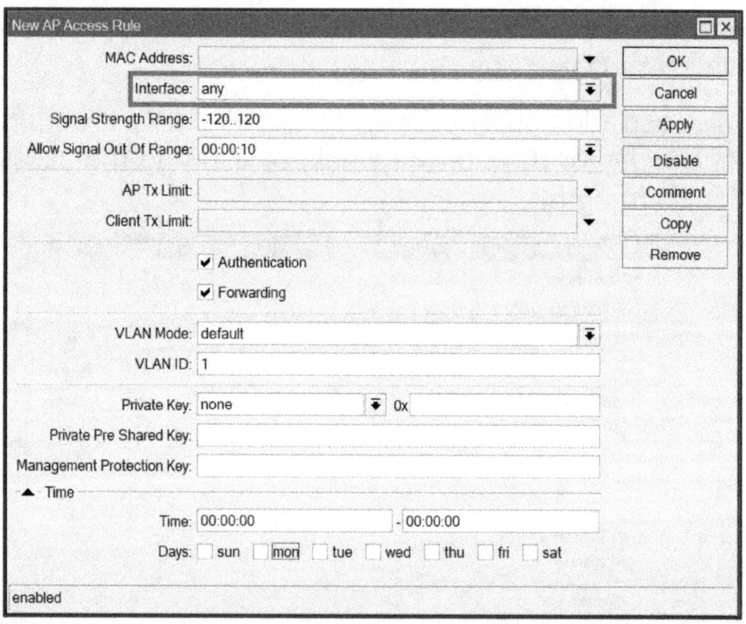

On the other hand, it is important to understand that if you do not specify a MAC address or use the address 00:00:00:00:00:00, the rule will be applied to any device.

You can also add a or create an AP access rule from the CLI using the following command:

```
interface wireless access-list add mac-address=[address]
authentication=[yes/no]
```

Where:

- [address] is the MAC address of the wireless station

For example:

```
interface wireless access-list add mac-address=74:4D:28:E6:9E:AD
authentication=no
```

```
Terminal <1>
[admin@MikroTik] >
[admin@MikroTik] >
[admin@MikroTik] >
[admin@MikroTik] > interface wireless access-list add mac-address=74:4D:28:E6:9E:AD authentication=no
```

To display the current AP access rules in RouterOS from the CLI use the following command:

```
interface wireless access-list print
```

```
Terminal <1>
[admin@MikroTik] >
[admin@MikroTik] > interface wireless access-list print
Flags: X - disabled
 0    mac-address=74:4D:28:E6:9E:AD interface=any signal-range=-120..120
      allow-signal-out-of-range=10s authentication=no forwarding=yes ap-tx-limit=0
      client-tx-limit=0 private-algo=none private-key="" private-pre-shared-key=""
      management-protection-key="" vlan-mode=default vlan-id=1
[admin@MikroTik] >
```

LAB

In this lab, you have two MikroTik devices. One device is configured to function as an access point (AP), and the other device is configured to function as a wireless station. You want to prevent the wireless station from connecting to the access point (AP) by using an access list in the access point (AP), (creating a new AP access rule by the MAC address of this station, and unchecking the Authentication checkbox).

To start the configuration:

- First: perform the basic configuration to set up the first device as an access point (AP) and the other device as a wireless station.

- Second: configure (or create) a new AP access rule in the access point (AP) to prevent the connection.

Basic Configuration

In the access point (AP) device:

Configure the wireless interface by setting its **mode** to ap bridge and enabling it.

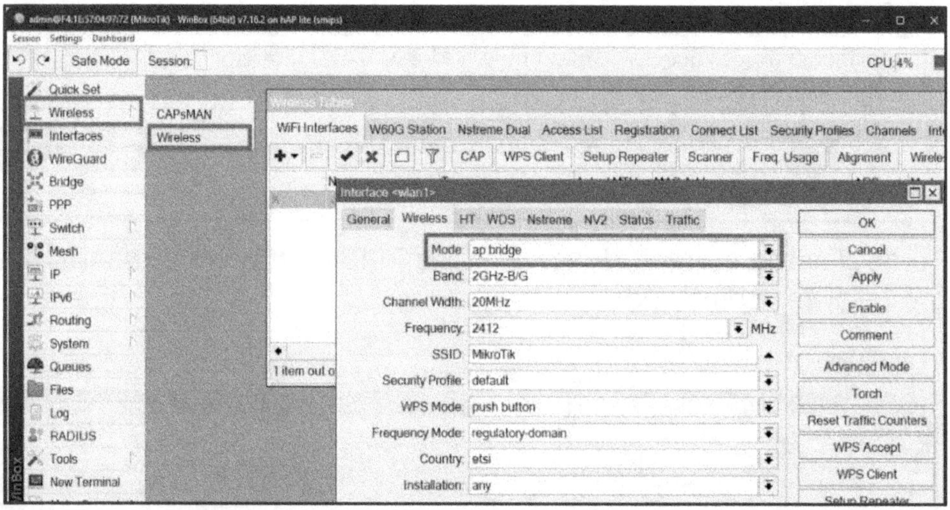

Assign the IP address 192.168.1.1/24 to the wireless interface.

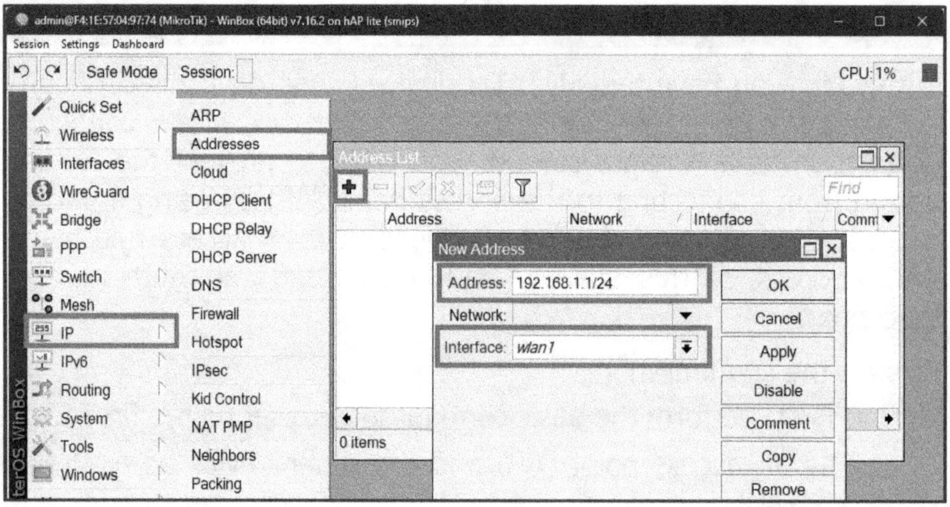

Configure a DHCP server on the wireless interface.

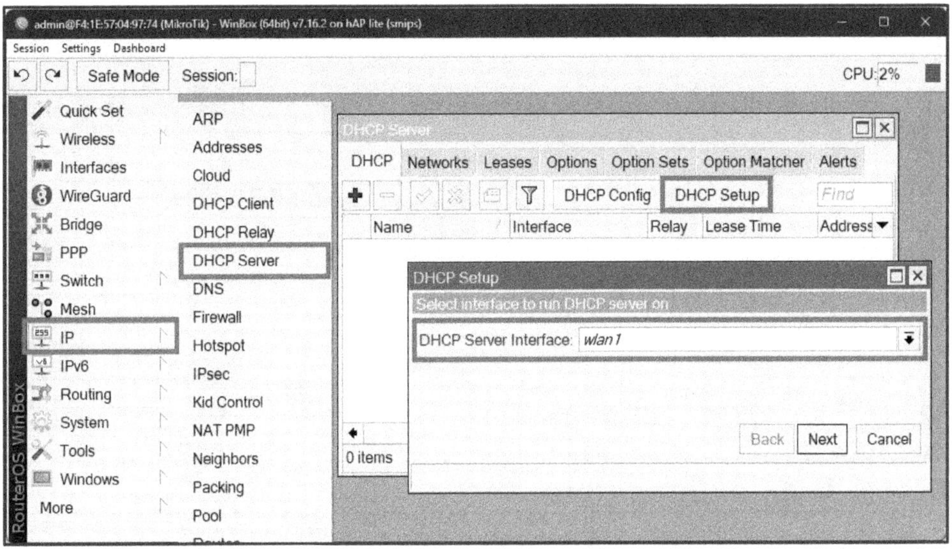

In the station device:

Configure the wireless interface by setting its **mode** to Station and enabling it.

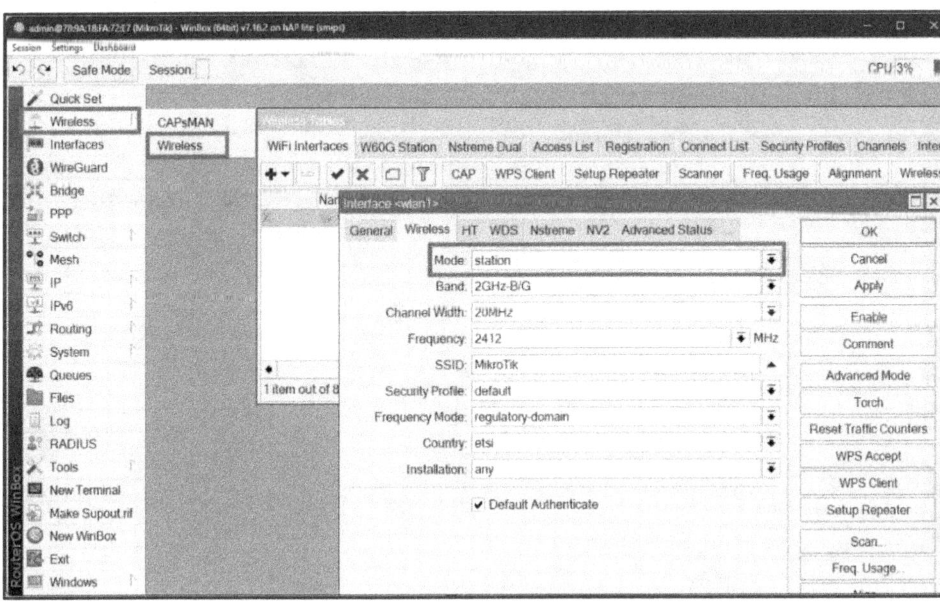

Configure a DHCP client on the wireless interface.

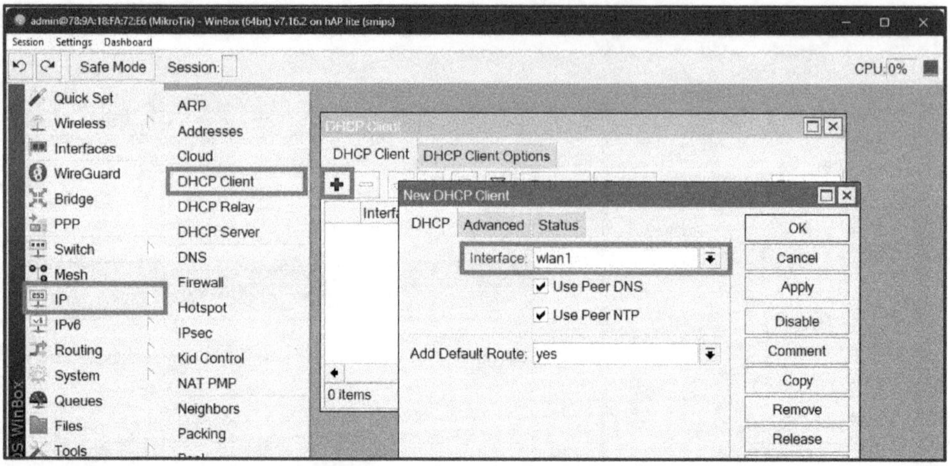

Access List Configuration

In the access point (AP) device:

To add a new AP access rule to prevent the wireless station from connecting to the access point (AP), click the **Add** button in the **Access List** tab of the **Wireless Tables** window to open the **New AP Access Rule** dialog box.

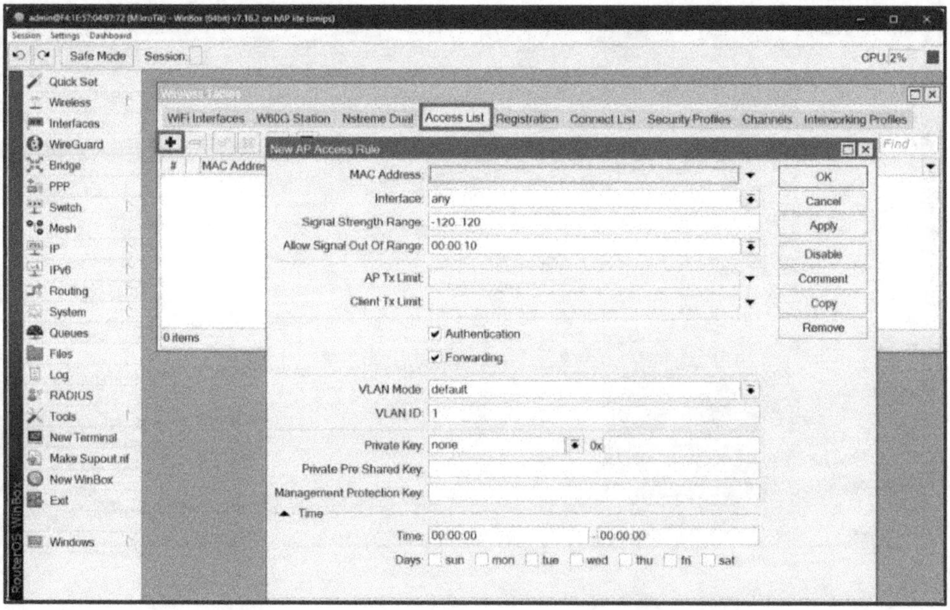

In the **MAC Address** field, enter the MAC address of the wireless station device, and uncheck the **Authentication** checkbox.

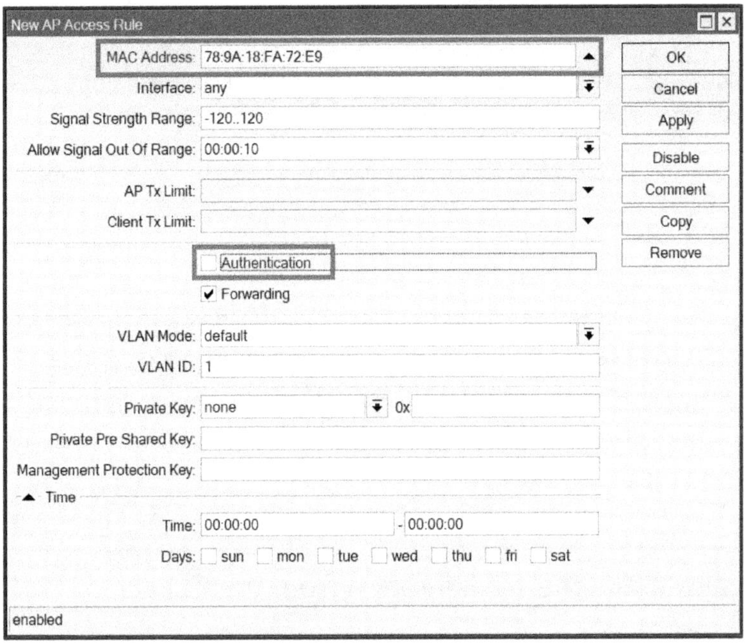

You can find the MAC address of the wireless station in the **General** tab of the wireless **Interface** settings dialog box on the wireless station device.

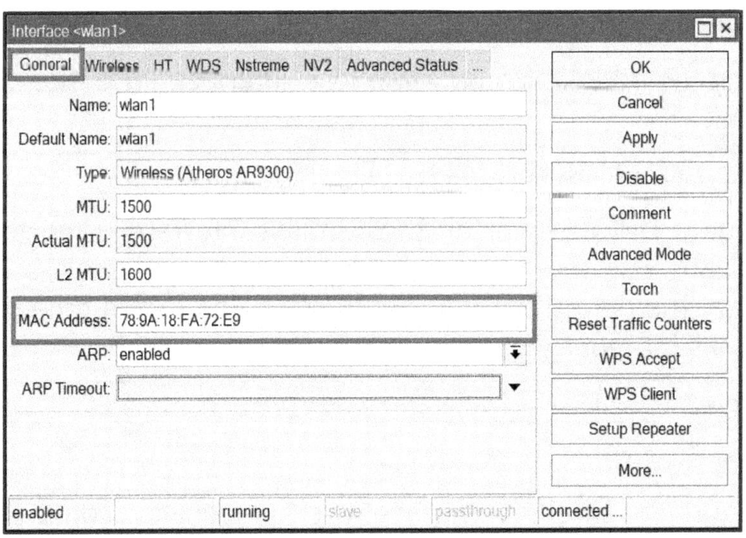

After adding the AP access rule, it will appear in the **Access List** tab.

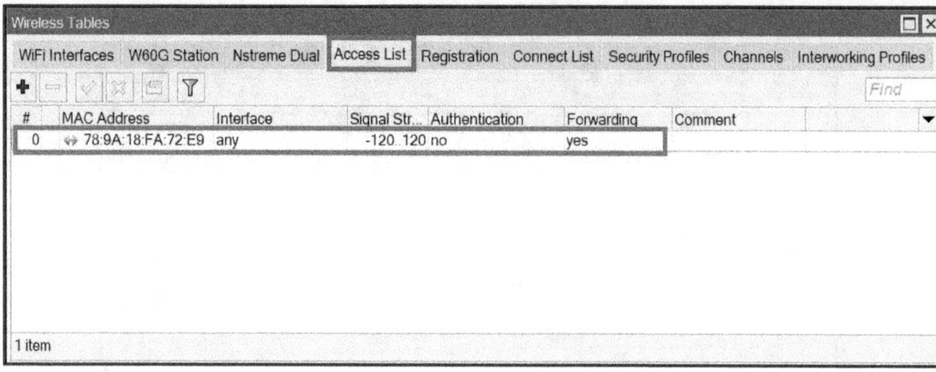

Now, if the wireless station device tries to connect to this access point (AP), the access point (AP) will check the access list and find rule matches this device. Since the rule prevents the connection, the connection will be denied.

CLI

You can also make the configuration from the CLI.

Access point (AP):

To configure the wireless interface, use the following commands:

```
interface wireless set wlan1 mode=ap-bridge
interface wireless enable wlan1
```

To assign IP address to the wireless interface, use the following command:

```
ip address add address=192.168.1.1/24 interface=wlan1
```

To configure DHCP server on the wireless interface using the DHCP setup wizard, use the following command, choose wireless interface and accept the default settings by pressing Enter each time the setup wizard asks for input

```
ip dhcp-server setup
```

Wireless Station:

To configure the wireless interface, use the following commands:

```
interface wireless set wlan1 mode=station ssid=MikroTik
interface wireless enable wlan1
```

To configure DHCP client on the wireless interface, use the following command:

```
ip dhcp-client add interface=wlan1
```

To create an AP access rule, first get the MAC address of the wireless station using the following command in the wireless station CLI:

```
interface wireless access-list print
```

Then use the following command to create an AP access rule in the access point (AP):

```
interface wireless access-list add mac-address=78:9A:15:FA:72:E9
authentication=no
```

5.14 Connect List

The Connect List is a tool used by the wireless station device to determine which access points (AP) are allowed or denied to connect to.

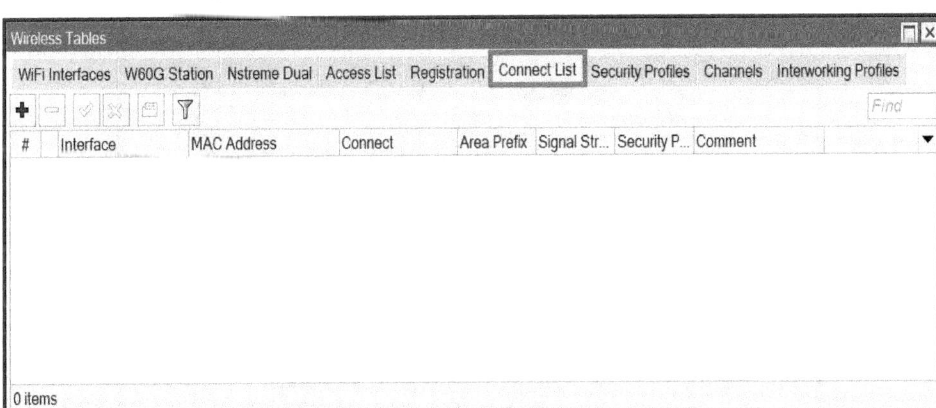

To add an access point (AP) to the Connect List, click the **Add** button in the **Connect List** tab of the **Wireless Tables** window to open the **New Station Connect Rule** dialog box.

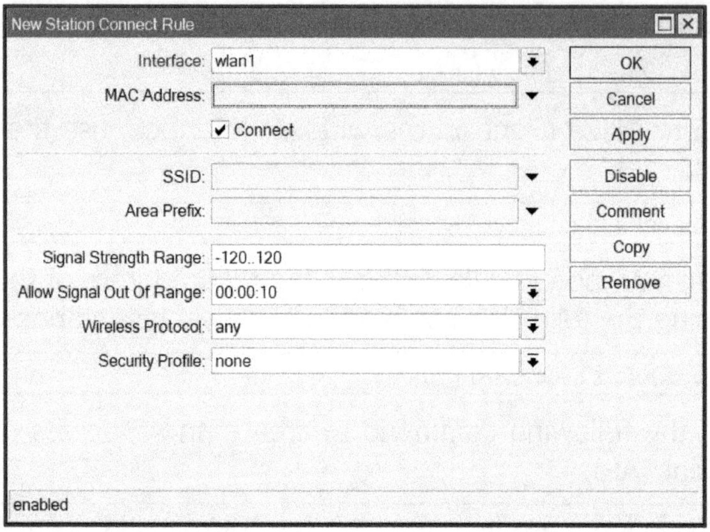

You can use this dialog box to create rules that control connections to the access point (AP), add the access point (AP) to the list to either allow or deny the connection, and configure different connection options.

To allow a connection to an access point (AP), add the access point (AP) to the connect list by its **MAC Address** or its **SSID**, and check the **Connect** check box, which permits the connection.

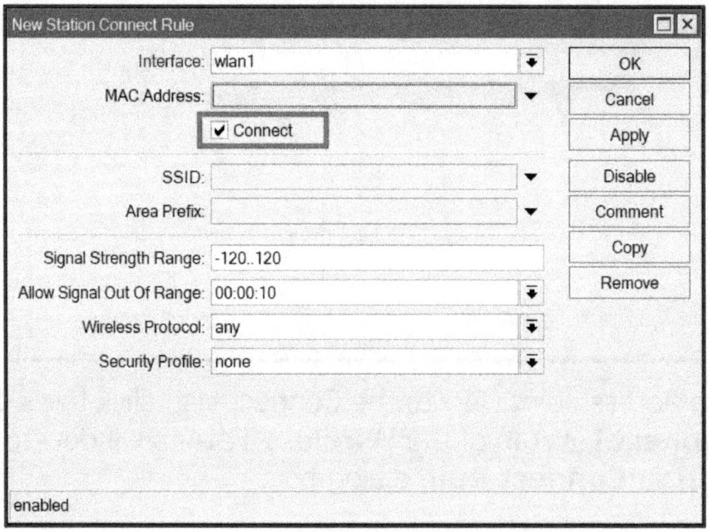

To deny the connection to an access point (AP), add it to the list and uncheck the **Connect** option. In this case the wireless station will not try to connect to this access point (AP).

Rules in the connect list are processed in sequential order. This means that RouterOS will start by checking the first rule:

- If the connection matches the rule, the action (allow or deny) will be applied.
- If it does not match, RouterOS will move to the next rule, continuing until it reaches the end of the list.

Therefore, the order of the rules is very important. For example, if the first rule denies the connection and the second rule allows it, the connection will be denied because the first rule will be applied.

You can use the order of rules to prioritize the preferred access points (AP) to connect to, by placing the preferred one at the top of the list.

When adding a station connect rule, you must specify the desired interface to which this rule will be applied by selecting the interface from the **Interface** field. (if the device has multiple wireless interfaces).

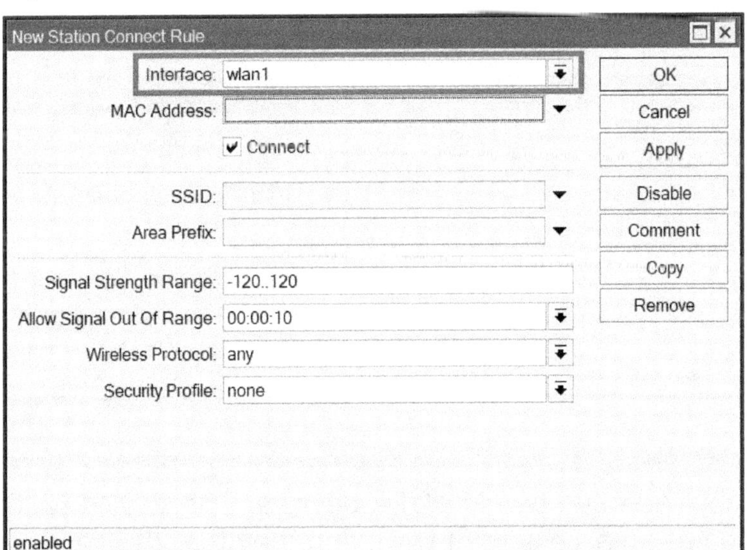

On the other hand, it is important to understand that if you do not specify an SSID, a MAC address or use the address 00:00:00:00:00:00, the rule will be applied to any device.

You can also add a or create a station connect rule to the connect list from the CLI using the following command:

```
interface wireless connect-list add mac-address=[address]
interface=[interface] connect=[yes/no]
```

Where:

- [address] is the MAC address of the access point (AP)
- [interface] is the interface to which this rule will be applied.

For example:

```
interface wireless connect-list add mac-address=74:4D:28:E6:9E:AD
interface=wlan1 connect=no
```

```
Terminal <1>
[admin@MikroTik] >
[admin@MikroTik] >
[admin@MikroTik] >
[admin@MikroTik] > interface wireless connect-list add mac-address=74:4D:28:E6:9E:AD interface=wlan1 connect=no
```

To display the current station connect rules in RouterOS from the CLI use the following command:

```
interface wireless connect-list print
```

```
Terminal <1>
[admin@MikroTik] >
[admin@MikroTik] > interface wireless connect-list print
Flags: X - disabled
 0   interface=wlan1 connect=no mac-address=74:4D:28:E6:9E:AD ssid=""
     signal-range=-120..120 allow-signal-out-of-range=10s
     area-prefix="" security-profile=none wireless-protocol=any
     interworking=any iw-network-type=wildcard iw-venue=any
     iw-hessid=00:00:00:00:00:00 iw-internet=any iw-asra=any
     iw-esr=any iw-uesa=any iw-hotspot20=any iw-hotspot20-dgaf=any
     iw-roaming-ois="" iw-ipv4-availability=any
     iw-ipv6-availability=any 3gpp=""
[admin@MikroTik] >
```

LAB

In this lab, you have two MikroTik devices. One device is configured to function as an access point (AP), and the other device is configured to function as a wireless station. You want to prevent the wireless station from connecting to this access point (AP) by using Connect List in the wireless station device, (creating a new Station Connect rule by the MAC address of this access point (AP), and unchecking the **Connect** checkbox).

To start the configuration:

- First: perform the basic configuration to set up the first device as an access point (AP) and the other device as a wireless station
- Second: configure (or create) a new station connect rule in the wireless station device to prevent the connection.

Basic Configuration

In the access point (AP) device:

Configure the wireless interface by setting its **mode** to ap bridge and enabling it.

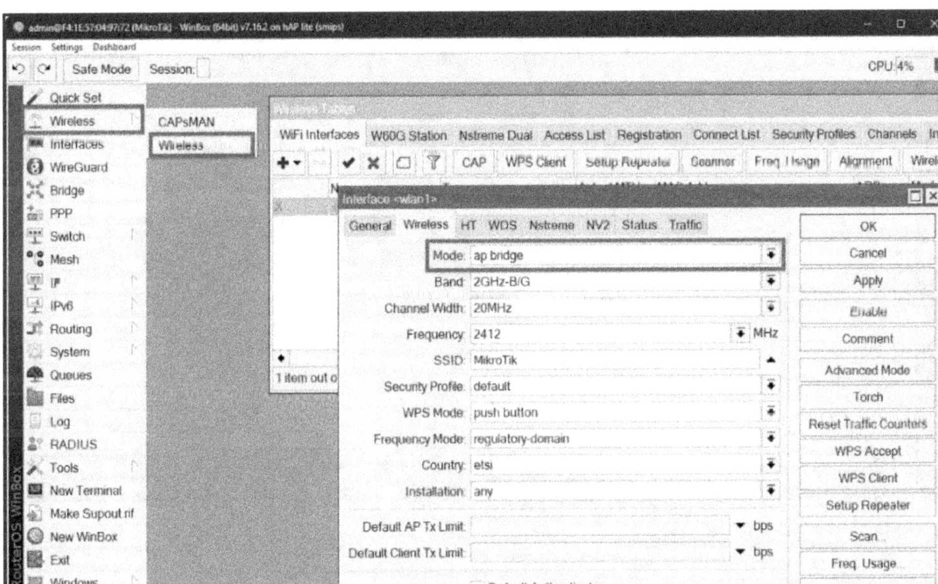

Assign the IP address 192.168.1.1/24 to the wireless interface.

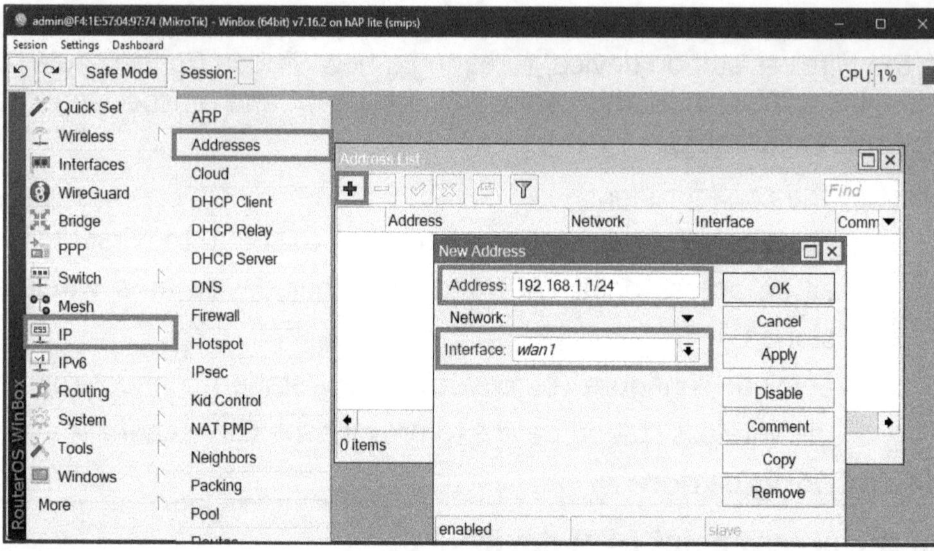

Configure a DHCP Server on the wireless interface.

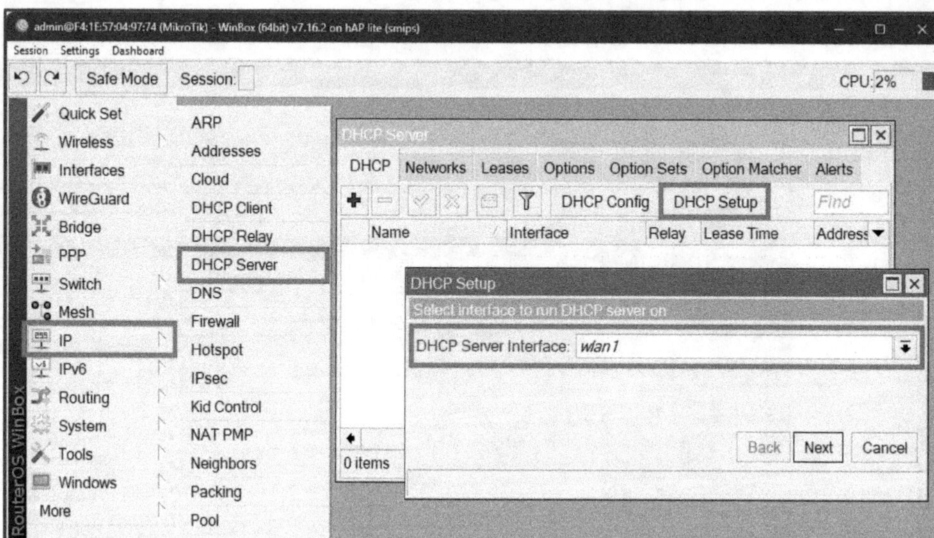

In the station device:

Configure the wireless interface by setting its **mode** to Station and enabling it.

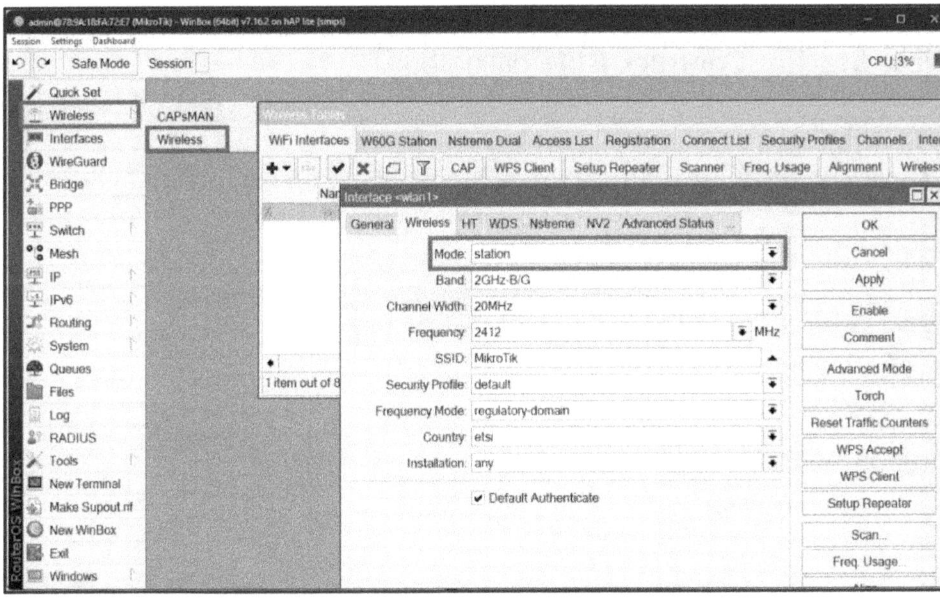

Configure a DHCP client on the wireless interface.

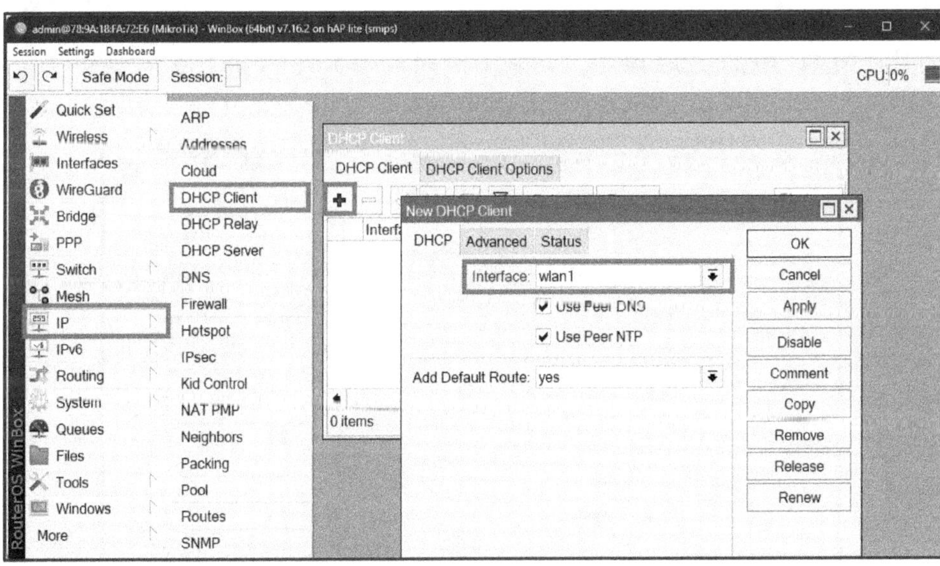

Connect List Configuration

In the wireless station device:

To add a new station connect rule to prevent the wireless station device from connecting to the access point (AP), click the **Add** button in the **Connect List** tab of the **Wireless Tables** window to open the **New Station Connect Rule** dialog box.

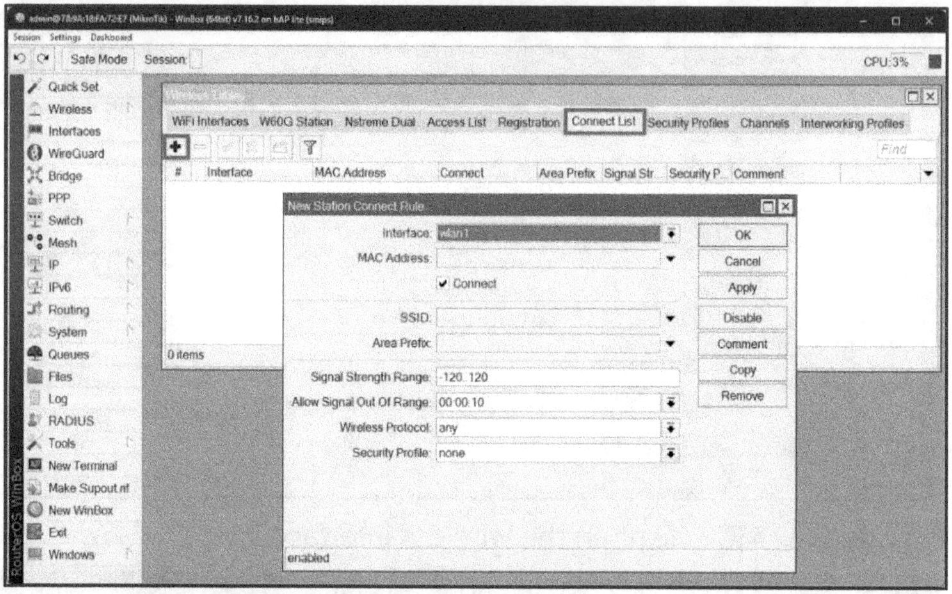

In the **MAC Address** field, enter the MAC address of the Access point (AP) device, and uncheck the **Connect** checkbox.

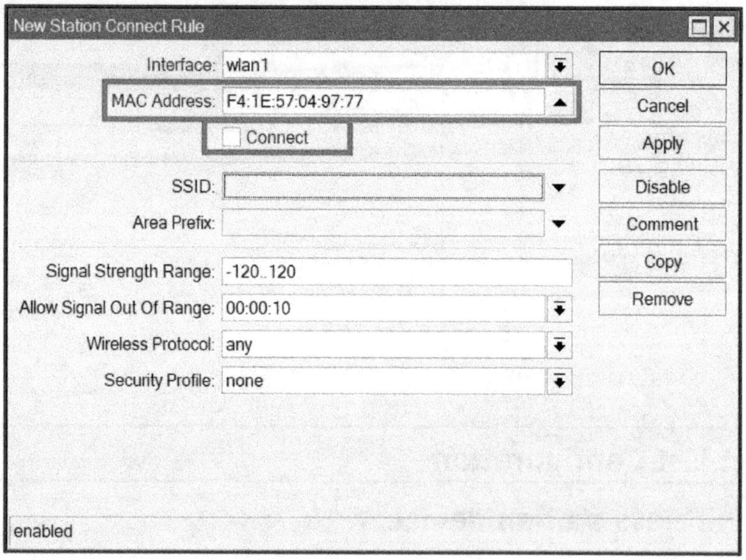

You can find the MAC address of the access point (AP) device in the **General** tab of the wireless **Interface** settings dialog box on the access point (AP) device.

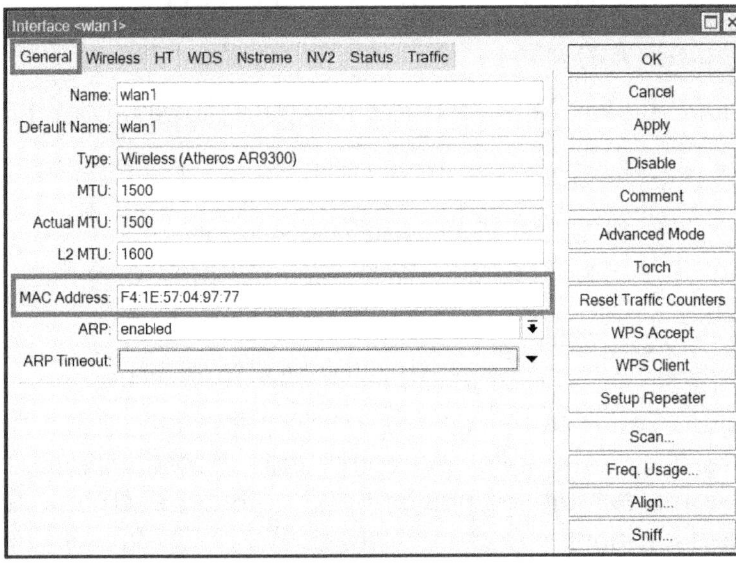

After adding the Station Connect rule, it will appear in the **Connect List** tab.

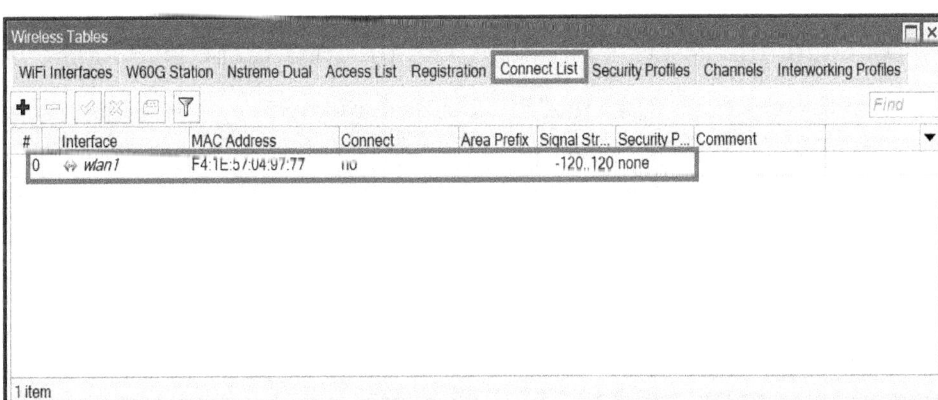

Now, if the wireless station device tries to connect to this Access Point (AP), the wireless station will check the connect list and find a rule matches this access point (AP). Since the rule prevents the connection, the connection will be denied.

CLI

You can also make the configuration from the CLI.

Access point (AP):

To configure the wireless interface, use the following commands:

```
interface wireless set wlan1 mode=ap-bridge
interface wireless enable wlan1
```

To assign IP address to the wireless interface, use the following command:

```
ip address add address=192.168.1.1/24 interface=wlan1
```

To configure DHCP server on the wireless interface using the DHCP setup wizard, use the following command, choose wireless interface and accept the default settings by pressing Enter each time the setup wizard asks for input

```
ip dhcp-server setup
```

Wireless Station:

To configure the wireless interface, use the following commands:

```
interface wireless set wlan1 mode=station ssid=MikroTik
interface wireless enable wlan1
```

To configure DHCP client on the wireless interface, use the following command:

```
ip dhcp-client add interface=wlan1
```

To create a station connect rule, first get the MAC address of the access point (AP) using the following command in the access point (AP) CLI:

```
interface wireless access-list print
```

Then use the following command to create a station connect rule in the wireless station:

```
interface wireless connect-list add mac-address= F4:1E:57:04:97:77
interface=wlan1 connect=no
```

5.15 Easy Way to Create Rules

Instead of writing the MAC address of the access point (AP) or the wireless station, you can use the **Registration** tab of the W**ireless Tables** window to easily create AP access rules and station connect rules. Simply double-click on the device in the **Registration** tab to open the **AP Client** dialog box, then click the **Copy to Access List** button or the **Copy to Connect List** button.

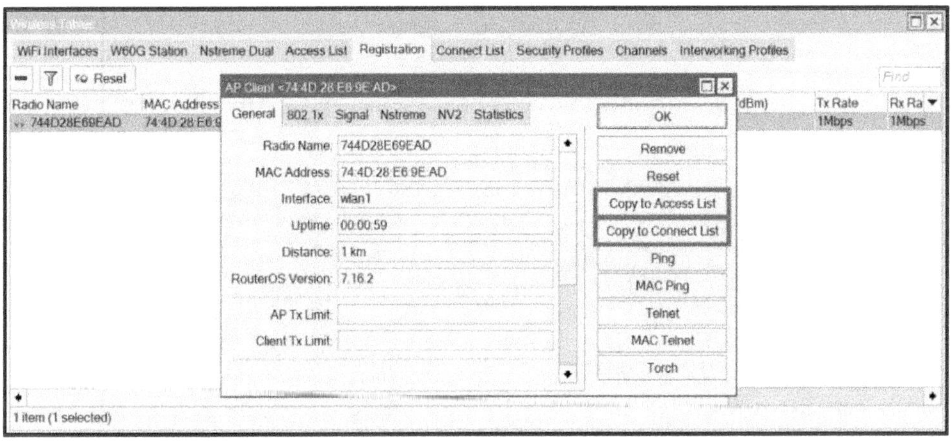

That will automatically create a rule with the details of this device. Then, you can open the rule to make any configuration changes.

5.16 Default Authenticate

From the Perspective of the Access Point

In the default settings, using default authentication option, when a wireless station device tries to connect to this access point (AP), the access point (AP) will check the Access List:

- If the device is added to the Access List and it is allowed to connect, the access point (AP) will allow the connection.
- If the device is added to the Access List but is not allowed to connect, the access point (AP) will deny the connection.

- If the device is not added to the Access List, the access point (AP) will allow the connection.

That means even if the wireless station device is not added to the Access List, it still can connect to the access point (AP).

If you want to allow only the wireless station devices added to the Access List, you need to uncheck the **Default Authenticate** checkbox in the **Wireless** tab of the wireless **Interface** settings dialog box.

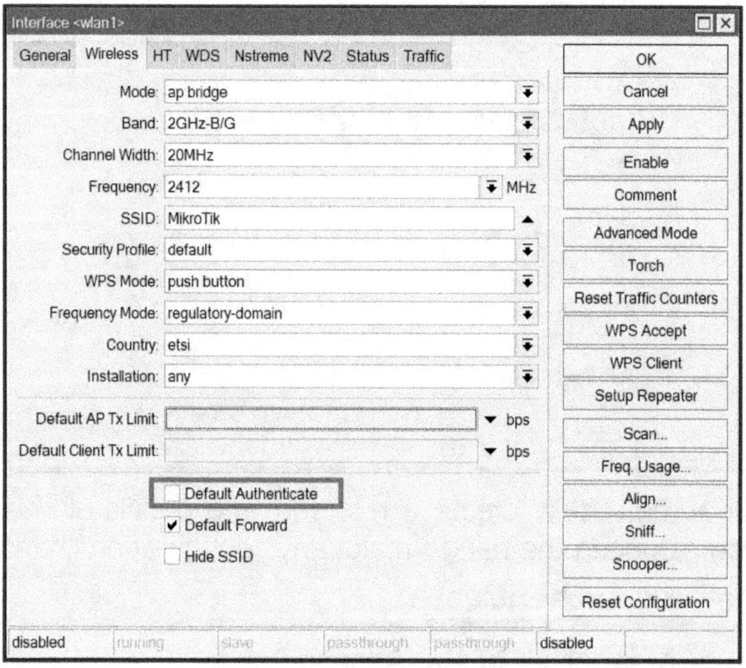

In this case when a wireless station device tries to connect to this access point (AP), the access point (AP) will check the Access List.

- If the device is added to the Access List and it is allowed to connect, the access point (AP) will allow the connection.
- If the device is added to the Access List but is not allowed to connect, the access point (AP) will deny the connection.
- If the device is not added to the Access List, the access point (AP) will deny the connection.

From the Perspective of the Station

In the default settings, using the default authentication option, when a wireless station device tries to connect to an access point (AP), the device will check the Connect List.

- If the access point (AP) is added to the Connect List and is allowed to connect to, the device will allow the connection.
- If the access point (AP) is added to the Connect List but is not allowed to connect to, the device will deny the connection.
- If the access point (AP) is not added to the Connect List, the device will allow the connection.

This means even if the access point (AP) is not added to the Connect List, the device still can connect to it.

If you want to allow the connection only to the access points (AP) that are added to the Connect List, you need to uncheck the **Default Authenticate** checkbox in the **Wireless** tab of the wireless **Interface** settings dialog box.

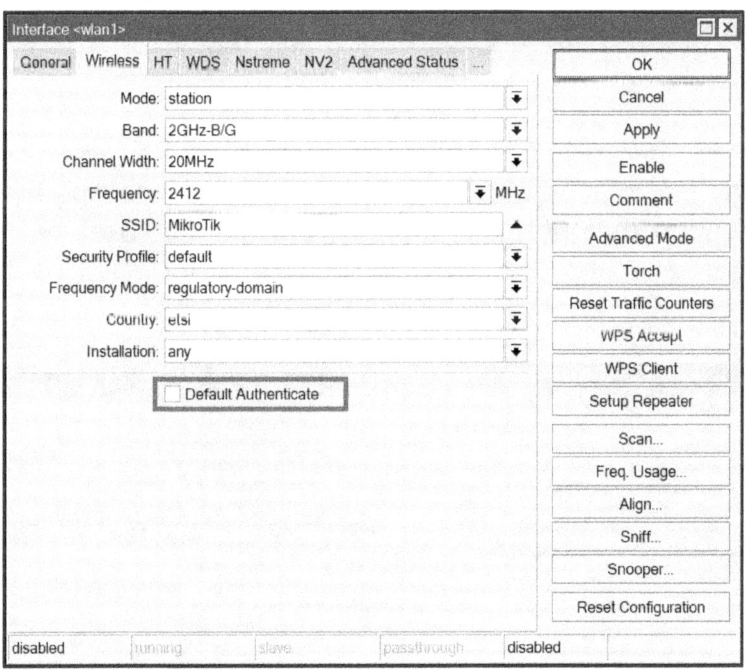

In this case, when the wireless station device tries to connect to an access point (AP), the device will check the Connect List.

- If the access point (AP) is added to the Connect List and is allowed to connect to, the device will allow the connection.
- If the access point (AP) is added to the Connect List but is not allowed to connect to, the device will deny the connection.
- If the access point (AP) is not added to the Connect List, the device will deny the connection.

You can also configure the default authentication option from the CLI using the following command:

```
interface wireless set [interface name] default-authentication[yes/no]
```

Where:

- [interface name] is the name of the wireless interface.

For example:

```
interface wireless set wlan1 default-authentication=no
```

```
Terminal <1>
[admin@MikroTik] >
[admin@MikroTik] >
[admin@MikroTik] >
[admin@MikroTik] > interface wireless set wlan1 default-authentication=no
```

To display information about wireless interfaces including the default authentication options in RouterOS from the CLI use the following command:

```
interface wireless print
```

```
Terminal <1>
[admin@MikroTik] > interface wireless print
Flags: X - disabled; R - running
 0    name="wlan1" mtu=1500 l2mtu=1600 mac-address=78:9A:18:FA:72:E9
      arp=enabled interface-type=Atheros AR9300 mode=ap-bridge
      ssid="Office_AP" frequency=2437 band=2ghz-onlyg
      channel-width=20mhz secondary-frequency="" scan-list=default
      wireless-protocol=any vlan-mode=no-tag vlan-id=1 wds-mode=disabled
      wds-default-bridge=none wds-ignore-ssid=no bridge-mode=enabled
      default-authentication=no default-forwarding=yes
      default-ap-tx-limit=0 default-client-tx-limit=0 hide-ssid=no
      security-profile=default compression=no
[admin@MikroTik] >
```

5.17 Default Forward

In the default settings, with the Default Forward option, wireless station devices connected to the same Access point (AP) can communicate with each other.

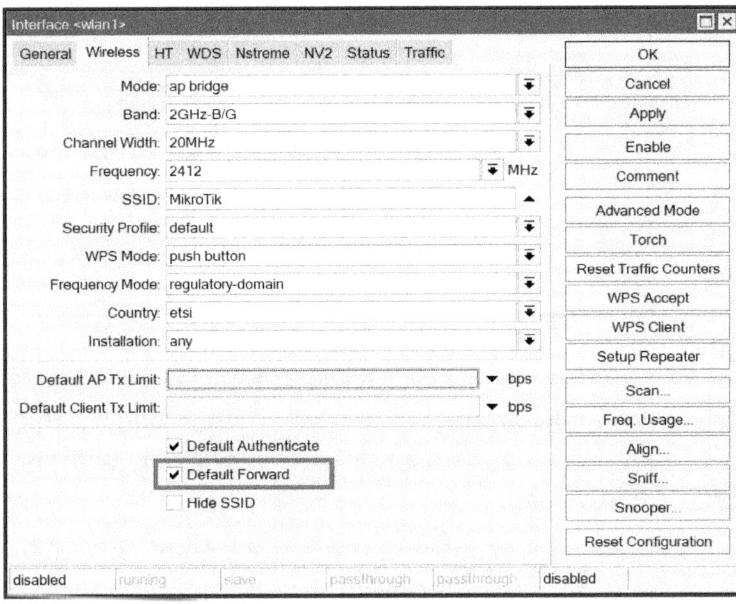

If you want to prevent wireless stations from communicating with each other, you need to uncheck the **Default Forward** checkbox in the **Wireless** tab of the wireless **Interface** settings dialog box on the Access point (AP) device.

Note: This checkbox is only available on the Access point (AP) device

You can also configure the default forwarding option from the CLI using the following command:

```
interface wireless set [interface name] default- forwarding [yes/no]
```

Where:

- [interface name] is the name of the wireless interface.

For example:

```
interface wireless set wlan1 default-forwarding=no
```

To display information about wireless interfaces including the default forwarding options in RouterOS from the CLI use the following command:

```
interface wireless print
```

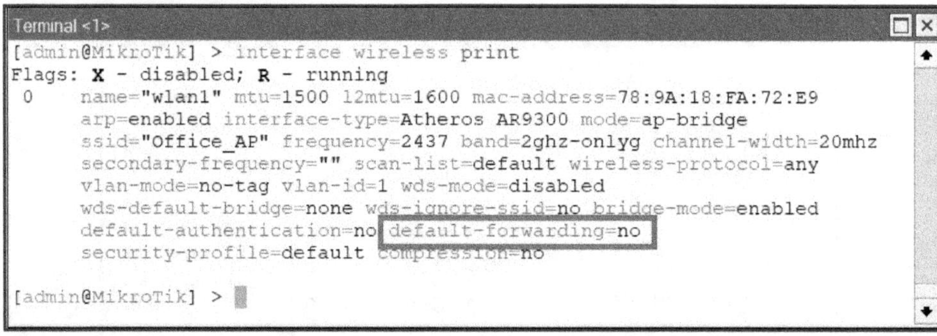

5.18 WPS

WPS (Wi-Fi Protected Setup) is a feature that allows the wireless station to connect to an access point (AP) very easily without entering a password or a key.

When pressing the WPS button on the access point (AP) device, it will allow the first WPS-supported device that tries to connect within two minutes without entering the password.

MikroTik RouterBOARD supports the WPS Access feature for access points (AP), and also supports WPS Client for clients.

5.18.1 WPS Access

In MikroTik devices, there are two types of WPS access buttons:

- Physical Button:

  This button is located on the device itself.

- Soft Button:

  This button can be found in the Wireless **Interface** Settings dialog box.

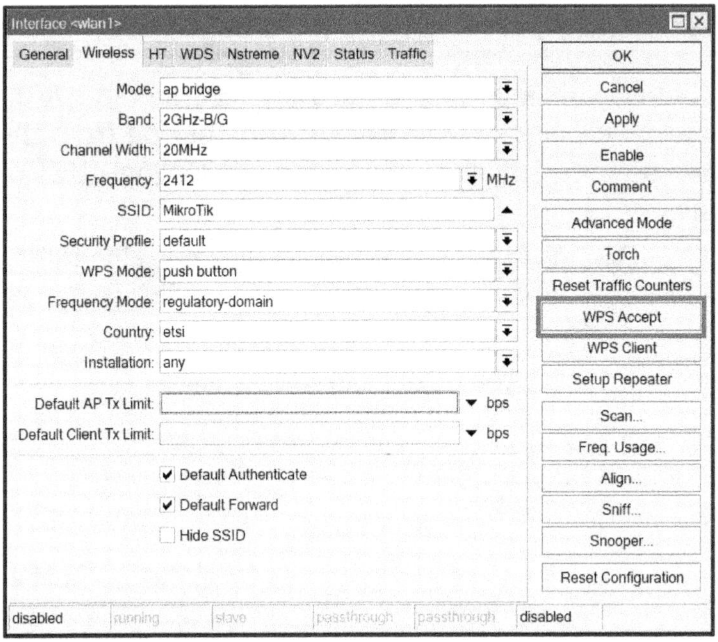

You can enable or disable the WPS button or adjust the default duration for WPS access from **WPS Mode** field.

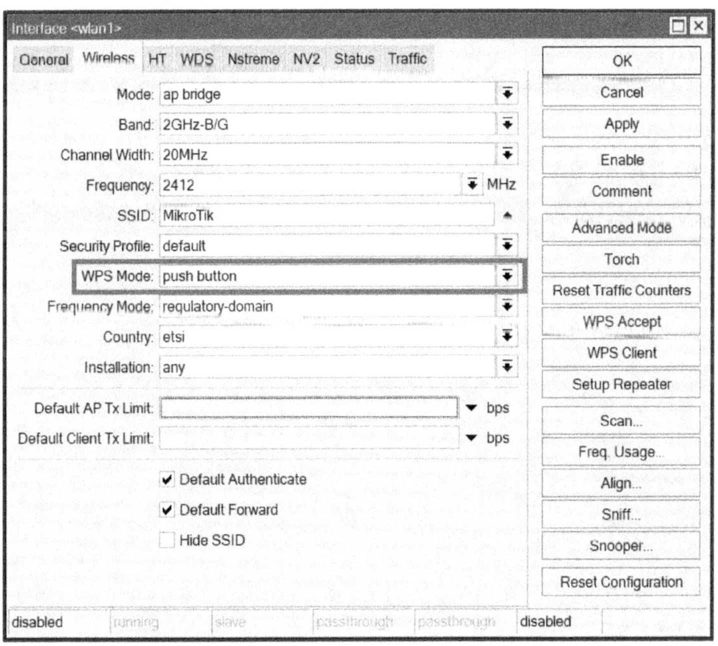

5.18.2 WPS Client

You can connect a MikroTik station to an access point (AP) using the WPS feature by clicking on the **WPS Client** button from the wireless **Interface** settings dialog box and following the on-screen instructions.

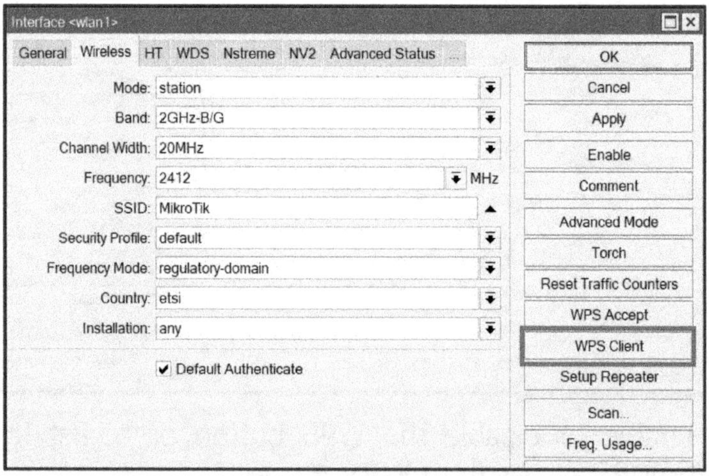

Note: for security reasons, it is recommended to disable WPS.

5.19 Snooper

The Snooper tool is used to display information about wireless networks in the area and their frequency usage.

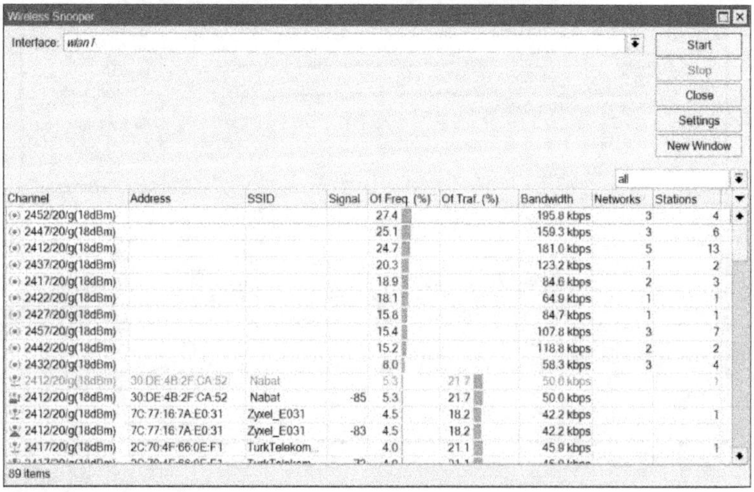

You can open the **Snooper** tool dialog box by clicking the **Snooper button** in the wireless **Interface** settings dialog box or the **Wireless Snooper** button in the **Wireless Tables** window.

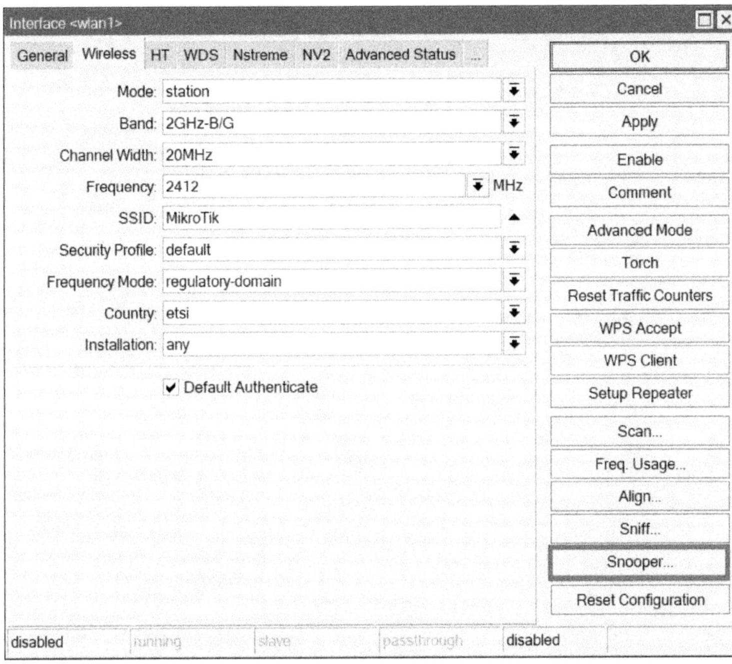

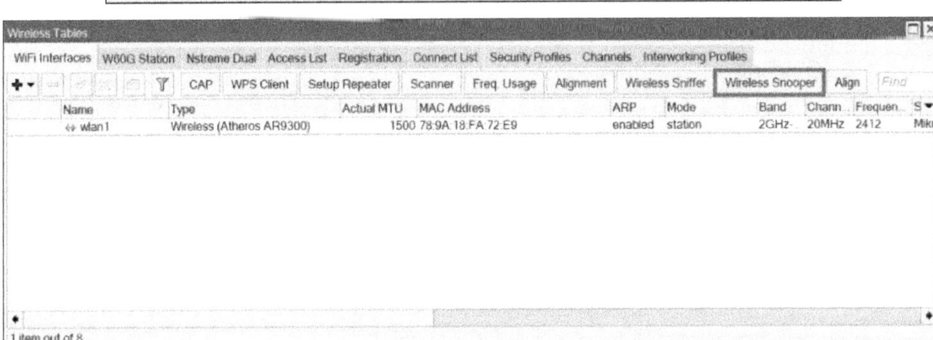

You will learn more about this tool and other wireless tools in the MTCWE course.

6

Module

FIREWALL

MTCNA

Module 6

This module provides an introduction to security and traffic control technology in MikroTik devices and explains how to configure the device as a firewall and perform NAT operations.

More advanced information about security and traffic control technologies is available in the MTCTCE and MTCSE courses.

This module covers the following course content topics:

- Firewall principles
    - Connection Tracking and States
    - Structure, Chains and Actions
- Firewall Filter in action
    - Filter Actions
    - Protecting Your Router (input)
    - Protection Your Customers (forward)
- Basic Address-List
- Source NAT
    - Masquerade and src-nat action
- Destination NAT
    - dst-nat and redirect action
- FastTrac
- Initial configuration (Internet access)
    - WAN DHCP-client
    - LAN IP address and default gateway

- Basic Firewall - NAT masquerade

Firewall

6.1 Firewall Overview and Key Concepts

To control the data flow through the network, a device called a firewall is used.

6.2 Firewall

The firewall is a device used to protect the network and control the data flow through it.

6.3 How Firewall Works

To control the traffic in the network, the firewall performs three stages or steps:

- Data Selection

  In this step, the device will specify, or select, the data to be controlled.

- Chain Choosing

  In this step, the device will specify, or choose, when to process the data, when it enters, exits, or passes through the device.

- Applying the Action:

  In this step, the device will specify the action to be applied to the data.

You can configure RouterOS to function as a Firewall by using the **Firewall** window and crate Firewall rules.

6.4 Firewall Rules

Firewall rules are instructions that tell MikroTik RouterOS how to handle the data: which data to control, when to control it, and what action should be applied to this data.

When multiple rules exist, the firewall processes them sequentially, starting from the first rule to the last, based on their sequence numbers. The processing stops as soon as the first matching rule is found.

6.5 Firewall Configuration

To configure RouterOS to function as a Firewall, use the **Firewall** Window.

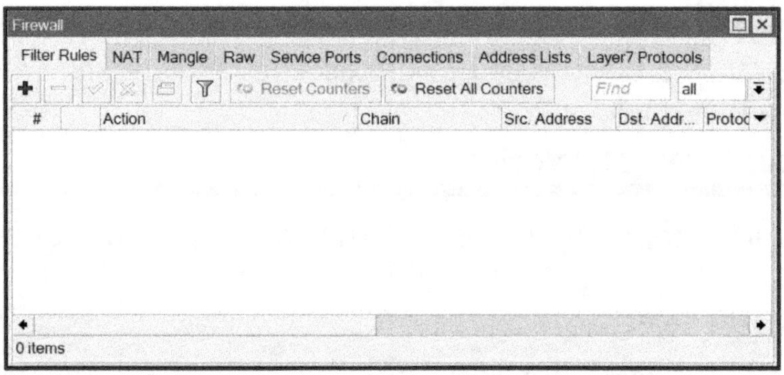

To open the **Firewall** window, click the **IP** menu, then select **firewall**.

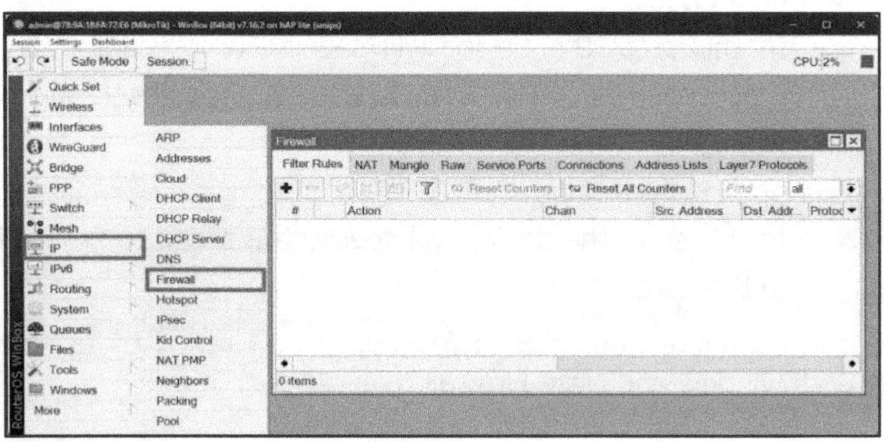

To add a firewall rule, or filter rule, click the **Add** button in the **Filter Rules** tab of the **Firewall** window to open the **New Firewall Rule** dialog box.

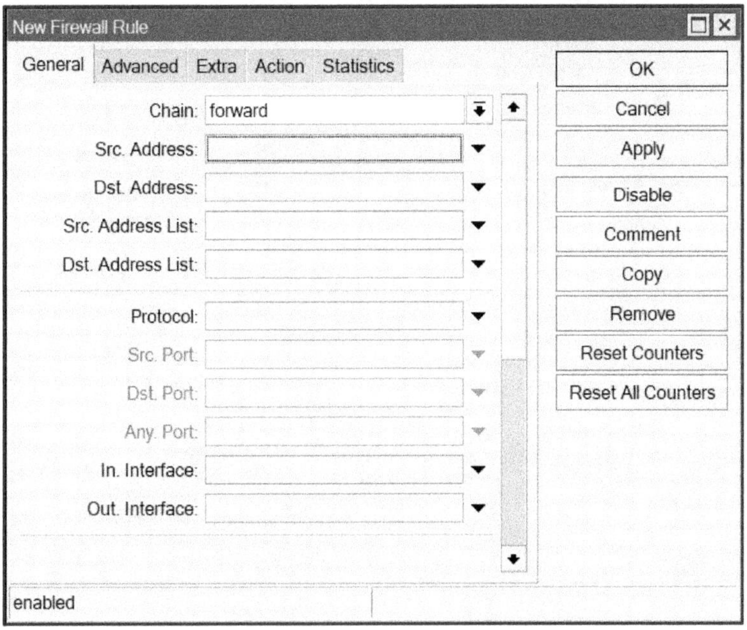

You can use this dialog box to create a new firewall rule and configure its settings.

As mentioned, the firewall performs three stages or steps:

- Data selection.
- Chain choosing.
- Appling the action.

You will configure these three steps when adding a new firewall rule.

6.6 Data Selection

In this step, specify, or select, the data you want to control.

You can select the data based on criteria such as source IP, destination IP, source port, destination port, incoming interface, outgoing interface, protocol, or other options provided by MikroTik RouterOS.

These options are available in the **General**, **Advanced**, and **Extra** tabs from the **New Firewall** dialog box.

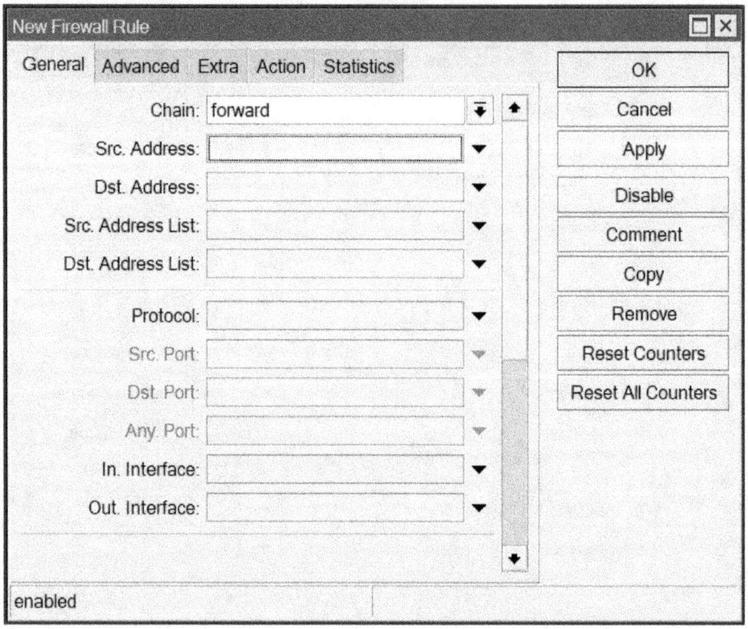

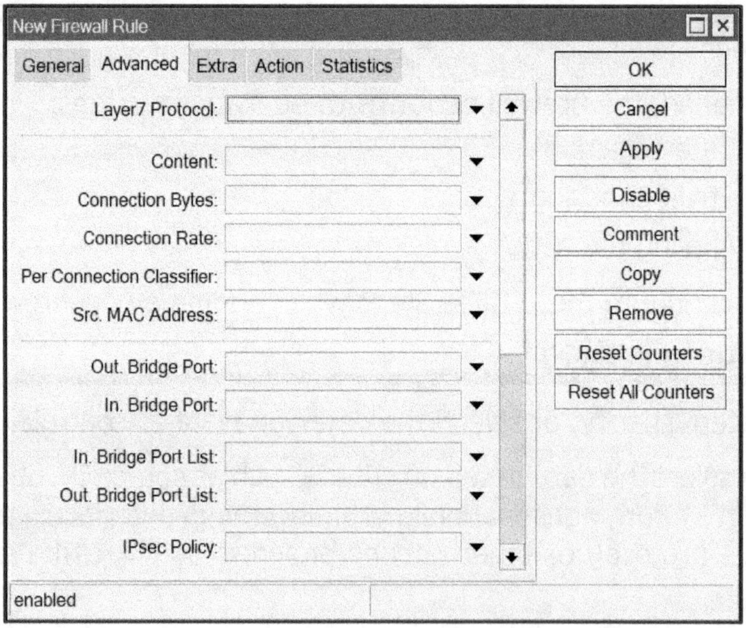

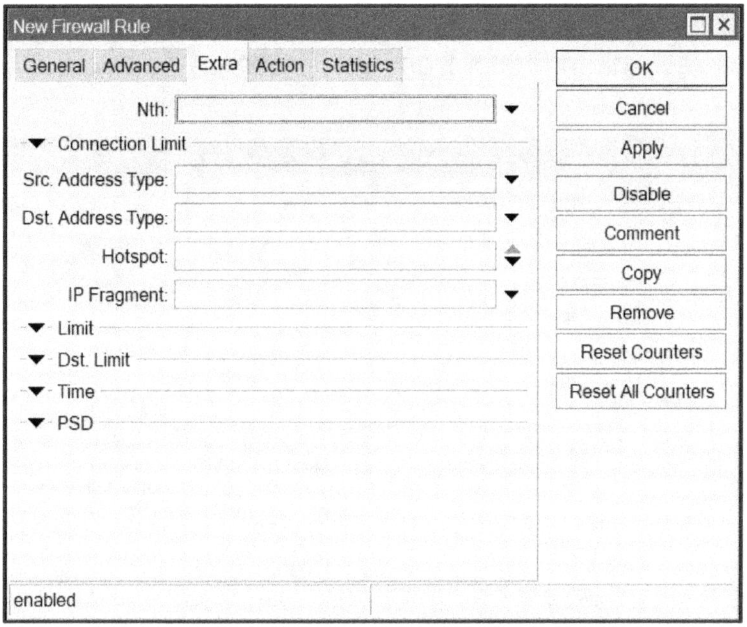

For example, if you want to control the data coming from a PC which has the IP address 192.168.1.15, you will enter this IP address in the **Src. Address** (or Source Address), field in the **General** tab.

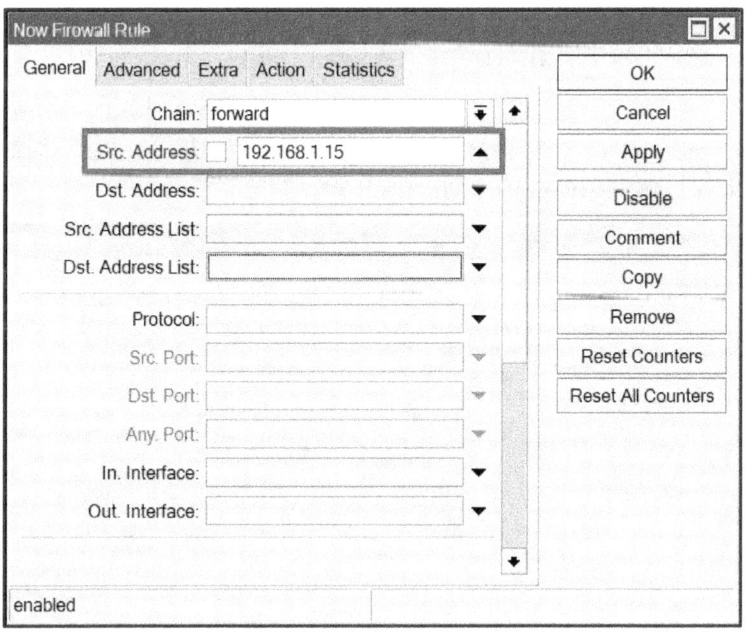

Likewise, if you want to control ICMP protocol data that comes from any PC, select this protocol from the **Protocol** field in the **General** tab.

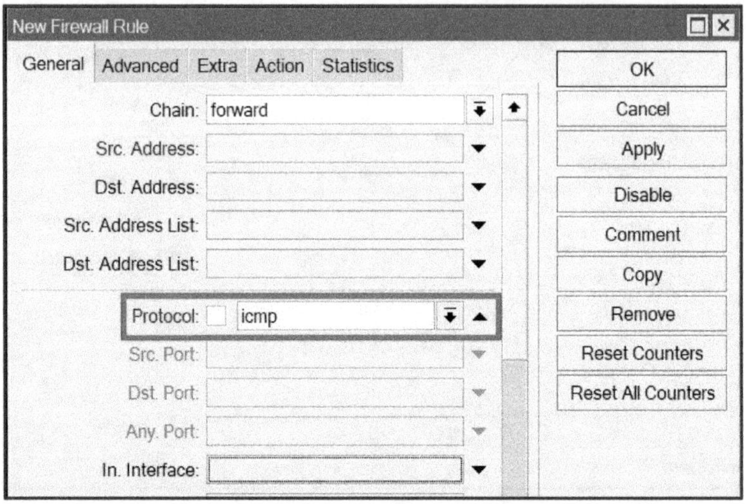

6.7 Chain Choosing

In this step, specify, or choose, when to process the data, when it enters, exits, or passes through the device. MikroTik RouterOS organizes this data into groups, called Chains.

When data enters the device, it will be placed in a chain; when it exits, it will be placed in another chain; and when it passes through the device, it will be placed in a third chain.

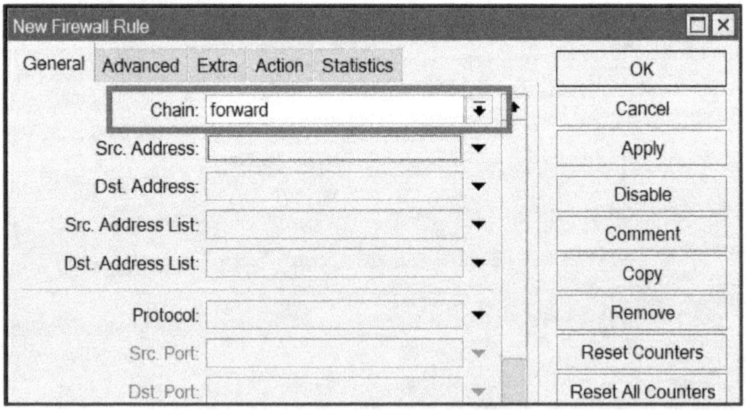

There are default predefined chains, and there are user-defined chains.

The default predefined firewall chains are:

- Input Chain:

  This chain processes data sent to the router itself, that means the destination address is the router address.

  For example, when you ping from a PC to the IP address of a router interface.

  You can use this chain to protect RouterOS.

- Output Chain:

  This chain processes data sent from the router itself, that means the source address is the router address.

  For example, when you ping from the router itself to the IP address of a PC.

- Forward Chain:

  This chain processes data that passes through the router, where neither the source nor the destination addresses are the router addresses.

  For example, when you ping from a PC to the IP address of another PC.

  You can use this chain to protect the other devices on the network.

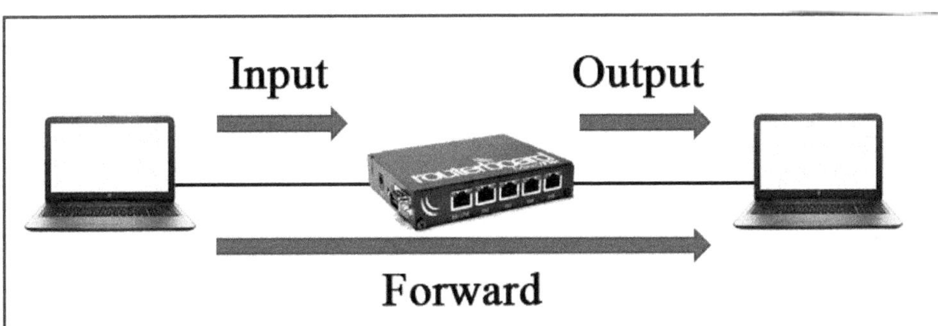

6.8 Applying the Action:

In this step, you specify the action to be applied to the data.

You can allow the data, block it, log it, or apply any other actions listed in the **Action** tab of the **New Firewall Rule** dialog box

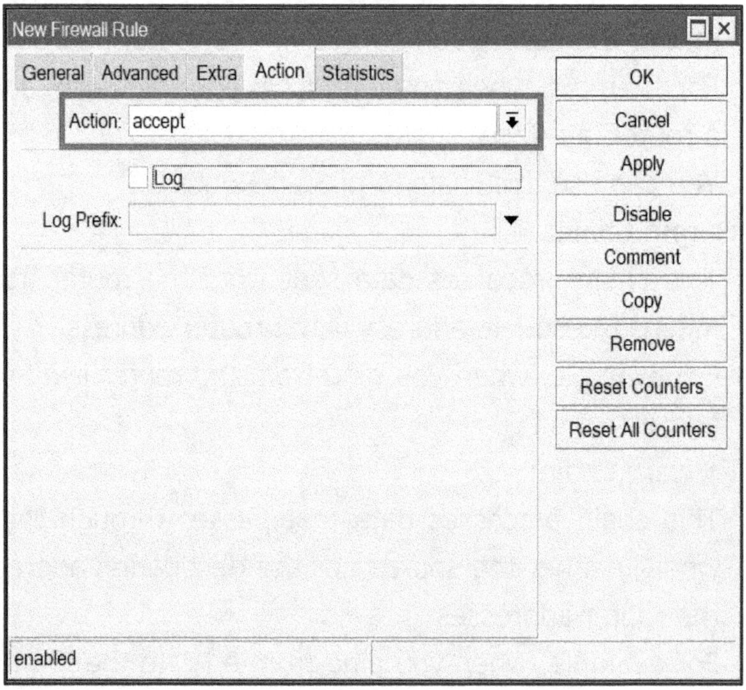

You can also add or create a firewall rule, or filter rule, from the CLI using the following command:

```
ip firewall filter add src-address=[address] chain=[chain] action=[action]
```

Where:

- [address] is the source IP address.
- [chain] is the chain of the rule
- [action] is the desired action

For example:

```
ip firewall filter add src-address=192.168.1.1 chain=forward action=drop
```

```
Terminal <1>
[admin@MikroTik] >
[admin@MikroTik] >
[admin@MikroTik] >
[admin@MikroTik] > ip firewall filter add src-address=192.168.1.1 chain=forward action=drop
```

You can also use other parameters to specify the destination address, protocol, port, and more.

To display the current filter rules in RouterOS from the CLI use the following command:

```
ip firewall filter print
```

```
Terminal <1>
[admin@MikroTik] >
[admin@MikroTik] > ip firewall filter print
Flags: X - disabled, I - invalid; D - dynamic
 0    chain=forward action=drop src-address=192.168.1.1
[admin@MikroTik] >
```

LAB

In this lab, the MikroTik device R1 is connected to two computers, each in a different subnet. PC1 has the IP address 192.168.1.2/24, is connected to the interface ether1, the PC2, has the IP address 192.168.2.2/24, is connected to the interface ether2.

You want to prevent the communication between those two computers by creating a firewall filter rule.

To start the configuration:

- First: you will perform the basic configuration to assign the IP addresses to MikroTik interfaces .
- Second: you will configure (or create) a firewall filter rule to prevent the communication between PC1 and PC2.

Basic Configuration

- Assign the IP address 192.168.1.1/24 to the interface ether1.
- Assign the IP address 192.168.2.1/24 to the interface ether2.

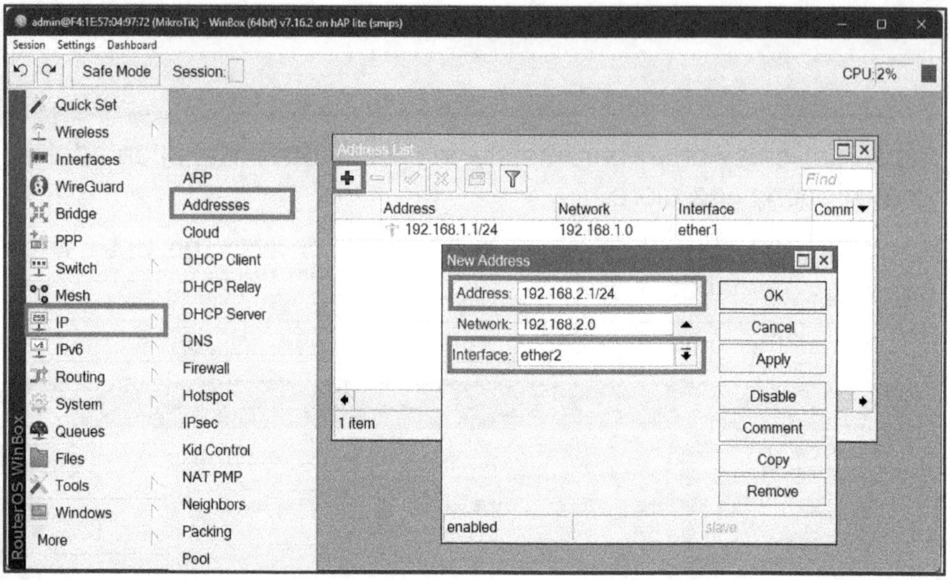

Firewall Configuration

To create a firewall filter rule, click the **IP** menu and select **Firewall** to open the **Firewall** window. Then, click the **Add** button in the **Filter Rules** tab to open the **New Firewall Rule** dialog box.

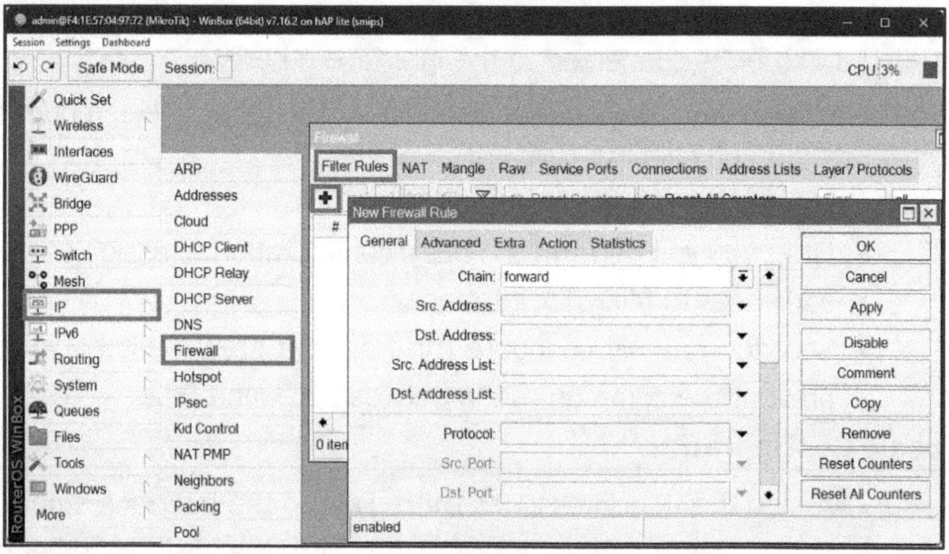

To configure the firewall filter rule, follow the three main steps:

Step 1: Data Selection

To select the data sourced from PC1 and destined for PC2:

- Enter the IP address of PC1 192.168.1.2 in the **Src. Address** (or Source Address) field.
- Enter the IP address of PC2 192.168.2.2 in the **Dst. Address** (or Destination Address) field.

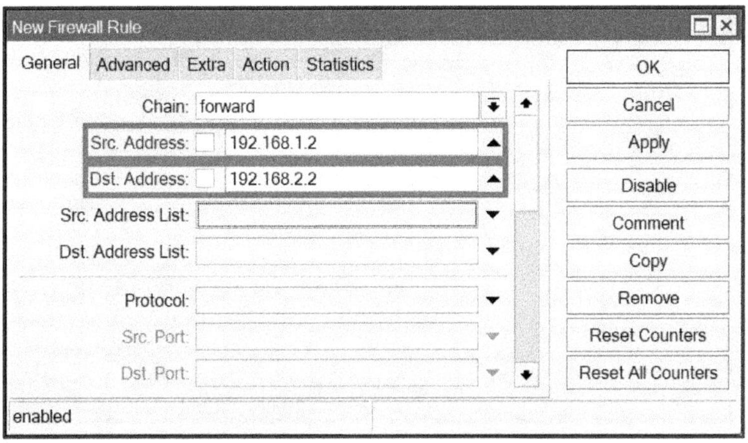

Step 2: Chain Choosing

Since neither the source IP nor the destination IP of the data sourced from PC1 and destined for PC2 belongs to the MikroTik device itself, so select the Forward chain from the **Chain** field.

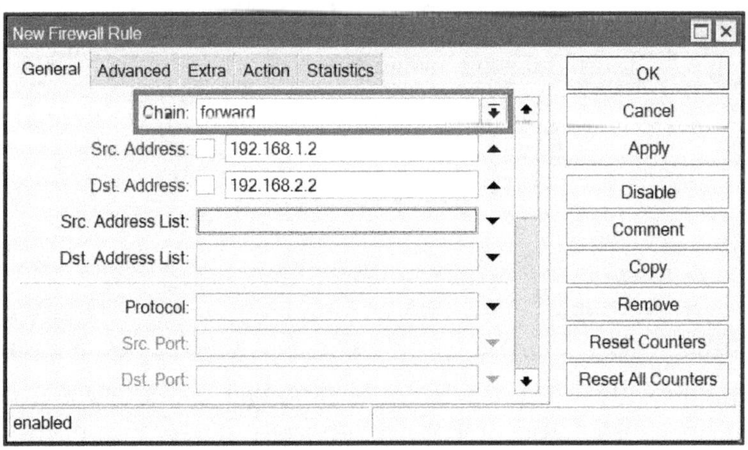

Step 3: Applying the Action

To prevent forwarding this data, select the Drop action from the **Action** field in the **Action** tab. And click the **Ok** button to close this dialog box.

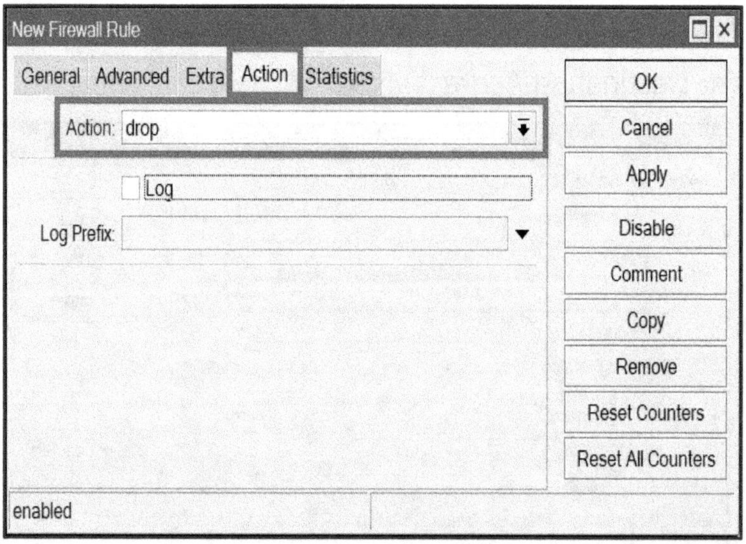

After creating the firewall filter rule, it will appear in the **Filter Rules** tab of the **Firewall** window.

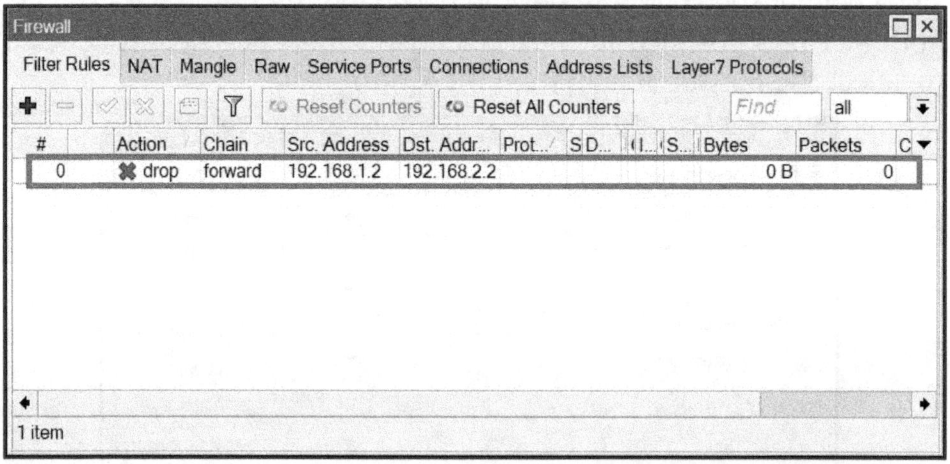

Now, when PC1 tries to ping PC2, the ping will fail because this firewall filter rule prevents communication between the two computers.

CLI

You can also make the configuration from the CLI .

To assign IP addresses to the interfaces, use the following commands:

```
ip address add address=192.168.1.1/24 interface=ether1

ip address add address=192.168.2.1/24 interface=ether2
```

To create the firewall filter rule, use the following command:

```
ip firewall filter add src-address=192.168.1.2 dst-address=192.168.2.2
chain=forward action=drop
```

6.9 Manage Firewall Rules

The **Filter Rules** tab displays the firewall rules created on the device. It is important to know how to read the filter rules and understand what each rule does.

In the previous lab, you created a filter rule. By looking at this rule in the **Filter Rules** tab, the **Src. Address** (or Source Address) and the **Dst. Address** (or Destination Address) fields tell you that this rule will be applied to data sourced from, (or coming from), the IP address 192.168.1.2 and destined for, (or going to), the IP address 192.168.2.2.

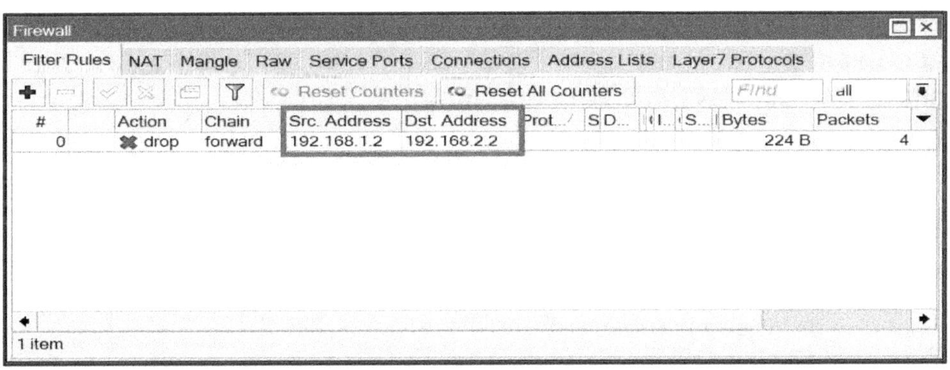

The **Chain** field tells you that the chain is forward. so this rule will be applied to data that comes from this IP and is destined for that IP when it passes through the device, with neither the source nor destination IP being any of the device IPs.

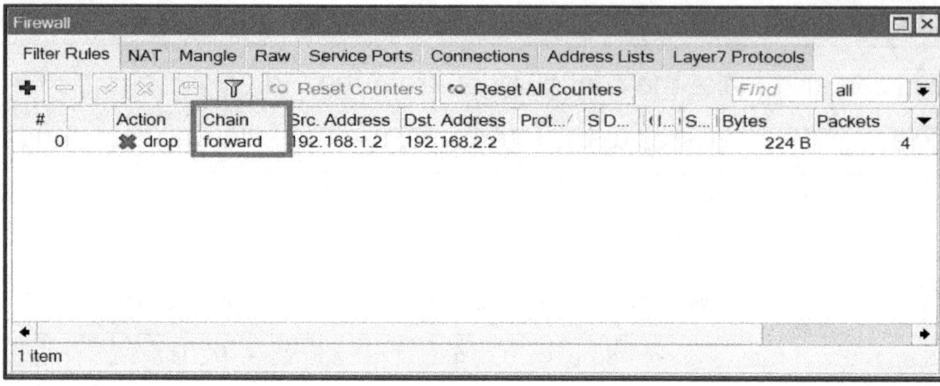

The **Action** field tells you that the action is Drop, so any data that matches this rule will be dropped.

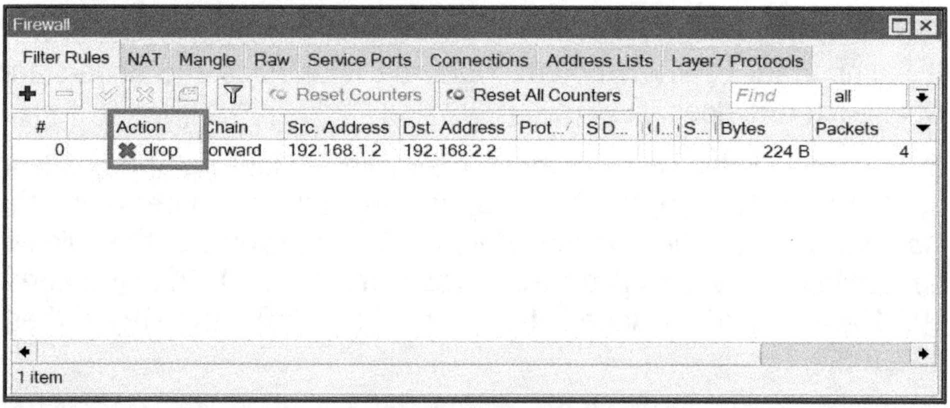

Another important field is the **Packets** field, which tells you how many times this rule has matched data and been applied

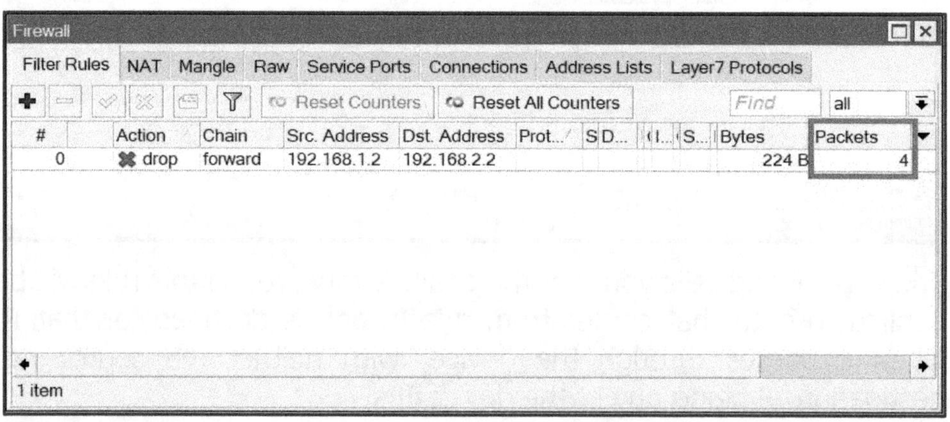

In this case, the packet counter is 4 because the ping sent 4 requests.

When you have multiple rules, they will be displayed in sequence order, starting from 0. The order field displays the sequence number of each rule.

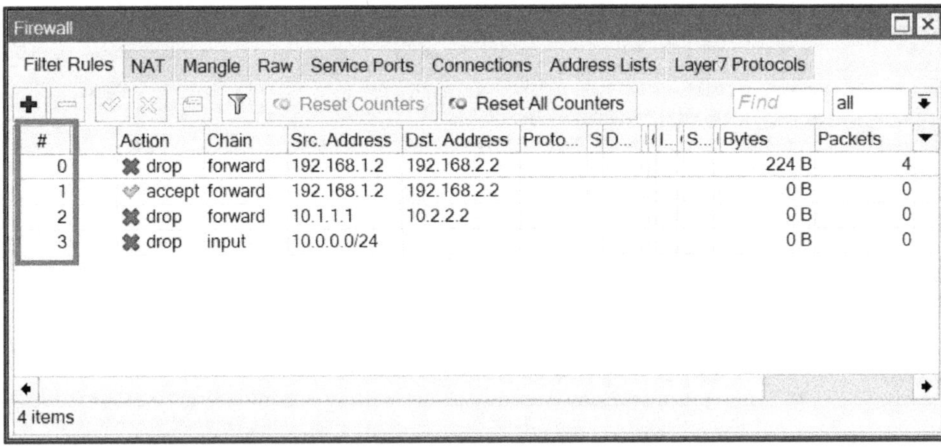

The firewall works on an If-Then concept. It checks the data against the first filter rule. If the data matches this rule, it will apply the action of this rule. If not, it will move to the next filter rule

The order of rules is very important because when the firewall analyzes the data against each rule to find a match, it follows the sequence number.

For example, if you create a filter rule to block the data comes from PC1 and goes to PC2 (by entering PC1 IP address in the source address field and PC2 IP address in the destination address field, choosing the forward chain, and setting the action to drop), this rule will appear in the **Filter Rules** tab with a sequence number of 0.

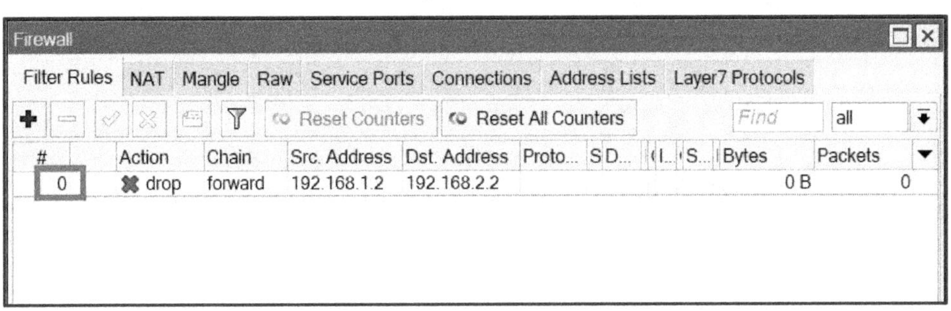

If you create another filter rule to allow data from PC1 to PC2, (setting the action to Accept), this rule will appear in the **Filter Rules** tab after the first rule, with a sequence number of 1.

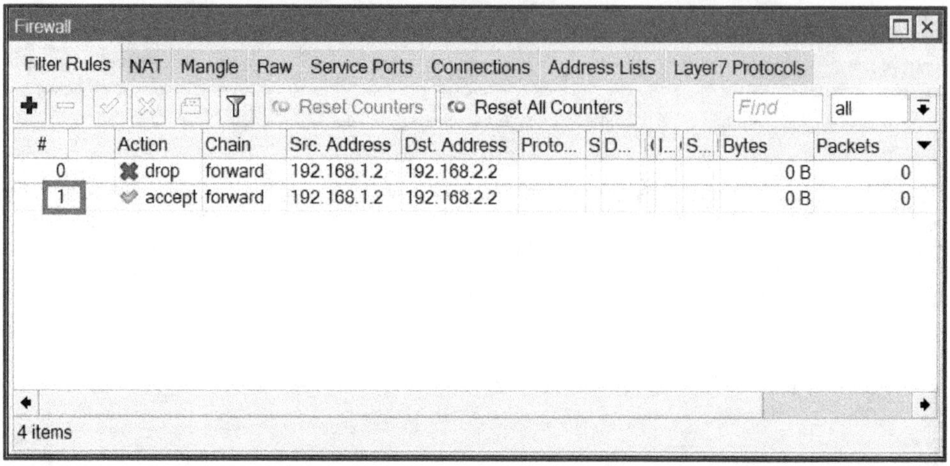

Now, when you try to ping from PC1 to PC2, the device will start analyzing the data against the rules, beginning with the first rule, which has a sequence number of 0. In this case, this rule matches the data, so it will block the data, and the ping will fail.

When you check the **Packets** counter field for each rule, you will find that the **Packets** counter field for the first rule has incremented, indicating that this rule was applied to the data.

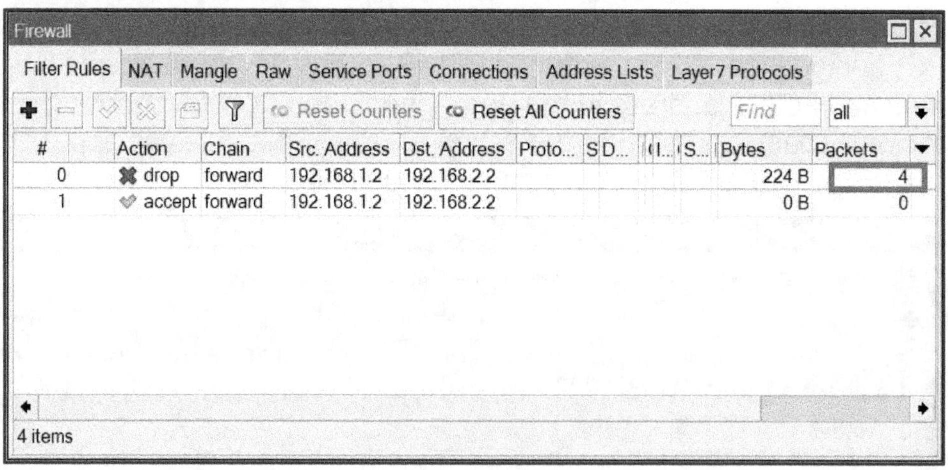

The **Packets** counter field for the second rule remains 0, indicating that this rule hasn't been applied yet.

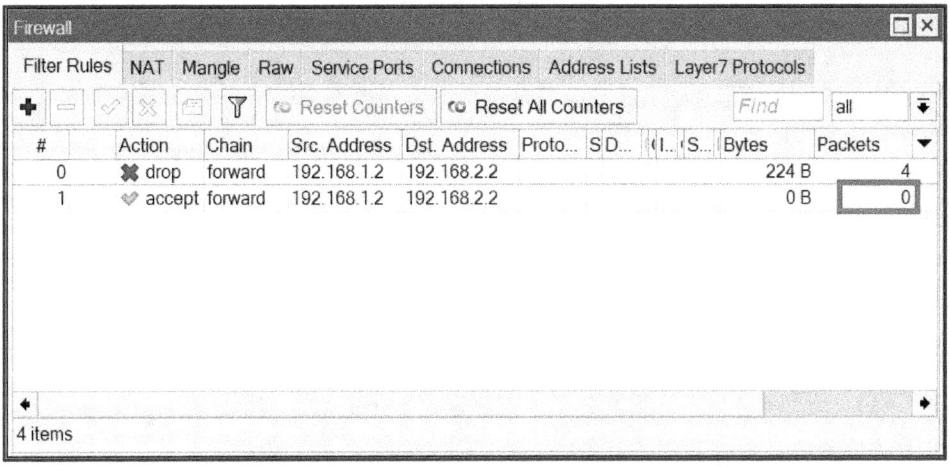

Although you can change the display order of the rules in the **Filter Rules** tab by clicking the header of any field, this does not change the sequence number.

For example, if you create four rules, the sequence number will start from 0, and they will appear as follows:

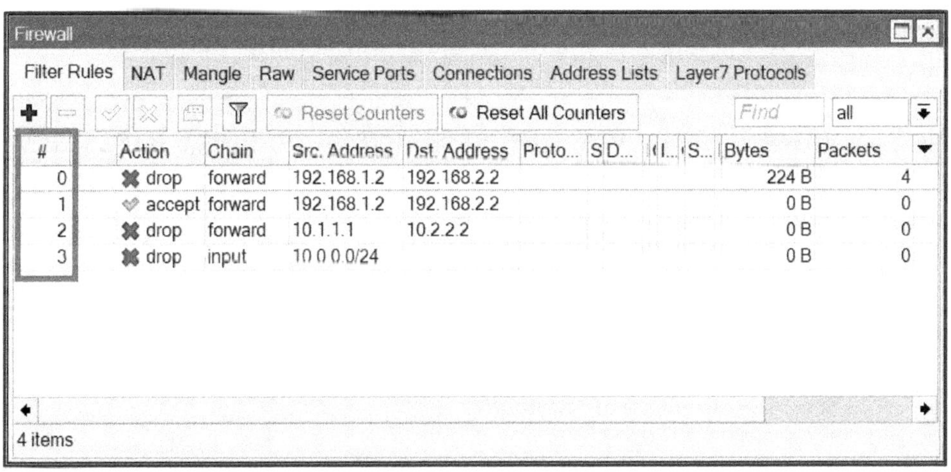

If you click the header of the **Action** field, the rules will be re-ordered, or resorted according to this field as follows:

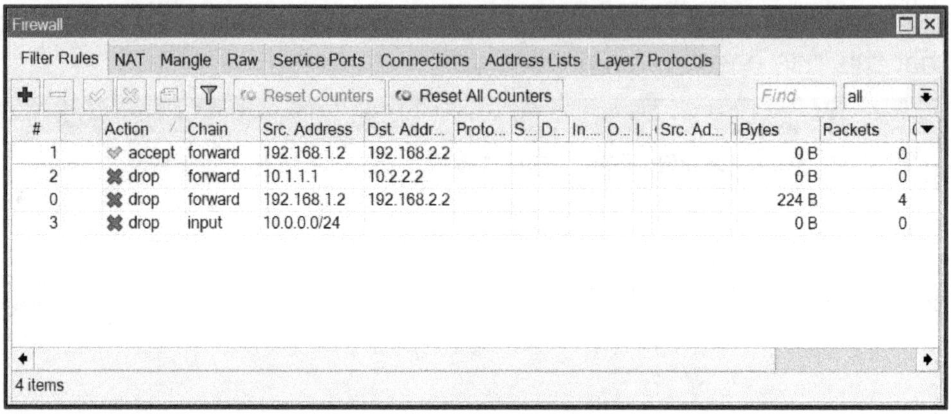

But that will not change the sequence number of each rule.

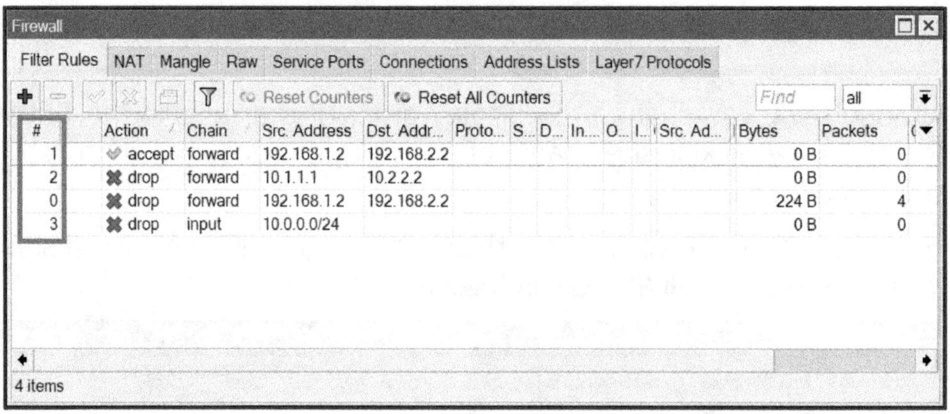

Here, you see that the first rule appearing in the **Filter Rules** tab is the rule accepting the data.

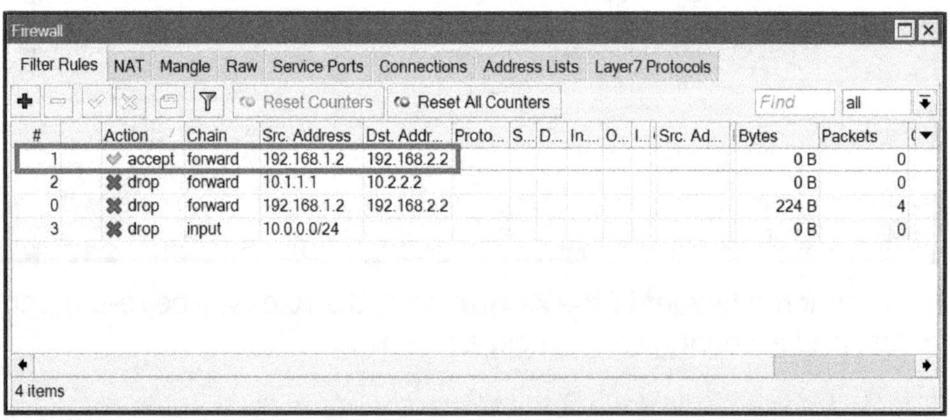

However, this rule is not the first one that will be analyzed, because, as mentioned, the device will start analyzing the rules based on their sequence numbers. So, the first rule to be analyzed is the rule with sequence number 0, which will drop the data here in this example.

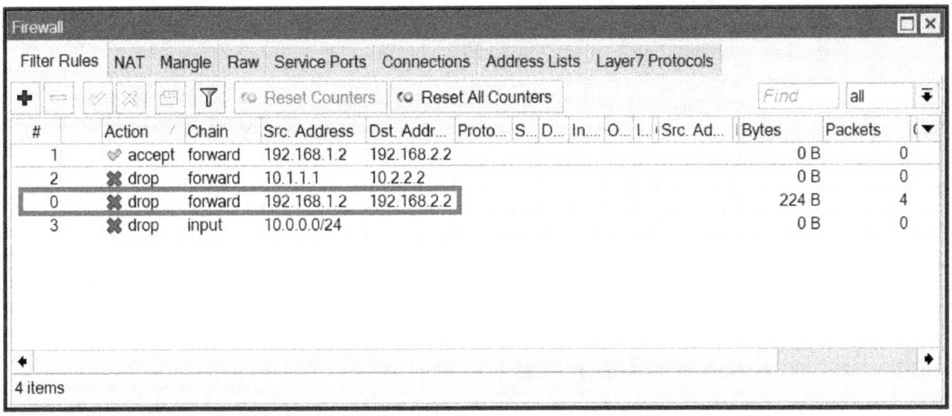

To re-order or sort the rules in the **Filter Rules** tab, click the header of the Sequence Number field.

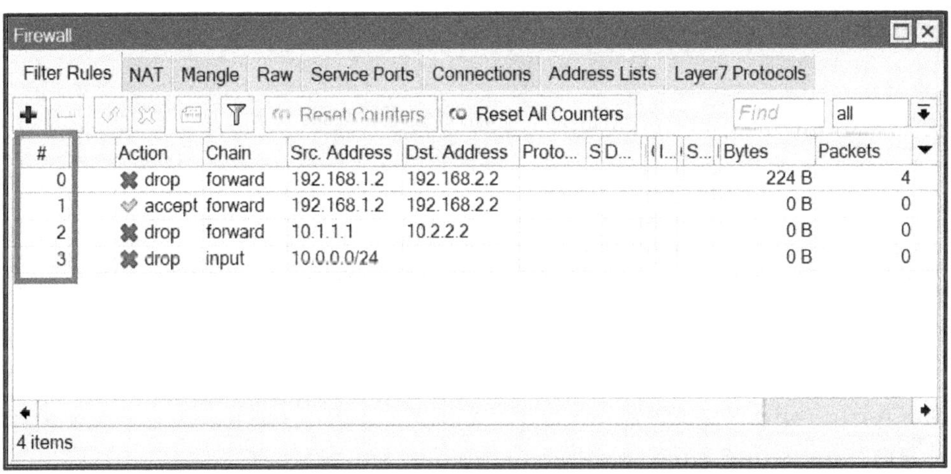

To change the sequence of the rules, you can drag and drop a rule by clicking and moving it up or down. The sequence number will be updated.

For example, you can drag and drop the second rule, which accepts the data and has a sequence number of 1, to the top.

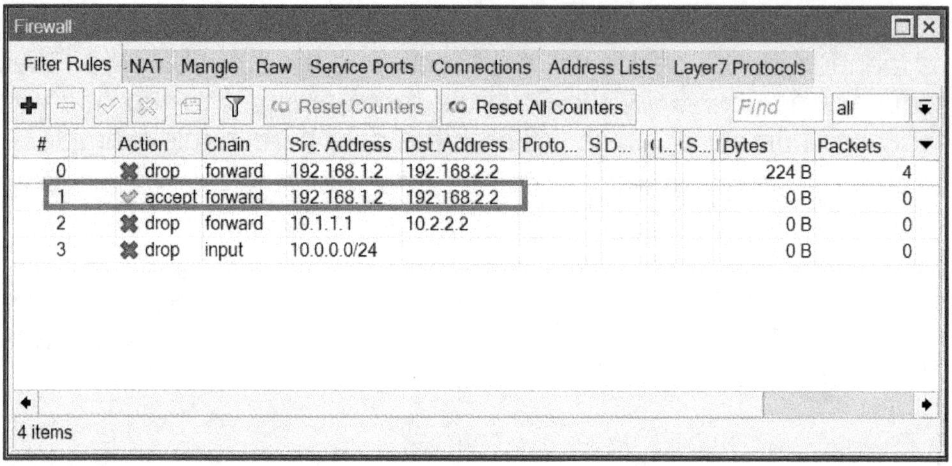

In this case, the sequence number of this rule will change to 0, making it the first rule in the **Filter Rules** tab.

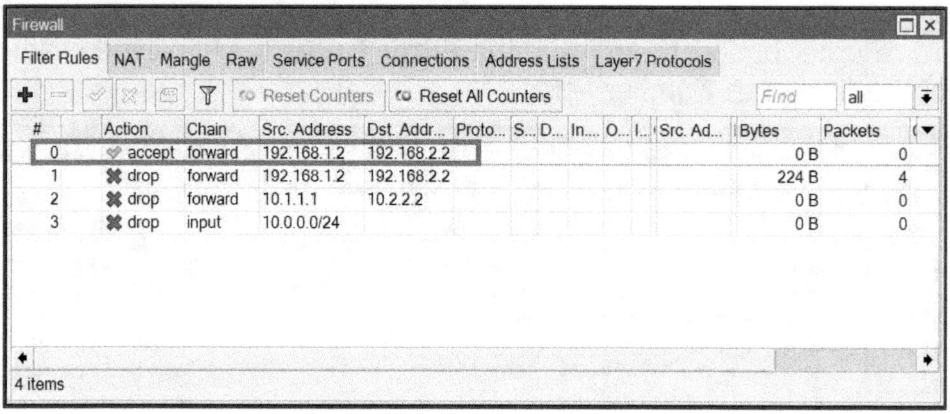

Also, it is important to understand that if the firewall does not find any rule that matches the data, it will allow the data. It will not drop or block the data.

6.10 Types of Firewalls

- Stateful Firewall:

  This firewall keeps information about the connections.

- Stateless Firewall:

  This firewall does not keep information about the connection.

You can configure MikroTik RouterOS to act as a stateful firewall or stateless firewall by using a feature called connection tracking.

6.11 Connection Tracking

Connection Tracking is the heart of the RouterOS firewall. It manages information about all active connections. To see the active connections in RouterOS, open the **Connections** tab of the **Firewall** window.

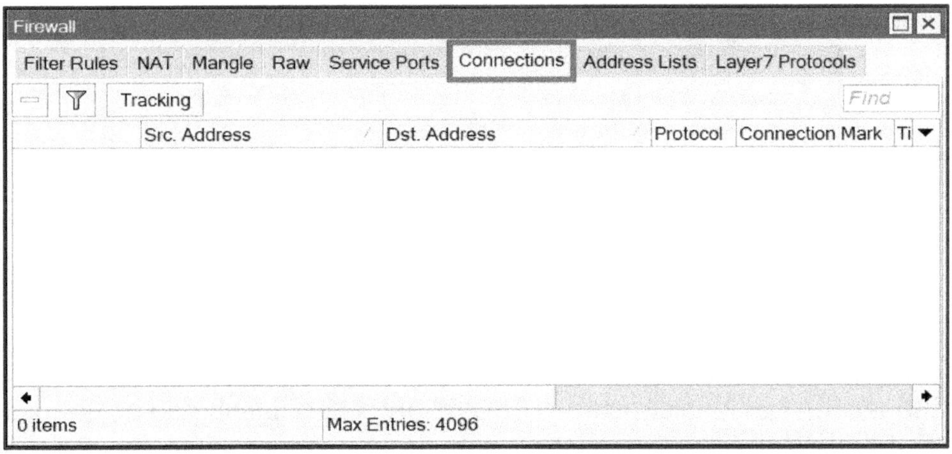

You can enable connection tracking by clicking the **Tracking** button in the **Connections** tab of the **Firewall** window, to open the **Connection Tracking** dialog box.

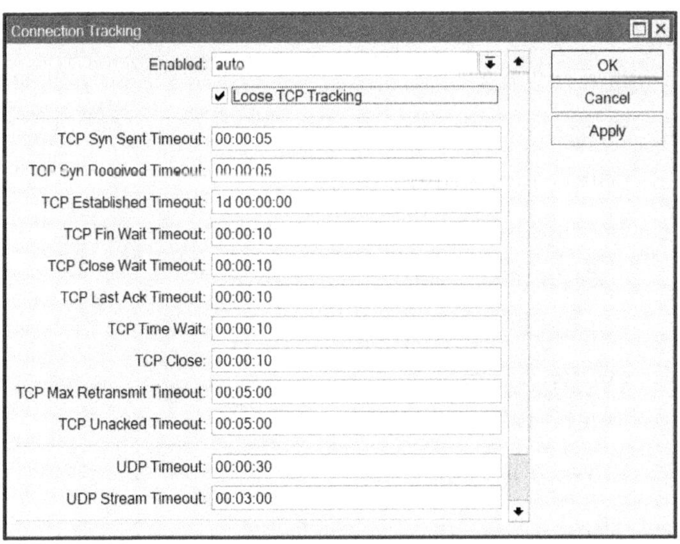

Then, choose Yes from the **Enable** field. To disable it, select No. You can also use Auto, which means that connection tracking will be automatically enabled when you add a firewall rule.

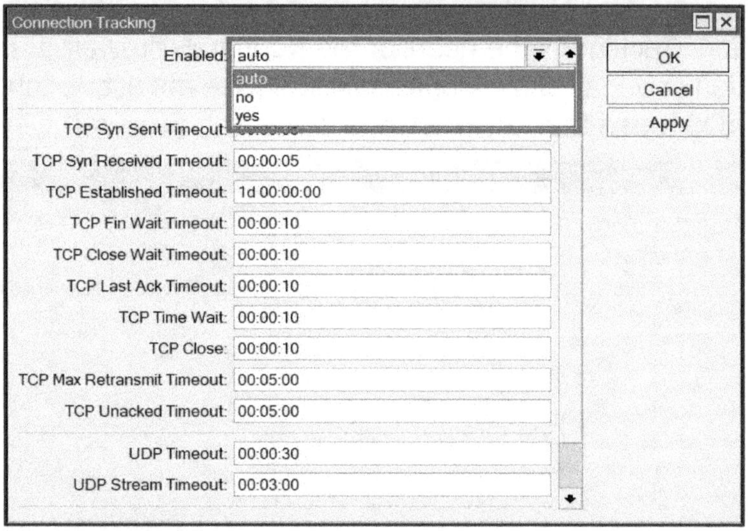

Connection tracking consumes CPU resources, but it should be enabled for firewall and NAT rules to work. If you do not use the firewall features in RouterOS, you can disable it.

However, by disabling connection tracking, many features in the RouterOS firewall will not work, such as:

- NAT
- firewall:
    - connection-bytes
    - connection-mark
    - connection-type
    - connection-state
    - connection-limit
    - connection-rate
    - layer7-protocol
    - new-connection-mark
    - tarpit

6.12 Connection State

When connection tracking keeps information about the active connections and lists them in the **Connections** tab, it assigns a property to those packets called connection state.

There are five connection states for the packet:

- New: This state means the packet starts a new connection.
- Established: This state means the packet belongs to an established connection.
- Related: This state means that the packet is related to an established connection.
- Invalid: This state means that the packet does not belong to any known connections.
- Untracked: This state means the packet is set to bypass connection tracking in the firewall **Raw** table.

You can find the connection state options in the **General** tab of the **New Filter Rule** dialog box.

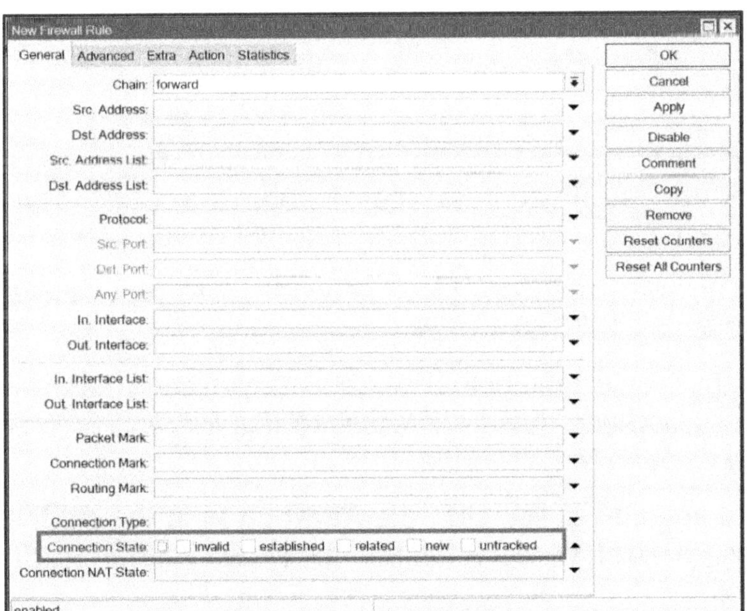

In most cases, it is recommended to drop the invalid packets and apply the filter rule to the new packets.

6.13 Address List

As mentioned before, to select data using an IP address, you enter this IP in the **Src. Address** field, (or Source Address), or in **Dst. Address** field, (or Destination Address), in the **New Firewall Rule** dialog box.

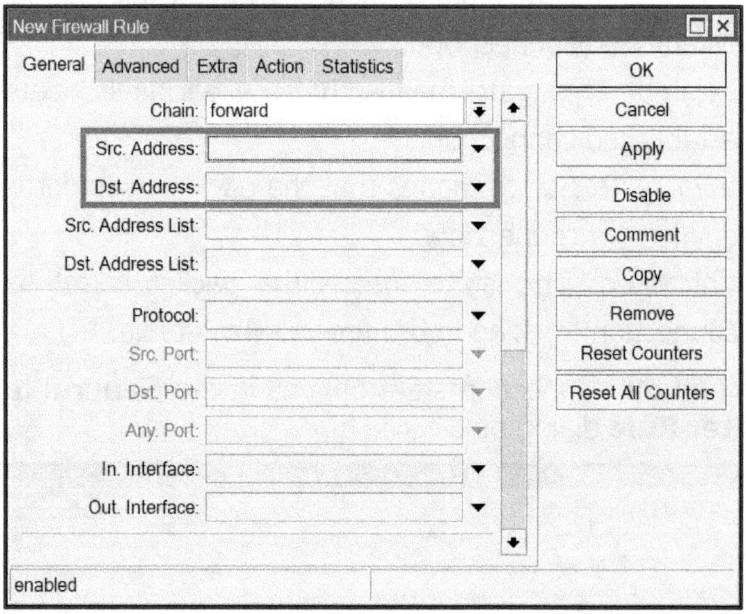

You can use an IP address representing a specific device, such as:192.168.1.2

Or you can use a network IP or network ID to represent an entire subnet, such as:192.168.1.0/24

If you want to select multiple IP addresses, you can create a list called an Address List, add those addresses to this list, and then select the list when creating the filter rule.

To create an address list, click the **Add** button in the **Address Lists** tab of the **Firewall** window, to open the **New Firewall Address List** dialog box.

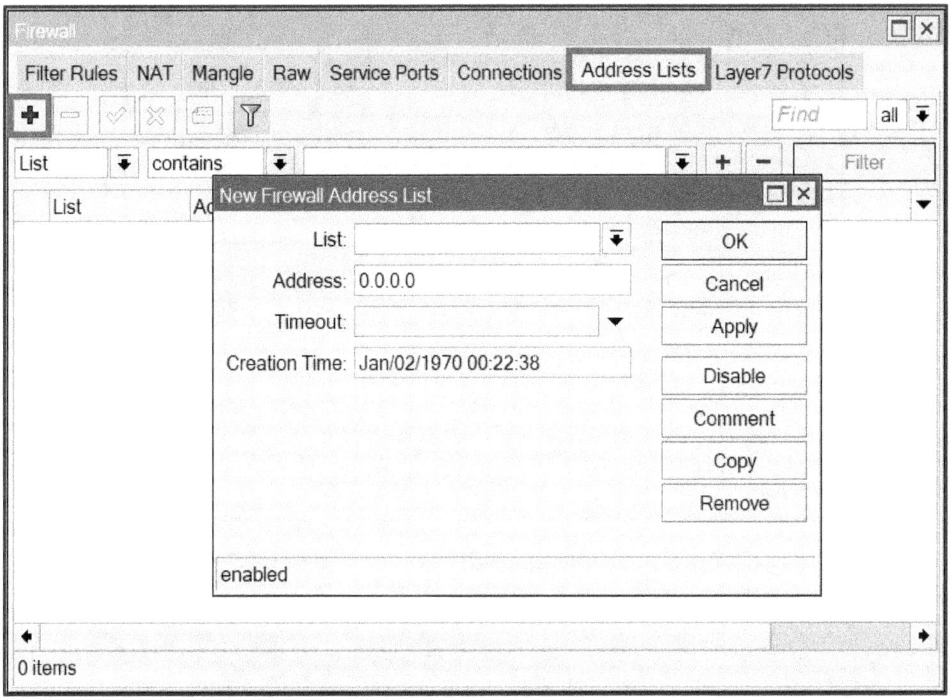

You can use this dialog box to create a new address list and configure its settings.

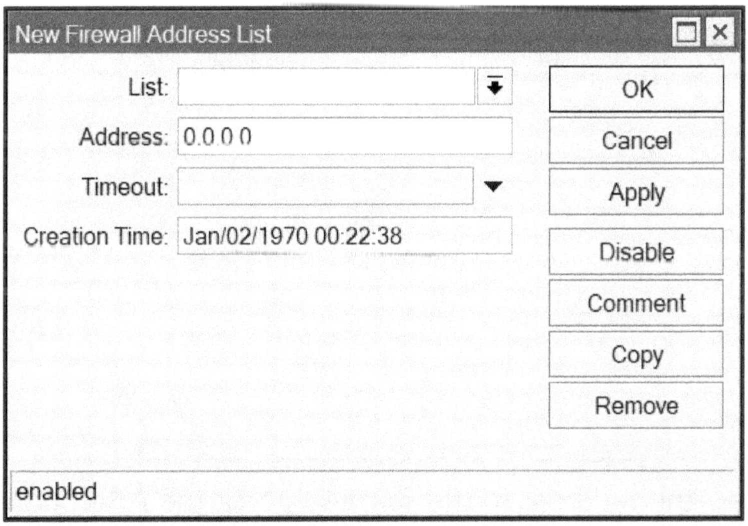

In the **List** field, enter a name for this list. In the **Address** field, enter the IP address you want to add to this list.

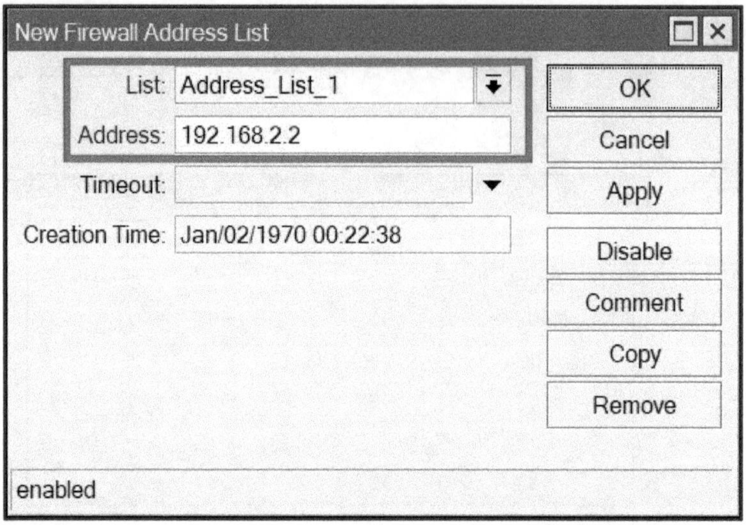

After creating the list, it will appear in the **Address Lists** tab of the **Firewall** window.

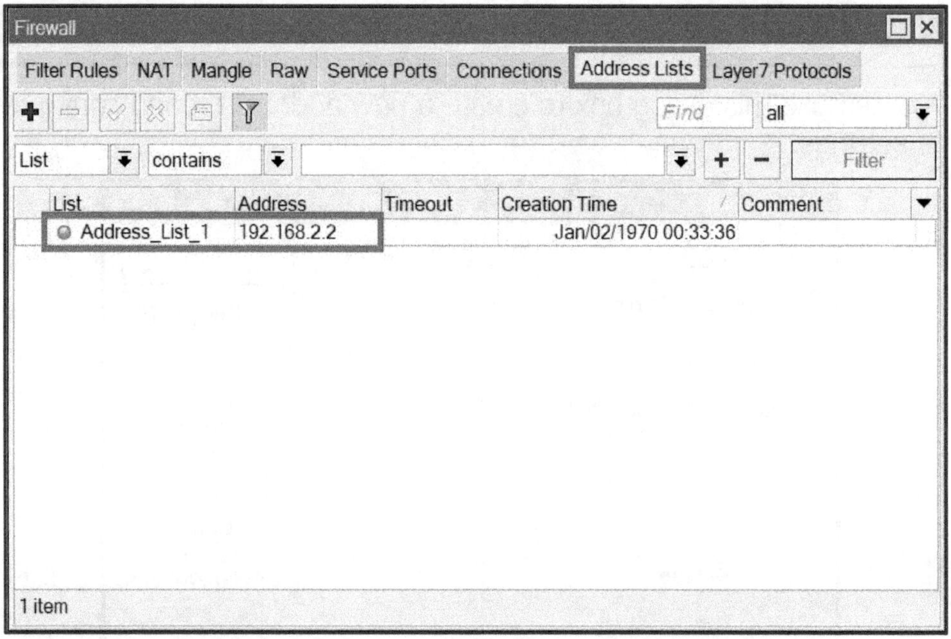

To add another address to the same list, click the **Add** button again, enter the same list name in the **List** field, and enter the IP address you want to add.

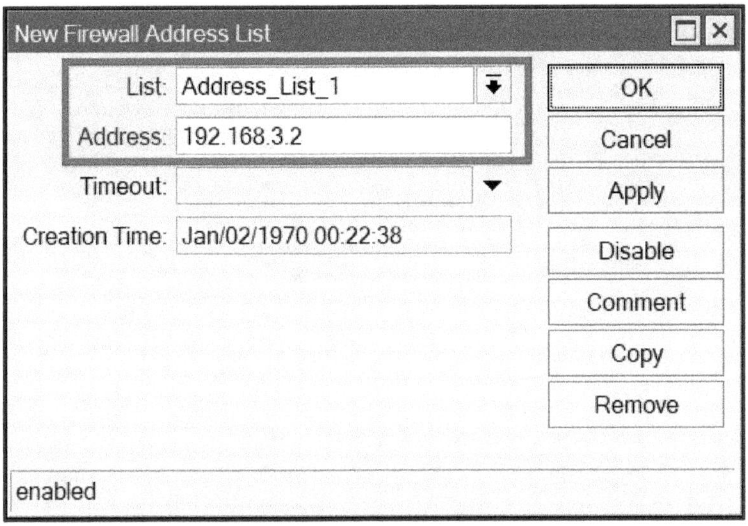

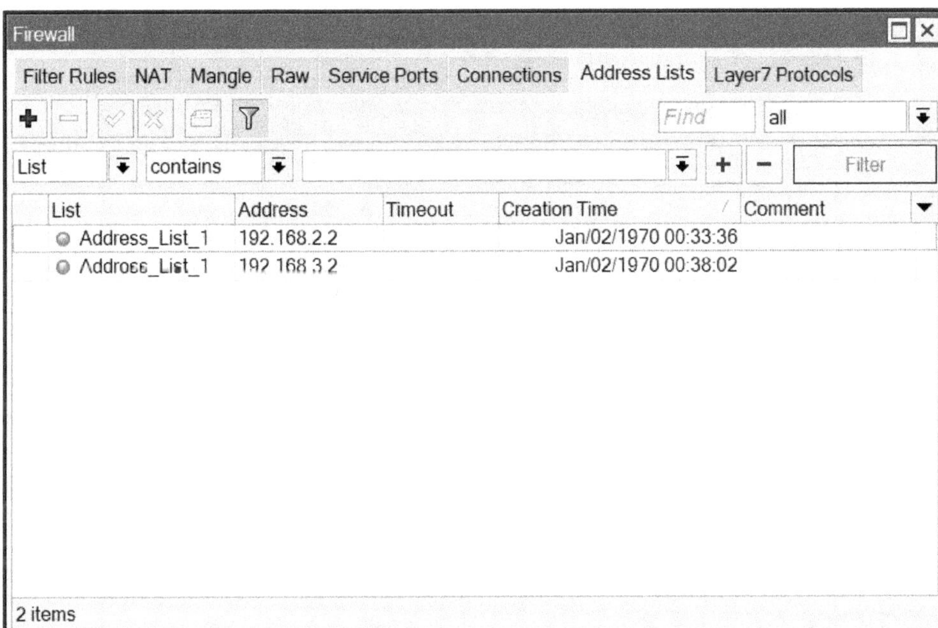

Now, you can select this list from the **Src. Address List** field, (or Source Address List), or **Dst. Address List** field, (or Destination Address List), in the **General** tab of the **New Firewall Rule** dialog box in RouterOS v7 or from the **Advanced** tab in RouterOS v6.

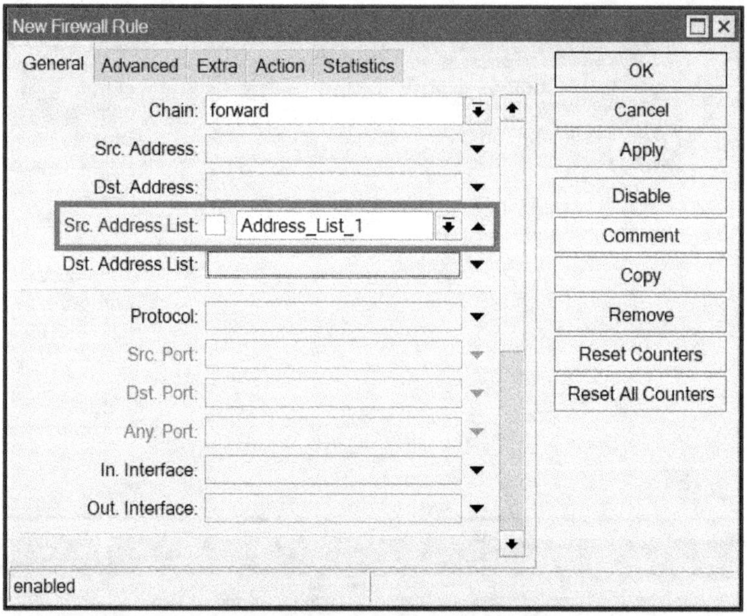

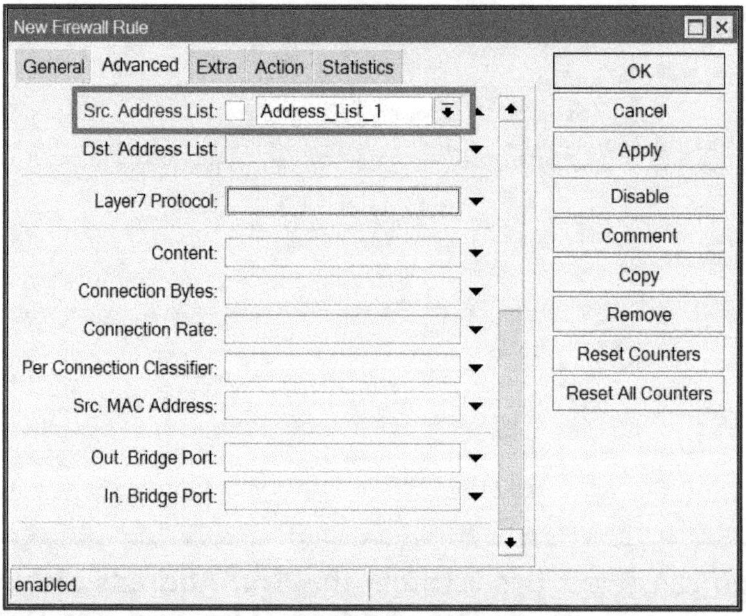

You can also create an address list and add addresses to it from the CLI using the following command:

```
ip firewall address-list add list=[name] address=[address]
```

Where:

- [name] is the name for the address list
- [address] is the IP address you want to add to this list.

For example:

```
ip firewall address-list add list=Address_List_1 address=192.168.2.
```

```
Terminal <1>
[admin@MikroTik] >
[admin@MikroTik] >
[admin@MikroTik] >
[admin@MikroTik] > ip firewall address-list add list=Address_List_1 address=192.168.2.2
```

To display the current address lists in RouterOS from the CLI use the following command:

```
ip firewall address-list print
```

```
Terminal <1>
[admin@MikroTik] >
[admin@MikroTik] > ip firewall address-list print
Columns: LIST, ADDRESS, CREATION-TIME
# LIST             ADDRESS       CREATION-TIME
0 Address_List_1   192.168.2.2   1970-01-03 03:48:59
[admin@MikroTik] >
```

LAB

In this lab, the MikroTik device R1 is connected to three computers, each in a different subnet. PC1 has the IP address 192.168.1.2/24, is connected to the interface ether1, PC2, has the IP address 192.168.2.2/24, is connected to the interface ether2, and PC3 has the IP address 192.168.3.2/24, is connected to the interface ether3.

You want to prevent the communication between PC1 and the two other computers by creating a firewall filter rule.

To start the configuration:

- First: perform the basic configuration to assign the IP addresses to MikroTik interfaces .
- Second, configure the firewall by adding a new filter rule to prevent the communication, using an address list.

Basic Configuration

- Assign the IP address 192.168.1.1/24 to the interface ether1.
- Assign the IP address 192.168.2.1/24 to the interface ether2.
- Assign the IP address 192.168.3.1/24 to the interface ether3.

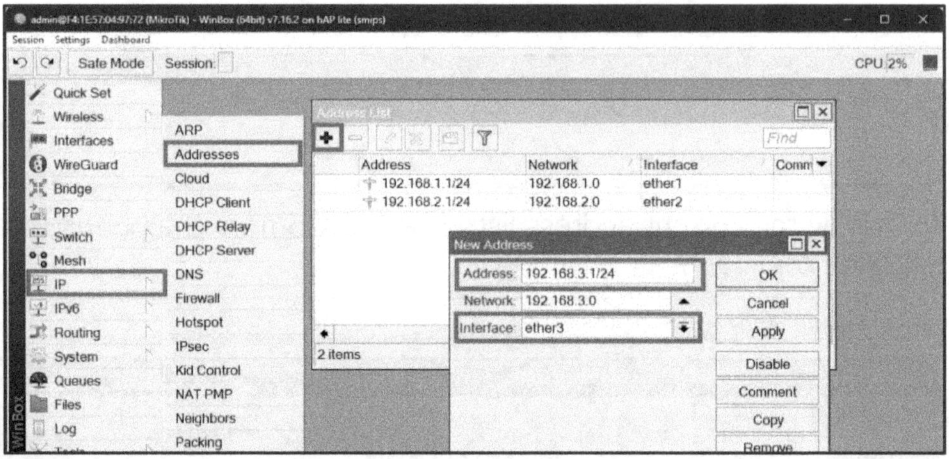

Firewall Configuration

To prevent the communication between PC1 and the other two computers, PC2 and PC3, instead of creating two filter rules, one for each computer, you will add the IP addresses of PC2 and PC3 to an Address List, then create only one filter rule and use this address list.

To create an address list, click the **IP** menu and select **Firewall** to open the **Firewall** window. Then, click the **Add** button in the **Address Lists** tab to open the **New Firewall Address List** dialog box.

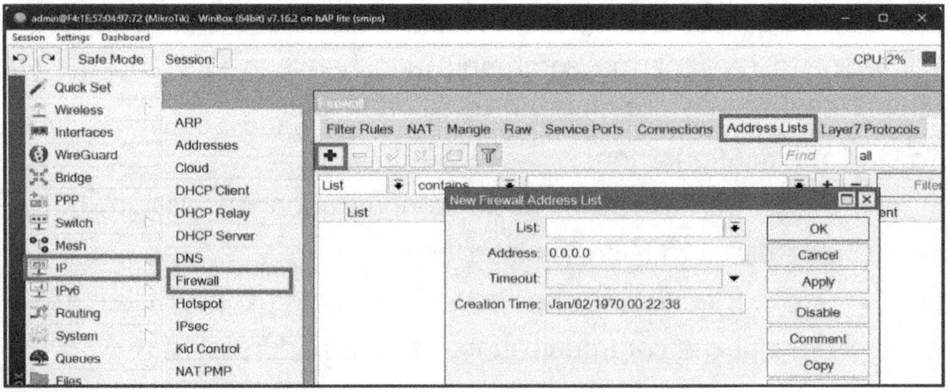

In the **List** field, enter a name for this list, Address_List_1. In the **Address** field, enter the IP address of PC2, 192.168.2.2, then click the **Ok** button to close this dialog box.

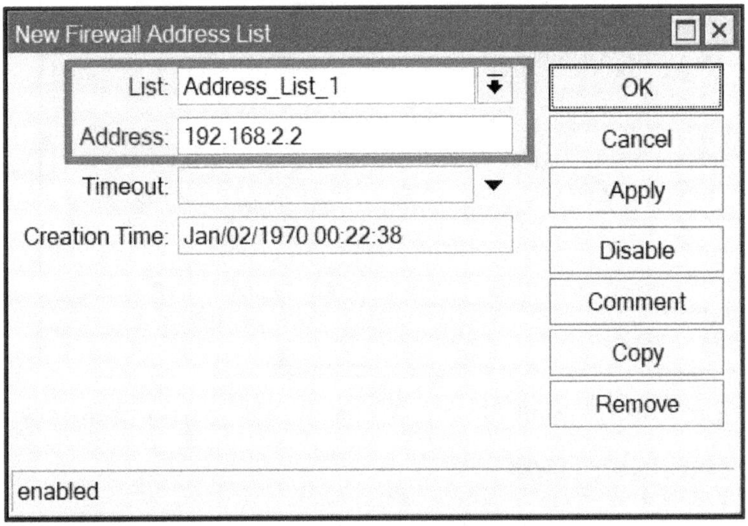

Repeat the same steps to add the IP address of PC 3, 192.168.3.2 by using the same address list name Address_List_1.

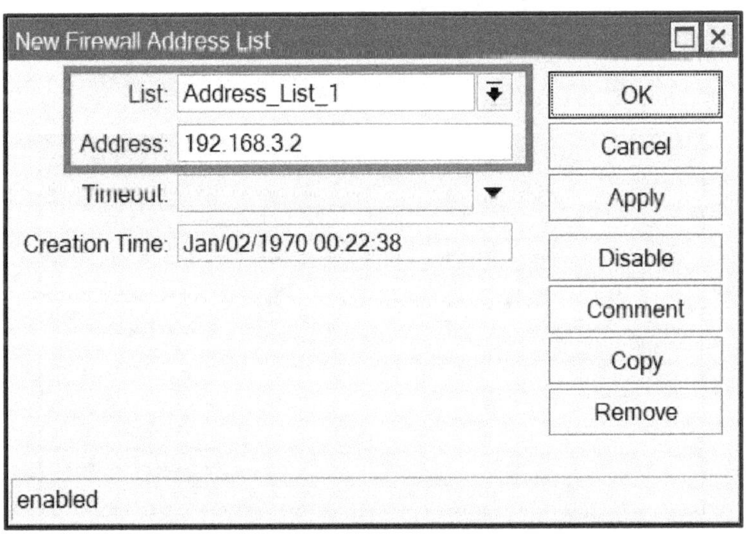

To create a firewall filter rule, click the **Add** button in the **Filter Rules** tab to open the **New Firewall Rule** dialog box.

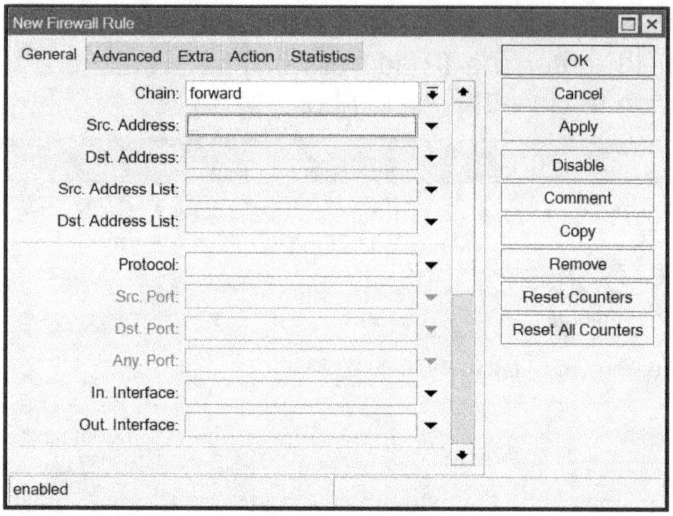

To configure the firewall filter rule, follow the three main steps:

Step 1: Data Selection

To select the data sourced from PC1 and destined for PC2 and PC3:

- Enter the IP address of PC1 192.168.1.2 in the **Src. Address** field, (or Source Address).
- Select the Address_List_1 from the **Dst. Address List** field, (or Destination Address List).

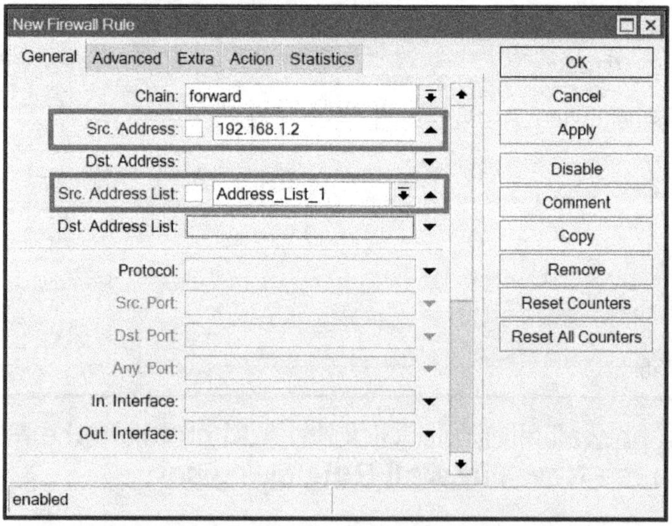

Step 2: Chain Choosing

Since neither the source IP nor the destination IPs of the data sourced from PC1 and destined for PC2 and PC3 belongs to the MikroTik device itself, so select the Forward chain from the **Chain** field.

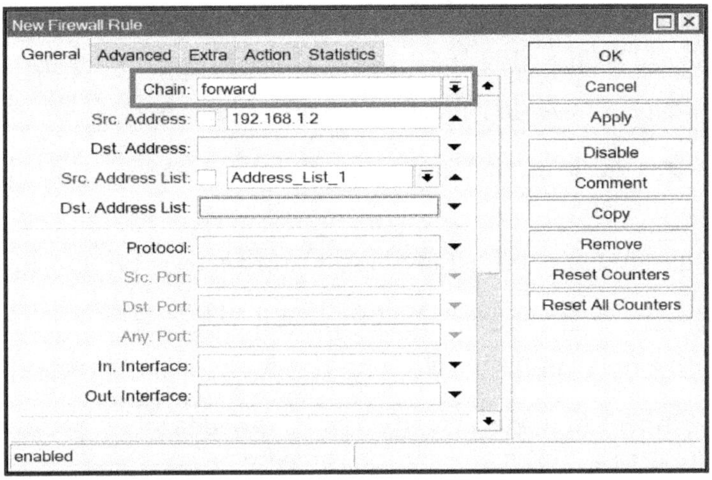

Step 3: Applying the Action

To prevent forwarding this data, select the Drop action from the **Action** field in the **Action** tab. And click the **Ok** button to close this dialog box.

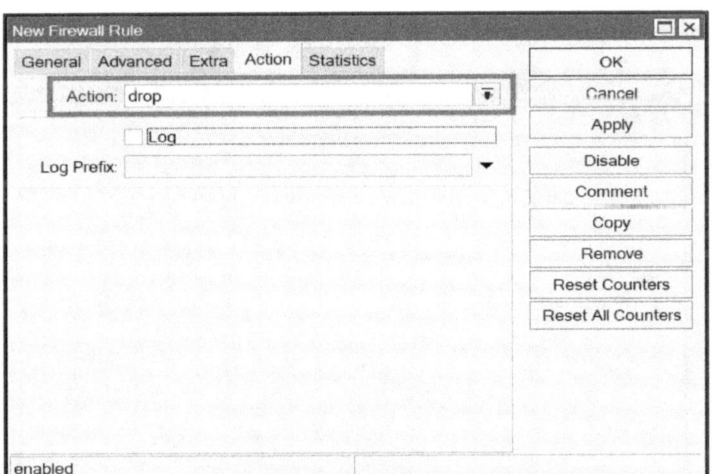

Now, when PC1 tries to ping PC2 or PC3, the ping will fail.

CLI

You can also make the configuration from the CLI.

To assign IP addresses to the interfaces, use the following commands:

```
ip address add address=192.168.1.1/24 interface=ether1
ip address add address=192.168.2.1/24 interface=ether2
ip address add address=192.168.3.1/24 interface=ether3
```

To create the address list and add the IP addresses to it, use the following commands:

```
ip firewall address-list add list=Address_List_1 address=192.168.2.2
ip firewall address-list add list=Address_List_1 address=192.168.3.2
```

To create the firewall filter rule, use the following command

```
ip firewall filter add src-address=192.168.1.2 dst-address-
list=Address_List_1 chain=forward action=drop
```

6.14 Add Address to Address List Automatically

You can add an IP address to an address list automatically or dynamically by creating a filter rule and choosing the action add src to address list (or add source address to address list) or add dst to address list (or add destination address to address list).

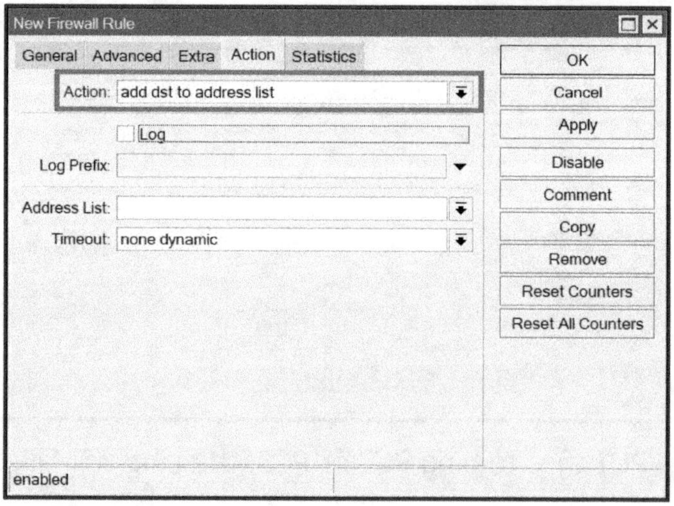

In the **Address List** field, enter the name of the address list to which you want to add the IP address.

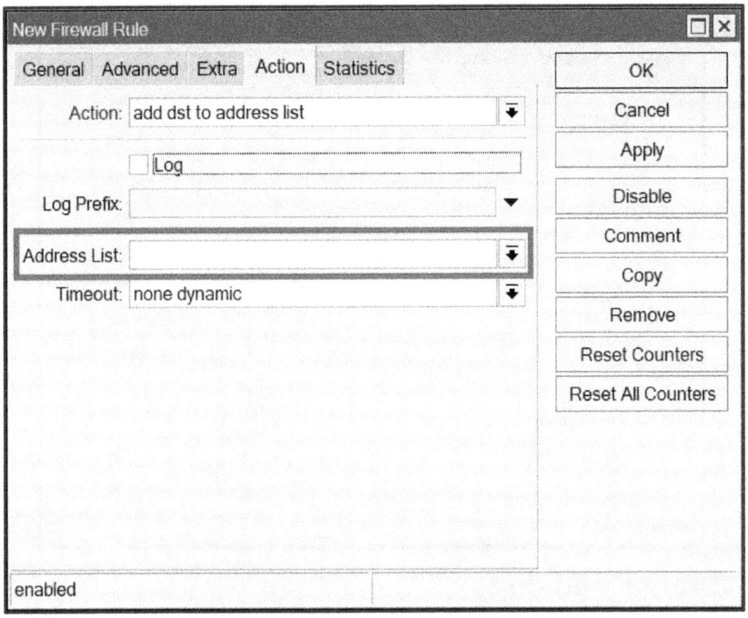

Note: The dynamically added IP address will be removed from the list after restarting the device.

LAB

In this lab, you want to add any IP address that PC1 tries to ping to the address list Address_List_1, which you created in the previous lab, by using a firewall filter rule.

To create a new firewall filter rule, click the **Add** button in the **Filter Rules** tab to open the **New Firewall Rule** dialog box.

To configure the firewall filter rule, follow the three main steps:

Step 1: Data Selection

To select the data of the ICMP protocol sourced from PC1:

- Enter the IP address of PC1 192.168.1.2 in the **Src. Address** field, (or Source Address).
- Select ICMP protocol from **Protocol** field

When you do not specify the destination address in a filter rule, it means this rule will be applied to the data sent to any destination.

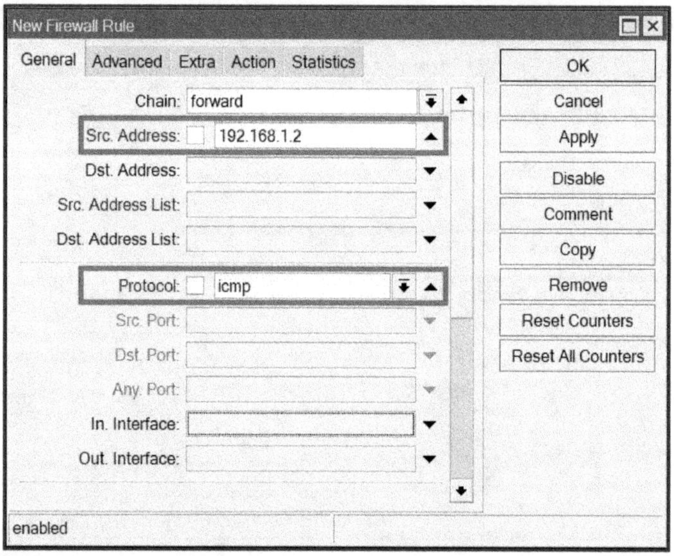

Step 2: Chain Choosing

Since you target the data where neither the source IP nor the destination IP belongs to the MikroTik device itself, select the Forward chain from the **Chain** field.

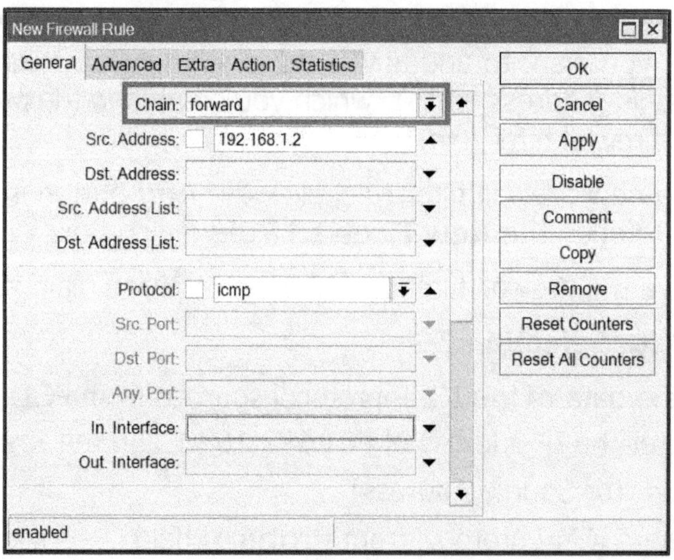

Step 3: Applying the Action

To add the destination IP address to the address list Address_List_1, select the add dst to address list (or add destination address to address list) action from the **Action** field in the **Action** tab. Enter the address list name Address_List_1 in **Address List** field, and click the **OK** button to close the dialog box.

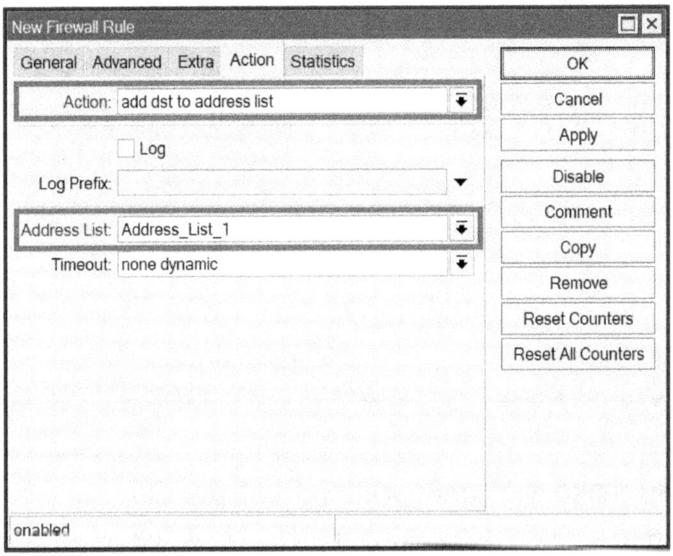

Now, when PC1 pings any IP address, such as:192.168.1.10 or 192.168.2.45, The firewall filter rule will add those IP addresses to the address list Address_List_1. They will then appear in the **Address Lists** tab.

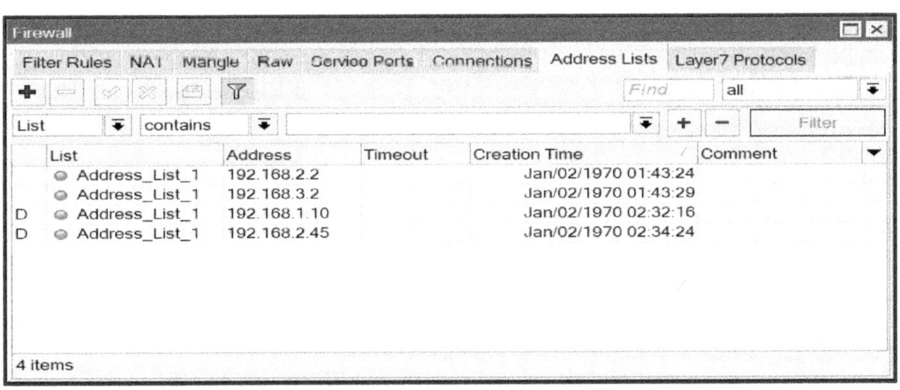

If you restart the MikroTik device, those dynamically added addresses will be deleted, and only the manually or statically added addresses, (which you added in the previous lab), will remain.

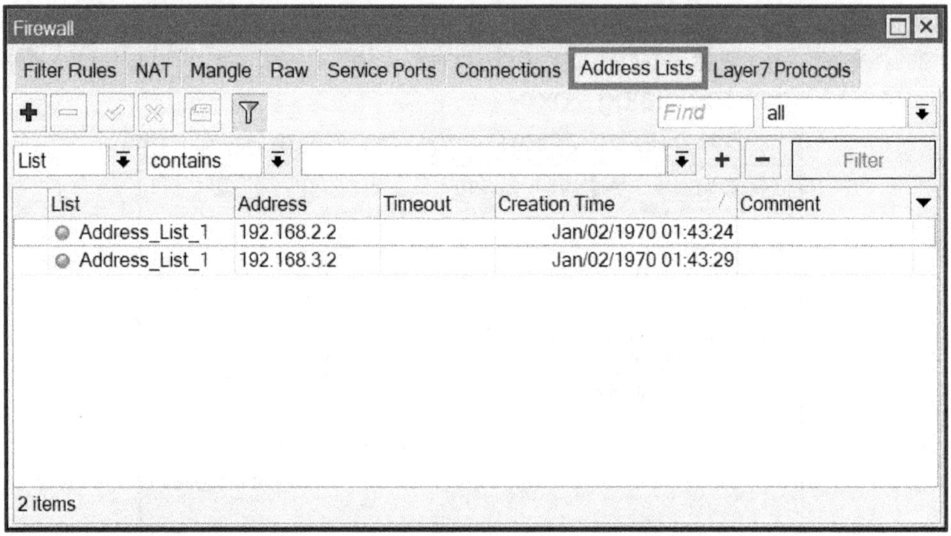

CLI

You can also make the configuration from the CLI.

To assign IP addresses to the interfaces, use the following commands:

```
ip address add address=192.168.1.1/24 interface=ether1
ip address add address=192.168.2.1/24 interface=ether2
ip address add address=192.168.3.1/24 interface=ether3
```

To create the address list and add the IP addresses to it, use the following commands:

```
ip firewall address-list add list=Address_List_1 address=192.168.2.2
ip firewall address-list add list=Address_List_1 address=192.168.3.2
```

To create the firewall filter rule, use the following command:

```
ip firewall filter add src-address=192.168.1.2 protocol=icmp
chain=forward action=add-dst-to-address-list address-list=Address_List_1
```

6.15 Create an Address List Automatically

You can create an address list automatically or dynamically when creating a firewall filter rule by entering the name of the new list in the **Address List** field in the **Action** tab.

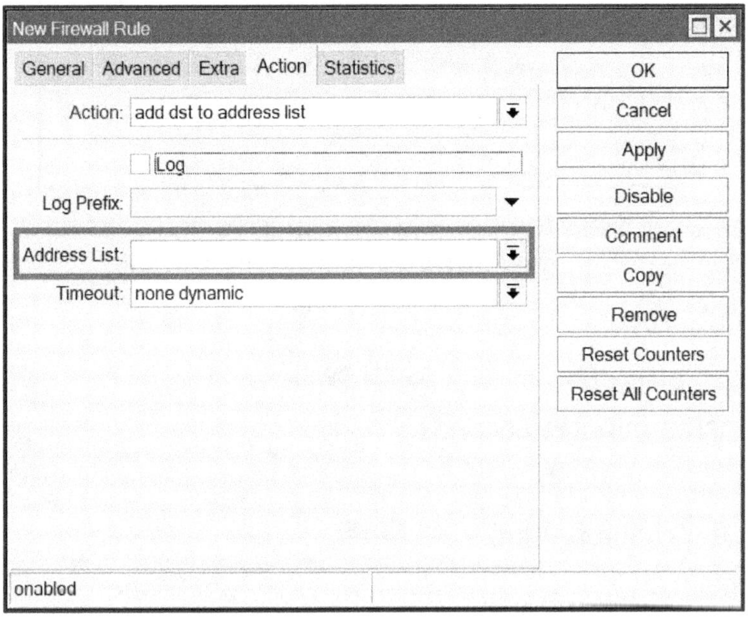

In this case, the firewall rule will create a new address list with the name you entered and add the source or destination IP address to this list.

So: if the name in the **Address List** field refers to an existing address list, the firewall filter rule will add the address to this list. If it is not an existing address list, the firewall filter rule will create a new address list by this name and add the address to it.

6.16 Address List Timeout

When you add an IP address to an address list, you can choose to add it permanently or temporarily for a specific period of time.

To add an IP address permanently to the address list, do not enter any values in the **Timeout** field. This means the IP address will remain in the address list permanently.

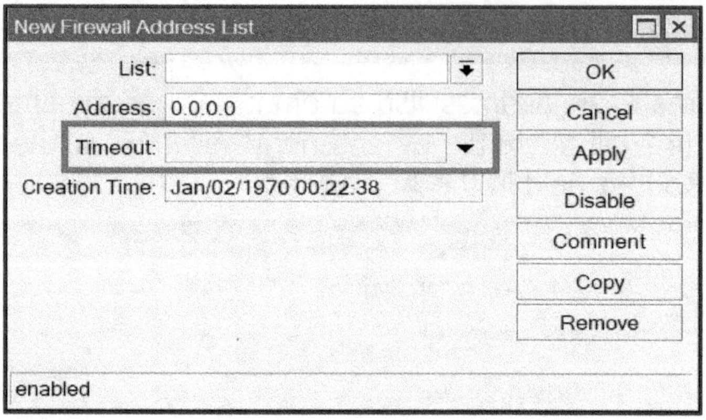

To add an IP address temporarily for a specific period of time, you can specify this period in the **Timeout** field in the format:

hour:minute:second

You can also use the day flag as follows:

[days]d hours:minutes:seconds.

where:

- [days] is the number of days

For example:

1d:10:15:20

In this case, the IP address will remain in the list for the specified period, and then it will be removed.

You can see a countdown timer next to the IP address in the **Address Lists** tab to know how long the IP will stay in the list.

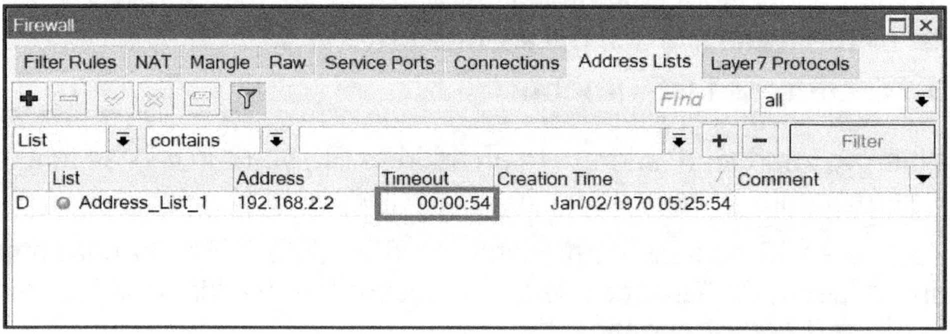

You can also specify the timeout period when dynamically adding an IP address to the address list by entering the period in the **Timeout** field.

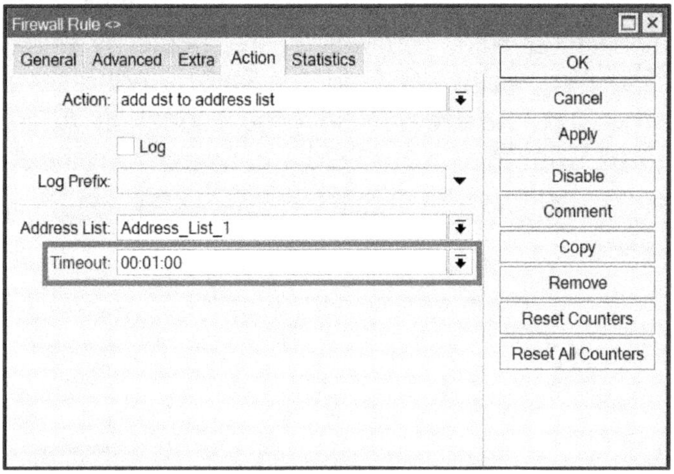

6.17 Some Important Firewall Actions

6.17.1 Drop Action

This action will silently drop the data. That means it will drop the data without notifying the source device.

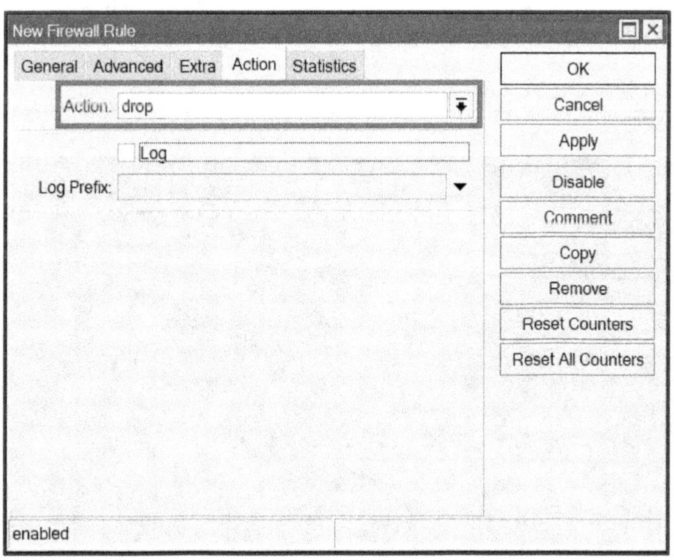

Example

If you want to prevent communication between PC1, which has the IP address 192.168.1.2, and PC2, which has the IP address 192.168.2.2, using a firewall filter rule, you will create a rule by entering PC1 IP address in the **Src. Address** field (or Source Address) and PC2 IP address in the **Dst. Address** field (or Destination Address). Then, select **Forward** from the **Chain** field and **Drop** from the **Action** field.

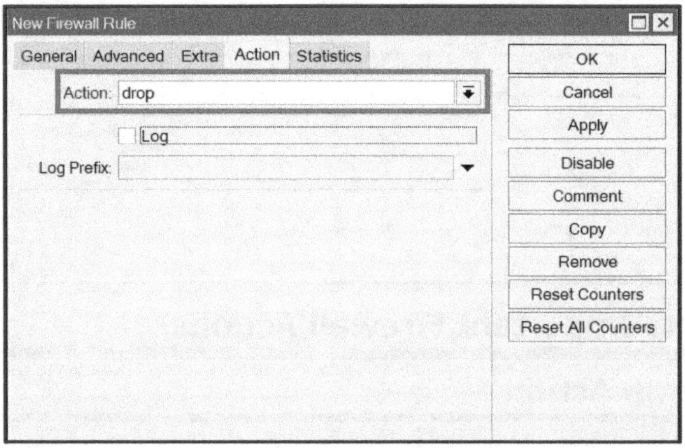

Now, when PC1 tries to ping PC2, the ICMP echo request will be dropped silently, and PC1 will not be informed that the packet was dropped. It will continue waiting for the ICMP echo reply until it times out.

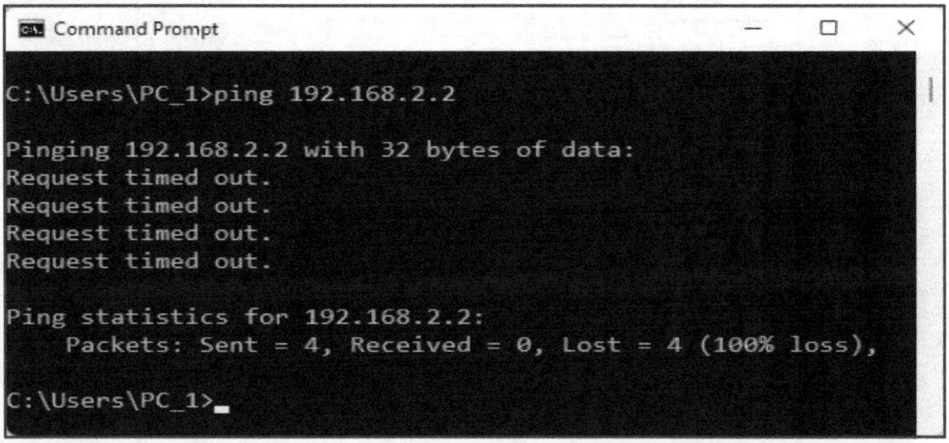

6.17.2 Reject Action

This action will drop the data and send an ICMP reject message to the source device.

You can choose the type of the reject message to send back from the **Reject With** field.

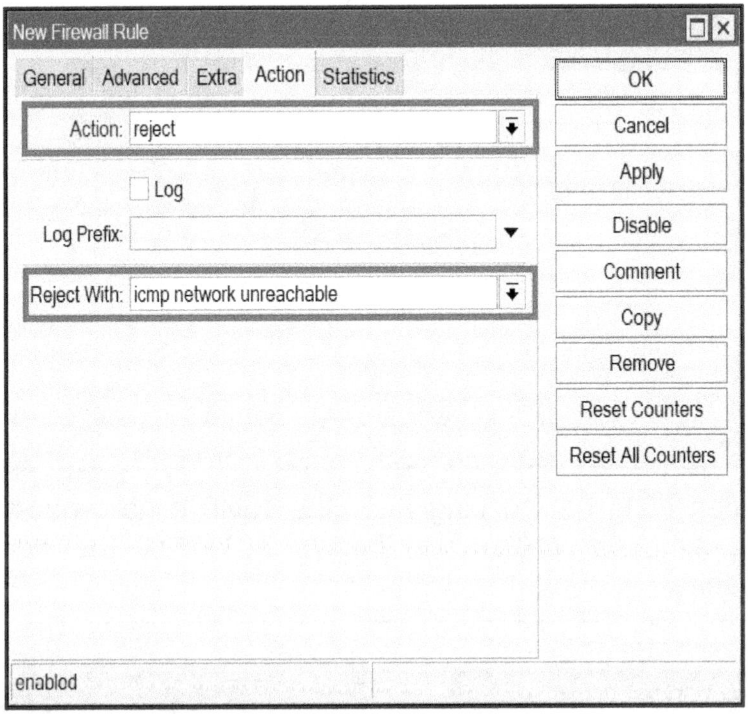

Example

If you want to prevent communication between PC1, which has the IP address 192.168.1.2, and PC2, which has the IP address 192.168.2.2, using a firewall filter rule, you will create a rule by entering PC1 IP address in the **Src. Address** field (or Source Address) and PC2 IP address in the **Dst. Address** field (or Destination Address). Then, select **Forward** from the **Chain** field and **Reject** from the **Action** field and icmp network unreachable from **Reject With** field.

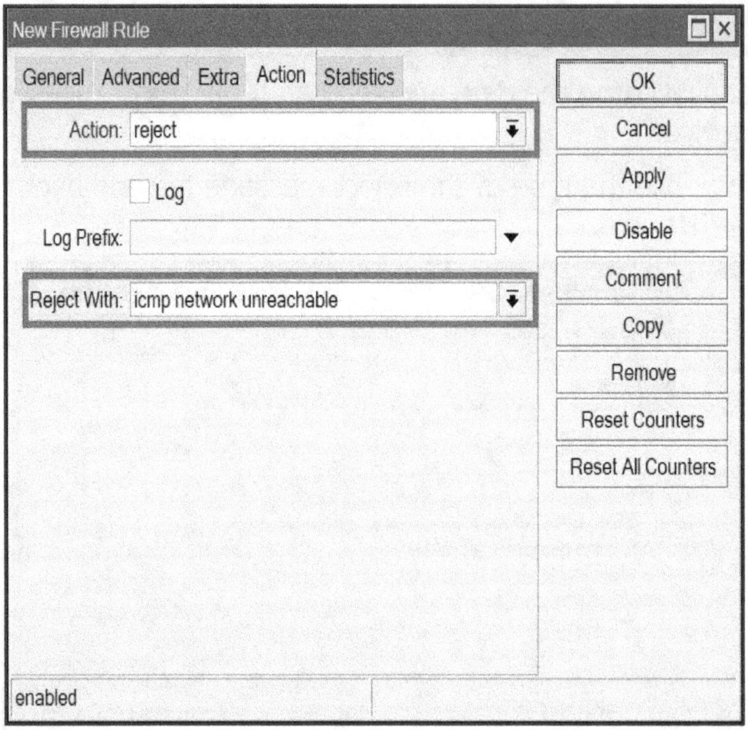

Now, when PC1 tries to ping PC2, the ICMP echo request will be dropped, and the router will inform PC1 that the network is unreachable.

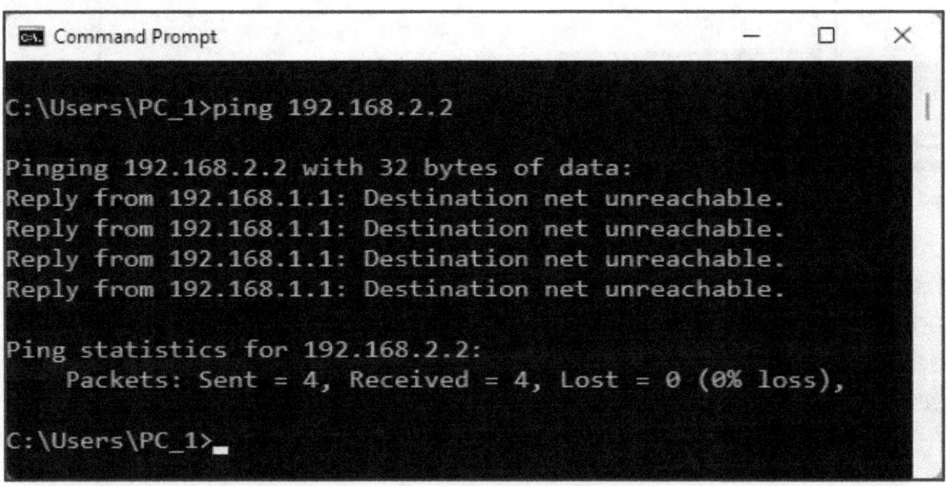

6.17.3 Accept Action

This action will forward the data.

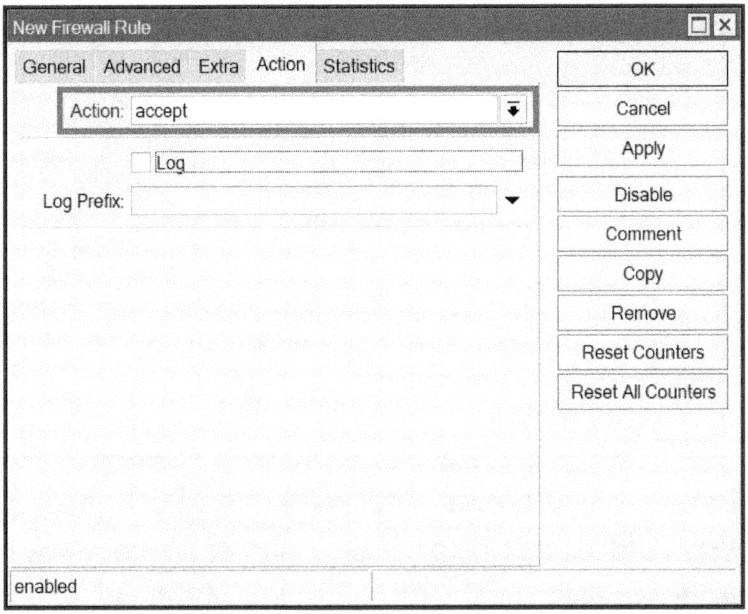

In general, this action is used to forward specific data when there is another rule that blocks or drops all the data. By default, the device forwards all data unless configured otherwise. So, there is no need to configure an Accept rule alone.

Example

If you want to allow PC1, which has the IP address 192.168.1.2, to communicate with PC2, which has the IP address 192.168.2.2, while preventing it from communicating with any other PC using a firewall filter rule, you will create two rules:

- In the first firewall filter rule, enter PC1 IP address in the **Src. Address** field (or Source Address) and PC2 IP address in the **Dst. Address** field (or Destination Address). Then, select **Forward** from the **Chain** field and **Accept** from the **Action** field.

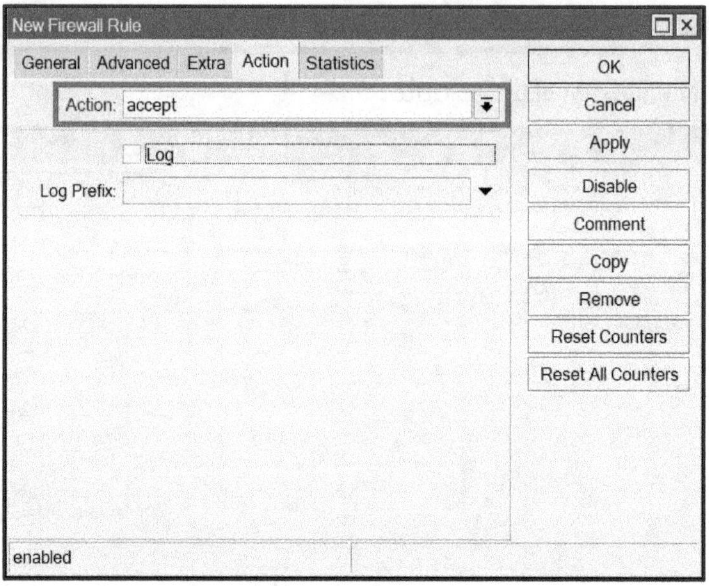

- In the second firewall filter rule, enter PC IP address in the **Src. Address** field (or Source Address) and leave the **Dst. Address** field (or Destination Address) empty, which means the destination is any IP address. Then, select **Forward** from the **Chain** field and **Drop** from the **Action** field.

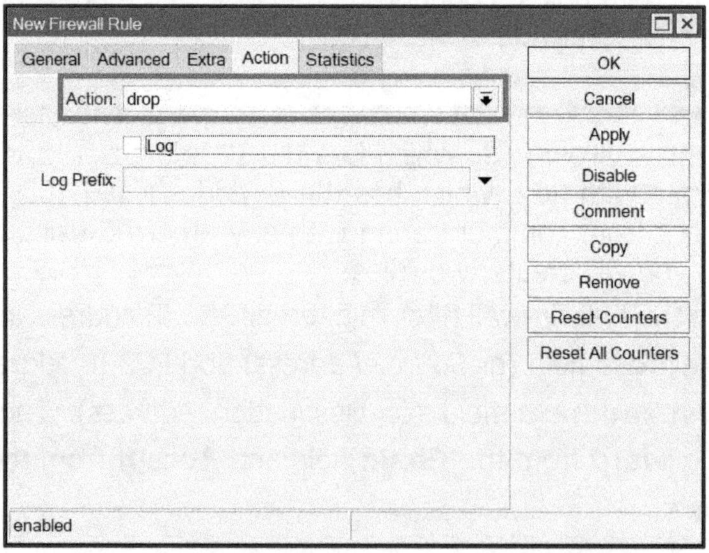

Those two rules will appear in the **Filter Rules** tab of the **Firewall** window.

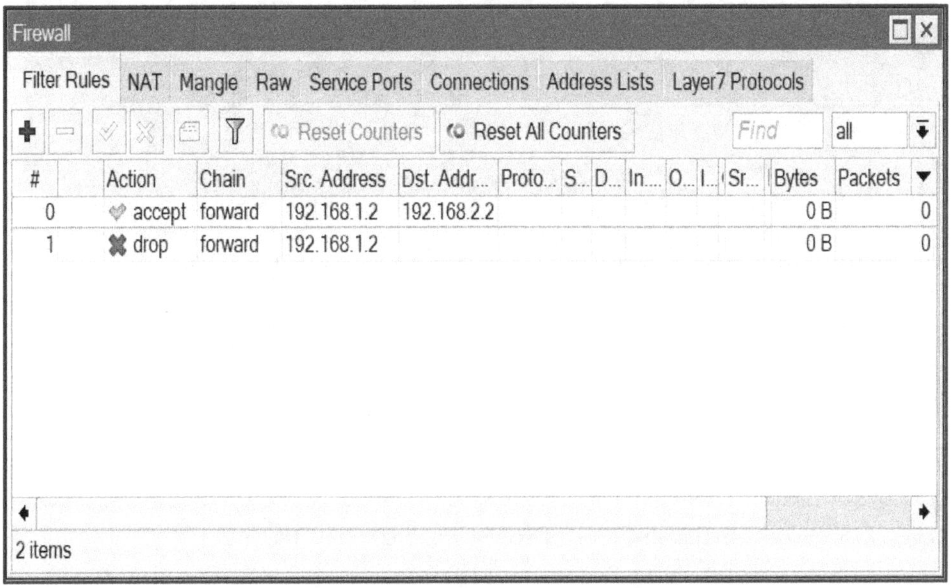

Now, when PC1 tries to ping PC2, the ping will succeed.

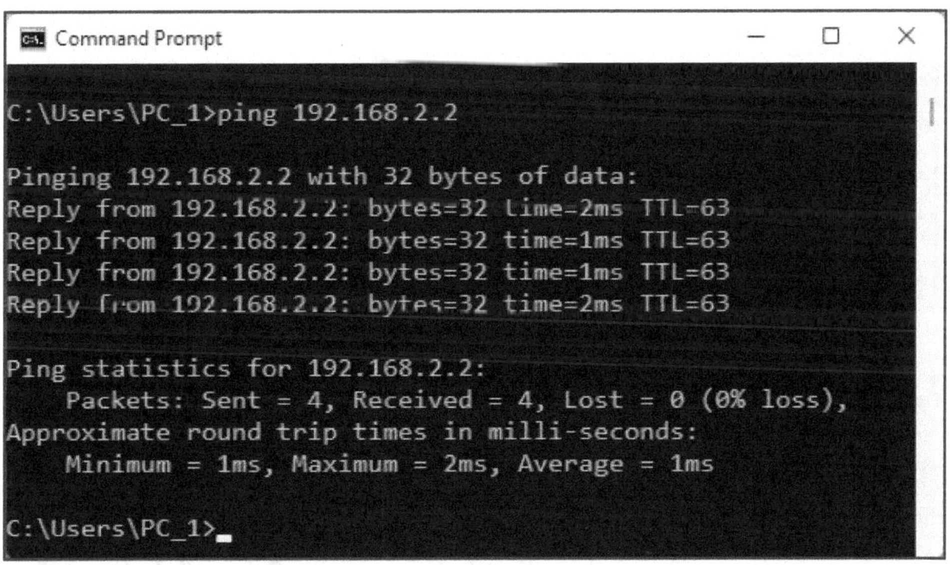

When PC1 tries to ping any other IP address, the ICMP echo request will be dropped silently.

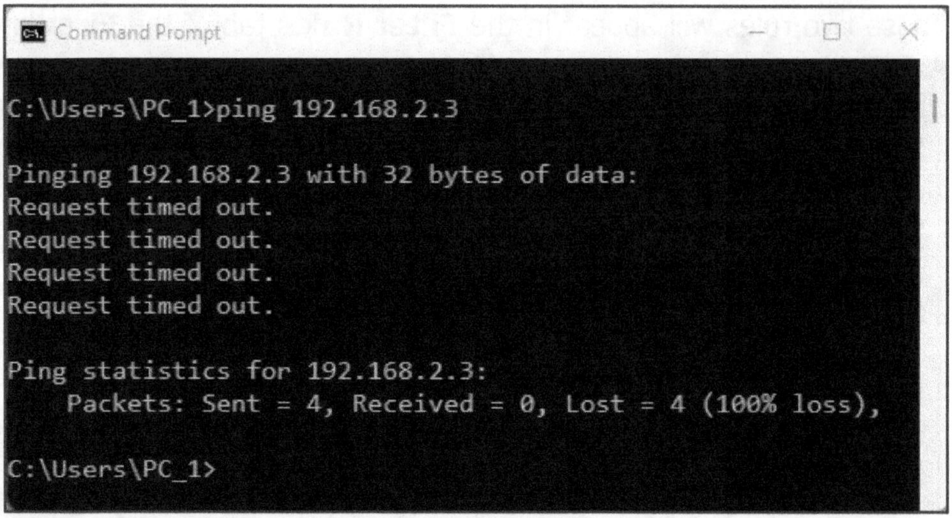

Note: in this example, the order of the rules is very important because the first rule allows communication from PC1 to PC2, while the second rule blocks all communication from PC1 to any PC.

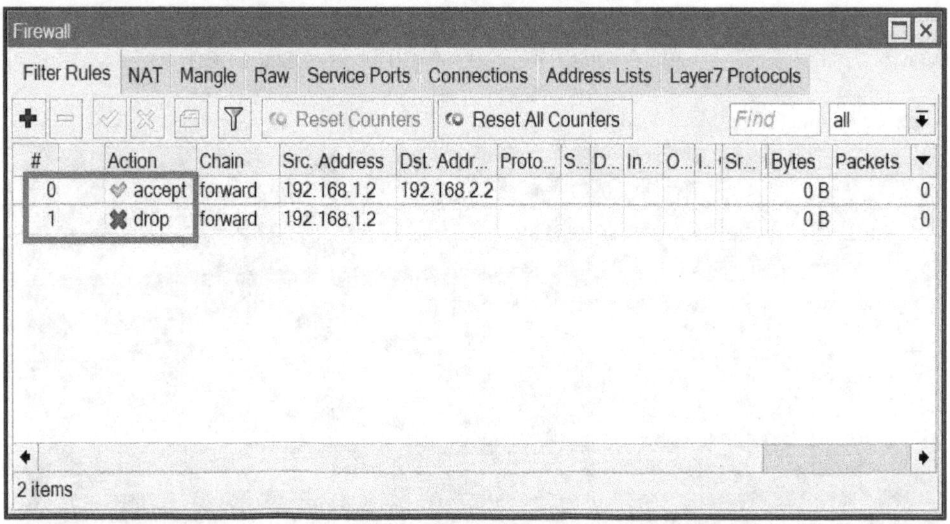

This is why when trying to ping PC2, it will succeed, but when trying to ping any other IP, it will not succeed.

If you place the second rule at the top, in this case, PC1 will not be able to ping any PC, including PC2.

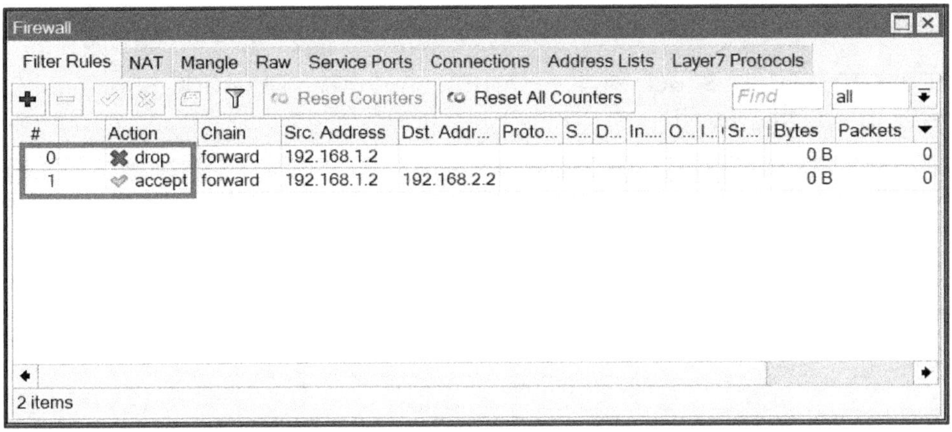

6.17.4 Log Action

This action adds a message to the system log containing information about the chosen data and then moves to the next rule in the firewall.

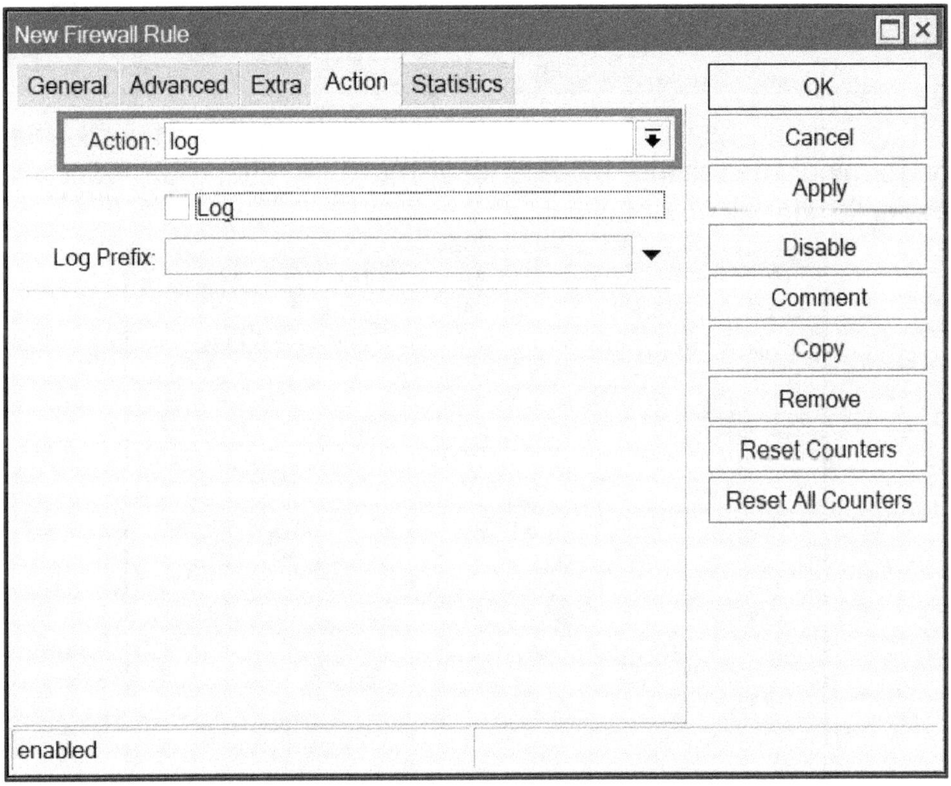

This action does not block or modify the data.

You can use this action for troubleshooting, network analysis, or tracing specific traffic.

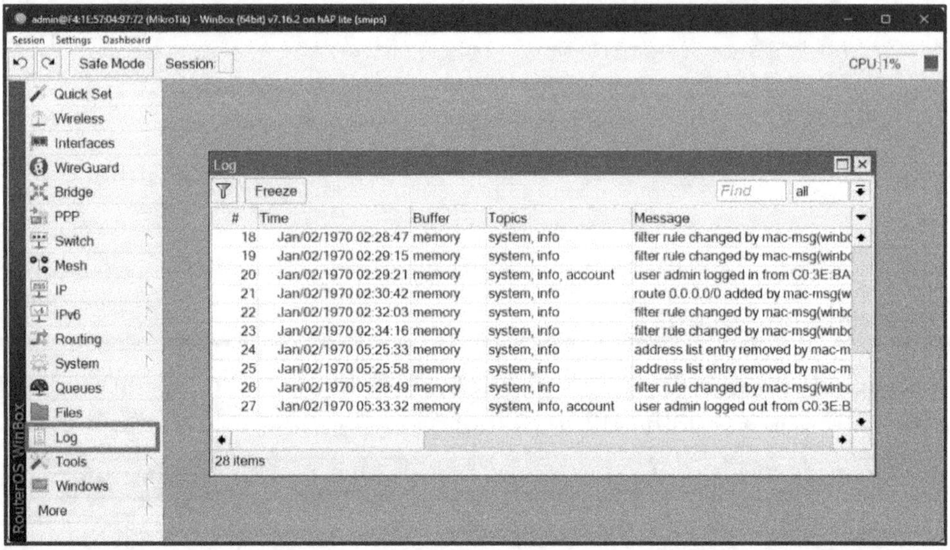

On the other hand, you can log all other actions as well after performing the action by checking the **Log** checkbox, which is available with all other actions.

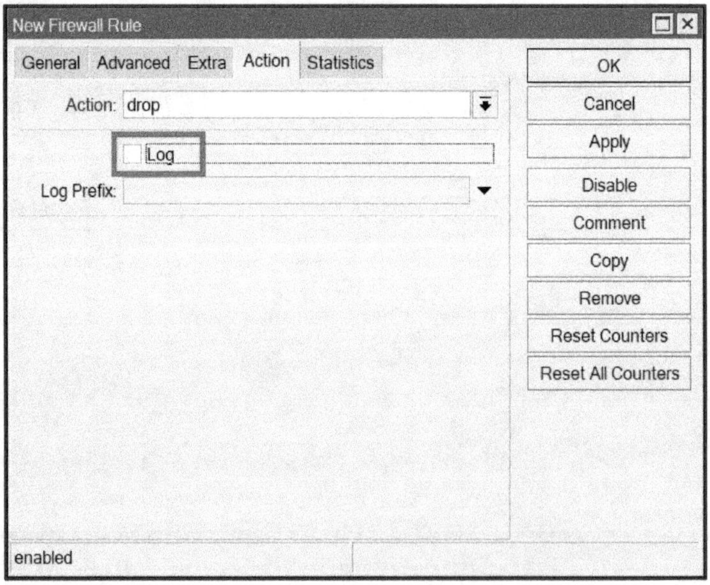

Example

If you want to add a note in the system log when PC1, which has the IP address 192.168.1.2, communicates with PC2, which has the IP address 192.168.2.2, using a firewall filter rule, you will create a rule by entering PC1 IP address in the **Src. Address** field (or Source Address) and PC2 IP address in the **Dst. Address** field (or Destination Address). Select **Forward** from the **Chain** field, then select the **Log** action from the **Action** field. To make it easier to recognize these logs in the system log window, add a note in the **Log Prefix** field, such as (PC1 to PC2 communications).

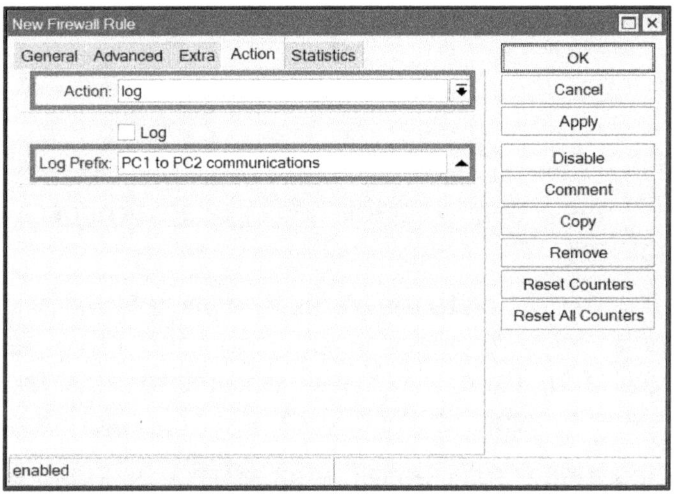

Now, when PC1 tries to ping PC2, log messages will be added to the **Log** window with the note you provided.

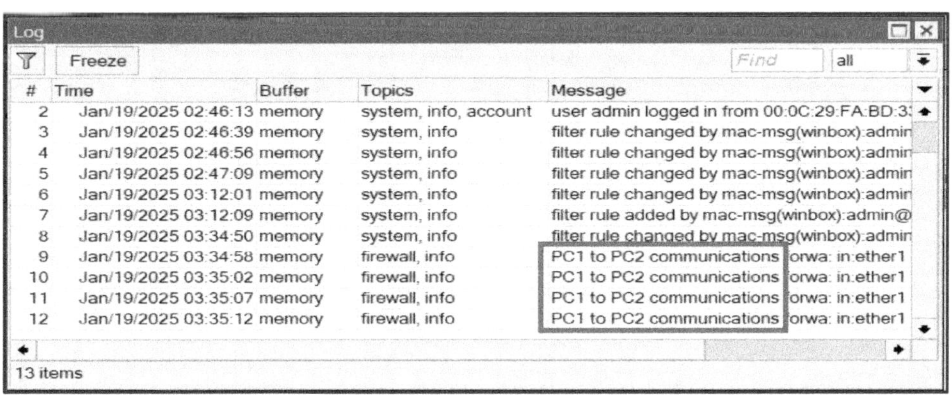

Note: the ping will succeed because this rule does not block the traffic, as mentioned.

6.17.5 FastTrack Action

This action accelerates packet flow through the RouterOS.

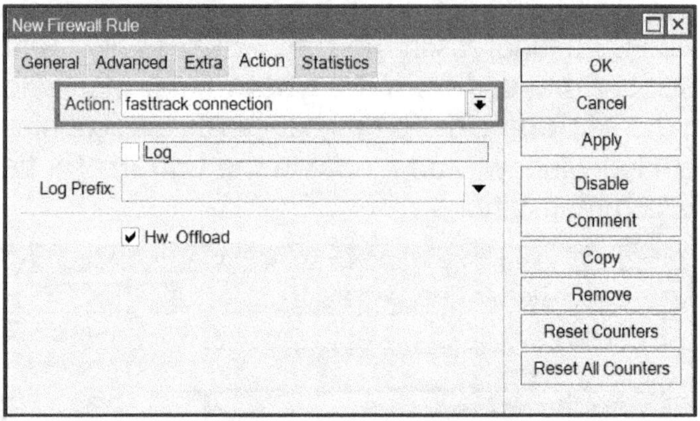

You can apply this action to established or related connections for TCP and UDP protocols.

When applying this action to the traffic, the packets will bypass firewall filters, mangle rules, connection tracking, and other features like simple queues and IPsec. So, it is important to consider that when using this action to avoid conflicts with other configurations.

When creating a filter rule using the Fast Track action, the device will automatically create another filter rule with the passthrough action.

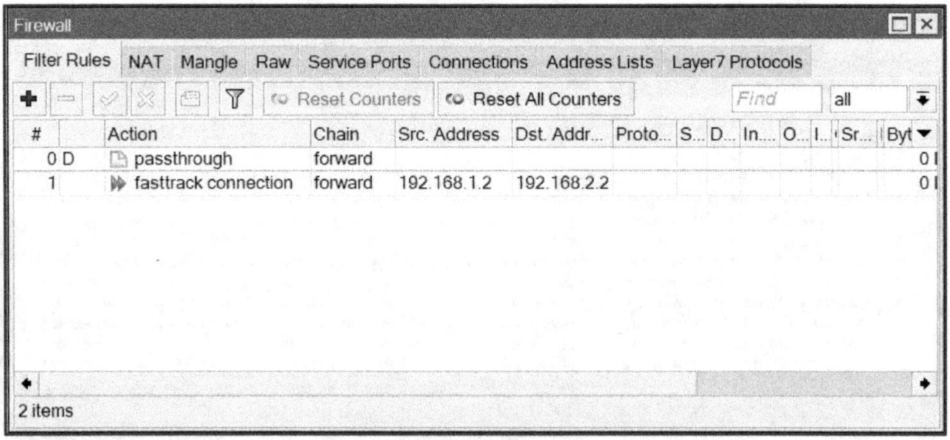

If you want to remove the Fast Track rule, first you need to delete the rule, and then you must reboot the device to remove the other automatically created rule.

Example

If you want to accelerate the communications between PC1, which has the IP address 192.168.1.2, and PC2, which has the IP address 192.168.2.2, using a firewall filter rule, you will create a rule by entering PC1 IP address in the **Src. Address** field (or Source Address) and PC2 IP address in the **Dst. Address** field (or Destination Address). Then, select **Forward** from the **Chain** field and **Fasttrack connection** from the **Action** field.

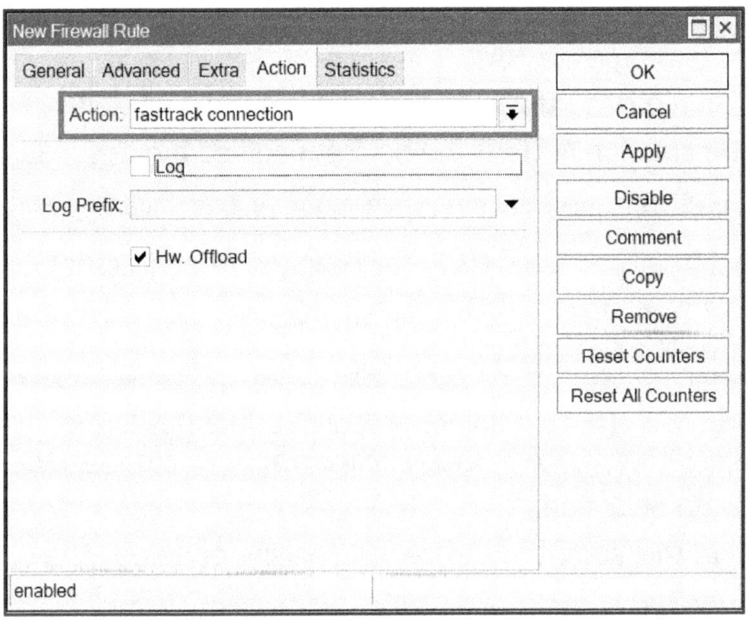

Now the communication between the PC1 and PC2 will be fast tracked.

NAT

6.18 NAT Overview and Key Concepts

Network Address Translation (NAT) is a technology used to modify the Source IP or the Destination IP of a packet.

There are two types of NAT:

- Source NAT: If the device modifies the source IP.
- Destination NAT: If the device modifies the destination IP.

The network that uses NAT technology is called a NATed network

The device that performs NAT, (or changes IP addresses), is called a NAT gateway or NAT router.

6.19 How NAT Works

To perform NAT, (or to modify the source or the destination IP address of a packet), the device follows similar stages or steps as the firewall

- Data Selection

  In this step, the device will specify, or select, the data to be NATed.

- Chain Choosing

  In this step, the device will specify, or choose, the type of NAT.

- Applying the Action:

  In this step, the device will specify the action to be applied to the data.

You can configure RouterOS to perform NAT operations by using the **NAT** tab of the **Firewall** window and creating NAT rules.

6.20 NAT Rules

NAT rules are instructions that tell the device how to perform the NAT: which data to be NATed, the type of NAT, and what action should be applied to this data.

When multiple rules exist, the device processes them sequentially, starting from the first rule to the last, based on their sequence numbers. The processing stops as soon as the first matching rule is found.

6.21 NAT Configuration

To configure RouterOS to perform NAT operations, use the **NAT** tab of the **Firewall** Window.

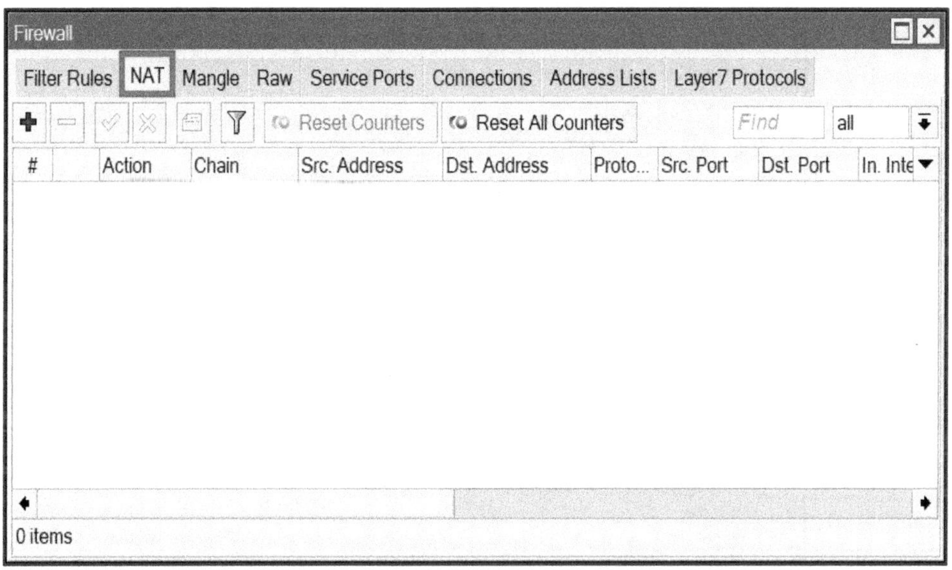

To open the **Firewall** window, click the **IP** menu, then select **Firewall**.

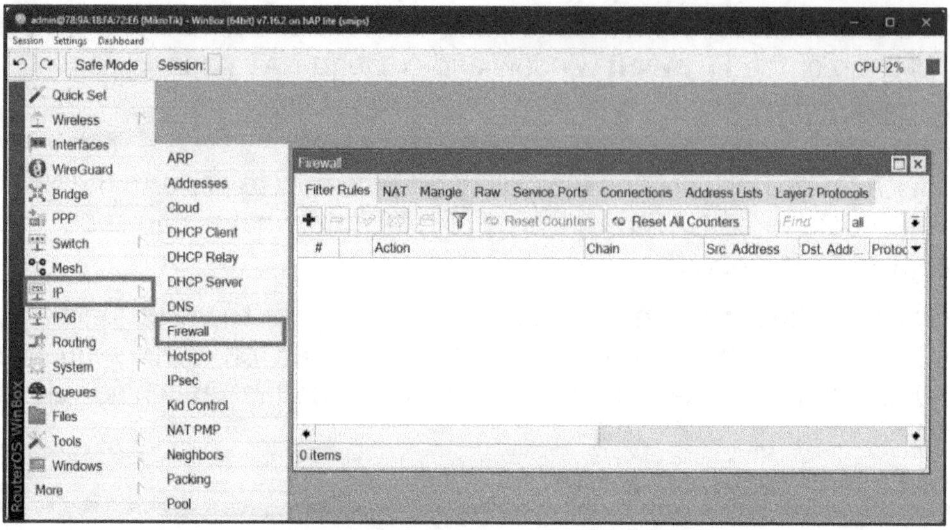

To add a NAT rule, click the **Add** button in the **NAT** tab of the **Firewall** window to open the **New NAT Rule** dialog box.

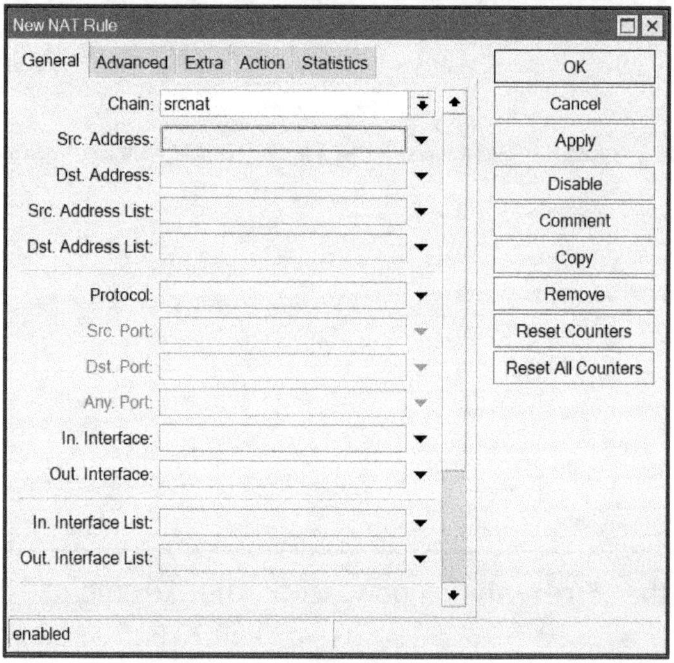

You can use this dialog box to create a new NAT rule and configure its settings.

As mentioned, the device performs NAT by following three stages or steps similar to the firewall:

- Data selection.
- Chain choosing.
- Appling the action.

You will configure these three steps when adding a new NAT rule.

6.22 Data Selection

In this step, specify, or select, the data you want to NAT, (or you want to change its source or destination IP address).

You can select the data based on criteria such as source IP, destination IP, source port, destination port, incoming interface, outgoing interface, protocol, or other options provided by MikroTik RouterOS. These options are available in the **General**, **Advanced**, and **Extra** tabs from the **New NAT Rule** dialog box.

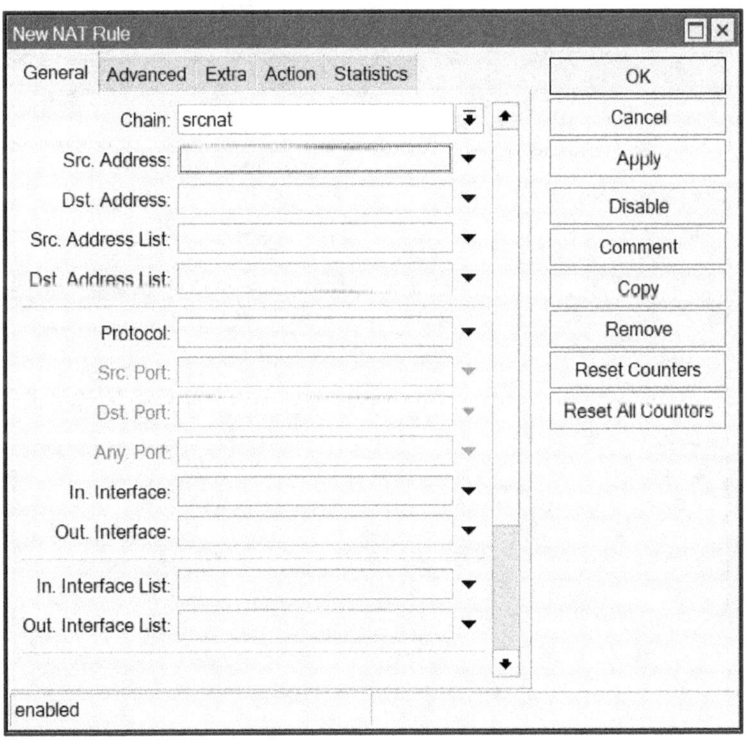

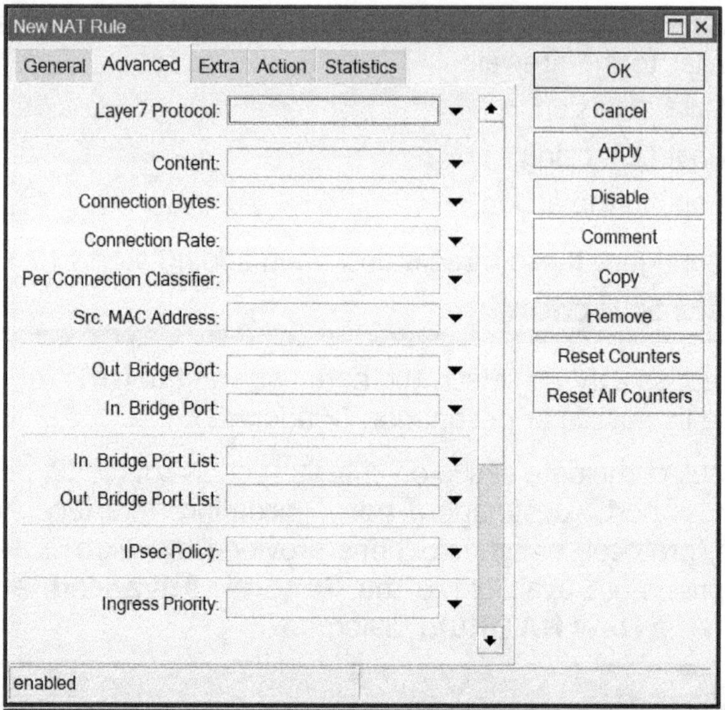
New NAT Rule
General
Advanced
Extra
Action
Statistics
Layer7 Protocol:
Content:
Connection Bytes:
Connection Rate:
Per Connection Classifier:
Src. MAC Address:
Out. Bridge Port:
In. Bridge Port:
In. Bridge Port List:
Out. Bridge Port List:
IPsec Policy:
Ingress Priority:
OK
Cancel
Apply
Disable
Comment
Copy
Remove
Reset Counters
Reset All Counters
enabled

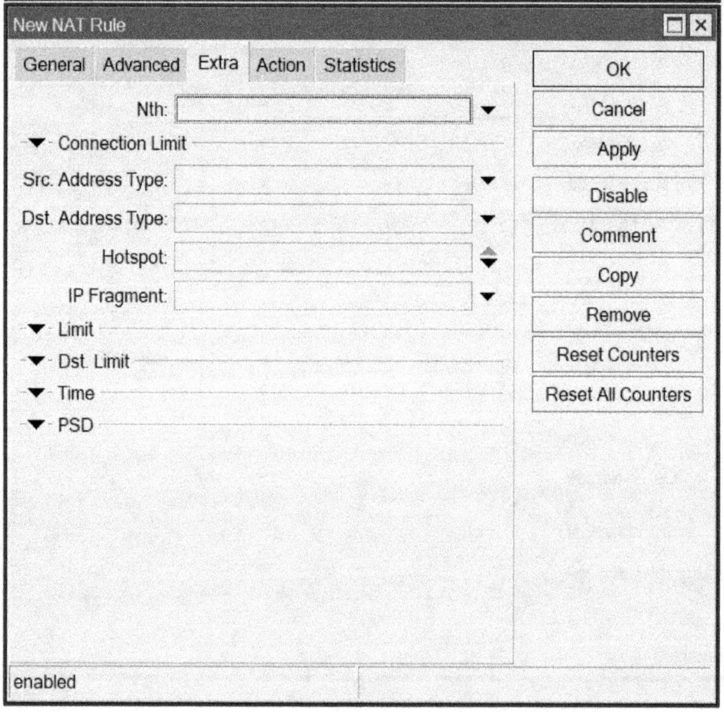
New NAT Rule
General
Advanced
Extra
Action
Statistics
Nth:
Connection Limit
Src. Address Type:
Dst. Address Type:
Hotspot:
IP Fragment:
Limit
Dst. Limit
Time
PSD
OK
Cancel
Apply
Disable
Comment
Copy
Remove
Reset Counters
Reset All Counters
enabled

For example, if you want to change the source IP address of the data coming from a PC which has the IP address 192.168.1.15, you will enter this IP address in the **Src. Address** field, (or Source Address), in the **General** tab.

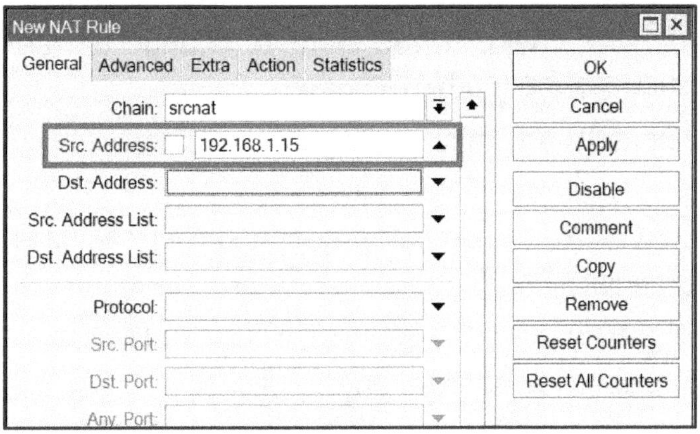

Likewise, if you want to change the source IP address of the data coming from the interface ether1, you will select this interface from the **In. Interface** field in the **General** tab

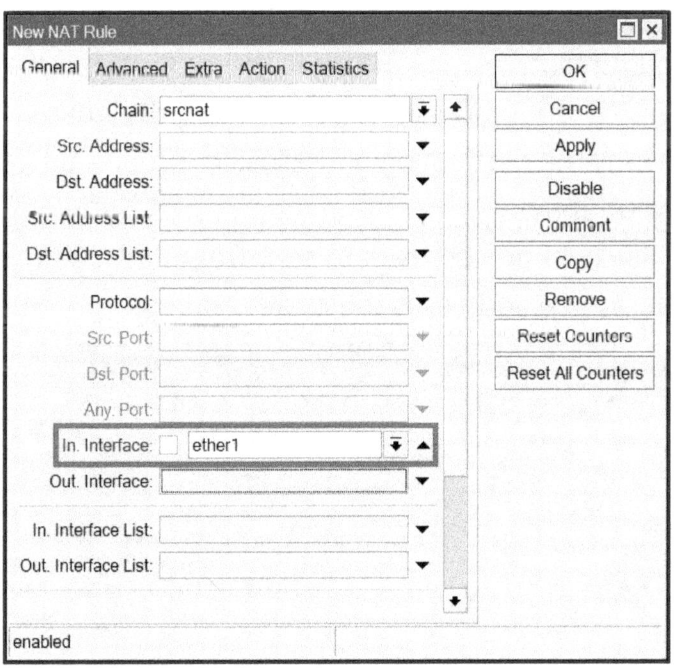

6.23 Chain Choosing:

In this step, specify, or choose, the type of NAT, In other words, determine what you want to change: the source IP address or the destination IP address. If you want to change the source IP address, select source NAT chain. If you want to change the destination IP address, select destination NAT chain.

There are default predefined chains, and there are user-defined chains.

In the Router OS V6, the default predefined NAT chains are:

- Source NAT

  This chain performs source NAT, so you can use it to change the source IP address on the packet
- Destination NAT

  This chain performs destination NAT, so you can use it to change the destination IP address on the packet

In Router Osv7, there are two new chains:

- Input Chain:

  This chain processes data sent to the router itself, that means the destination address is the router address.
- Output Chain:

  This chain processes data sent from the router, that means the source address is the router address.

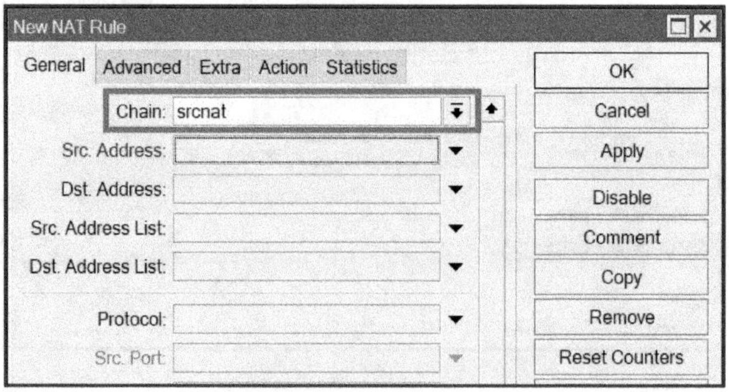

6.24 Applying the Action

In this step, specify the action to be applied to the data.

You can change the source IP address, or the destination IP address, or apply any other actions listed in the **Action** tab of the **New NAT Rule** dialog box

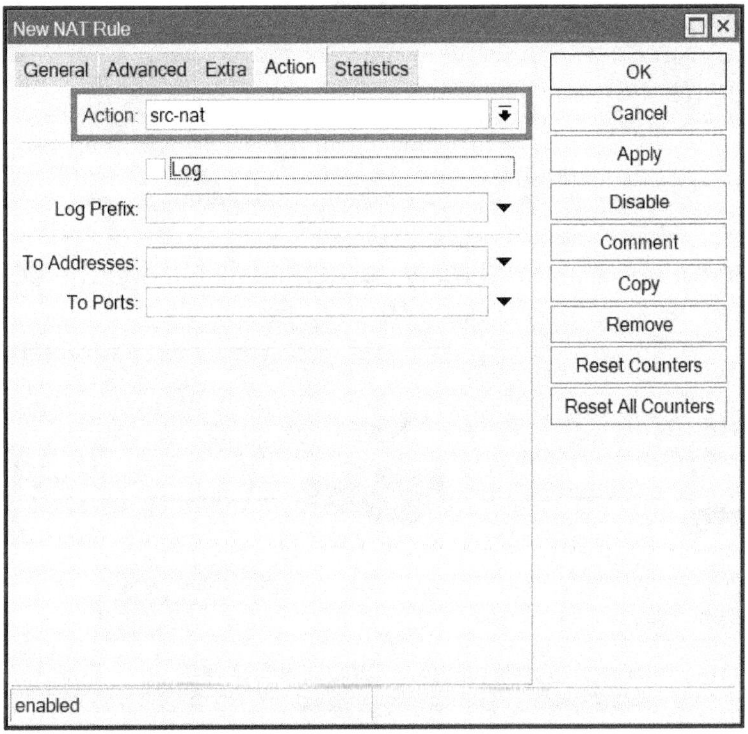

When creating a NAT rule, it checks the first packet of the chosen connection, and the connection tracking tool will remember this action, applying it to all packets belonging to the same connection.

It is very important to understand that if you change a NAT rule, you should clear the old entries in the **Connections** tracking tab to allow the NAT rule to function correctly.

Also, it is important to understand that when performing NAT to change the source or destination IP address of a packet, a reverse operation will be applied to the reply packets.

For example, if the router changes the source IP address of the packet from 192.168.1.2 to 200.0.0.3.

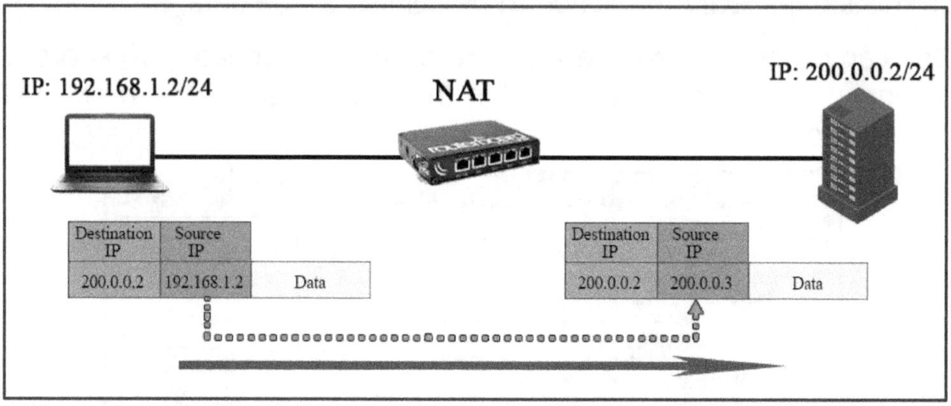

When the router receives a reply packet, it will change the destination IP address back from 200.0.0.3 to 192.168.1.2

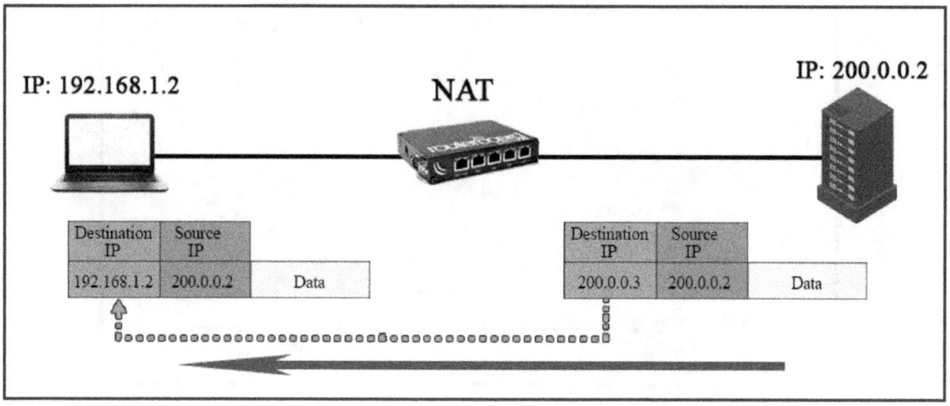

You can also add, or create, a NAT rule from the CLI using the following command:

```
ip firewall nat add src-address=[address] chain=[chain] action=[action]
```

Where:

- [address] is the source IP address.
- [chain] is the chain of the rule
- [action] is the desired action

Note: when using an action, you may need to specify additional parameters for it.

For example:

```
ip firewall nat add src-address=192.168.1.2 chain=srcnat action=src-nat to-addresses=200.0.0.3
```

```
Terminal <1>
[admin@MikroTik] >
[admin@MikroTik] >
[admin@MikroTik] > ip firewall nat add src-address=192.168.1.2 chain=srcnat
action=src-nat to-addresses=200.0.0.3
```

You can also use other parameters to specify the destination address, protocol, port, and more.

To display the current NAT rules in RouterOS from the CLI use the following command:

```
ip firewall nat print
```

```
Terminal <1>
[admin@MikroTik] >
[admin@MikroTik] > ip firewall nat print
Flags: X - disabled, I - invalid; D - dynamic
 0    chain=srcnat action=src-nat to-addresses=200.0.0.3 src-address=192.168.1.2
[admin@MikroTik] >
```

LAB

In this lab, the MikroTik device R1 is connected to two computers, each in a different subnet. PC1 has the IP address 192.168.1.2/24, is connected to the interface ether1, Server 1, has the IP address 200.0.0.2/24, is connected to the interface ether2.

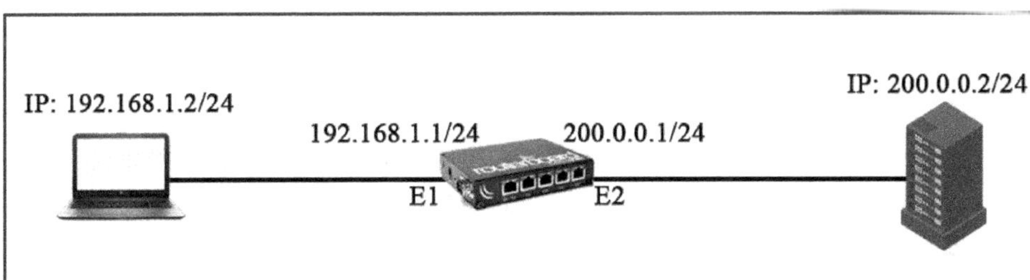

You want to change the IP address of PC1 when it tries to connect to the server from 192.168.1.2 to 200.0.0.3

To start the configuration:

- First: perform the basic configuration to assign the IP addresses to MikroTik interfaces .
- Second: configure (or create) a NAT rule to change the IP address of PC 1

Basic Configuration

- Assign the IP address 192.168.1.1/24 to the interface ether1.
- Assign the IP address 200.0.0.1/24 to the interface ether2.

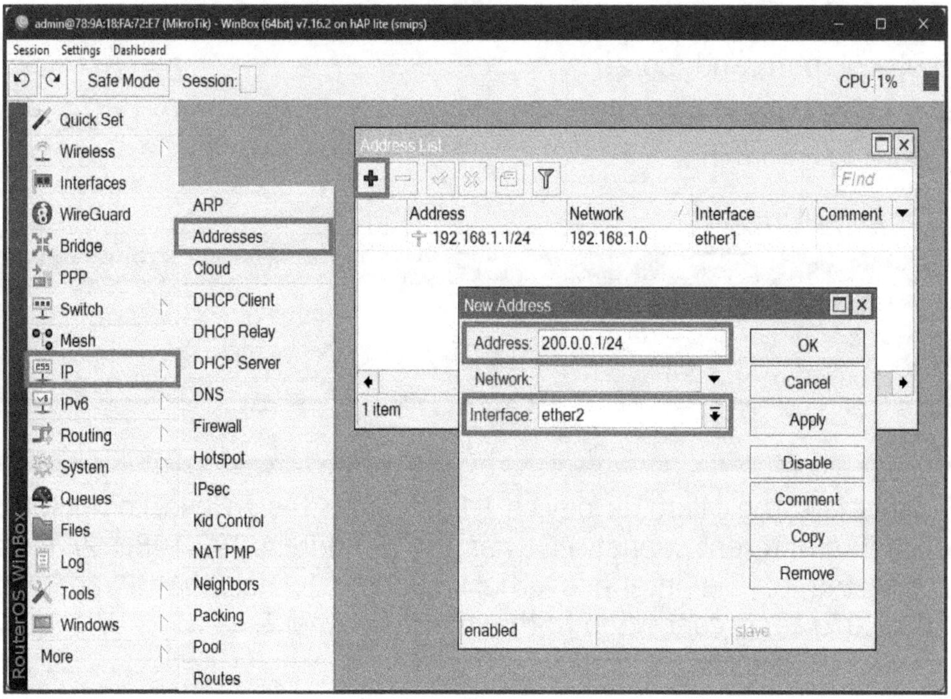

NAT Configuration

To create a NAT rule, click the **IP** menu and select **Firewall** to open the **Firewall** window. Then, click the **Add** button in the **NAT** tab to open the **New NAT Rule** dialog box.

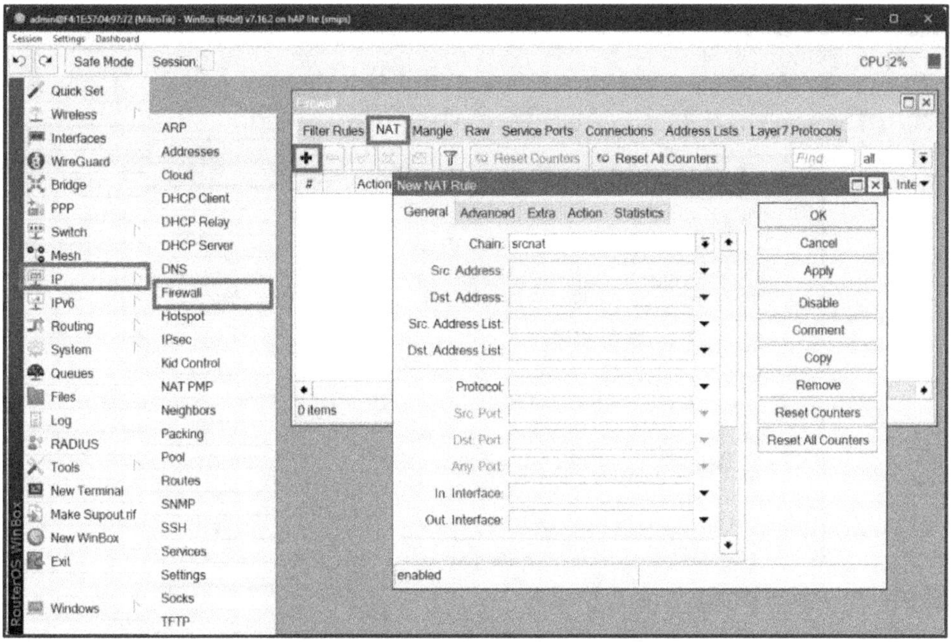

To configure the NAT rule, follow the three main steps:

Step 1: Data Selection

To select the data sourced from PC1 and destined for Server1:

- Enter the IP address of PC1 192.168.1.2 in the **Src. Address** filed, (or Source Address).
- Enter the IP address of Server1 200.0.0.2 in the **Dst. Address** field, (or Destination Address).

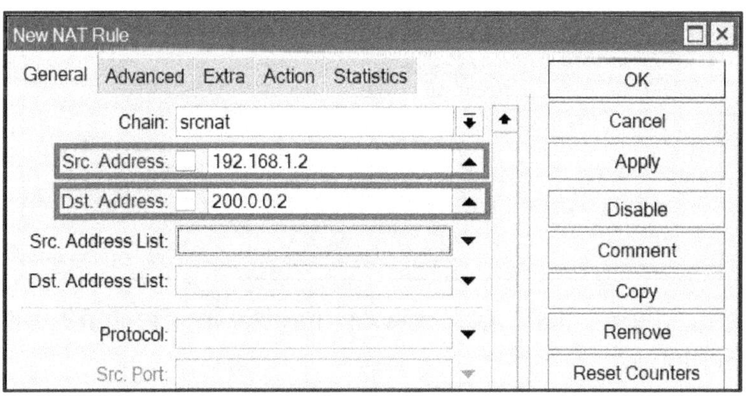

Step 2: Chain Choosing

Since you want to change the source IP address of PC1, select the **srcnat** (or source NAT) chain from the **Chain** field.

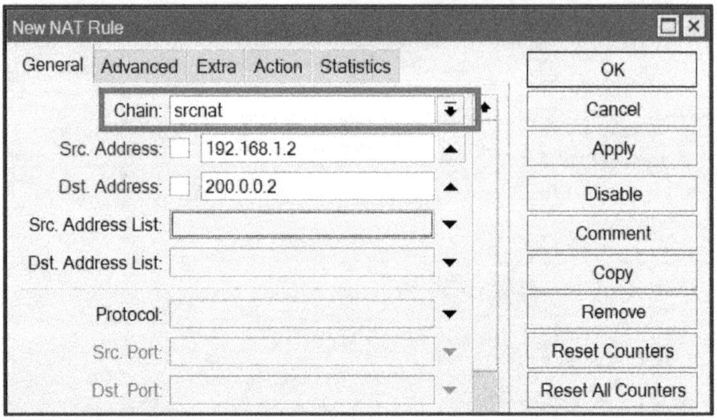

Step 3: Applying the Action

To change the source IP address, select the **src-nat** (or source NAT**)** action from the **Action** field in the **Action** tab. In the **To Address** field, enter the IP address 200.0.0.3, and click the **Ok** button to close this dialog box.

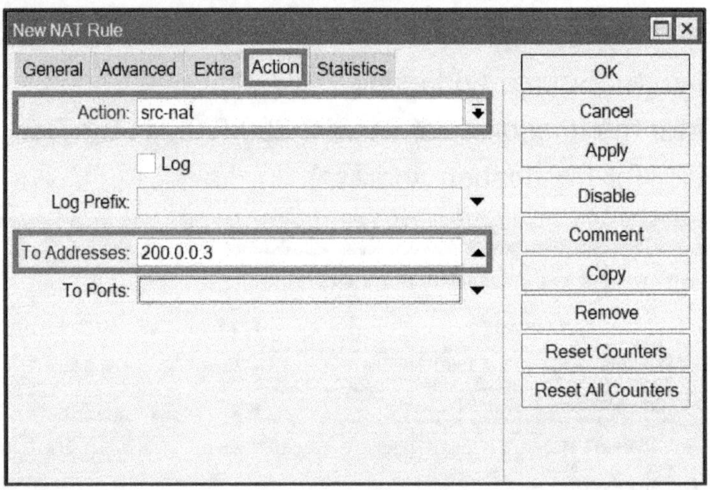

After creating the NAT rule, it will appear in the **NAT** tab of the **Firewall** window.

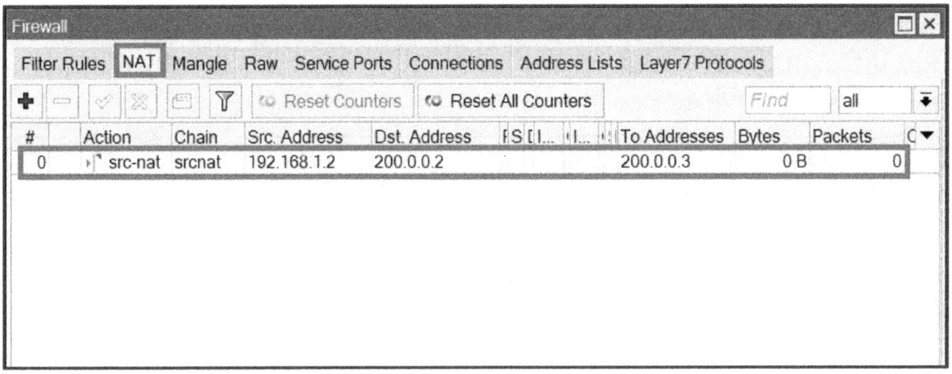

Now, when PC1 tries to ping Server1, PC1 will create a packet and write its IP address as the source IP 192.168.1.2 and the server IP address as the destination IP 200.0.0.2 in this packet.

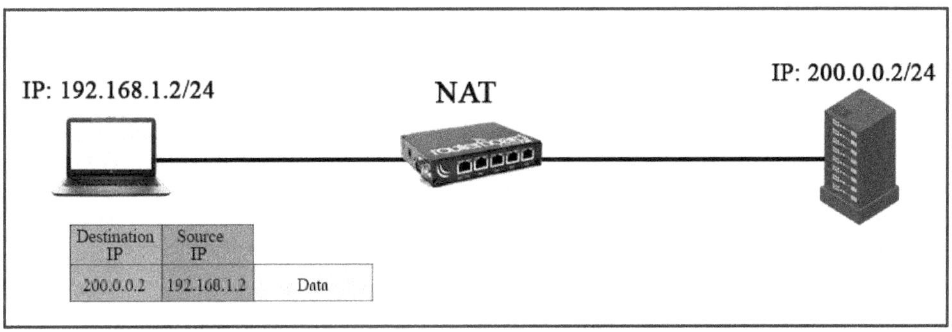

When this packet reaches the MikroTik device, it will perform a NAT operation, changing the source IP from 192.168.1.2 to 200.0.0.3, and then send it to Server1.

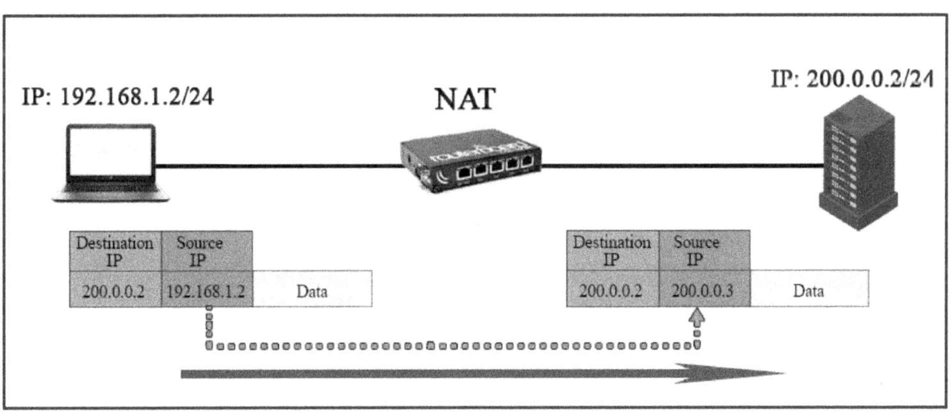

When the server replies, it will write its IP address as the source IP 200.0.0.2 and 200.0.0.3 as the destination IP, then send the reply to the MikroTik device.

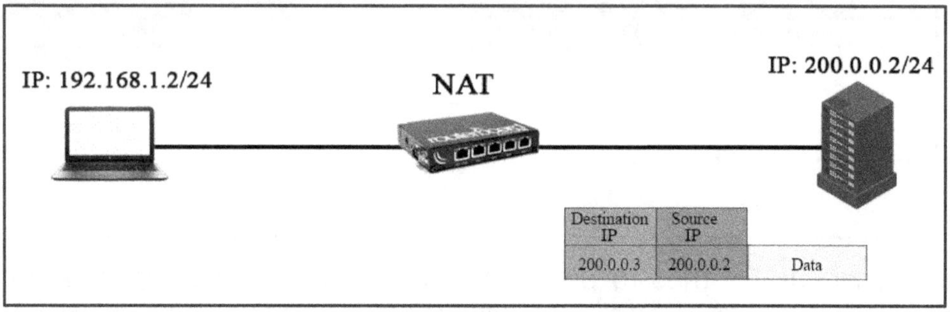

As mentioned before, the MikroTik device will perform a reverse operation when it receives this reply. It will change the destination IP address from 200.0.0.3 back to PC1 IP address, 192.168.1.2, and send it to PC1.

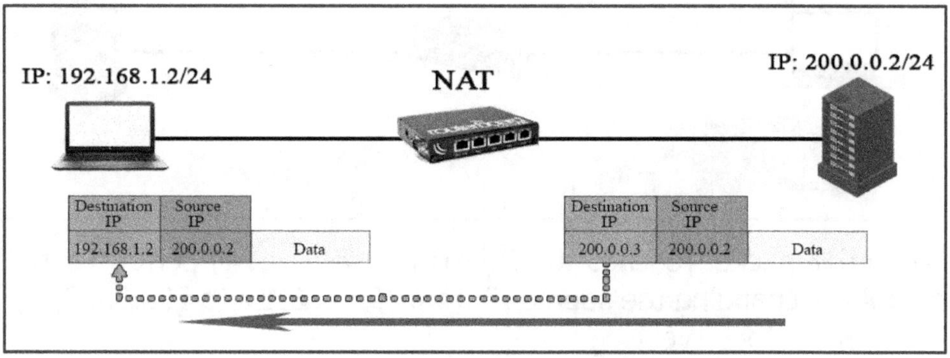

CLI

You can also make the configuration from the CLI .

To assign IP addresses to the interfaces, use the following commands:

```
ip address add address=192.168.1.1/24 interface=ether1

ip address add address=200.0.0.1/24 interface=ether2
```

To create the NAT rule, use the following command:

```
ip firewall nat add src-address=192.168.1.2 dst-address=200.0.0.2
chain=srcnat action=src-nat to-addresses=200.0.0.3
```

6.25 Manage NAT Rules

NAT rules work very similarly to firewall rules, and the **NAT** tab displays the NAT rules created on the device. It is important to know how to read the NAT rules and understand what each rule does

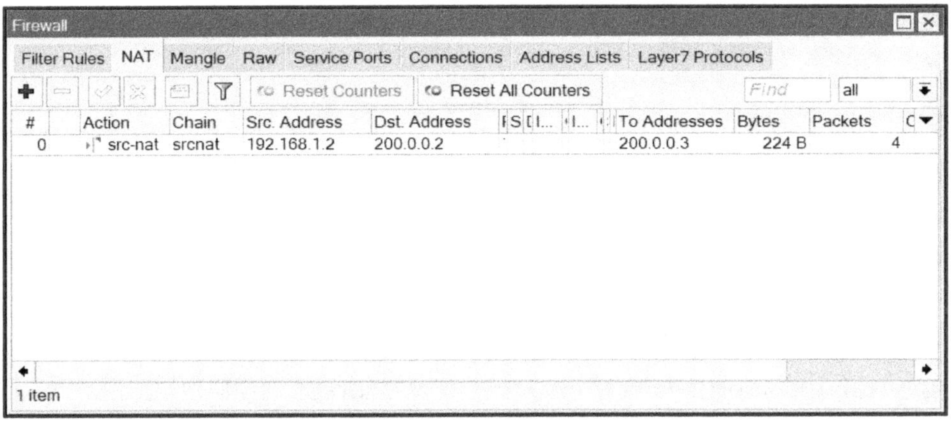

In the previous lab, you created a NAT rule. By looking at this rule in the **NAT** tab, the **Src. Address** (or Source Address) and the **Dst. Address** (or Destination Address) fields tell you that this rule will be applied to data sourced from, (or coming from), the IP address 192.168.1.2 and destined for, (or going to), the IP address 200.0.0.2

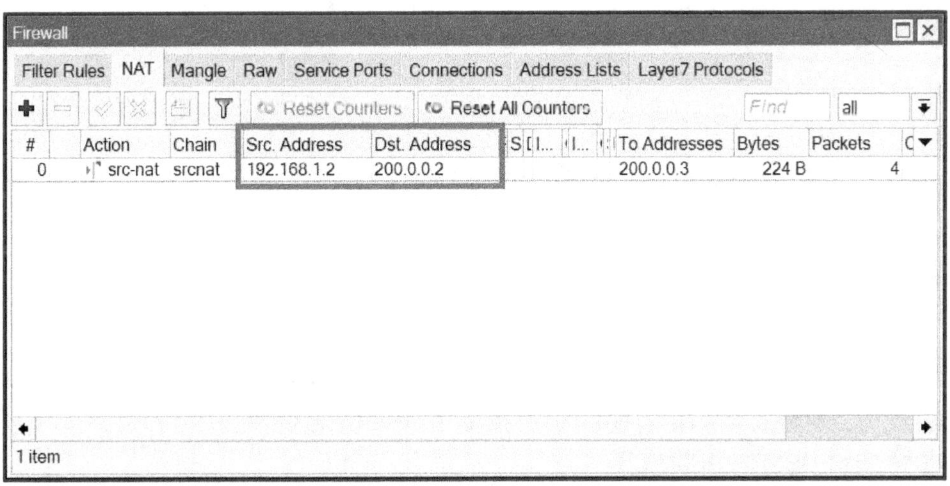

The C**hain** field tells you that the chain is **srcnat** (or source NAT), so this rule will change the source IP address.

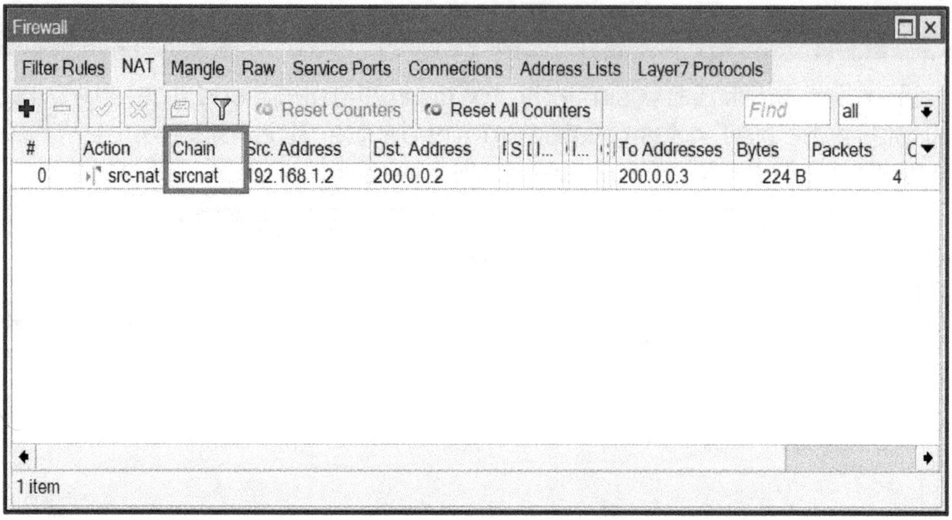

The **Action** field and **To Addresses** field tell you that the action is **src-nat** (or source NAT), and the new address is 200.0.0.3 so it will change the source IP address to the address entered in the **To Addresses** field.

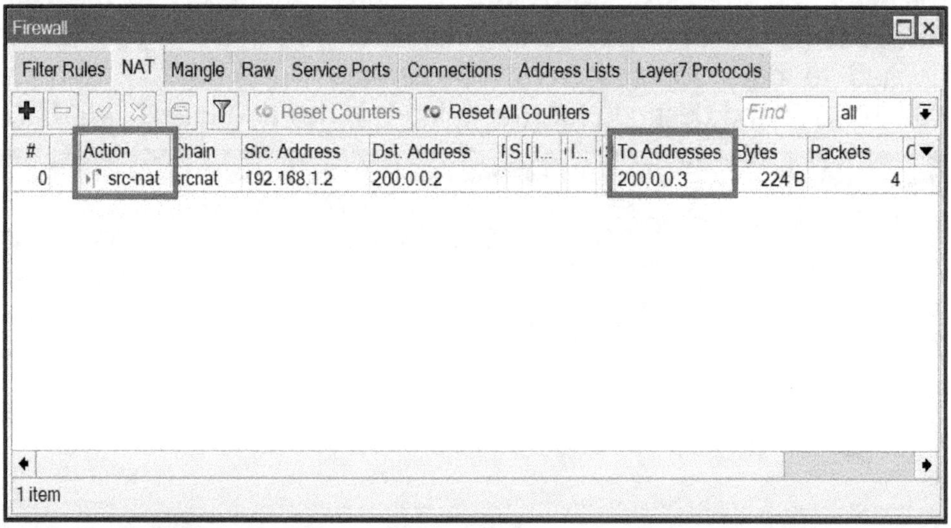

Also, the **Packets** field tells you how many times this rule has matched data and been applied.

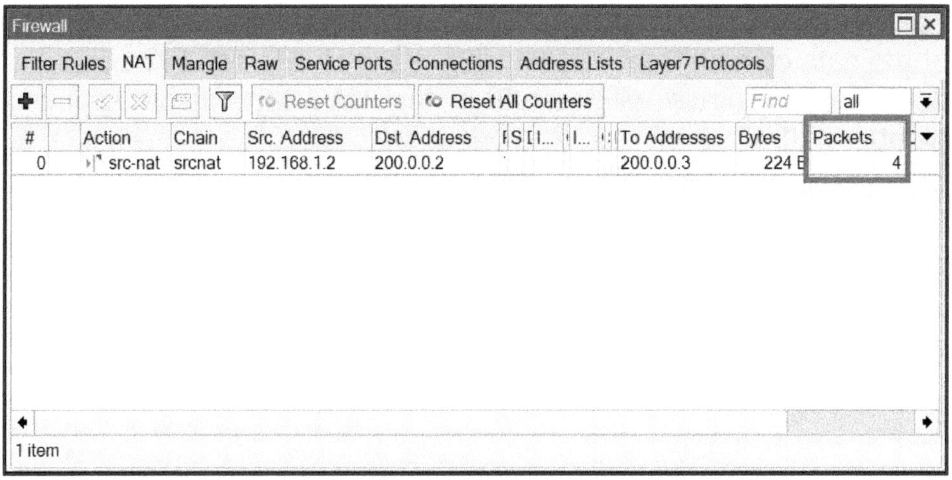

In this case, the packet counter is 4 because the ping sent 4 requests.

When you have multiple rules, they will be displayed in sequence order, starting from 0. The order field displays the sequence number of each rule.

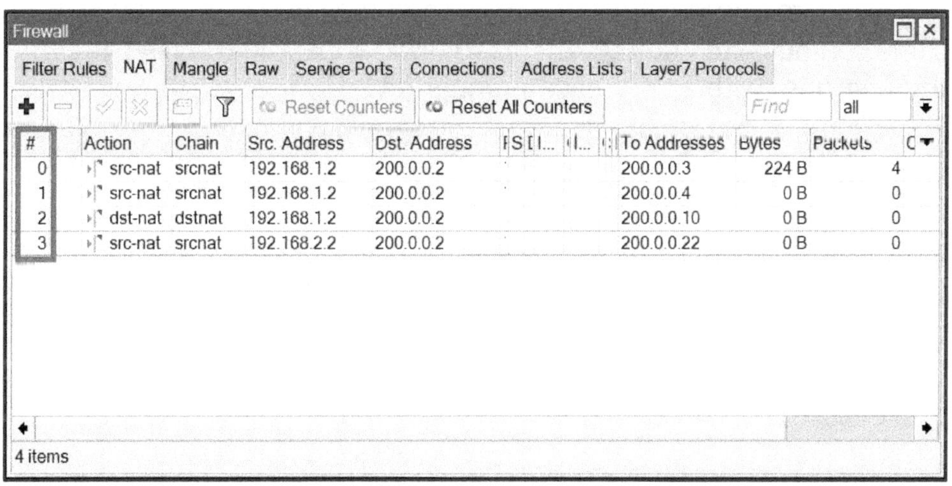

The NAT rule also works on an If-Then concept. It checks the data against the first rule. If the data matches this rule, it will apply the action of this rule. If not, it will move to the next filter rule

Like the firewall filer rules, the order of NAT rules is very important because when the device analyzes the data against each rule to find a match, it follows the sequence number.

For example, if you create a NAT rule to change the source IP address of the data coming from PC1 which has the IP address 192.168.1.2 to 200.0.0.3. This rule will appear in the **NAT** tab with a sequence number of 0.

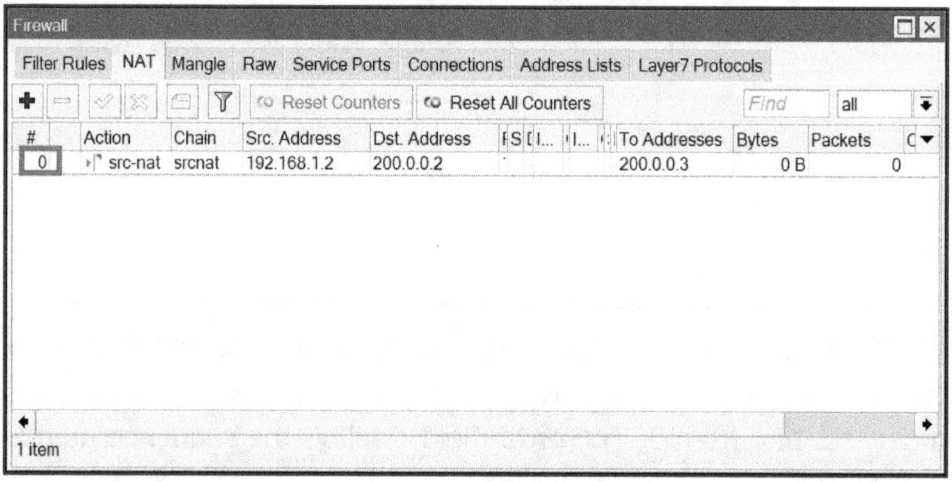

If you create another NAT rule to change the source IP address of the same computer to 200.0.0.4. This rule will appear in the **NAT** tab after the first rule, with a sequence number of 1.

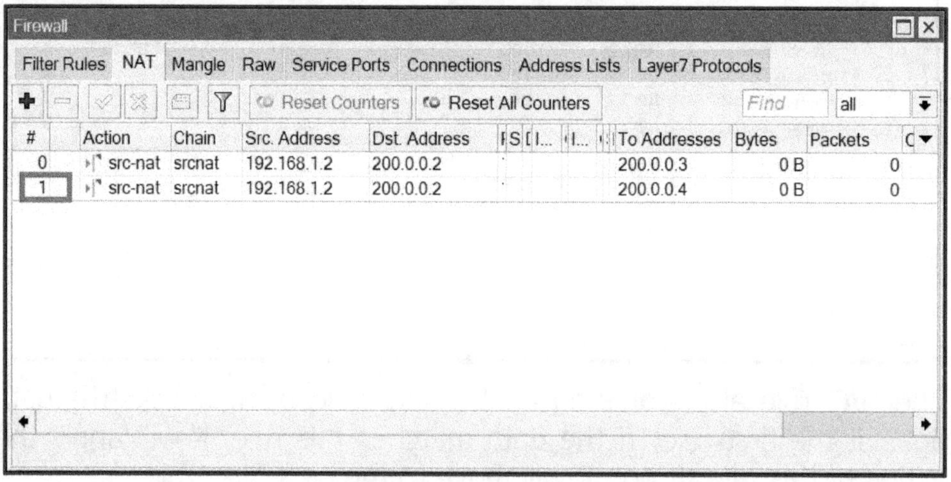

Now, when you try to ping from PC1 to Server1 which has the IP address 200.0.0.2, the MikroTik device will start analyzing the data against the rules, beginning with the first rule, which has a sequence number of 0. In this case, this rule matches the data, so it will NAT the data, (or it will change the source IP address to 200.0.0.3).

When you check the **Packets** counter field for each rule, you will find that the **Packets** counter field for the first rule has incremented, indicating that this rule was applied to the data.

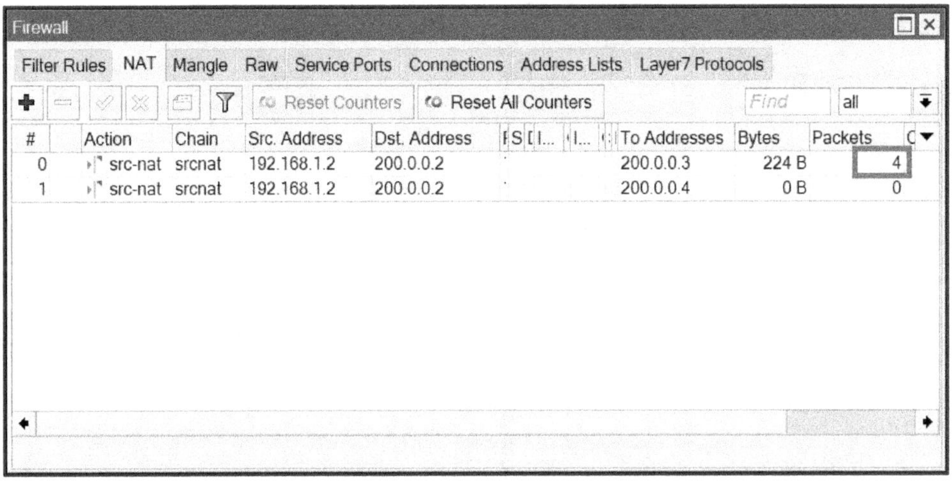

The **Packets** counter field for the second rule remains 0, indicating that this rule hasn't been applied yet.

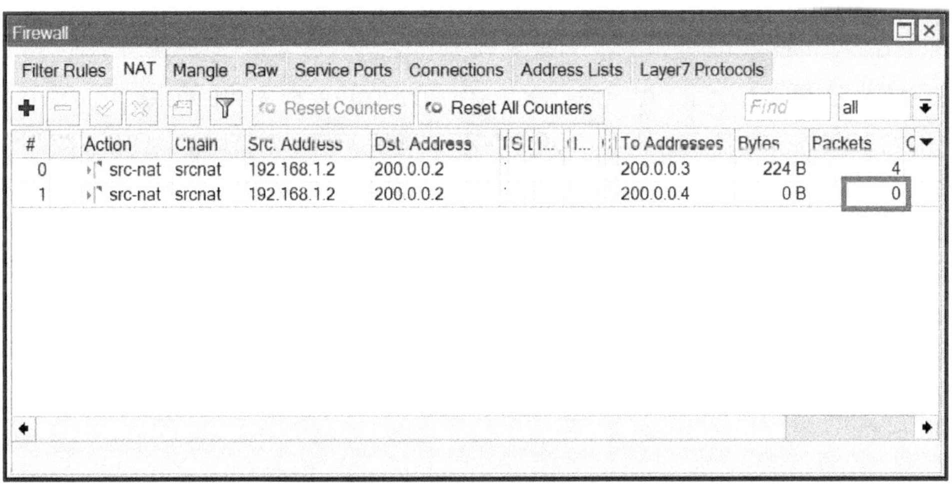

Although you can change the display order of the rules in the **NAT** tab by clicking the header of any field, this does not change the sequence number.

For example, if you create four rules, the sequence number will start from 0, and they will appear as follows:

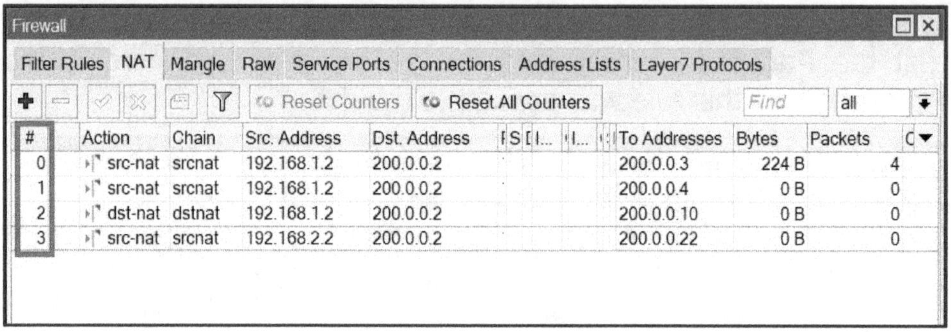

If you click the header of the Action field, the rules will be re-ordered, or resorted according to this field as follows:

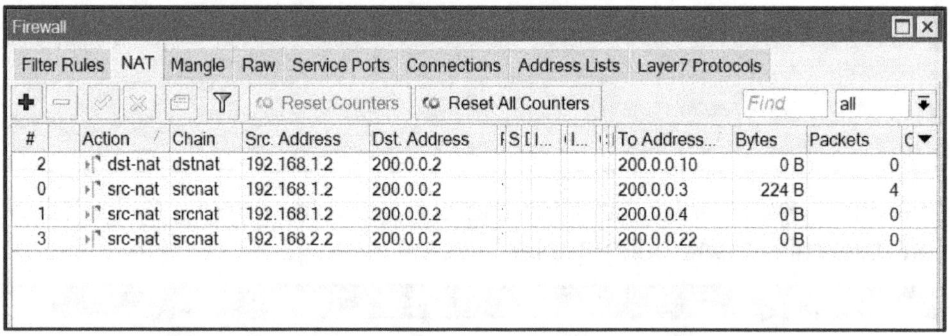

But that will not change the sequence number of each rule.

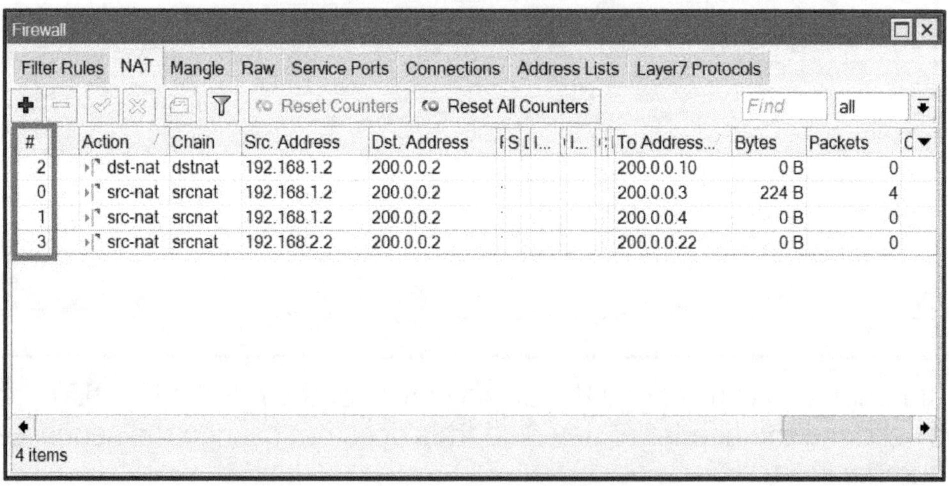

Here, you see that the first rule appearing in the **NAT** tab is the rule changing the destination IP address, applying **dst-nat** (or Destination NAT).

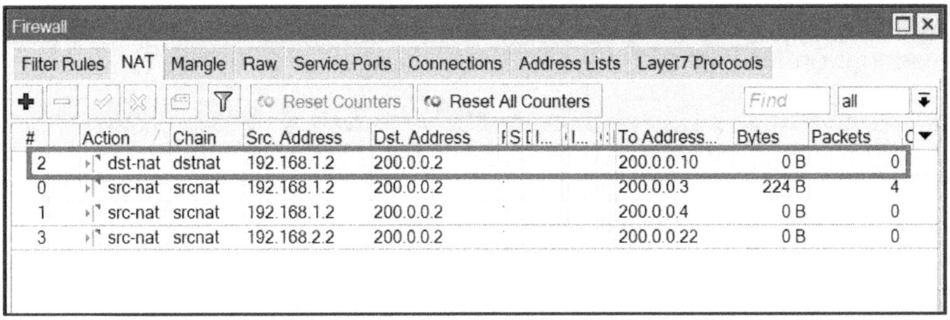

However, this rule is not the first one that will be analyzed, because, as mentioned, the device will start analyzing the rules based on their sequence numbers. So, the first rule to be analyzed is the rule with sequence number 0, which will apply a source NAT to 200.0.0.3

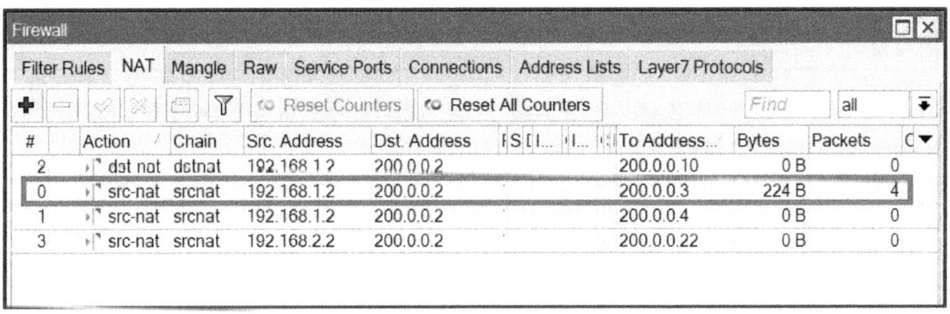

To reorder or sort the rules in the **NAT** tab, click the header of the Sequence Number field.

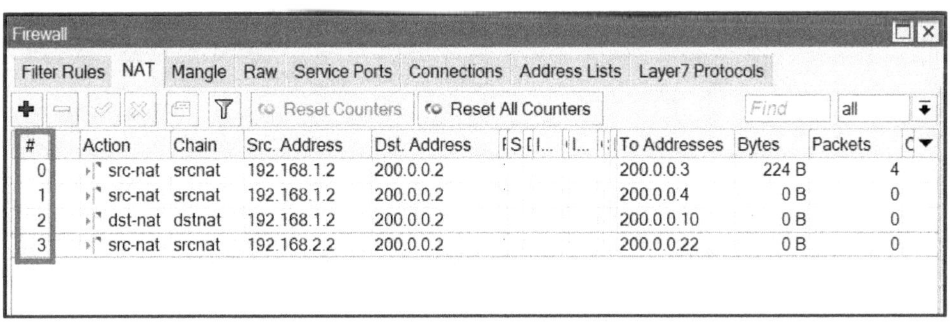

To change the sequence of the rules, you can drag and drop a rule by clicking and moving it up or down. The sequence number will be updated.

For example, you can drag and drop the third rule, which applies Destination NAT and has a sequence number of 2, to the top.

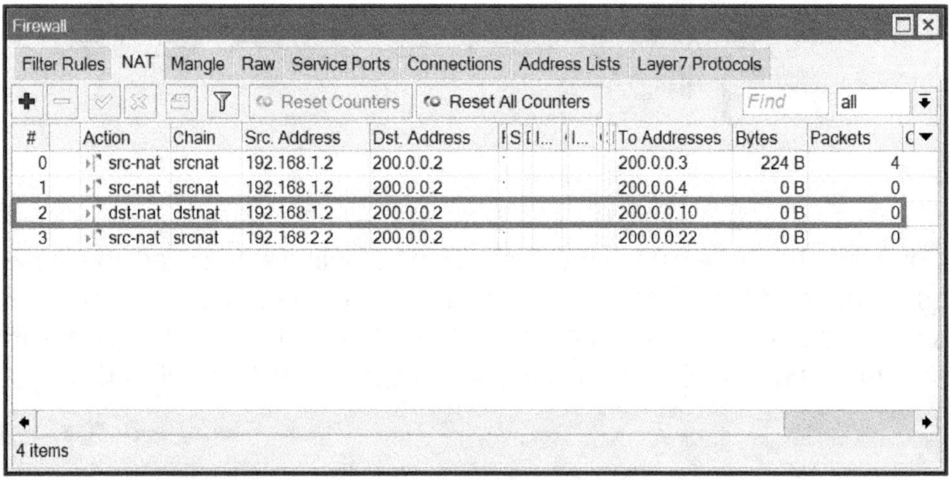

In this case, the sequence number of this rule will change to 0, making it the first rule in the NAT tab.

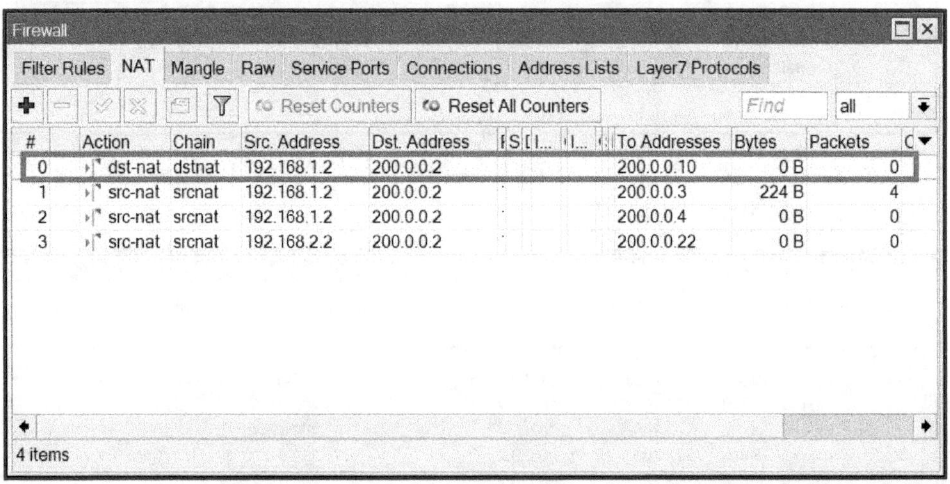

Note: as mentioned, when changing a NAT rule, you should clear the old entries in the Connection Tracking, **Connections** tab, to allow the NAT rule to function correctly.

6.26 NAT Helper

The connection between hosts behind the NATed network is not a real end-to-end connection, so some protocols and services may not work properly. To solve this issue, you can use a technique called NAT helpers, which allow these protocols to work in NATed networks.

NAT helpers are displayed in the **Service Ports** tab of the **Firewall** window, where you can enable, disable, or change their ports as needed.

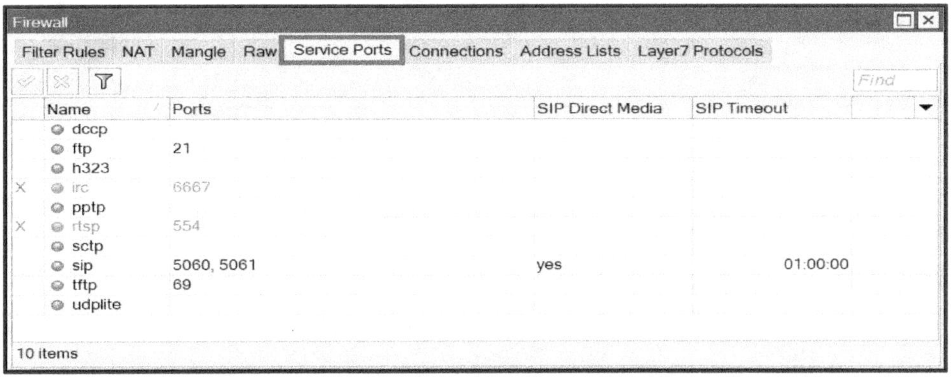

6.27 Some Important NAT Actions

6.27.1 Masquerade and src-nat Action

The Masquerade action is a special action for the source NAT chain.

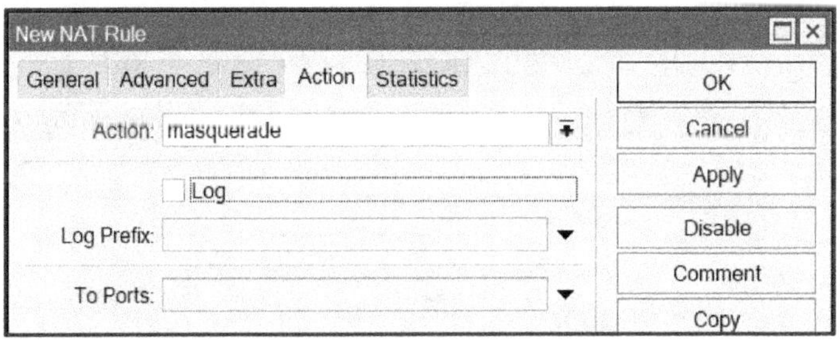

This action usually is used to allow hosts to connect to the internet.

Instead of using the source NAT action and specifying the IP address to use, you can simply choose the **Masquerade** action, and the MikroTik device will handle the rest.

LAB

In this lab, the MikroTik device R1 is connected to two computers, each in a different subnet. PC1 has the IP address 192.168.1.2/24, is connected to the interface ether1, Server 1 , has the IP address 200.0.0.2/24, is connected to the interface ether2.

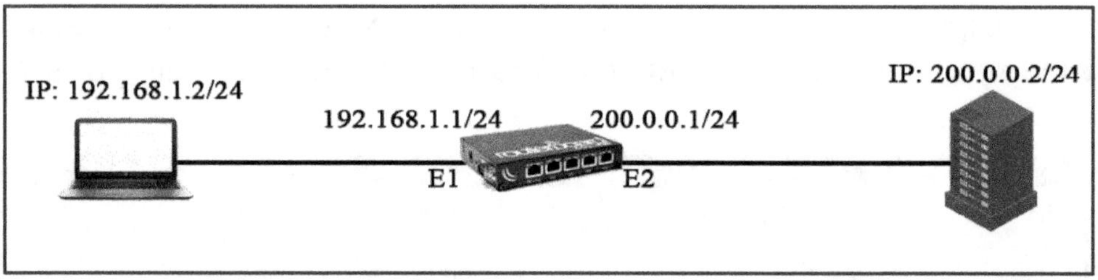

You want to do exactly as in the previous lab (to change the IP address of PC1 when it tries to connect to the server) but this time, you will use the **Masquerade** action instead of the **Source NAT** action.

To start the configuration:

- First: perform the basic configuration to assign the IP addresses to MikroTik interfaces .
- Second: configure (or create) a NAT rule to change the IP address of PC 1 using **Masquerade** rule.

Basic Configuration

- Assign the IP address 192.168.1.1/24 to the interface ether1.
- Assign the IP address 200.0.0.1/24 to the interface ether2.

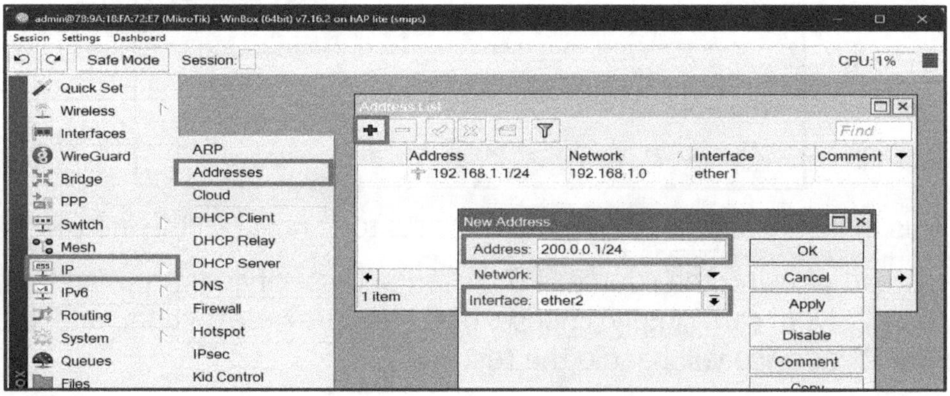

NAT Configuration

To create a NAT rule, click the **IP** menu and select **Firewall** to open the **Firewall** window. Then, click the **Add** button in the **NAT** tab to open the **New NAT Rule** dialog box.

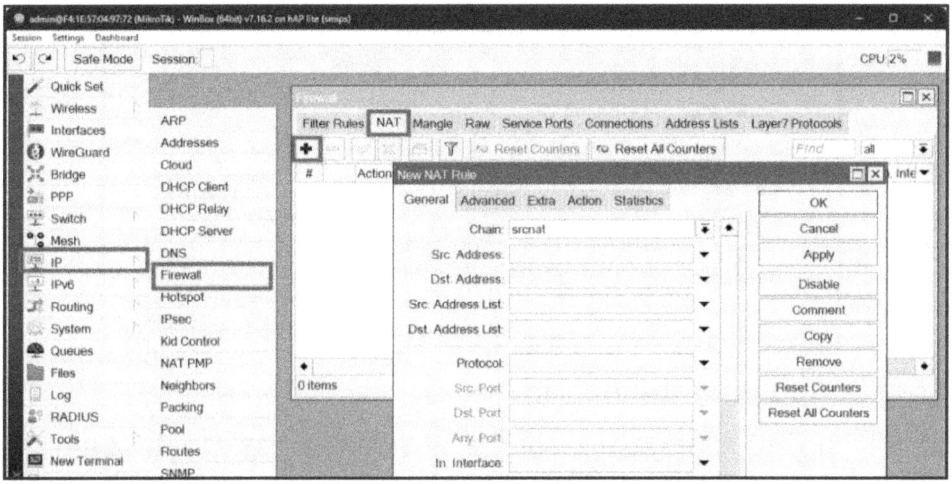

To configure the NAT rule, follow the three main steps:

Step 1: Data Selection

To select the data sourced from PC1 and destined for Server1:

- Enter the IP address of PC1 192.168.1.2 in the **Src. Address** (or Source Address) field.
- Enter the IP address of Server1 200.0.0.2 in the **Dst. Address** (or Destination Address) field.

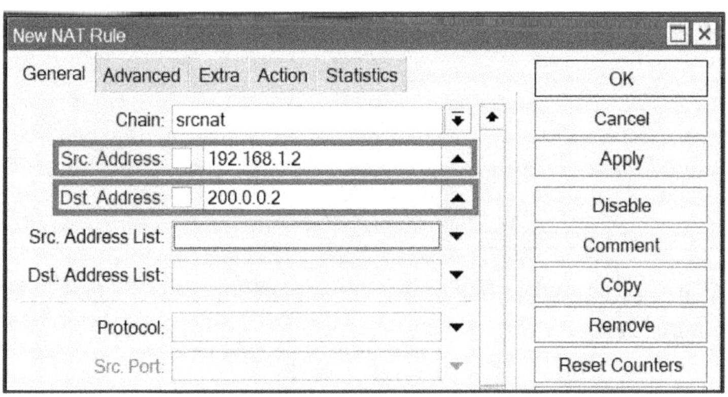

Step 2: Chain Choosing

Since you want to change the source IP address of PC1, select the **srcnat** (or source NAT) chain from the **Chain** field.

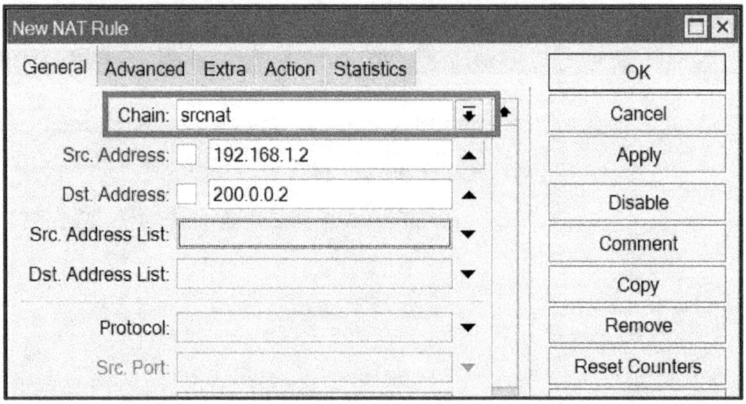

Step 3: Applying the Action

In this lab, to change the source IP address, select **Masquerade** action from the **Action** field in the **Action** tab, and click the **Ok** button to close this dialog box.

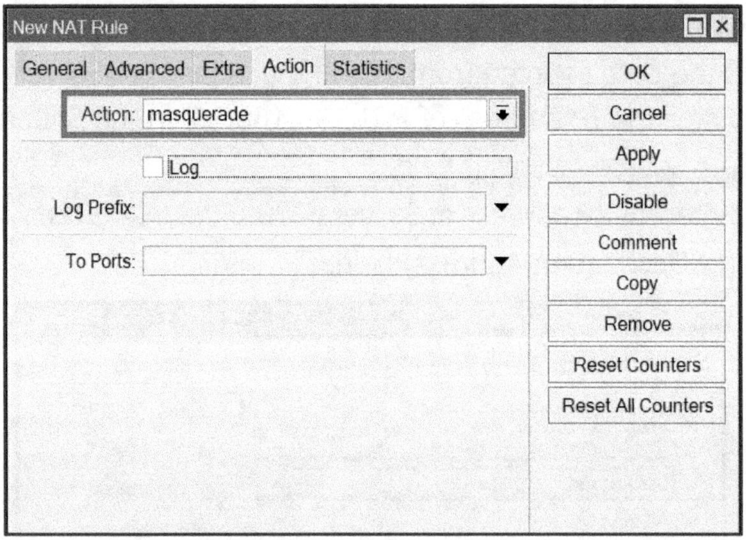

After creating the NAT rule, it will appear in the **NAT** tab of the **Firewall** window.

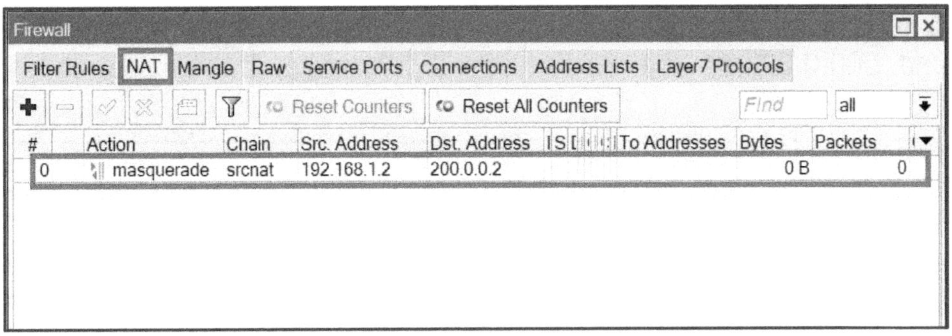

Now, when PC1 tries to ping Server1, PC1 will create a packet and write its IP address as the source IP 192.168.1.2 and the server IP address as the destination IP 200.0.0.2 in this packet.

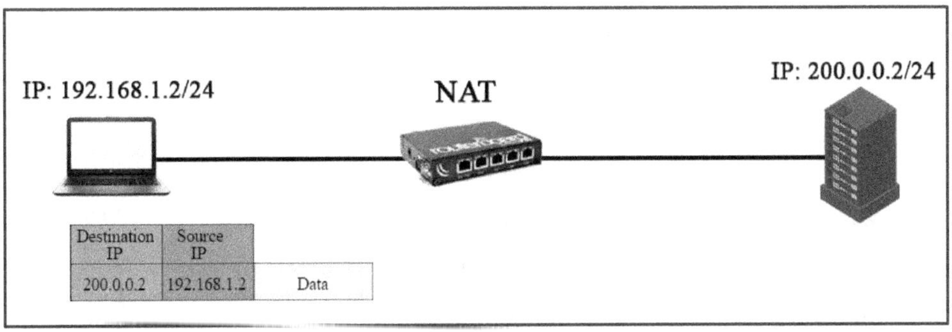

When this packet reaches the MikroTik device, it will perform a NAT operation. The action, in this case, is **Masquerade**, so it will change the source IP address from 192.168.1.2 to the outgoing interface IP address, which in this case is 200.0.0.1 (the IP address of ether2), and then send it to Server1.

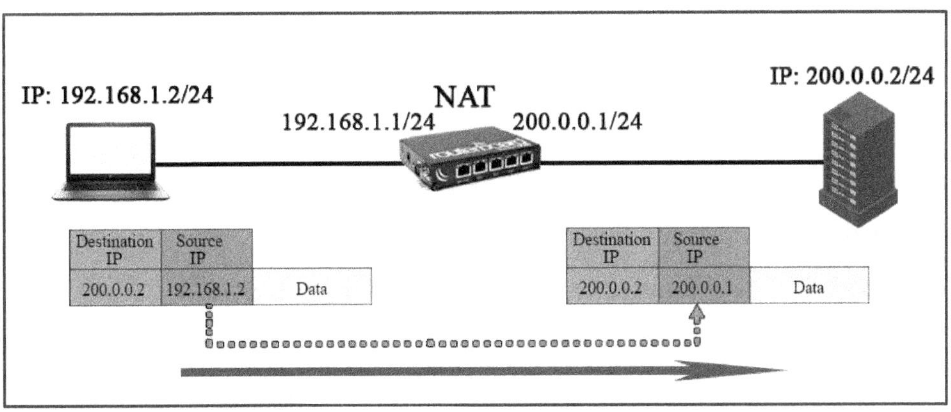

When the server replies, it will write its IP address as the source IP and 200.0.0.1 as the destination IP, then send the reply to the MikroTik device.

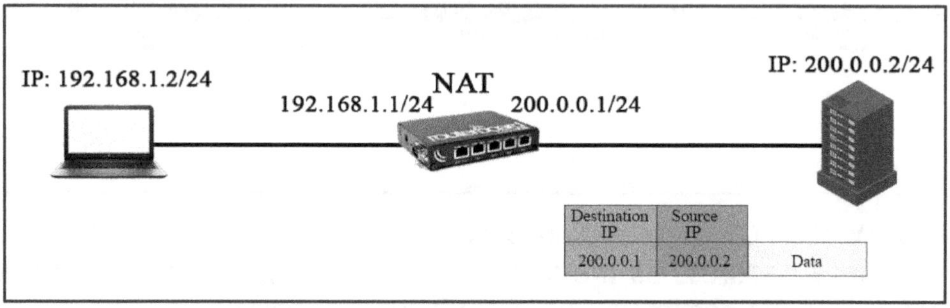

As mentioned before, the MikroTik device will perform a reverse operation when it receives this reply. It will change the destination IP address from 200.0.0.1 back to PC1 IP address, 192.168.1.2, and send it to PC1.

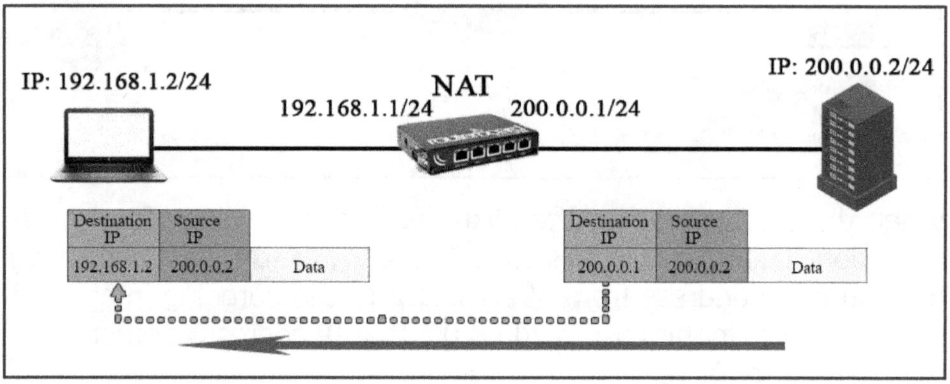

CLI

You can also make the configuration from the CLI.

To assign IP addresses to the interfaces, use the following commands:

```
ip address add address=192.168.1.1/24 interface=ether1
ip address add address=200.0.0.1/24 interface=ether2
```

To create the NAT rule, use the following command:

```
ip firewall nat add src-address=192.168.1.2 dst-address=200.0.0.2
chain=srcnat action=masquerade
```

LAB

This lab is a real-life scenario. you have a MikroTik devices R1 which is connected to a local network ,(or LAN), 192.168.1.0/24 via ether1, and connected to the internet, (or WAN), via ether2.

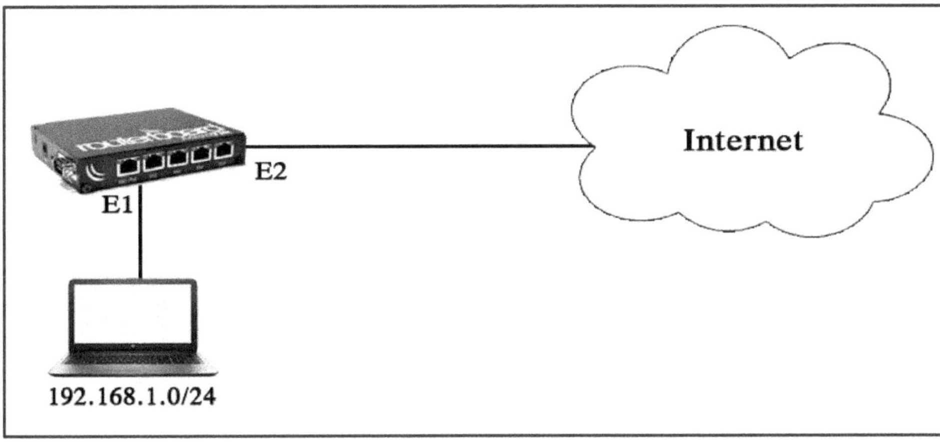

To allow computers in the local network (LAN) to connect to the internet, you will perform two steps:

- Connect the device to the internet:

  Configure a DHCP Client on ether2 (which is connected to the internet) to obtain the IP address, subnet mask, DNS, and default gateway from the ISP router.
- Allow MikroTik to distribute the internet:

  Assign the IP address 192.168.1.1/24 to ether1 (which is connected to the local network) and configure a DHCP Server on this interface to distribute IP addresses to any computer connects to it. Then, create a NAT rule using **masquerade** action to enable these computers to access the internet

Connect the Device to the Internet

To configure DHCP Client on ether2, click **IP** menu, then select **DHCP Client** to open **DHCP Client** window, then click the **Add** button in the **DHCP Client** window to open the **New DHCP Client** dialog box.

In the **Interface** field, select the ether1 and click the **OK** button to close this dialog box.

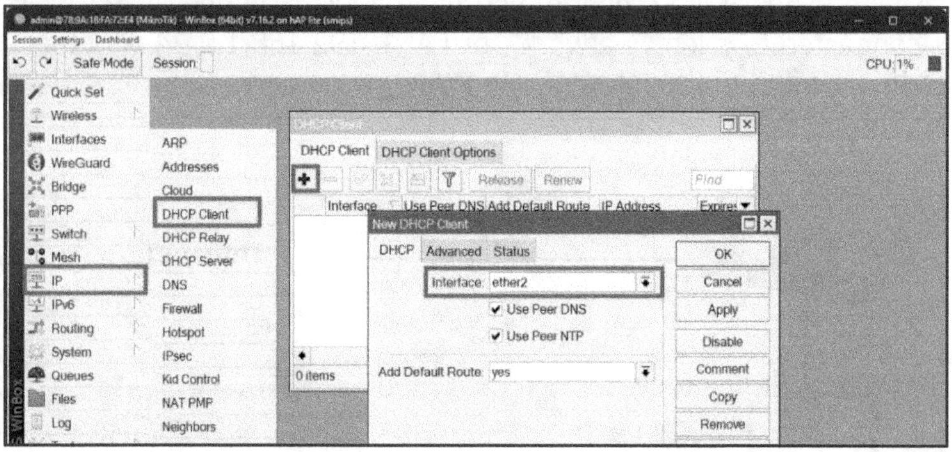

As mentioned, after the interface obtains an IP address from the ISP DHCP server, it receives four main pieces of information:

- The IP address
- The subnet mask
- The default gateway
- The DNS

You can see the IP address and subnet mask in the **Address List** window.

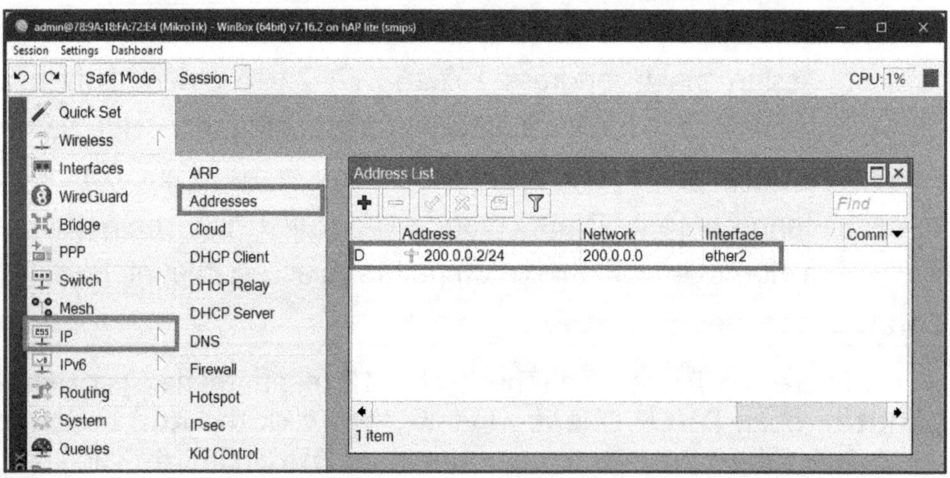

The default gateway is listed in the **Routing Table**.

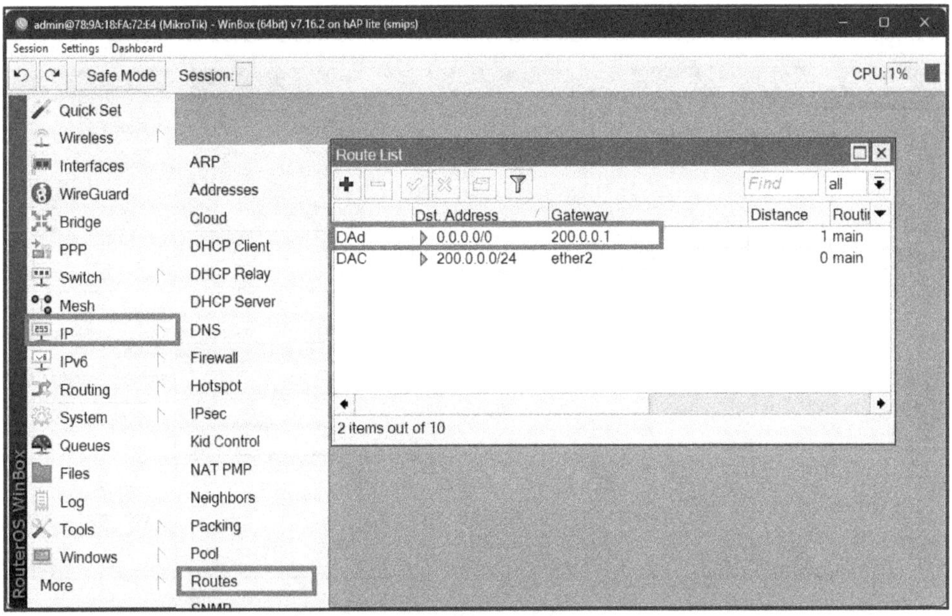

The DNS can be seen in the **DNS** window.

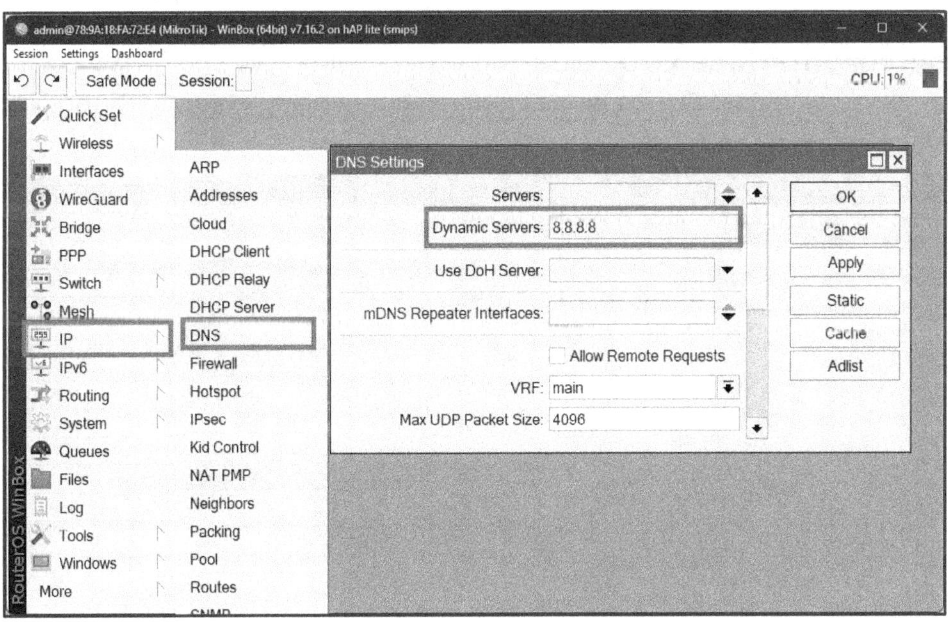

Allow the Device to Distribute Internet

Assign the IP address 192.168.1.1/24 to the interface ether1.

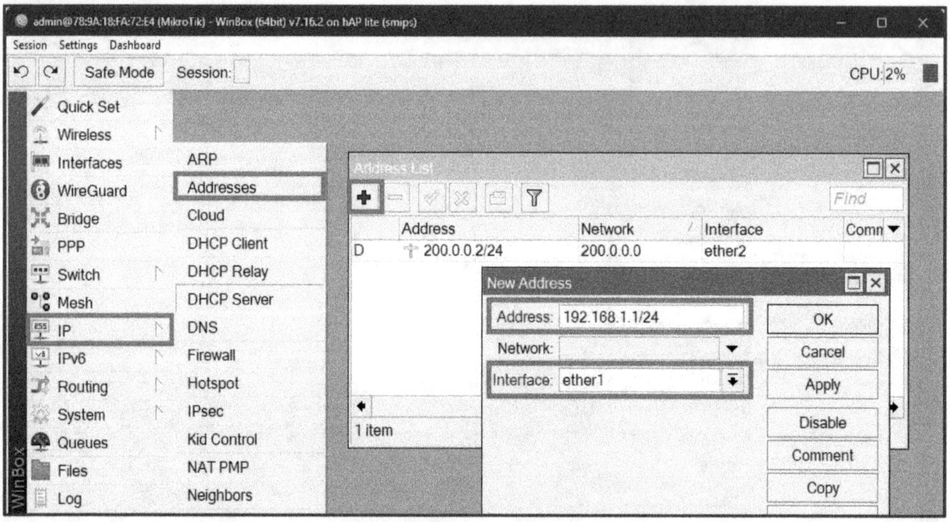

To configure DHCP Server on the interface ether1, click the **IP** menu, then select **DHCP Server** to open the **DHCP Server** window. click the **DHCP Setup** button to open **DHCP Setup** dialog box. In **DHCP Server Interface** field Select the ether1, and click the **Next** button in all other messages to accept the default settings and configure the DHCP Server.

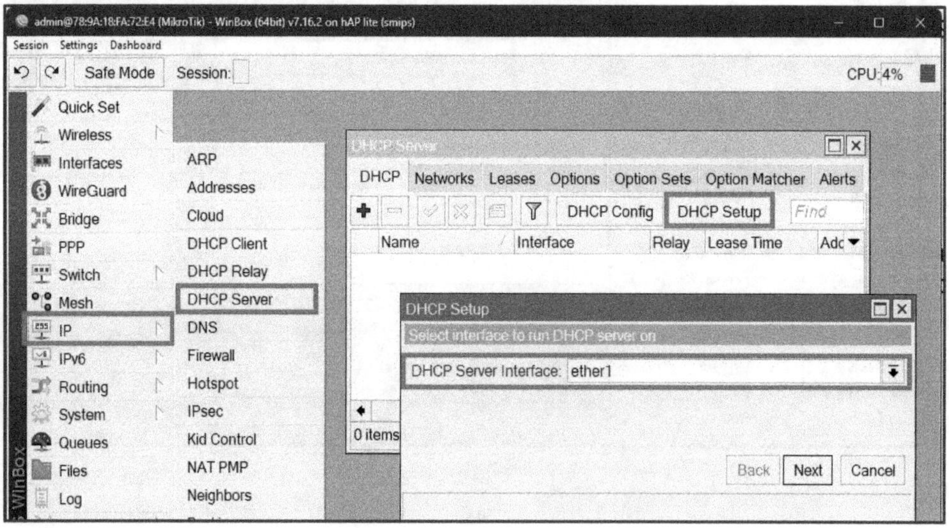

To create a NAT rule with **Masquerade** action, click the **IP** menu and select **Firewall** to open the **Firewall** window. Then, click the **Add** button in the **NAT** tab to open the **New NAT Rule** dialog box.

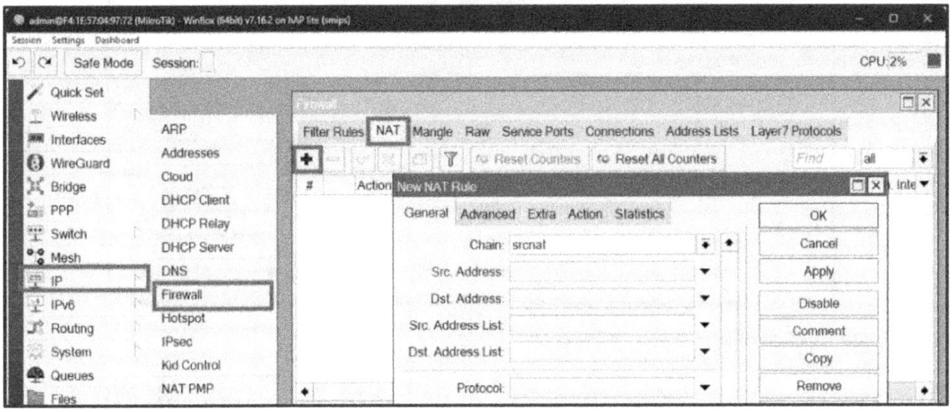

To configure the NAT rule, follow the three main steps:

Step 1: Data Selection

To select the data sourced from the local network**:**

- Enter the network ID 192.168.1.0/24 in the **Src. Address** (or Source Address) field.

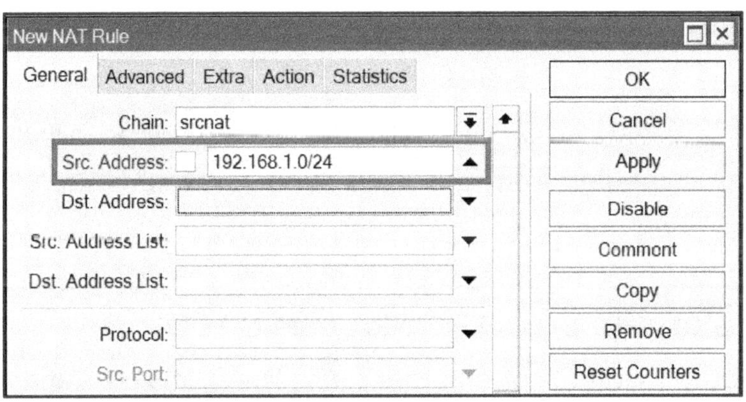

Step 2: Chain Choosing

Since you want to change the source IP address using **Masquerade** action, select the **srcnat** (or source NAT) chain from the **Chain** field.

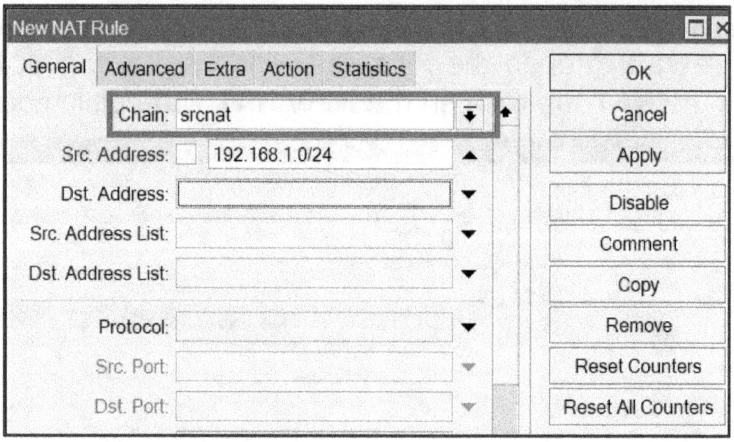

Step 3: Applying the Action

In this lab, to change the source IP address, select **Masquerade** action from the **Action** field in the **Action** tab, and click the **Ok** button to close this dialog box.

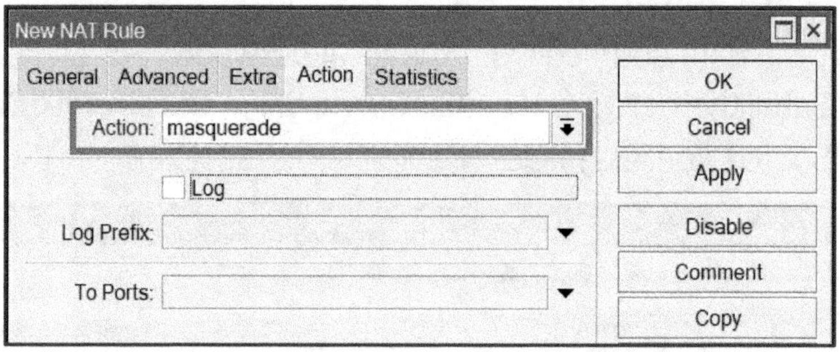

Now, any computer from the local subnet will have access to the internet.

CLI

You can also make the configuration from the CLI.

To configure DHCP Client on ether2, use the following command:

```
ip dhcp-client add interface=ether2
```

To assign IP addresses to ether1, use the following command:

```
ip address add address=192.168.1.1/24 interface=ether1
```

To configure DHCP server on ether1 interface using the DHCP setup wizard, use the following command, choose ether1 interface and accept the default settings by pressing Enter each time the setup wizard asks for input

```
ip dhcp-server setup
```

To create the NAT rule, use the following command:

```
ip firewall nat add src-address=192.168.1.0/24 chain=srcnat
action=masquerade
```

6.27.2 Redirect and src-nat Action

The Redirect action is a special action for the destination NAT chain to redirect data to the router itself.

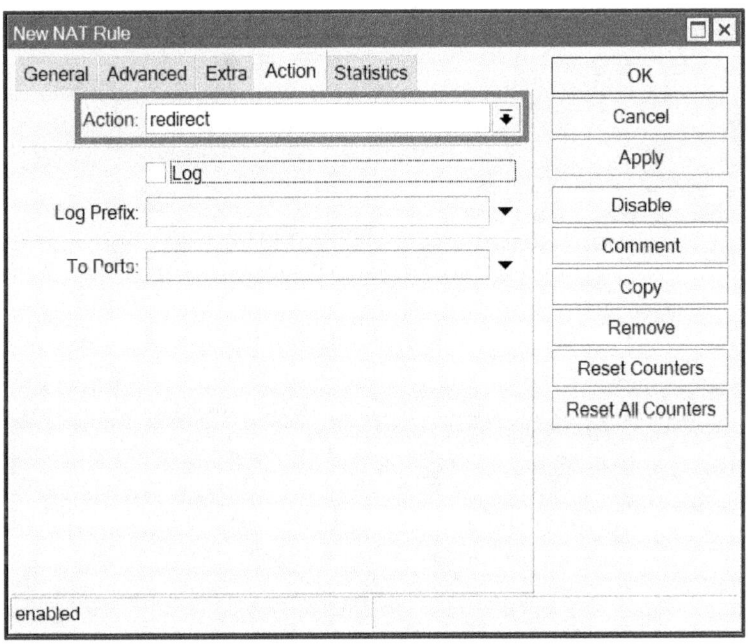

This action usually is used to redirect data to the router to act as a transparent proxy for network services like DNS or HTTP.

You will learn more about this in the MTCTCE course.

MikroTik | MTCNA

7

Module

QoS

MTCNA

Module 7

This module provides an introduction to Quality of Service (QoS) technology in MikroTik devices and explains how to configure the device to perform bandwidth limitation operations.

More advanced information about Quality of Service (QoS) technologies is available in the MTCTCE course.

This module covers the following course content topics:

- Simple Queue
  - Target
  - Destinations
  - Max-limit and limit-at
  - Bursting
- One Simple queue for the whole network (PCQ)
  - pcq-rate configuration
  - pcq-limit configuration

QoS

7.1 QoS Overview and Key Concepts

Quality of Service (QoS) is a generic term that refers to the performance of a service provided by the network.

There are various mechanisms, methods, or tools used to control this performance and determine how the data for this service is transmitted through the network. These mechanisms or methods are referred to as QoS mechanisms.

For example, you can guarantee a specific bandwidth to a host or prioritize certain protocol traffic over others.

7.2 Bandwidth Limiting Concepts

You can use two concepts to limit bandwidth

- MIR (Maximum Information Rate)
- CIR (Committed Information Rate)

7.2.1 MIR (Maximum Information Rate)

MIR (Maximum Information Rate) is the maximum bandwidth limit that should not be exceeded in the best conditions. In RouterOS, it is called **Max Limit**.

For example, if the main bandwidth in the network is 100 Mbps, and one PC connects to this network, under normal conditions, when no QoS rules are applied, this host will get the full 100 Mbps bandwidth.

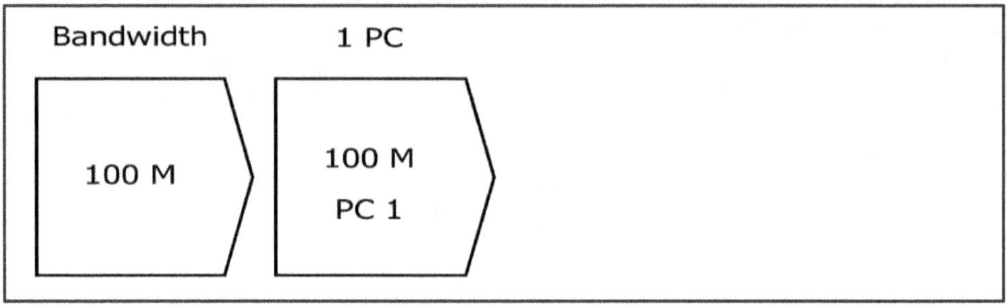

If you limit the bandwidth by setting the Maximum Information Rate (MIR) for this PC to 50 Mbps. In this case the PC will not get the full bandwidth, it will not receive more than 50 Mbps in the best conditions.

Here (in the best conditions) means that there is enough bandwidth available to satisfy the MIR limit, in other words, enough bandwidth to allocate 50 Mbps to this host.

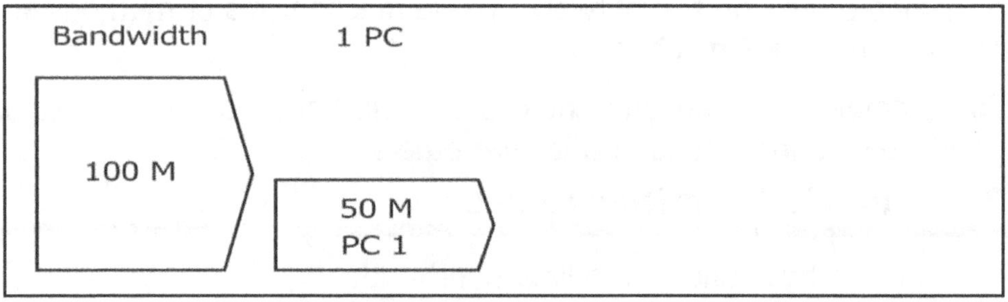

If there are many hosts connected to this network, and there is not enough bandwidth to allocate 50 Mbps to PC1, then this PC will receive less than the MIR limit. This is because the MIR is not a guaranteed limit, it is the maximum bandwidth the host can get if there is enough available bandwidth.

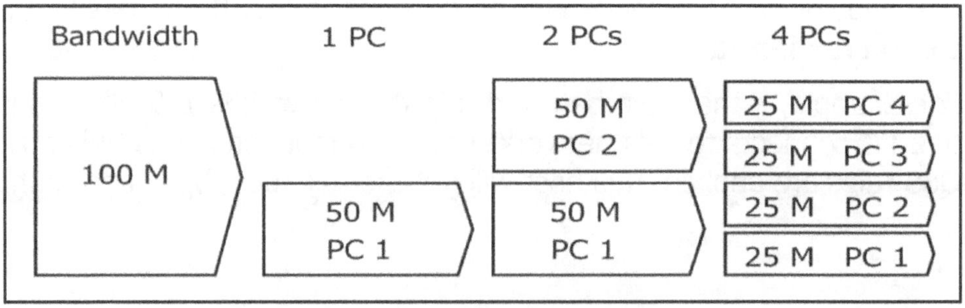

7.2.2 CIR (Committed Information Rate)

CIR (Committed Information Rate) is a guaranteed bandwidth limit that should be allocated even in the worst conditions. In RouterOS, it is called **Limit At**.

For example, if the main bandwidth in the network is 100 Mbps and 4 hosts connect to this network, under normal conditions, when no QoS rules are applied, each host will get almost 25 Mbps.

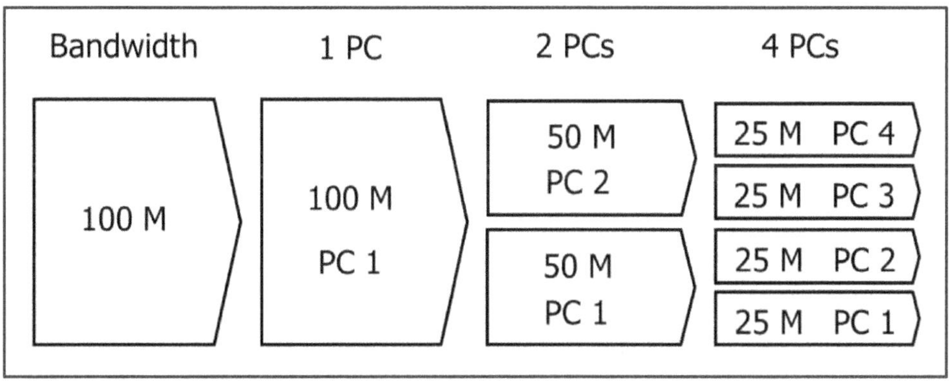

If you set the Committed Information Rate (CIR) for PC1 to 50 Mbps, this PC will receive 50 Mbps even in the worst conditions, as this is a guaranteed bandwidth.

Here (the worst conditions) means that the full bandwidth is consumed, in other words, when many hosts are connected to the network.

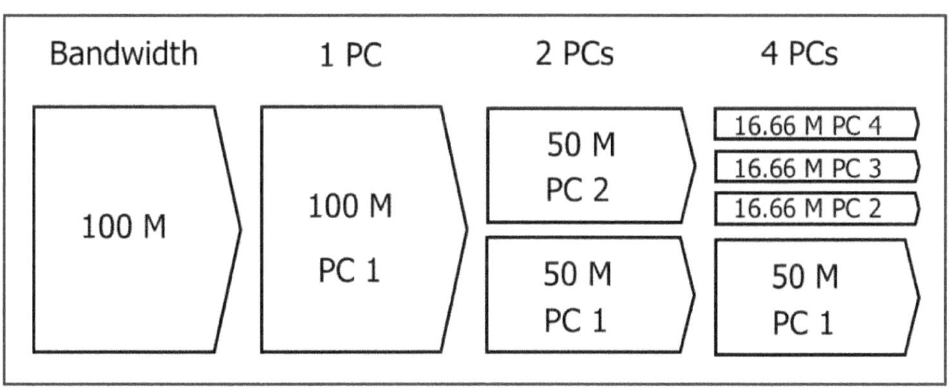

7.2.3 MIR and CIR Together

You can use both the MIR and CIR concepts to set limits in the network, depending on the required scenario.

For example, if the main bandwidth in the network is 100 Mbps, and one PC connects to this network, as mentioned before, under normal conditions, when no QoS rules are applied, this PC will get the full 100 Mbps bandwidth.

If there are 4 hosts connected to this network, each host will get almost 25 Mbps.

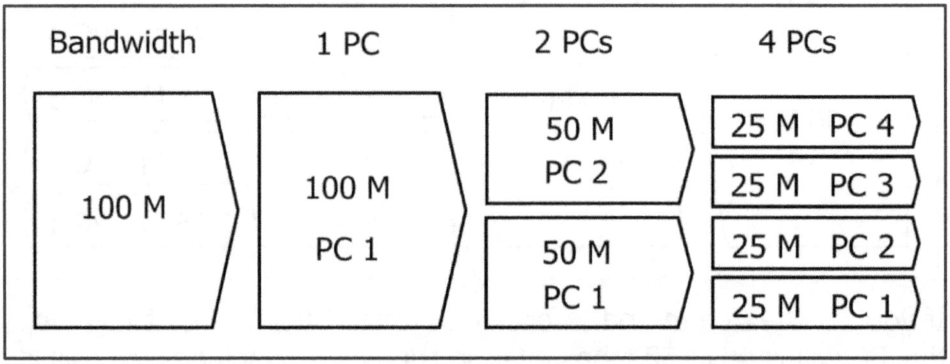

You can set the MIR to 80 Mbps and the CIR to 50 Mbps for PC1. This means that if PC1 is the only connected host to the network, it will not take the full bandwidth, it will get a maximum bandwidth of 80 Mbps. If there are multiple hosts connected to the network, PC1 will get the guaranteed bandwidth of 50 Mbps, and the remaining bandwidth will be distributed to the other hosts

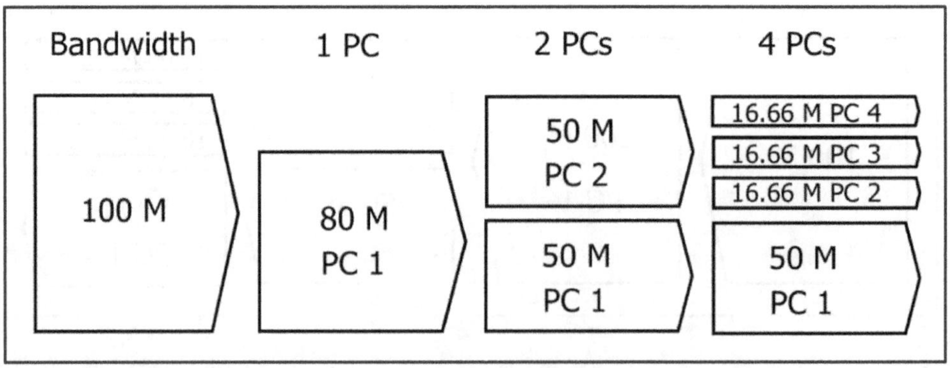

You can configure RouterOS to perform QoS operations, limit bandwidth, and set priorities by using the **Queue List** window and adding a Simple Queue.

7.3 Simple Queue

To configure RouterOS to perform QoS operations, use the **Queue List** window.

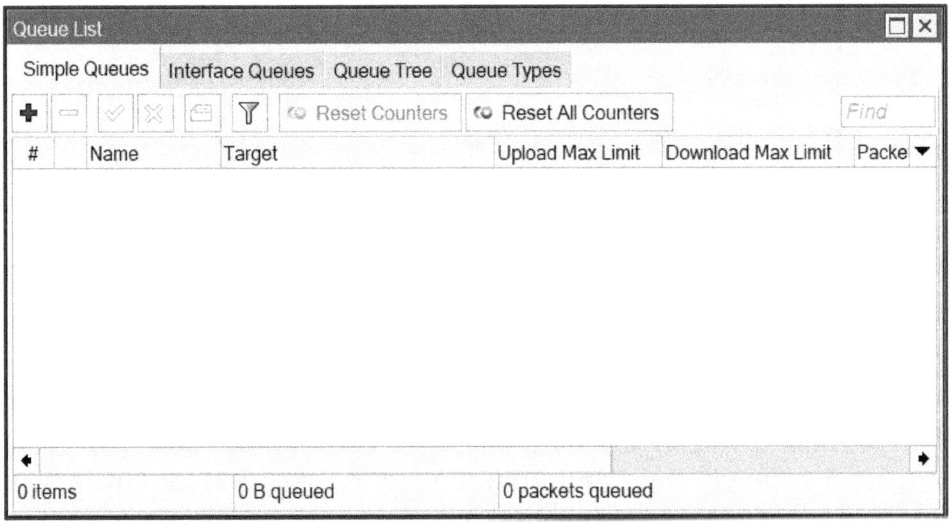

To open the **Queue List** window, click the **Queues** menu.

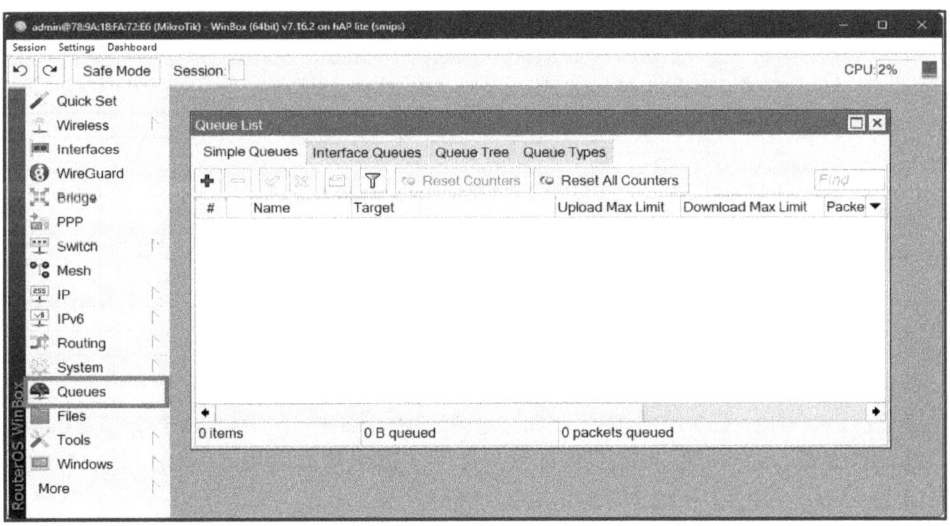

To add a Simple Queue, click the **Add** button in the **Simple Queues** tab of the **Queue List** window to open the **New Simple Queue** dialog box.

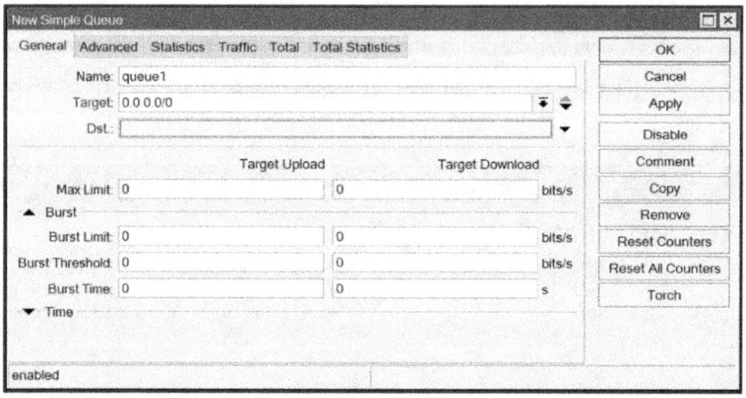

You can use this dialog box to create a new simple queue and configure its settings.

To apply the Maximum Information Rate (MIR) limit to a host, network, or interface, use the **General** tab of this dialog box. In the **Target** field, you can specify the host, network, or interface on which you want to apply the bandwidth limitation. In the **Max Limit** field, you can specify the target upload and download limits.

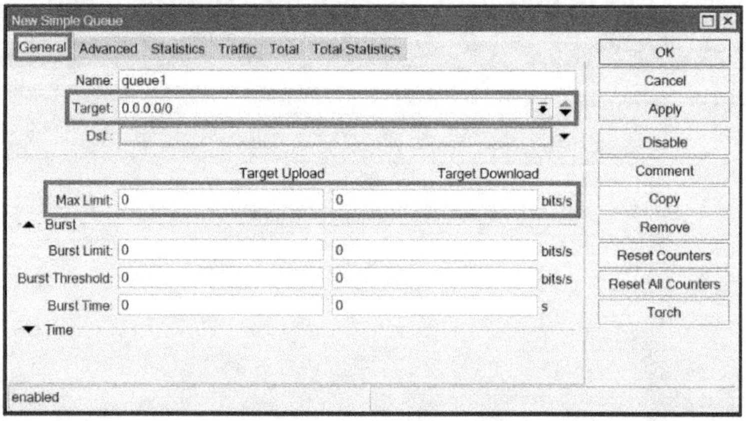

To apply the Committed Information Rate (CIR) limit, use the **Advanced** tab of this dialog box. In the **Limit At** field, you can specify the target upload and download limits.

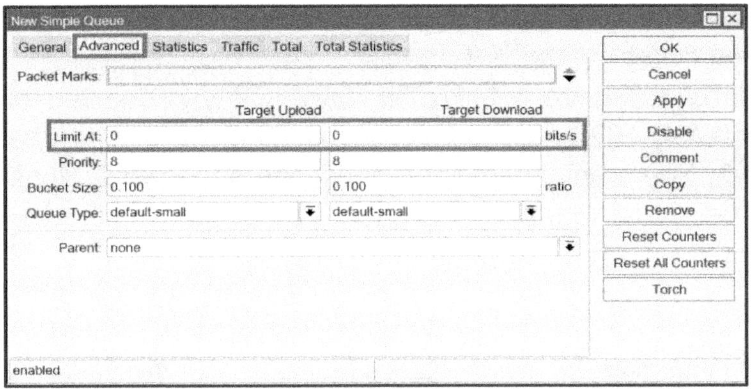

Note: to use Simple Queue, you should disable the firewall FastTrack rules if there are any.

You can also add or create a simple queue from the CLI using the following command:

```
queue simple add target=[address] max-limit=[upload/download]
```

Where:

- [address] is the target IP address.
- [upload/download] are the upload limit and the download limit

For example:

```
queue simple add target=192.168.1.0/24 max-limit=1M/2M
```

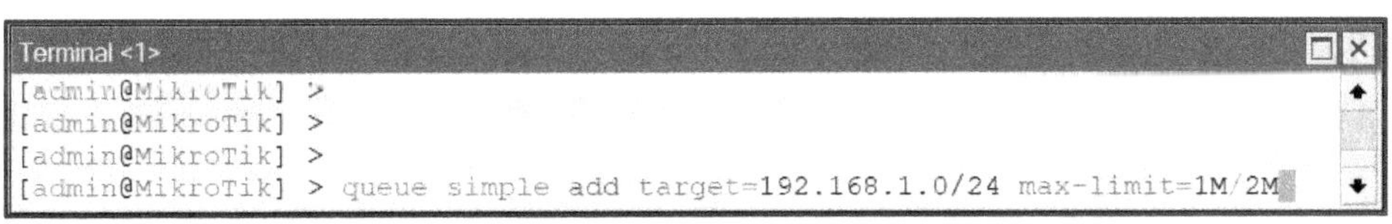

To display the current simple queues in RouterOS from the CLI use the following command:

```
queue simple print
```

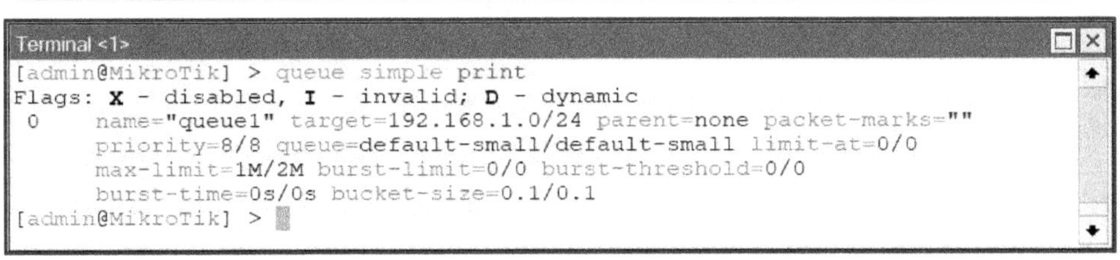

LAB

In this lab, you have a MikroTik device, R1, connected to a local network (LAN) 192.168.1.0/24 via ether1 and to the internet (WAN) via ether2. You want to limit the download speed to 2 Mbps and the upload speed to 1 Mbps for this subnet by using simple queue.

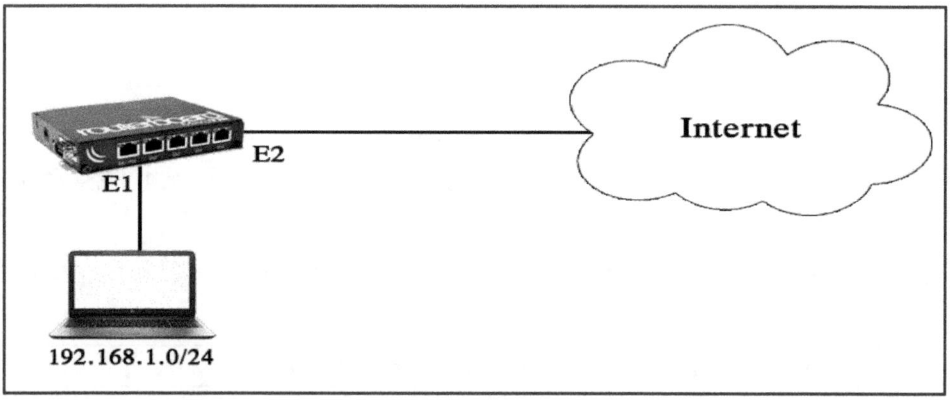

To start the configuration:

- First: perform the basic configuration to allow the connection to the internet.
- Second: configure a simple queue to limit the bandwidth.

Basic Configuration

Insall DHCP Client on ether2 to obtain an IP address from the ISP.

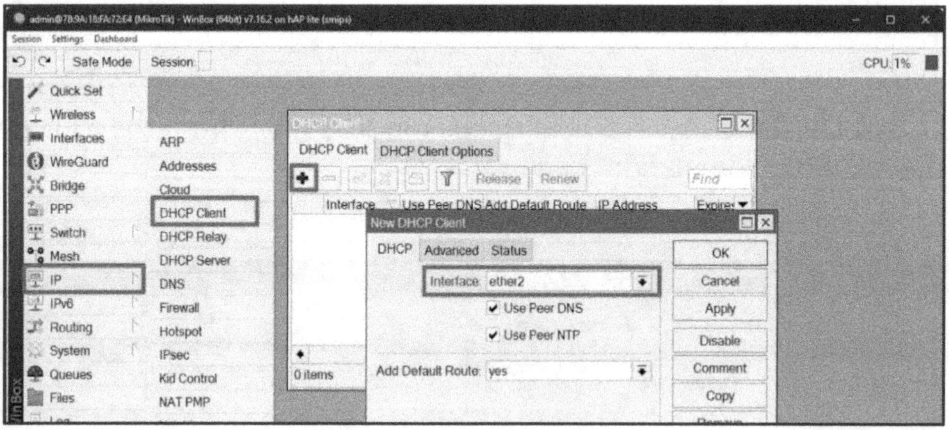

Assign the IP address 192.168.1.1/24 to the interface ether1.

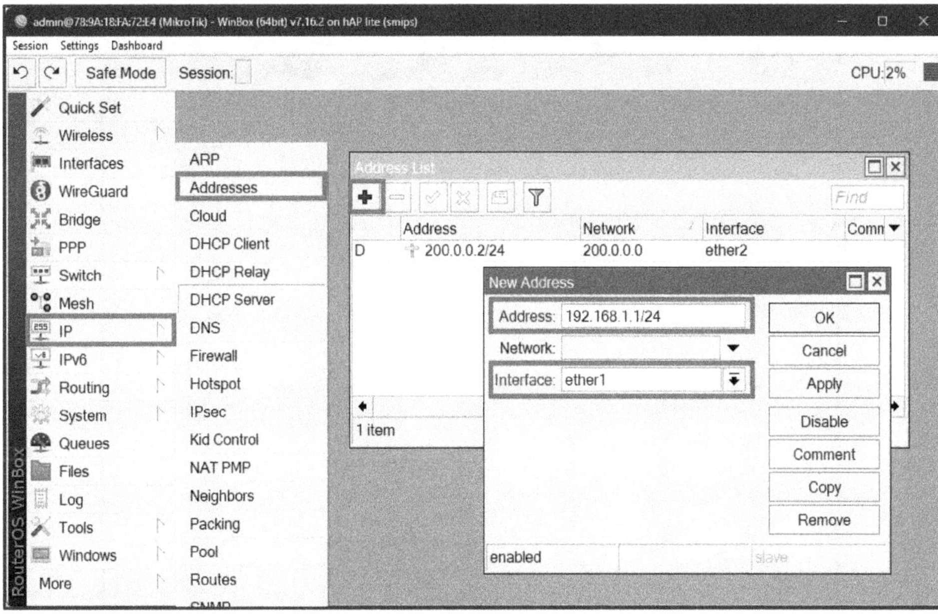

Configure DHCP Server on the interface ether1, to distribute IP addresses to any computer connects to it.

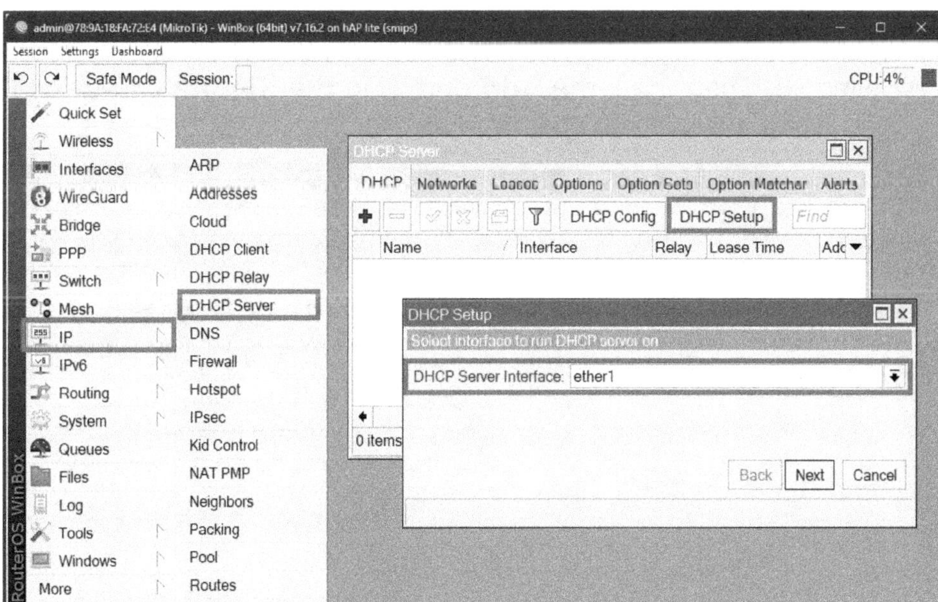

Create a NAT rule with the **Masquerade** action, for the subnet 192.168.1.0/24

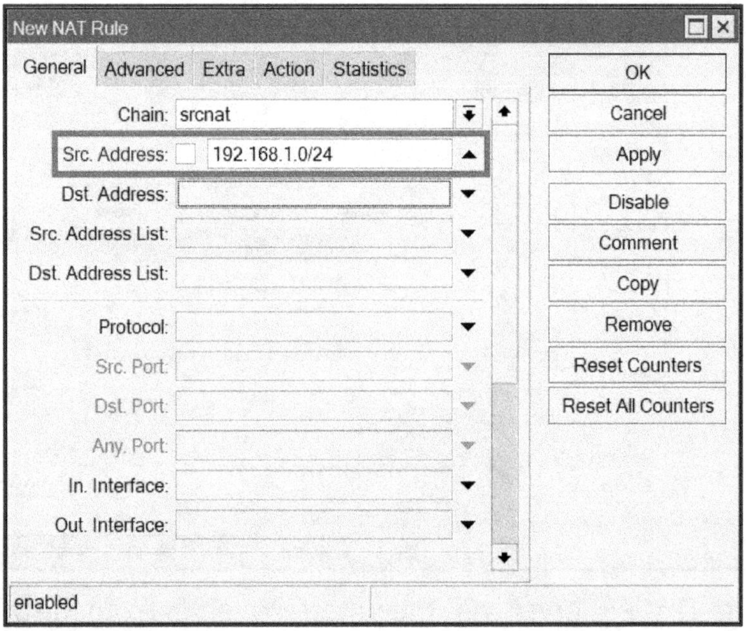

Queue Configuration

To create a simple queue, click the **Queues** menu to open the **Queue List** window. Then, click the **Add** button in the **Simple Queues** tab to open the **New Simple Queue** dialog box.

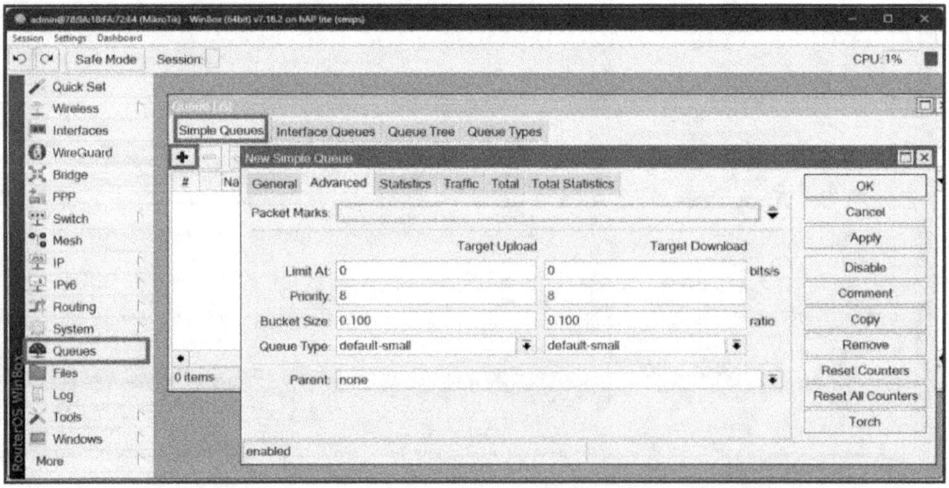

In the **Target** field in the **General** tab, enter the network ID 192.168.1.0/24. In the **Max Limit** enter 1M in **Target Upload** and 2M in **Target Download**. then, click the **OK** button to close the dialog box.

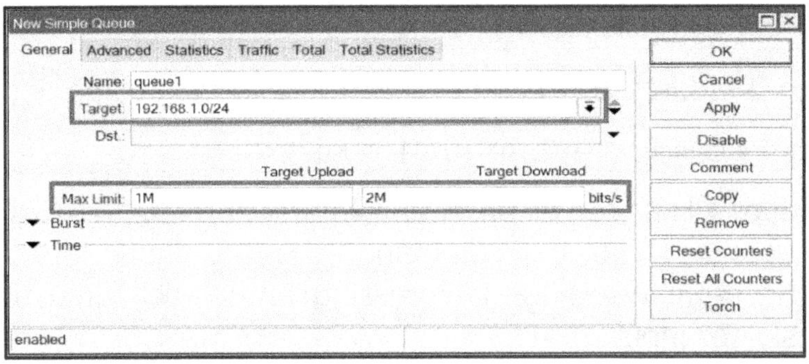

Also, you can select the interface ether1 from the **Target** field. It will give the same result in this lab.

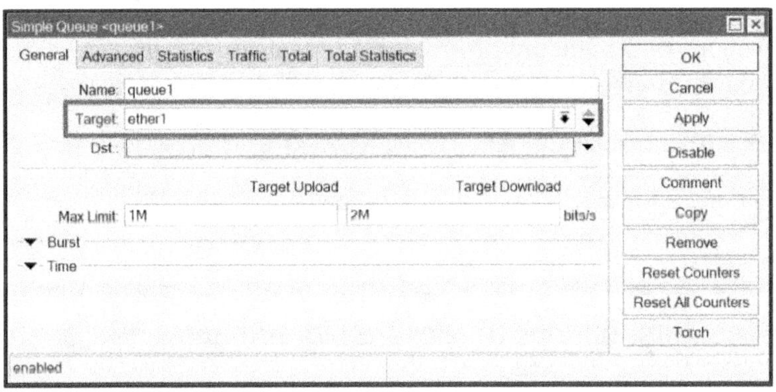

Now, if any computer connects to the local subnet, it will have a maximum bandwidth of 1 Mbps for the upload and 2 Mbps for the download.

It is important to understand that by using Simple Queues, all devices from the target subnet will share this limit.

For example, if there is one computer in this subnet, it will have a maximum bandwidth of 1 Mbps for the upload and 2 Mbps for the download. If there are two computers, they will share this limit, so they may each have a maximum bandwidth of 0.5 Mbps for upload and 1 Mbps for download.

CLI

You can also make the configuration from the CLI.

To configure DHCP Client on ether2, use the following command:

```
ip dhcp-client add interface=ether2
```

To assign IP addresses to ether1, use the following command:

```
ip address add address=192.168.1.1/24 interface=ether1
```

To configure DHCP server on ether1 interface using the DHCP setup wizard, use the following command, choose ether1 interface and accept the default settings by pressing Enter each time the setup wizard asks for input

```
ip dhcp-server setup
```

To create the NAT rule, use the following command:

```
ip firewall nat add src-address=192.168.1.0/24 chain=srcnat
action=masquerade
```

To create simple queue, use the following command:

```
queue simple add target=192.168.1.0/24 max-limit=1M/2M
```

7.4 Bursting

You can use burst options to allocate higher bandwidth for a period of time.

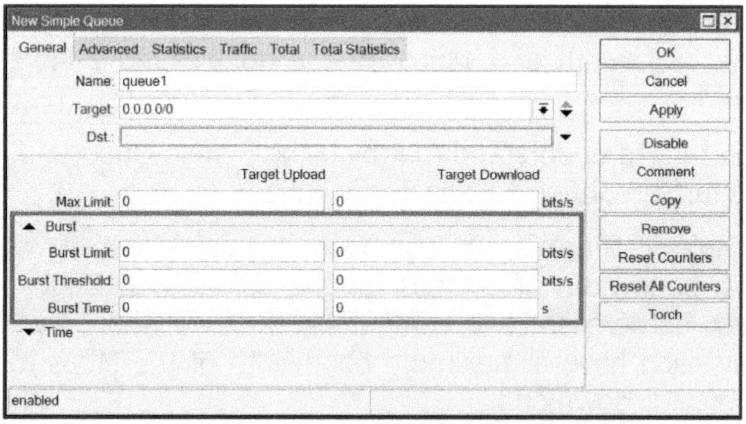

In the **Burst Limit** field, you can specify the upload and download bandwidth. In the **Burst Time** field, you can set a value for the time in seconds to be used in calculating the average data rate. This time is not the actual burst time.

In the **Burst Threshold** field, you can specify a bandwidth value when the average data rate exceeds or drops below this threshold, the burst will switch off or on.

You will learn more about this topic in the MTCTCE course.

7.5 Parent and Child Queues

You can create a queue and link it to another queue. In this case, the main queue is called the Parent queue, and the linked queue is called Child queue. When you create multiple child queues, you can prioritize one child queue over another by using the child queue priority.

7.6 Queues Priority

There are 8 different priority values for queues, starting from 1 to 8. 8 is the lowest priority, and 1 is the highest. These priorities work only for child queues.

A queue with a higher priority will have the chance to satisfy its Maximum Information Rate (MIR), (or max-limit) before other queues.

You will learn more about this topic in the MTCTCE course.

7.7 Queue Kinds

When sending data, the device will first arrange those packets in lines or rows, then start sending the packets one by one.

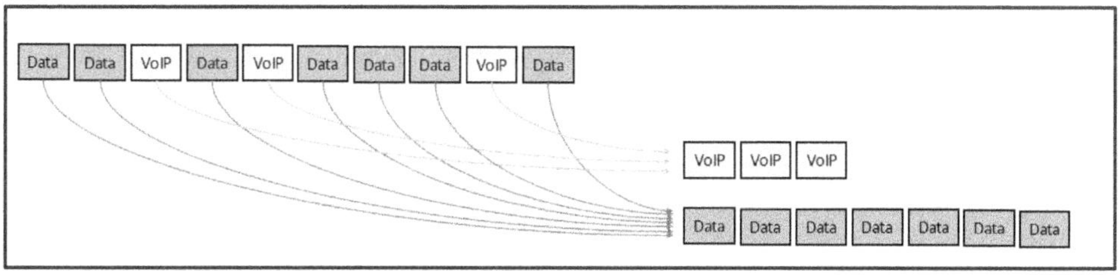

These lines or rows are called queues.

The method or mechanism of sending the packets that are waiting in the line is called the queue type.

The process of arranging those packets in lines or queues is called classification.

You can arrange, or classify ,the packets in different lines or queues using many criteria.

For example, you can place the data belonging to a specific protocol in one queue and the data of other protocol in another queue.

Or you can place the data sourced from a specific PC in one queue and the data from another PC in another queue.

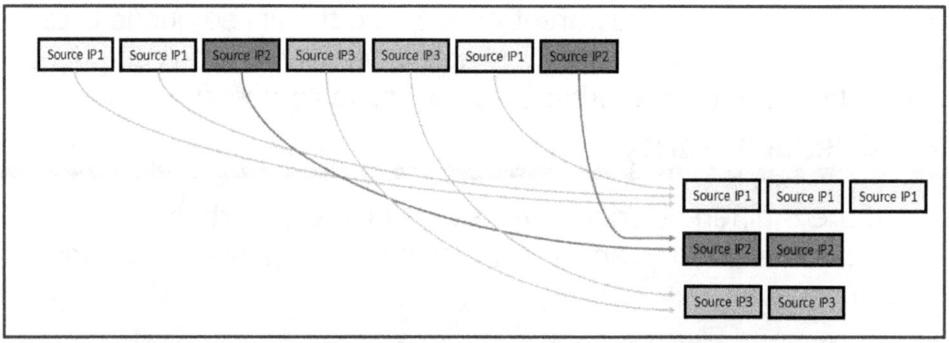

When processing, or sending, data from these queues, you can use various methods (or queue types) to do that. For example, you can send the packet that arrives first before other packets that arrive later. In some other cases, the last-arrived packet might be more important to be sent before the first-arrived one.

MikroTik RouterOS supports various methods or queue types for sending data:

- FIFO (BFIFO, PFIFO, MQ PFIFO)
- RED
- SFQ
- PCQ

7.8 Per Connection Queuing

You can create one Simple Queue for the entire network using PCQ queues.

The concept of using PCQ queues is to divide the main data stream into sub-streams, lines, or queues, based on specific classification criteria. Then, when sending the data, the first packet from each queue will be sent.

For example, you can place the data of each host in a separate line or queue by classifying it based on the source IP.

To configure PCQ in RouterOS:

- First: create the PCQ
- Second: apply it to the interface.

To create a PCQ, use the **Queue Types** tab of the **Queues List** window.

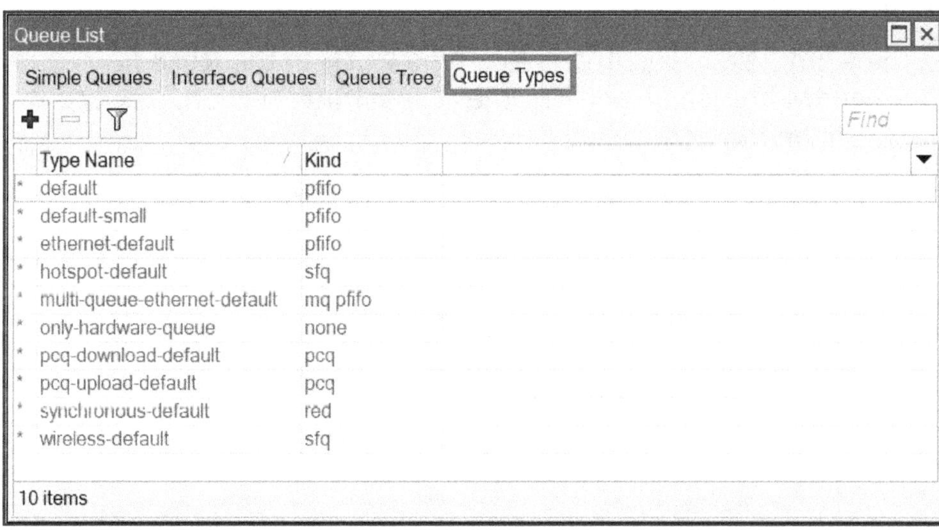

To add a new PCQ, click the **Add** button to open the **New Queue Type** dialog box.

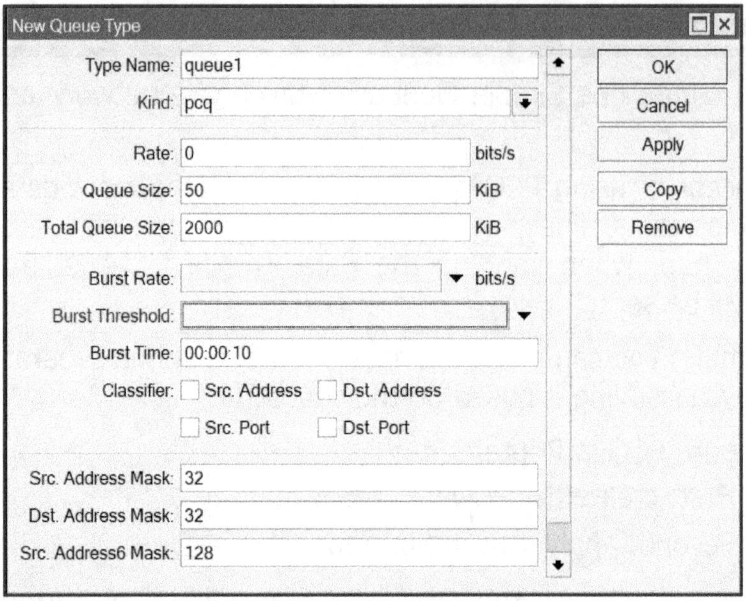

You can use this dialog box to create different queue types and configure their settings.

In the **Kind** field, select the queue type **PCQ**. In the **Rate** field, enter the bandwidth limit, and in the **Classifier** section, choose the classification method.

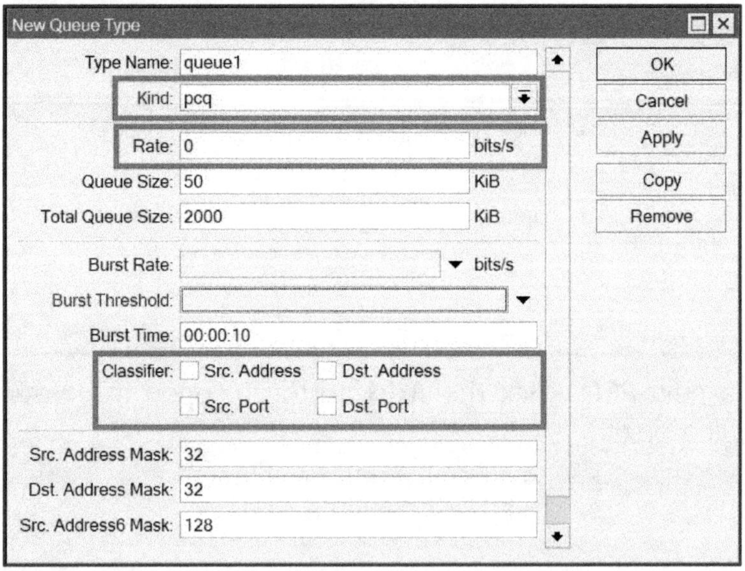

To apply the PCQ to an interface, use the **Interface Queues** tab of the **Queues List** window.

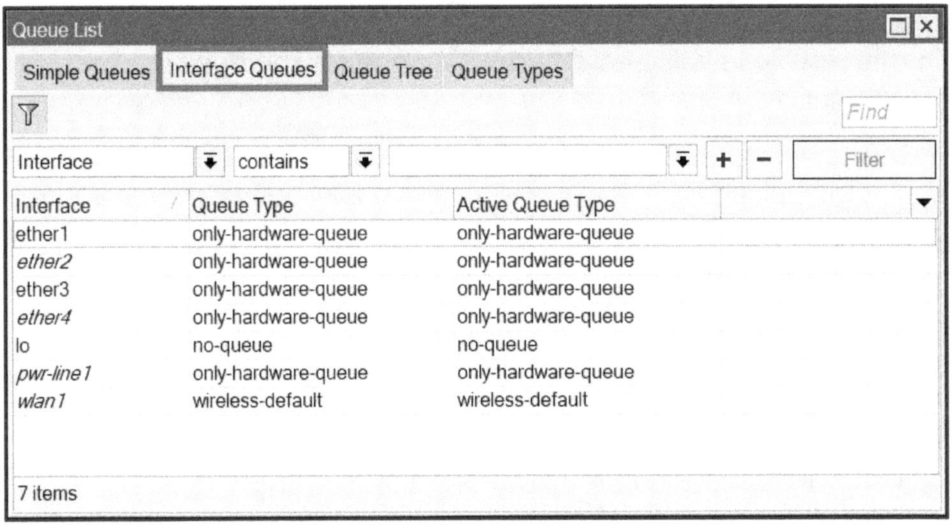

Double-click the desired interface to open the **Interface Queue** dialog box.

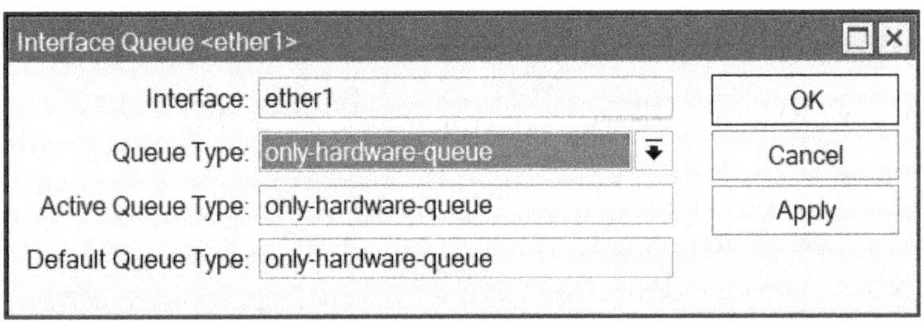

In the **Queue Type** field, select the PCQ you've just created.

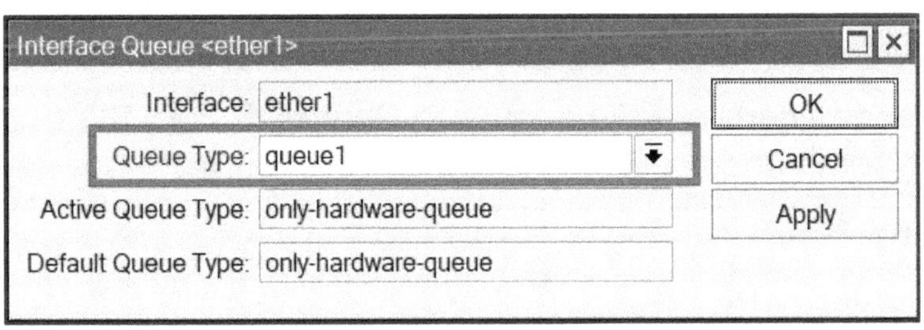

One common scenario of using PCQ is to limit the bandwidth (download and upload) for each computer in the local network and distribute the bandwidth evenly among them.

In this case, you will create two PCQs: one for the download and one for the upload.

In the download PCQ, use classification based on destination address, and in the upload PCQ, use classification based on the source address.

When applying the PCQ to an interface, the download PCQ will be applied to the interface connected to the local network, and the upload PCQ will be applied to the interface connected to the internet

You can also add or create a PCQ queue from the CLI using the following command:

```
queue type add name=[name] kind=pcq pcq-rate=[rate] pcq-classifier=[classification method]
```

Where:

- [name] is the name for the PCQ.
- [rate] is the bandwidth limit.
- [classification method] the classification method.

For example:

```
queue type add name=queue1 kind=pcq pcq-rate=2M pcq-classifier=dst-address
```

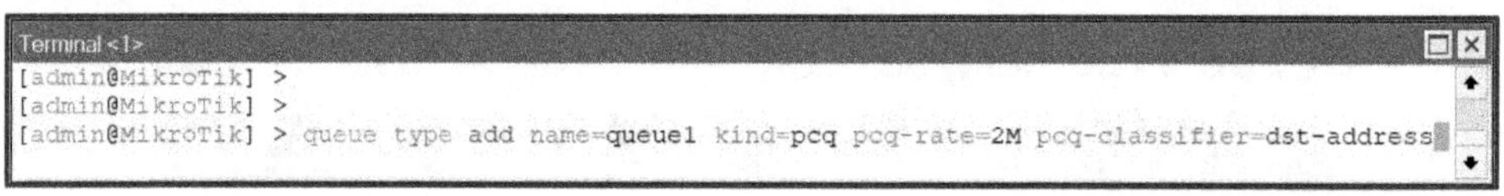

To display the current PCQ queues in RouterOS from the CLI use the following command:

```
queue type print
```

```
Terminal <1>
    red-max-threshold=50 red-burst=20 red-avg-packet=1000

 4 * name="hotspot-default" kind=sfq sfq-perturb=5 sfq-allot=1514

 5   name="queue1" kind=pcq pcq-rate=2M pcq-limit=50KiB pcq-classifier=dst-address
     pcq-total-limit=2000KiB pcq-burst-rate=0 pcq-burst-threshold=0 pcq-burst-time=10s
     pcq-src-address-mask=32 pcq-dst-address-mask=32 pcq-src-address6-mask=128
     pcq-dst-address6-mask=128

 6 * name="pcq-upload-default" kind=pcq pcq-rate=0 pcq-limit=50KiB pcq-classifier=src-addres>
     pcq-src-address-mask=32 pcq-dst-address-mask=32 pcq-src-address6-mask=128
     pcq-dst-address6-mask=128

 7 * name="pcq-download-default" kind=pcq pcq-rate=0 pcq-limit=50KiB
     pcq-classifier=dst-address pcq-total-limit=2000KiB pcq-burst-rate=0
     pcq-burst-threshold=0 pcq-burst-time=10s pcq-src-address-mask=32
     pcq-dst-address-mask=32 pcq-src-address6-mask=128 pcq-dst-address6-mask=128

 8 * name="only-hardware-queue" kind=none

 9 * name="multi-queue-ethernet-default" kind=mq-pfifo mq-pfifo-limit=50

10 * name="default-small" kind=pfifo pfifo-limit=10

[admin@MikroTik] >
```

To apply the PCQ to an interface from the CLI use the following command:

```
queue interface set [interface] queue=[queue]
```

Where:

- [interface] is the name for the interface.
- [queue] is the name of the PCQ.

For example:

```
queue interface set ether1 queue=queue1
```

```
Terminal <1>
[admin@MikroTik] >
[admin@MikroTik] >
[admin@MikroTik] >
[admin@MikroTik] > queue interface set ether1 queue=queue1
```

LAB

In this lab, you have a MikroTik device, R1, connected to a local network (LAN) 192.168.1.0/24 via ether1 and to the internet (WAN) via ether2. You want to limit the download speed to 2 Mbps and the upload speed to 1 Mbps for each computer in the local network to distribute the bandwidth evenly among them using a PCQ.

To start the configuration:

- First: perform the basic configuration to allow the connection to the internet.
- Second: configure PCQ by creating two PCQs, One for download, using the classification based on the destination address, and applying it to the interface connected to the LAN interface. The second for upload, using the classification based on the source address, and applying it to the WAN interface.

Basic Configuration

Insall DHCP Client on ether2 to obtain an IP address from the ISP.

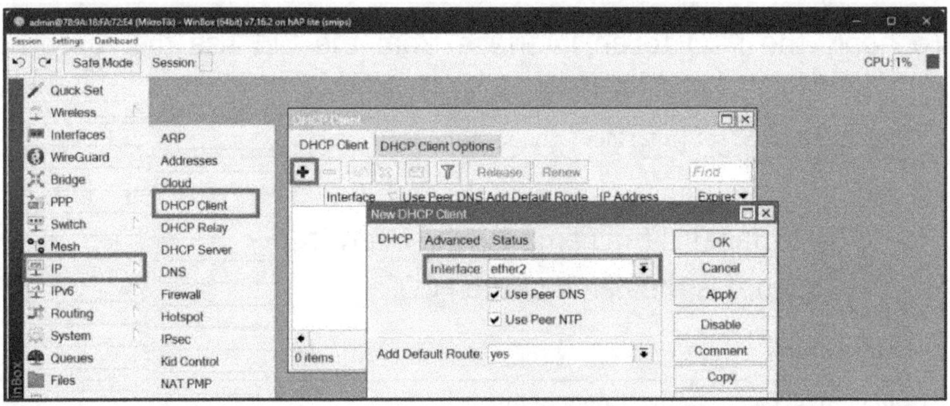

Assign the IP address 192.168.1.1/24 to the interface ether1.

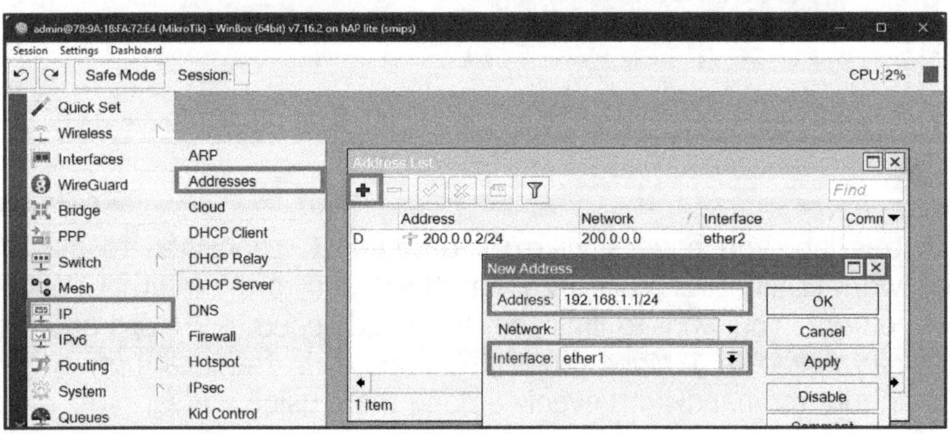

Configure DHCP Server on the interface ether1, to distribute IP addresses to any computer connects to it.

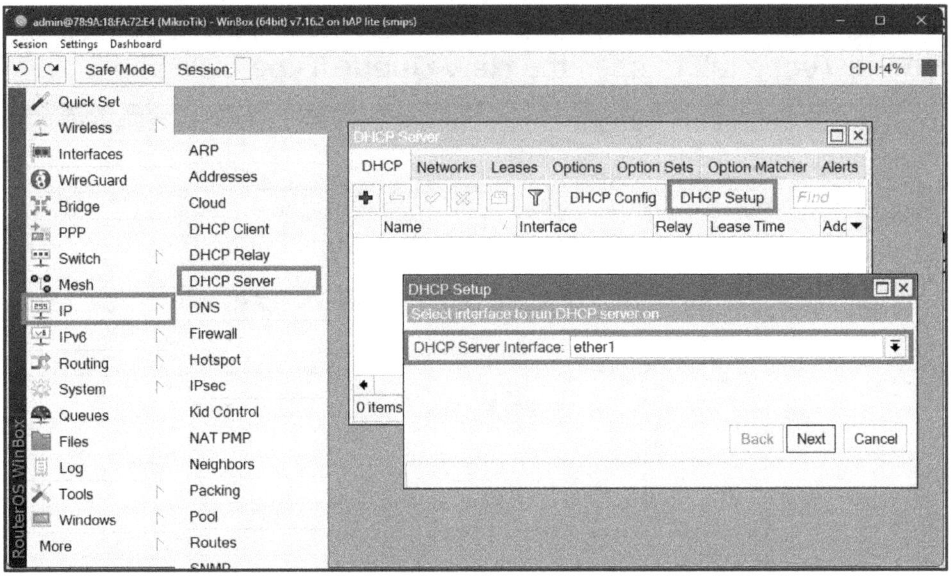

Create a NAT rule with the **Masquerade** action, for the subnet 192.168.1.0/24

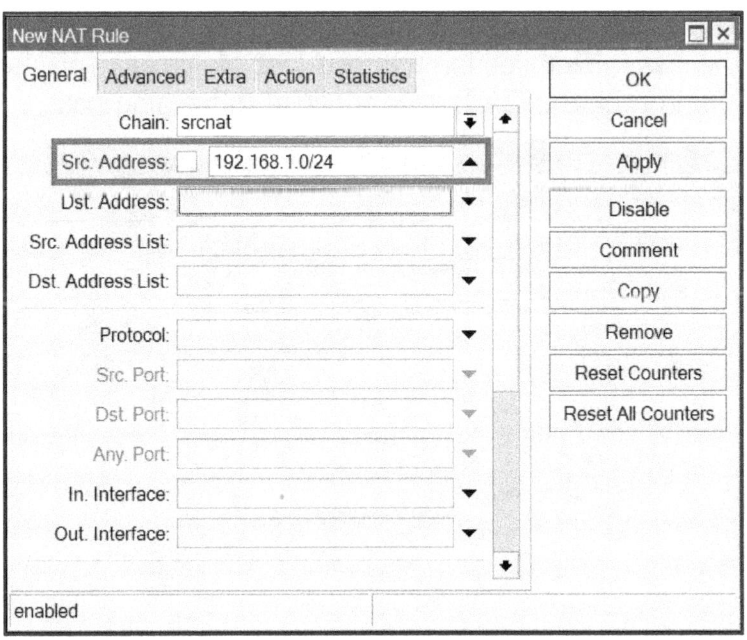

PCQ Configuration

To create the first PCQ for the download, click the **Queues** menu to open the **Queue List** window. Then, click the **Add** button in the **Queue Types** tab to open the **New Queue Type** dialog box.

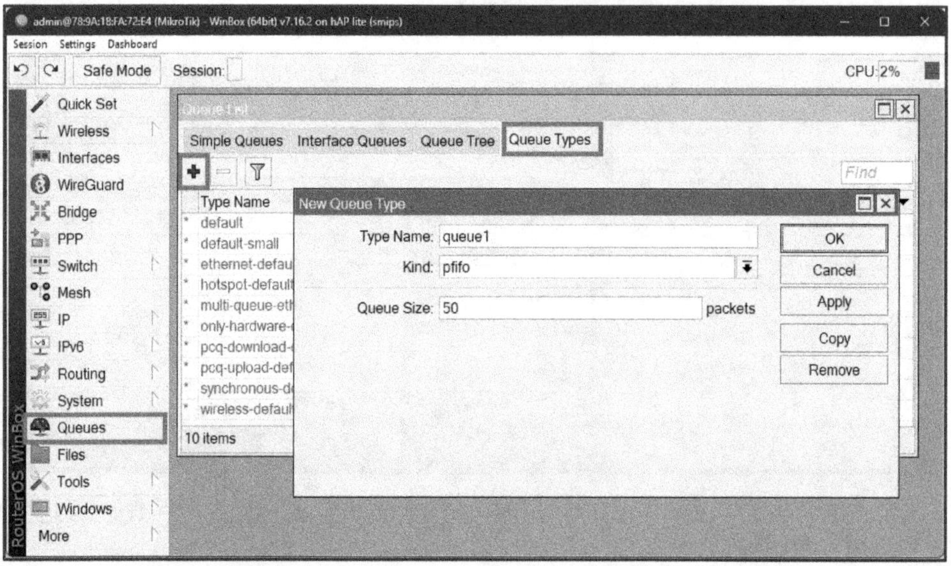

In the **Kind** field, select the queue type PCQ. In the **Rate** field, enter **2M**. In the **Classifier** section, choose **Dst. Address** (or Destination Address), and click the **OK** button to close this dialog box.

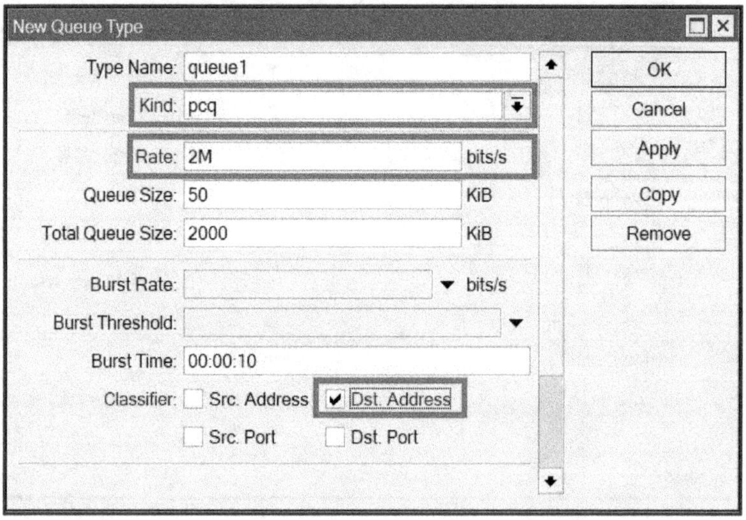

After creating the PCQ, it will appear in the **Queue Types** tab.

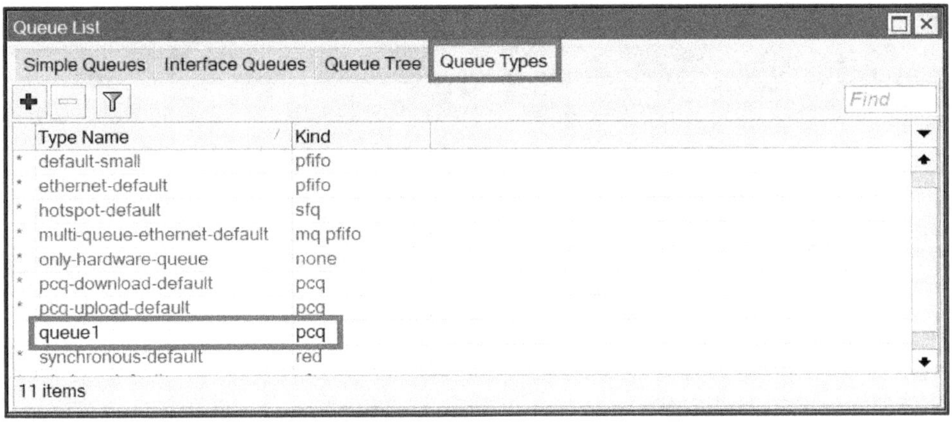

To apply this PCQ to the LAN interface (ether1), double-click the ether1 interface in the **Interface Queues** tab of the **Queues List** window to open the **Interface Queue** dialog box.

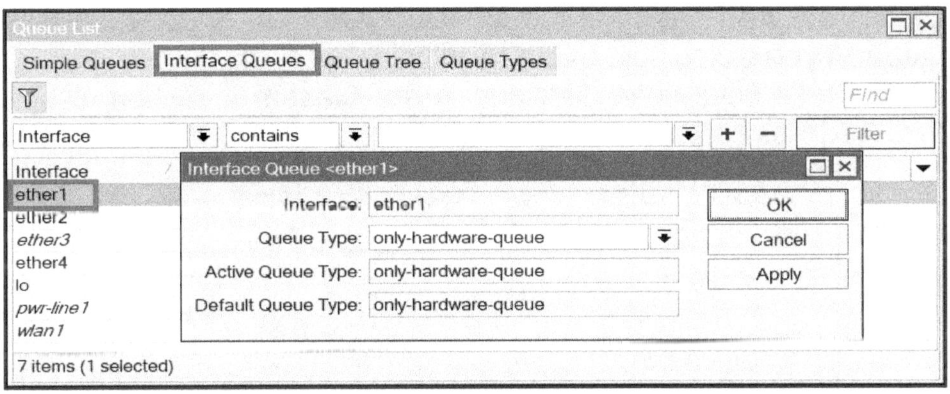

In the **Queue Type** field, select queue1 (the PCQ you've just created), and click the **OK** button to close this dialog box.

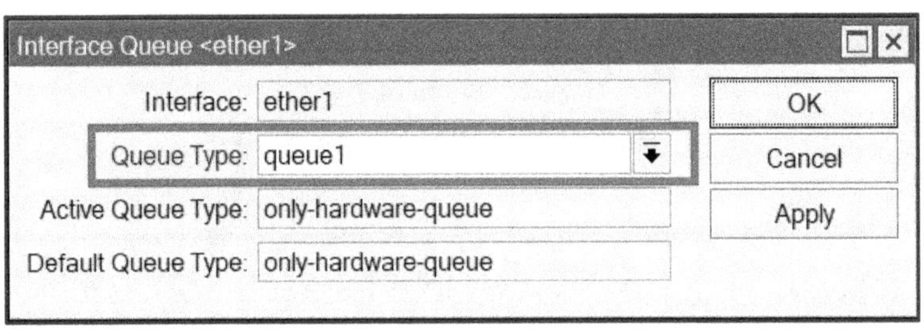

The new configuration for ether1 will appear in the **Interface Queues** tab.

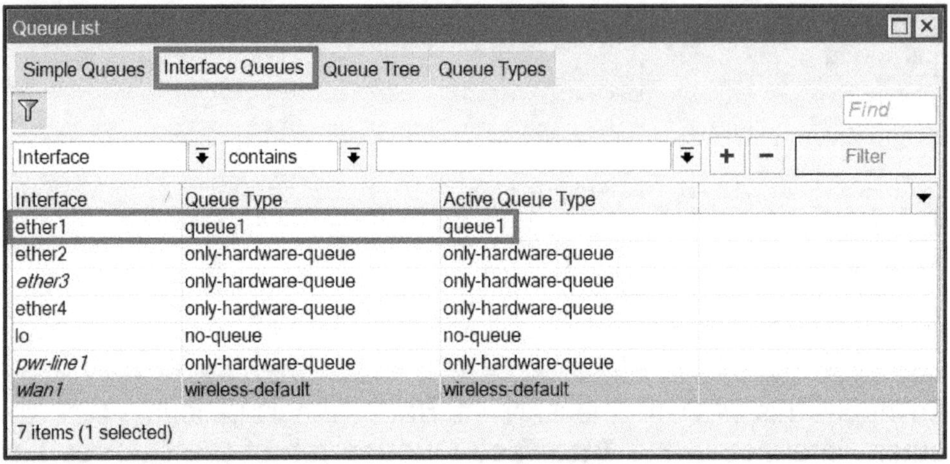

Repeat the same steps again to create the second PCQ for the upload, clicking the **Add** button in the **Queue Types** tab to open the **New Queue Type** dialog box. In the **Kind** field, select the queue type PCQ. In the **Rate** field, enter **1M,** and in the **Classifier** section, choose **Src. Address** (or Source Address).

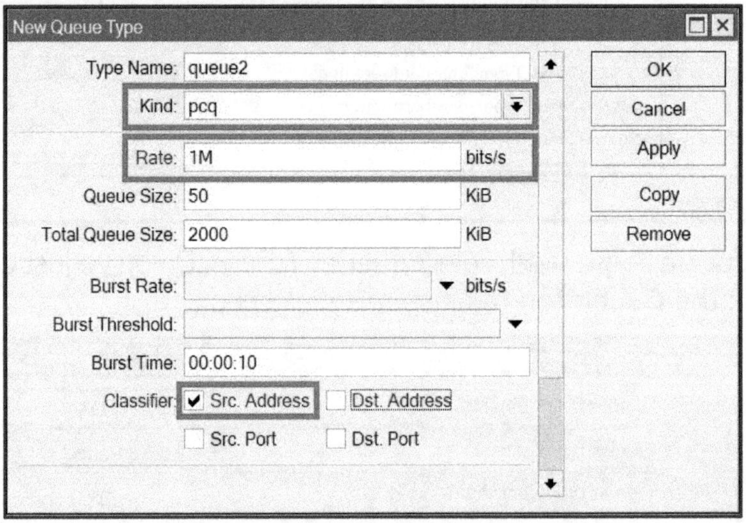

Then to apply this PCQ to the WAN interface (ether2), double-click the ether2 interface in the **Interface Queues** tab to open the **Interface**

Queue dialog box. In the **Queue Type** field, select queue2, and click the **OK** button to close this dialog box.

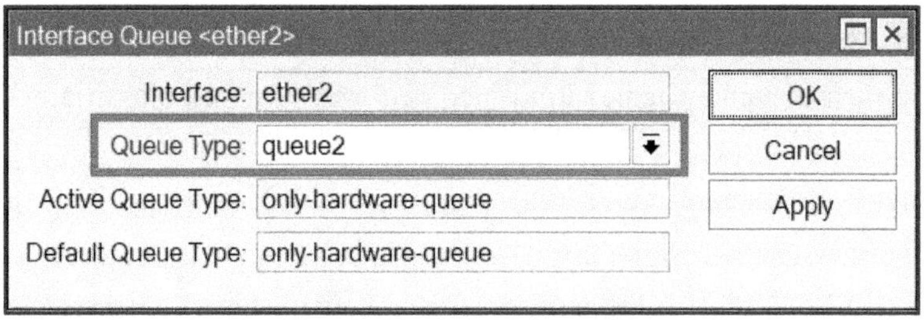

Now, each computer connects to the local network will have a maximum bandwidth of 2 Mbps for download and 1 Mbps for upload.

It is important to understand that in this lab by using PCQ, the bandwidth limit will be applied to each computer individually.

For example, if there is one computer in this network, it will have a maximum bandwidth of 2 Mbps for download and 1 Mbps for upload. If there are two computers, each one will have a maximum bandwidth of 2 Mbps for download and 1 Mbps for upload, (for sure if there is enough bandwidth available).

CLI

You can also make the configuration from the CLI.

To configure DHCP Client on ether2, use the following command:

```
ip dhcp-client add interface=ether2
```

To assign IP addresses to ether1, use the following command:

```
ip address add address=192.168.1.1/24 interface=ether1
```

To configure DHCP server on ether1 interface using the DHCP setup wizard, use the following command, choose ether1 interface and accept the default settings by pressing Enter each time the setup wizard asks for input:

```
ip dhcp-server setup
```

To create the NAT rule, use the following command:

```
ip firewall nat add src-address=192.168.1.0/24 chain=srcnat
action=masquerade
```

To create PCQ queues, use the following commands:

```
queue type add name=queue1 kind=pcq pcq-rate=2M pcq-classifier=dst-
address

queue type add name=queue2 kind=pcq pcq-rate=1M pcq-classifier=src-
address
```

To apply the PCQ to the interfaces ether1 and ether2, use the following command:

```
queue interface set ether1 queue=queue1

queue interface set ether2 queue=queue2
```

8

Module

TUNNELS

MTCNA

Module 8

This module provides an introduction to tunneling and virtual private network (VPN) technology in MikroTik devices and explains a simple method to configure the VPN.

More advanced information about VPN technologies is available in the MTCTCE and MTCUME courses.

This module covers the following course content topics:

- PPP settings
  - PPP profile
  - PPP secret
  - PPP status
- Secure local network
  - PPPoE service-name
  - PPPoE client
  - PPPoE server
- Point-to-point addresses
- Secure remote networks communication
  - PPTP client and PPTP server (Quick Set)
  - SSTP client

Tunnels

8.1 Tunnels Overview and Key Concepts

A tunnel, or VPN (Virtual Private Network), is a technology that allows remote devices to appear as if they are directly connected to each other. This technology is used to establish a secure connection between devices over the internet.

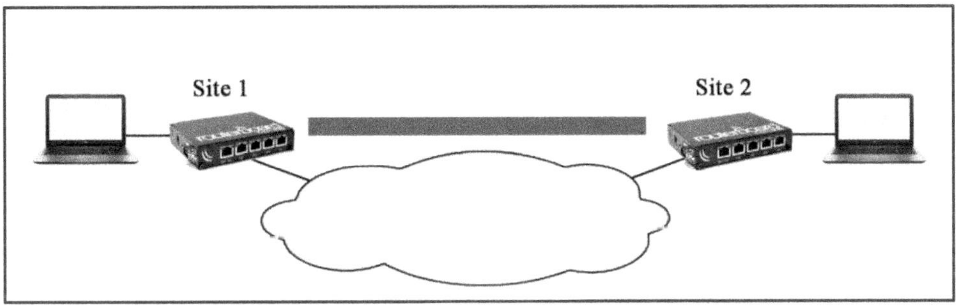

8.2 How Tunnel Works

The concept behind using tunnels or VPNs is to configure a virtual link, or virtual tunnel, between two remote devices and then use this link to carry data of a specific subnet.

You can configure this virtual link using different methods or protocols, called VPN protocols, to create different types of VPNs.

When using certain protocols to create a VPN, you configure one device to act as the VPN server and the other as the VPN client.

- On the server, perform two main steps:
    - Enable the protocol.
    - Create an account.

- On the client, perform one main step:
  - Establish the connection

With some other protocols, both devices are configured in the same way.

8.3 Types of VPNs

There are two main types of VPNs:

8.3.1 Site-to-Site VPN

Where two remote sites, or remote routers, are configured to appear as if they are directly connected to each other,

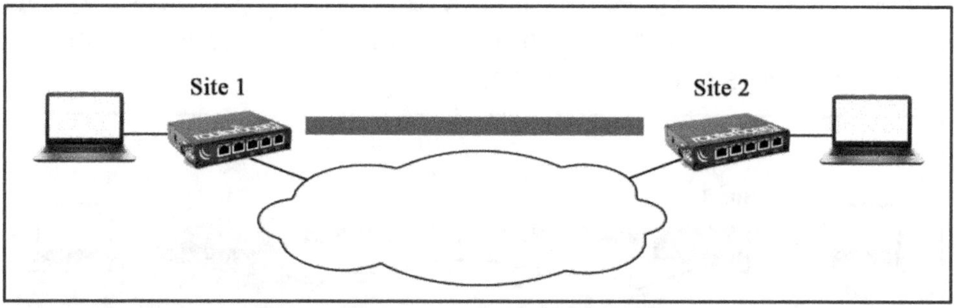

8.3.2 Client-to-Site VPN (Remote Access)

Where a client device, or a host device, is connected to a remote site, or remote router, appearing as if they are directly connected to each other.

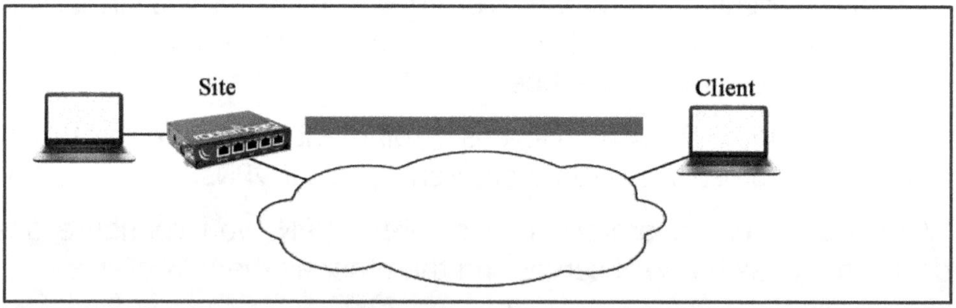

8.3.4 Other Types of VPNs

VPNs can also be categorized into different types based on:

- Topology, such as:
    - Point-to-point VPN.
    - Point-to-multipoint VPN.
- OSI Layer, such as:
    - Layer 2 (L2) VPN.
    - Layer 3 (L3) VPN

8.4 Point-to-Point Addresses

To connect a device to another device, you need at least 4 IP addresses:

- One for the first device.
- One for the second device.
- One for the network ID.
- One for the broadcast IP.

In this case, you will use a subnet mask of /30. Although you only want to connect two devices, you have to use 4 IP addresses.

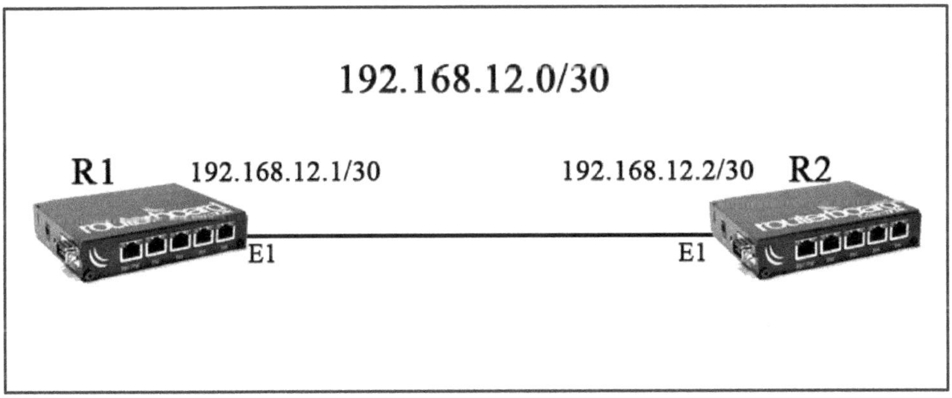

If you want to connect one device to 10 other devices using 10 links, you will need at least 40 IP addresses. This is because each link requires 4 IP addresses, using a subnet mask of /30.

If you want to connect one device to 100 other devices using 100 links, you will need at least 400 IP addresses. This is because each link requires 4 IP addresses, using a subnet mask of /30.

Instead of wasting IP addresses like that, you can use the point-to-point addressing method with a subnet mask of /32. In this case, to connect one device to another, you will use only two IP addresses, one for each device.

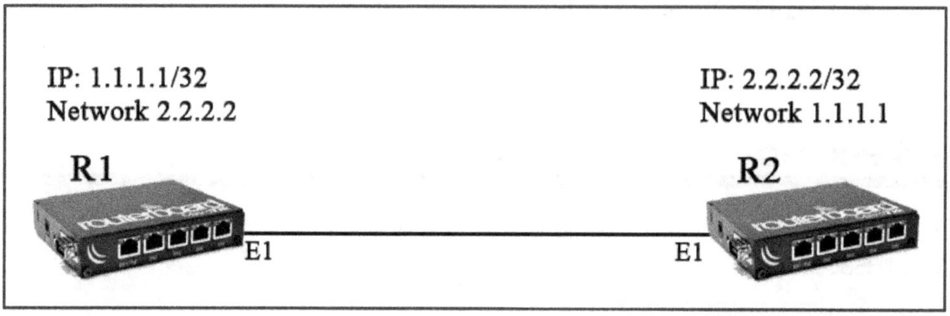

To connect a device to 10 other devices, you will need 11 IP addresses, one for each device.

To connect a device to 100 other devices, you will need 101 IP addresses, one for each device.

When configuring VPNs, or tunnels, the point-to-point addresses are used to avoid wasting IP addresses.

LAB

In this lab, router R1 is connected to three routers: R2, R3, and R4. Since each link is in a separate subnet, you will need at least 16 IP addresses when using the subnet mask of /30, which gives 4 IP addresses for each link.

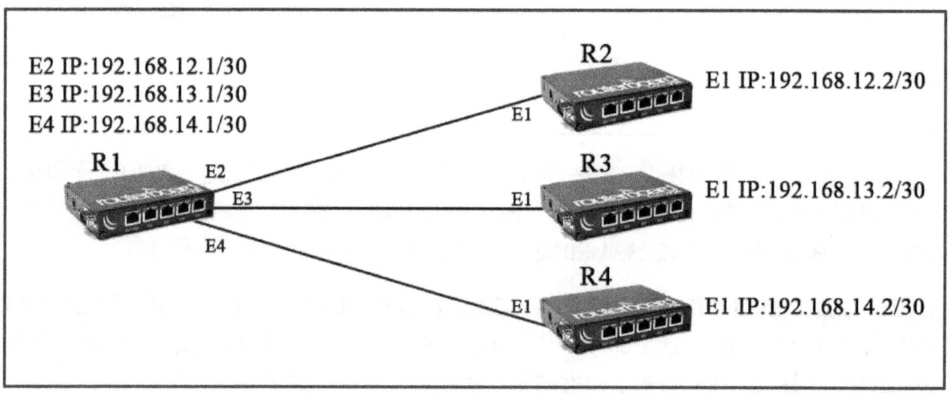

Instead of using 16 IP addresses, you can use point-to-point addresses. In this case, you will need only 4 IP addresses, one for each device.

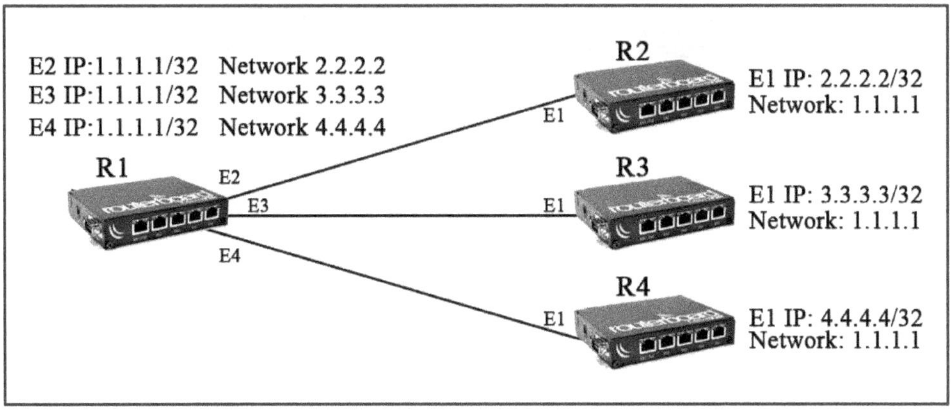

So, you will assign:

- R1 the IP address 1.1.1.1/32,
- R2 the IP address 2.2.2.2/32
- R3 the IP address 3.3.3.3/32
- R4 the IP address 4.4.4.4/32.

To start configuring the first link between R1 and R2, Open the **Address List** window, then click the **Add** button to open the **New Address** dialog box. In the **Address** field, enter the IP address of R1 along with the subnet mask:

1.1.1.1/32

Or you can write the IP address without the subnet mask:

1.1.1.1

In both cases, the device will understand that this is an IP address with a /32 subnet and will remove the mask when saving the IP.

In the **Network** field, enter the IP address of R2:

2.2.2.2

In this lab, R1 is connected to R2 via interface ether2. So, in the **Interface** field, select ether2, then click the **OK** button to close the dialog box.

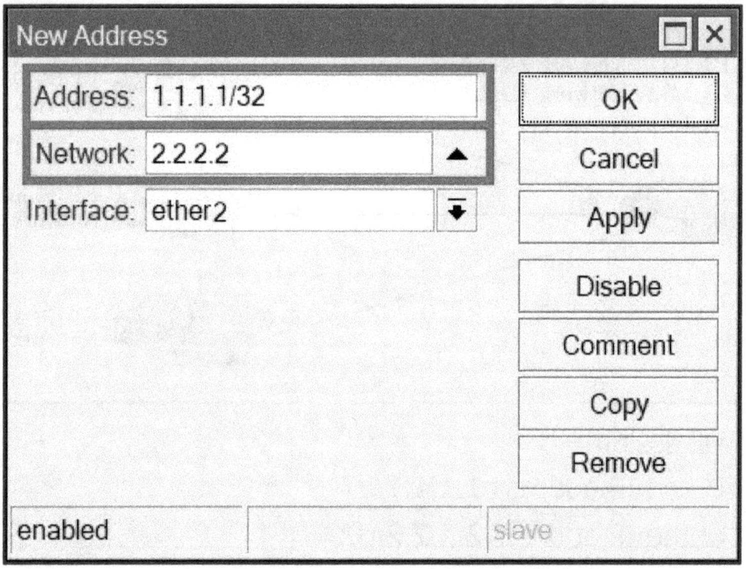

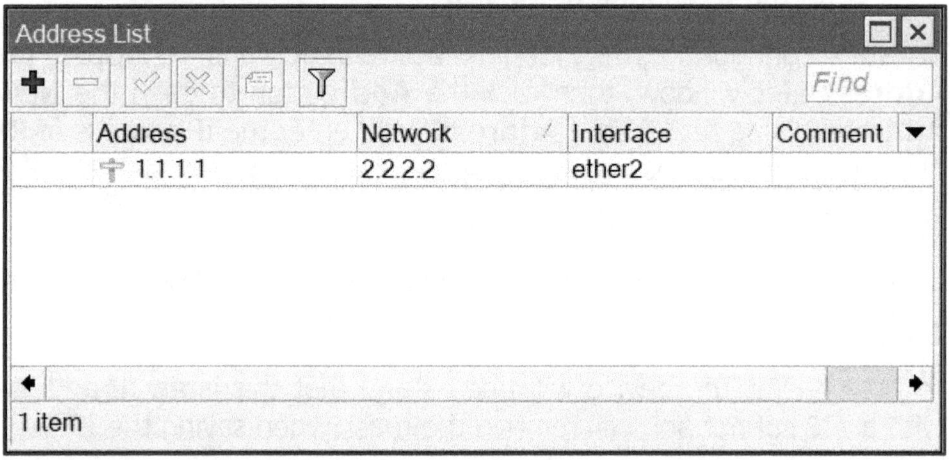

Then in R2, open the **Address List** window. Click the **Add** button to open the **New Address** dialog box. In the **Address** field, enter the IP address of R2 along with the subnet mask:

2.2.2.2/32

In the **Network** field, enter the IP address of R1:

1.1.1.1

In this lab, R2 is connected to R1 via interface ether1. So, in the **Interface** field, select ether1, then click the **OK** button to close the dialog box.

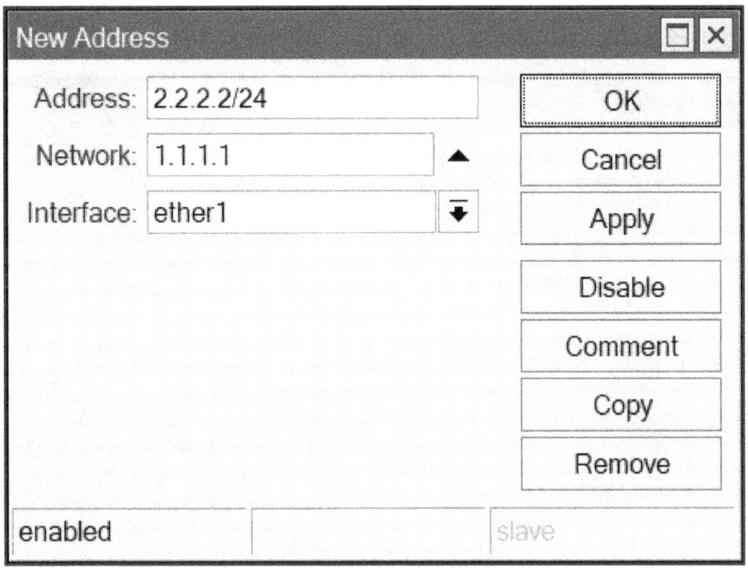

The configuration of the point-to-point address on the link between R1 and R2 is complete. Now, you can check the connectivity between these routers by pinging the IP address of R2 from R1, or the IP address of R1 from R2.

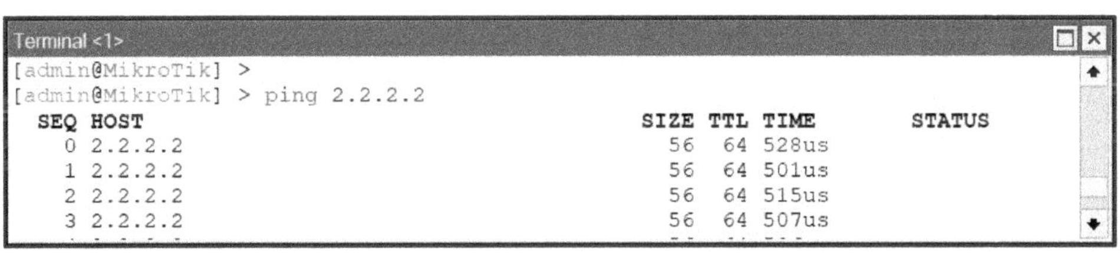

Repeat the same steps to assign IP addresses to the link between R1 and R3, noting that you will use the same IP address of R1 1.1.1.1/32 for this link as well. However, it is not mandatory; you can use a different IP if you want, depending on the network requirements.

So, in R1, in the **Address** field enter the IP address of R1 along with the subnet mask:

1.1.1.1/32

In the **Network** field, enter the IP address of R3:

3.3.3.3

In the **Interface** field, select ether3, which connects R1 to R3.

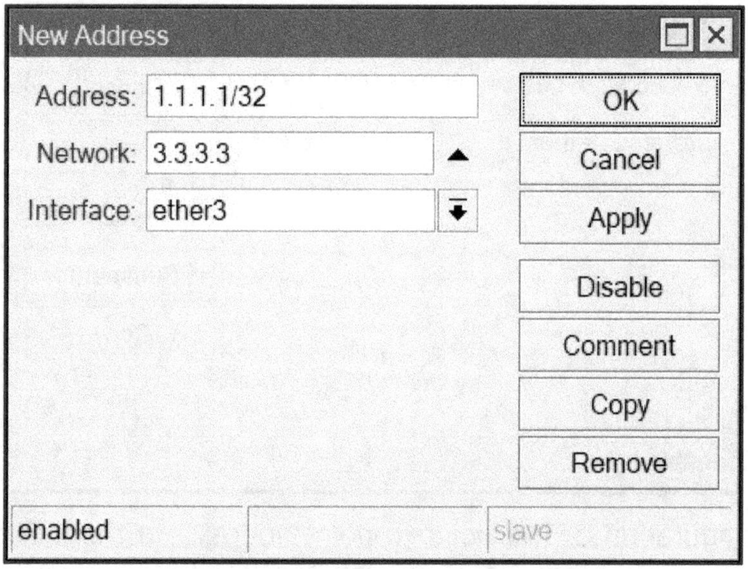

Then in R3, in the **Address** field, enter the IP address of R3 along with the subnet mask:

3.3.3.3/32

In the **Network** field, enter the IP address of R1:

1.1.1.1

In the **Interface** field, select ether1, which connects R3 to R1.

Then, repeat the same steps again to assign IP addresses to the link between R1 and R4.

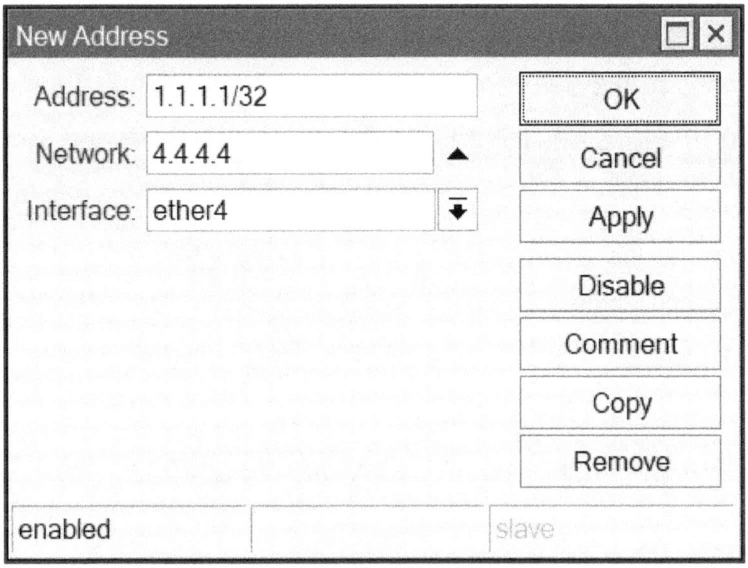

Note: in R1, you've used the same IP address 1.1.1.1/32 on all three interfaces: ether2, ether3, and ether4. By doing that, you preserved the IP addresses and used only one IP address for each device.

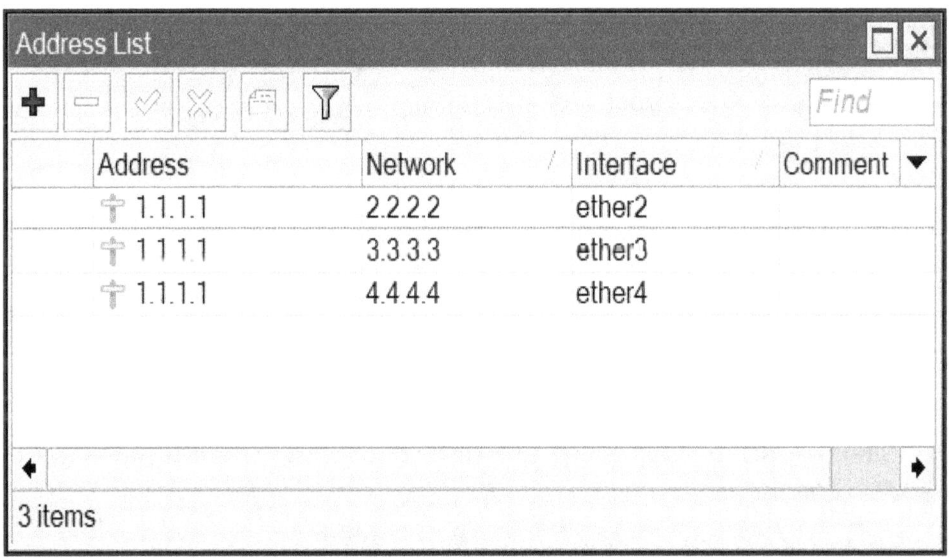

The same concept is used when assigning IP addresses to tunnels or VPNs.

CLI

You can also make the configuration from the CLI.

To assign IP addresses to the interfaces, use the following commands:

R1

```
ip address add address=1.1.1.1/32 network=2.2.2.2 interface=ether2
ip address add address=1.1.1.1/32 network=3.3.3.3 interface=ether3
ip address add address=1.1.1.1/32 network=4.4.4.4 interface=ether4
```

R2

```
ip address add address=2.2.2.2/32 network=1.1.1.1 interface=ether1
```

R3

```
ip address add address=3.3.3.3/32 network=1.1.1.1 interface=ether1
```

R4

```
ip address add address=4.4.4.4/32 network=1.1.1.1 interface=ether1
```

8.5 VPN Protocols

You can configure a VPN using different protocols such as:

- SSTP
- PPTP
- L2TP
- IPIP
- EoIP
- IPsec

In MikroTik RouterOS, there are different ways to configure various VPN protocols.

Some protocols are configured using the **PPP** window, such as:

- PPTP
- L2TP
- SSTP

- OVPN
- PPPoE

Some protocols are configured using the **Interface List** window, such as:

- GRE
- IPIP
- EoIP

Other protocols are configured using their own windows, such as:

- IPsec
- WireGuard

For the objectives of the MTCNA course, you will use the PPP window to make a basic PPP configuration. You will learn more about VPNs in the MTCRE course.

8.6 Tunnel Configuration

To configure a tunnel, or a VPN, in RouterOS, use the **PPP** Window.

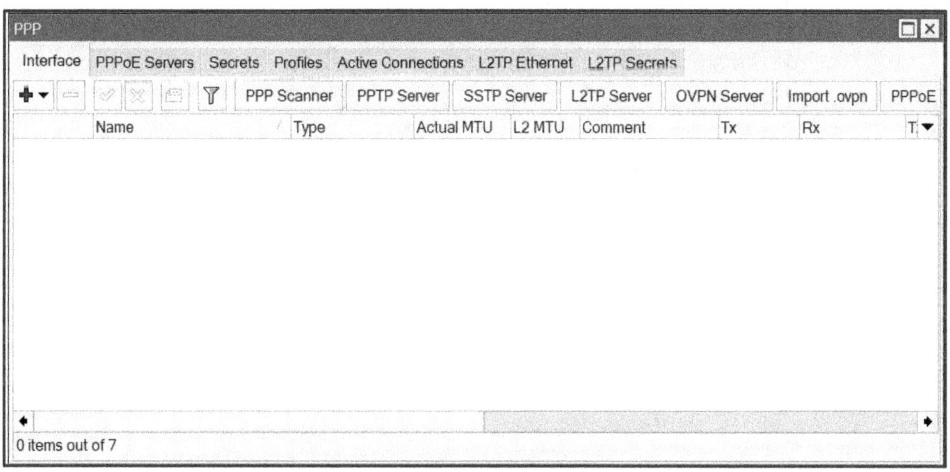

To open the **PPP** window, click the **PPP** menu.

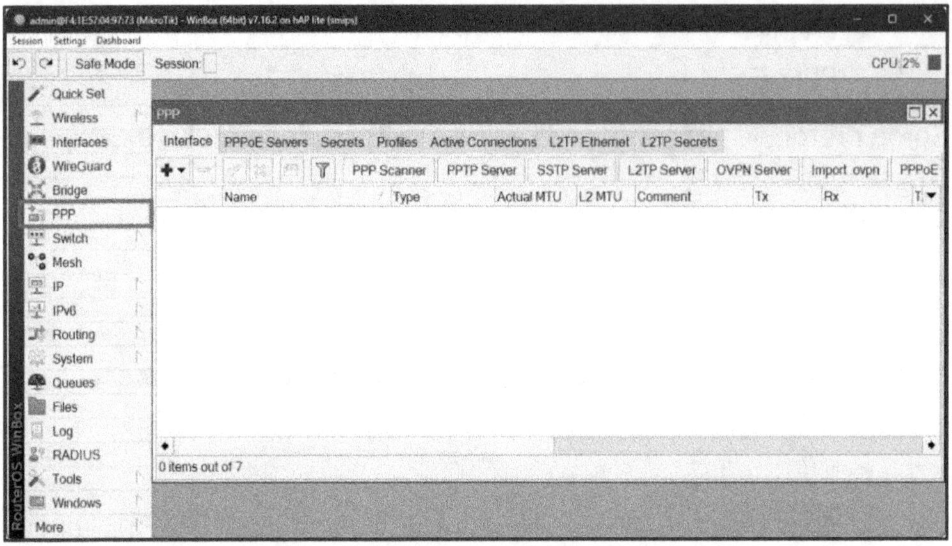

You can use this window to create a tunnel using PPP protocols such as PPTP, L2TP, SSTP, OVPN, and PPPoE, and configure its settings

Note: In RouterOS v6, before configuring PPP, make sure that the PPP package is installed. In RouterOS v7, this package is already included in the main package.

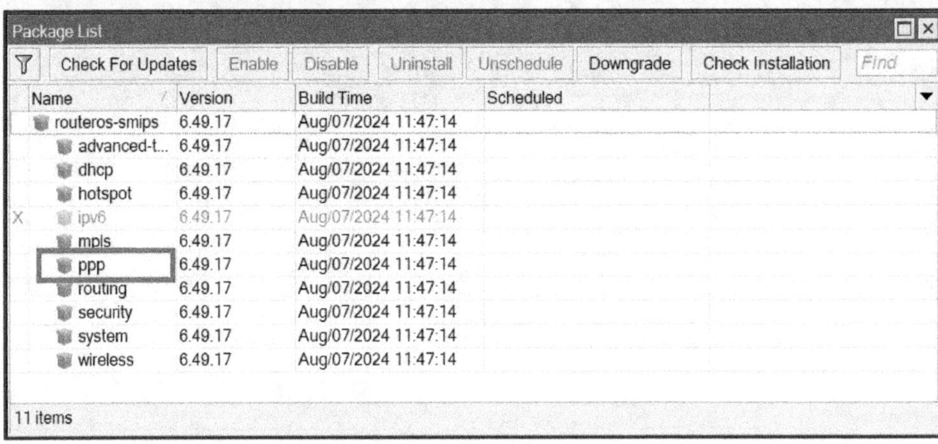

When using the **PPP** window to create a tunnel or VPN, configure one device to act as the VPN server and the other device to act as the VPN client.

On the server, perform two main steps:

- Enable the Protocol

  In this step, enable the protocol and configure its properties and features.
- Create an Account

  In this step, create an account to be used by the VPN client device to establish a connection with the server. This includes setting a username, password, and other properties for the account, such as IP addresses.

  In RouterOS, this account is called a Secret or PPP Secret.

On the client, perform one main step:

- Establish the connection.

  In this step, establish the connection to the server using the username and password created on the server.

To manage multiple accounts and set their properties, you can use a tool called a Profile, or PPP Profile. When a property is set in the profile, it is applied to all linked or connected accounts or secrets.

MikroTik RouterOS makes it simple and easy to create VPNs using various protocols. You can enable multiple PPP protocols in almost the same way, create an account, or PPP secret, to be used by those protocols, and manage multiple accounts with a PPP Profile.

8.6.1 Enable PPP Protocols

To enable, or activate, different PPP protocols like PPTP, SSTP, L2TP, or OVPN use the **Interface** tab of the **PPP** window.

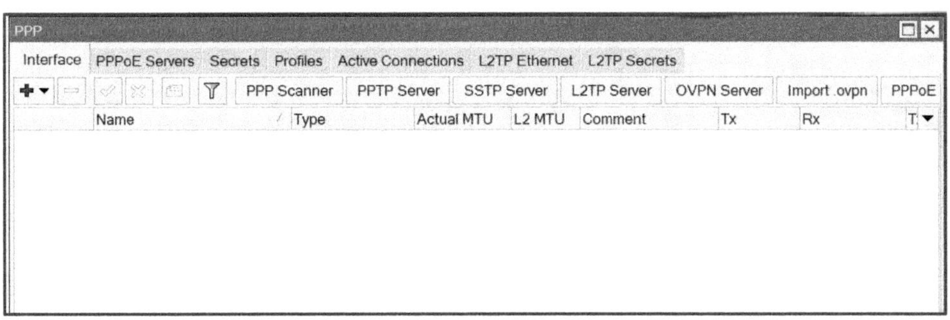

To enable a protocol, click the protocol button to open its dialog box.

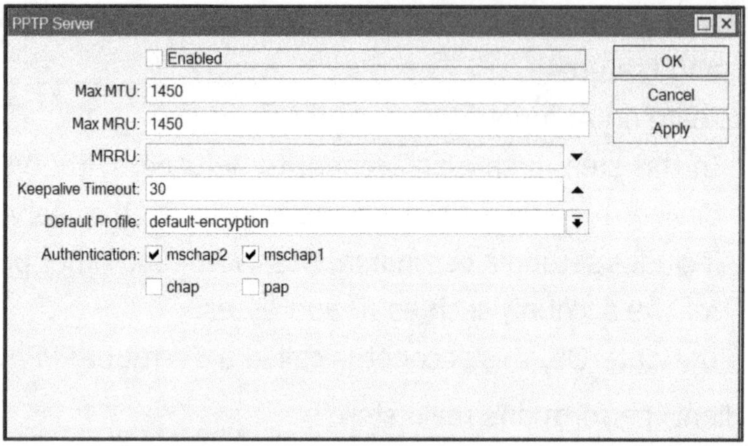

You can use this dialog box to enable the protocol and configure its settings.

8.6.2 Create an Account

To create an account, or PPP secret, use the **Secrets** tab of the **PPP** window.

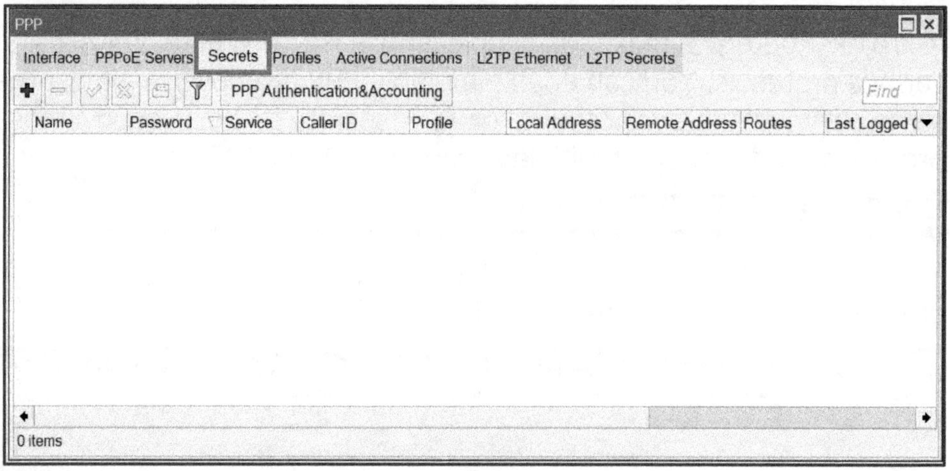

To add a new account, or a new PPP Secret, click the **Add** button to open the **New PPP Secret** dialog box.

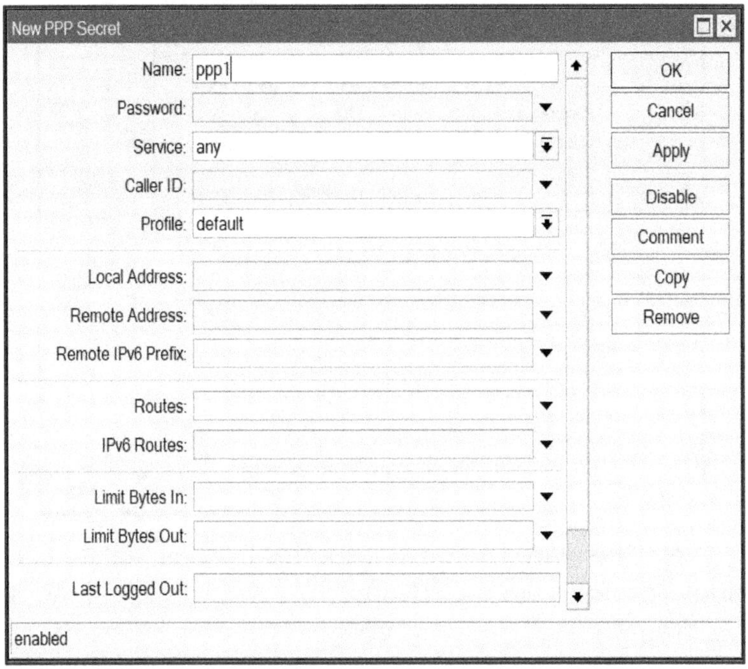

You can use this dialog box to create a new PPP Secret and configure its settings and properties, such as the username, password and IP addresses.

This account, or PPP Secret, will be used by the VPN client device to connect to the VPN server.

In the **Name** field, enter the username for this account. In the **Password** field enter the password.

When the client device connects to the server and creates a tunnel, or VPN, a new virtual interface, or tunnel interface, will be dynamically created, and both ends of this tunnel interface will be assigned IP addresses.

In the **Local Address** field, enter the IP address that will be assigned to the server end, and in the **Remote Address** field, enter the IP address that will be assigned to the client end.

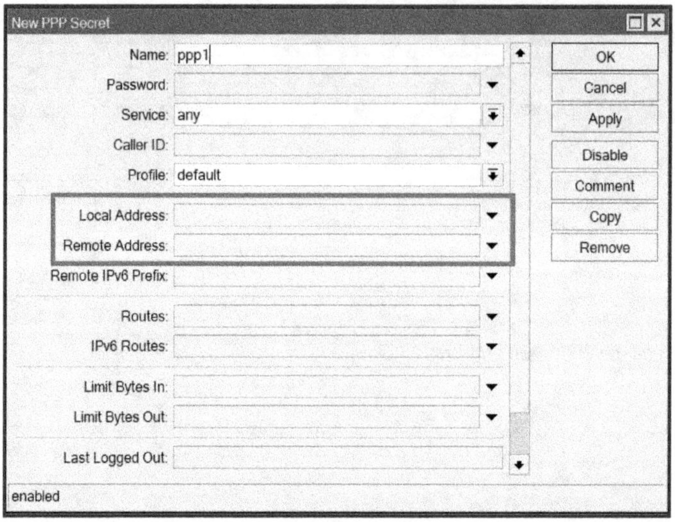

In most cases, these are the most important properties to configure in the account, or PPP Secret, (Name, Password, Local Address and Remote Address)

You can also configure other settings, such as using the **Service** field to set this account to be used by a specific PPP protocol only. or to be used by any PPP protocols.

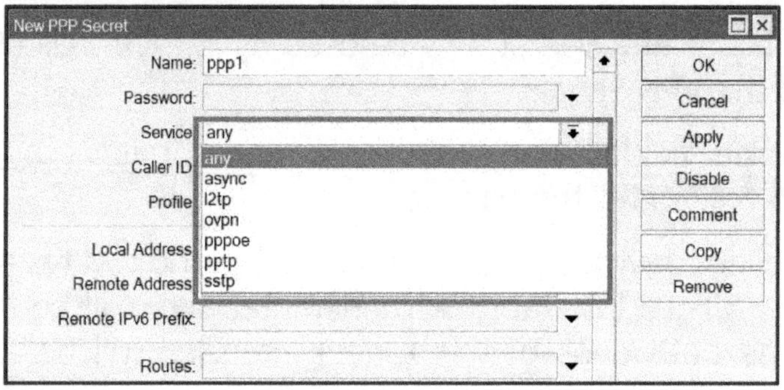

PPP Secrets can be used by the following protocols:

- PPTP
- L2TP
- SSTP
- OVPN
- PPPoE

You can also apply quota limits for this account by using the **Limit Bytes In** and **Limit Bytes Out** fields.

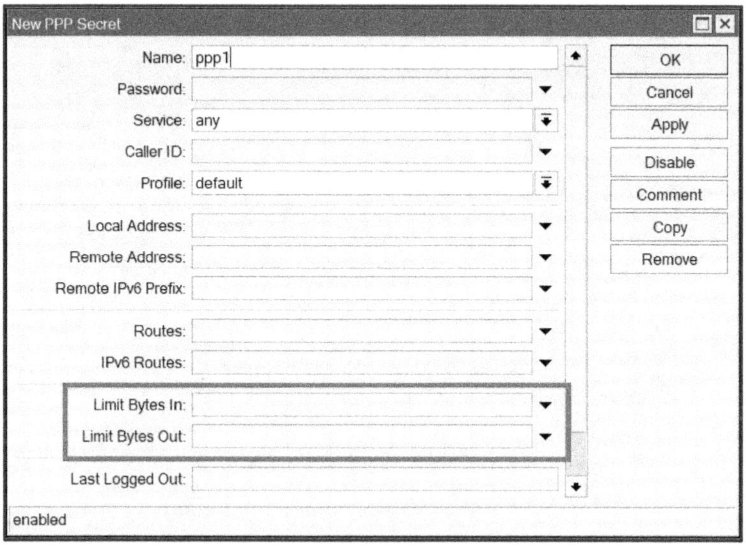

8.7 PPP Profile

A PPP profile is used to manage multiple accounts, or multiple PPP secrets, and to set their properties easily.

To create a profile, or a PPP profile, use the **Profiles** tab of the **PPP** window.

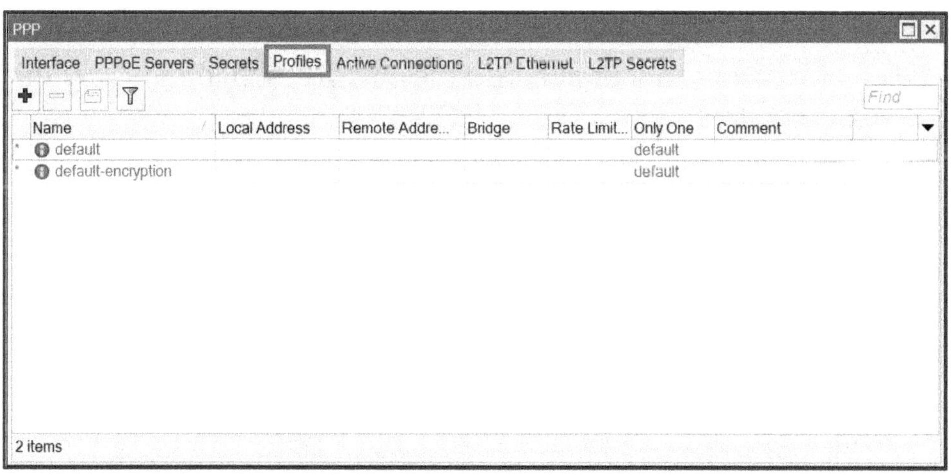

By default, there are two predefined profiles. To add a new PPP profile, click the **Add** button to open the **New PPP Profile** dialog box.

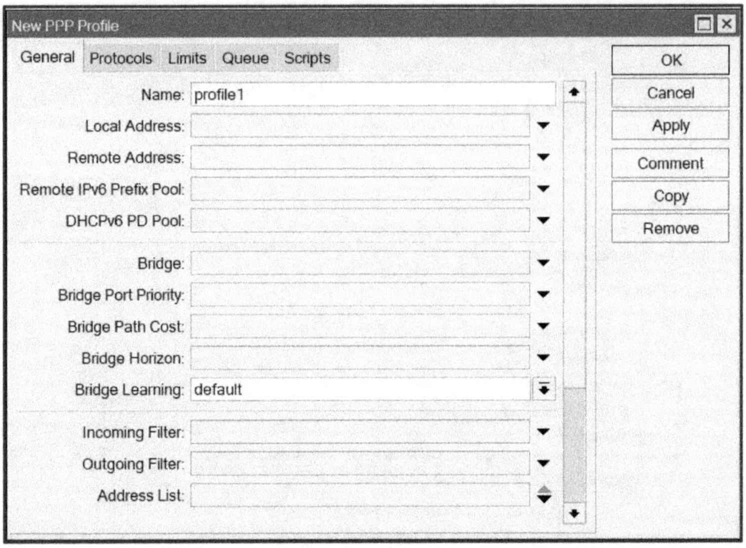

You can use this dialog box to create a new PPP profile, configure its settings and properties.

For example, if you have many accounts and want to set the Local IP and Remote IP for those accounts, instead of configuring those IP addresses in each account manually, you can enter the Local IP in the profile once, create an IP pool, and link this pool to the profile. Then, connect or link those accounts to this profile.

To link an account to a profile, use the **Profile** field in the **New PPP Secret** dialog box.

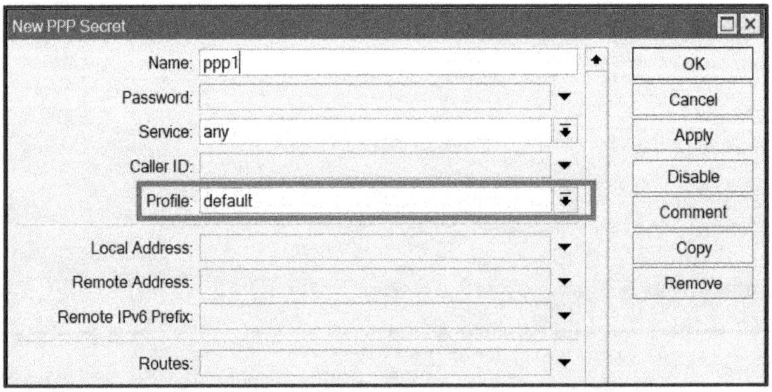

You can also configure additional settings using the **Limits** tab of the **New PPP Profile** dialog box.

For example, you can use the **Session Timeout** field to specify how long the client will stay connected to the server, the **Rate Limit** field to control the bandwidth for those accounts, or the **Only One** field to prevent the same account from being used on multiple devices.

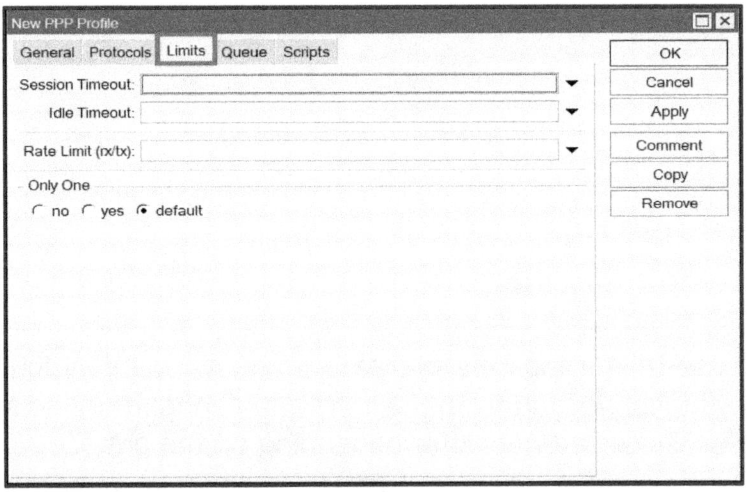

8.8 Establish the Connection.

To establish a connection from the client to the server and create a VPN virtual interface using different PPP protocols like PPTP, SSTP, L2TP, or OVPN, use the **Interface** tab of the **PPP** window.

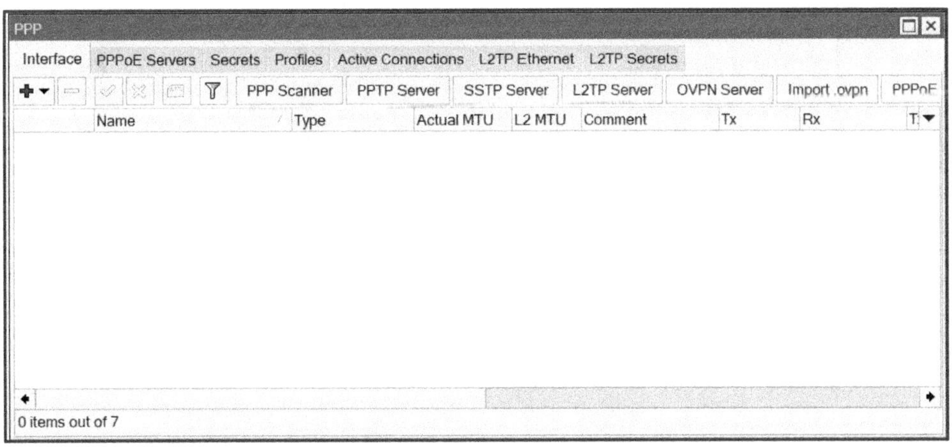

To establish the connection, (or to add a new VPN interface), click the **Add** menu, and select the protocol client interface to open the **New Interface** dialog box.

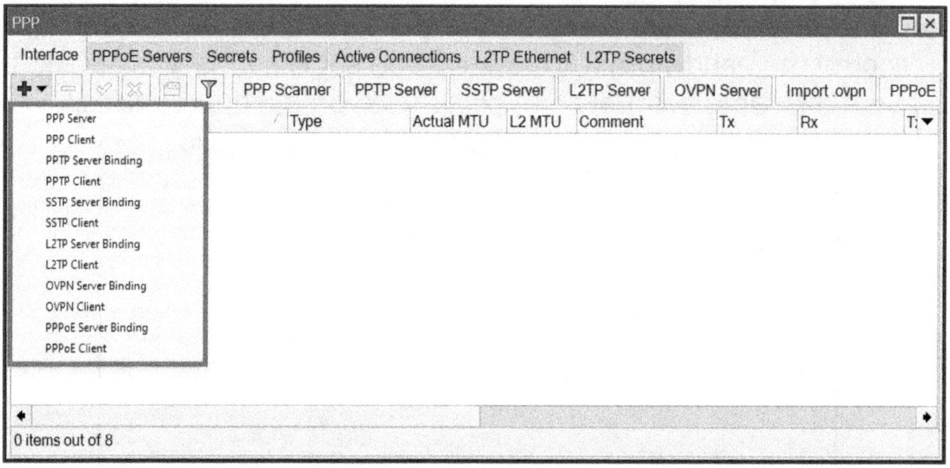

You can use this dialog box to create a new virtual VPN interface to establish the connection to the server, and configure its settings and properties. These settings differ depending on the protocol.

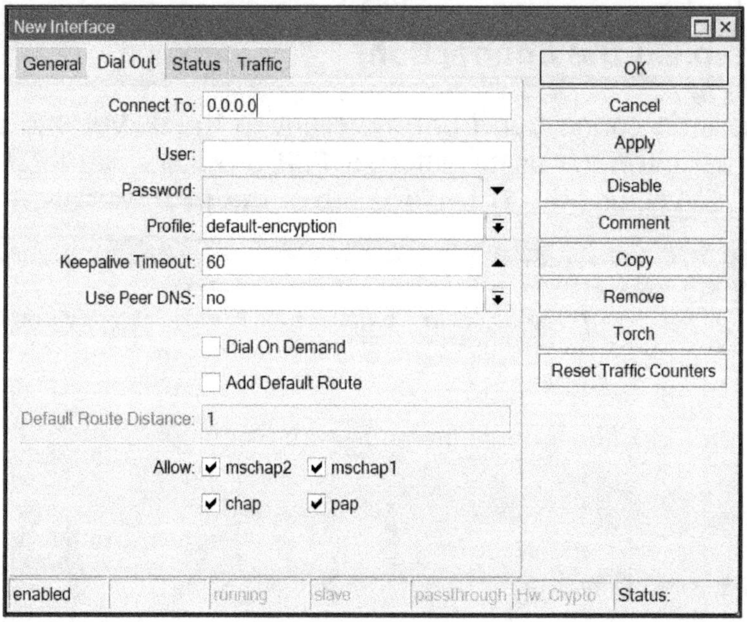

For example, to establish a VPN connection using the PPTP protocol, click the **Add** menu and select **PPTP Client**.

In the **Connect To** field in the **Dial Out** tab, enter the IP address of the server. In the **User** and **Password** fields, enter the username and the password created in the account, or PPP secret, on the server.

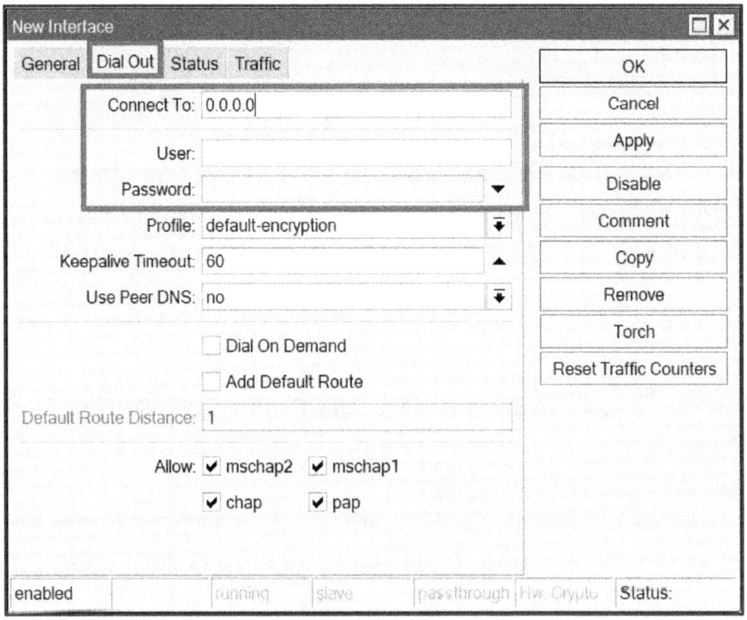

PPPTP Protocol

8.9 PPTP Protocol

Point-to-Point Tunneling Protocol (PPTP) is a protocol used to create VPNs. It uses port 1723 TCP and IP protocol ID 47 (GRE).

In networks that use NAT, NAT helpers should be used to support this protocol.

(This protocol is outdated and not recommended for use in industrial networks).

8.10 PPTP Configuration

To configure a VPN using PPTP protocol, use the **PPP** window to configure one device as the VPN server and the other as the VPN client, as mentioned before.

- On the server, perform two main steps:
  - Enable the protocol.
  - Create an account.
- On the client, perform one main step:
  - Establish the connection.

8.11 PPTP Server

In PPTP Server, to enable the PPTP protocol, click the **PPTP Server** button in the **Interface** tab of the **PPP** window to open the **PPTP Server** dialog box.

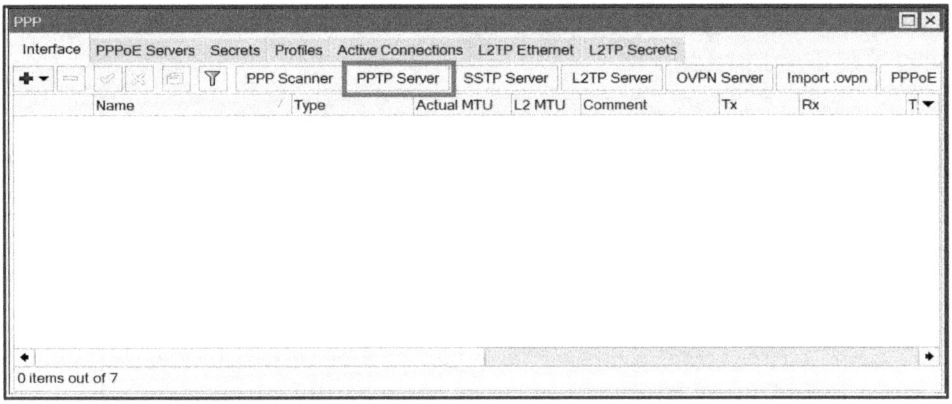

Then, check the **Enable** checkbox in this dialog box.

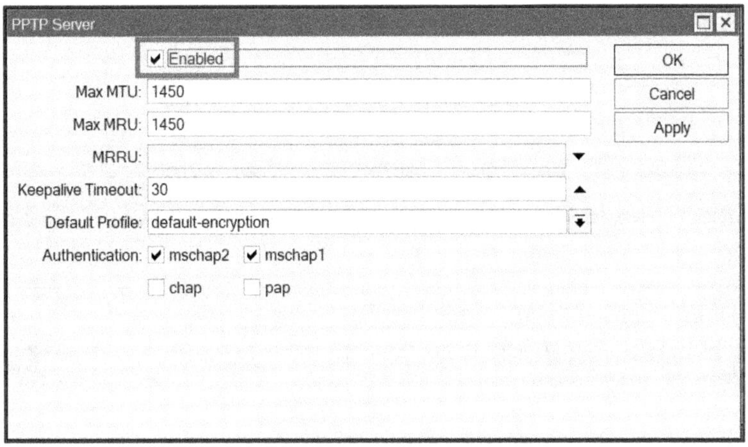

To create an account, or PPP secret, click the **Add** button in the **Secrets** tab to open the **New PPP Secret** dialog box.

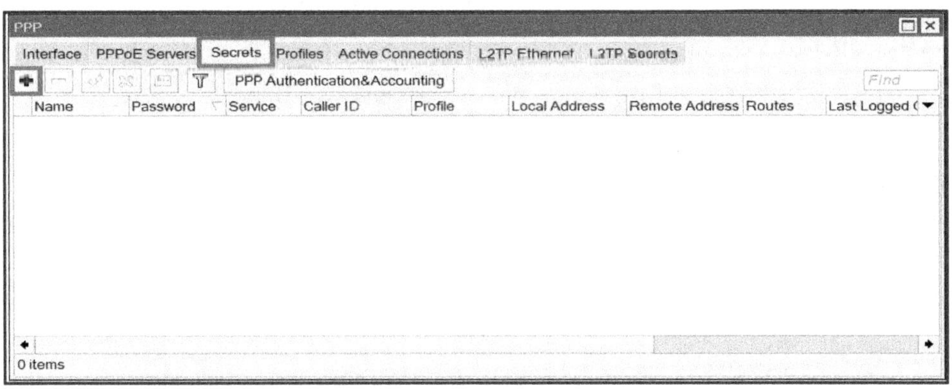

Then, set the account properties, such as the username, password and the IP addresses.

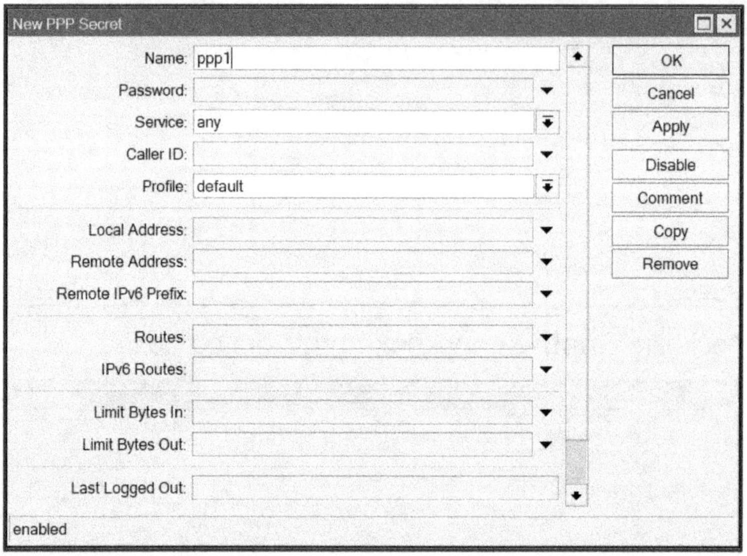

You can also enable the PPTP protocol from the CLI using the following command:

```
Interface pptp-server server set enable=yes
```

To create an account, or a PPP secret, from the CLI, use the following command:

```
ppp secret add name=[username] password=[password] local-address=[server IP] remote-address=[client IP]
```

Where:

- [username] is the username for this account.
- [password] is the password.
- [server IP] is the server end IP address.
- [client IP] is the client end IP address.

For example:

```
ppp secret add name=user1 password=1234 local-address=10.0.0.1
remote-address=10.0.0.2
```

```
Terminal <1>
[admin@MikroTik] >
[admin@MikroTik] >
[admin@MikroTik] >
[admin@MikroTik] > ppp secret add name=user1 password=1234 local-address=10.0.0.1 remote-address=10.0.0.2
```

To display information about PPTP protocol use the following command:

```
Interface pptp-server server print
```

```
Terminal <1>
[admin@MikroTik] > interface pptp-server server print
                   ;;; PPTP connections are considered unsafe, it
                       is suggested to use a more modern VPN
                       protocol instead
            enabled: yes
            max-mtu: 1450
            max-mru: 1450
               mrru: disabled
     authentication: mschap1,mschap2
  keepalive-timeout: 30
    default-profile: default-encryption
[admin@MikroTik] >
```

To display the current PPP secrets in RouterOS use the following command:

```
ppp secret print
```

```
Terminal <1>
[admin@MikroTik] >
[admin@MikroTik] > ppp secret print
Columns: NAME, SERVICE, PASSWORD, PROFILE, REMOTE-ADDRESS
# NAME   SERVICE  PASSWORD  PROFILE  REMOTE-ADDRESS
0 user1  any          1234  default  10.0.0.2
[admin@MikroTik] >
```

8.12 PPTP Client

In the PPTP Client, to establish a connection to the PPPTP server and create a virtual VPN interface using the PPTP protocol, click the **Add** menu in the **Interface** tab of the **PPP** window, and select **PPTP Client** to open the **New Interface** dialog box.

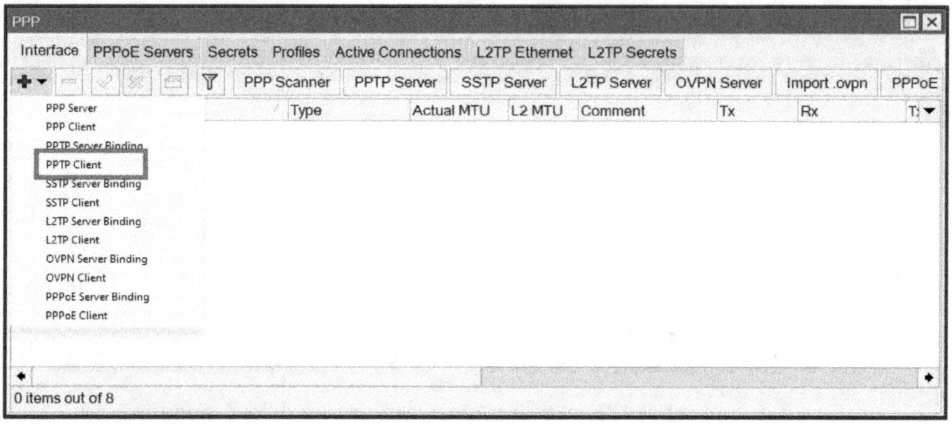

Then, set the virtual interface properties, such as the IP address of the server, the username, and the password.

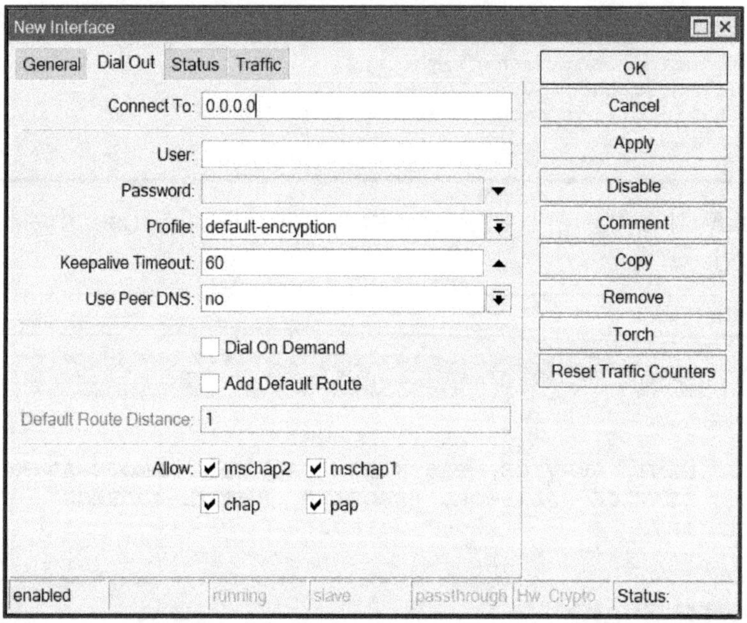

You can also establish the connection to the PPPTP server from the CLI using the following command:

```
interface pptp-client add connect-to[server IP] user=[username]
password=[password]
```

Where:

- [server IP] is the server IP address.
- [username] is the account username.
- [password] is the account password.

For example:

```
interface pptp-client add connect-to=192.168.12.1 user=user1
password=1234
```

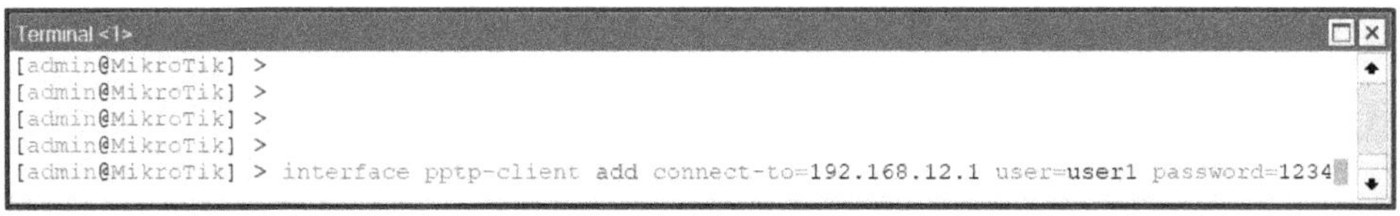

LAB

In this lab, you want to create a tunnel between R1 and R3 using the PPTP protocol. Then, use this tunnel to send data between LAN 1 and LAN 3.

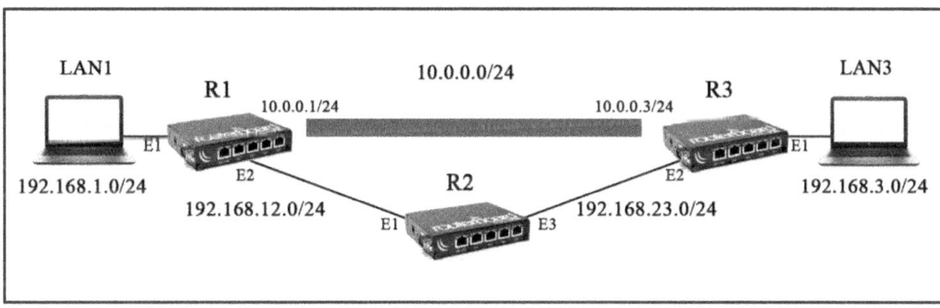

To start the configuration:

- First: perform the basic configuration by assigning IP addresses, setting up basic routes, and configuring the identity for each router
- Second: configure the **PPTP tunnel**.

Basic Configuration

R1

- Set the router name to R1_PPTP_Server.

- Assign IP address 192.168.1.1/24 to ether1, which is connected to LAN 1.
- Assign IP address 192.168.12.1/24 to ether2, which is connected to R2. This interface plays the role of the WAN interface, which is connected to the internet. In real-life scenarios, this IP is a public IP address.
- Add a default route through ether2 (WAN interface) using the next hop IP of R2.

R2

- Set the router name to R2_ISP.
- Assign IP address 192.168.12.2/24 to ether1, which is connected to R1.
- Assign IP address 192.168.23.2/24 to ether3, which is connected to R3.

This router plays the role of the ISP cloud.

R3

- Set the router name to R3_PPTP_Client.
- Assign IP address 192.168.3.1/24 to ether1, which is connected to LAN 3.
- Assign IP address 192.168.23.3/24 to ether2, which is connected to R2. This interface plays the role of the WAN interface, which is connected to the internet. In real-life scenarios, this IP is a static public IP address.
- Add a default route through ether2 (WAN interface) using the next hop IP of R2.

PPTP configuration

R1

This router will act as PPTP Server, so to configure it, perform two steps:

- Enable the Protocol
- Create an Account

To enable the PPTP protocol, click the **PPTP** button in the **PPP** window to open the **PPTP Server** dialog box, then check the **Enable** checkbox.

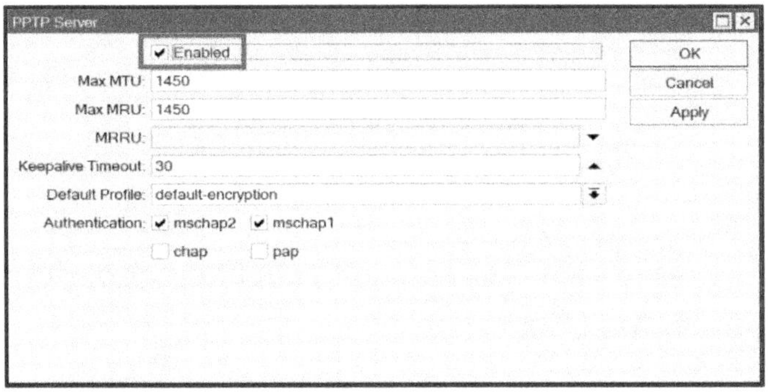

To create an account, or PPP secret, click the **Add** button in the **Secrets** tab of the **PPP** window to open the **New PPP Secret** dialog box.

- In the **User** field, enter user1.
- In the **Password** field, enter 1234.
- In the **Local Address** field, enter 10.0.0.1.
- In the **Remote Address** field, enter 10.0.0.3.

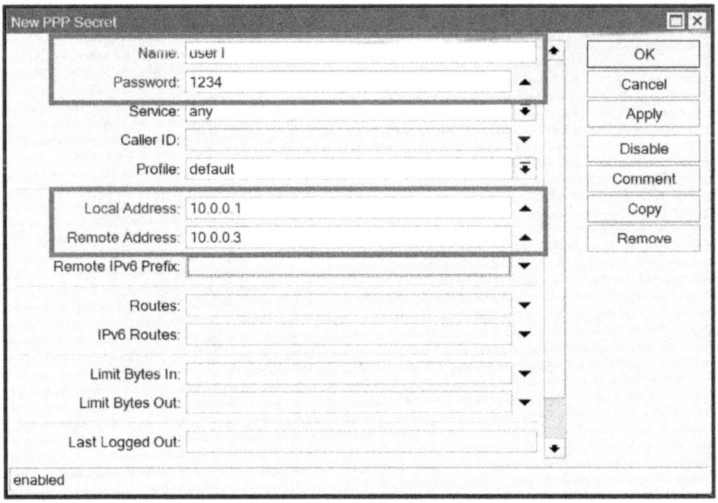

After creating the PPP secret, it will appear in the **Secrets** tab of the **PPP** window.

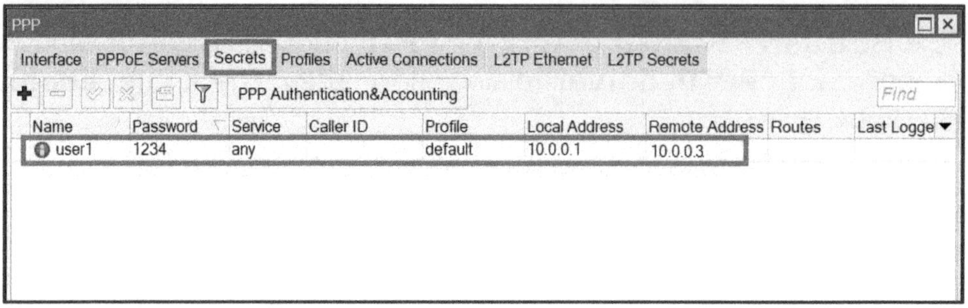

R3

This router will act as PPTP Client, so to configure it perform one step:

- Establish the Connection

To establish the connection and create the tunnel interface, click the **Add** button in the **Interface** tab of the **PPP** window and select **PPTP Client** to open the **New Interface** dialog box.

- In the **Connect To** field in the **Dial Out** tab, enter the server IP address: 192.168.12.1.
- In the **User** field, enter user1.
- In the **Password** field, enter 1234

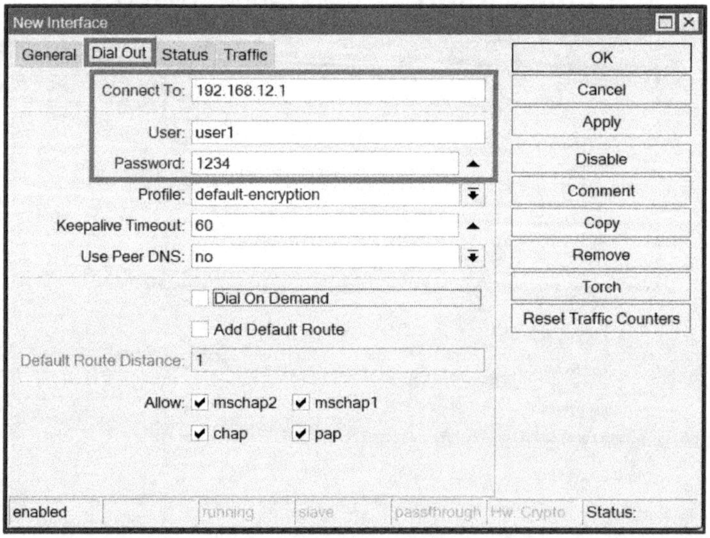

After adding the interface in the client device R3, it will appear in the **Interface** tab of the **PPP** window.

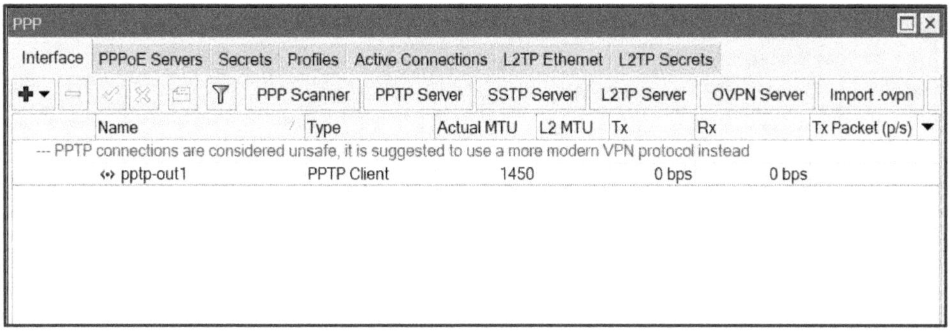

After establishing the connection, an **R** flag will appear next to this interface, indicating that the connection has been successfully established and the interface is now running.

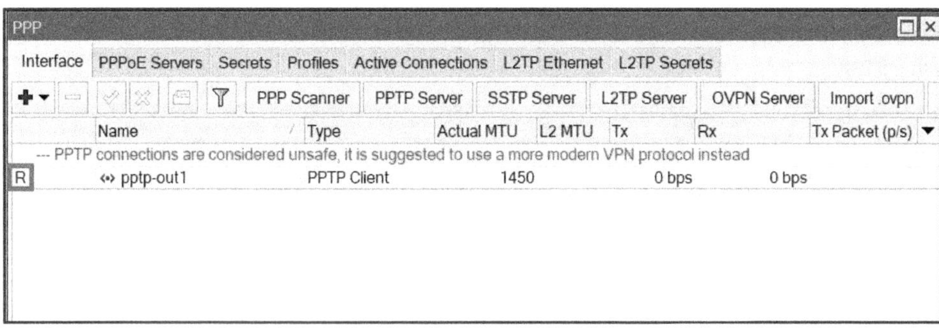

On the server device R1, a new virtual PPP interface will be automatically, or dynamically, created and appear in the **Interface** tab of the **PPP** window with **DR** flags, indicating that the interface is dynamically created and is now running.

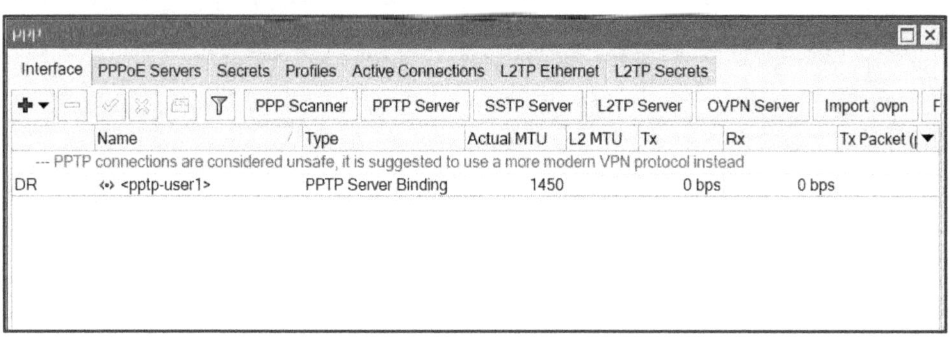

This interface will also appear in the **Interface** tab of the **Interface List** window.

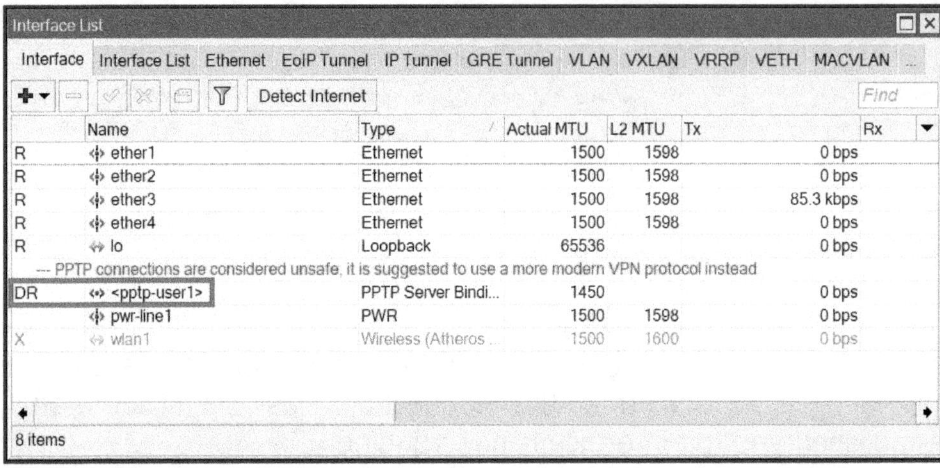

The IP address of this new interface will appear in the **Address List** window.

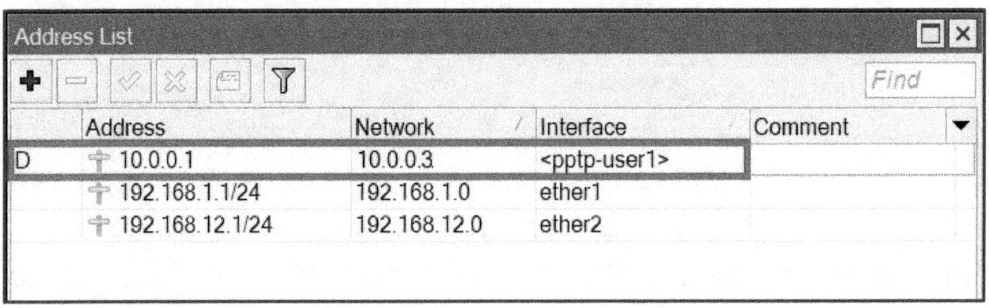

Also, this active connection will appear in the **Active Connections** tab of the **PPP** window.

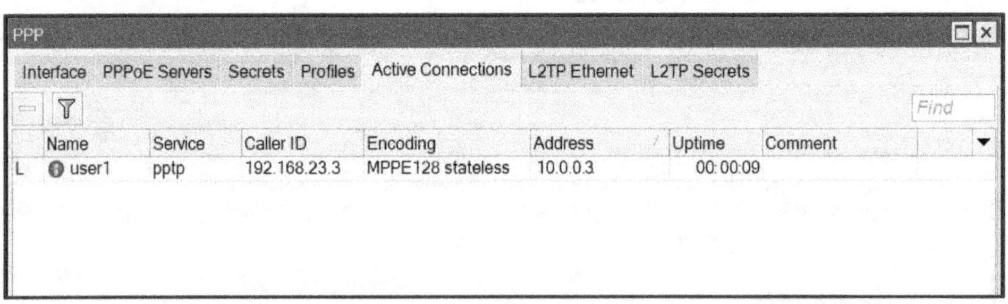

Now, you have a virtual connection, or virtual tunnel interface, that connects R1 and R3. You want to use this interface to send data

between LAN 1 and LAN 3. To achieve this, create a static route on R1 for the remote subnet LAN 3, through this tunnel. Then, create a static route on R3 for the remote subnet LAN 1 through the same tunnel

R1

To create a static route for LAN 3, click the **IP** menu and select **Routes** to open **Route List** window, then click the **Add** button to open the **New Route** dialog box.

- In the **Dst. Address** (or destination address) field, enter the remote subnet LAN 3 network ID 192.168.3.0/24.
- In the **Gateway** field, enter the next hope IP address of the tunnel 10.0.0.3.

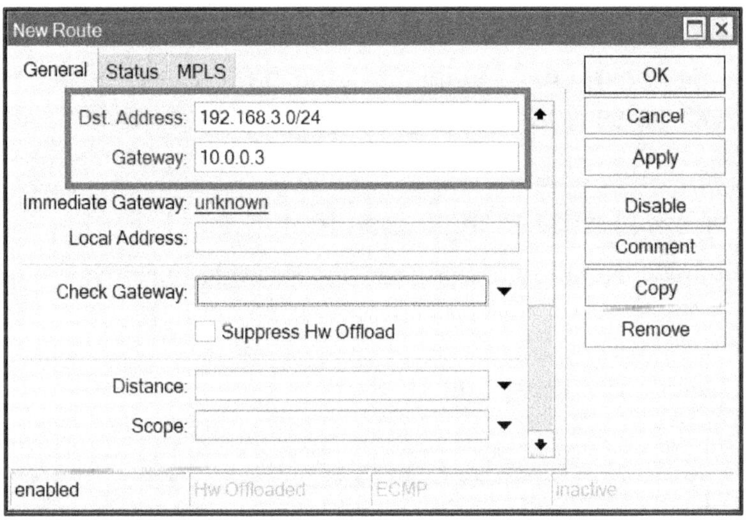

R3

To create a static route for LAN 1, click the **IP** menu and select **Routes** to open **Route List** window, then click the **Add** button to open the **New Route** dialog box.

- In the **Dst. Address** (or destination address) field, enter the remote subnet LAN 1 network ID 192.168.1.0/24.
- In the **Gateway** field, enter the next hope IP address of the tunnel 10.0.0.1.

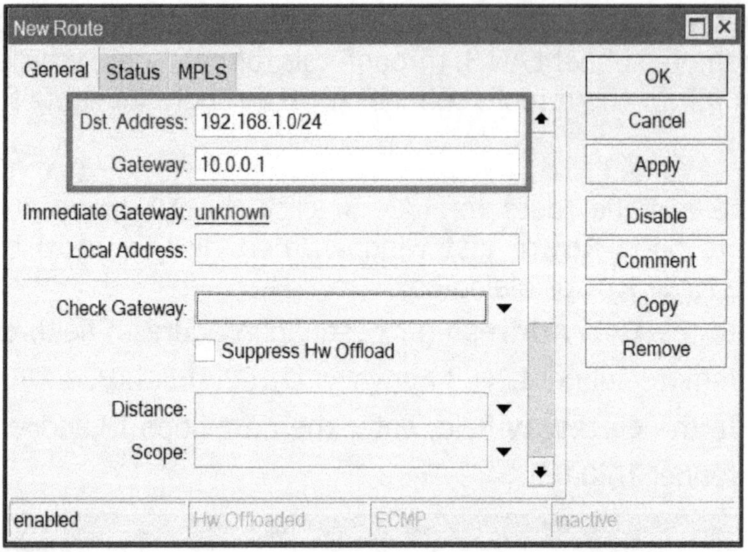

Now, any device in LAN 1 wants to send data to any device in LAN 3, the data will be sent through the tunnel, and vice versa.

CLI

You can also make the configuration from the CLI.

To set the identity for each device, use the following commands:

R1

```
system identity set name=R1_PPTP_Server
```

R2

```
system identity set name=R2_ISP
```

R3

```
system identity set name=R3_PPTP_Client
```

To assign IP addresses to the interfaces, use the following commands:

R1

```
ip address add address=192.168.1.1/24 interface=ether1
ip address add address=192.168.12.1/24 interface=ether2
```

R2

```
ip address add address=192.168.12.2/24 interface=ether1
ip address add address=192.168.23.2/24 interface=ether3
```

R3

```
ip address add address=192.168.3.1/24 interface=ether1
ip address add address=192.168.23.3/24 interface=ether2
```

To create a default route, use the following commands:

R1

```
ip route add dst-address=0.0.0.0/0 gateway=192.168.12.2
```

R3

```
ip route add dst-address=0.0.0.0/0 gateway=192.168.23.2
```

To enable the PPTP protocol in R1, use the following command:

```
interface pptp-server server set enable=yes
```

To create an account, or a PPP secret, in R1, use the following command:

```
ppp secret add name=user1 password=1234 local-address=10.0.0.1
remote-address=10.0.0.3
```

To establish the connection to the PPPTP server from R3, use the following command:

```
interface pptp-client add connect-to=192.168.12.1 user=user1
password=1234
```

To create a static route for the remote subnets, use the following commands:

R1

```
ip route add dst-address=192.168.3.0/24 gateway=10.0.0.3
```

R3

```
ip route add dst-address=192.168.1.0/24 gateway=10.0.0.1
```

SSTP Protocol

8.13 SSTP Protocol

Secure Socket Tunneling Protocol (SSTP) is a protocol used to create VPNs. It uses port 443 TCP. In general, SSTP traffic passes through firewalls without additional configuration because it uses the same port as HTTPS.

8.14 SSTP Configuration

To configure a VPN using SSTP, use the **PPP** window to configure one device as the VPN server and the other as the VPN client, as mentioned before

- On the server, perform two main steps:
    - Enable the protocol.
    - Create an account.
- On the client, perform one main step:
    - Establish the connection.

8.15 SSTP Server

In SSTP Server, to enable the SSTP protocol, click the **SSTP Server** button in the **Interface** tab of the **PPP** window to open the **SSTP Server** dialog box.

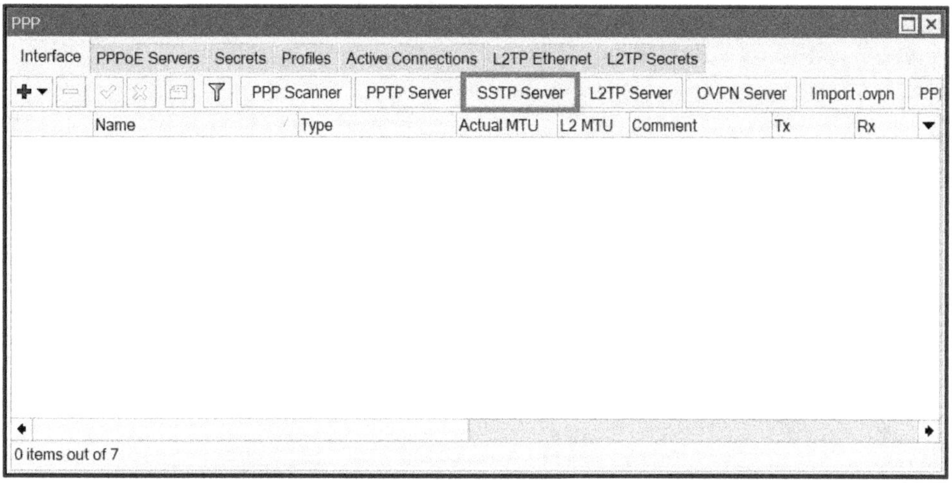

Then, check the **Enable** checkbox in this dialog box.

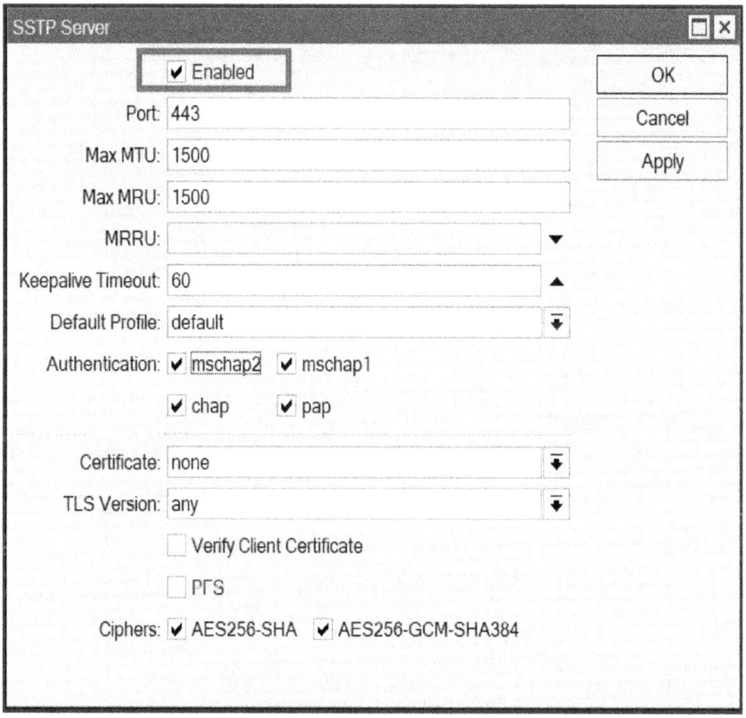

To create an account (or PPP secret), click the **Add** button in the **Secrets** tab to open the **New PPP Secret** dialog box.

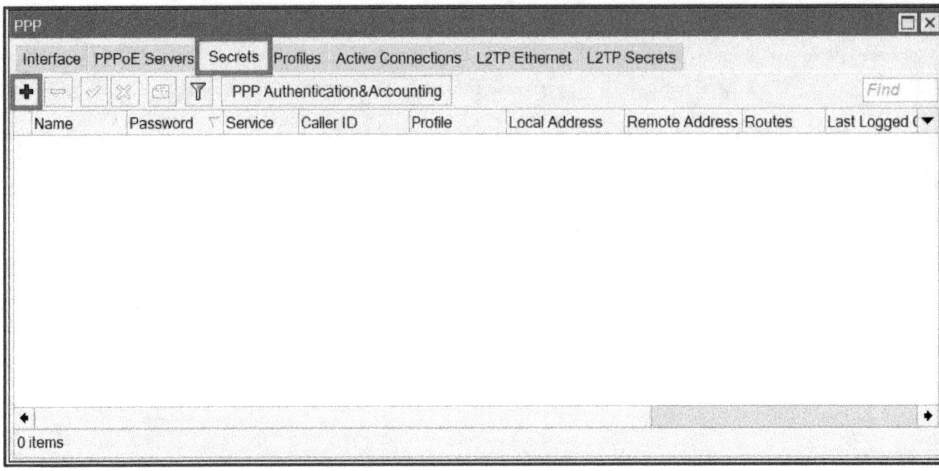

Then, set the account properties, such as the username, password and the IP addresses.

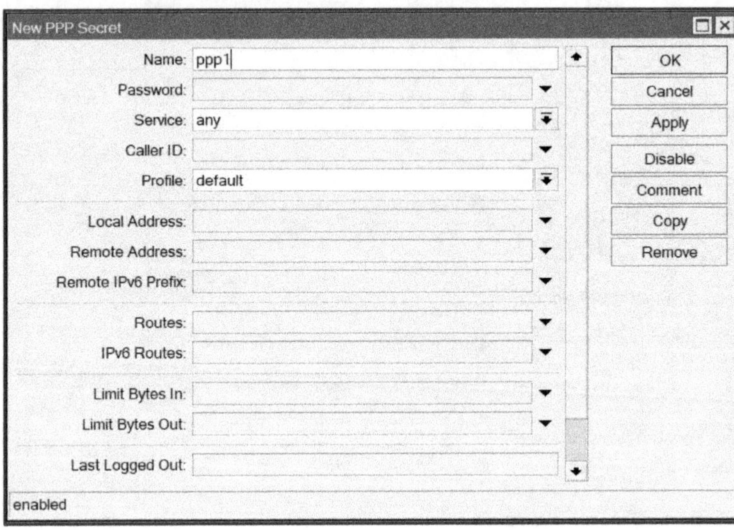

You can also enable the SSTP protocol from the CLI using the following command:

```
Interface sstp-server server set enable=yes
```

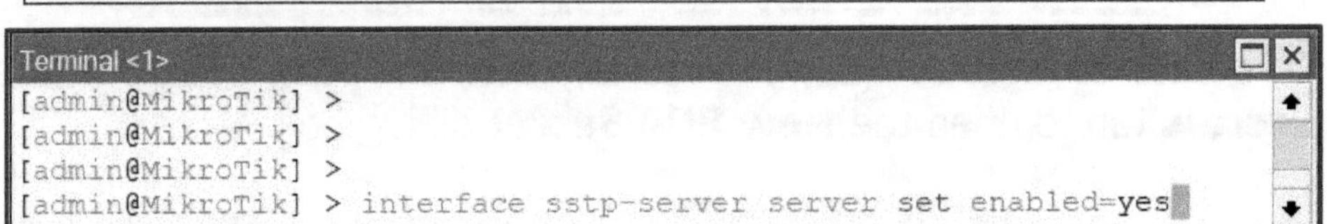

To create an account, or a PPP secret, from the CLI, use the following command:

```
ppp secret add name=[username] password=[password] local-
address=[server IP] remote-address=[client IP]
```

Where:

- [username] is the username for this account.
- [password] is the password.
- [server IP] is the server end IP address.
- [client IP] is the client end IP address.

For example:

```
ppp secret add name=user1 password=1234 local-address=10.0.0.1
remote-address=10.0.0.2
```

To display information about SSTP protocol use the following command:

```
Interface sstp-server server print
```

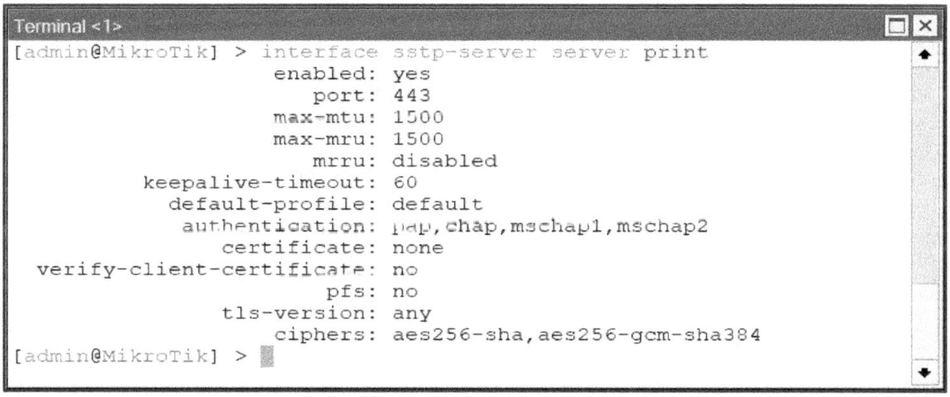

To display the current ppp secrets in RouterOS use the following command:

```
ppp secret print
```

```
Terminal <1>
[admin@MikroTik] >
[admin@MikroTik] > ppp secret print
Columns: NAME, SERVICE, PASSWORD, PROFILE, REMOTE-ADDRESS
# NAME   SERVICE  PASSWORD  PROFILE  REMOTE-ADDRESS
0 user1  any          1234  default  10.0.0.2
[admin@MikroTik] >
```

8.16 SSTP Client

In the SSTP Client, to establish a connection to the SSTP server and create a virtual VPN interface using the SSTP protocol, click the **Add** menu in the **Interface** tab of the PPP window, and select **SSTP Client** to open the **New Interface** dialog box.

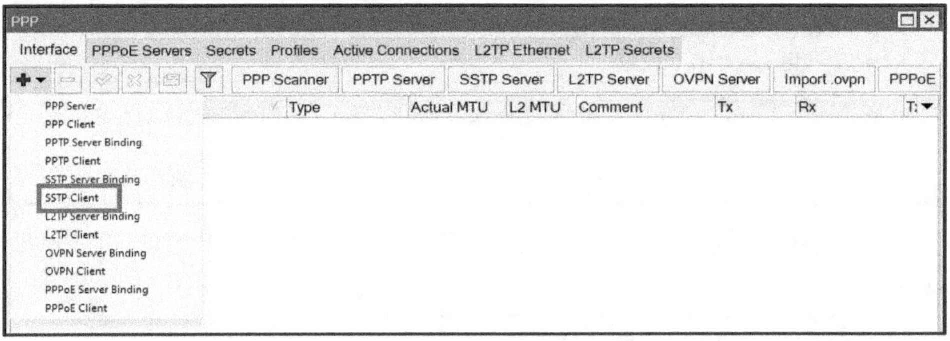

Then, set the virtual interface properties, such as the IP address of the server, the username, and the password.

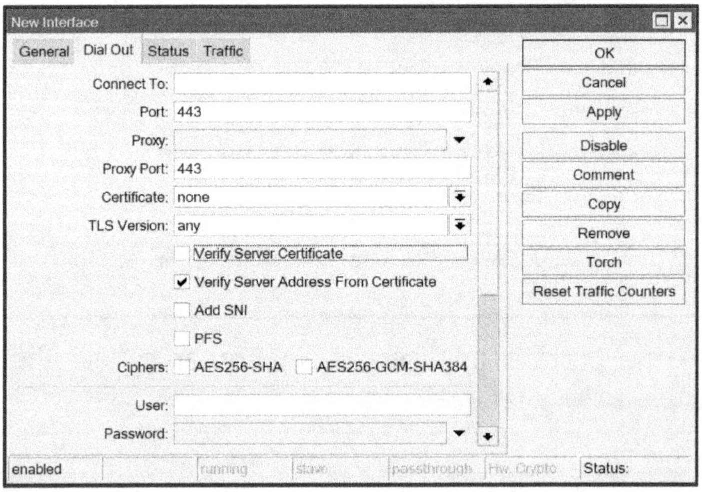

You can also establish the connection to the SSTP server from the CLI using the following command:

```
interface sstp-client add connect-to[server IP] user=[username]
password=[password]
```

Where:

- [server IP] is the server IP address.
- [username] is the account username.
- [password] is the account password.

For example:

```
interface sstp-client add connect-to=192.168.12.1 user=user1
password=1234
```

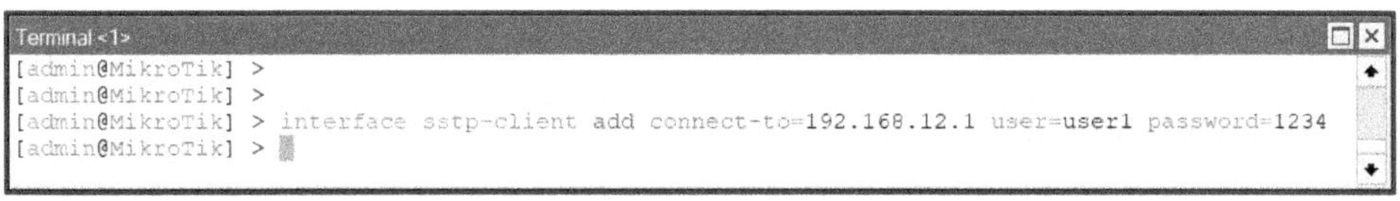

LAB

In this lab, you want to create a tunnel between R1 and R3 using the SSTP protocol. Then, you want to use this tunnel to send data between LAN 1 and LAN 3.

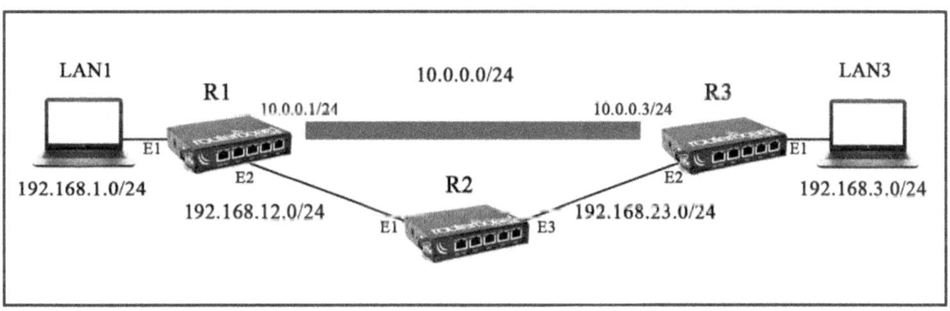

To start the configuration:

- First: perform the basic configuration by assigning IP addresses, setting up basic routes, and configuring the identity for each router
- Second: configure the **SSTP tunnel**.

Basic Configuration

R1

- Set the router name to R1_SSTP_Server.
- Assign IP address 192.168.1.1/24 to ether1, which is connected to LAN 1.
- Assign IP address 192.168.12.1/24 to ether2, which is connected to R2. This interface plays the role of the WAN interface, which is connected to the internet. In real-life scenarios, this IP is a public IP address.
- Add a default route through ether2 (WAN interface) using the next hop IP of R2.

R2

- Set the router name to R2_ISP.
- Assign IP address 192.168.12.2/24 to ether1, which is connected to R1.
- Assign IP address 192.168.23.2/24 to ether3, which is connected to R3.

  This router plays the role of the ISP cloud.

R3

- Set the router name to R3_SSTP_Client.
- Assign IP address 192.168.3.1/24 to ether1, which is connected to LAN 3.
- Assign IP address 192.168.23.3/24 to ether2, which is connected to R2. This interface plays the role of the WAN interface, which is connected to the internet. In real-life scenarios, this IP is a static public IP address.
- Add a default route through ether2 (WAN interface) using the next hop IP of R2.

SSTP configuration

R1

This router will act as a SSTP Server, so to configure it, perform two steps:

- Enable the Protocol
- Create an Account

To enable the SSTP protocol, click the **SSTP** button in the **PPP** window to open the **SSTP Server** dialog box, then check the **Enable** checkbox.

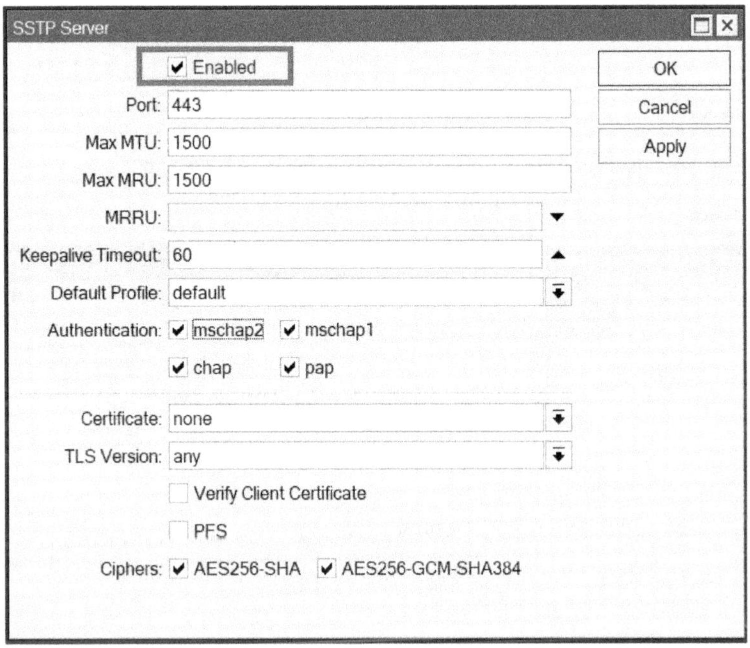

To create an account, or PPP secret, click the **Add** button in the **Secrets** tab of the **PPP** window to open the **New PPP Secret** dialog box.

- In the **User** field, enter user1.
- In the **Password** field, enter 1234.
- In the **Local Address** field, enter 10.0.0.1.
- In the **Remote Address** field, enter 10.0.0.3.

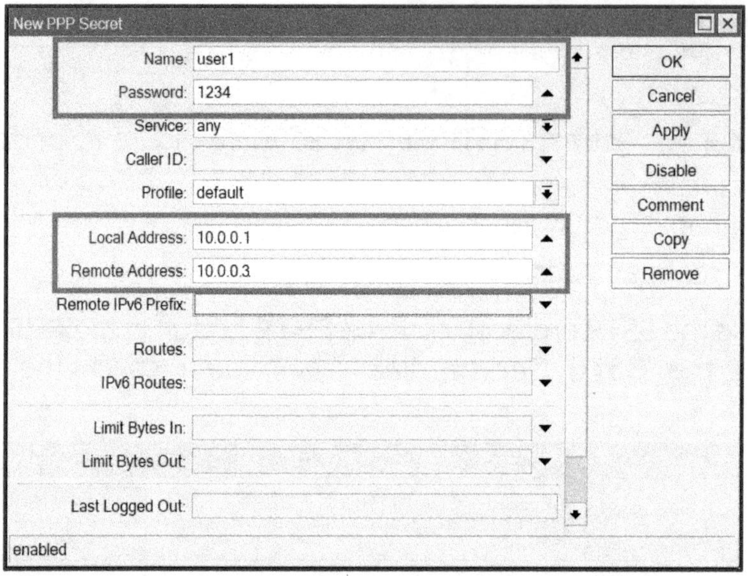

After creating the PPP secret, it will appear in the **Secrets** tab of the **PPP** window.

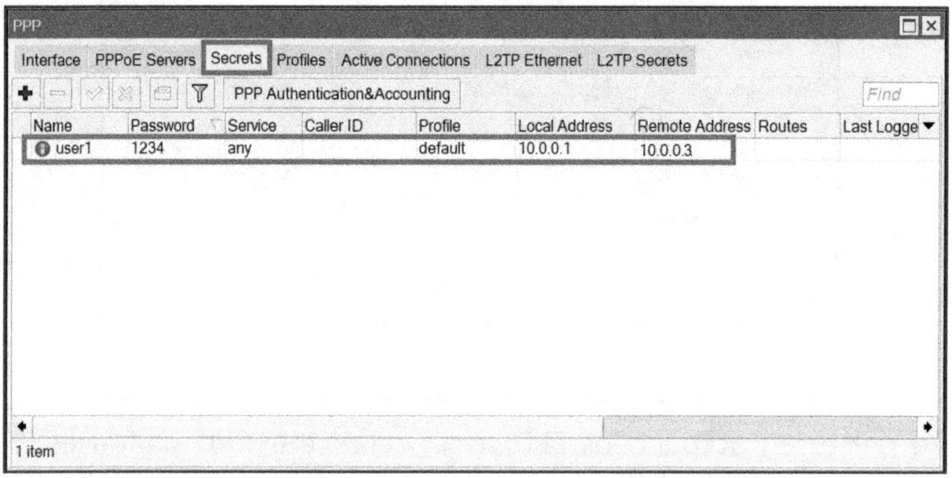

R3

This router will act as SSTP client, so to configure it perform one step:

- Establish the Connection

To establish the connection and create the tunnel interface:

Click the **Add** button in the **Interface** tab of the **PPP** window and select **SSTP Client** to open the **New Interface** dialog box.

- In the **Connect To** field in the **Dial Out** tab, enter the server IP address: 192.168.12.1.
- In the **User** field, enter user1.
- In the **Password** field, enter 1234

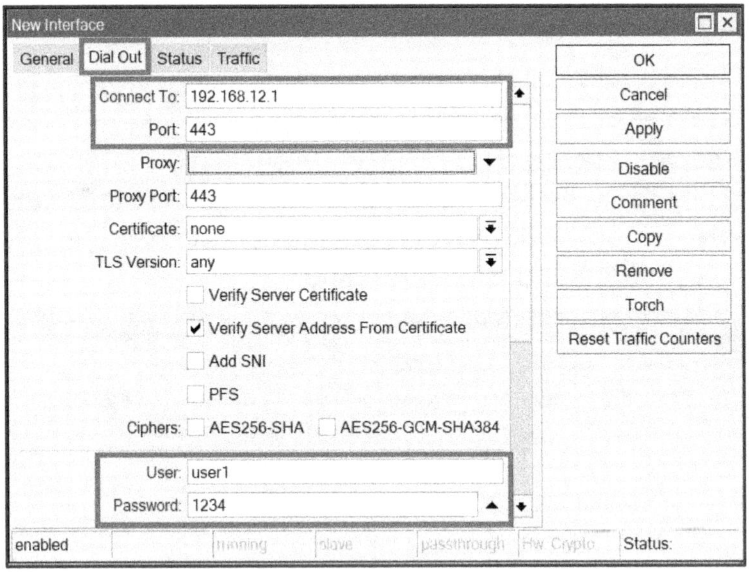

After adding the interface in the client device R3, it will appear in the **Interface** tab of the **PPP** window.

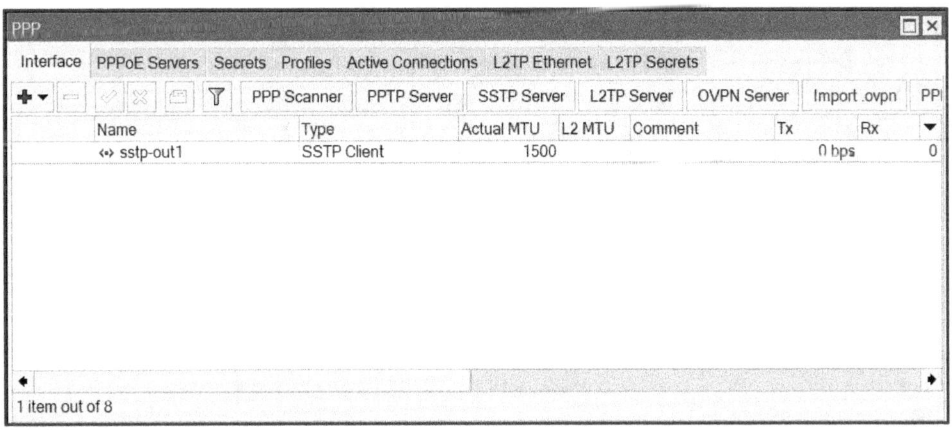

After establishing the connection, an **R** flag will appear next to this interface, indicating that the connection has been successfully established and the interface is now running.

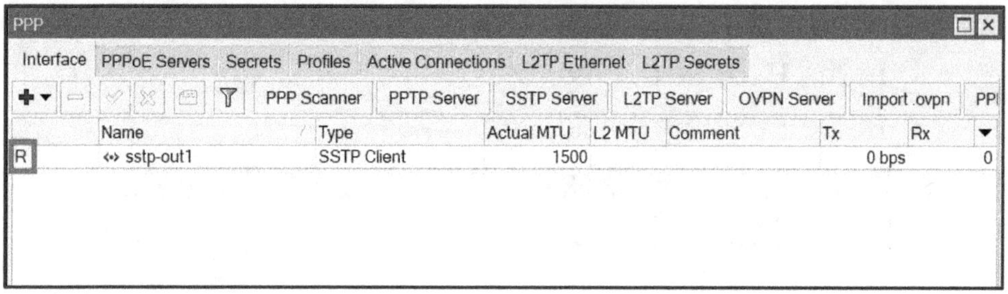

On the server device R1, a new virtual PPP interface will be automatically or dynamically created and appear in the **Interface** tab of the **PPP** window with **DR** flags, indicating that the interface is dynamically created and is now running.

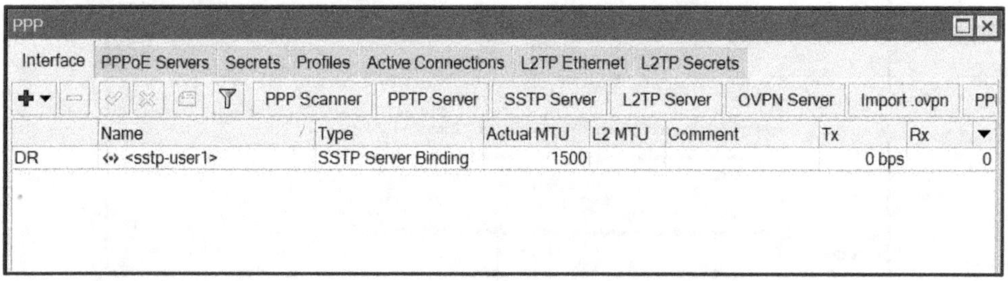

This interface will also appear in the **Interface** tab of the **Interface List** window.

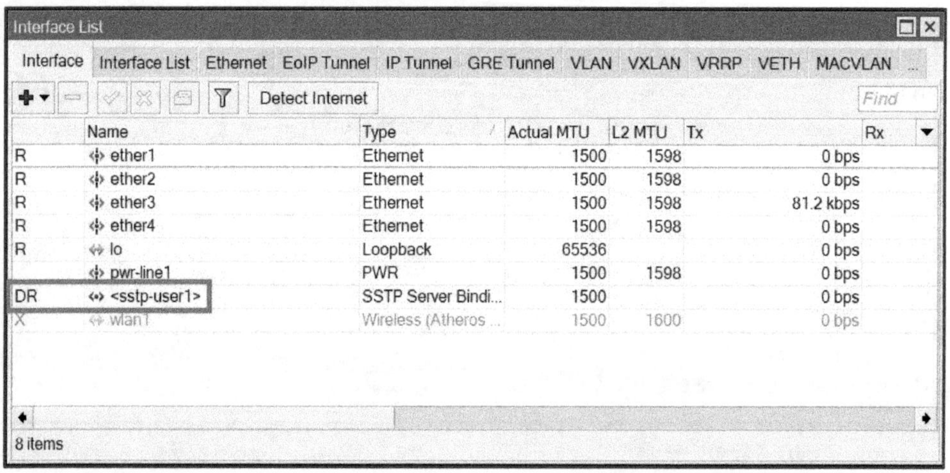

The IP address of this new interface will appear in the **Address List** window.

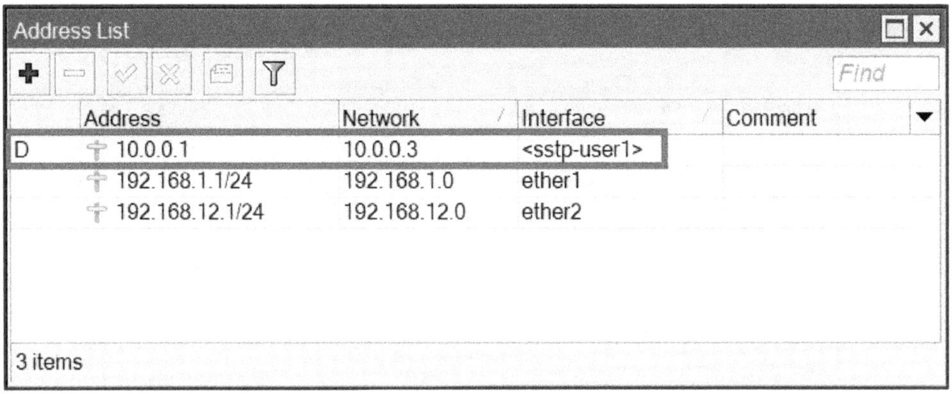

Also, this active connection will appear in the **Active Connections** tab of the **PPP** window.

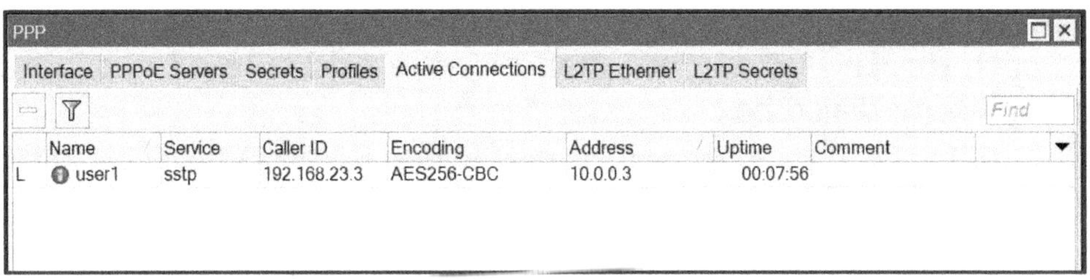

Now, you have a virtual connection, or virtual tunnel interface, that connects R1 and R3. You want to use this interface to send data between LAN 1 and LAN 3. To achieve this, create a static route on R1 for the remote subnet LAN 3, through this tunnel. Then, create a static route on R3 for the remote subnet LAN 1 through the same tunnel

R1

To create a static route for LAN 3 click the **IP** menu and select **Routes** to open **Route List** window, then click the **Add** button to open the **New Route** dialog box.

- In the **Dst. Address** (or destination address) field, enter the remote subnet LAN 3 network ID 192.168.3.0/24.
- In the **Gateway** field, enter the next hope IP address of the tunnel 10.0.0.3.

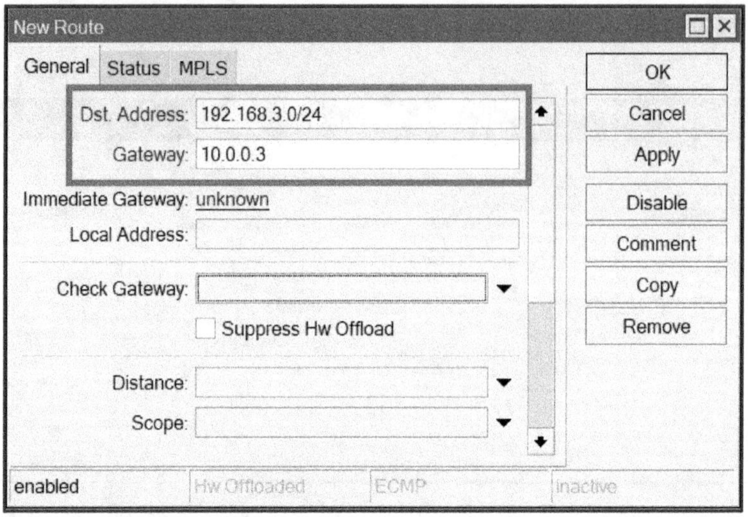

R3

To create a static route for LAN 1 click the **IP** menu and select **Routes** to open **Route List** window, then click the **Add** button to open the **New Route** dialog box.

- In the **Dst. Address** (or destination address) field, enter the remote subnet LAN 1 network ID 192.168.1.0/24.
- In the **Gateway** field, enter the next hope IP address of the tunnel 10.0.0.1.

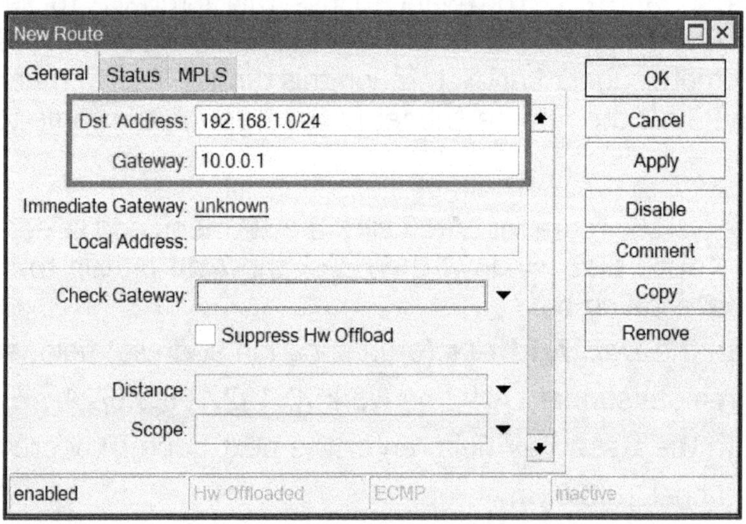

Now, any device in LAN 1 wants to send data to any device in LAN 3, the data will be sent through the tunnel, and vice versa.

CLI

You can also make the configuration from the CLI.

To set the identity for each device, use the following commands:

R1

```
system identity set name=R1_SSTP_Server
```

R2

```
system identity set name=R2_ISP
```

R3

```
system identity set name=R3_SSTP_Client
```

To assign IP addresses to the interfaces, use the following commands:

R1

```
ip address add address=192.168.1.1/24 interface=ether1
ip address add address=192.168.12.1/24 interface=ether2
```

R2

```
ip address add address=192.168.12.2/24 interface=ether1
ip address add address=192.168.23.2/24 interface=ether3
```

R3

```
ip address add address=192.168.3.1/24 interface=ether1
ip address add address=192.168.23.3/24 interface=ether2
```

To create a default route, use the following commands:

R1

```
ip route add dst-address=0.0.0.0/0 gateway=192.168.12.2
```

R3

```
ip route add dst-address=0.0.0.0/0 gateway=192.168.23.2
```

To enable the SSTP protocol in R1, use the following command:

```
interface sstp-server server set enable=yes
```

To create an account, or a PPP secret, in R1, use the following command:

```
ppp secret add name=user1 password=1234 local-address=10.0.0.1
remote-address=10.0.0.3
```

To establish the connection to the SSTP server from R3, use the following command:

```
interface sstp-client add connect-to=192.168.12.1 user=user1
password=1234
```

To create a static route for the remote subnets, use the following commands:

R1

```
ip route add dst-address=192.168.3.0/24 gateway=10.0.0.3
```

R3

```
ip route add dst-address=192.168.1.0/24 gateway=10.0.0.1
```

8.17 Using Quick Set to Configure PPP Server

MikroTik RouterOS provides a very quick and easy way to configure a PPP server using the **Quick Set** tool. With this tool, you can enable the protocol and create an account, or PPP secret, from one window: the **Quick Set** window.

To open the **Quick Set** window, click the **Quick Set** button.

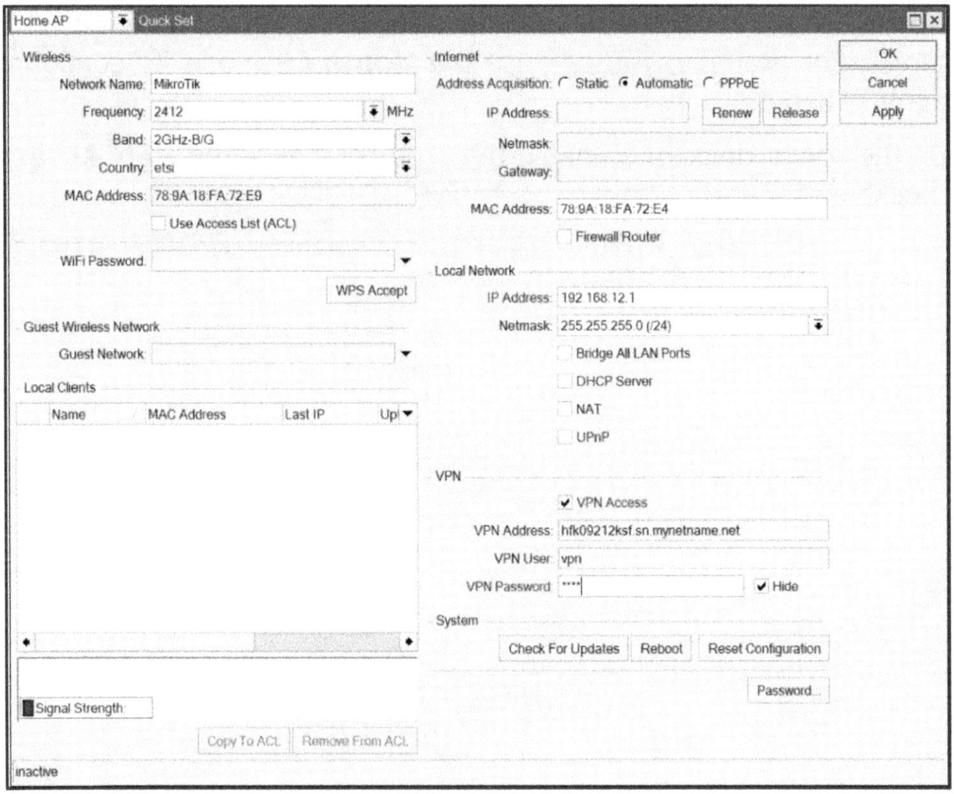

Then, choose a predefined configuration set from the **Quickset** dropdown menu.

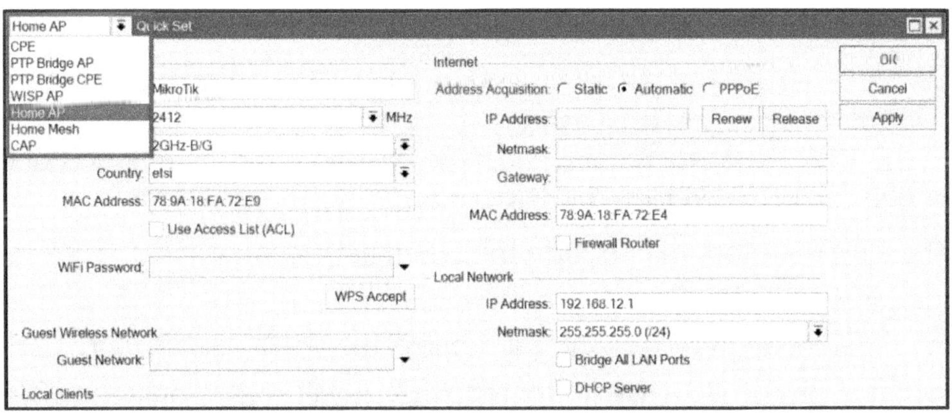

Note: Not all configuration set modes will allow you to configure VPN server. For example, you can use the **Home AP** mode, to configure the VPN server.

On the server device, to enable the protocol, check the **VPN Access** checkbox.

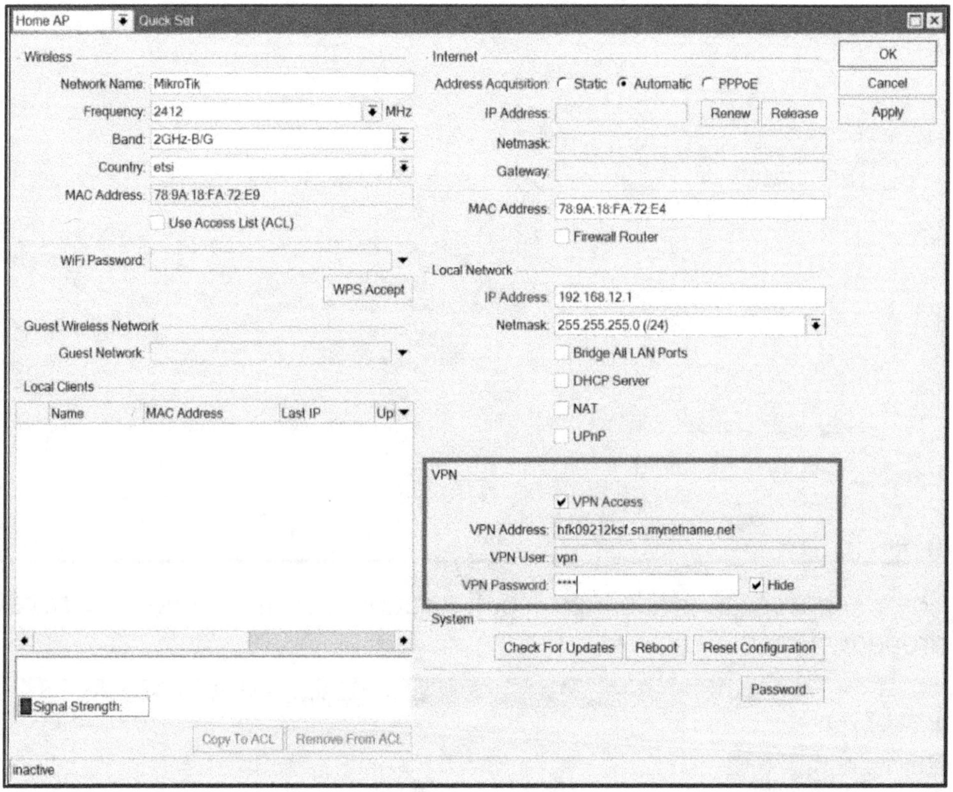

In the **VPN Password** field, enter the password for the PPP account, or PPP secret. Then click the **OK** button to close this window.

The Quick Set tool will perform the two main steps:

- Enable the Protocol

  In RouterOS v6, it will enable the PPTP, SSTP, and L2TP protocols, while in RouterOS v7, it will enable only the L2TP protocol (as of the latest versions at the time of publishing this book: v6.49 and v7.18).

- Create an Account

  It will create a PPP secret linked to the default PPP profile and an IP pool linked to this default PPP profile.

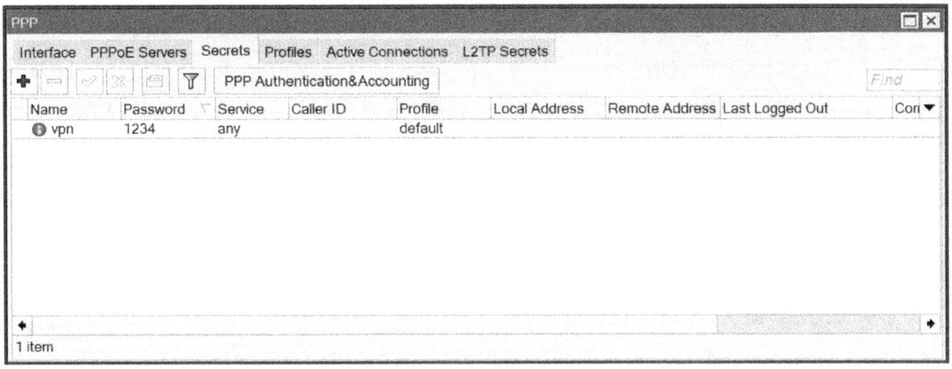

Now, on the client device, you can establish a connection using this PPP secret.

LAB

In this lab, you want to create a tunnel between R1 and R3 using the Quick Set tool.

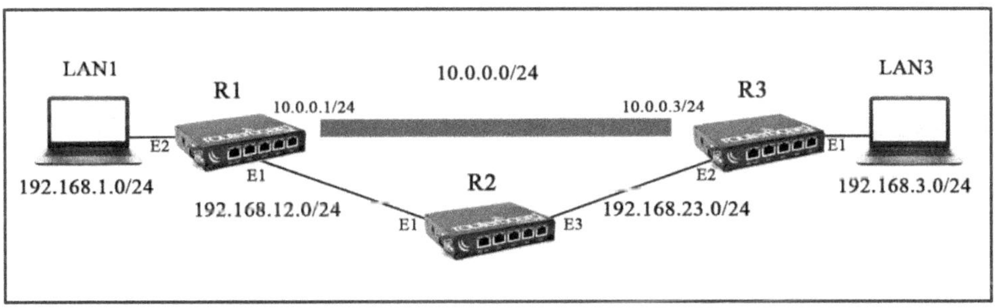

To start the configuration:

- First: perform the basic configuration by assigning IP addresses, setting up basic routes, and configuring the identity for R2 and R3 router
- Second: use Quick Set tool to configure R1 performing the basic configuration and the VPN configuration too.
- Third, configure the VPN tunnel on R3.

Basic Configuration

R2

- Set the router name to R2_ISP.
- Assign IP address 192.168.12.2/24 to ether1, which is connected to R1.
- Assign IP address 192.168.23.2/24 to ether3, which is connected to R3.

  This router plays the role of the ISP cloud.

R3

- Set the router name to R3_SSTP_Client.
- Assign IP address 192.168.3.1/24 to ether1, which is connected to LAN 3.
- Assign IP address 192.168.23.3/24 to ether2, which is connected to R2. This interface plays the role of the WAN interface, which is connected to the internet. In real-life scenarios, this IP is a static public IP address.
- Add a default route through ether2 (WAN interface) using the next hop IP of R2.

Using Quick Set Tool

R1

In this lab, you want to configure R1 using the Quick Set tool to set the basic configuration, and the VPN configuration as well.

To open the **Quick Set** window, click the **Quick Set** button. Then from the **Quickset** dropdown menu select **Home AP** mode.

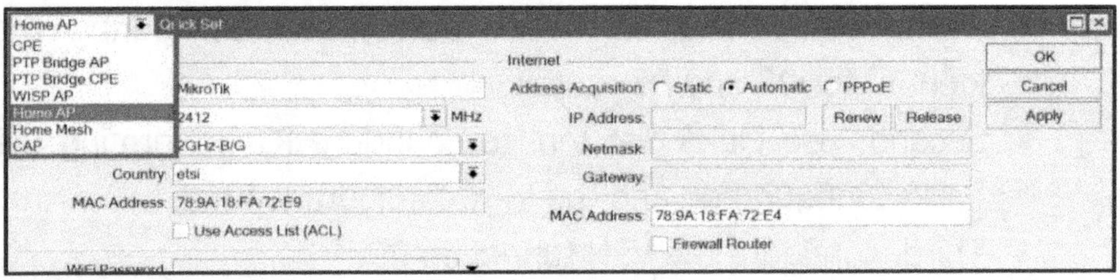

From the **Internet** section in the **Quick Set** window, choose the **Static** option and in the **IP Address**, **Netmask, Gateway** and **DNS Server** fields enter the following:

- IP Address: 192.168.12.1
- Netmask: 255.255.255.0
- Gateway: 192.168.12.2
- DNS Server: 8.8.8.8

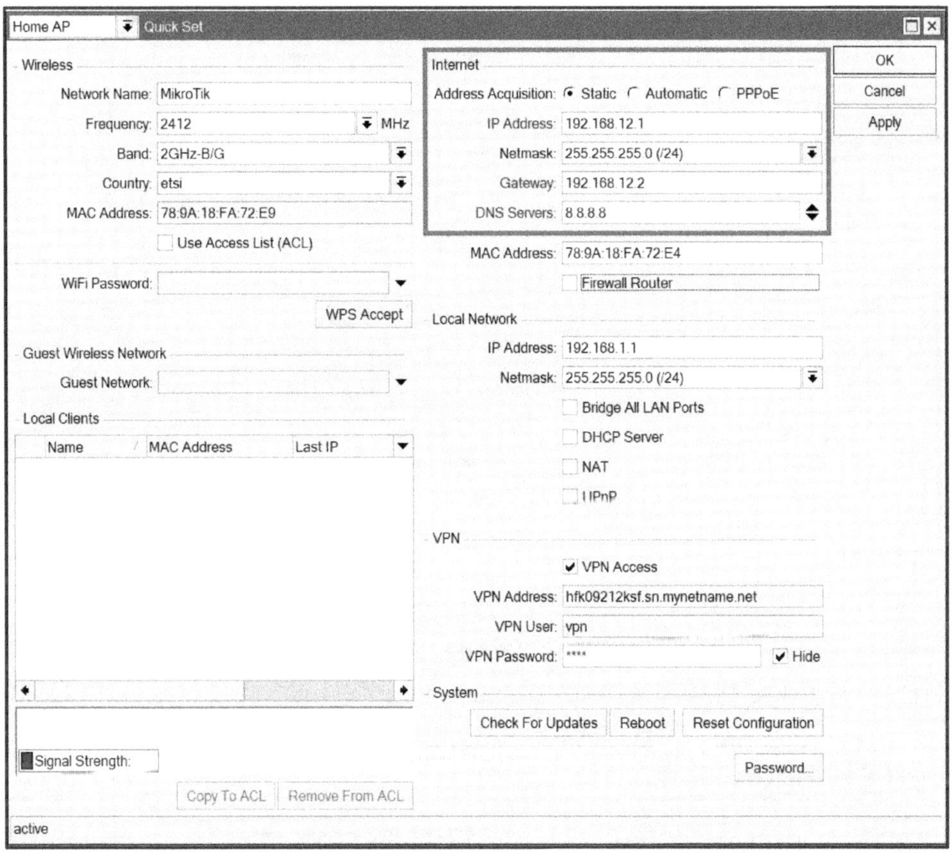

These settings play the role of the WAN interface settings, which is connected to the internet. The Quick Set tool will assign these settings to ether1. In real-life scenarios, you would choose the **Automatic** option to get the IP settings from the ISP, or you could enter them manually. It would be a static public IP address.

From the **Local Network** section in the IP Address 192.168.1.1 in the **IP Address** field, and the subnet mask 255.255.255.0 in the **Netmask** field.

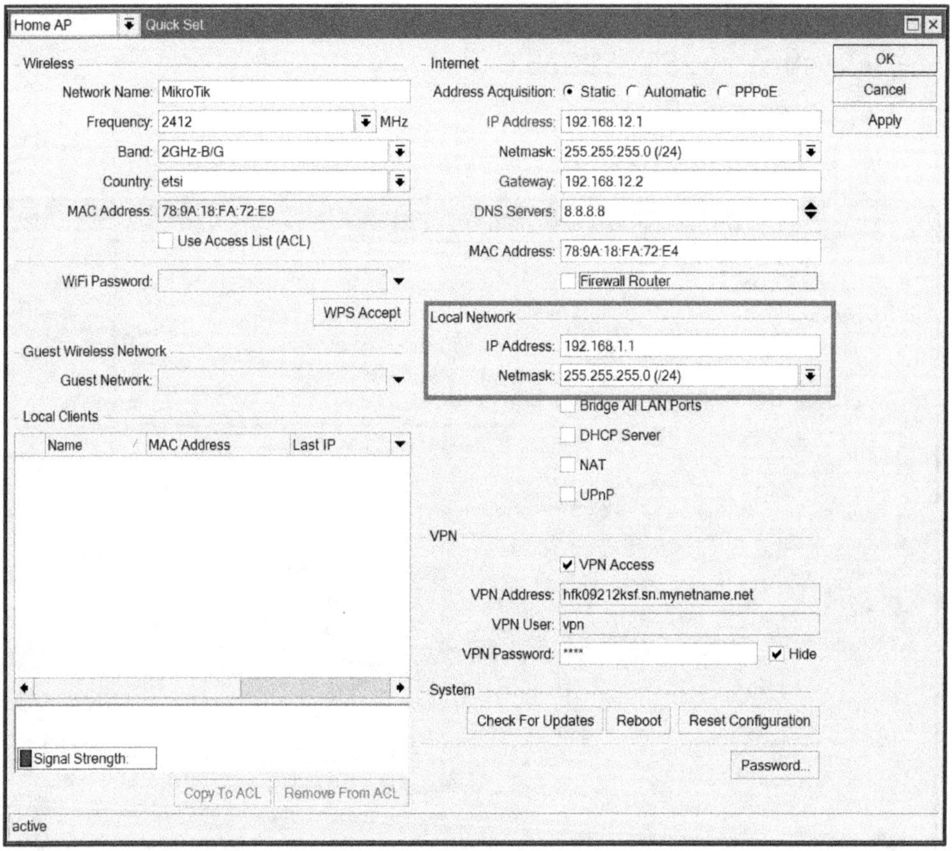

These settings play the role of the LAN interface settings. The Quick Set tool will assign these settings to ether2.

VPN Configuration

From the **VPN** section, check the **VPN Access** checkbox, and in the **VPN Password** field, enter the password 1234. Then click the **OK** button to close this window.

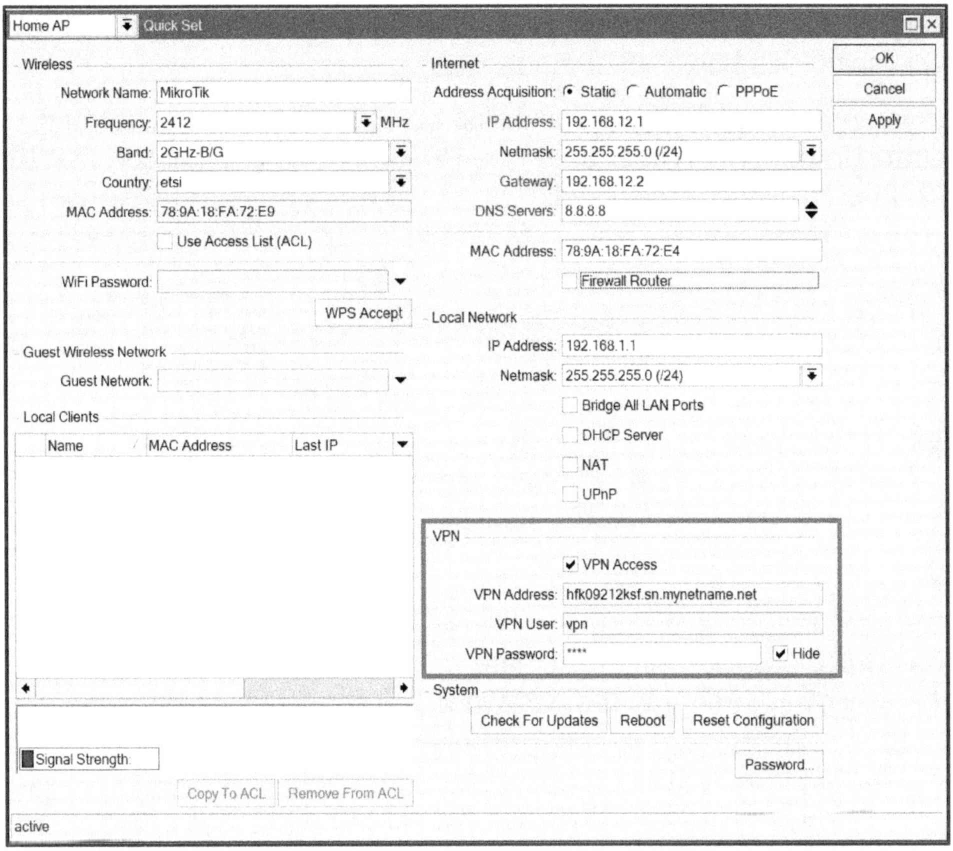

This information is very important as you will use it in the VPN client device to connect to the server (VPN Address, VPN User, and VPN Password).

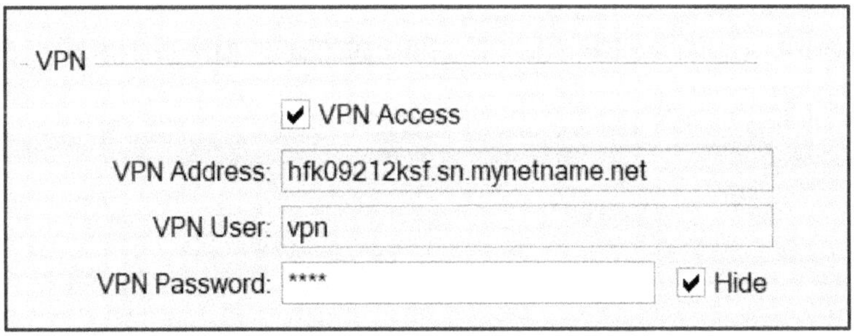

As mentioned, the Quick Set tool will automatically enable the PPTP, SSTP, and L2TP protocols in RouterOSv6, while in RouterOS v7, it will enable only the L2TP protocol. (as of the latest versions at the time of publishing this book: v6.49 and v7.18).

If you open the **L2TP Server** dialog box by clicking the **L2TP Server** button in the **Interface** tab of the **PPP** window, you will see that the **Enable** checkbox is checked.

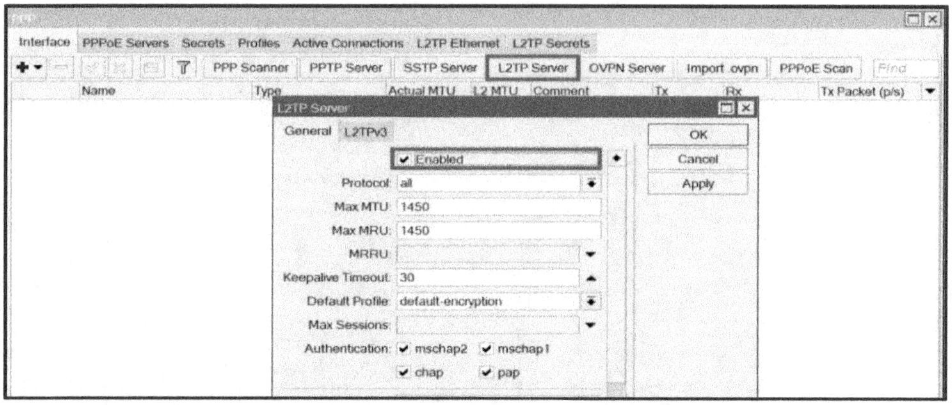

The Quick Set tool will also create an account, or a PPP secret, with the username: vpn and the password you specified: 1234.

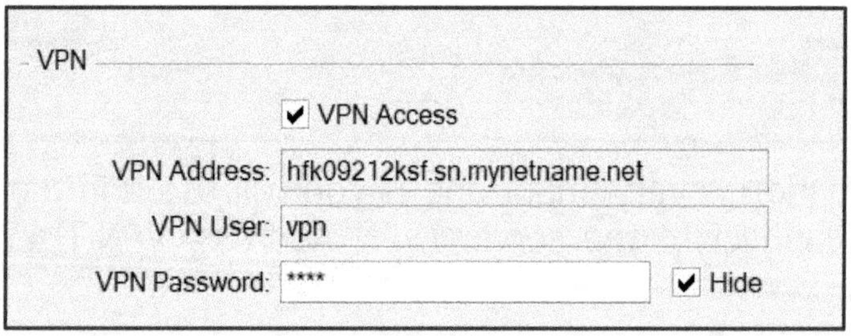

This account, or this PPP secret, will appear in the **Secrets** tab of the **PPP** window.

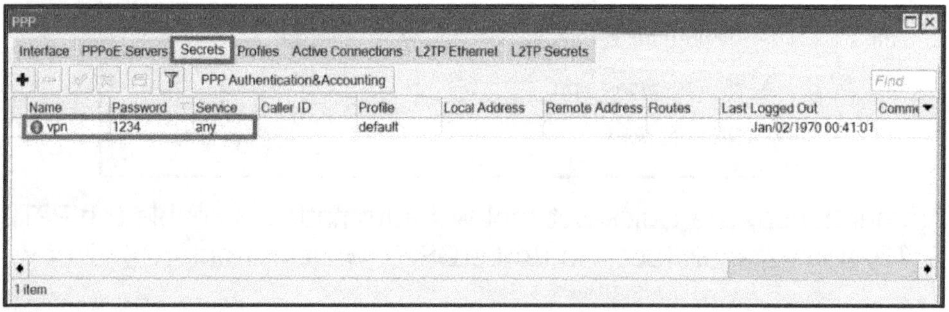

The Quick Set tool will also create an IP pool, using the range of 192.168.89.2-192.168.89.255. It will appear in the **Pools** tab of the **IP Pool** window.

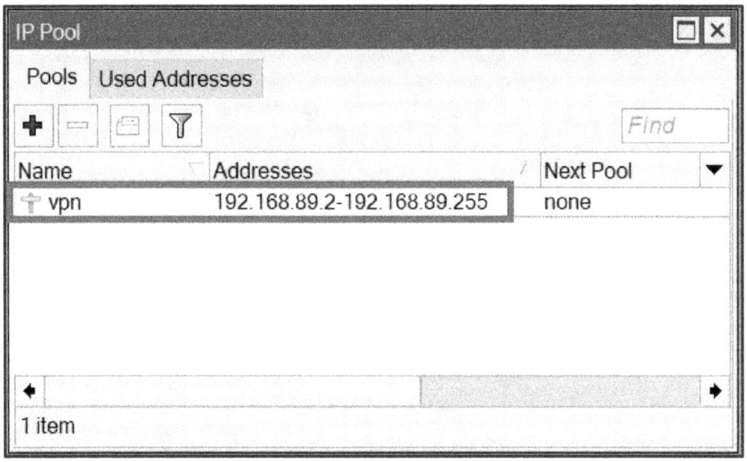

And it will link this pool to the default-encryption profile. You can open this profile from **Profiles** tab of the **PPP** window.

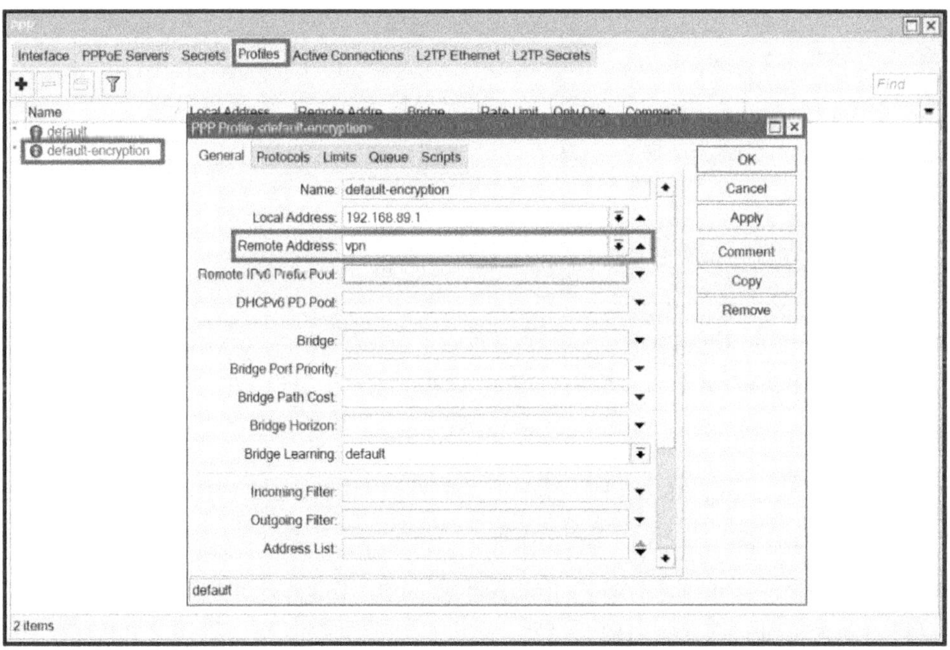

Also, the Quick Set tool will enable DDNS, to allow the connection to this VPN server using the address displayed in the VPN address field.

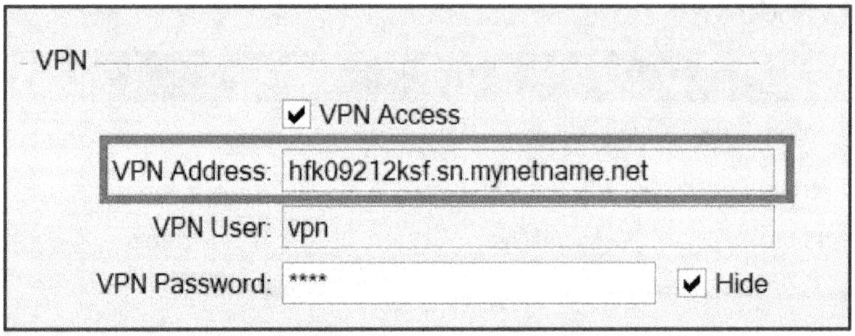

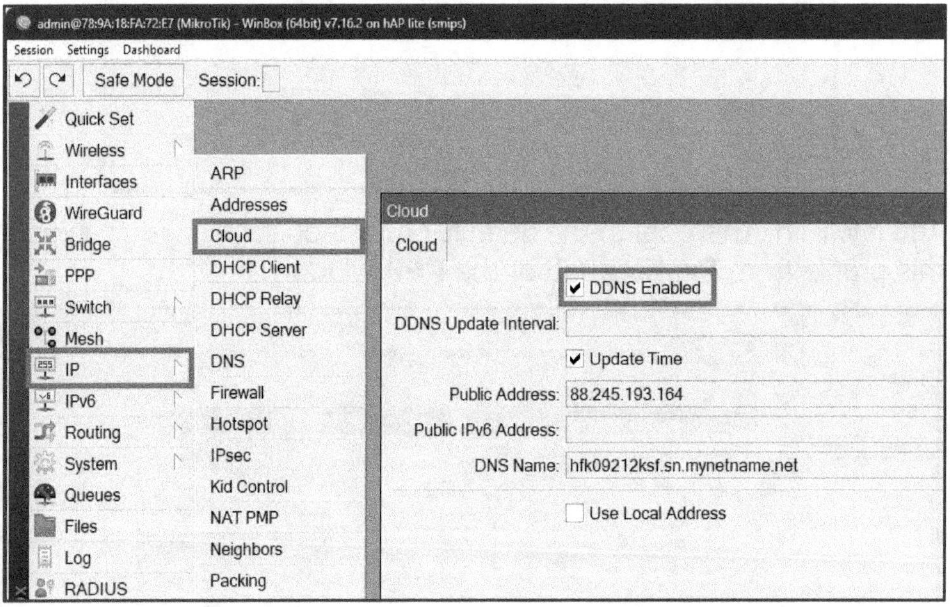

As you can see, the Quick Set tool has added many configurations with just a small amount of information entered in one window

R3

This router will act as a VPN client, so to configure it perform one step:

- Establish the Connection

As mentioned before, the Quick Set tool enables the PPTP, SSTP, and L2TP protocols in RouterOS v6, while in RouterOS v7, it enables the L2TP protocol (as of the latest versions at the time of publishing this book: v6.49 and v7.18). To establish a connection from the VPN client device, you can use any of these protocols depending on the RouterOS version. In this lab, the version used is RouterOS v7, so you will use the L2TP protocol.

To establish the connection using L2TP protocol and create the tunnel interface click the **Add** button in the **Interface** tab of the **PPP** window and select **L2TP Client** to open the **New Interface** dialog box.

In the **Connect To** field in the **Dial Out** tab, enter the VPN address displayed in the Quick Set window.

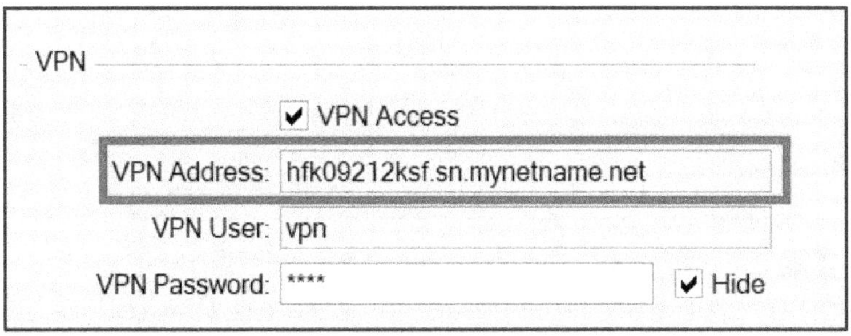

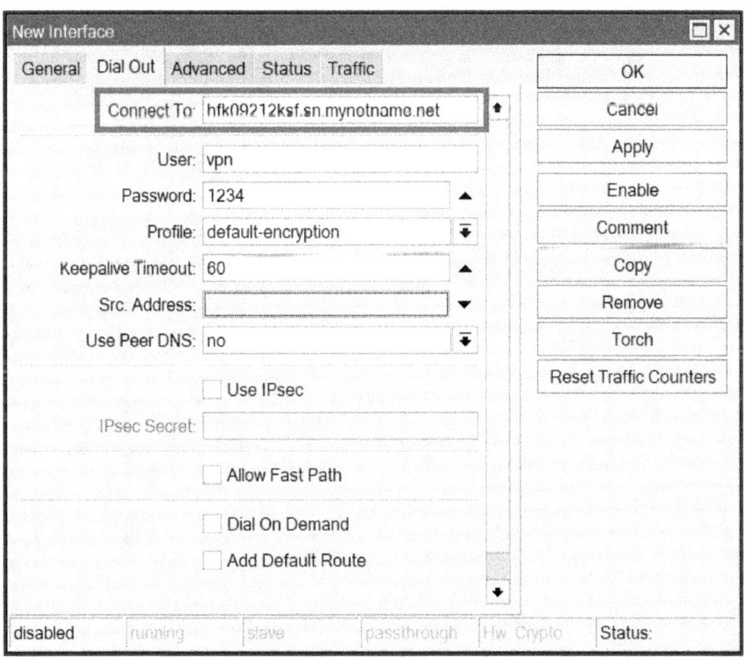

If your connection to the internet is behind the NAT, the VPN connection might not work.

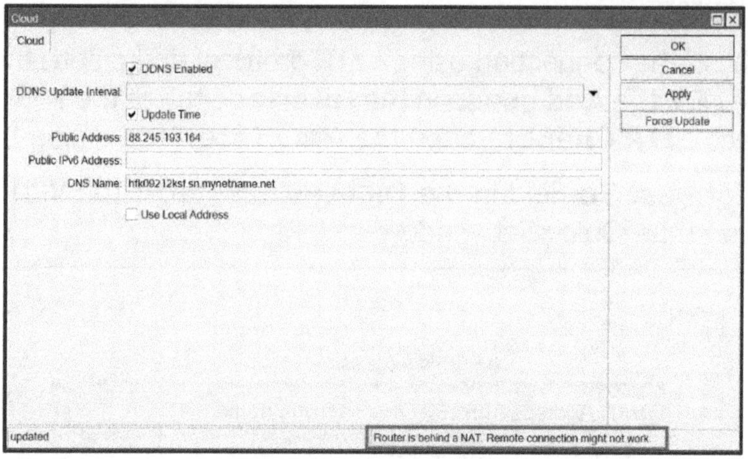

For the sake of training, you can perform this lab without an internet connection by using the VPN server IP address 192.168.12.1.

- In the **User** field, enter vpn.
- In the **Password** field, enter 1234

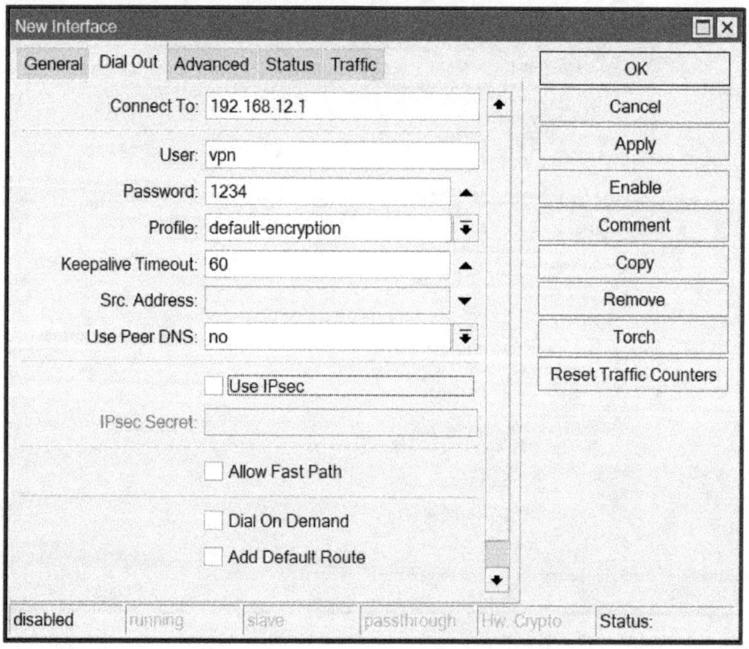

After adding the interface and establishing the connection, an **R** flag will appear next to this interface, indicating that the connection has been successfully established and the VPN interface is now running.

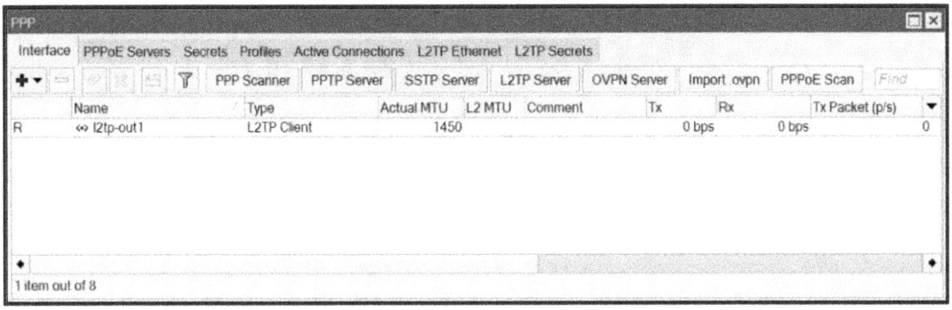

PPPoE Protocol

8.18 PPPoE Protocol

Point-to-Point Protocol over Ethernet PPPoE is a protocol used to provide an authenticated way to assign IP addresses to clients. It is a layer 2 protocol that provides authentication, encryption and compression.

8.19 How PPPoE Protocol Works

The concept of using PPPoE is as follows: a device on the network is configured to act as a PPPoE Server, and another device to act as a PPPoE Client.

The communication between the PPPoE Server and the PPPoE Client happens in four steps:

- The client sends a message called PPPoE Active Discovery Initialization (PADI).
- The server replies with a message called PPPoE Active Discovery Offer (PADO).
- The client sends a message called PPPoE Active Discovery Request (PADR).
- The server replies with a message called PPPoE Active Discovery Session Confirmation (PADS).

8.20 PPPoE Configuration

To configure a PPPoE, use **PPP** window to configure one device as the PPPoE server and the other as the PPPoE client, as mentioned before

- On the server, perform two main steps:
    - Enable the protocol.
    - Create an account.
- On the client, perform one main step:
    - Establish the connection.

8.21 PPPoE Server

The PPPoE server, called also Access Concentrator, is configured on an interface. This interface should not be a bridge interface. And it is recommended to do not assign an IP address on the interface.

In PPPoE Server, to enable the PPPoE protocol and create or add PPPoE Server, click the **Add** button in the **PPPoE Servers** tab of the **PPP** window to open the **New PPPoE Server** dialog box.

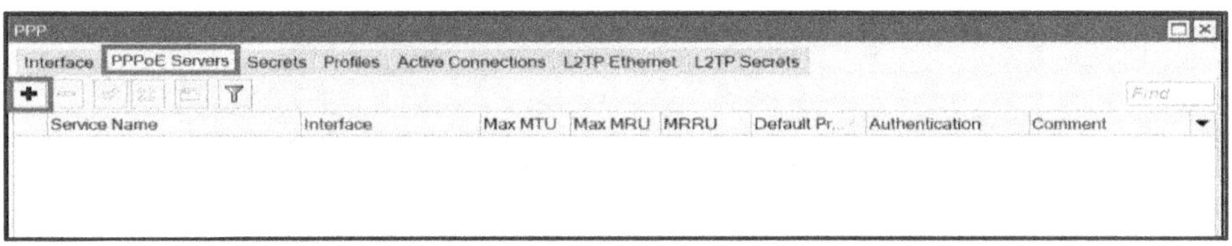

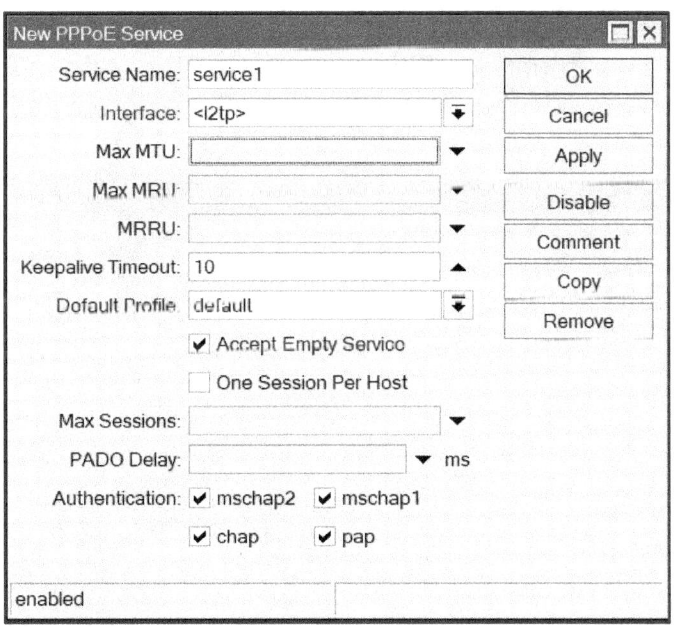

In the **Interface** field, select the interface on which PPPoE will be configured.

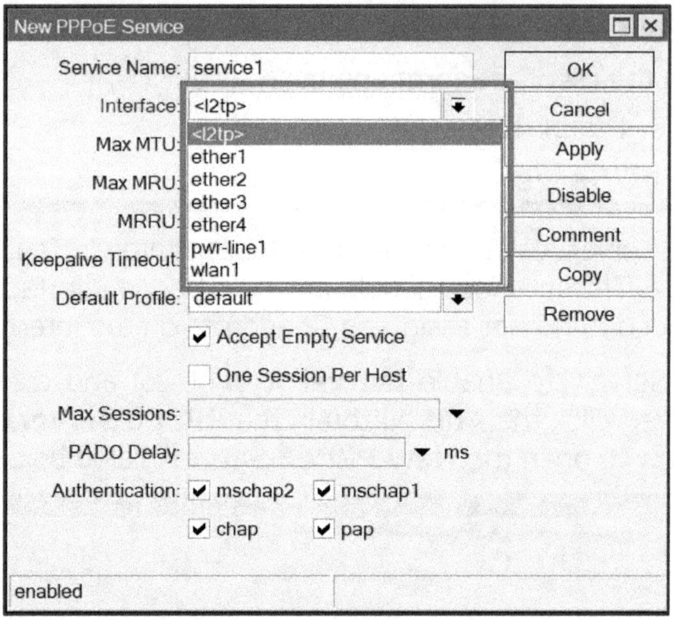

You can use the **Service Name** field to enter a name for this server, or you can leave the default name.

To create an account, or PPP secret, click the **Add** button in the **Secrets** tab to open the **New PPP Secret** dialog box, as mentioned before.

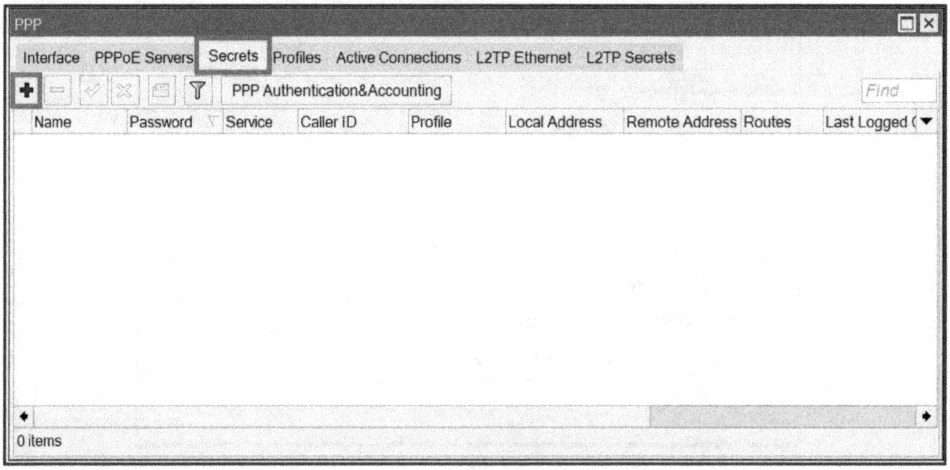

Then, set the account properties, such as the username, password and the IP addresses.

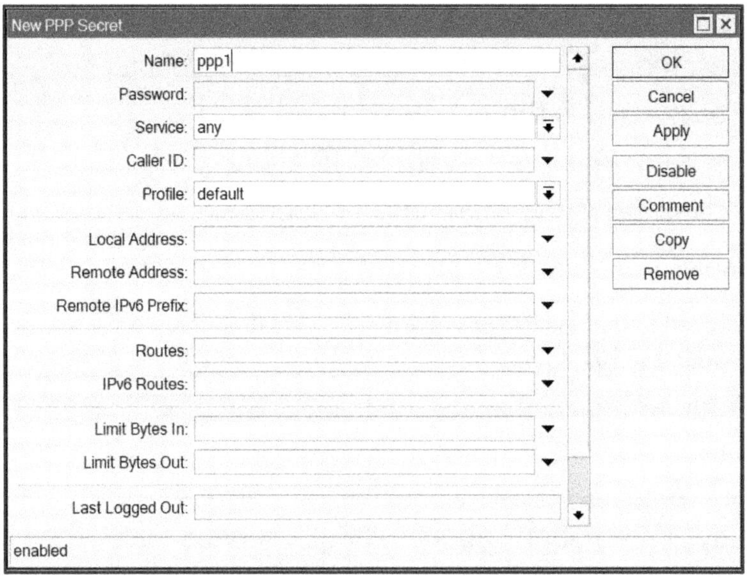

You can also create a PPPoE server from the CLI using the following command:

```
interface pppoe-server server add service-name=[name]
interface=[interface] disabled=no
```

Where:

- [name] is the name of this service.
- [interface] is the interface on which the server will be configured.

For example:

```
interface pppoe-server server add service-name=service1 interface=ether1
disabled=no
```

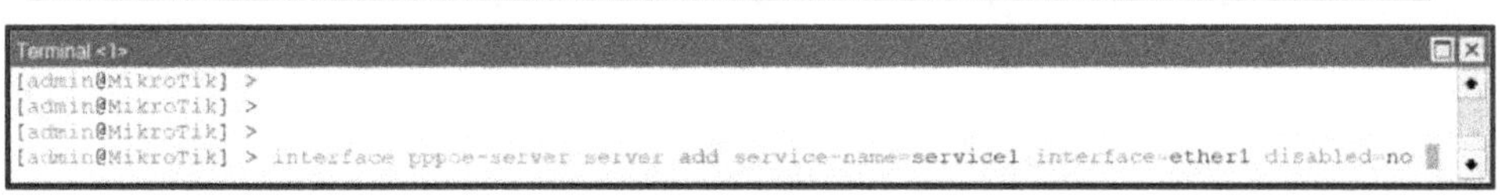

To create an account, or a PPP secret, from the CLI, use the following command:

```
ppp secret add name=[username] password=[password] local-
address=[server IP] remote-address=[client IP]
```

Where:

- [username] is the username for this account.
- [password] is the password.
- [server IP] is the server end IP address.
- [client IP] is the client end IP address.

For example:

```
ppp secret add name=user1 password=1234 local-address=10.0.0.1
remote-address=10.0.0.2
```

```
Terminal <1>
[admin@MikroTik] >
[admin@MikroTik] >
[admin@MikroTik] >
[admin@MikroTik] > ppp secret add name=user1 password=1234 local-address=10.0.0.1 remote-address=10.0.0.2
```

To display information about PPPoE servers use the following command:

```
Interface pppoe-server server print
```

```
Terminal <1>
[admin@MikroTik] >
[admin@MikroTik] > interface pppoe-server server print
Flags: X - disabled, I - invalid
 0   service-name="service1" interface=ether1 max-mtu=auto
     max-mru=auto mrru=disabled
     authentication=pap,chap,mschap1,mschap2
     keepalive-timeout=10 one-session-per-host=no
     max-sessions=unlimited pado-delay=0
     default-profile=default
[admin@MikroTik] >
```

To display the current ppp secrets in RouterOS use the following command:

```
ppp secret print
```

```
Terminal <1>
[admin@MikroTik] >
[admin@MikroTik] > ppp secret print
Columns: NAME, SERVICE, PASSWORD, PROFILE, REMOTE-ADDRESS
# NAME   SERVICE  PASSWORD  PROFILE  REMOTE-ADDRESS
0 user1  any          1234  default  10.0.0.2
[admin@MikroTik] >
```

8.22 PPPoE Client

In the PPTP Client, to establish a connection to the PPPoE server and create a virtual interface using the PPPoE protocol, click the **Add** menu in the **Interface** tab of the **PPP** window, and select **PPPoE Client** to open the **New Interface** dialog box.

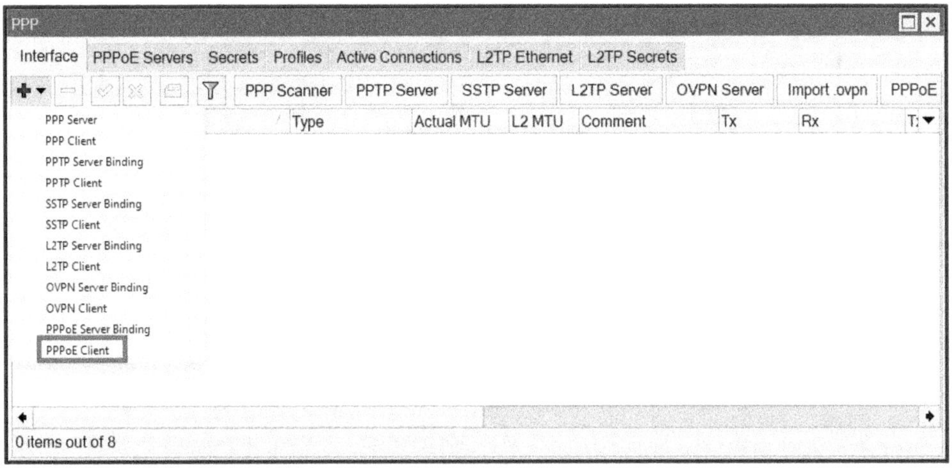

In the **Interface** field in the **General** tab of the **New Interface** dialog box, select the interface on which the **PPPoE Client** will be configured.

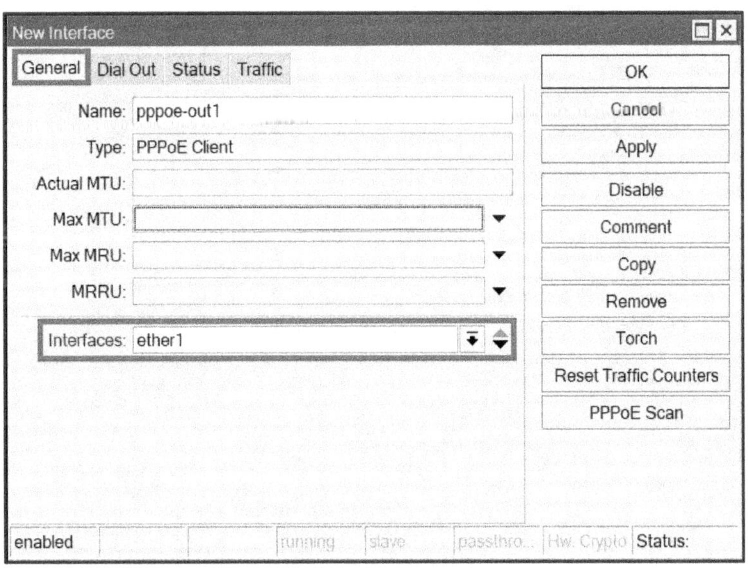

In the Username and Password fields of the Dial-Up tab, enter the username and password.

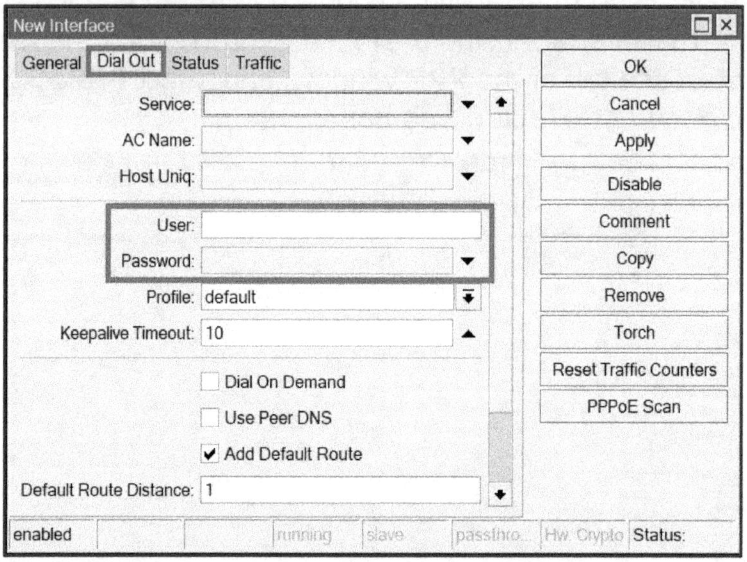

You can also specify the name of the PPPoE server if there are multiple PPPoE servers on the same broadcast domain connected to this interface and you want to connect to a specific PPPoE server by entering the name in the **Service Name** field.

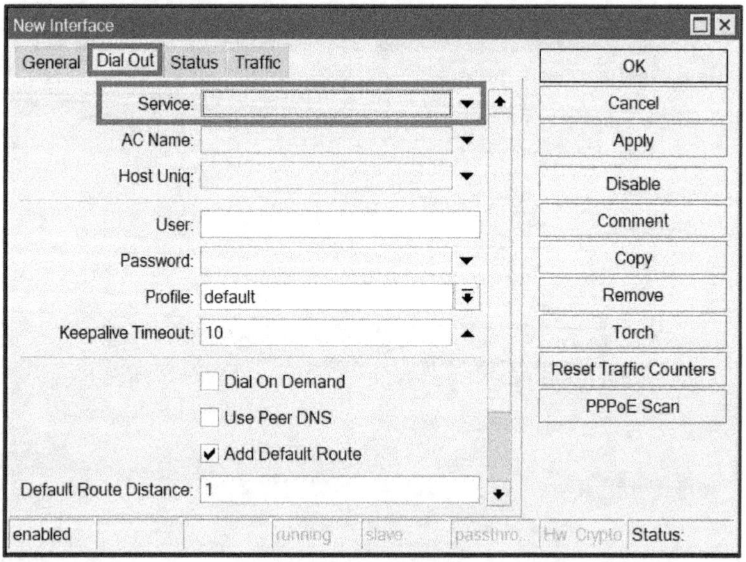

You can also use the **AC Name** field (or Access Concentrator Name), to specify the server device name.

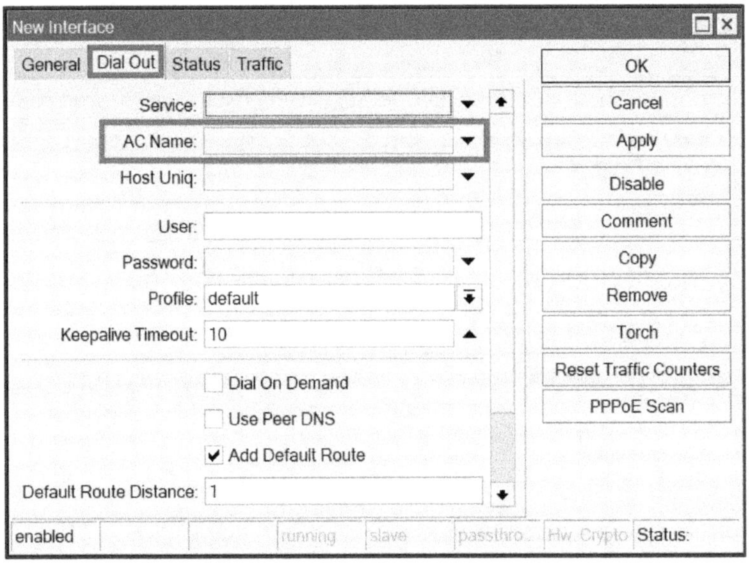

Note: the server device name is the name, or the identity, of the server set by the **System Identity**.

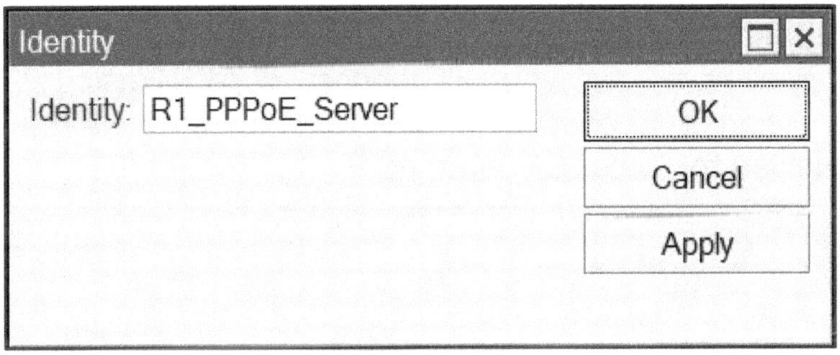

You can also establish the connection to the PPPoE server from the CLI using the following command:

```
interface pppoe-client add interface=[interface] user=[username]
password=[password] disabled=no
```

Where:

- [interface] is the interface on which the client will be configured

- [username] is the account username.
- [password] is the account password.

For example:

```
interface pppoe-client add interface=ether1 user=user1 password=1234
```

```
Terminal <1>
[admin@MikroTik] >
[admin@MikroTik] >
[admin@MikroTik] >
[admin@MikroTik] > interface pppoe-client add interface=ether1 user=user1 password=1234 disabled=no
```

To display information about PPPoE client use the following command:

```
interface pppoe-client print
```

```
Terminal <1>
[admin@MikroTik] > interface pppoe-client print
Flags: X - disabled, I - invalid; R - running
 0  R name="pppoe-out5" max-mtu=auto max-mru=auto mrru=disabled
      interface=ether1 user="user1" password="1234" profile=default
      keepalive-timeout=10 service-name="" ac-name=""
      add-default-route=no dial-on-demand=no use-peer-dns=no
      allow=pap,chap,mschap1,mschap2

[admin@MikroTik] >
```

LAB

In this lab, R1 is connected to the internet. You want to allow R2 to have internet access, so you will connect R2 to R1 using PPPoE. R1 will then assign an IP address to R2 via PPPoE from a NATed IP range that is allowed to access the internet.

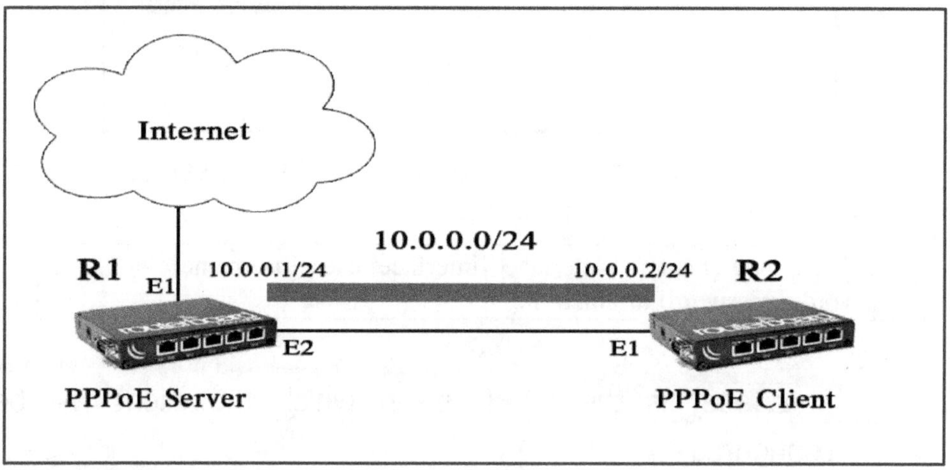

To start the configuration:

- First: perform the basic configuration.
- Second:, configure the **PPPoE**.

Basic Configuration

R1

- Set the router name to R1_PPPoE_Server.
- Insall DHCP Client on ether1 to obtain an IP address from the ISP.

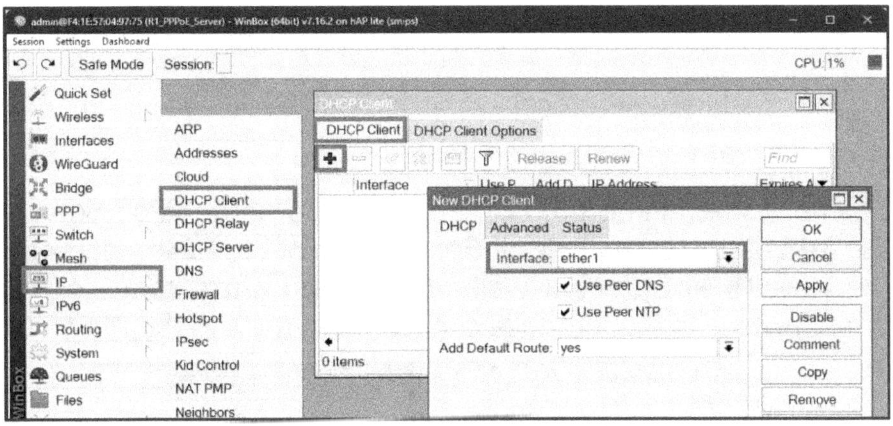

- You want this router to assign IP addresses to R2 using the PPPoE protocol and NAT this range to allow access to the internet. To do that create a NAT rule using the range 10.0.0.0/24 and set the action to Masquerade

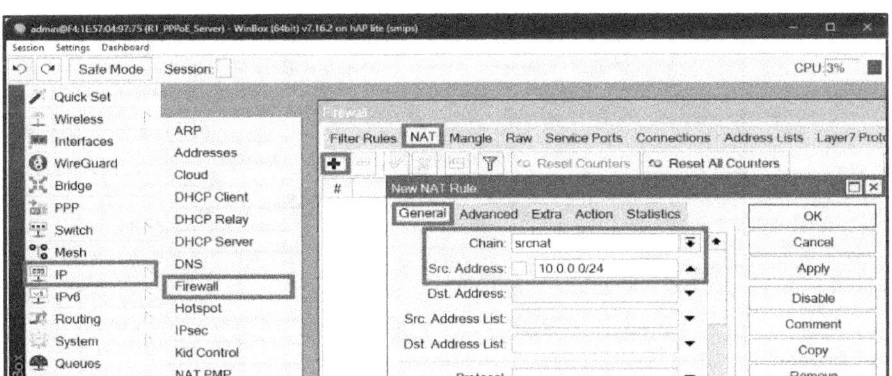

Note: you do not need to assign any IP address to the interface that is connected to R2.

R2

- Set the router name to R2_PPPoE_Client.

Note: you do not need to assign any IP address to the interface that is connected to R1.

PPPoE configuration

R1

This router will act as PPPoE Server, so to configure it, perform two steps:

- Enable the Protocol
- Create an Account

To enable the PPPoE protocol and create or add PPPoE Server, click the **Add** button in the **PPPoE Servers** tab of the **PPP** window to open the **New PPPoE Server** dialog box, then in **interface** field choose ether2, which is the interface connected to the R2, the PPPoE Client.

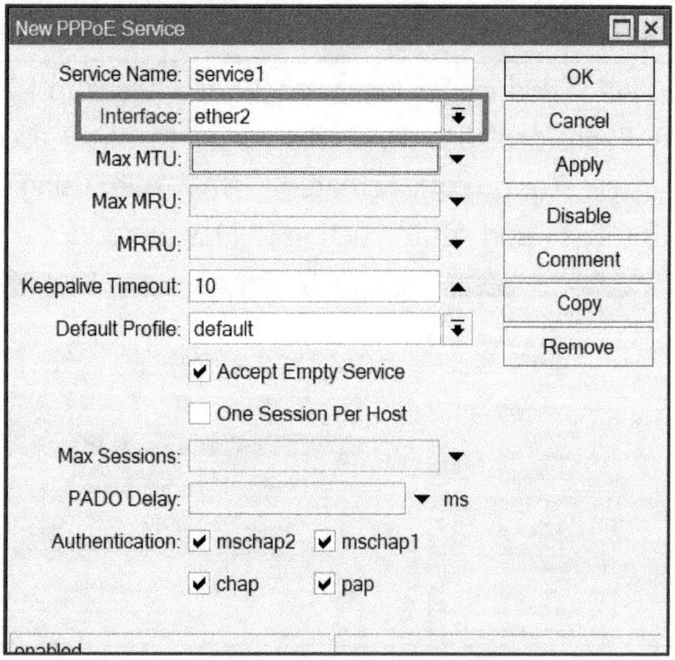

After creating the PPPoE Server, it will appear in the **PPPoE Servers** tab of the **PPP** window.

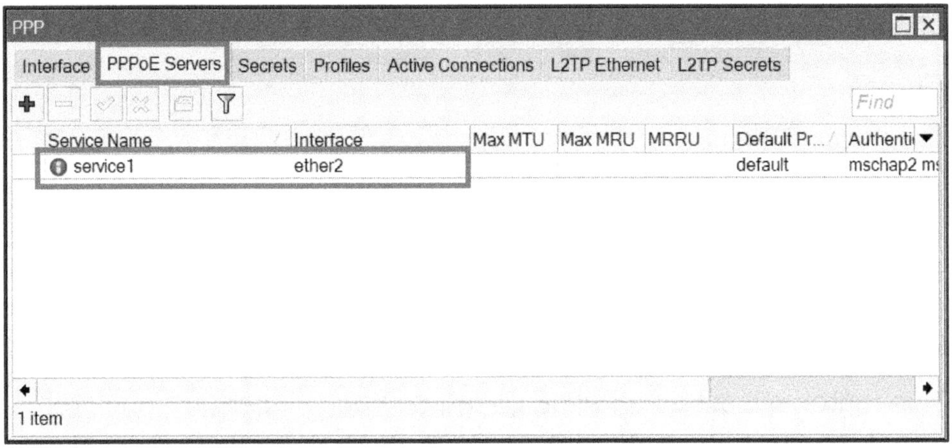

To create an account, or PPP secret, click the **Add** button in the **Secrets** tab of the **PPP** window to open the **New PPP Secret** dialog box.

- In the User field, enter user1.
- In the Password field, enter 1234.
- In the Local Address field, enter 10.0.0.1.
- In the Remote Address field, enter 10.0.0.2.

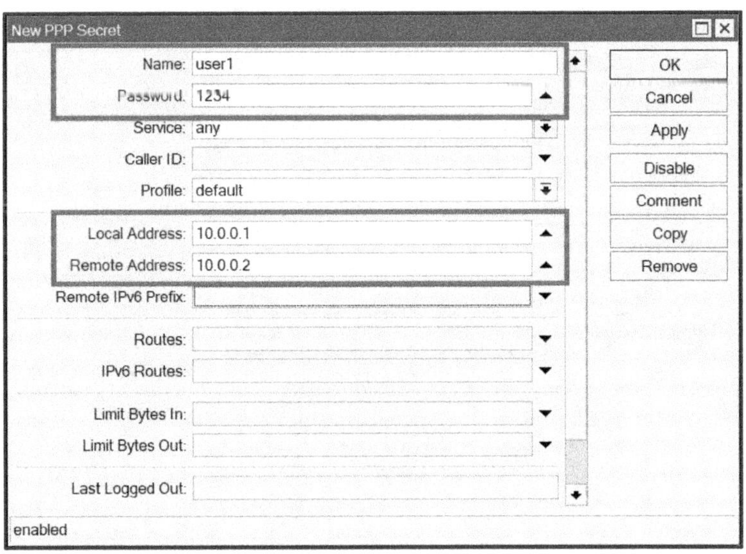

After creating the PPP secret, it will appear in the **Secrets** tab of the **PPP** window.

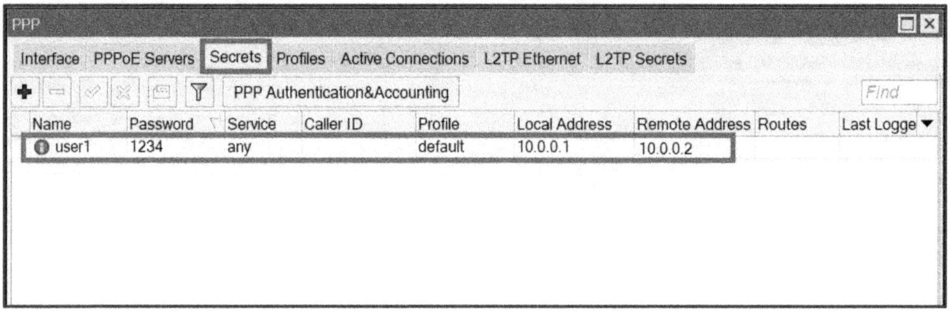

R2

This router will act as a PPPoE Client, so you will perform one step:

- Establish the Connection

To establish the connection and create the tunnel interface:

- Click the **Add** button in the **Interface** tab of the **PPP** window and select **PPPoE Client** to open the **New Interface** dialog box.
- In the **Interface** field in the **General** tab, select ether1, which is connected to the R1, the PPPoE Server.

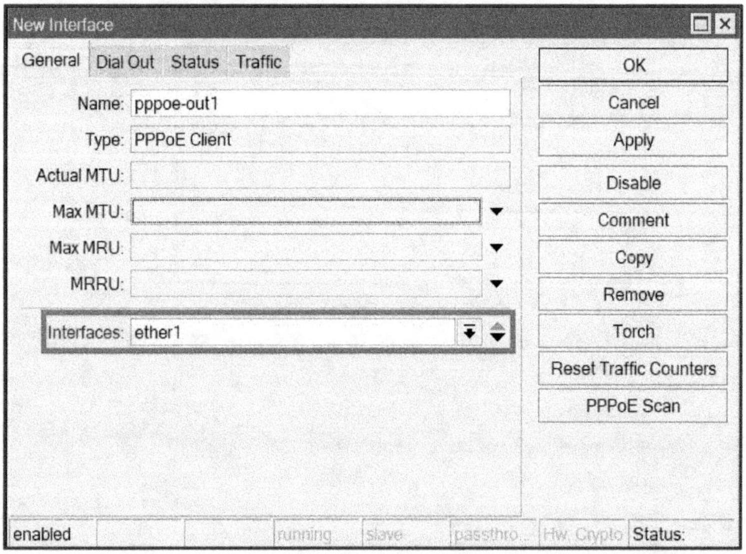

- In the **User** field, in the **Dial Out** tab enter user1.
- In the **Password** field, enter 1234

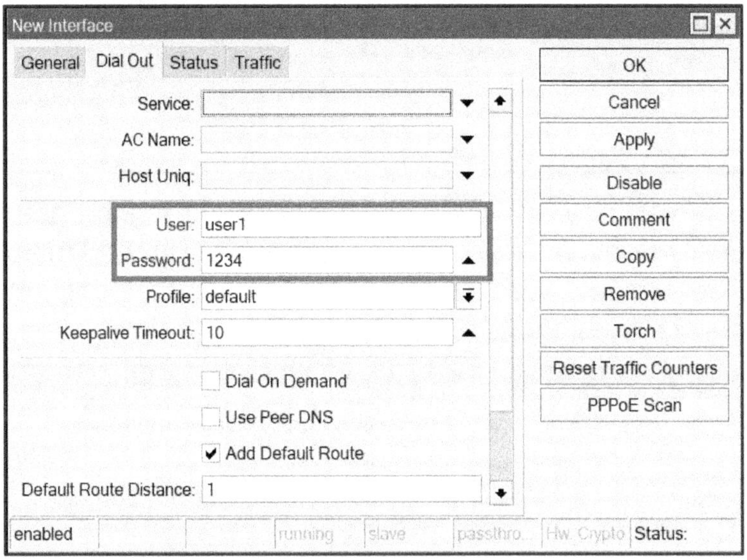

After adding the interface in the client device R2 , it will appear in the **Interface** tab of the **PPP** window.

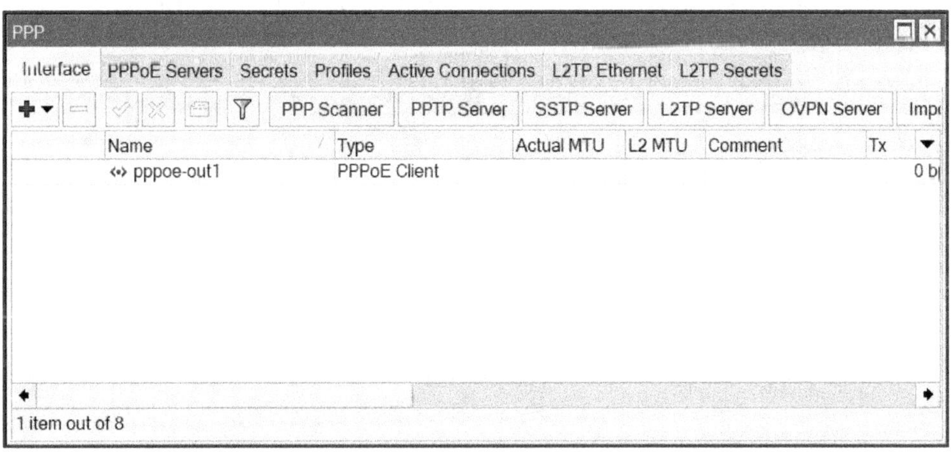

After establishing the connection, an **R** flag will appear next to this interface, indicating that the connection has been successfully established and the interface is now running.

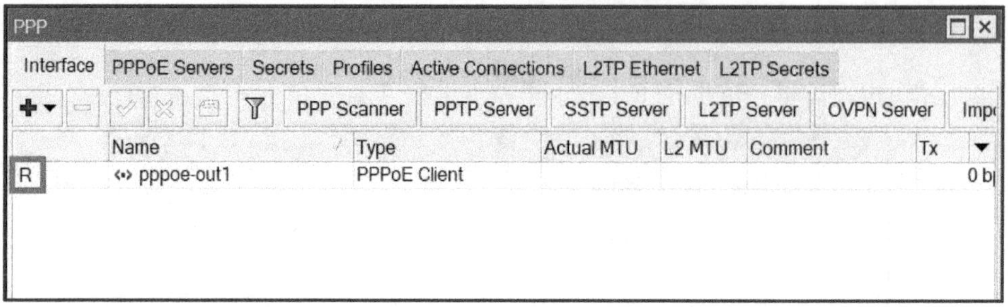

On the server device R1, a new virtual PPP interface will be automatically or dynamically created and appear in the **Interface** tab of the **PPP** window with **DR** flags, indicating that the interface is dynamically created and is now running.

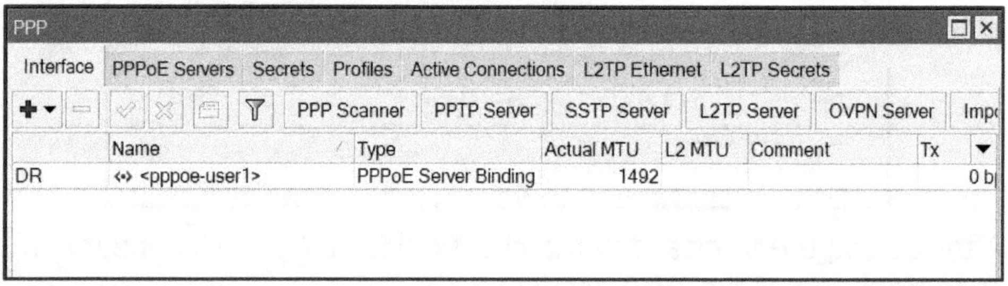

This interface will also appear in the **Interface** tab of the **Interface List** window.

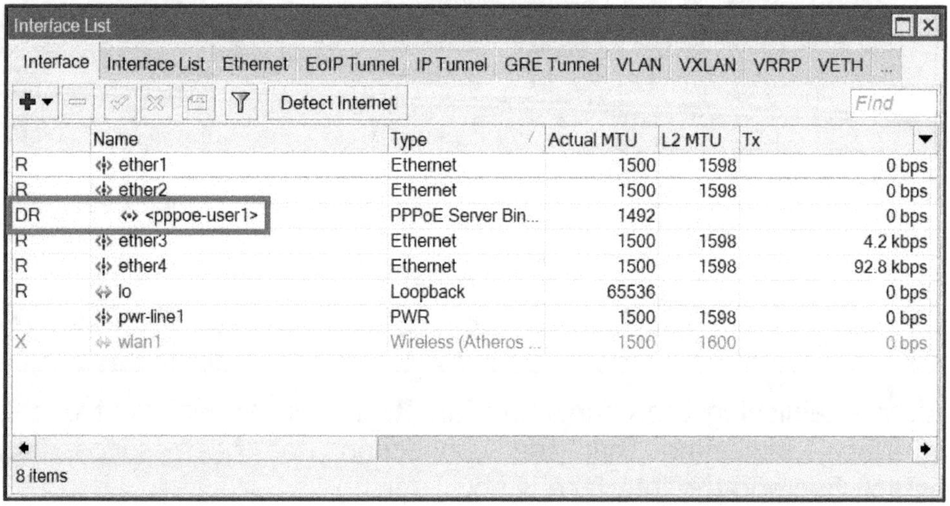

The IP address of this new interface will appear in the **Address List** window.

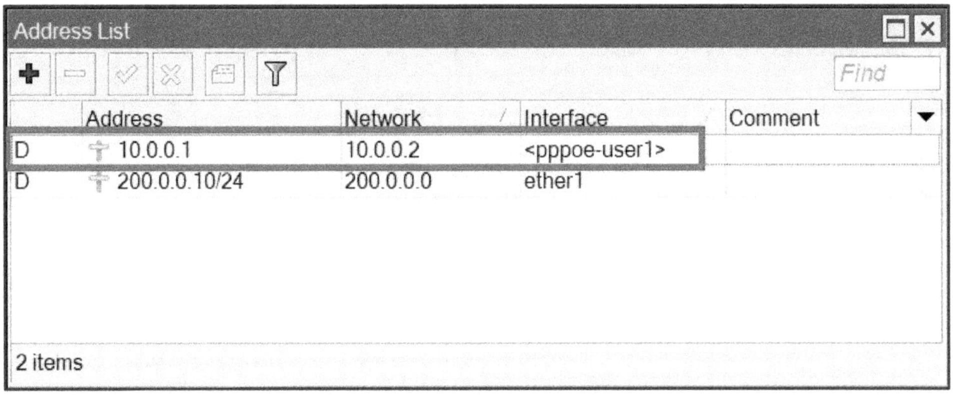

Also, this active connection will appear in the **Active Connections** tab of the **PPP** window.

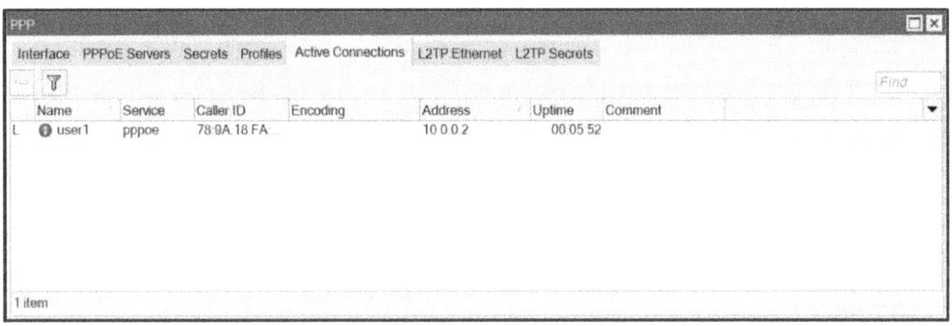

Now, R2, the PPPoE Client, has internet access.

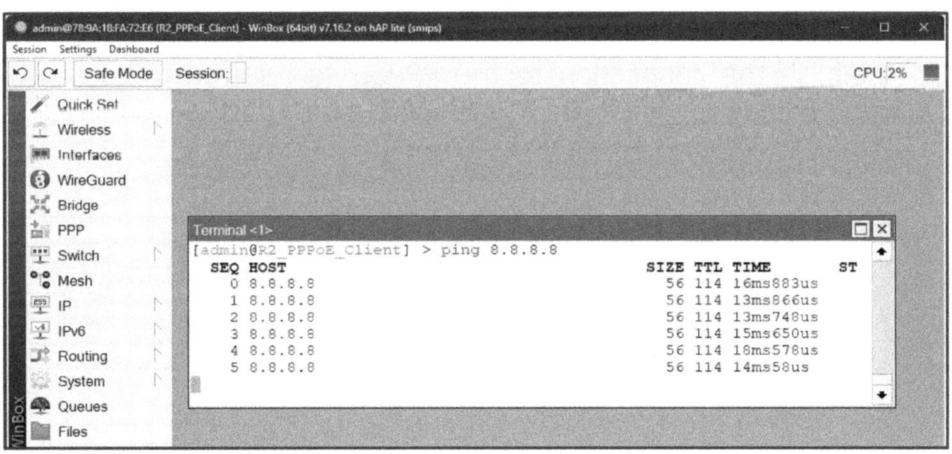

CLI

You can also make the configuration from the CLI.

To set the identity for each device, use the following commands:

R1

```
system identity set name=R1_PPPoE_Server
```

R2

```
system identity set name=R2_PPPoE_Client
```

To configure DHCP Client on ether1 in R1, use the following command:

```
ip dhcp-client add interface=ether1
```

To create the NAT rule in R1, use the following command:

```
ip firewall nat add src-address=10.0.0.0/24 chain=srcnat
action=masquerade
```

To enable the PPPoE protocol, or create a PPPoE server, on ether2 in R1, use the following command:

```
interface pppoe-server server add service-name=service1 interface=ether2
disabled=no
```

To create an account, or a PPP secret in R1, use the following command:

```
ppp secret add name=user1 password=1234 local-address=10.0.0.1
remote-address=10.0.0.2
```

To establish the connection to the PPPoE server from R3, use the following command:

```
interface pppoe-client add interface=ether1 user=user1 password=1234
```

Module 9

MISCELLANEOUS

MTCNA

Module 9

This module provides information about some important tools that RouterOS provides and their usage.

Up-to-date information about other tools and new tools is available on the MikroTik website.

This module covers the following course content topics:

- RouterOS tools
  - E-mail
  - Netwatch
  - Ping
  - Traceroute
  - Profile (CPU load)
- Monitoring
  - Interface traffic monitor
  - Torch
  - Graphs
  - SNMP
  - The Dude
- Contacting support@mikrotik.com
  - System logs, enabling debug logs
  - readable configuration (item comments and names)
  - network diagrams

Miscellaneous

9.1 RouterOS tools

MikroTik RouterOS offers many useful tools that can be used to manage and monitor the network. You can access most of these tools from the **Tools** menu.

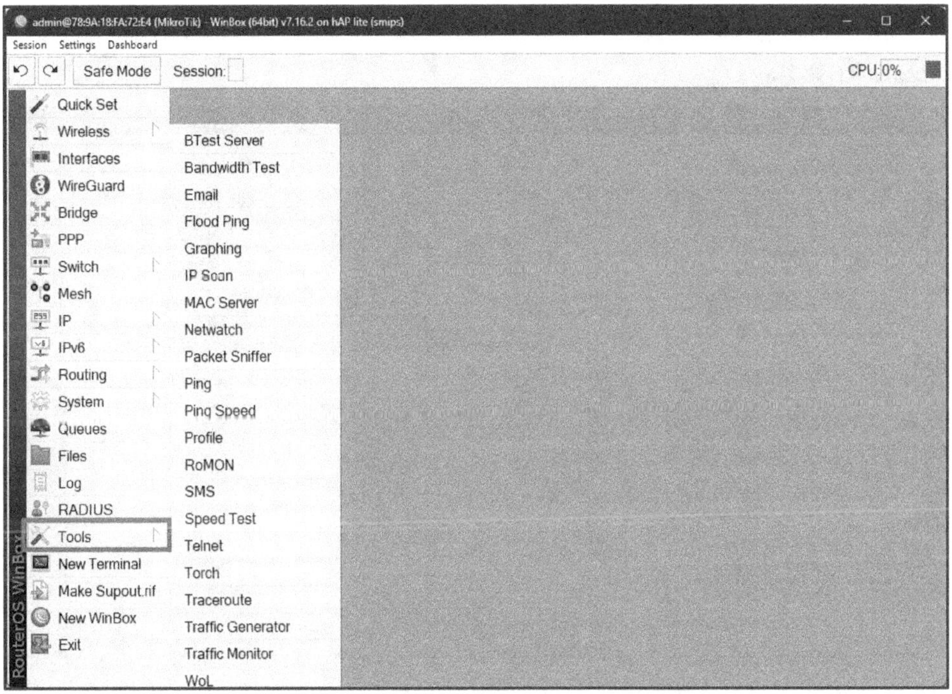

MikroTik adds new tools with RouterOS update from time to time. Some tools are included in the main package, you can get them by updating the main package. Other tools are provided in separate packages.

9.2 Email Tool

You can use the email tool to configure RouterOS to send emails.

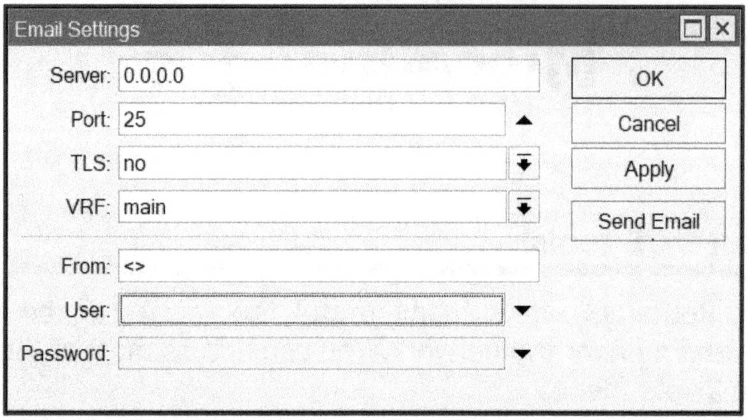

To open the **Email Settings** dialog box, click the **Tools** menu, then select **Email**.

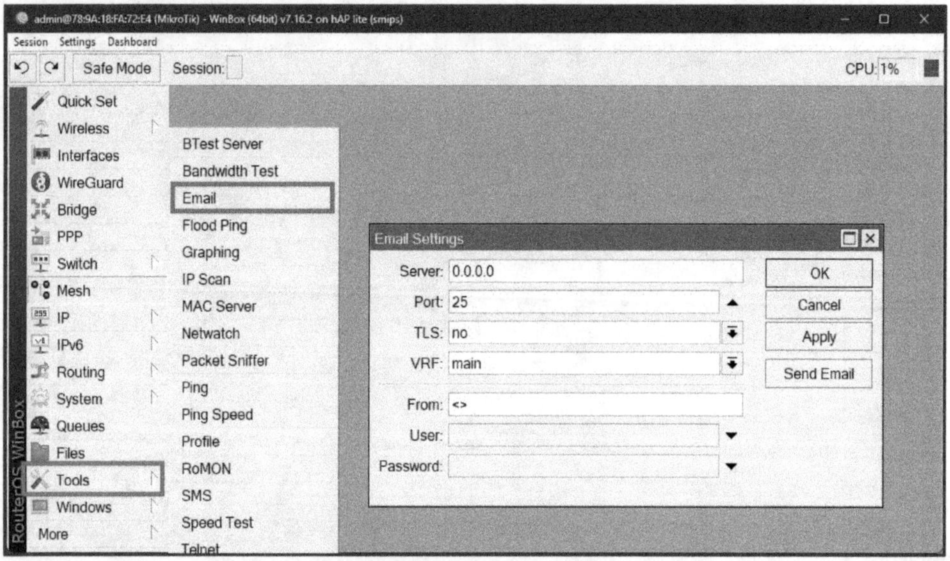

To configure the **Email Settings** tool on RouterOS, enter the SMTP outgoing server settings:

- The server IP address or web address (URL) in the **Server** field.

- The server port in the **Port** field.
- The TLS (Transport Layer Security) settings in the **TLS** field.

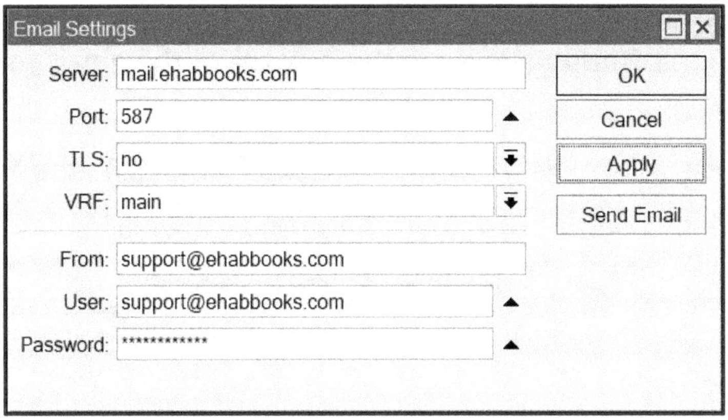

- In the **From** field, enter the email address you want to use. In the **Username** and **Password** fields, enter the username and password for this email account. Then, click the **OK** button to close the dialog box.

After configuring the email settings, you can manually send emails using this email tool, or you can configure other tools to use the email service for automatically sending emails either periodically or in response to specific events.

To manually send an email, click the **Send Email** button in the **Email Settings** dialog box to open the **Send Email** dialog box.

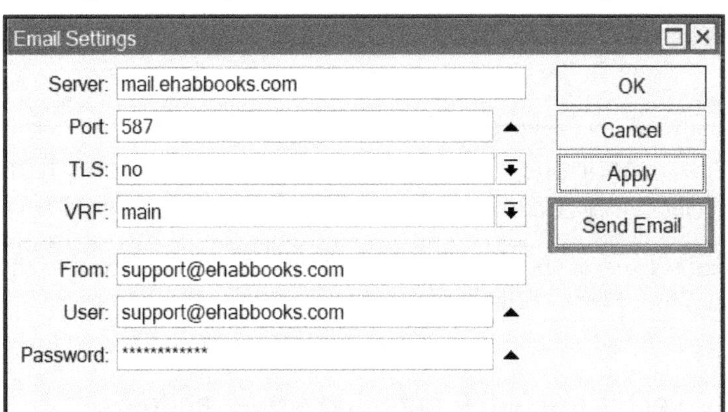

- In the **To** field, enter the recipient email address.
- In the **From** field, enter the email address you want to use.
- In the **Subject** field, enter the subject of the email.
- In the **Body** field, write the content of the email you want to send.

You can also attach files, (such as a backup file), using the **Files** field. Then, click the **Send Email** button to send the email.

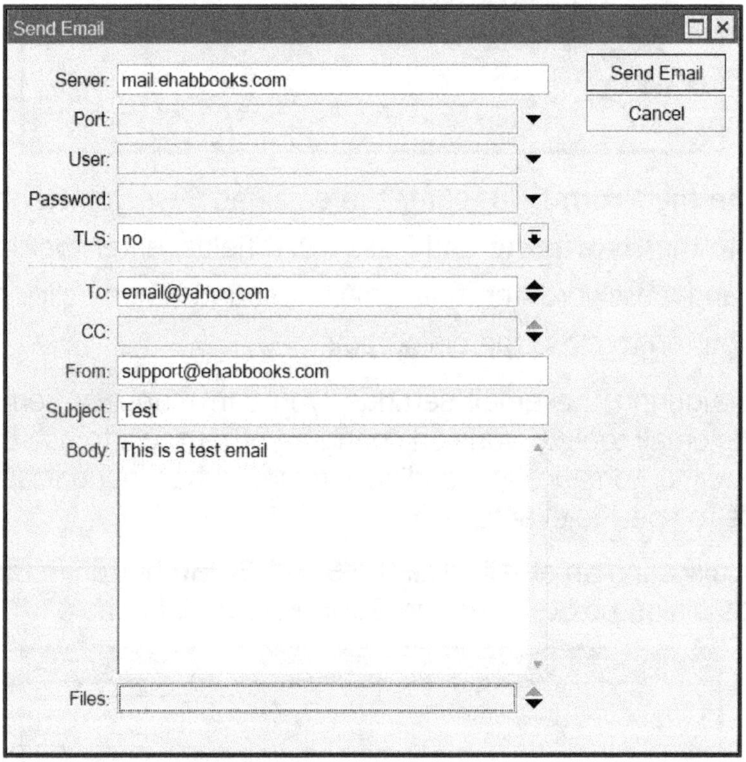

You can also configure the email settings in RouterOS from the CLI using the following command:

```
tool e-mail set server=[server] port=[port] tls=[tls settings] from=[email]
user=[username] password=[password]
```

Where:

- [server] is the SMTP outgoing server address.

- [port] is the server port.
- [tls settings] is the TLS settings.
- [email] is the email address that will appear to the recipient.
- [username] is the username of the email.
- [password] is the password of the email.

For example:

```
tool e-mail set server=mail.ehabbooks.com port=587 tls=no
from=support@ehabbooks.com user=support@ehabbooks.com
password=12345678
```

```
Terminal <1>
[admin@MikroTik] >
[admin@MikroTik] >
[admin@MikroTik] >
[admin@MikroTik] > tool e-mail set server=mail.ehabbooks.com port=587 tls=no
from= support@ehabbooks.com  user=support@ehabbooks.com password=12345678
```

To display information about email settings, use the following command:

```
tool e-mail print
```

```
Terminal <1>
[admin@MikroTik] > tool e-mail print
         server: mail.ehabbooks.com
           port: 587
            tls: no
            vrf: main
           from: support@ehabbooks.com
           user: support@ehabbooks.com
       password: 12345678
    last-status: succeeded

[admin@MikroTik] >
```

To send an email from CLI use the following command:

```
tool e-mail send to=[email] subject=[subject] body=[message]
```

Where:

- [email] is the In the recipient email address.
- [subject] is the subject of the email.
- [message] is the content of the email.

For example:

```
tool e-mail send to=email@yahoo.com subject="Test" body="This is a test email"
```

9.3 Netwatch Tool

The **Netwatch** tool allows you to monitor the connection state of a device on the network, to check if it is connected to the network and reachable or not. Then you can take some action depending on its state.

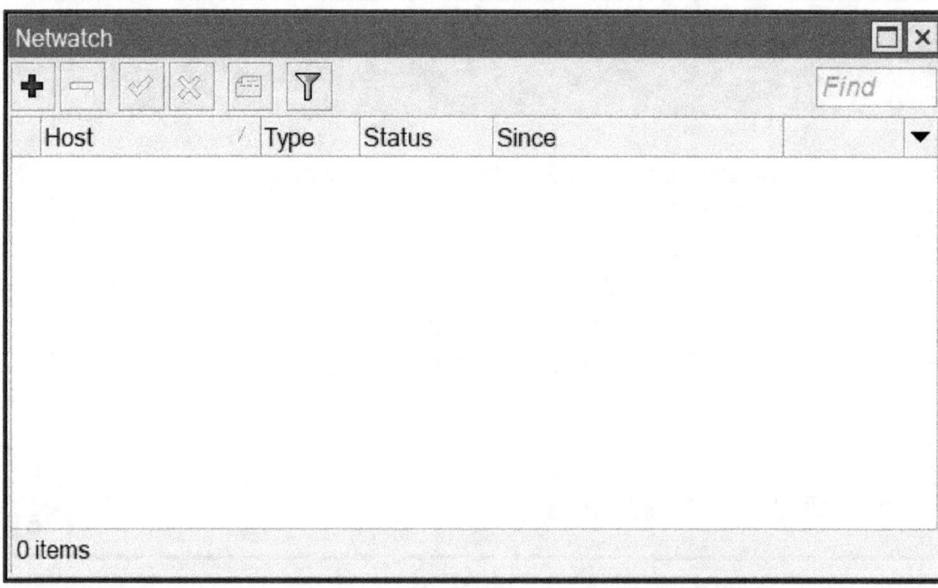

To open the **Netwatch** tool dialog box, click the **Tools** menu, then select **Netwatch**.

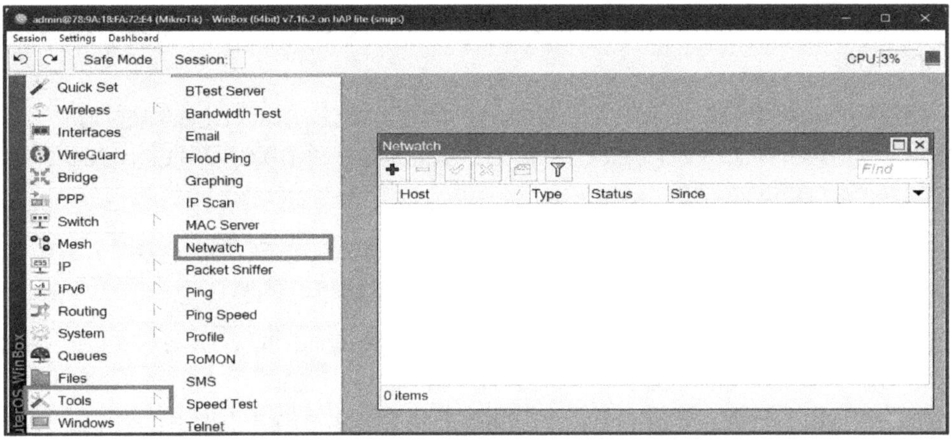

The tool works by using ICMP messages in a way similar to the ping command. When an ICMP echo request message is sent to the target device and an ICMP echo reply is received, it means the device is connected to the network and is reachable. If the ICMP echo reply is not received, it means that the device is either not connected to the network or unreachable.

This tool can be used to execute commands (or scripts) in response to the device status.

For example, you can configure this tool to send an email when a server fails.

To add a device to **Netwatch** tool, click the **Add** button in the **Netwatch** window to open the **New Netwatch Host** dialog box.

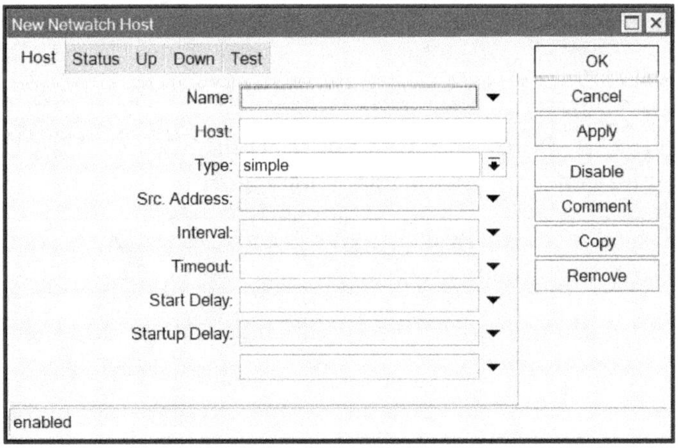

In the **Host** field enter the IP address of the device you want to monitor.

In the **Type** field, you can choose the check or probe method you want to use. You can select the default type simple, which uses ping to check connectivity.

In the **UP** and **Down** tabs, you can write the scripts you want to execute when the device state changes to up or down.

For example, if you want to monitor the reachability of a server with the IP address 192.168.1.100, in case this server becomes unreachable, you want to receive an email notification about this failure, enter the IP address of the server in the **Host** field.

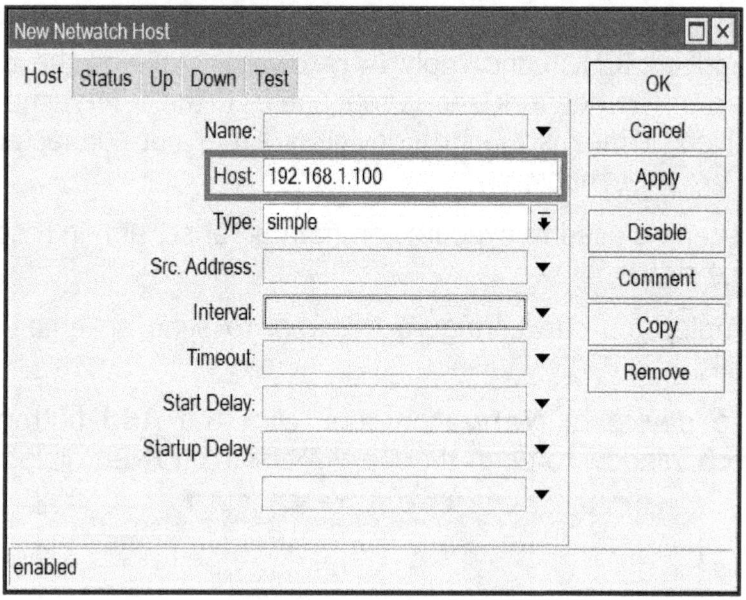

In the **Down** tab, enter the following command, or script, which will send an email notifying you about this failure:

```
tool e-mail send to=email@yahoo.com subject="Server Down" body="The server 192.168.1.100 is down"
```

Note: you should configure the email tool first before using it here.

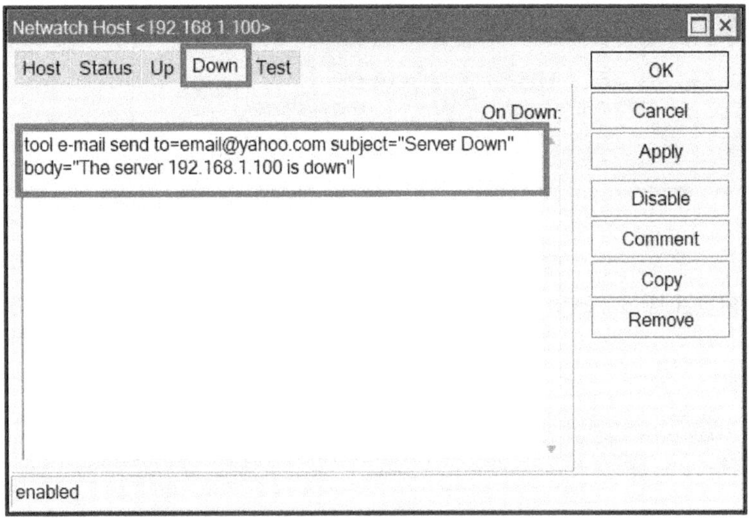

You can also configure the Netwatch settings in RouterOS from the CLI using the following command:

```
tool netwatch add host=[IP] down-script=[script]
```

Where:

- [IP] is the IP address of the device you want to monitor
- [script] is the scripts you want to execute

For example:

```
tool netwatch add host=192.168.1.100 down-script={tool e-mail send
to=email@yahoo.com subject="Server Down" body="The server
192.168.1.100 is down"}
```

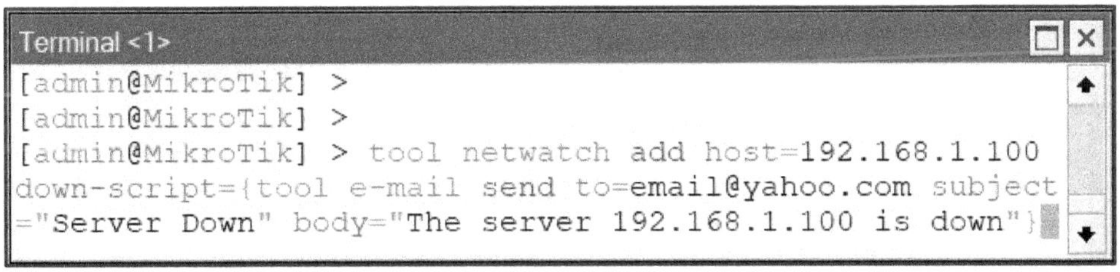

To display information about Netwatch settings use the following command:

```
tool netwatch print
```

9.4 Ping Tool

The Ping tool is a very useful tool that is used to check the reachability of a device on the network. It also measures the round-trip time to that device.

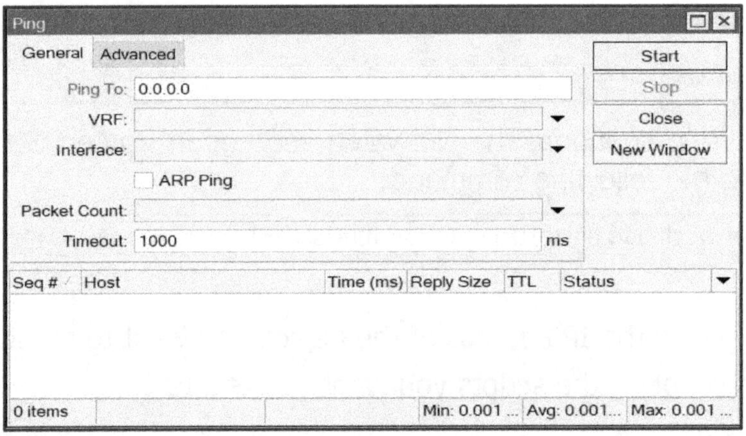

To open the **Ping** tool dialog box, click the **Tools** menu, then select **Ping**.

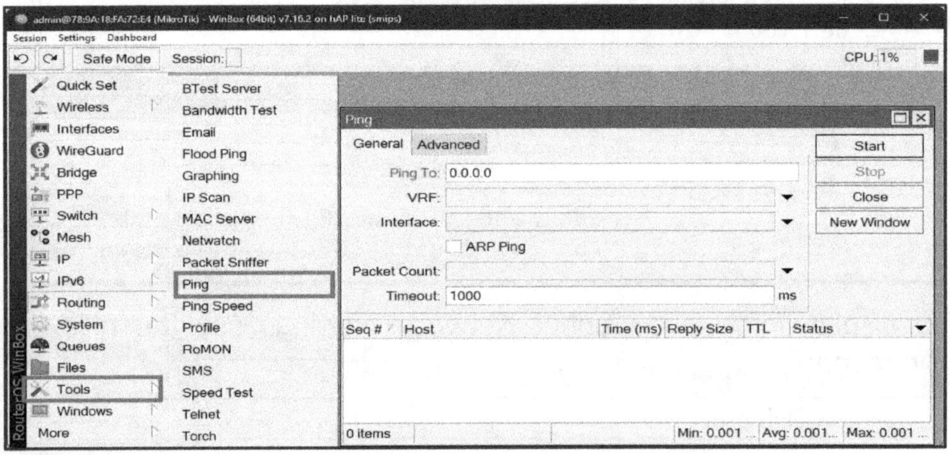

9.4.1 How Ping Works

Because this tool is used in troubleshooting, it is important to understand some details about how it works and how to use it.

The concept of using the Ping tool is as follows: to check the reachability of a device, it uses the ICMP protocol, sending an ICMP echo request to the device and waiting for an ICMP echo reply from this device.

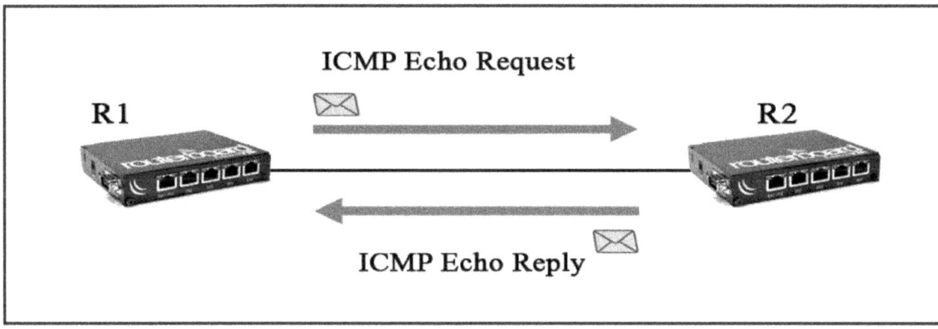

If it does not receive the reply within a specific period of time, called a timeout interval, the ping is considered unsuccessful

For example, if you want to ping the IP address 192.168.1.2, you will write this IP address in the **Ping To** field in the **General** tab.

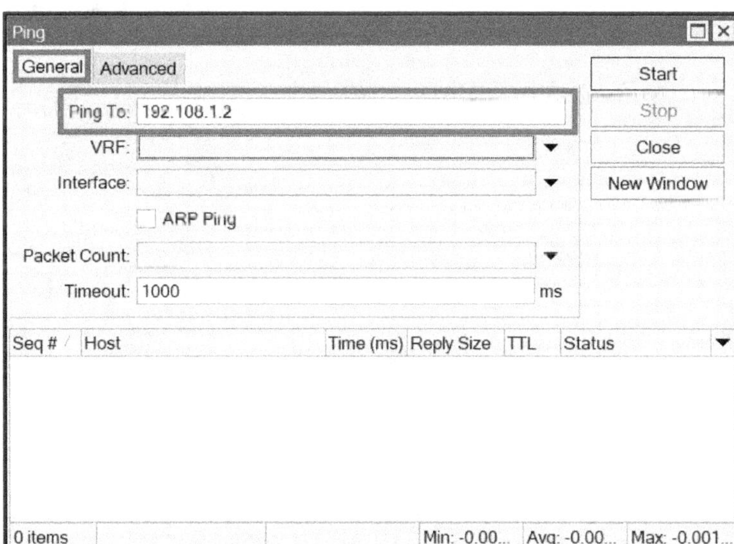

When clicking the **Start** button, the Ping tool will continuously send ICMP echo request packets to this IP address, wait for ICMP echo reply packets, and display information about those packets in the dialog box.

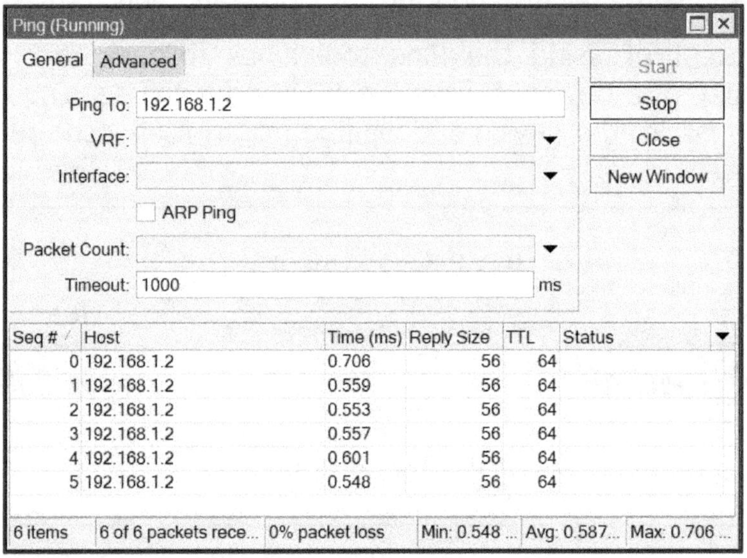

If the reply is not received within the Timeout interval specified in the **Timeout** field, a timeout message will be displayed, and the packet will be considered lost.

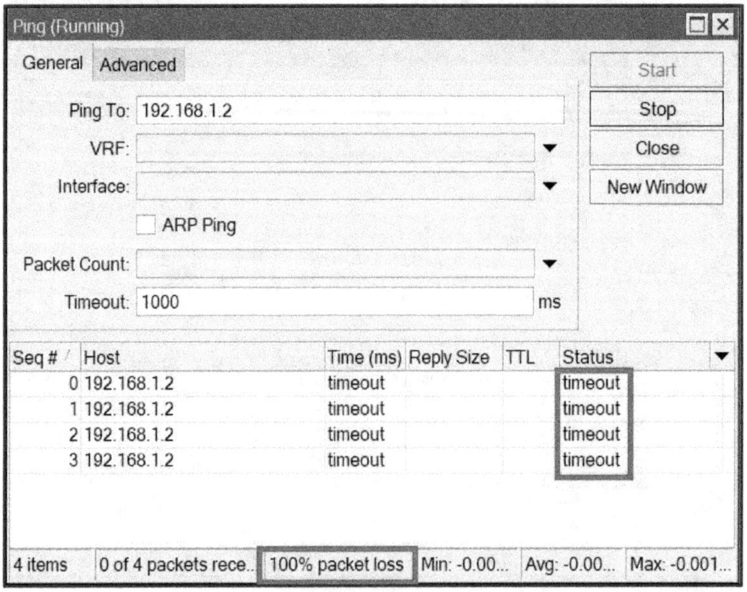

To stop the ping, click the **Stop** button.

To change the timeout interval, enter the desired value in the **Timeout** field.

You can also specify the number of ICMP echo request packets to be sent instead of continuously sending packets by entering the desired number in the **Packet Count** field. In this case, the Ping tool will send the specified number of packets and then stop.

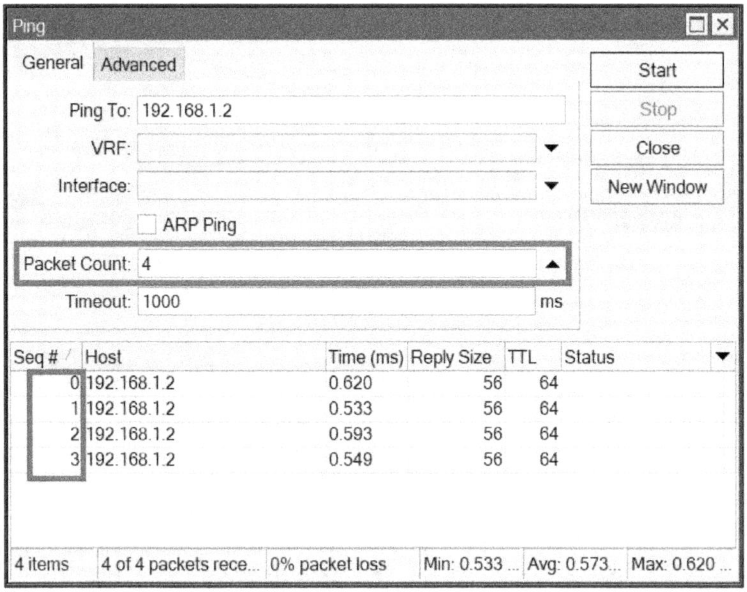

It is important to understand that when sending an echo request, the Ping tool will first look up the routing table for a route to this IP address to determine which interface it should use to send the data.

Then it will create an ICMP echo request packet, writing the IP address of the outgoing interface as the source IP on this packet, and forward it through the interface.

The step of choosing the source IP for the echo request is crucial because the destination device will reply to this IP. If the destination device does not recognize this IP (does not have a route for it in its routing table), it will not reply, and the ping will fail.

For example, if the device R1 is connected to three subnets:

- The interface ether1 is connected to the subnet 192.168.1.0/24 and has the IP address 192.168.1.1/24.
- The interface ether2 is connected to the subnet 192.168.2.0/24 and has the IP address 192.168.2.1/24.
- The interface ether3 is connected to the subnet 192.168.3.0/24 and has the IP address 192.168.3.1/24.

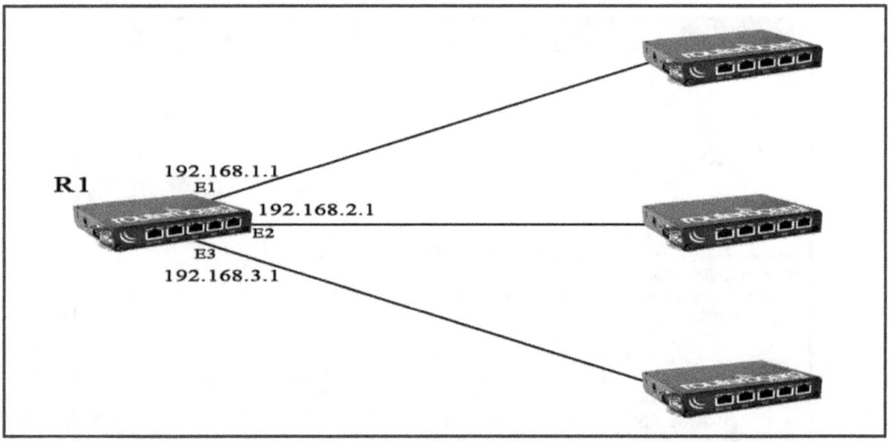

If you ping the IP address 192.168.1.2, the Ping tool will check the routing table for a route to this IP. In this case, it will find a route to this IP through ether1, so it will use the IP address of ether1 192.168.1.1 as the source IP on ICMP echo request packet and send it from this interface.

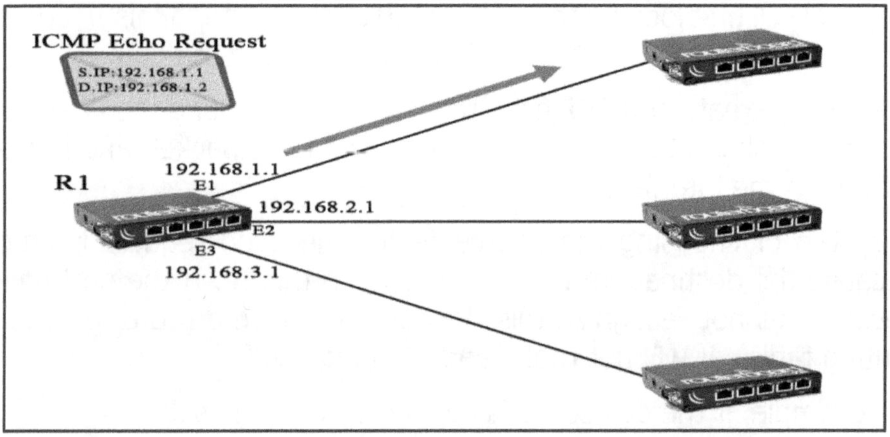

Likewise, If you ping the IP address 192.168.2.2, it will check the routing table for a route to this IP, and find a route through ether2, so it will use the IP address of ether2 192.168.2.1 as the source IP on ICMP echo request packet and send it from this interface.

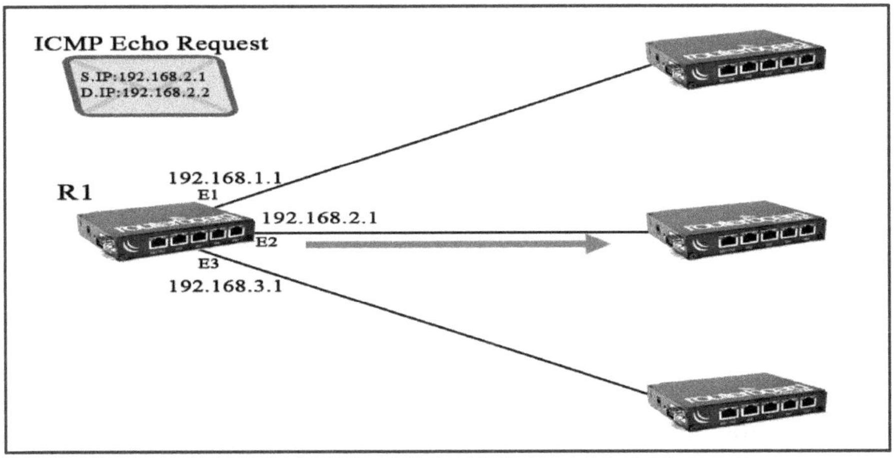

You can specify which routing table the Ping tool should use to look up the IP, (in case there are multiple routing tables, or VRFs, on the device), by selecting the table from the **VRF** field, in RouterOS v7, or from **Routing Table** field in **Advanced** tab in RouterOS v6.

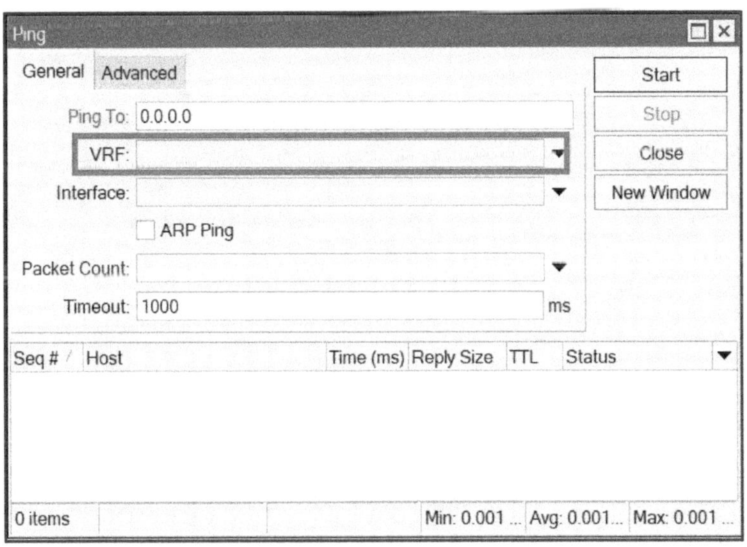

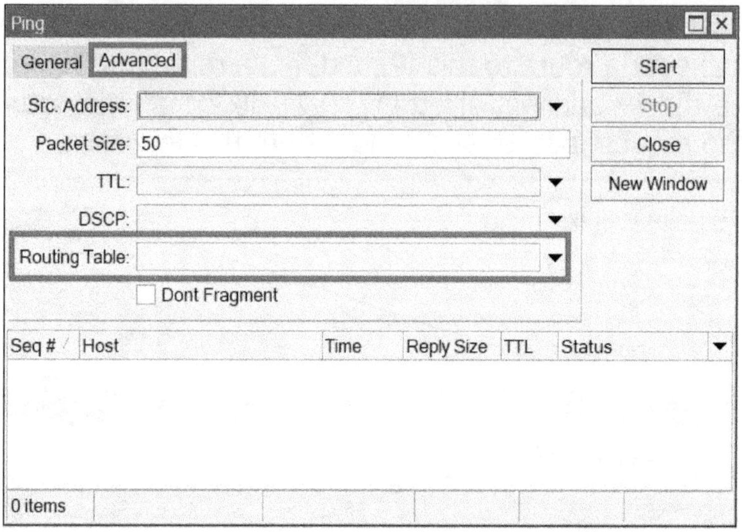

You can also manually choose the source IP for the ICMP echo request packet by entering this IP in the **Src. Address** field (or Source Address) in the **Advanced** tab of the **Ping** dialog box.

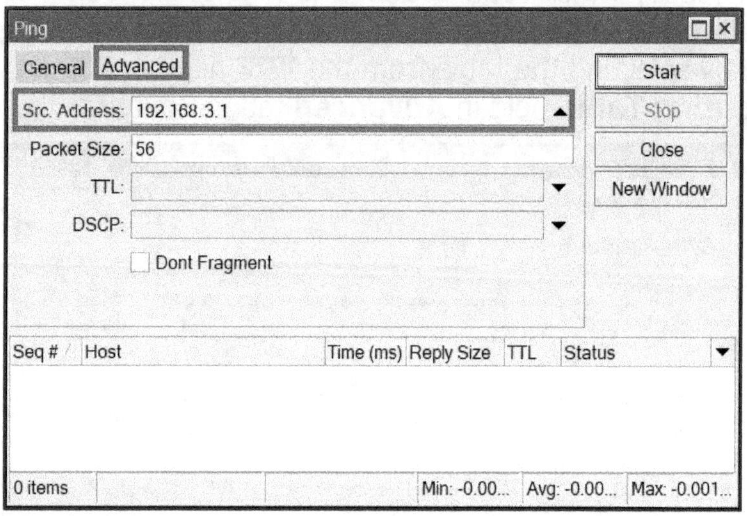

This IP address can be any IP of the device interfaces.

For example, if you ping the IP address 192.168.1.2 and specify the source IP 192.168.3.1, the Ping tool will check the routing table for a route to this IP to determine which interface to send it from, and it will use the source IP you specified.

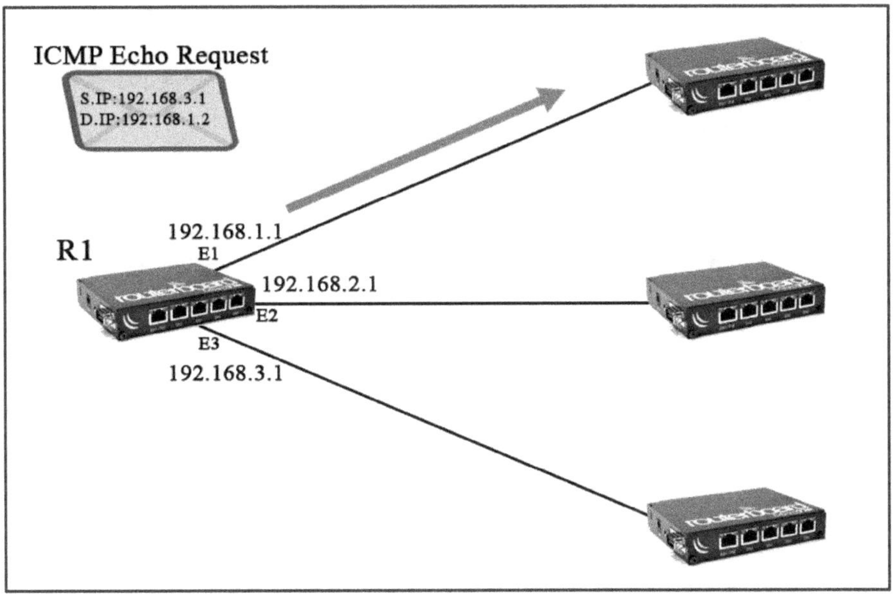

You can also force the Ping tool to send the packets from a specific interface, instead of looking up the route in the routing table. In this case, the IP address of this interface will be used as the source IP.

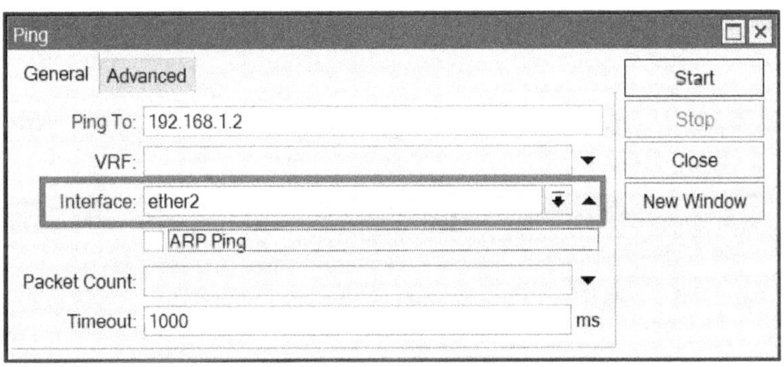

For example, if you ping the IP address 192.168.1.2 and choose the outgoing interface ether2 from the **Interface** field, the Ping tool will use the IP address of this interface, 192.168.2.1, as the source IP for the ICMP echo request packet and also send the packet from this interface.

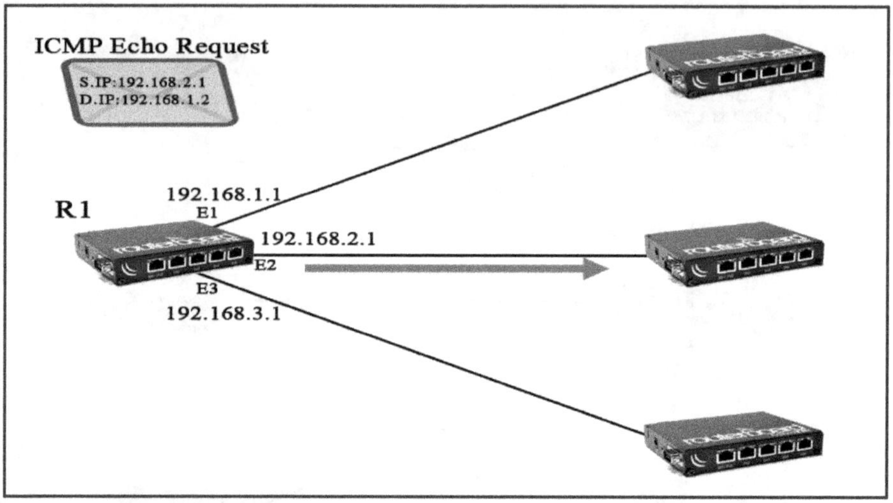

Also, you can specify both outgoing interface and the source IP by using those fields, **Interface** field an **Src. Address** field. In this case the IP you specified will be used as the source IP for the ICMP echo request packet.

On the other hand, you can use ARP ping to send an ARP request instead of sending an ICMP echo request by checking the **ARP Ping** checkbox.

In this case, you must specify the outgoing interface you want to use from the **Interface** field.

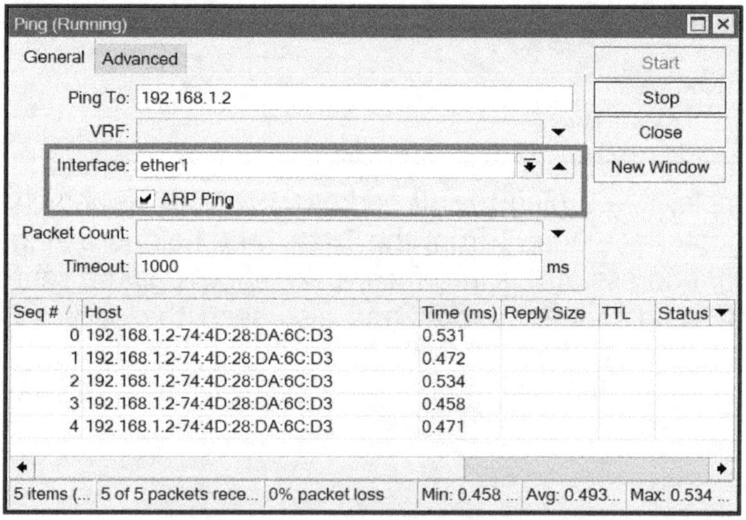

You can also specify other options like the **Packet Size**, **TTL**, **DSCP** value, and the **Don't Fragment** option from the Advanced tab.

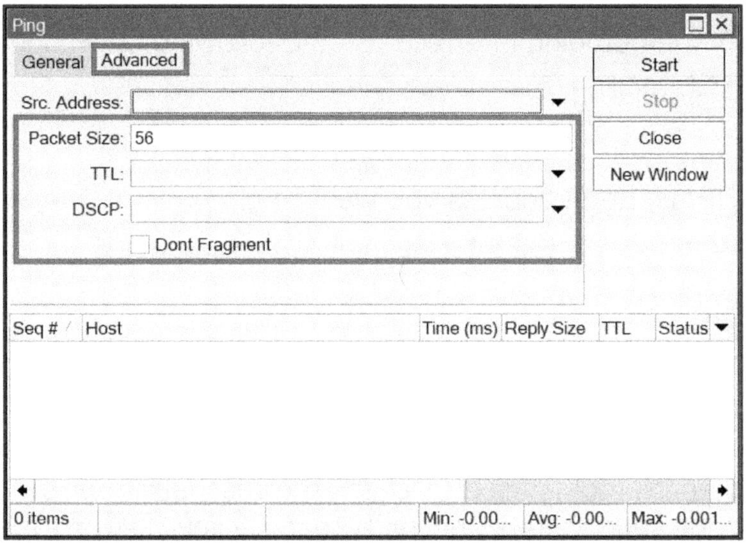

You can run Ping from the CLI using the following command:

```
ping [IP]
```

or

```
ping address=[IP]
```

where:

- [IP] is the IP address you want to ping.

For example:

```
Ping 192.168.1.2
```

To stop the ping, press **Control+C** on the keyboard.

To specify the source address, use the following command:

```
ping [IP] src-address=[source IP]
```

where:

- [IP] is the IP address you want to ping.
- [source IP] is the source IP address you want to use.

For example:

```
Ping 192.168.1.2 src-address=192.168.4.1
```

To specify the outgoing interface use the following command:

```
ping [IP] interface=[interface]
```

where:

- [IP] is the IP address you want to ping.
- [interface] is the interface you want to use.

For example:

```
Ping 192.168.1.2 interface=ether2
```

9.5 Traceroute Tool

The Traceroute tool is used to check the reachability of a device on the network and displays the path that packets take to reach that device.

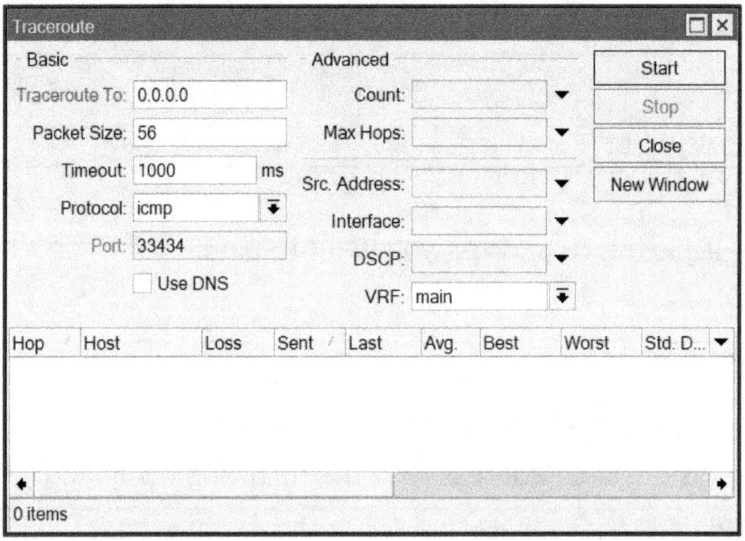

To open the **Traceroute** tool dialog box, click the **Tools** menu, then select **Traceroute**.

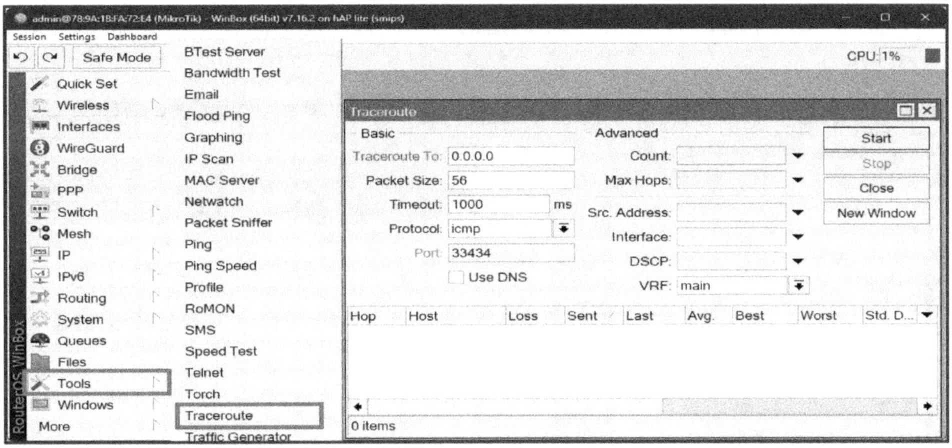

You can use this tool in troubleshooting to determine the point where the packets reach and stop, so you can begin troubleshooting from that point.

This tool also provides similar options to the Ping tool. You can have control over the count, timeout, source IP, interface, and packet size.

This tool can use both the ICMP protocol and the UDP protocol.

9.6 Profile (CPU load)

The Profile tool displays the amount of resources consumed by different processes on the device.

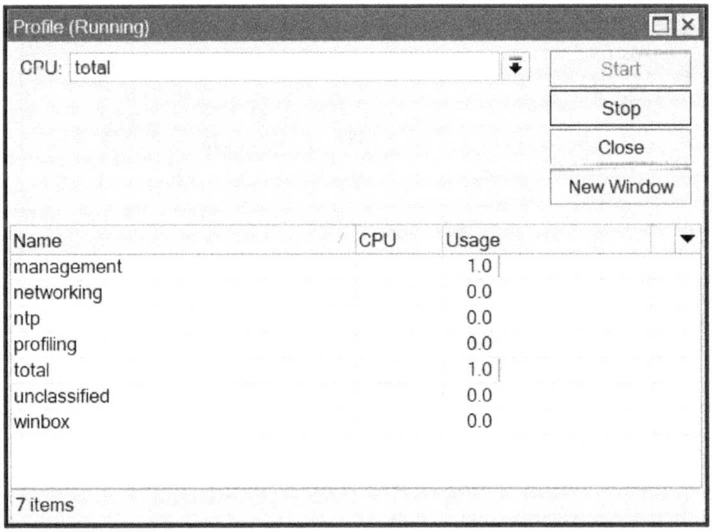

To open the **Profile** tool dialog box, click the **Tools** menu, then select **Profile**.

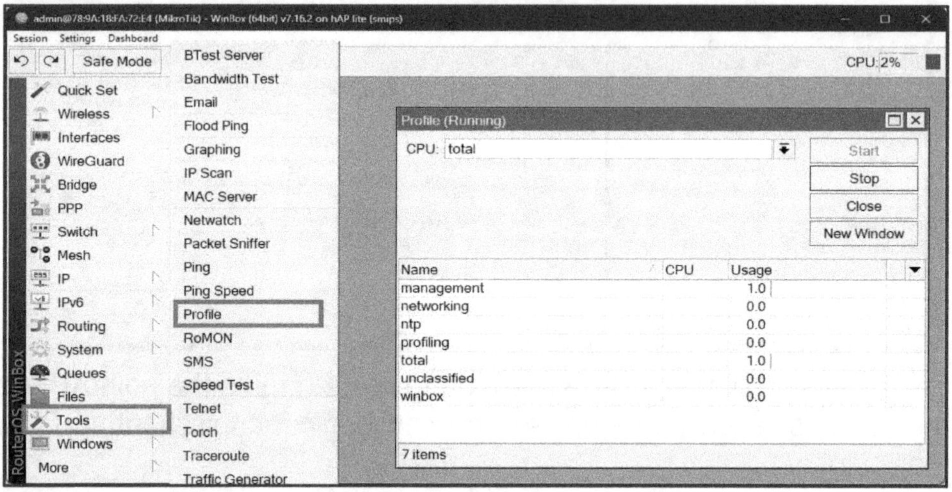

9.7 Interface Traffic Monitor

The **Interface Traffic Monitor** tool displays the real-time amount of traffic passing through an interface and provides some details about this traffic, such as the sending and receiving rates or speeds.

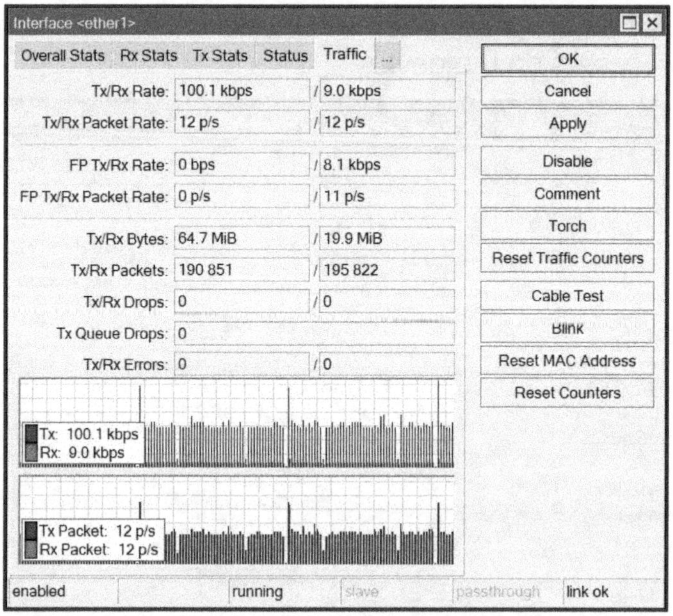

To open the Interface Traffic Monitor tool, click on the **Interface** menu to open the **Interface list** window, then double-click on the desired interface to open the **Interface** settings dialog box. Then click the **Traffic** tab.

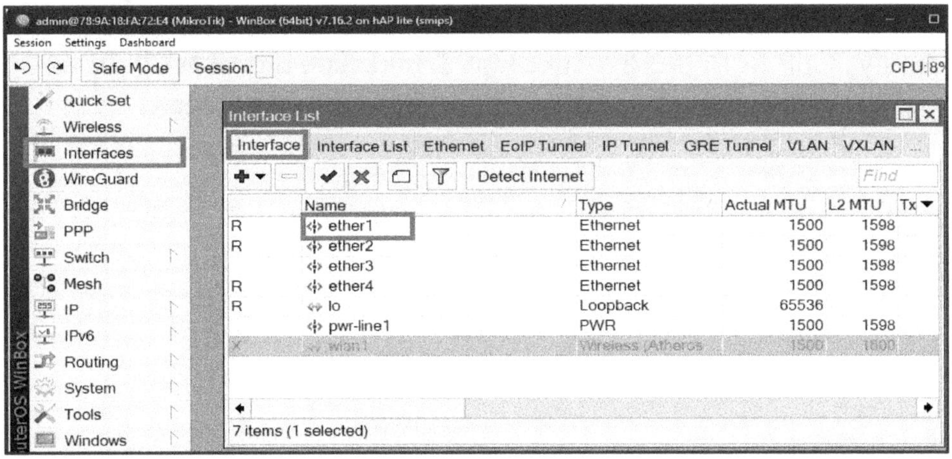

9.8 Torch Tool

The **Torch** tool is a very useful tool that can be used to monitor traffic in real-time through an interface. It can be useful for troubleshooting and diagnostic, as well as for training and learning purposes.

To open the **Torch** tool dialog box, click the **Tools** menu, then select **Torch**.

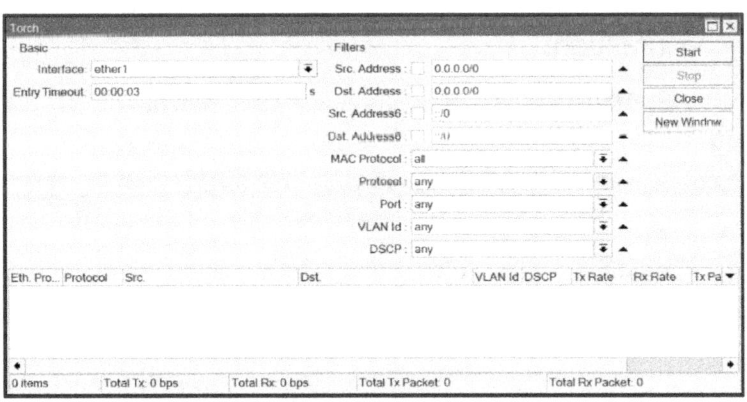

To monitor the interface traffic, select the interface from the **Interface** field and click the **Start** button.

You can specify the traffic you want to monitor by using the different fields and options this tool provides, such as monitoring a specific protocol or data coming from a specific device.

For example, if you want to monitor the incoming ping through interface ether1, choose this interface from the **Interface** field, specify ICMP from the **Protocol** field, and click the **Start** button.

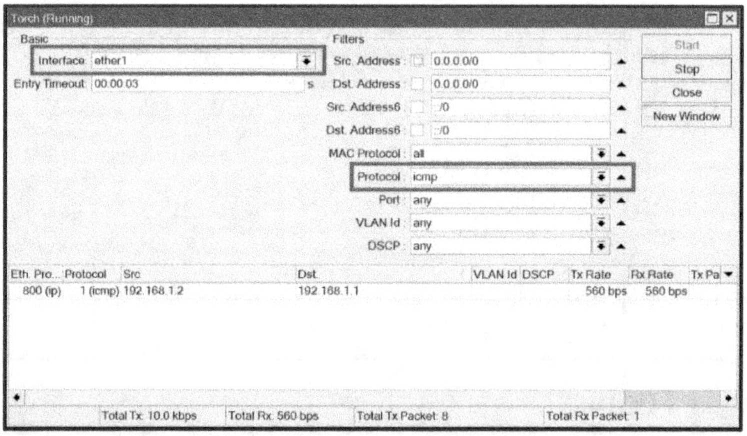

9.9 Graphs Tool

The **Graphs** tool is used to display reports in a graphical format, making it easier to compare and analyze the data.

For example, this tool can display the amount of traffic passing through a specific interface or queue, and the resource usage, CPU or memory consumption.

To open the **Graphing** tool window, click the **Tools** menu, then select **Graphing**.

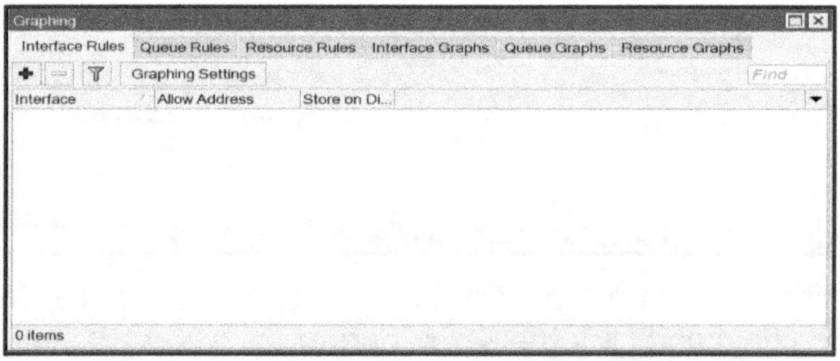

To display a graphical report about interface traffic, first add the interface to the graphing tool by clicking the **Add** button in the **Interface Rules** tab of the **Graphing** window to open the **New Interface Graphing Rule** dialog box. Then, select the interface you want to monitor.

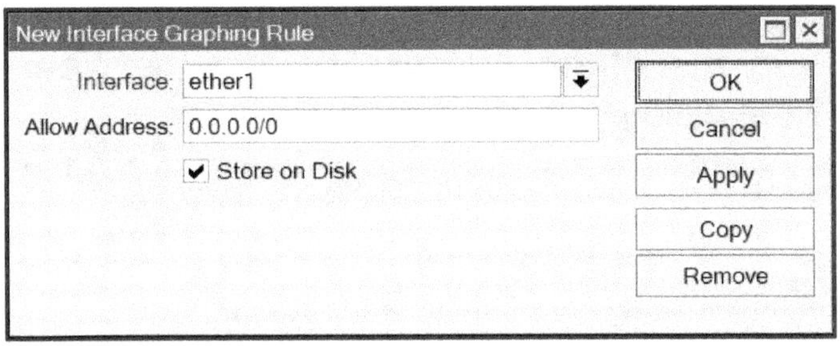

The device will start collecting data of this interface in the background.

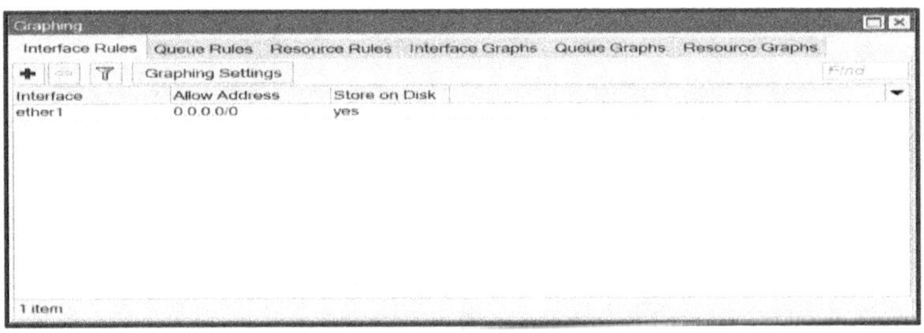

Now, to display the graphical report, double-click the interface in the **Interface Graphs** tab.

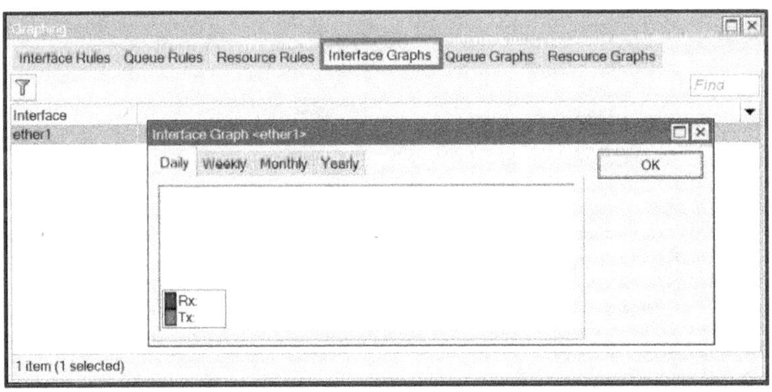

The graphical report can also be displayed remotely using a web browser by entering the graphs page URL of the device in the following format:

http://[router_ip]/graphs

where:

- [router_ip] is the IP address of the RouterOS .

To ensure that only authorized users can access and view the graphical report, you can specify the allowed IP address or subnet by entering the address in the **Allow Address** field in the **New Interface Graphing Rule** dialog box.

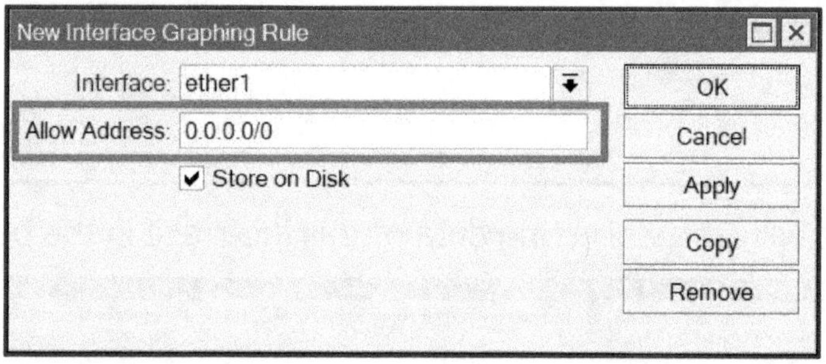

9.10 System logs

The **Log** window displays system messages about different device events, activities, and statuses. These log messages provide information about what is happening inside the device. You can use this information for monitoring and troubleshooting.

To open the **Log** window, click the **Log** menu.

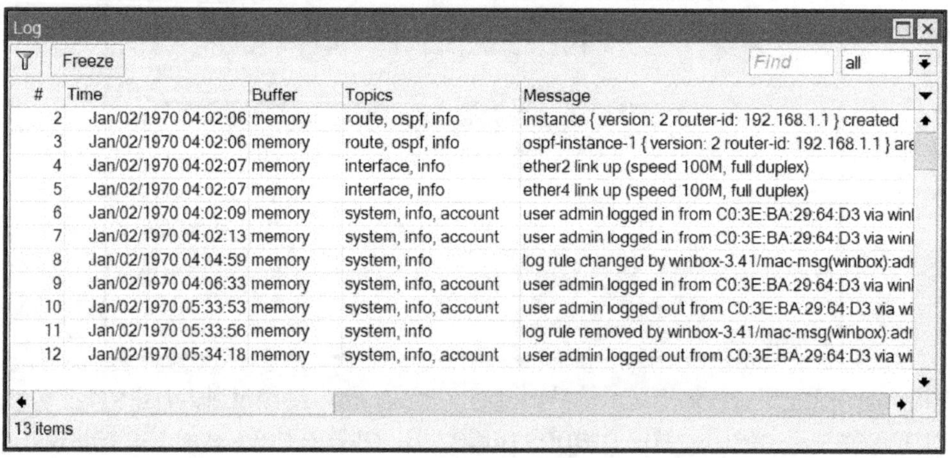

In the default settings, there are some log rules collect information about some events and display this information in **Log** window. You can disable these rules or add new rules to collect information about other events, tools, or protocols. You can also choose to store this information (or these log messages) temporarily in the device memory (RAM), save them to the device disk, or send them by email or to a remote syslog server by using **Logging** window.

To open the **Logging** window, click the **System** menu, then select **Logging**.

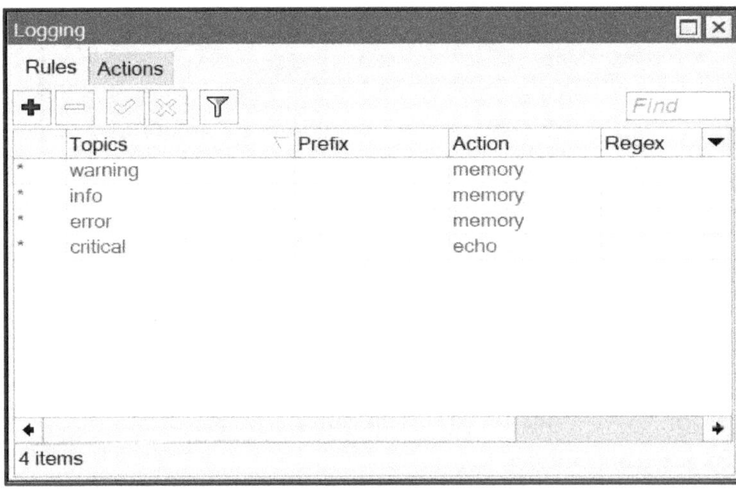

To add a new log rule, click the **Add** button from the **Rules** tab to open the **New Log Rule** dialog box.

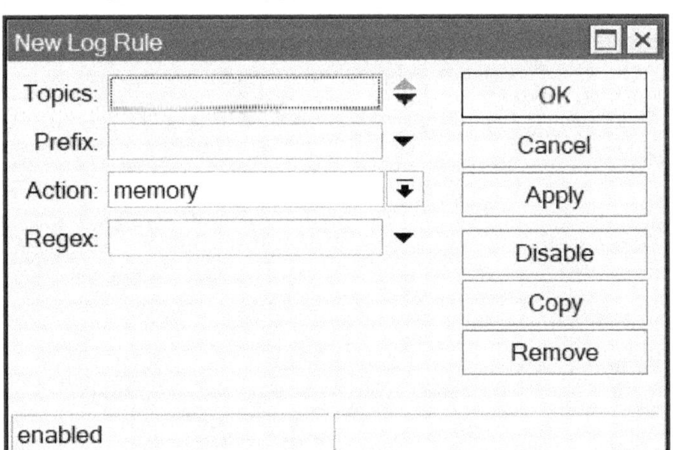

You can use this dialog box to add a new log rule and choose where to save it.

From the **Topics** field, select the topic, protocol, tool, or activity which you want to collect information about.

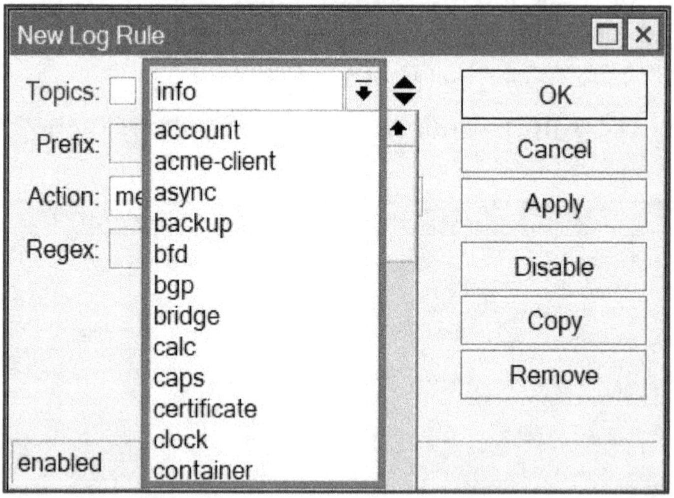

From the **Action** field, select where to save this information, (or these log messages), by choosing one of the preconfigured actions. You can also add your own actions which specify more details about where to save these log messages.

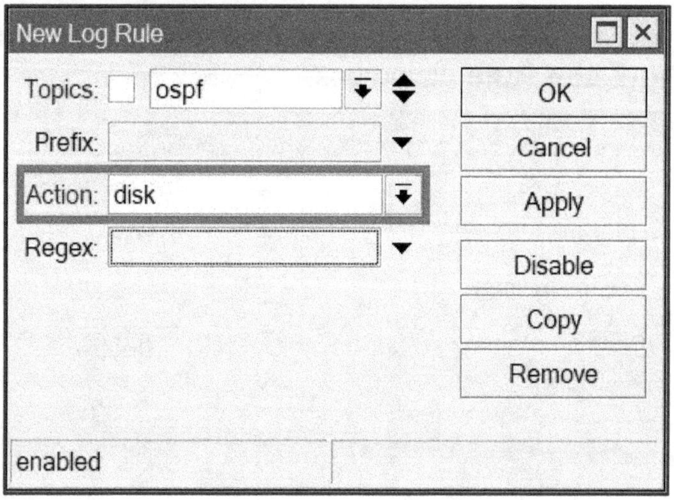

In the **Prefix** field, you can add a note to the log to make it easier to recognize in the system log. In the **Regex** field, you can use a code or script for advanced logging and analysis

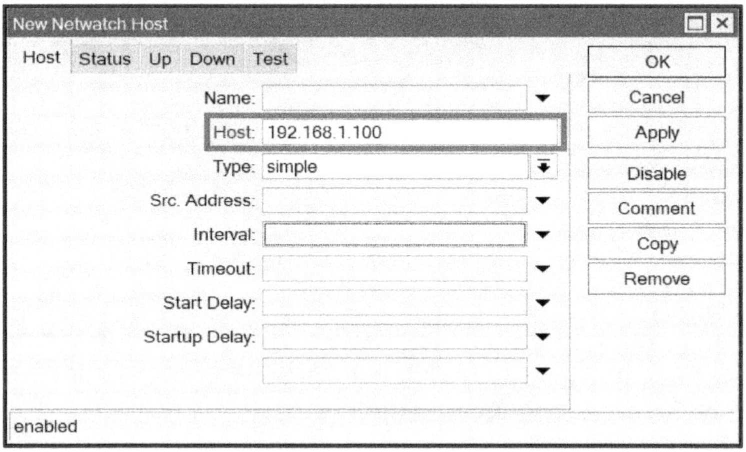

To save this information, (or these log messages), in the device disk, choose **disk** from the **Action** field. In this case, the information will be saved in a text file, which will appear in the **File List** window. You can then download it to your computer

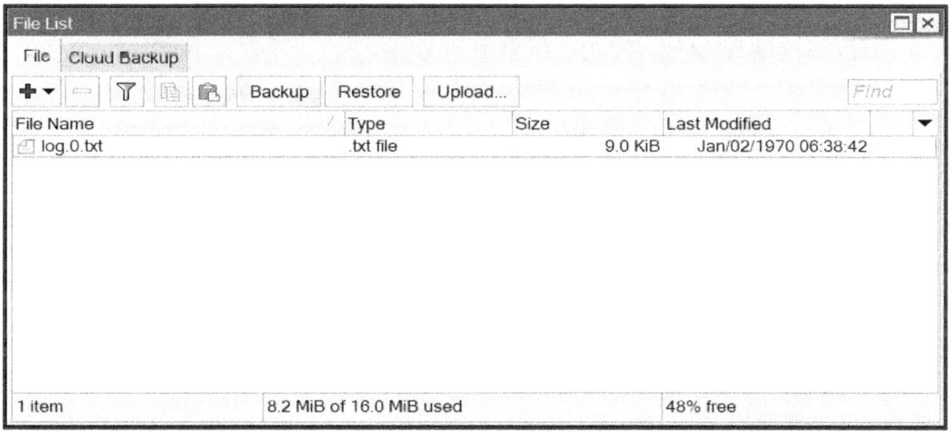

To save this information temporarily in the device memory (RAM), choose **memory** from the **Action** field. In this case, the information (or these log messages) will appear in the **Log** window. They will be deleted when the device is rebooted or when they reach a specific limit that you can specify too.

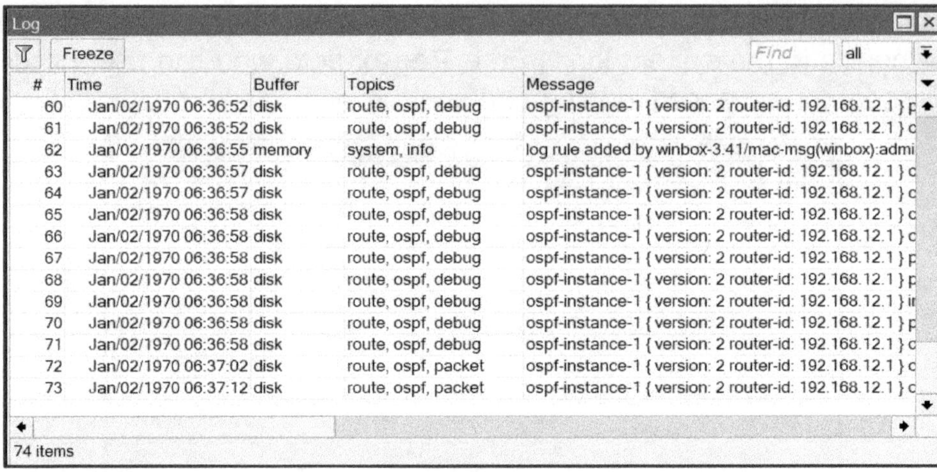

Or you can also choose to display these log messages on CLI by selecting **echo** from the **Action** field.

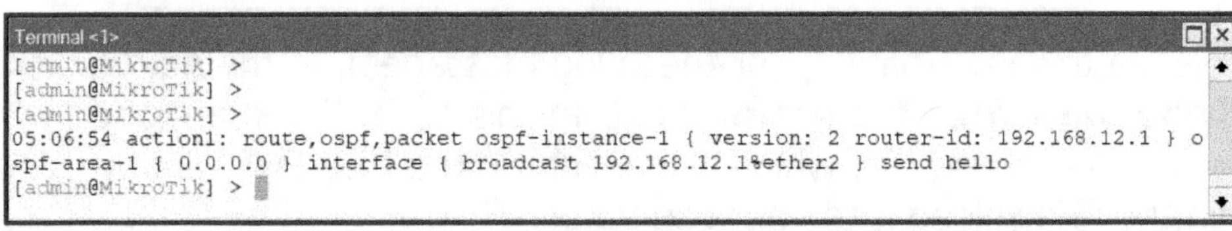

To send the log messages to a remote syslog server, choose **remote** from the **Action** field. Then, edit the server details by double-clicking the **remote** action in the **Action** tab of the **Logging** window.

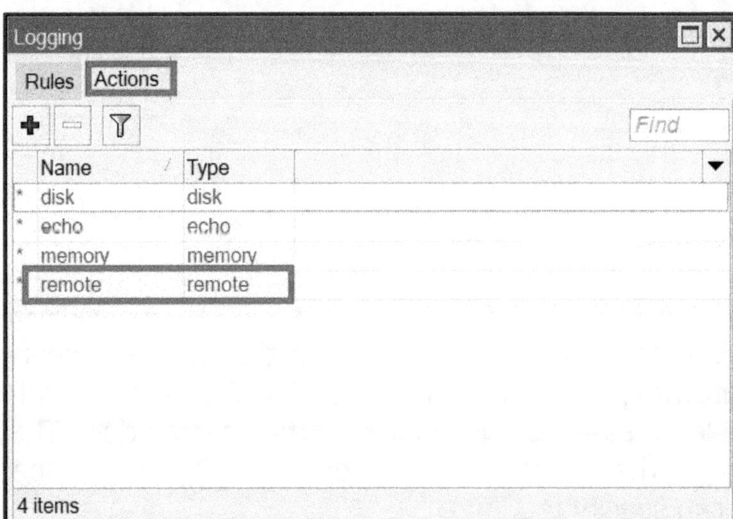

Then enter the server details.

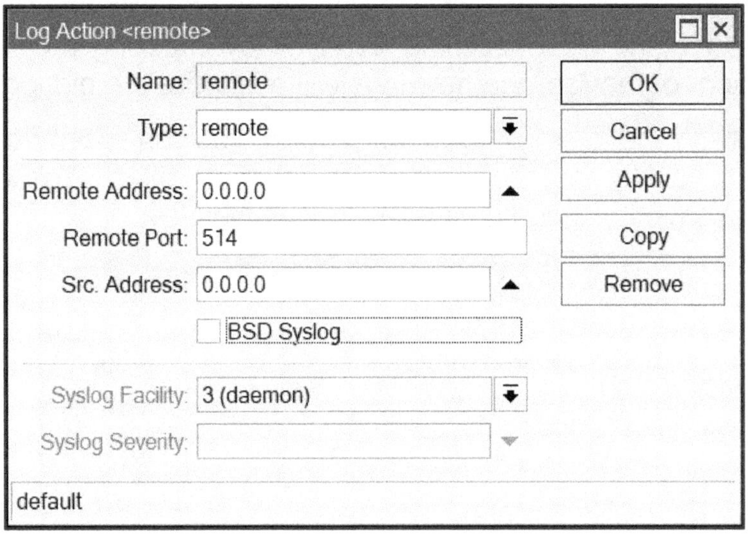

You can also add a new customized action to specify where to save the information (in RAM, on the disk, send it by email, or send it to a remote server) and edit more details by clicking the **Add** button in the **Action** tab to open the **New Log Action** dialog box.

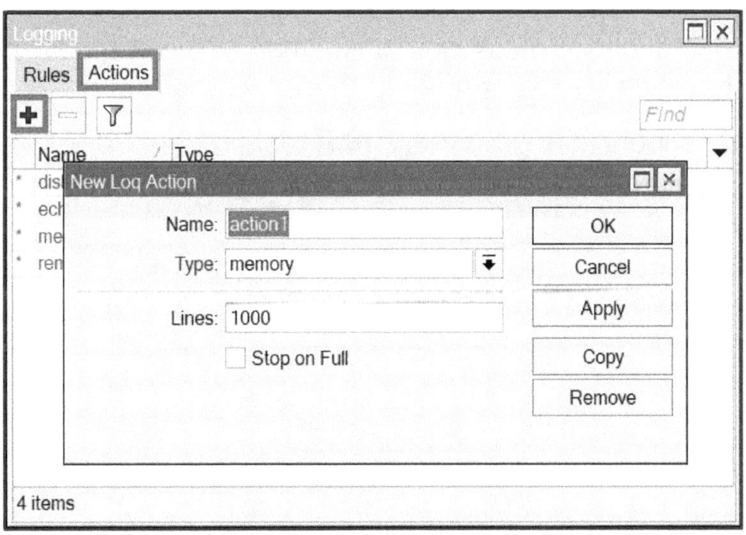

You can use this dialog box to add a new log action and configure its settings.

When saving the log messages in the memory, (RAM), you can specify the length of the log you want to collect using the **Lines** field. You can also stop logging after reaching this limit by checking the **Stop On Full** option, otherwise, the new logs will overwrite the old logs

When saving the log messages on the disk, you can specify the name of the saved file and the limit of log lines to collect. You can also choose to save these log messages in multiple files.

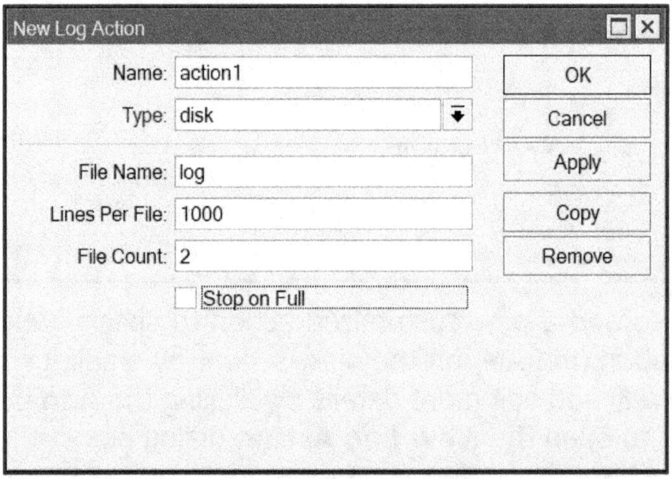

When sending the log messages to an email, you can specify the email address to which you want to send these messages.

Note: you should configure the **Email** tool first before using it here.

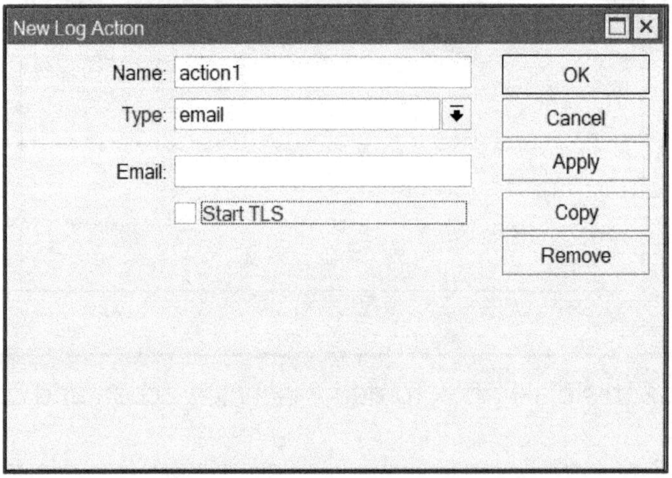

When sending the log messages to a remote syslog server, you can specify the server details.

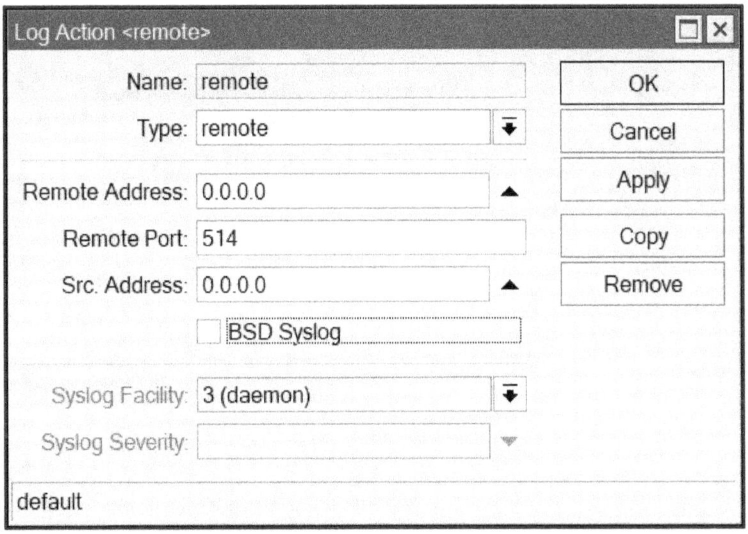

For example, if you want to collect information about the OSPF protocol activities and save it to the device disk, select the protocol from **Topics** field, and select **disk** from the **Action** field. Then click the **OK** button.

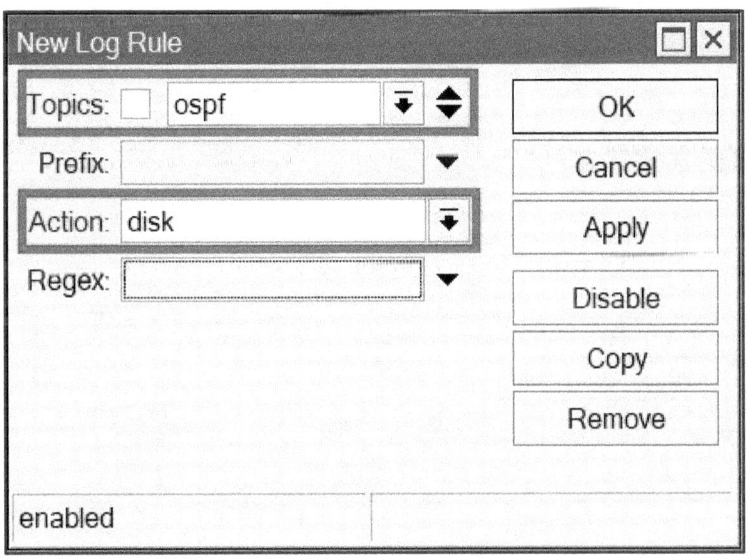

The new log will now appear in the **Logging** tab.

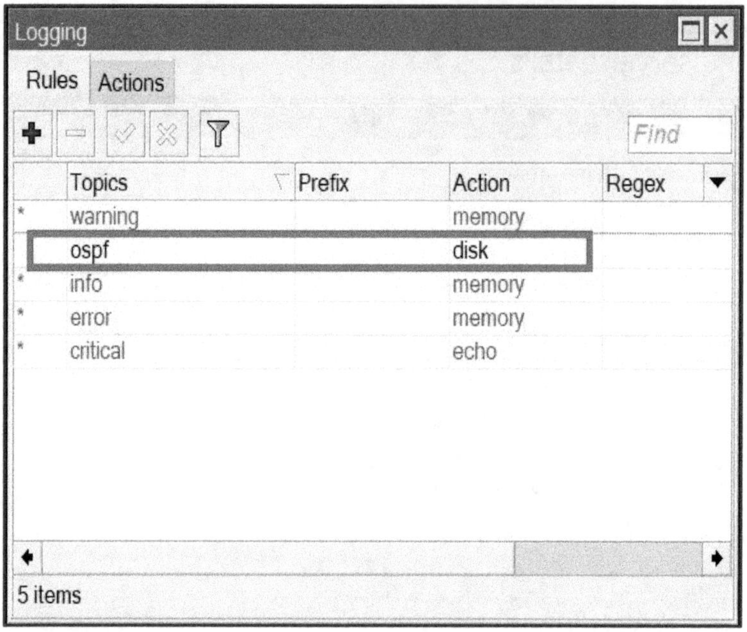

Now, the device will collect information about the OSPF protocol and display this information in the **Log** window and in a file stored in the **File List** window.

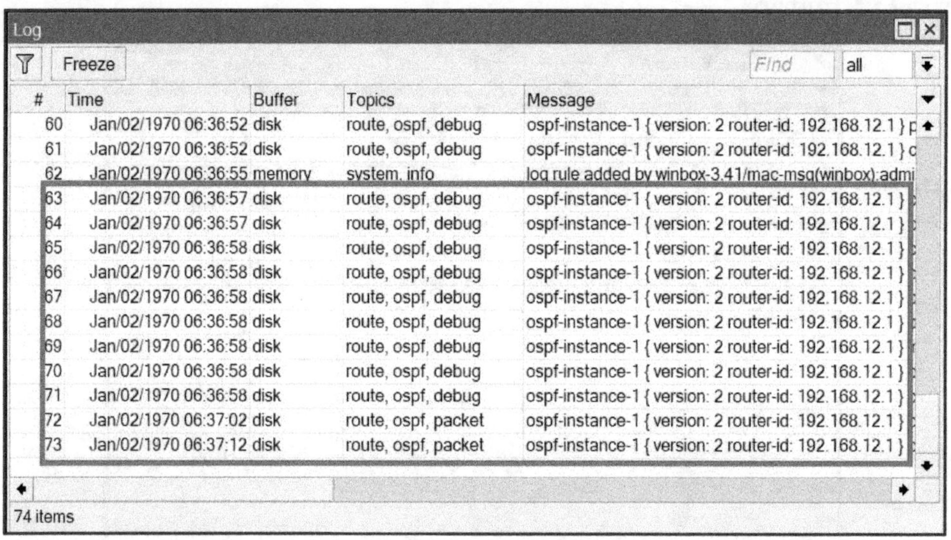

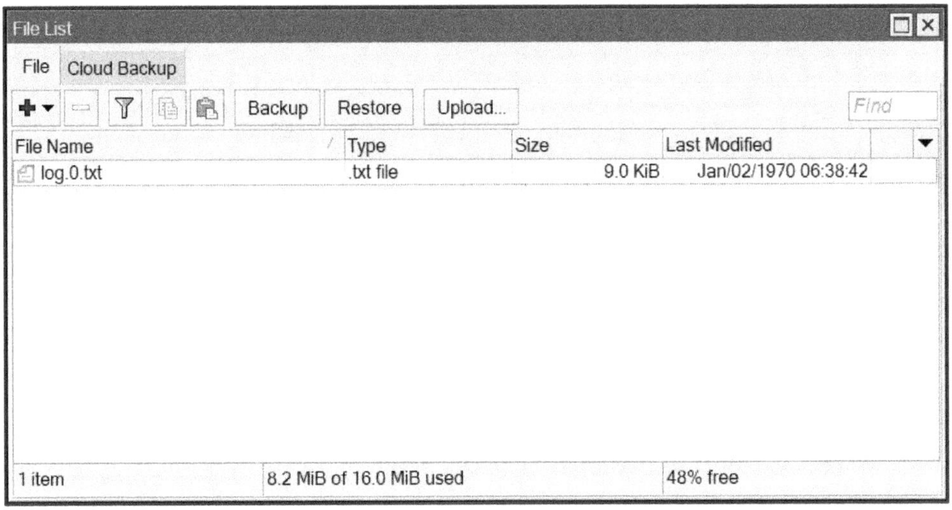

For detailed and up-to-date information about each topic or activity that you can log using the **Logging** window, visit MikroTik website.

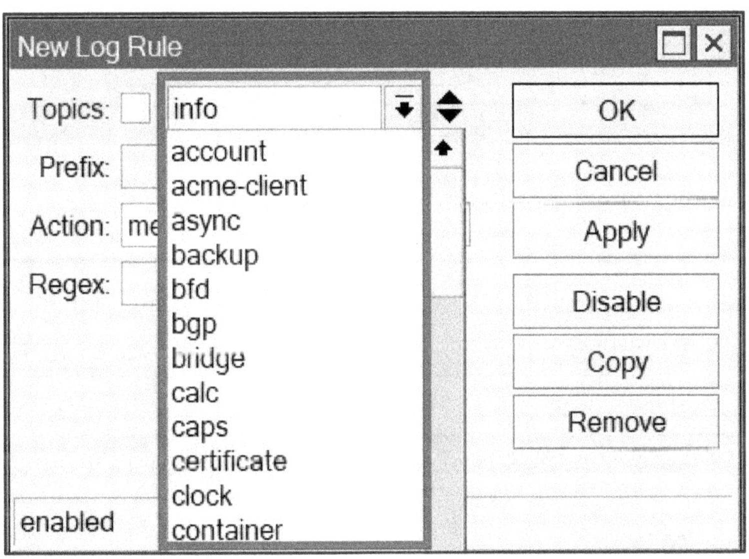

You can also display the log messages in RouterOS from the CLI using the following command:

```
log print
```

```
Terminal <1>
[admin@MikroTik] >
[admin@MikroTik] >
[admin@MikroTik] > log print
 1970-01-02 07:38:49 system,info router rebooted by winbox-3.41/mac-msg(winbox):admin@C0:3E:BA:29:64:D3
 1970-01-02 07:38:51 interface,info lo link up
 1970-01-02 07:38:52 interface,info ether2 link up (speed 100M, full duplex)
 1970-01-02 07:38:52 interface,info ether4 link up (speed 100M, full duplex)
 1970-01-02 07:39:10 system,info,account user admin logged in from C0:3E:BA:29:64:D3 via winbox
 1970-01-02 07:39:13 system,info,account user admin logged in from C0:3E:BA:29:64:D3 via winbox

[admin@MikroTik] >
```

To create or add a new log rule from the CLI use the following command:

```
system logging add topics=[topic] action=[action]
```

Where:

- [topic] is the topic, protocol, tool, or activity which you want to collect information about
- [action] is where to save this information

For example:

```
system logging add topics=ospf action=disk
```

```
Terminal <1>
[admin@MikroTik] >
[admin@MikroTik] >
[admin@MikroTik] >
[admin@MikroTik] > system logging add topics=ospf action=disk
```

To display information about the current logging rules, use the following command:

```
system logging print
```

```
Terminal <1>
[admin@MikroTik] >
[admin@MikroTik] > system logging print
Flags: * - DEFAULT
Columns: TOPICS, ACTION
#   TOPICS    ACTION
0 * info      memory
1 * error     memory
2 * warning   memory
3 * critical  echo
4   ospf      disk
[admin@MikroTik] >
```

9.11 Console Modes

In RouterOS, there are multiple modes for the Console or CLI.

9.11.1 Normal Mode

Normal mode is the default mode for the CLI. You can use this mode to execute different commands to configure the device. It has a normal prompt (>).

```
Terminal <1>
[admin@MikroTik] >
[admin@MikroTik] >
[admin@MikroTik] >
[admin@MikroTik] >
[admin@MikroTik] >
```

9.11.2 HotLock Mode

You can use HotLock mode to autocomplete commands, helping you write commands faster.

To enable HotLock mode, press the **F7** key, in RouterOS v7, or **Control + V** in RouterOS v6. To exit HotLock mode, press the **F7** key again, or **Control + V.**

When this mode is enabled, the prompt will change to (>>).

```
Terminal <1>
[admin@MikroTik] >
[admin@MikroTik] >
[admin@MikroTik] >
[admin@MikroTik] >>
[admin@MikroTik] >>
```

9.11.3 Lock Mode

You can use the Lock mode to lock the screen and protect access to the CLI. This can be useful when you log in using SSH or Telnet and want to keep the session open but prevent anyone from accessing the CLI while you are away. To return to normal mode, you need to enter your account password.

To enable the Lock Mode, type the following command:

```
lock
```

```
Terminal <1>

  MMM      MMM       KKK                          TTTTTTTTTTT      KKK
  MMMM    MMMM       KKK                          TTTTTTTTTTT      KKK
  MMM MMMM MMM  III  KKK  KKK   RRRRRR     OOOOOO      TTT     III  KKK  KKK
  MMM  MM  MMM  III  KKKKK      RRR  RRR  OOO  OOO     TTT     III  KKKKK
  MMM      MMM  III  KKK KKK    RRRRRR    OOO  OOO     TTT     III  KKK KKK
  MMM      MMM  III  KKK  KKK   RRR  RRR   OOOOOO      TTT     III  KKK  KKK

  MikroTik RouterOS 7.18beta2 (c) 1999-2025       https://www.mikrotik.com/

Session is locked       (Ctrl-D to Quit)

 password for admin:
```

9.11.4 Safe Mode

You can use safe mode to maintain your access to RouterOS in case you mistakenly block your access to it due to incorrect configuration.

The concept of using safe mode is as follows: When you enable the safe mode and make a configuration:

- If this configuration blocks your access to RouterOS, the system will automatically undo, or remove, the configuration to restore your access.
- If the configuration does not block you and you want to keep it, you can save the configuration and exit the safe mode.

You can enable the safe mode from the GUI by clicking the **Safe Mode** button.

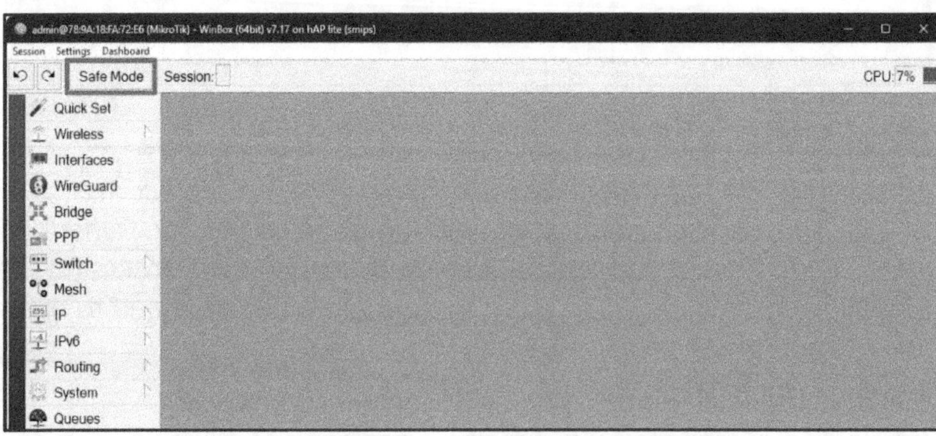

To exit the safe mode, click the button again. This will apply the configuration you made.

To enable the safe mode from the CLI, press **Control + X** or **F4** key. A note will appear in the CLI prompt indicating that the safe mode is on. (<SAFE>)

To exit the safe mode and apply the configuration you made, press **Control + X** again or **F4** key.

To exit the safe mode without applying the configuration, press **Control + D**. That will exit the safe mode and close the CLI window, or the terminal window.

For example, if you enable the safe mode and then create a firewall rule that blocks all connections to RouterOS using the following command:

```
ip firewall filter add chain=input action=drop
```

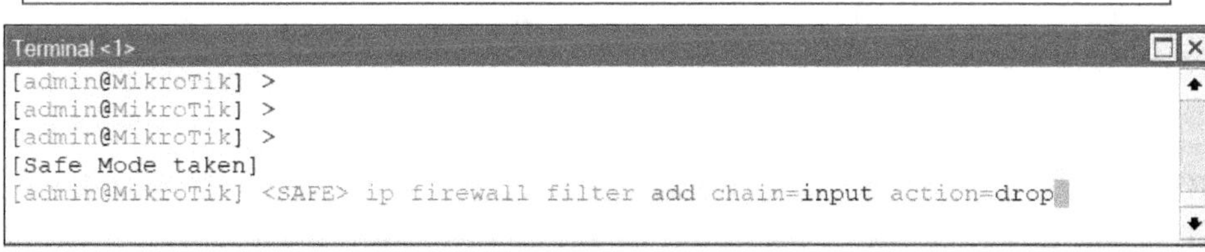

After a short period of time, (approximately 10 seconds), RouterOS will automatically undo, or remove, this rule to restore your access to the device.

9.12 RoMON Tool

You can use RoMON tool (Router Management Overlay Network) to login to devices that is not directly connected to your computer using WinBox.

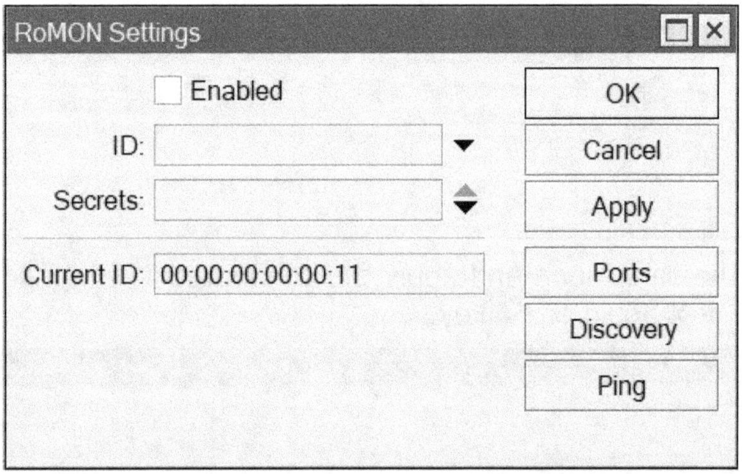

For example, if you are connected to a MikroTik device, R1, and this device is connected to another device, R2, which is also connected to another device, R3.

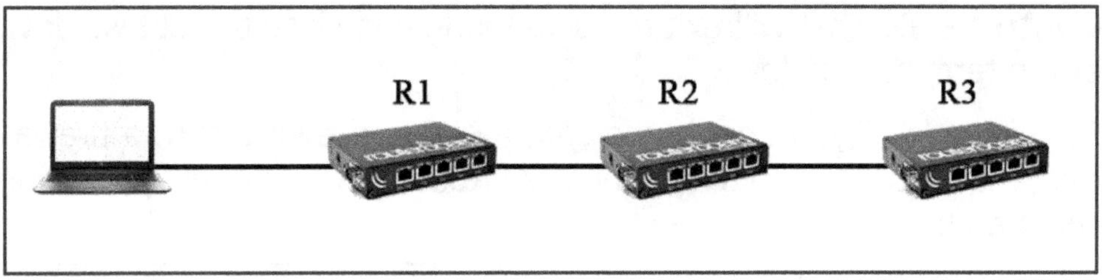

In a normal situation, if you want to configure R2 using WinBox, you would unplug your device from R1 and connect it to R2. Similarly, if you want to configure R3, you would do the same.

Instead of connecting to each device like that, you can use the **RoMON** tool, enable it on those devices, and then just connect to one device, R1 for example. This way, you will be able to reach all other devices.

To open the **RoMON** tool, click the **Tools** menu, then select **RoMON**.

To enable the RoMON, check **Enabled** checkbox from the **RoMON Settings** dialog box.

In the **ID** field, you can enter an ID for the device to make it easier to recognize when using RoMON to log into it. The ID should be in the form of MAC address, consisting of 12 hexadecimal digits. If you don't specify an ID, the device will use its MAC address.

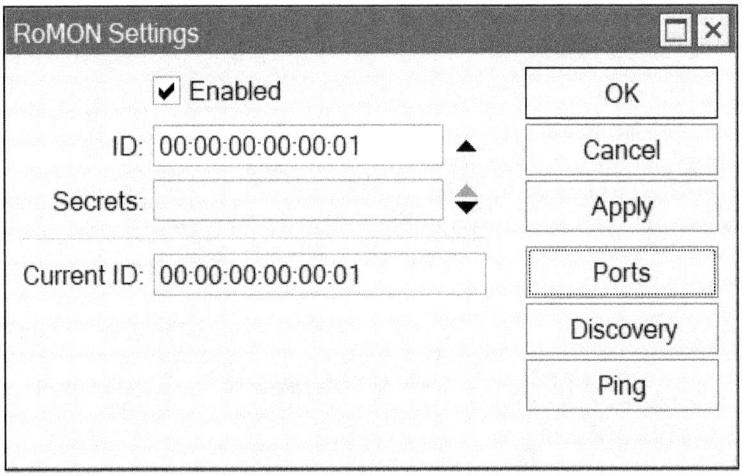

After enabling RoMON on the other devices, now connect to R1 by clicking the **Connect to RoMON** button in the **WinBox** window.

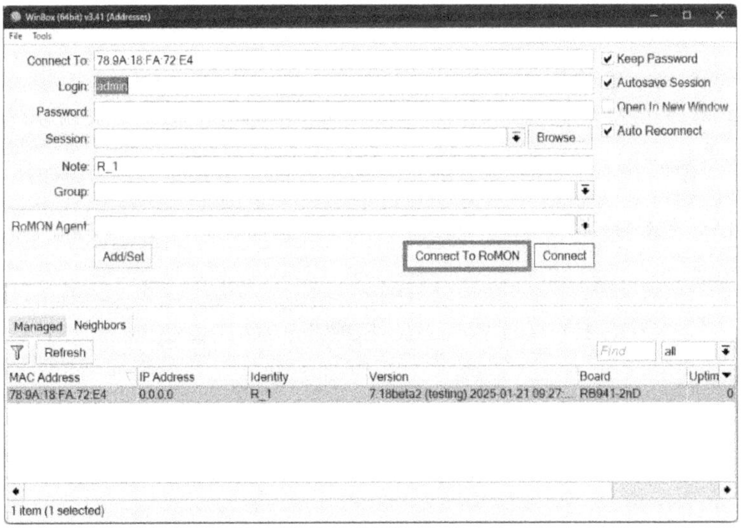

You will see the other two devices, R2 and R3, in the **WinBox** window. You can select any one of them to log in to it.

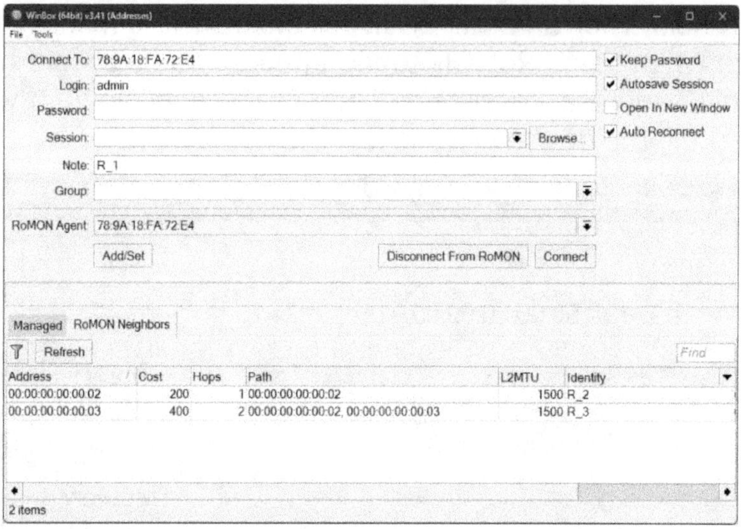

You can also enable the RoMON in RouterOS from the CLI using the following command:

```
tool romon set enabled=yes
```

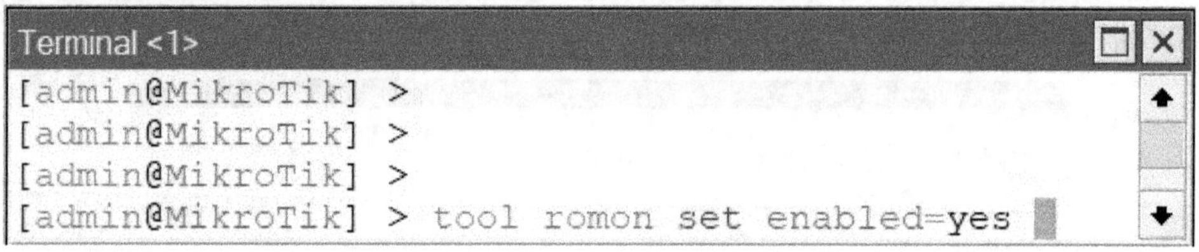

To specify an ID for the device, use the following command:

```
tool romon set id=[id]
```

Where:

- [id] is the ID you want to specify to the device.

For example:

```
tool romon set id=00:00:00:00:00:01
```

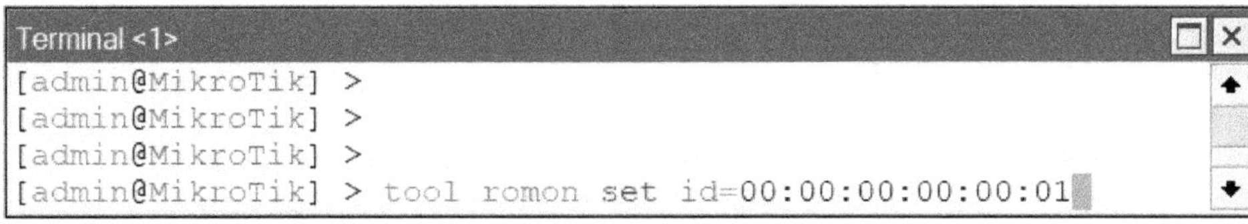

To display information about the RoMON tool use the following command:

```
tool romon print
```

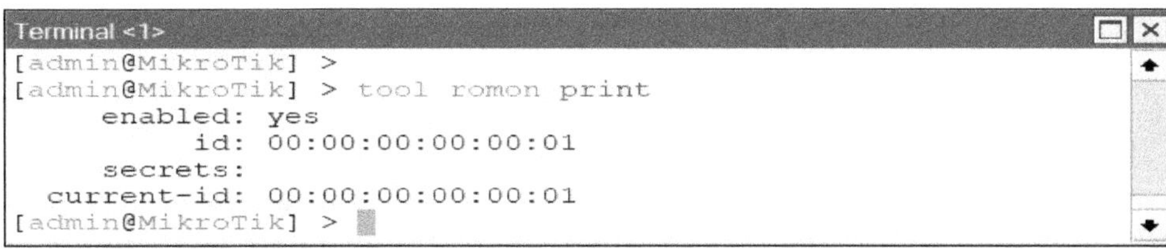

9.13 Scheduler Tool

You can use the **Scheduler** tool to execute codes or scripts at specific times. For example, you can configure this tool to run a script that takes a backup and sends it to your email every week.

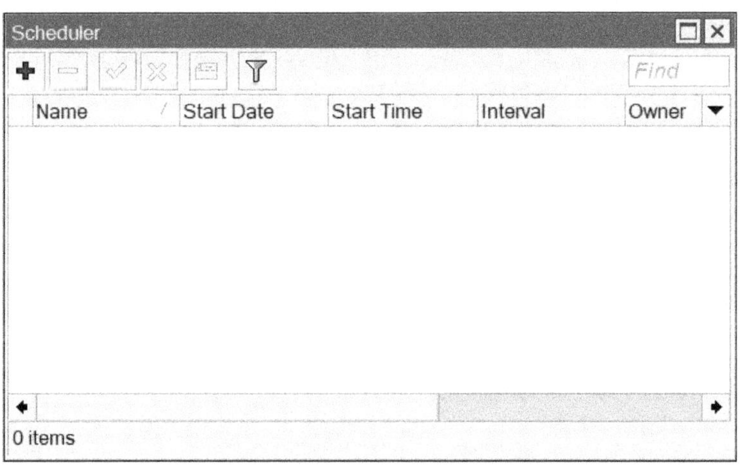

To open the **Scheduler** window, click the **System** menu, then select **Scheduler**.

To add a new Schedule, or task, click the **Add** button in the **Scheduler** window to open the **New Schedule** dialog box. Write the script you want, set the starting time, and interval for this task.

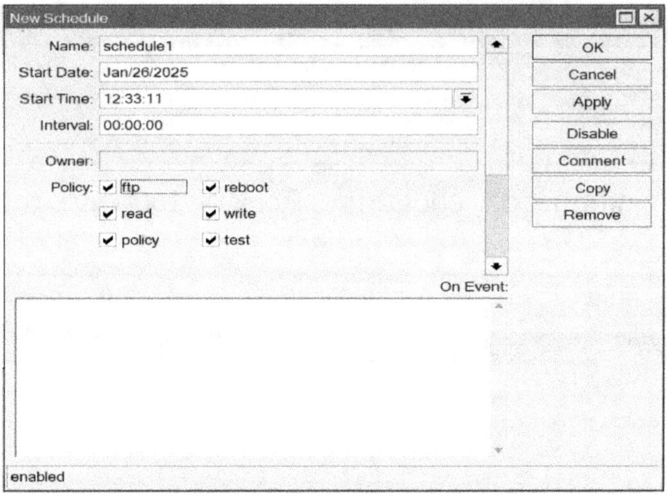

For example, if you want to take a backup every week and send it to your email, enter the interval as follows in the **Interval** field:

7d 00:00:00

In the **On Event** field, write the following script

```
export file=backup
tool e-mail send to=email@yahoo.com subject="Backup" body="This is the weekly backup " file=backup.rsc
```

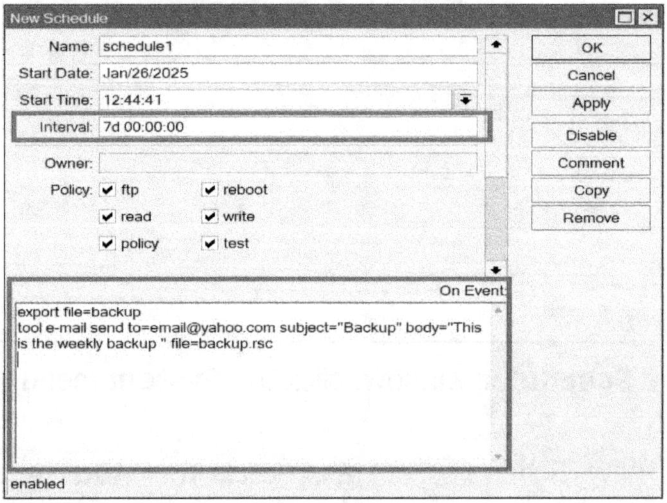

Note: you should configure the email tool first before using it here.

9.14 Scripts Tool

You can use the **Scripts** tool to easily manage codes or scripts on the device. You can add scripts to this tool and then call them from different places using other tools. Later, if you want to edit those scripts or make any changes, you simply edit them from a central place using the **Scripts** tool, in this case there is no need to make any changes in the other tools that use these scripts.

To open the **Script List** window, click the **System** menu, then select **Scripts**.

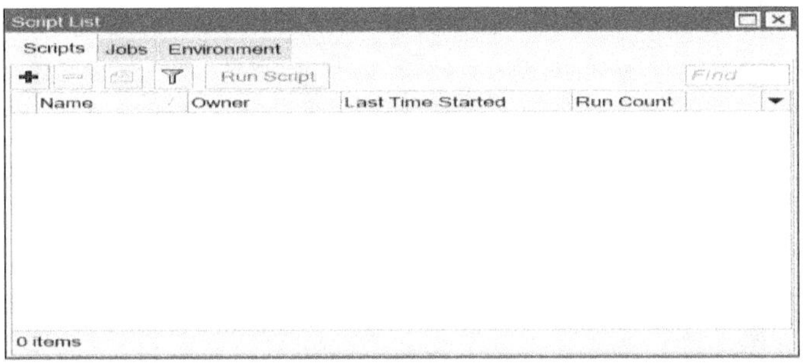

To add a new script, click the **Add** button in the **Script List** window to open the **New Script** dialog box. And write the script you want.

9.15 Neighbors Tool

The **Neighbors** tool displays the connected devices and some information about them, such as the interface they are connected to, their IP address, and the platform, (the operating system). It uses CDP, LLDP, and MNDP protocols to collect this information. You can use this tool to know which device is connected to which interface.

To open the **Neighbor List** window, click the **IP** menu, then select **Neighbors**.

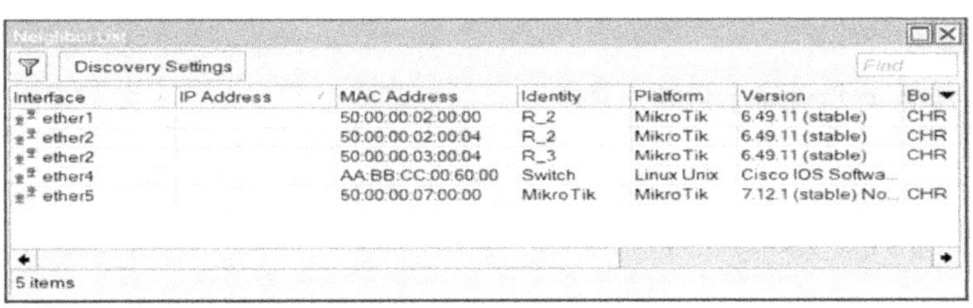

9.16 SNMP Tool

You can use the **SNMP** tool to configure SNMP protocol settings on a MikroTik RouterOS. This protocol is used for monitoring and managing various network devices.

The MikroTik RouterOS supports SNMPv1, SNMPv2 and SNMPv3

To open the **SNMP Settings** dialog box, click the **IP** menu, then select **SNMP**.

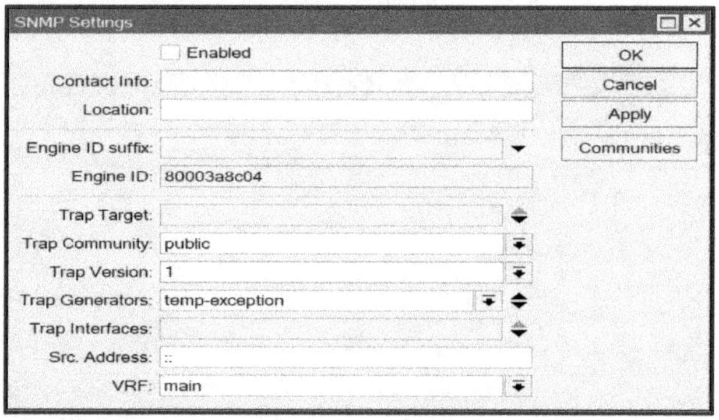

9.17 The Dude

The Dude is a free tool developed by MikroTik that can be used to monitor and manage the network. This tool supports various methods for network monitoring using multiple protocols such as SNMP, ICMP, DNS, and TCP.

The concept of using the Dude is to install a version called the Dude Server on a RouterOS device, and another version called the Dude Client on a Windows operating system to display information about the entire network.

The details of using this application are beyond the scope of the MTCNA course.

9.18 Support Output File

If you need technical support from MikroTik, you can create a file containing the device information and settings and send it to the support team to allow them to analyze the configurations and identify the issue. This file is called the Support Output File (supout.rif).

To create the Support Output File, click the **Make Supout.rif** menu. Then, enter a name for the file in the **File Name** field and click the **Start** button.

After creating the file, it will appear in the **File List** window. To open **File List** window, click the **Files** menu.

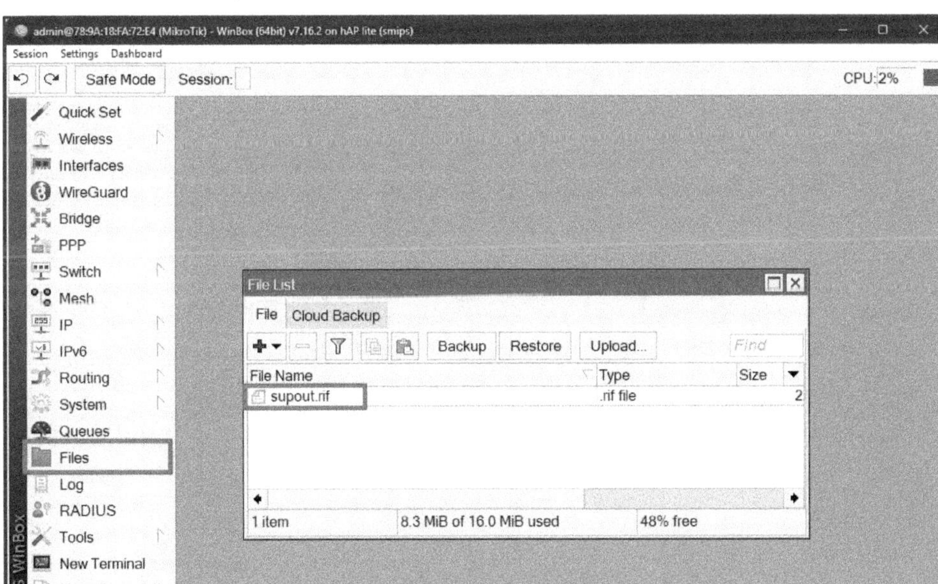

Now you can download this file to your computer and send it to MikroTik technical support team at the following email:

support@mikrotik.com.

MikroTik advises taking the following steps before creating the Support Output File (supout.rif) and contacting technical support:

- Add meaningful and helpful comments to the rules and configurations that have been created so the support team can understand their purpose.
- Explain the details as much as possible.
- Provide a diagram of the network design.

Table of Contents

www.ingramcontent.com/pod-product-compliance
Lightning Source LLC
LaVergne TN
LVHW082012200926
848481LV00010B/2846

* 9 7 8 1 7 3 9 7 9 3 1 2 8 *